WHEN JOHNNY
CAME
MARCHING HOME

William H.

2012

WHEN JOHNNY
CAME
MARCHING HOME

a novel by

William Heffernan

Published by Akashic Books
©2012 William Heffernan

Hardcover ISBN-13: 978-1-61775-127-1
Paperback ISBN-13: 978-1-61775-135-6
Library of Congress Control Number: 2012939263

First printing

Akashic Books
PO Box 1456
New York, NY 10009
info@akashicbooks.com
www.akashicbooks.com

This book is dedicated to the memory of Stewart Dickson: journalist, novelist, stalwart Scotsman, and above all a true and loyal friend.

I'll miss ye, laddie.

Acknowledgments

A special thanks to Gloria Loomis and Johnny Temple for their continued encouragement and support; to my sons and daughters, who give me a sense of reality and never allow me to take myself too seriously; and to Nancy Williams, whose friendship keeps me sane.

Author's Note

Liberties were taken in the writing of this novel that at times may seem to bend historical fact. This was done purely for dramatic effect.

PROLOGUE

We were eleven years old when we found the old man's body.

It was the dead of winter and just about as cold as it gets in Vermont, and the body was frozen solid, a thin film of ice covering the eyelids and nose and mouth, making the man's dark brown skin seem eerily lighter than it had been in life.

"Tha's ol' Jesse, ain't it?" Johnny asked.

We both turned to look at Abel Johnson. Abel's father ran the town store and Jesse Brown was the old Negro who worked for him stocking shelves and unloading delivery wagons.

Abel nodded, his gaze fixed on the clouded, milky, dead eyes that stared back at him. He was a heavy boy, with plump cheeks that were now red with the cold. "I was jus' talkin' ta him this mornin'," he said. "He tol' me he was goin' out ta hunt up a squirrel fer his supper." Abel's voice was faint and distant, sounding as if he were talking more to himself than to us; his lips began to quiver as he spoke.

It was midafternoon and we were in the woods about a hundred yards up from the dirt road that runs along the river, a favorite hunting ground for squirrel and rabbit and the deer that move down the mountain at night to graze in the open meadows below.

The river cuts through our town of Jerusalem's Landing. It is a cold, fast waterway, fed by streams that live off the eleven-month snowmelt that runs off Camel's Hump Mountain. The town sits in the foothills of the mountain, its five hundred–odd souls forging a living mostly from dairy farming or logging, with the spring maple sugar season adding a few more necessary dollars. It is not a wealthy community, nor is it poor, and the people are largely content with their lives despite the hardships they endure.

"Jubal, ya better go an' get yer daddy," Johnny said. "An' ya better have him tell my pa what happened. He'll be a wantin' to come pray over Jesse."

"Ya better have him stop by the store an' tell my daddy too," Abel said.

My father, Jonas Foster, is the town constable. Johnny's father is the minister of the Baptist church. The town store sits between my house and the parsonage, so we all live within walking distance of each other.

"I'll tell him," I said. "You two better stay with the body to keep any varmints off him." I looked down at the old squirrel gun that Jesse had been carrying. "You better not touch nothin' less you have to," I said, trying to think what my father would want.

"Okay, sheriff," Johnny said. His blond hair peeked out from under his cap and splayed across his forehead and he was grinning at me, adding to the teasing quality of his voice. I wondered then, as I still do now, how he could be so light-hearted with a man we had all known lying dead at his feet.

An hour later I led four men up the wooded slope. They walked in a line behind me, my father first; Abel's dad, Walter Johnson, next; then Johnny's father, the Reverend Virgil Harris; bringing up the rear was the town doctor, Brewster Pierce, the one man we boys had forgotten. My father had not.

Dr. Pierce went to the body straight off and confirmed what we already knew. He opened Jesse Brown's coat, did a cursory check of his torso, then removed his hat and checked his head and neck. "I don't see any signs of violence," he said, still looking over the body. "My best guess until we do an autopsy is that he had a heart attack or stroke." He glanced up at Walter Johnson. "How old was he, Walter?"

Walter Johnson gave a small shrug. He was a moderately short, stocky man, with a prominent chin and deep brown eyes, a picture of what his son, Abel, would probably look like one day. He toed the ground as if the question embarrassed him. "Sixty, maybe, but tha's jus' a guess. I reckon I never axed him his age. Don't know why, but I never did." He paused, thinking about what he had just said, then quickly added: "He was strong, though; could unload a delivery wagon good as any man half his age."

"He was sixty-two," Virgil Harris said. "He cleared some tree limbs from the church grounds after that storm we had in September, and we got to talking. He moved here three years ago, as I recall, from somewhere in Connecticut. Said he had no family . . . just had himself to look after." Reverend Harris spoke with his chin elevated, just as he did when he was giving his Sunday sermon. He was tall and slender with unruly blond hair that he had passed on to his son, along with piercing blue eyes.

"Was he an escaped slave?" my father asked. My father is a big man, a good four inches over six feet and heavy through the chest and shoulders, and he seemed to tower over the other three. I, too, was big for my age, and I hoped one day to be as big as he.

"Never said that he was," Walter Johnson responded. "I always figured he was jus' like the other nigs who live hereabouts."

The Negroes who live in Jerusalem's Landing—slightly more than one hundred—were never slaves, but the offspring of former slaves who had escaped to the North years before. It is a tight-knit community whose members have their own small church, but who send their children to school with the rest of us. One, Josiah Flood, was in our class and usually ran the ridges with the three of us when he wasn't doing chores at the Billingsley farm.

My father stepped forward and placed the litter they had brought next to the body. He looked at Jesse for a long moment, then turned to Reverend Harris. "You go ahead an' offer yer prayer, Virgil," he said. "Then we'll load the old fella up an' take 'em down to Doc's office."

We all removed our hats as Reverend Harris offered his prayer. It was short and simple.

"Dear Lord, we didn't know this man well, but by all accounts he was a good soul, who worked hard and always offered his help when needed. We ask that You accept him as a favored child and offer him a place in the glory of Your heavenly kingdom. Amen."

My father had been standing beside me and now he placed a hand on my shoulder. "You boys should go on down an' get yerselves warm," he said. "We kin take care of the rest of it."

"Go on down ta the store," Mr. Johnson said. "My wife has some hot chocolate brewin' on the woodstove. It'll warm ya up quick."

We started down the hill, the wind cutting sharply into our faces. The sun had begun to fade, as the night comes upon you quickly in a Vermont winter, and soon the cold would become even more bitter, more cutting. Before we were too far away I glanced back. My father and Doc Brewster were just lifting the body onto the litter. It was rigid and ramrod straight, like a board being loaded onto a pallet.

When we got to the Johnsons' store Abel's mother fussed over us, concerned that coming across Jesse Brown's body had somehow been a terrible experience. Despite her mother's hovering concern, Abel's nine-year-old sister Rebecca kept asking us questions about the body and how we had come across it, and Mrs. Johnson repeatedly hushed her.

Partly to get us warm, and partly to distract us, Mrs. Johnson fed us all cup after cup of hot chocolate. Later, when she went to take care of customers who had come into the store, Rebecca started in on us again. She was a gangly girl, with long legs and skinny arms, and her small jaw jutted defiantly when she spoke to us.

"Tell me what happened, Abel," she demanded. Her voice had an edge to it, almost as if she were ready to stamp her foot.

"Ma said not ta talk about it," Abel said, glancing off to where his mother had gone.

Rebecca turned to me. "Jubal, you tell me," she insisted. "You gotta."

I shook my head no.

A large grin broke out on Johnny's face and he leaned forward and whispered into Rebecca's ear.

Rebecca had inherited her mother's soft green eyes and strawberry-blond hair, and now those eyes became as large as saucers and her cheeks took on the tint of her hair, and she spun on her heels and hurried off to the front of the store where her mother was working.

"What'd you say to her?" I asked, angry that Johnny had frightened her off that way.

Johnny grinned at me. "I tol' her that old nig was as white as a ghost an' as stiff as a board. Then I tol' her they was puttin' his body in Doc's icehouse an' that I'd take her down there later an' show her."

"You shouldn't of scared her," Abel said.

"No, you shouldn't of. That was dumb and mean-spirited," I snapped.

"Heck, it weren't nothin' ta be scared of," Johnny said. He was still grinning at us, unmoved by our anger. "It was jus' a dead man. It's the ones still walkin' aroun' ya gotta worry 'bout, least that's what my daddy always says."

Reluctantly, Abel and I nodded in agreement, thinking it the manly thing to do, yet deep inside something told me we were wrong. But we were too young to know that. We were only eleven and right then none of us knew how many dead men we would one day see.

CHAPTER ONE

I came down the stairs using the banister for support, what remained of my left arm hanging limp and useless in the folded-up sleeve of my wool shirt. I had been home from the war for nearly six months, living off my father's charity, accepting his offer of a job as the town's deputy constable, and returning to my boyhood room in our small house.

My mother had died giving birth to a stillborn brother when I was only a child, so there had always been just the two of us in the house, and it had created a strong bond between my father and me. Yet the idea of accepting his—or anyone's—charity ground at me. Of course my father refused to think of it as charity. But it was. In addition to the occasional police duties, for which he received a small stipend, a town constable earns his keep by collecting delinquent taxes and settling disputes over fence lines or the ownership of livestock. He receives a small percentage of the taxes collected and fees from the county for his mediation of disputes, which otherwise would have to go to the courts in Burlington. As the elected constable he is allowed to hire deputies when needed, but the number of disputes and the amount of taxes remain constant and all concerned get paid out of the same pot. So in reality my father was giving his crippled son half his income, a fact he justified as something that gave him much needed time off in his approaching old age.

I entered the kitchen and went to the coffee pot my father had started earlier. He had left a note on the kitchen table, which also served as our office, explaining that he had ridden up to Richmond, a larger town to our north, to deposit tax revenues into the town bank account. It was a fairly long trip by horseback and it would be well into the afternoon before he returned.

I finished my coffee and decided to make myself useful and ride up to the Billingsley farm to iron out a dispute about some stray cattle. I slipped on a red-and-black checked jacket and a broad-brimmed Stetson and went out to the barn behind the house to saddle up my horse. As soon as I stepped outside the crisp autumn air assaulted my senses. There is nothing like autumn in Vermont's mountains. We were still a week or two from peak color, but already the hillsides were awash in the red and yellow and orange of the changing leaves. Those that had already fallen lay stiff with the early-morning frost and crunched underfoot as I made my way to the barn.

My horse, Jezebel, was an old bay mare who gave me a sad look as I pulled her saddle from a hook on the wall.

"Don't want to go out yet, eh, girl," I said, soothing her. "It's too early for you, is it? Well, it is for me too, but it's gotta be done." I noted that my father had given her oats and fresh hay before leaving, and I patted her side. "You need the exercise," I said. "You lay about the barn too much and you're getting to be a fat old lady."

Saddling a horse with one arm is a tricky proposition and had taken some practice to learn. But everything was a chore with one arm. Even half a missing limb affected your balance, sometimes making you stumble, always making you feel clumsy and inept. I was setting myself to heave the saddle onto Jezebel's haunches when a voice stopped me.

"Ya need ta be comin' with me, Jubal."

I turned and found Josiah Flood standing in the doorway of the barn. His brown face, under his old Union military cap, had a fearful look spread across it, something I had not seen since I lay wounded in his arms in a Virginia meadow.

"What's wrong?" I asked.

"It's Johnny Harris. He's dead. Somebody's gone an' kilt him."

Johnny's body lay in the rear of the barn behind his father's church. He was on his back, a large bloodstain covering the front of his white shirt. I reached down and needlessly felt for a pulse in his neck. His arms were thrown out, making a cross of his body, and his upturned face held an expression of surprise. The deep blue eyes he had inherited from his father had not yet begun to fade, but they were no longer the eyes I had known since childhood, full of life and laughter and cynicism.

I could feel Josiah standing behind me, feel him staring past me at the body. When I turned back to him a look of angry satisfaction filled his face.

"I ain't sorry he's dead," he said. "I wished 'em dead ever since that day in Spotsylvania."

I nodded, knowing I felt much the same, although it was something I had never spoken aloud. "Don't go saying that to anybody else. They weren't there with us. They wouldn't understand."

He nodded, then looked down at his boots. "I'll keep my place," he said.

His words stung, but they were true enough that no reply was warranted.

"How did you happen on Johnny's body?" I asked, pushing past the unintended insult.

"I ran into Reverend Harris over ta the Johnsons' store las' night, an' he axed me if I could do some work here in the barn. When I came ta do it a bit ago, I found Johnny layin' here dead."

"Is Reverend Harris here?"

Josiah shook his head. "He tol' me him and his missus was goin' outta town las' night, an' that they wasn't gonna be back till tonight aroun' suppertime. Said I could come git my money then."

I bent over and unbuttoned Johnny's shirt. The wound beneath was in the center of his chest. It was thin and circular, but I couldn't tell if it had been caused by a small-caliber handgun or a puncture from a round-bladed tool or knife. I sat back on my haunches.

"You want I should run down the road an' git Doc Pierce?" Josiah asked, almost as if he were reading my thoughts.

"Yes, that would be good. We're gonna need him here to look at the body."

When Josiah left I began searching the area around the body to see if any weapon had been discarded. There was a pile of hay several feet away and I picked up a pitchfork that was leaning against a nearby wall and began raking through the top layer. Nothing appeared. Using the pitchfork to clear away any debris I encountered I searched the far reaches of the barn to see if anything had been thrown into a dark corner. Again, nothing.

A sound behind me caused me to turn. Rebecca Johnson stood framed by the opened double doors of the barn. One hand cupped her brow as she tried to see into the darkened interior. I hurried forward to stop her from entering.

"Jubal, it's you," she said as I came into the light. "Is it true? I met Josiah on the road and he told me Johnny Harris was dead."

I had loved Rebecca Johnson for years but had never mustered the courage to tell her. Yet, I believe she knew. When the war had come and her brother and Johnny and I had gone off to fight she had hugged me fiercely as we prepared to leave and made me promise I would come home to her. And she had written to me as well. Every time Abel received a letter there was one for me written in her graceful hand, telling me all the news from home and urging me to keep myself safe, and with each letter the love I felt for Rebecca deepened. Then came Spotsylvania, and what the generals called the Battle of the Wilderness, the place where Abel was killed and I was wounded, and where Johnny was captured and taken to Andersonville Prison. When I came home, half the man who had left four years earlier, I had barely spoken to Rebecca, not wanting to see the hurt and pity in her eyes as she looked at my mutilated body, not wanting to expose the love I felt for her and then await the rejection that was certain to come.

When I had left for the war, Rebecca was a nineteen-year-old girl who had already caught the eye of every young man in the surrounding towns. When I returned four years later, a deep maturity had taken hold of her, making her even more appealing, and I wondered if it was brought about by the death of her only brother and the subsequent loss of her grieving mother. But then, we had all matured. Death seems to have that effect.

Now, framed by the wide doorway, she was even more beautiful than I remembered, tall and slender, her delicate features framed by flowing reddish-blond hair and set off by soft green eyes.

I towered over her, having inherited much of my father's size, and I stood slightly to the side as I spoke to her, keeping my crippled arm away from her and as much out of view as possible. "Yes, it's true," I said. "It looks as though someone killed him."

She stared into my face, then glanced at the Navy Colt I had strapped to my hip after Josiah told me that someone had killed Johnny. She gazed past me into the darkened interior of the barn. "I'm not surprised someone killed him," she said. She looked back at me and took in the wonder that her words must have covered my face with. "He left here a pleasant boy and came home a very cruel man. Certainly you saw the difference."

I didn't know how to respond and was saved from further comment by the arrival of Josiah and Doc Pierce.

After directing Doc to the body I turned back to Rebecca. "I can't have anyone inside the barn," I said softly. "But I would like you to do me a favor."

She looked at me curiously. "What is that, Jubal?"

"I'd like to soften the blow for Reverend and Mrs. Harris as much as possible. They're due to return home this evening, and I wonder if you could keep a watch for them and send word to me when they get back. It would also be good if you and your father could be there when I tell them."

Rebecca nodded. "Yes, of course. I'll go sit with Mrs. Harris and I'm sure my father will want to go to Reverend Harris. Neither of them should be alone when you tell them."

I thanked Rebecca and began to turn away when she reached out and placed her hand on my right arm, stopping me. She stared into my face. "Jubal, have I done something to offend you?" she asked.

I was stunned by the unexpected question and I gave a clumsy, stammering reply. "Why no, no, you haven't . . . done anything."

"Then why do you avoid me, Jubal? Certainly you know how much I care for you. I grew up caring for you. But you've been so distant since you returned from the war."

I studied my boots, then spoke without raising my eyes to her. "Things are different. I'm different."

Her eyes became sad. "If your feelings for me have changed, I can accept that. I have no choice but to accept it. But if you're avoiding me because of your wound—"

I spoke quickly, stopping her before words of pity reached her lips. "I have to get back inside."

Rebecca kept her eyes fixed on mine. Then she reached up and brushed an unruly strand of curly brown hair from my forehead. "I understand, Jubal. I'll send for you when Reverend and Mrs. Harris get home."

I watched her turn and walk away, and I wondered if she could ever truly understand—if anyone could.

Doc Pierce was finishing his examination of the body when I squatted beside him. He glanced at me and shook his head. "It was a single wound, straight to the heart," he began.

Doc had aged over the years. Now close to sixty, his body had grown thick, while his hair had turned a snowy white and thinned considerably. His full cheeks were rosy, in part from the autumn chill, in larger part from a growing use of brandy in the evenings. Since the war began he had worked several days a week in a Burlington hospital, treating the returning wounded, and he told me after I too had returned that the insane waste he had witnessed had filled him with near total despair for the human race.

"Was it a small-caliber pistol?" I asked.

"No, definitely not a pistol. My best guess, until I can examine him more thoroughly, is a handheld weapon with a thin, round blade, perhaps an awl or an ice pick. Could even have been a fencer's foil, although I've never heard of one in these parts. But one thing's certain: it was a single thrust, straight through the breastbone and into the heart."

I peered down at Johnny's body. He still had traces of frailty from the months he had spent in Andersonville Prison, and the look of surprise was still frozen on his face. Did he know the person who had killed him? Was that the cause of the surprise?

"All those years of war, months and months in that wretched prison," Doc said. "And now, to have it end here in his own barn. It doesn't seem right. You'd think the boy had earned himself a long, quiet life."

I had always admired Doc. He was the most educated man in our village and one of the smartest I had ever known, and even at an early age I had recognized that and had tried to pattern my actions, even the way I spoke, after him. But his intelligence had failed him this time. Johnny had not earned himself a long, quiet life. This is what he'd earned. I glanced up at Josiah, standing behind Doc Pierce, and I could tell he was thinking the same thing.

CHAPTER TWO

The two young women had stripped down to their shifts and waded into the water. We had seen two farm horses tied to a tree on the road that ran along the top edge of the Huntington Gorge, and figured we'd find a couple of farm boys swimming in one of the many deep pools that dotted the river.

We had not expected this and the three of us were now lying on a ledge high above the deep pool in which the women were swimming, staring down at them, at the way their wet shifts pressed against their breasts and thighs as they climbed out of the pool and laid back on a large boulder.

We glanced at each other then back at the women. It was mid-July and ungodly hot and the sight of the women made it seem even hotter. We were fourteen and had seen very little of women's bodies and certainly nothing as erotically pleasing as this.

"I'm gonna jump in," Johnny whispered.

The ledge was thirty feet above the pool, which was a good twelve feet deep, and we normally entered it by jumping from the ledge rather than climb down the twisting, rocky trail that led to the river.

"You can't," Abel whispered back.

"We'll all jump," Johnny insisted. "One at a time, just like always."

"They'll skin us if we do," I said.

"We'll jus' tell 'em we never saw 'em down there." Johnny grinned at us. "Don' ya wanna see 'em up close?" He paused, putting on a serious face. "Anybody who don' jump after me is a sissy fer all time."

With that he scrambled to his feet, let out a whoop, just as he always did, and leaped from the ledge, his thin arms flailing in the air. As soon as he hit the water, Abel was up whooping and jumping after him, and I wasn't sure if it was from fear of being a sissy for all time, or really wanting to see the women up close. I jumped third, and deep down I knew my reason and it had nothing to do with being called a sissy.

By the time I surfaced the young women were screaming at us, calling us peeping Toms and claiming that their brothers would come after us and thump us good. Close up I recognized them. They were from a farm that lay halfway along the road to Richmond that I had stopped at once with my father. They did indeed have brothers, one that was well into his twenties, an unlikely sort to hunt down the sons of a local lawman, a minister, and a storekeeper, and a second one who was younger and smaller than us.

Johnny immediately started to smooth things over, his eyes never leaving the women. "We never saw ya. Honest ta God, we never did. We always come here an' jump straight in," he pleaded.

One of the women followed his gaze which was fixed on the outline of her breasts and the erect nipples that pressed against her wet shift. She got to her feet and brazenly put her hands on her hips. "Well, ya sure are seein' us now," she snapped. "So ya better turn away while we get ourselves dressed. I know who ya are; I know who yer daddy is too. I've been ta his church. An' I've got a mind ta ride on down ta Jerusalem's Landing an' tell him whatcha done."

Johnny was treading water, but raised his hands in surrender. "I'm turnin' aroun', I'm turnin' aroun'." He glanced at us, fighting to keep a grin off his face. "You boys turn aroun' too," he said. "We gotta give these here ladies some privacy."

The women got dressed, whispering to each other as they did, and I was confident there would be no consequences for our prank, and certainly no brothers coming to thump us. Women and girls who grew up on farms had seen pretty much everything when it came to animals going at each other, so there was very little that embarrassed them. We, however, were village boys and anything even hinting at sex was a great curiosity.

Later, when the women were gone, we were still laughing and talking about our adventure. Johnny summed it all up in typical fashion.

"Did ya see the bosoms on that one who was yellin' at us?" he asked. "I'm surprised her pa ain't put her in the barn an' turned her into a milker."

Jerusalem's Landing, Vermont, 1865

I answered the knock on my door and found Rebecca standing there.

"Reverend Harris and his wife just got home," she said. "My father and his new wife are waiting for you to get there and then they'll stop by to be with them."

"I thought you were going with your father," I said.

"He preferred that his wife go with him." There was an edge to her voice and I thought I understood why.

Rebecca's mother had died seven months ago. When word had come about Abel's death she'd become deeply depressed. Some said she'd died of a broken heart, others believed that her son being buried in far-off Virginia had driven her to despair. In any event she had jumped or fallen into the river and drowned. I had been in a military hospital for almost a year, recovering from my wounds, then assigned as a clerk to the medical staff, and by the time I returned home Rebecca's father had remarried, telling friends that he needed a wife to help him with the store.

Rebecca's stepmother was a war widow herself, her young husband having died early in the conflict. She was not much older than I, and Walter Johnson's remarriage to a young widow so soon after his first wife's death had set local tongues wagging. It was something that had obviously hurt his only remaining child as well.

Seeing Rebecca's pain I wanted to reach out to her, draw her close to me with my one good arm, and comfort her, but knew I could not, certain Rebecca would not favor such an awkward gesture from a one-armed man.

"I'll walk you to the store," I said.

I had hoped my father would be back before the Harris's returned, but it was already nearing eight and I concluded that he had decided to spend the night in Richmond. There was a woman there he favored and I didn't begrudge him time with her. Still, telling the Harris's that their son had been murdered was something I would have liked to pass on to someone else.

The distance between my home and the Johnsons' store is no more than fifty yards, with the church and parsonage almost directly across the road. When we reached the store I stared at the lighted windows of the parsonage, trying to imagine what I would say when Reverend Harris or his wife answered the door.

Rebecca, who had not spoken since we started out, now seemed to intuitively understand my concern.

"Just tell them as simply as you can, Jubal," she said. "They'll be shocked by what you say, just as my family and I were shocked when we learned about Abel. They won't need details. They'll be too numbed to understand them anyway. Later, if they want to know more, you or your father can tell them." She paused and reached out to touch my good arm. "I'll tell my father and his wife that it's time for them to go to the Harris's."

I nodded, realizing that I didn't know Walter Johnson's new wife very well. I had spoken to her in their store, but only casually, and I suddenly wished there was some way Rebecca could take her place.

Walter Johnson and his wife Mary were already crossing the road when I knocked on the parsonage door, still wondering how I would deliver this terrible message to people I had known all my life.

I had spoken to Doc Pierce late in the afternoon and he confirmed that Johnny had been killed by a slender, rounded weapon akin to an ice pick or an awl, one thrust to the heart. Awls are used to make holes in wood or leather and I had not noticed any wood- or leather-work in the barn, and I knew the Harris's icebox was in a shed off the kitchen. I would check the barn again, but if nothing was found it would mean that whoever killed Johnny had probably brought the weapon with them, not picked it up in a moment of anger. I had thought about that for some time, and the more I did the more sense it seemed to make. Someone had brought a weapon with them out of fear that they might need it to defend themselves, or out of simple, cold-blooded hatred.

When the door opened Walter Johnson and his new wife were already standing behind me. They both seemed very nervous and distraught. Reverend Harris smiled at us, his eyes curious but not concerned.

"Jubal, Walter, Mary, what a surprise. Is something wrong? Do you need me to go somewhere with you?"

I realized what a natural response that was coming from a minister, given all the times people must have knocked at his door, asking him to come to the bedside of a sick or dying member of his church.

"I'm afraid I have bad news, Reverend," I began, deciding to heed Rebecca's advice.

Reverend Harris began to stutter. "Wha, what is it?" His eyes had grown fearful, his body rigid.

"It's about Johnny," I said. "He was killed today . . . murdered, by the looks of it. Josiah found him in the barn when he came to do some work for you."

Mrs. Harris had caught my words and came rushing across the room. "Virgil, what is he saying? Virgil! Not our Johnny. It's not our Johnny who's dead. Tell him it's not our Johnny!"

Reverend Harris put his arms around his wife, and Walter and his wife Mary immediately went to their sides. Mrs. Harris began to sob uncontrollably and Mary placed trembling hands on her back and arm, leading her to a sofa. Reverend Harris watched her for several moments, not seeming to know what to say or do. Finally he turned back to me.

"Where is my boy?" he asked.

"Doc has the body at his office," I said.

"I want to go to him."

I nodded, lowering my voice. "Doc has already . . . examined him . . . internally," I said. "It might be best if Mrs. Harris didn't come."

My words struck him like a slap and I saw him wince in pain. "Yes, I understand." He turned to Walter. "Can you and Mary stay with my wife?"

"Of course, Virgil," Walter said.

Johnny lay on an examination table, his body drained of color. Virgil Harris wept over his son as Doc Pierce briefly explained what had happened.

"I know it's of little comfort, Virgil, but I'm certain the boy died quickly and did not suffer."

The minister slowly nodded. "When can I take him for services and burial?" he asked, his voice soft and hoarse.

Doc glanced at me. "I have no further need of the body," he said. "I'm certain about the cause of death."

I turned to the minister. "I'll need to have access to your barn, but I won't need the body."

Doc stepped forward and placed his hands on Virgil Harris's shoulders. "You go ahead and get ready to bury your boy. I'll keep the body here until you're in need of it."

CHAPTER THREE

We could hear them screaming as the flames roared all around. The wounded lay in the no-man's-land between the two armies, awaiting the next assault that would allow us to drag them to safety. Then the fire had started. I don't know if it was caused by a stray artillery shell, or if it was deliberately set by one side or the other. The Wilderness in Spotsylvania County was a nearly impenetrable area of scrub brush and forest, covering more than seventy square miles, and chosen as a point of conflict by Lee's Army of Northern Virginia to limit the effectiveness of the Union's superior artillery.

Abel and Johnny and I were holed up behind a fallen tree awaiting the command to again charge the Confederate line. But the fire had ended that. Now we just waited and listened as the wounded, Union and Rebels alike, screamed in horror as they burned to death in the raging brush fire.

"Somebody's gotta go help them boys." Abel was staring at me as he spoke, his face covered with dirt and ash, his eyes wide with the terror of what he was proposing. He looked behind us. "Where the hell's all our officers? Why ain't they sendin' us out ta git 'em?"

"They're keepin' their asses safe, jus' like always," Johnny snapped. "Jus' like all of us gotta do, else we'll be layin' out there gettin' burned up too."

Another scream reached my ears as the fire reached another soldier.

It was long and sustained and filled with terror, and it cut me to my gut. "We gotta go and get anybody we can," I said. I looked at Abel and saw the fear in his eyes, the same fear I felt myself. Abel gave a short, brusque nod and I knew he was ready to go with me. I turned to Johnny, who stared at me as though I were speaking in a foreign tongue. I kicked him in the thigh. "Come on, while there's still smoke to give us cover." I had been promoted to sergeant several months earlier, so I outranked them both, and I made it sound as much like an order as I could.

Abel and I eased ourselves over the fallen tree and began to crawl forward. When we were halfway to the flaming brush I looked back and saw that Johnny had finally begun to follow.

Miraculously, no one fired a shot in our direction. Maybe the thick smoke hid us from the Rebels; maybe they were just glad to see someone going to the dying men, hoping just like us that the screaming would stop.

When we reached the fire we used our canteens to wet our bandannas and cover our noses and mouths. Even so the smoke pressed into our lungs and burned our eyes, and the heat from the burning brush made us feel like we were being roasted on a spit.

Abel and I each grabbed a soldier by the collar. Their uniforms were covered in ash and soot and you couldn't tell if they wore blue or gray, or even where or how badly they were wounded. They were breathing and peering up at us with pleading, fear-filled eyes, and that was all that mattered.

As I dragged my soldier back I passed Johnny. "Go get somebody. Nobody's shooting at us."

"Nobody's shootin' at *you*," Johnny growled back. "They're waitin' to blow *my* ass ta hell an' back."

We had made three trips to the fire before some officer saw us and ordered others to help, but by then the flames had overtaken the battlefield and the screams began to lessen and finally stop, and we knew there was no point in going out again, that there would be no one left to save.

When the smoke cleared the shooting started again, each side taking potshots at the other, the mercy we had felt an hour earlier disappearing with the smoke. We stayed low behind the log and I looked back at the boys we had pulled to safety. There were nearly a dozen and I could tell now that at least two wore Rebel uniforms. One of the Rebs stared back at me, a mixture of gratitude and confusion in his eyes. He had a wound in his belly and I could see his intestines oozing out from a tear in his shirt, and I knew the man would die. But at least he hadn't burned to death.

Johnny crawled up beside me and followed my gaze. "We sure wasted our time savin' him," he said.

I turned back to the field. The smoke was largely gone now, and I could see the burned bodies still steaming from the fire, and the smell of charred meat floated back to me. I drew a long, weary breath and then regretted that I had.

Jerusalem's Landing, Vermont, 1865

My father came home the next morning. I explained what had happened, told him what I had done so far. He seemed satisfied, which pleased me, and we walked down the road to the Harris's barn so he could see where Johnny had been killed.

Aside from my mutilated arm, I had grown into a fair-sized man, tall and rawboned with my father's broad shoulders. But I was still half a head and a good thirty pounds smaller than he. My father also had wide, heavy features, while mine were more delicate and pronounced and came, along with my curly brown hair and hazel eyes, from the mother I could barely remember. But there was no question we were father and son, and people often said that my movements and manner of walking mimicked his. I do not know if this was from heredity or by unconscious design.

When we reached the parsonage my father went inside to speak with Reverend Harris and his wife. When I had left the Harris's yesterday I asked them to keep everyone away from the barn until I had searched it more thoroughly, and I went there now to make sure nothing had been disturbed.

I was standing near the spot where I had first seen Johnny's body, and I stared down at the dirt floor and scattered straw still heavily stained by the blood that had poured from his body.

My father came up beside me. "I take it this is where Josiah found him," he said. He paused. "Are ya sure he din' have nothin' more ta do with it?"

"As sure as I can be," I said.

He thought that over. "Well, ya went through four years a war wit the boy, so I figure ya know him better'n all of us." He turned to face me. "Ya got any ideas 'bout who mighta done it?"

I shook my head slowly. "Johnny and I haven't stayed close since I got back home. But I've heard some things, stories about him making eyes at women he should have stayed away from. To be honest, I kind of ignored it."

"Married women?" my father asked. "Who'd ya hear this from?"

"It was just talk going around. You know how that is. Everybody knows everybody's business here. And with some, what they don't know they make up."

He nodded. "Yeah, I heard some things too. But it was mostly cracker-barrel talk 'bout how the boy came back even wilder than afore he left. I just chalked it up ta the boy blowin' off steam he'd built up in that Rebel prison he ended up in."

I thought about that, about Johnny's time in Andersonville Prison and all the horrors I'd heard about the place, the starving, malnourished prisoners, the rampant disease. But I also knew what Johnny had done before he was captured. I decided I'd keep that to myself for now.

My father and I searched the barn to no avail. Whoever killed Johnny had obviously taken the weapon with him. As we prepared to leave he placed a hand on my shoulder. "I want ya ta follow up on what Johnny was doin' since he got back. You'll do better talkin' to the younger folks than I will. Ya find yourself dealin' with older folks who ain't talkin' too freely, or if ya think ya need my help on anything, ya just let me know." He glanced down at the pistol on my hip. "I'm glad ta see ya had the sense to strap that on. You keep wearin' it. Right now we don't know who killed that boy or what he's gonna do when we find out who he is. But ya kin be sure of one thing: he ain't gonna wanna be caught."

Johnny's open coffin lay in the Harris's sitting room. He had been dressed in his Union uniform, the two medals he'd earned pinned to his breast. They were simple unit citations, but his parents were obviously proud he had received them and someone had taken care to polish them until they shined brightly.

It was early evening and the oil lamps were already lit, giving the sitting room a hazy glow. I stood quietly before the bier. Josiah Flood stood beside me. Josiah had been with the three of us throughout the war, assigned as a litter-bearer for the medical unit that followed our regiment into battle. It was one of the more dangerous jobs. Litter-bearers were lightly armed, usually carrying only a pistol, and of necessity they often performed their duties out in the open where they were easy targets for the Rebs. Many Union officers preferred to use Negroes because they considered them expendable.

After expressing our condolences to the Harris's, Josiah and I by-passed the food that had been laid out for guests and moved to the wide veranda that ran along three sides of the parsonage.

"Johnny sure is lookin' like a reg'ler hero in his uniform," Josiah said, his words laden with sarcasm.

I nodded, but said nothing. The air was crisp and cold and, as with any change in weather, I could feel a tingling that seemed centered in my missing arm. The doctors told me to expect it, warning I would even feel pain or muscle spasms where none could possibly exist. When this happened I rubbed the stump and it usually went away, although that was something I refused to do when anyone else was present.

"There's been some talk about Johnny acting wild since he got back home," I said. "I know you hear things that are being said. You hear anything about that?"

Josiah smiled and looked out into the night. "Those two years ya spent at the college done made ya sly, ya know that, Jubal?"

With Doc Pierce's help I had gotten a scholarship to the University of Vermont and had attended for two years before the war broke out. When I returned, despite my father's and Doc Pierce's urging, I found I had little interest in going back.

"Sly or not, tell me what you've heard."

Josiah stared at me for several moments. He had grown into a tall, thin, wiry man, with a broad nose and heavy lips that broke into an easy smile whenever something pleased him. He had carried me to safety after a mortar shell had blown me halfway across a Virginia meadow, and I knew without question that I owed him my life. He was also a Ne-gro, and as such someone the good white people of Jerusalem's Landing spoke in front of as though he did not exist.

"What I heard, or what I seen?" he asked.

I inclined my head to the side, questioning his response.

"Ya tellin' me ya ain't heard 'bout Johnny an' my sister Heddy?"

"Not a word."

Josiah smiled at me. It was not a warm smile. "Well, maybe ya ain't as sly as I was thinkin'."

Josiah's sister Heddy was seventeen years old, a plain but pleasant young girl who earned a living doing domestic chores for some of the town's more prosperous families. She was slightly dull-witted and Josiah provided her a room in his small cabin in exchange for some basic cooking and cleaning.

"Why don't you tell me what you're talking about?" I said.

Josiah drew a long breath. "It was 'bout two months ago, durin' tha' week when it gots so hot."

I nodded, urging him to continue.

"Well, I quit work early, the heat was so bad, and when I got ta my cabin I found Johnny forcin' hisself on my sister."

"Raping her?" I asked.

He studied his shoes, then looked up and shook his head. "Ya know Heddy's a bit slow, that it don' take much ta talk her inta anythin'. Well, Johnny, he done talked her inta takin' off her shirt, an' when I gots there he had her up against the back a my ol' shed an' he was runnin' his hands all over her. Weren't no question where he wanted ta go, an' woulda iffen I din' come home early."

"So what did you do?"

A slow, unhappy smile formed on Josiah's face. "I threw his ass offen my sister an' my land."

"Did you two fight?"

"Wasn't much of a fight," Josiah said. "I grabbed him an' pulled him off Heddy an' threw him onna groun'." He paused, then continued, "An' maybe I kicked him a time or two."

"That must of riled him up a bit," I said.

"A bit, but there was an ol' pitchfork leanin' up against the shed an' I took hold of it, an' he moved off right smart . . . said he'd make me answer fer what I done later."

"And did he?"

"Never said another word ta me, an' whenever we came across each other he jus' looked right through me . . . like I wasn't even there."

I thought over what Josiah had said. "Why'd you think I knew about this?" I asked.

"I figured Johnny woulda tol' ya."

"Why?"

"Yer his frien' . . . his white frien'," he said.

"Johnny and I haven't been friends since that time in Spotsylvania. You know that, Josiah."

He looked at me and I could see regret in his eyes. "Truth is, there's times when I don't know nothin' 'bout white people," he said.

I remained on the veranda after Josiah left. Walter Johnson and his wife Mary arrived to pay their respects, although Rebecca was noticeably absent. I asked after her and was told she'd been delayed at the store and would be along presently. Rebecca arrived a short time later, nodded a greeting to me, and went inside. I decided to wait so I could speak to her about Johnny, about something she had said about him.

While I waited I glanced in the window and noticed that Rebecca had chosen not to sit with her father and stepmother, but was quietly speaking to Reverend Harris and his wife.

When she came outside I asked if I could have a moment of her time. The question brought an odd look to her face.

"You're always welcome to my time, Jubal," she said. "I hope you will always remember that."

I took her elbow and guided her to the far end of the veranda where we could find some privacy. Standing in the muted light that came from a nearby window I was again struck by Rebecca's beauty, the soft glow that seemed to radiate from her face, the gentleness that flowed from her emerald eyes, and I had to force myself to speak quickly or risk becoming mute and appearing like some lovesick schoolboy.

"You said something the other day, something about Johnny," I began. "You said he left for the war as a pleasant boy and returned a cruel man." I paused, but she said nothing. "What happened to make you feel that way?"

She stared at me with open curiosity. "Didn't you notice the change in him? You grew up with Johnny, we both did. He was mischievous, just as we all were. But none of us were cruel. When Johnny came home you could see the cruelty in him. It flowed out of his eyes when he looked at you. When you got home you must have seen that. Haven't you heard things about him since you got home?"

I felt suddenly embarrassed. I had had one very brief, very violent confrontation with Johnny shortly after I returned home, and I had found little satisfaction in it. I had spent almost a year in a military hospital in Virginia, not only recovering from my wounds but also nursing the overwhelming pity I felt for myself. Since returning home, that pity had only grown and I hadn't paid much attention to anything but myself. Now that realization reached out and shook me.

I studied my boots for a moment. "I guess I haven't noticed a lot of things. And I haven't paid attention to the things I've heard, especially things about Johnny. To be honest, I avoided Johnny, and everything about him, as much as I possibly could."

"You've avoided everyone, Jubal." She touched the empty sleeve of my shirt, and it startled me and made me take a step back. She stared at me. "Just as you are now," she said, her voice becoming little more than a whisper. "Come back to us, Jubal. Come back to *me*. My brother never came home. You lost your arm, don't lose everything else because of it."

I looked out into the night. "It's very hard, Rebecca."

"Yes, I'm certain it is. But the war took Abel away from me. I don't want it to take you too."

I turned back to her, but had difficulty meeting her eyes. "Tell me about the cruelty you saw in Johnny," I said.

She shook her head, but I couldn't tell if it was about Johnny, or because I had avoided what she had said to me. I suspected it was the latter. She turned and now it was she who stared out into the dark night. "He came into the store quite often, especially over the last few months. It was the way he looked at people, Jubal, almost as if he had contempt for everyone he met, people he had known all his life. And it was also the things he said. We spoke about Abel right after he came home, and I asked him if he was with my brother when he died. He said he wasn't, but he knew what had happened. He said Abel died because he was a fool." She turned back to me, her eyes filled with tears. "Is that true, Jubal?"

Rage built inside me. I had been with Abel, had seen him draw his final breath. I knew why he had died. But I could tell Rebecca none of it, not now . . . perhaps never.

"No, it's not true," I said. "It was a stupid thing for him to say . . . stupid and cruel. Did he ever say that to your father?"

"No, not that I ever heard." Her jaw had tightened when I mentioned her father.

"Did he speak to your mother?"

Again, her jaw tightened. "Yes, he did. He came home two weeks before she drowned, and she went to him to ask him about Abel's grave. She was deeply, deeply wounded that her son's body was buried so far away. So she went to him looking for some comfort. But Johnny had nothing to offer except more pain, and my mother told me that he seemed to take great pleasure in the terrible things he told her, in the suffering it caused her." She lowered her eyes. "Two weeks later she was dead."

"What exactly did he say?"

"He said the boys who died at the Wilderness were all thrown into a pit together, Rebels and Union alike, and then covered over. It was a lie. I wrote to the army and they told me exactly where Abel is buried. They assured me it is a solitary, marked grave that our family can visit. But my mother was already dead by the time that letter arrived."

My rage was still boiling, yet I could think of no way to comfort her. "I'm sorry," I said. It was all I could manage.

CHAPTER FOUR

dgar Billingsley plucked his banjo and Cory Jimmo sawed away at his country fiddle in a rousing rendition of "Oh! Susanna." They were seated on the bandstand on our small town green where more than three hundred townspeople had gathered, some slapping their thighs or stomping their feet to the music, others forming lines at tables tended by women from the Baptist church, each one laden with home-cooked food.

My house was opposite the green and my father had set up picnic tables on the wide front porch so people could sit in the shade and eat their Fourth of July lunches. It was something he did every year, always winking at me and telling me it was "good politics."

Abel and Johnny and I wandered through the crowd, our pockets stuffed with fireworks, mostly miniature explosives called "salutes," that we would drop behind young girls as we passed by and then laugh raucously as they squealed with mostly false fear. We were sixteen and full of ourselves and even the stern looks we got from some of the older women had little effect on us. All that mattered was getting the attention of the girls we were trying to impress.

"The three of you are being very annoying." The soft yet stern voice had come from behind us, and when I turned I found Abel's sister Rebecca staring at us. "If you're not careful you're going to hurt someone with those dumb salutes," she added.

Rebecca was fourteen and something miraculous had begun to happen to her. The skinny, awkward little sister who had tagged along after us for years had experienced a physical transformation. Almost overnight, or so it seemed, breasts had begun to appear, hips suddenly became more rounded, and there was a new graceful sway to her movements that I had never noticed before. Abel said she had also become impossible to live with, and would get mad or just burst into tears at the drop of a hat.

"It don' matter whatcha say ta her. Either she's mad, or she's cryin'. Then my ma gits mad an' I git it from both ends. My ma says Rebecca's developin' early, whatever that means, and that I gotta be extra nice ta her." He rolled his eyes. "I don' remember nobody bein' extra nice ta me when I was fourteen."

Now she stood before us and I was afraid to answer, not wanting to make her mad, and certainly not wanting to make her cry.

"We're just havin' fun," I said.

"Well, maybe everybody doesn't think it's fun." She tilted her head to one side and her voice had become almost haughty.

"The girls don't seem to mind," I said, a bit defensively.

"They just want the same thing you want, a chance to show off."

Her words defeated me and I didn't know how to respond without saying something mean.

"Look, we have a plan for a real good prank that we're gonna pull off as soon as it gets dark." I glanced at Johnny and Abel. "How about we let Rebecca help us?" I asked the others.

"Why do ya wanna include a girl, especially one who's still a little kid?" Johnny said.

I turned to Abel for support. He just shrugged and I wondered if he feared driving Rebecca to tears and having to deal with his mother.

Rebecca was glaring at Johnny, and it made him squirm a bit; now she turned back to me. "What are you talking about?" she demanded.

I glanced around at the crowd. "Let's get somewhere where nobody can hear us," I suggested.

"Where ya wanna go?" Abel asked.

Rebecca looked at me with suspicion. "What are you up to, Jubal?"

"Let's go to my barn and we can show you what we've got," I said.

We had hidden our special firework in the hayloft. One of the drummers who sold goods to Abel's father had offered it to Abel on the sly. All Abel had to do was say how much he liked the cheddar cheese the drummer was trying to get his father to lay in. Abel had taken the bribe, and a wheel of the drummer's cheddar now sat on the counter of the town store.

I climbed down from the hayloft carrying the special firework. The drummer had told Abel that it was called a Roman candle, and while we weren't really certain what it would do, he had assured Abel that "folk's jaws will surely drop" when we set it off.

I held up the firework for Rebecca to see. It had a flat base with a foot-long tube rising out of it.

"What does it do?" Rebecca asked. "Does it explode?"

"I hope not," Johnny replied. "It's as big as a stick a dynamite."

"It don't explode," Abel said. "The drummer said it sets off a kinda display of bright lights. A real shocker, he said, but it ain't gonna blow anythin' up. But that's why we wanna do it after dark. It sure as heck is gonna surprise a lot of people."

"We'll be Fourth of July heroes," Johnny said. There was a wide grin spread across his face and his eyes glittered, but I couldn't tell if he was being serious, or making fun of us all, himself included.

"Where are you gonna set it off?" Rebecca asked.

"Right on the bandstand," Abel said.

"And you can help us do it," I suggested.

"How?" Rebecca's voice held a note of suspicion, but her eyes sparkled with excitement.

"You could help sneak it up on the bandstand," Johnny said. "Kinda hide it under yer skirt."

"Yeah," I added. "Then kind of ease it down on the floor, someplace where we can sneak up along the outside of the bandstand and light it up."

A slow smile spread across Rebecca's face. "I can do that," she said.

Full dark came at eight o'clock and we waited patiently for Edgar Billingsley and Cory Jimmo to take a break from their music and clear the bandstand. As soon as they did Rebecca slowly climbed the stairs acting as if she just wanted to be able to look out over the crowd. When she got to the far end of the bandstand she stooped down as though picking up something she had dropped, then quickly stood, walked to the stairs, and climbed back down into the crowd. At the back of the bandstand, where no one could easily see it, stood the Roman candle she had left behind.

Abel and Johnny and I approached that side of the bandstand as casually as we could.

"I'm gonna light it," Abel said, opening a box of wooden matches he had taken from his father's store.

"Why you?" Johnny demanded. "We should pull straws or somethin'."

"Cause I'm the one who got it," Abel said. "I even got the matches."

"Well I got matches too," Johnny countered.

"No, Abel's right," I said. "He got us the firework, so he gets the right to light it up."

Johnny grumbled but finally agreed. Rebecca had joined us and now she and Johnny and I stood shoulder to shoulder so we could shield Abel from view as he lit the fuse. As soon as the fuse was going all four of us moved back.

Josiah Flood came up to us. "Whatcha all doin'?" he asked.

"Shh," Johnny hissed. "Jus' watch."

It took several long seconds for the fuse to burn down and for the Roman candle to begin to spit out its balls of colored flame, each one coming with a whoosh of air that shot it up into the rafters of the bandstand.

"Oh, shit," Abel whispered.

We watched in horror as the bandstand caught fire.

"You boys in trouble now," Josiah said. "I don' wanna be no place near ya." He turned and moved quickly away from us.

"Abel, what have you done?" Rebecca asked. Her eyes were wide in disbelief.

"Oh my God," Johnny said. "We are gonna get skinned fer sure."

As the Roman candle spit its last fiery ball, I saw my father race up onto the bandstand. He had a blanket in his hands that he had plucked from the lawn and he began beating back the flames. Others came up behind him with buckets of water and within minutes the fire had been extinguished.

The four of us were slowly easing back into the crowd when my father's voice boomed down at us: "You kids jus' hold it right there. Don't ya take another step."

My father hurdled the bandstand railing with one hand and took two long strides to where we stood.

"It was them, constable," one of the churchwomen snapped, pointing a finger in our direction. "It was them boys fer sure. They been settin' off firecrackers all day."

My father towered over us, his eyes hard and angry. "You three boys intendin' ta burn this whole town to the ground, or was the bandstand gonna be enough?"

No one said anything. I glanced at Rebecca who stood off to one side. She looked back at me. She seemed terrified. Then her back stiffened. "Mr. Foster, I helped too," she said. "It was supposed to be a display of pretty lights. It wasn't supposed to do anything bad."

My father stared down at Rebecca and shook his head. "Well it sure did light up the night." He turned back to us boys. "You all see the damage ya done?" he asked.

We all nodded.

"Well, it looks ta me like the three of ya"—he paused and peered back at Rebecca—"like the *four* of ya are gonna have some work ta do this summer."

Martinsburg, Virginia, 1861

We moved through a tree line on the outskirts of Hoke's Run, searching out the Confederate force that was retreating before our advancing line. It was early summer in the first year of the war and it was our first battle. Johnny and Abel and I had been among several hundred Vermonters who had been seconded to Major General Robert Patterson's division on the Maryland border as it prepared to cross the Potomac River and engage Rebel forces at Martinsburg, Virginia.

On July 2, two Union brigades crossed the river near Williamsport and marched on the main road toward Martinsburg, where we encountered a single Confederate brigade that almost immediately began to fall back before our superior force. Later we would learn that it had been nothing more than a delaying tactic, luring us to the west and diverting our southerly advance, thereby taking pressure off Confederate forces in the Shenandoah Valley. In three weeks those delaying tactics would help secure a Confederate victory at the First Battle of Bull Run near Manassas, while our force was benignly encamped at Harper's Ferry.

We, of course, knew nothing of the tactics. We were just three boys exhilarated by our first encounter with Rebel troops who fled before us.

"These Rebs are just gonna wear us out chasin' 'em," Johnny said as he moved through the tree line, his rifle at port arms.

"Maybe that's their victory plan," Abel said. "Just get us so damn tired chasin' their asses that we up an' quit an' head on home."

Before I could add my own comment to the mix a minie ball struck a tree inches from Abel's head and we all hit the ground.

Abel spit dirt out of his mouth. "Sumbitch, I think they heard what I said."

A sergeant crawled up beside us. "There's a Rebel company massing behind that hedgerow over yonder. I expect they'll be charging us, so get yourselves ready. Check your loads and fix bayonets."

We had been issued muzzle-loading Springfield muskets, with the promise that they'd soon be replaced with breech-loading Spencer carbines. Our cap-and-ball sidearms were a hodgepodge of varying calibers. Mine was a six-shot .36-caliber Navy Colt, while Abel and Johnny carried the heavier .44-caliber 1860 Colts. In short, we had gotten whatever the quartermaster had at that given moment, and ammunition for all weapons was severely limited.

I rolled over on my back and fixed my bayonet to my Springfield, then checked to make sure my Colt revolver was fully loaded. I glanced over at Johnny and Abel and they each looked as fearful as I felt. Tremors moved along my legs and arms and I rolled over on my stomach and tried to ignore it.

The reason Vermonters had been seconded to General Patterson's division as sharpshooters was our demonstrated ability as marksmen. Almost every boy in Vermont grows up hunting deer, which is a mainstay of our winter meat, and as such we could usually be counted on to hit what we aimed at. Of course the deer we hunted didn't charge us in force, or shoot back, and combined with the trembling in my arms, I wasn't certain how all that would affect the accuracy of my aim.

The Rebel attack came without warning, as several hundred surged out into the small meadow that separated us, screaming like wild men when they moved into the open ground. Only fifty of us had set off into the tree line to flush out Rebel forces, but now fire erupted on both of our flanks and I realized that more troops had been brought up out of our sight.

I fired my first shot of the war and missed my target. Rolling over on my back I quickly began to reload. As I did I heard the concussion of artillery in the rear, and when I looked back the meadow erupted with three successive blasts as twelve-pound howitzer rounds, loaded with grapeshot, sliced into the advancing Rebs like a scythe. The howitzers were devastating at 250 yards or less, the favored grapeshot having the same effect as a giant scattergun.

I watched in disbelief as the Rebels who had not been hit rose to their feet and resumed their charge. They were no more than twenty-five yards from us now and I fired again, this time hitting my target in the chest and hurling him back. Fire from our line came from all sides now, howitzers and rifles alike, and within seconds where there had once been some two hundred Rebs, fewer that twenty-five remained.

With no time to reload I drew my Navy Colt and shot another Reb as he reached our position. He screamed, spun in a half circle, and fell to the ground. Now a second Reb breached the line where Abel and Johnny lay. He swung his rifle butt at Abel as he and Johnny struggled to reload their Springfields, barely missing his head. Afraid to fire my pistol into our line I jumped on the Reb's back, pulled my knife from my belt, and plunged it into his chest. He let out a grunt that seemed to come from deep inside him, ending in a gurgling sound when blood bubbled up into his mouth, and as I fell to the ground on top of him I felt bile rising in my throat.

"It's over. It's over."

I heard Johnny's voice as I rolled off the dead Reb and looked back into the meadow. It was true. The Rebs were finished, the attacking force all dead or wounded. I rolled onto my back again and looked up through the trees. The sky was obscured by a haze of burnt gunpowder. It seemed that night was about to fall, but it was only ten o'clock in the morning. Ten in the morning, I thought, and I just killed three men.

I looked back at Johnny. He was kneeling over a Reb he had killed with his bayonet, the blade still buried in the man's chest. Suddenly, he spun away and vomited.

As I watched I heard Abel's voice next to me, although it sounded like it came from far off. "Oh God, it was so fast, so fast," he said. "I thought we was dead fer sure."

CHAPTER FIVE

Mary Johnson was helping a customer when I got to the store so I busied myself among the dry goods. She was a tall, slender, rather plain-looking woman, perhaps twenty-six or twenty-seven years of age and easily thirty years younger than her husband. She wore a checked gingham dress and her dull brown hair was pulled back in a severe bun; her eyes were the washed-out blue of someone who had seen their share of pain, and as I rummaged among the winter wool shirts those eyes kept glancing back at me. When the customer she'd been waiting on paid for her goods and left I walked to the front counter.

"Hello Mrs. Johnson," I began. "I wonder if I could speak to you for a moment."

"Of course, Jubal, but please call me Mary, or you'll make me feel very old. Is it something about the shirts you were looking at?"

"No, Mary. I want to talk to you about Johnny Harris."

She shifted her weight, nervously. "What about Johnny?"

"How well did you know him?" I asked.

"Not well, really. Walter and I only married a short time ago. My first husband—he was killed during the first year of the war, you know—well, he and I lived in Richmond before he died, so I'm afraid I never met many people from Jerusalem's Landing."

"Rebecca mentioned that Johnny came into the store quite a lot over the past few months, so I wondered if you or Mr. Johnson had seen or heard anything that might help me understand what happened."

"Do you mean about who killed him?" Her eyes were wide and fearful, and she turned and quickly busied herself with things behind the counter. "Lord, I certainly never heard anyone threaten him, if that's what you mean."

"Did you ever hear any talk about Johnny having trouble with anyone?"

She shook her head, then seemed to realize that probably wasn't enough. "I work in the store in the mornings with my husband, but then I leave to take care of our home"—she raised her eyes to the upper floor where the Johnsons had their living quarters—"and my husband works here in the afternoons, so he'd probably hear more than I would, him being here a lot more than I am."

I had a strong feeling that she didn't want to talk and I decided not to push her. "Is Mr. Johnson here?"

"Yes, Walter's out in the barn unpacking some stock." She spoke the words with a clear sense of relief.

I thanked her and went to the rear door that led outside to the barn.

Despite the morning chill, Walter Johnson was sweating as he wrestled a crate from a stack near the barn's wide front door. He was short and stocky and his soft brown eyes and prominent chin made me feel I was again looking at Abel, grown older that he would ever be.

"Good morning, Mr. Johnson."

"Good morning, Jubal. Something I can do fer ya?"

"I just wanted to talk to you about Johnny."

He withdrew a red handkerchief from a rear pocket and mopped his brow. "Sad thing," he said, but there was little sadness in his voice. "You three boys grew up in this quiet valley and then that damnable war came along, and now you're the only one left." He glanced at my missing arm as he spoke the final words and I knew what he was thinking.

"You believe the war had something ta do with Johnny's death?" I asked.

He gave his head a small shake. "I don't know, Jubal. I jus' know Johnny weren't the same boy came back as left." He paused, his eyes growing sad. "But at least he come back. God, I miss that boy of mine, miss him every day."

"I miss him too, Mr. Johnson."

The man drew a deep breath as if it might drive all the sadness away. He seemed to get hold of himself and went on. "Anyways, what can I tell ya 'bout Johnny that ya don't already know?"

"Well, sir, I know there's always a lot of talk going on when people get together in your store, and I was wondering if you overheard anything about Johnny, about any trouble he might have been having with anyone."

Walter Johnson chuckled softly. "Yeah, we are a good ol' buncha gossips, ain't we?" He scratched his head. "I did hear that he was havin' some trouble with Rusty LeRoche, but then ever'body has trouble with Rusty one time or another, don't ya know?"

"Did you hear what the trouble was about?"

He offered up a small shrug. "Well, I heard he was up on Rusty's land, doin' some huntin' a few weeks back. Well, ya know, Rusty's got that young daughter who folks say has a bit of trouble keepin' her britches on, an' I guess Rusty caught Johnny on his land and figured the kind of huntin' he was doin' didn't require no gun. I guess Rusty made it pretty clear that he might do some huntin' hisself if he caught Johnny up there again." He shook his head. "From what I heard that didn't scare Johnny none, an' he was up there a couple more times when Rusty was out loggin' his timber."

I toed the ground with my boot. "You know Rusty a lot better than I do. You think he's the kind to come looking for Johnny?"

He shrugged his shoulders. "I don't know, Jubal. He's a crazy Frenchman, fer sure, an' strong as a bull, an' I sure wouldn't want ta meet him alone in the woods iffen he was mad at me. But I can't see him doin' more then maybe give somebody a good thumpin'." He paused, thinking that over. "Unless he was awful, awful mad."

I went back to the store, and as I came through the rear door I heard sharp words being exchanged. Rebecca and Mary Johnson were face-to-face and both sets of eyes were flashing anger at each other, but at the sound of the rear door, they stopped and Mary turned away from her stepdaughter.

"Good morning, Jubal," Rebecca said. "I heard you were out back talking to my father. Was he able to help?"

"A bit," I said. "At least he gave me someone else to talk to. That's about the most I can expect right now."

She nodded. A bit curtly, I thought, and her eyes flashed defiance at her stepmother's back. "Are you going to Johnny's funeral tomorrow?" she asked, as she turned back to me.

"Yes, I am."

"I wonder if you'd be kind enough to escort me there."

The brazenness of her request startled me. Rebecca had always been a willful girl, and I now saw that it had carried well into her adulthood. And asking me in front of her stepmother had left me little choice but to agree to her request. Yet, I have to admit, though slightly unnerving, it gave me more than a little pleasure.

"Of course," I said.

Her stepmother had turned back to her, a look of surprise spread across her face. Rebecca gave her a sharp, defiant stare in return.

She looked back to me with softer eyes. "Thank you," she said. "The service starts at ten. I'll wait for you here at the store."

I guided Jezebel off the main road and onto the track that led to Sherman Hollow. It was past noon, and I hoped to catch Rusty LeRoche at home having his afternoon meal. The road into the hollow rose steeply and was only wide enough for one wagon, making it necessary to pull off the track if you met another coming the other way. But these were sparsely populated lands and that was something that rarely happened.

There were only a handful of cabins in Sherman Hollow, all of whose occupants forged a living by logging the thick pine forest that covered the area, or hunting and trapping the abundance of game that lived there. There were vegetable gardens, of course, but the land with its high, rocky hills was not suited to serious farming or raising a dairy herd.

The LeRoche cabin was a good two miles into the hollow. It was a simple four-room structure, barely big enough for LeRoche, his wife, his two sons, and one daughter. I wondered about LeRoche's supposed concern that Johnny had designs on his daughter, thinking that Johnny would have had to get her off into the woods somewhere if that was his intent. But the concern certainly fit what I knew of Johnny, at least the Johnny who had come home from that "great civil war" our dead Mr. Lincoln had spoken of.

After about a twenty-minute ride I turned Jezebel into the dooryard of the LeRoche cabin. Rusty's young daughter Chantal was outside, drawing water from the well. She had brown hair that fell below her shoulders and doelike brown eyes that looked up at me with what I could only describe as hunger. She had been a child when I left for the war. Now she was seventeen and had the body of a grown woman, and she was dressed to show it at its best advantage. Standing before me, she wore a skirt and a loose-fitting blouse that was open to expose an ample cleavage. I hadn't seen her since I returned home, and I could see why Johnny had wanted to hunt LeRoche's land.

"You're Jubal Foster, ain't ya?" she asked, smiling.

"Yes, and you must be Chantal. I remember you from before the war."

Her smile widened. "I've changed a bit, don't ya think?"

Before I could answer the cabin door opened and Rusty LeRoche stepped out into the dooryard. He was a big bull of a man—not as tall as my father, but even wider—and he had the largest hands I had ever seen. LeRoche had a full black beard and long, scraggly hair streaked with gray, and his eyes, brown like his daughter's, bore no sense of warmth or friendship.

"Who are ya?" he snapped. "An' whaddaya want? Yer interruptin' my meal."

"I'm Jubal Foster," I said. "I'm the deputy town constable and I need to take a moment of your time."

Rusty looked me up and down and offered me a derisive snort. "Then ya better git yerself down offen that horse." He turned to his daughter. "Git back in the house. Yer mother's waitin' fer that water."

LeRoche watched his daughter return to the cabin, his eyes hardening at the sway she put in her hips; then he led me to a nearby woodpile and seated himself on the chopping block. "All right, git to it," he said.

"Have you heard about Johnny Harris's murder?"

"I heard. What about it?" LeRoche's eyes bore into my face and then he looked at my missing arm as if measuring me by it. "Ya lose that arm in the war?"

"Yes."

"Goddamn stupid war; all 'bout a bunch a niggers. Wouldn't let my boys go." His words carried the sneer that filled his face.

I had heard that sentiment before and wanted to challenge it, but knew any attempt would be useless.

"I'm investigating Johnny's death," I said instead, "and I heard you had some words with him a few weeks back. I need to ask you about that."

LeRoche stared at me with cold eyes. "Just throwed him off my land is all," he said at length.

"Why was that?"

LeRoche snorted. "Didn't those gossipy bastids who tol' ya the rest tell ya that too?"

"I need to hear it from you, Mr. LeRoche."

"You kin call me Rusty, boy. I ain't fancy like them folks live down in the village."

"All right, Rusty. What I heard was that you felt Johnny was up here chasing after your daughter."

"That what they said?" He let out a grunt. "Didn't think none of 'em was smart enough ta figure that out."

I remained silent and he gave me a long stare. He looked at the pistol on my hip and his lips curled into a renewed sneer. "Course that's what he was up cheer fer. You don't have ta travel five miles ta hunt in rough country like we got cheer. Not when ya got deer an' rabbit and squirrel right on t'other side a the river, huntin' grounds a village boy kin walk ta."

"So you think he came up here to see your daughter?"

"I *know* he was up here lookin' ta see my daughter."

"Why is that?"

"My daughter an' me was in ta the store 'bout a month back an' that there Johnny Harris, he waltzes over from the church an' starts eyein' her. Then, next thing I know, he's up cheer in my dooryard askin' my daughter if it's okay ta hunt my land, an' iffen she'll show him the best trail ta take. Well, he din' know I was in the barn an' I heard him as I was comin' out. He jus' 'bout shit his pants when he saw me. An' I tol' him straight out ta git his ass outta there an' if I caught him in my dooryard agin, he was gonna be the one what got hunted."

"I heard he came back." I watched Rusty's face redden.

"Yeah, I know he did—the sumbitch."

"What did you do about it?"

"I made my daughter tell me when he was plannin' ta come on up cheer agin. I was gonna lay fer him and give that Bible-thumpin' little shit what he deserved. But I never got the chance, cause somebody took care of it fer me."

Rusty was smirking, as if he knew I lacked any information to challenge his story.

"When's the last time you were down in the village?" I asked.

"Go there 'bout ever week," he said. "Always somethin' ta do. Bring some lumber down ta the mill, or some hides fer Walter Johnson ta sell. I don't much keep track of what day I'm there an' what day I'm not."

"Were you there two days ago?"

"Don't rightly remember. Either then, or the day afore it, or the day afore that. Like I said, don't much keep track. Only thing certain is I drive my wife down on Sundays, so as she kin git herself ta church."

"Do you go to church with her?"

"I'm French Catholic and there ain't no church a mine close by. My wife, she'll go ta any damned church."

"When you went to town two or three days ago, did you think to look in on Johnny? Sort of tell him you weren't too happy with him?"

LeRoche offered up a cold smile. "Can't say I din' think on it. You have ta pass by his house ta get ta the mill."

"But you didn't stop?"

"No."

"Why not?"

"Better ta see him when he come up cheer agin." The chilling grin returned. "That way there wouldn't be no witnesses ta the ass-kickin' I was gonna give him."

When I got back to the village I checked with Walter Johnson, who said he hadn't seen Rusty in more than a week, and then with the yard manager at the sawmill, who said Rusty had delivered a load of cut timber the day Johnny was killed. While there I looked out into the yard and watched several men moving logs with cant hooks, long hickory poles with slender, pointed metal tips and a hook hanging about six inches down on one side. I asked the yard manager if Rusty LeRoche owned such a tool and was told he certainly did. The man said he'd never known a logger who didn't own at least one. I decided I'd bring Doc Pierce to the yard to tell me if that logging tool could have been the weapon that ended Johnny's life.

——— ——

Jerusalem's Landing, Vermont, 1856

Johnny led the way up the hill. We had built a hunting blind in the woods up behind the church, using rocks and fallen tree limbs and filling the holes with hard mud. Thirty yards to the east there was a cold stream that came off the hillside, and the fresh sign left by the deer told us they were watering there most every morning. We had scouted the surrounding area farther out and had found numerous rubs on trees— places were bucks had rubbed their antlers to remove the summer felt and sharpen the tips. In a few weeks, when the rut started, we would again scout the area and search out scrapes the bucks had left on the ground, patches of earth that had been freed of any snow or leaves or twigs that the bucks would then mark with their urine in an effort to attract passing doe.

Up ahead, Johnny stopped and raised a hand, then pointed up the slope to his left. It was late autumn and the leaves were off the trees, but there had not been any snow yet. I scanned the area he had pointed to and it took me almost a minute to spot a well-hidden deer standing behind a pile of brush.

Abel and Josiah came up beside me and I whispered: "About seventy, seventy-five yards up on the left, standing behind that pile of brush. Johnny's an eagle eye."

"I see it," Abel said, "but I can't tell if it's a buck or a doe."

"Too far," Josiah said. "Need us a long glass."

"I'd shoot it anyway," Abel said. "We don't eat the horns at my house."

"Shoot some little deer's momma would ya," I teased. "I'd tell Rebecca and she'd fix your fat ass, fer sure."

"She sure would," Abel said. "She raises hell with Pa and me even when we bring a buck home. But it ain't never stopped her from eatin' the venison."

"Ain't never gonna unnerstan' how ya white folks think," Josiah said, shaking his head. "My peoples believe if it runs on four legs ya better eat it afore it eats ya instead, 'cept if it's a dog or cat, or maybe a skunk."

Abel and I laughed and the sound spooked the deer we'd been watching. As it bolted away we could see it was a doe.

Johnny came down the hill and joined us. He was grinning. "You boys ain't exactly Davy Crockett when it comes ta huntin'," he said. "I hope ya ain't gonna be whoopin' it up when we got our rifles with us."

"Don't you worry, Johnny boy," I said. "You just be ready to help me drag my buck home."

Johnny's grin widened. "Okay, Mr. Crockett. Ya make sure ya git yerself a coonskin hat an' I'll bring the rope."

"You better bring another one fer me too," Abel said. "I ain't missin' out this year."

We continued on up the hill until we reached our blind. It was laid out to Johnny's plan and could hold two of us comfortably. The blind was set up facing a wide draw between two outcroppings of rock, and the tracks we'd found made clear it was a regular path the deer followed.

Johnny pointed to each of the outcroppings. "I figure the deer also run along those small ridges, so I think we need ta have somebody on each one. We can split up the time in the blind. Two here in the mornings starting at sun-up, two on the ridges, then switch in the afternoon until sundown."

"Sounds good to me," I said. "We better find us places to sit on both of them."

"Tha's what I was thinkin'," Johnny agreed. He pointed to the westerly ridge. "Abel, why don't ya take Josiah an' check that ridge, an' me an' Jubal will check the other."

"Tha's where I wanna be," Abel said. "It'll be an easy drag pullin' a big buck off that steep slope."

Johnny and I climbed the easterly outcropping. It was a difficult climb and we had to traverse in several places to work our way up. Near the top we split up to check for signs, finally joining together again and choosing a spot behind a deadfall that overlooked a heavily traveled deer trail.

"It's a good place," I said. "Hell to get to, but worth the climb."

Johnny pointed to the deer trail some twenty yards below us. "Should be a nice easy shot. Oughta be able ta see 'em comin' a good fifty yards off. I'll be surprised we don't get us a nice fat buck right here. Let's get back on down. It's gettin' close ta suppertime."

We started down the outcropping and had gone about halfway

when my foot caught a tree root hidden by some leaves, and it pitched me forward, twisting my leg. I called out in pain, then scrabbled with my hands to keep from sliding down the ridge.

Johnny was there in a second to grab hold of me. When I looked behind me I saw that he had stopped me from sliding over a ridge and into a sixty-foot drop to the rocks below. I struggled to my feet and winced in pain as I tried to put pressure on my leg.

"You're gonna make me carry your sad ol' ass, ain't ya?" Johnny said. With that he dipped his shoulder and hoisted me onto his back. "Jus' hang on. This is gonna be a little tricky."

Abel and Josiah had seen Johnny hauling me down and they were waiting at the base of the outcropping when we got there.

"What happened?" Abel asked.

"Jubal jammed up his leg so's he could get an easy ride down," Johnny said. He eased me off his shoulder. "Abel, you and me gotta put him between us and walk him down. He's too damn heavy ta carry all the way." He glanced at me, grinning. "What's yer daddy feedin' ya, Jubal? Whatever it is, it's turnin' ya inta a regular ol' horse."

CHAPTER SIX

Across the road people had begun filing into the church. Rebecca was waiting for me outside the store. She was wearing a pale gray dress with a matching bonnet, a gray shawl draped over her shoulders. I had put on the one suit I owned, a dark gray tweed my father bought me when I went off to the University of Vermont. It was six years old now and a little tight through the shoulders. The last time I'd worn it the left sleeve had not been pinned up.

Rebecca smiled at me. "You look very handsome in your suit, Jubal," she said. "You look like a young businessman."

We were standing outside the store. Walter Johnson and his wife Mary had already left for the church and had hung a *Closed* sign on the front door. I wanted to ask Rebecca about the argument she and her stepmother had the previous day, but decided it would be better to wait until after the services. As we stood there the church bell tolled, indicating that Johnny's funeral was about to start.

"We better go," Rebecca said.

Johnny's open coffin had been placed on a bier just below the pulpit. The church was close to overflowing and Rebecca and I were forced to sit in the rear, which suited me fine, but even from there you could tell that Johnny had begun to go a bit gray and needed to be put under the ground.

During the war I had seen enough bodies that had been left out on the battlefield, or laid out at field hospitals, and the stench that came off them was something that grew upon them quickly and one I would never forget.

The choir finished a hymn I did not recognize and Reverend Harris stepped up to the pulpit and began the service with the Lord's Prayer. When he had finished he looked out over the congregation, smiling weakly or nodding recognition at various members of his flock.

"Thank you for coming on this sad occasion. But it is only sad for my wife and me, and for Johnny's many friends." He extended an arm toward the coffin. "For my son it is a day of peace and happiness, a day that finds him sitting before the throne of our Lord and Savior, Jesus Christ, basking in all His glory . . ."

Spotsylvania County, Virginia, 1864

Abel and Josiah and I moved out into the open meadow, heading away from the small farm we'd just been driven from, seeking cover from the Rebs we knew were still in the area.

Abel's face was boiling with anger, and he stopped and peered back at the farm, at the blue uniforms clustered in the front yard.

"That sumbitch, that goddamn sumbitch." He turned again. "You'll pay fer this, Johnny Harris!" he shouted. "Sure as there's a God in heaven, you'll pay fer it."

The first shell hit the meadow some fifty feet away from us and we all dove for the ground, fearful of any grapeshot that might be coming our way.

"Forget about Johnny," I hissed. "Just get yourselves to cover." I pointed across the meadow toward the thick woods of the Wilderness. "We gotta get into those trees or these shells are gonna cut us to pieces."

"We should still be at that goddamned farmhouse," Abel said. "We had all the cover we needed there. Johnny and his bastard friends had no right ta drive us off jus' so they could—"

"Stop it," I shouted. "We'll take care of Johnny and his friends later. Let's just get our asses over to those trees."

Another shell exploded, and then another.

Jerusalem's Landing, Vermont, 1865

The choir was singing "Amazing Grace" with the congregation joining in. I held a hymnbook and sang in a barely audible voice, my eyes blindly staring at the long-familiar verses. Rebecca sang at my side, her voice high and sweet, and I thought it sad that she had not been able to sing a hymn or say a prayer at her own brother's funeral.

I had visited his grave in Spotsylvania County before I'd headed home. The war was over then, although it was hard to tell in the still-ravaged Virginia towns I passed through.

I rode my horse into areas where we had fought, passing places where men I had known so well had died. It was all I had left of them, remembrances of their deaths, and as I rode I thought I could still smell the stench of the battlefields and forests where their lives had ended.

Abel's grave was in a small Union cemetery near Chancellorsville and I thought one day I would like to take Rebecca there, let her see with certainty that her brother's body had not been thrown into a pit with dozens of others, let her kneel before his grave as I had to weep over his loss.

My father was among the men who carried Johnny's body from the church, placing the coffin on a flatbed wagon for the short drive to the town cemetery. The mourners followed on foot, led by Reverend Harris and his wife. Rebecca and I walked at the rear of the line, where we were joined by Josiah.

"I didn't see you in church," I said.

"Tha's cause I wasn't there," he said. "I don' mind seein' him put inna ground. Fact is I kinda like the idea. But I din' have no need ta pray over him."

Rebecca stared at Josiah, but said nothing. I wondered what she thought, hearing the bitterness in his voice, knowing he had been with Johnny throughout the war, remembering how different it had been as we all grew up together.

"What happened to us?" she finally asked, almost as if she had read my mind.

Neither Josiah nor I answered her.

It was not a military burial, just a simple ceremony of townspeople burying a man who had lived among them for most of his life.

Reverend Harris prayed over his son's body, tears running down his cheeks. His wife fell to her knees and sobbed into clasped hands. Others wept openly, perhaps recalling the boy they had known for so many years.

Rebecca leaned into my arm. "Oh Jubal, I wish Abel could have been buried this way, surrounded by people who loved him."

Doc Pierce and I stood in the yard at the sawmill as he examined a cant hook. "This blade looks a bit thick to me," he said, "but I believe these tools come in different sizes." He turned it in his hand and studied it further. "Yes, a smaller one or one with a thinner blade could have been the murder weapon, I suppose. But we really won't know unless we come up with the actual tool and find traces of human blood on it." He looked me in the eye. "You got somebody particular in mind?"

"Rusty LeRoche had a squabble with Johnny, and he does a bit of logging."

Doc nodded, thinking this over. "Yes, Rusty's a hard one, that's for sure. But I heard something today that you and your father need to know. Edgar Billingsley told me that a fella stopped by his farm about a week back, asking directions to Johnny's house. Said this fella told him that he and Johnny had fought together in the war, and had both been captured and sent to Andersonville Prison. Ed said he'd just heard about Johnny when he came to town, and he asked me if I thought he should tell your daddy about it. I told him I'd pass it on, and that somebody would likely be out to see him."

"Why the hell didn't he just come to us?"

Doc chuckled. "He came into my office this morning to have me lance a boil on his backside, and had to hurry on home to tend to his cows, least that's what he said. But you know how folks are hereabouts. They don't want to cause trouble for people without good reason."

"Did he tell you the man's name?"

"He did. The man told him his name was Bobby Suggs."

I stiffened at the sound of the name. The last time I had seen Bobby Suggs he was standing behind the barrel of a Navy Colt that was leveled at my head.

"Looks like you know the name," Doc said.

"Yes, I sure do know it. And he's somebody I'll need to talk to."

I found Rebecca down by the river, close to the place where her mother had drowned. I had brought her home from the cemetery, telling her that there was someone I needed to see, but that I would like to talk to her later. She had said she was going for a walk and told me where she would likely be.

"Do you come here often?" I asked as I came up beside her.

She was staring into the river and didn't look at me. "No, not often. Being at Johnny's funeral made me think of my mother and how she died."

I asked why.

"Because Johnny was responsible for her death." She turned to face me. "I don't mean that he pushed her into the river." She stared into the water again. "You see, I accept the fact that my mother took her own life. But Johnny drove her to it. That cruel lie he told her about Abel being thrown into a pit with dozens of others was more than she could bear, more than she should have had to bear." Her jaw tightened. "Oh Jubal, I'm so glad he's dead, so very, very glad. And I know how terrible it is to feel that way."

I took her arm and led her away from the river. We were halfway back to the store before I brought up the subject I had wanted to talk to her about.

"The other day, after I finished speaking to your father out in the barn, I came back into the store and interrupted what seemed like an angry conversation between you and your stepmother—"

"Please don't call her my stepmother," Rebecca cut in. "Just call her by her name."

"All right." I stopped and waited until she met my eyes again. "As I was saying, when I came back into the store, I had the feeling I was interrupting an argument, and that it had something to do with me coming to the store to question her about Johnny."

Rebecca hesitated, then let out a long breath that had the feel of surrender to it. "You were right, she was upset about that. She knew I told you that Johnny had spent a lot of time at the store the past few weeks, and she said it was wrong of me to let on about that. She said it couldn't do anything but cause trouble for her and my father."

"Why did she think that?"

She turned away again. "Because she was afraid you'd find out that she and Johnny were lovers."

"She said that?"

"No, but I know that's the reason."

"How can you be certain?"

Rebecca stopped and stared at me, her eyes harder than I had ever seen them. "Oh, she denies it. But I saw them coming out of his barn one night, when my father was still working in the store, and I saw the way she looked at him." She drew a long breath. "But it's Johnny Harris I blame, that . . . miserable, miserable man. First he killed my mother; then he seduced my father's new wife."

CHAPTER SEVEN

My father looked me up and down, a small smile playing at the corners of his mouth making me feel a touch nervous.

"Do I look all right? I asked.

He nodded. "Ya look jus' fine, son."

"Then why are you smiling like you're seeing something funny?" I was wearing my newest pair of trousers and my newest shirt, and I was thinking I appeared the best I possibly could.

"Tha's not what's makin' me smile," my father said. "I'm just marvelin' at how big ya've gotten, how yer almost a full growed-up man. I guess it just makes me happy ta see it."

I felt my face heating up under the compliment. My father must have seen it too, because he glanced away, not wanting to embarrass me further.

"I expect all the town kids will be at the church dance," he said. "That should mean you'll have a good time." He paused as if considering what else he wanted to say. "Will Rebecca Johnson be there?"

"I guess she will. Why do you ask?"

"I just noticed the way ya been lookin' at her lately. An' the way she looks at you."

My lips began to form a denial, but the words wouldn't come. My father's next comment let me off the hook.

"I can't imagine any young buck not bein' taken with her. She sure is a beautiful girl, sweet as can be too; should grow inta a fine young woman any man would be proud ta know."

"Yes sir."

"Well, ya git yerself off now. An' don' forget ta ask that young girl ta dance."

"I don't know how to dance."

"Ain't nothin' to it. Jus' tell her yer jus' learnin' an' she'll help ya out. Womenfolk are like that. Then jus' take her right hand in your left hand, put your right hand on her waist, and move yer feet ta the music. Also, it's best ta pick somethin' slow till ya learn yer steps." He smiled broadly. "You'll do jus' fine, son."

The dance was in the barn behind the church, the beams and rafters now draped in bunting, the dirt floor cleared and raked. A makeshift plank stage had been hammered together up against the rear wall, and Edgar Billingsley and Cory Jimmo had added to their usual banjo-and-country-fiddle duo by bringing in Lester Blow and his squeeze-box. Beside the open front doors long tables had been set up and the ladies of the church had filled them with a spread of homemade food and jugs of cold apple cider. It was autumn, the leaves having just filled the hillsides with color, and the dance was a celebration of the season, in itself a quiet acknowledgment of the long, cold winter that lay ahead and the fact that many of the townspeople would see little of each other until spring.

Inside the barn boys of varying ages were gathered to one side, while girls banded together on the other, each group casting furtive glances across the width of the building. Johnny Harris, Abel Johnson, and I stood together as always.

"Hey, Abel, I think Jubal is eyein' yer lil' sister," Johnny said. He was smirking, trying to goad me into a denial.

Abel slipped his arm around my shoulder. "He always does. But so do you. Ya just won't fess up ta it."

Johnny let out a scoffing laugh but I could tell that Abel's remark embarrassed him. "No offense, partner," he said, trying to recover, "but that sister a yours is a bit of a goodie-goodie, an' I like ladies when they're a bit wilder, if ya know what I mean."

Abel punched me in the arm and we both started to laugh. "Well, ya sure got a big choice of wild and wanton women right cheer," Abel said.

I raised my chin toward one of the food tables, where Edith Summers was serving up her baked beans. She was in her early seventies and skinny as a rail. "I hear old Edith has a real wide wild streak," I said. "Maybe you ought to mosey on over there, get a plate of her beans, then see if you can get her up in the hayloft."

Johnny squared his shoulders and wiggled his eyebrows comically. "I'll be up in *somebody's* hayloft long afore either of you are," he said.

Abel winked at me. "The great lover, Johnny Harris, has spoken. Say, Johnny, I hear tell there's a woman up ta Richmond who takes in visitors by the hour. They say she weighs two hundred pounds, but she's available fer some quick lovin'. Maybe she'd be worth a try."

Johnny let out a cold laugh. "Don't need no whore," he said. He was still grinning, still having fun with the teasing. When it stopped being fun, his mood would quickly change. I'd seen it happen before. Johnny puffed himself up. "Now, I'm not sayin' I wouldn't mind a loose lady like that, but I'll leave the ones who weigh two hundred pounds ta Abel here. Big as he is, I'd be pleased jus' ta look in the window an' watch 'em break the bedsprings."

I couldn't help laughing at the image. It even made Abel laugh. I'd never been with a whore, but I'd imagined how it might be, and deep down I found the idea a bit intimidating. I secretly believed the others probably felt the same way.

"Shh," Abel hissed. "Rebecca's comin' over."

I watched her approach. She was wearing a simple white dress that was modestly buttoned to the neck, but which still couldn't hide the lovely lines of her sixteen-year-old body. I raised my eyes to the soft contours of her face, her vivid green eyes, and I felt my breath catch just looking at her.

"Why are you just standing here?" she asked as she stopped in front of us. "Aren't the three of you going to ask anyone to dance?" She turned pointedly to me.

I began to stutter. "I'm . . . I'm just learning, Rebecca . . . I'm not very good at it yet . . . Somebody else . . . well, they might be more fun to dance with."

She reached out and took my hand. "I think you'll be just fine," she said. "Come and show me what you can do."

I saw Abel roll his eyes and heard Johnny give out a big guffaw, and as Rebecca led me out to the center of the barn I could feel my heart beating in my chest, and I thought I hadn't felt it beat so wildly since I was eleven and first saw a buck in my rifle sights.

Rebecca smiled up at me as she took my left hand in her right, and placed my right hand on her waist. There was a faint smell of lilac rising about her and it overwhelmed my senses. It took a moment before I heard the music and I was immediately grateful it was a slow rendition of "When I Saw Sweet Nellie Home."

I heeded my father's advice and moved my feet to the music, feeling clumsy and awkward. At the same time, Rebecca moved as though her feet weren't even touching the ground.

"You're going to be a good dancer, Jubal," she whispered up at me. "You just have to learn to relax."

I wondered if that would ever be possible. Maybe it would happen with some other girl, but never with her. Certainly not when I felt her so close to me, her body moving under my hand as it sat on her waist; my nostrils filled with her scent, and her beautiful green eyes staring up at me. No, that would surely never happen.

———— ————

Manassas, Virginia, 1862

It had been a slaughter. Rumor had it we had lost nearly 10,000 men, killed and wounded, while the Reb's had lost just over 8,000. We had stormed Stony Ridge with 62,000 men under Major General John Pope, the new commander of the Union Army of Virginia, to which we were now assigned. Just before the assault began our officers had told us we had Confederate General Stonewall Jackson trapped on the ridge and we were going to crush him and his army—the very same one that had defeated us at the First Battle of Bull Run the previous year. But by the time the battle ended it was our left flank that had been crushed by the unexpected arrival of Confederate General James Longstreet and his force of 25,000, who took up position on Jackson's right and sent us into a full retreat toward Centreville. Only a bitter rearguard action had kept our entire army from falling victim to the slaughter.

Johnny, Abel, Josiah, and I were seated under a stand of pine, trying with little success to soak some strength back into our bodies. For myself, I was amazed we were all still alive, the battle having been that fierce.

Abel was seated across from me. He stared at me, shook his head, and let out a long sigh. "I'm ready ta call this war a draw an' head on home," he said. His face was covered in gunpowder residue and streaked with sweat. "Every day I'm here the less sense it all makes." He glanced at Josiah. "I know the slavery part makes sense, I don' mean ta say it don'. But this killin' each other by the thousands, an' all of it dependin' on where you was born, that jus' makes no sense at all."

"I know what *I'm* fightin' for," Johnny said. "I'm fightin' to keep myself alive. I don't intend to let some Johnny Reb blow my ass to kingdom come."

"Amen," I said. "Let's keep all our asses in one piece and get ourselves back home."

A tall, lanky soldier came slouching along the dirt lane we'd been traveling down on our way to Centreville. When he reached us he pulled up short and grinned down at Johnny.

"Glad ta see ya made it outta that shithole," he said.

"Barely," Johnny replied. He turned to us. "This here's Bobby Suggs. He's assigned ta the company that was on our left flank. Bobby, this is Jubal Foster, Abel Johnson, and Josiah Flood, all boys from back home in Vermont." He raised his chin toward Suggs. "Bobby here is the best scrounger in the unit. You wanna find somethin' the quartermaster ain't got, he's your man."

Suggs stared down at Josiah. "Didn't know ya had niggers up in Vermont," he said. "Ya enlist, boy?"

I felt my blood turn hot. "Josiah's our friend," I said. "He's our *longtime* friend. We don't call him a nigger and we sure as hell don't call him a boy."

"Ta each his own," Suggs smirked, then turned to Johnny. "Speakin' of scroungin', there's an ol' farmhouse back yonder that 'peers ta be abandoned. Ya wanna come along with me an' have a look-see?"

Johnny struggled to his feet. "Might as well," he said.

"We're gonna be pullin' out soon," Abel warned him.

"Don't worry," Johnny said. "Ya pull out afore I'm back, I'll sure as hell catch up ta ya. After goin' through that meat grinder back there, I ain't about ta get myself shot fer a deserter."

We watched them head back down the road. I had an uneasy feeling about Suggs, and from the look on Abel and Josiah's faces I could tell they felt the same way.

"You ever meet this Suggs before?" I asked them.

Abel shook his head. "Don't think I have."

"I seen him," Josiah said. "Ain't never talked ta him. If I had I'm thinkin' he woulda axed me ta shine his boots or kiss his skinny white ass."

"I woulda liked ta see that," Abel said. "Just ta see how far ya shoved his rifle up that ass."

I let out a short, harsh laugh. "Next time you start pullin' wounded bodies off a battlefield, you make sure you take a real close look. You find him lyin' out there, you just tell him you're not gonna offend his white sensibilities by putting your sorry black hands on him."

Josiah fought off a smile. "Had one like that t'other day. Kept screamin', *Come git me, boy! You do what I tell ya an' git on over here, boy!* Just had a graze on his leg, but he was yellin' like it was blowed clear off. An' there I was wif minie balls wizzin' by my ears." He let out a snort. "Well, I jus' went stone-cold deaf. Musta been some artillery shell went off too close an' plugged up my ears, an' I left that sumbitch layin' there screamin' at me and moved off an' took care a the ones what really needed help." He raised his chin in the direction Suggs and Johnny had gone. "Whatcha think Johnny sees in that one, he'd go off wif him like that?"

Abel shook his head. "Johnny's gettin' stranger by the day."

"This war is makin' us all strange," I said. "Yesterday I saw our sergeant sittin' on a Reb body while he smoked a cigar, just using it for a stool."

"Yeah, I know what yer sayin'. It's like the dead ain't really people, an' never was," Abel said. He drew a long breath. "T'other day I saw a Reb no older'n us shot down right in front a me, an' it was like he din' really exist, even though I saw him runnin' across a meadow jus' a minute afore a minie ball lifted him off the ground." He shook his head and looked across at me. "Why ya think that is, Jubal? Ya think we're jus' gettin' cold inside?"

"I heard one a the docs talkin' at the hospital," Josiah responded. "He said our minds jus' block things out. Said we see so much terrible stuff that we'd go plum crazy iffen our minds din' shut it off like that."

"I hope he's right," I said.

"Yeah, me too," Abel said. "Cause if he ain't there's gonna be an army of monsters goin' home when this here war is finally over."

The sergeant came through and got us up and moving toward Centreville again. Josiah went back to his hospital unit and Abel and I were sent to join a rearguard unit that would make sure the Rebs didn't sneak up behind us.

Back at the rear I watched Johnny and Suggs cutting across a field, hurrying to get back to the column. Each had a sack in his hand and I assumed they had found things worth taking from the abandoned farmhouse. I hoped it was something good that we could all share, like a slab of bacon or a salted ham. We had been taught early on that it wasn't stealing. It was living off the land, taking food the Rebs would use if we didn't confiscate it. I smiled at the thought. Seemed like you could justify anything in war, or almost anything, and I wondered what my father would say about it. I remembered back when we were seven and Abel and Johnny and I raided a neighbor's apple tree. The neighbor had complained to my father, who sent us to do chores for the neighbor to make up for the apples we had taken. "Stealin' is stealin'," he had said then. I suspected he'd say the same thing now.

This made me think of home and I reached into my pocket and pulled out a letter I had gotten just before we went into battle. It was from Rebecca, and I had already read it three or four times. I read it again now. It ended with the words: *I miss you, Jubal. Stay safe for me and come home soon.* I hoped that I would.

Jerusalem's Landing, Vermont, 1865

My father and I rode out to Ed Billingsley's farm to question him about Bobby Suggs. When I had told my father about Suggs he had volunteered to go along.

"It ain't that Ed don' respect ya, son, it's jus' that he might still think of ya as a boy, cause that's how he's known ya all yer life. If so, he'll be expectin' ta talk ta me, so if ya don' mind, I'll jus' go along sort of as yer helper an' let him know yer runnin' this here investigation."

I tried not to smile at my father's words, but in the end I had to turn away to hide it. I'd had a professor at the university who'd been a great advocate of a new science called psychology, and I wondered what he would have said about my father's attempt to soothe my psyche.

We dismounted in Ed Billingsley's dooryard where we were greeted by his wife, offered something cold to drink, and, when we declined, told we'd find Ed in the milking barn.

Entering the barn brought back memories of the first time I'd been in one. The smell was overwhelming, and back then it had put me off drinking milk for almost a month.

Cows are strange creatures. They come in from grazing and go straight to the same stall each day, and if another cow is confused and has taken their stall, they'll stand behind it, stomping their hooves and bellowing a complaint until the farmer removes the offender and puts it in its proper place. Then they'll stand there eager to be milked, all the while shitting and pissing into the narrow ditch that runs behind each row of stalls. The ditches are mucked out twice a day, but the smell never leaves, and after my first visit to a cow barn I'd been sure the same smell came off the next glass of milk I tried to drink.

"Ho, Ed," my father called out now.

Ed Billingsley rose up behind the haunches of a cow he'd been milking and waved us over. "Ya come ta help me git my milkin' done?" he said with a grin.

"Not likely," my father replied, reaching across to shake his hand. "Ya remember my boy Jubal, don' ya?"

"I do," Ed said. "Though I'd hardly recognize him, he's gotten so big. Back home from the war I hear," he added, trying but not succeeding in keeping his eyes off my pinned-up sleeve.

"Yes sir." I reached my good hand across the cow to shake his.

"Well, Jubal's the deputy town constable now," my father explained. "An' he's investigating the murder of Johnny Harris. I jus' wanted ta let ya know that he's in charge of that, cause I know he's got some questions ta ask ya."

Ed nodded; then he grinned at me. "The deputy constable, eh? That there's a far cry from burnin' up the town bandstand like you and yer friends did a couple Fourth of July's back, now ain't it?"

My father let out a loud guffaw and I lowered my eyes and smiled at my boots.

"Yes sir, it is. I guess I'm never gonna live that one down."

"Not in this town, ya ain't. Now what kin I do fer ya, son?" Billingsley was a large man, almost as big as my father. He had a round belly that pushed out against his overalls, but like the rest of him it looked hard as a rock. He was wearing a straw hat, which I knew had little hair beneath it, and a full beard flecked with gray that covered most of his round face. His blue eyes always seemed to have a smile in them, and I'd always thought of the man as one of the happiest people in the town.

"Well, sir," I began, "I was talking to Doc the other day and he told me you'd had a man by here asking after Johnny Harris."

"Sure enough did. Said his name was Bobby Suggs. I 'membered it, cause it sounded strange ta me. Suggs, that is. Don't have no people named Suggs up hereabouts. Least none I ever heard of. Said he was from Pennsylvania, an' that he fought with you boys in the war. Even mentioned ya by name, Jubal."

"I remember Suggs," I said. "He was more Johnny's friend than mine."

"Well, he sounded real anxious ta meet up with Johnny agin. Said he'd had a devil of a time findin' this here town. Din' like the way he said that, kind of smart, ya know, so I din' offer him no help findin' young Johnny. Then when I heard 'bout Johnny gettin' kilt I thought I better pass the information on."

"Did this Suggs say where he was staying?" I asked.

"No, never did. I got the idea he might be stayin' up ta Richmond, but not because he tol' me that. He did axe if there was any work hereabouts. I tol' him ta try some of the other dairy farms, maybe the sawmill, and some a the loggin' camps. Said he'd do that; then he left."

I thanked him and asked that he let me know if Suggs came back, and after some neighborly gossip my father and I started out for home.

"I'm headed up ta Richmond tomorra," my father said as we rode back toward town. "Got some more tax money ta deposit in the town account. While I'm there I'll check fer any strangers stayin' in any of the roomin' houses. Meantime, why don't ya ride out ta the local farms, the sawmill, an' the logging camps?"

"I'll start with the sawmill as soon as we get back to town, then I'll set up a route that'll take me by all the farms and camps. Should be able to do it in a day, a day and a half."

My father nodded agreement. "You'll be earnin' yer money an' more this week," he said.

The sawmill manager, Jesse Barton, told me that a man named Suggs had indeed been by looking for work, but there had been none he could offer him. "I tol' him ta try some a the local loggin' camps an' gave him directions on how he might find 'em. Did the same fer some a the bigger farms who take on workers from time ta time."

Barton was a short, stocky man with a face that was deeply weathered from years of working out in the open. He had a gruff manner about him, but my father claimed he had the softest heart in town. He ran a hand through steely gray hair, and thoughtfully rubbed an equally gray beard. "Ya know, Jubal, there was somethin' 'bout that fella I jus' din' like. Kind of a shifty sort, he was. Scraggly beard, battered old Union cap, and all the time actin' like he was owed sumthin'."

"Did he ask you about Johnny Harris?"

"Oh, he was here a good week afore we lost poor Johnny," he said. "If that's whatcha was thinkin'. But no, he din' ask me nothin' 'bout nobody in particular."

That told me one thing: Suggs had probably already located Johnny by then. I thanked Jesse, and decided I'd try the store to see if Suggs had stopped by there.

Rebecca was behind the counter when I got there and it gave me a rush of pleasure to see her look up at me and smile.

"Hello, Jubal, I was hoping I'd see you today."

"Why was that?" I asked, thinking she had something specific in mind.

"I always hope I'll see you. Certainly you know that."

Her words added to my pleasure but left me floundering for a response. "You're very kind to say so," I said weakly. I shifted my weight and hurried on. "I'm trying to track the movements of a stranger who came to town about a week ago. His name is Suggs, Bobby Suggs. He's a tall, lanky fellow about my age, has a scruffy beard, and was supposed to be wearing an old Union cap. He knew Johnny and me during the war, and Ed Billingsley said he came by his farm asking where Johnny lived. I wondered if he might have stopped at the store."

Rebecca thought about it and slowly shook her head just as her stepmother came behind the counter.

"Who are you asking about, Jubal?" Mary Johnson asked. She was wearing a gingham dress and her hair was pulled back severely, a sharp contrast to Rebecca, whose pale blue dress seemed to make her long, reddish-blond hair all the more striking.

I repeated the description of Bobby Suggs and thought I saw a hint of alarm come into Mary Johnson's eyes.

"No, I don't believe I saw anyone like that, but I'll ask Walter, and if he did, I'm sure he'll tell you what he knows."

"Is Mr. Johnson around now?" I asked.

"No, he's not. He took the buckboard up to Richmond to pick up some goods that came in on the train."

"He should be back late this afternoon," Rebecca added quickly, casting a glance at her stepmother.

"Good. I'll be by then," I said. I turned to go, but Rebecca's words stopped me.

"I was just going to have my lunch, sort of a picnic down by the river," she said. "Would you care to join me, Jubal? It's just apples and cheddar and a bit of cider, but it's all very good."

I still had several stops to make in my search for Bobby Suggs, but I took her words as a signal that there was more she wanted to tell me. "I'd like that," I said. "But I can't stay too long. There are several other places I have to stop at today."

Rebecca spread a small blanket on a flat rock just above the river and set out her basket. I used my knife to cut up two apples and slice two slabs of cheese, while she poured us cider.

"You know that Mary was lying to you, don't you?" she said at length. Her voice was harsher than I expected and that surprised me.

I knew Rebecca didn't like her stepmother, but her tone bordered on something more.

"I had a feeling she wasn't telling me everything she could have," I said.

"She thinks she's a very good liar, that she can fool people quite easily, but she can't. Oh, she fools my father, but it's only because he wants to believe her. But I always know when she's not telling the truth."

"How is that?" I asked.

"She has to turn her eyes away from me and that's when I know. And that's what she did to you when you asked her about that Suggs man. As soon as you described him, she knew who he was."

I'd noticed the same thing. "Why do you think she did that?"

"I think she's fearful that Johnny told Suggs about their affair, and that when you find Suggs he'll tell you."

"Still, it would be her word against his," I said. "And he's a shiftless sort, just passing through. When he asked Jesse Barton for some work at the sawmill Jesse wouldn't touch him, and you know what kind of rough characters he's like to hire."

Rebecca's eyes hardened. "She wouldn't take the chance. Not Mary. She believes in protecting herself at all cost, and she knows she'd be in danger if my father believed what Suggs said. If he did, he might very well throw her out. And then she'd have no place to go, no one to take care of her. When Johnny was alive I think she held out hope that *he'd* go off with her if they got caught."

"If she thought that, she didn't know Johnny very well. At least not the man who came back from the war."

"No, she didn't."

I guided my horse Jezebel up Sherman Hollow. Recent rains had left the path rougher than usual, and I took care to keep her well away from the many potholes. By the time I reached Rusty LeRoche's dooryard it was nearing on two o'clock.

Rusty's daughter Chantal came out of the cabin, her hair tousled, her breasts swaying beneath the thin blouse she wore. She looked up at me and gave me an impish smile. "You come back ta see me, deputy?"

"I'm afraid not. I'm looking for your daddy."

"He's out in the woodlot," she said, grinning again. "Don't expect him back till suppertime. Yer welcome ta come inside an' wait fer him."

I could imagine Rusty's reaction if I accepted her offer. "Can you tell me what path to take to get out to your woodlot?" I asked.

"You afraid of me, deputy?"

"I just want to respect your daddy's wishes. I also need to see him now, so I can get home in time for my own supper."

She shook her head. "My, my. I'm startin' ta wonder if that war hurt more'n yer arm. You all right everywheres else?"

"I'm fine, Chantal. But thank you for your concern. Now why don't you stop teasing me and tell me what path to take?"

"I don't mean ta tease ya, deputy. It just gets real lonely out cheer, if you know what I mean. I'd just enjoy the company of a good-lookin' young fella."

"I take it as a compliment, Chantal. But I've got some work I've gotta get done." I hesitated, then thought I'd ask her about Suggs.

"Did a fella named Suggs come by here looking for work?" I asked.

"Bobby Suggs? Yeah, he came by. But as soon as Daddy found out he was a frienda Johnny's he tol' him ta get off his land an' not ta show hisself agin."

"Did he ever come back?"

Chantal offered up a coy smile. "He came back one time when Daddy was out workin' the woodlot. Took me for a little walk in the woods, he did."

"Did he say where he was staying?"

"He din' say it, but I heard Daddy tell Momma that he'd taken a job at Billy Lucie's place. Ain't seen him since I heard that, so I suppose it's true."

Lucie's place was located on a high, flat ridge that overlooks the Huntington Gorge. "I still need to talk to your daddy," I said. "Can you point me in the right direction?"

I could hear the axes long before I saw the clearing where Rusty and his sons were working. I rode in slowly, taking care not to veer into the path of a falling tree. Rusty noticed me, buried his axe blade into the tall pine he'd been working, and approached.

"Whatcha lookin' fer now?" he said as a way of greeting. His face and beard were covered in grit and dripping sweat.

"Fella named Bobby Suggs. A scraggly-looking man, might of been wearing—"

"Yeah, he was by here coupla weeks back. Lookin' fer work, he said. Friend of Johnny Harris, he said. Soon's I heard that I throwed his ass offen the place. Birds of a feather, I figured, an' I don't need none of that hangin' aroun' Chantal."

"Did you ever see him again?"

"No, but I heard he came back. My missus saw someone looked like him sneakin' out of the woods; saw Chantal sneakin' out a few minutes later."

"What did you do?"

Rusty's face turned into a snarl. "Whatcha think I did? I figured he was stayin' with his friend in town, so next time I was droppin' off a load of timber I went ta the parsonage an' asked the reveren' iffen he was there. That skinny ol' Bible-thumper tol' me Suggs'd taken a job up at Lucie's wood-lot. Lucie's got a cabin fer his workers so's I figured he was stayin' there."

"Did you go on up to Lucie's place?"

"Don't have time to go runnin' all over creation after some no-account drifter." His eyes hardened. "I figured he came sneakin' aroun' my place agin I'd sure enough catch up ta him."

"Did you see Johnny when you were at the parsonage?"

"No, he weren't there." He gave me a cold stare. "Now I gotta git back ta work."

"Thank you, Mr. LeRoche. You've been a help and I appreciate it." I turned to remount my horse, hesitated, and turned back. "If you do run into Suggs again I'd appreciate it if you'd let me or my father know."

LeRoche let out a snort. "I run inta him up cheer on my land, I'll deliver him ta ya in a basket. Whatever's lefta him, that is."

It was three thirty when I turned Jezebel into the gorge road and headed toward the skid slash that would mark the route up into Lucie's wood-lot. Billy Lucie had a house along the road, but there was little chance of finding him there this early in the day. He'd most likely be up with his men making sure he was getting a full day's work out of each of them.

The land rose steeply behind Lucie's house, angling up steadily for at least three hundred yards until it leveled out into a wide, flat wood-lot. I'd hunted bear there with my father years ago and I knew how dense and isolated the land was, pocked with rock outcroppings and riddled with caves that coyotes and bobcats used until a bear claimed it for its winter den.

I stopped at Lucie's house just in case he was there, but was told by his wife that he was up in the woodlot. She was a stocky woman in a homespun dress, with a broad smile and twinkling blue eyes, and she gave me a cold glass of cider, which I accepted gratefully.

"He should be headed down soon, iffen ya want ta wait," she said.

I thanked her for her kindness and explained there was a man up in the woodlot I wanted to see, then went back out to remount Jezebel.

Halfway up the slope I met Billy Lucie headed down as his wife had predicted.

"Ya lookin' fer me, young Jubal?" he asked.

I tipped my hat out of respect. "It's a pleasure to see you, Mr. Lucie, but actually I'm here to see one of your men."

Lucie was about average height, but thick in the arms and body like most loggers. He had a weatherworn face, marked by a large, drooping mustache and warm brown eyes. Now the eyes took on a look of worry. "One of my boys in trouble with the constable's office?"

"Not that I know for certain," I said, trying to put his mind at ease. "I'm looking for a man named Bobby Suggs. I knew him during the war, though not well. But he was a particular friend of Johnny Harris, and I'm told he was trying to locate him a week or so before Johnny was killed."

Lucie nodded. "He's up in the woodlot, but I wouldn't be surprised if all them boys have headed ta the bunkhouse early now that I'm gone." He looked at me steadily. "Ya think he mighta had somethin' ta do with young Johnny's killin'?"

"I don't know, sir. Right now I just want to talk to him."

"You want me to go back on up with ya? He's kind of a rough sort, a little shifty too, if ya ask me. I only took him on because one of my regular boys busted a leg and I was shorthanded."

"I think I'll be all right, sir." I smiled at him. "But if you hear any shooting come right on up."

Lucie laughed. "Don't allow no guns up there. Don't want those boys poachin' deer, or shootin' each other over a poker hand. Bad enough they punch each other up now an' agin, or cut each other when somebody ends up with five aces. Stop by and see me when ya come back down. You'll be welcome ta supper."

I thanked Billy and turned Jezebel back up the steep slope. When we reached the plateau I could see the bunkhouse across a wide swath that had already been clear cut. I turned in my saddle and looked down into the valley below. The Huntington River moved through the land like a winding blue line, and you could see where the gorge cut deep into the rock, the white foam from the rapids and the small waterfalls that moved it steadily down and on toward Richmond. It was a special place for me, had been since I was a small boy. And I drew in a deep breath, almost as though I could taste it if I tried hard enough.

CHAPTER EIGHT

I held Rebecca's hand as we climbed down the narrow trail that led deeper into the gorge. It was mid-July and as hot as it ever gets here in the foothills of our mountains.

The others were already there when we reached the bottom, along with some other young people who lived on outlying farms.

I had finished my first year at the University of Vermont and was enjoying the freedom of having put my books away for the summer months, and the opportunity to be with my father and my friends again, and especially with Rebecca.

"Hey there, Jubal!" Abel shouted. "I was wonderin' where ya got off ta with my lil' sister. 'Bout ta send out a search party ta see whatcha was up to."

"Took my father's buggy," I explained, "and my horse put up a fuss about getting hitched up to it."

Johnny Harris had just risen out of the water like a river otter and was grinning up at me. "Tha's a good one, Jubal. I gotta remember me that excuse."

"Why don't you just slide on back under the water and soak your head some more, Johnny Harris?" Rebecca had placed both hands on her hips and it made her look like an angry schoolmarm.

"Don't pay him any mind," I said. "Nobody else does. Same goes for your brother."

Both Abel and Johnny started to laugh and Rebecca turned away from them, took my hand, and said: "Take me for a walk, Jubal. I don't need to stand here listening to their nonsense."

She pulled me and we started down a rock-strewn path that ran along the river, accompanied by hoots from Abel and Johnny.

"Idiots," Rebecca said. "It must be a pure pleasure to go off to the university and talk to people who have brains in their heads."

I squeezed her hand and smiled. "Actually, I couldn't wait to get home and see you all."

"Well, I'm glad you include me."

"You most of all," I said.

Rebecca stopped, glanced over her shoulder to make sure we were out of view from the others, and rose up on her toes and kissed me lightly on the lips.

My hands went to her waist and I gently pulled her toward me and returned the kiss. Heat immediately rushed through me, and I could feel it rush through Rebecca as well, and she was breathing deeply as she raised her hands to my chest and pushed me away.

"We have to stop, Jubal." I pulled her toward me again and heard her whisper, "Please, Jubal," in my ear.

I stepped back. "I sure don't want to stop."

"And I don't want you to, but we have to."

"Let's walk on down a bit more," I suggested, hoping if we got farther away from the others Rebecca would change her mind and I could start kissing her again.

She smiled up at me as though she knew what I had planned. "I think we should head on back," she said. "The other girls from school will be here soon, and I don't want them telling everyone we were off in the bushes."

I looked around me, then back at her. "They sure are awful nice bushes," I said.

A small smile spread across her mouth. "Yes, they are." She took my hand and started us back along the path. "Maybe someday we'll come back and see just how nice they are."

"Someday? When is that?"

"I don't know," she said. "When we're more sure about each other, I suspect."

Jerusalem's Landing, Vermont, 1865

I rode Jezebel across the swath of clear-cut toward the bunkhouse on the opposite side. Billy Lucie's suspicions had proved correct. The men who worked for him had already abandoned their axes and saws and were lazing about on the shaded bunkhouse porch. When I was halfway across the swath I saw one man break off from the others and head to the rear of the ramshackle building. I was too far away to identify him as Bobby Suggs, but I suspected it was he.

As I rode up to the cabin a man I knew only as Jimmy stood and stepped off the porch to meet me.

"You lookin' for Suggs, Jubal?" he asked.

"I am."

Jimmy was a slender, wiry man, with a ragged beard and unkempt black hair. He was dressed in heavy wool trousers and a red-and-black checked flannel shirt, and like all loggers there were deep scars on his hands and arms from various misadventures with axes and saws.

"Well, Jubal, I don't think yer gonna git ta see him. Leastways not today," he said. "When he saw ya ridin' up, he axed if I knew who ya was, an' I tol' him ya was Jubal Foster, the deputy constable." Jimmy let out a laugh. "Said he knew ya from the war an' had no plan on seein' ya agin. I guess ya saw him head off."

I nodded slowly. "I think I'll take a ride into the woods and see if I can spot him."

"He in trouble with the law?"

"Not that I know of. But I do have to talk to him."

"Woods are pretty thick back there," Jimmy said. "Lotta pucker brush, could tear up yer horse's legs."

"I'm not goin' in very far," I said.

I rode Jezebel to the rear of the cabin and looked back into the tree line. Light was fading quickly and there was no point in heading farther back. The chance of finding a lone man in the dark was minimal, especially one who didn't want to be found.

I rode back to the front of the bunkhouse. Jimmy was sprawled on the porch again and this time he didn't bother to rise. "Ya see him?" he asked.

I shook my head. "When he comes back, you tell him I need him to stop by and see me the next time he's in town."

"I'll tell him, but I wouldn't count on him comin' by."

I nodded, but said nothing. I had no intention of waiting for Bobby Suggs. On the way home I'd stop by and ask Billy Lucie what time the men started work in the morning, and I'd be back here waiting when Bobby Suggs dragged his sorry self out of bed.

———

Centreville, Virginia, 1862

We were encamped outside the town on land surrounding a large plantation house that our officers had already commandeered. I had been promoted to corporal, replacing a man who'd been killed during the rearguard action covering our retreat. We were a badly battered army and our field hospital was still trying to tend to all the wounded we had brought with us.

I had been assigned to head a detachment of litter-bearers to carry the wounded into surgery and to remove the severed limbs that lay scattered about the surgery floor. The limbs were taken to a pit where they would later be burned, or buried, and seeing them laying there together, the mismatched arms and legs varying in size, had put all of us off our dinners.

Now, seated before a campfire, I could do little more than stare into the flames.

"I was listenin' ta two of them doctors talk," Abel said. "One was sayin' how he could cut off an arm or a leg in two minutes flat." He stopped to draw a breath. "Jesus, ta think that they're timin' how fast they kin do it, like it's some kinda race or somethin'."

I kept my eyes on the flames. "It's because they don't have any medicine to kill the pain. All they can give you is a shot of whiskey. It must seem like two days, not two minutes, when they start cutting, so the faster they can do it . . ." The words died in my mouth, the thought too grim to finish.

Jemma, a young Negro girl who had become a camp follower and now worked for her keep, asked me if I wanted water or coffee. She was a pretty girl, tall and lean, with light skin and large, round, wonder-filled eyes, and not more than fifteen years old, I guessed. She had run away from a plantation farther south and had attached herself to our unit to keep out of the hands of the Rebs.

I shook my head and declined. "I'm too tired to raise a cup to my lips."

She asked the same of Abel and he agreed to a drink of water.

"Yo young massahs done has yo'sefs a powful, bizzy day, I 'spect. Furs fightin' dem Rebs, den carryin' all dem wounded boys ta da docta's tent so's de kin git de arms an' legs chopped off." She paused, her large eyes blinking. "Why dey do dat, Massah Jubal? Why dey don' fix 'em up? Why dey jus' chop off de arms an' legs?"

"The wounds are too bad to fix," I explained. "If they didn't cut them off, they'd die from the infection that would set in."

"Dem po' boys," Jemma said, shaking her head. "Dey be betta off daid. Dey git home ain't no woman gonna wants dem. Ain'ts no work dey gonna be able ta do. It's jus' pow'ful sad, Massah Jubal, pow'ful sad."

Jemma's observations were cut short by the arrival of Johnny and Bobby Suggs.

"Johnny, where the hell have you been?" I demanded. "I was looking for you to be part of the litter detail and I couldn't find you anywhere."

Johnny grinned down at me. "Well, look at this. Ol' Jubal Foster is a corporal for less than a day an' he's already barkin' out orders an wantin' ta know where ever'body is." He let out a laugh. "Reason ya couldn't find me is that I knew ya was gonna put me ta work, so me an' Bobby headed out ta do some scroungin' instead." He raised his chin toward the sack Bobby was carrying. "We found some ol' nigger who works on this plantation an' made him show us where their masters buried their foodstuffs. We got us some ham, some beans, some bacon. Bobby, ya give that sack ta Jemma. We're gonna have us a *good* breakfast tomorrow." He raised a cautioning finger to Jemma. "Don' ya go givin' any of that away ta any of yer friends. Ya keep it safe fer us."

"Here you go, good lookin'," Bobby said, handing the sack to Jemma. "When ya gonna break down an' give me a kiss?"

Jemma shied back as she took the sack from Bobby, but her eyes quickly started to glitter over what was inside. "I'z hides it in my tent," she said. "I sleep wit it unda my head. Don' yo go an' worry. It's gonna be safe wit me. Oh Lordy, I ain't had no bacon since I cain't 'member when. We be cookin' in bacon grease fo' a week, I betcha."

I got up and walked over to Bobby. The smell of liquor surrounded him like a mist. I stepped up to Johnny and smelled the same. "Looks like you boys found something to drink too," I said. "You better get your asses in your bedrolls before some officer comes by and smells it on you."

"It was jus' a little tipple." Johnny started to chuckle.

"Is it all gone or is there more?" I asked.

"Oh, it's all gone," Bobby said, laughing around his words. "We woulda brought ya some, *corporal*, but there jus' wasn't enough."

"Get some sleep," I said, and returned to the fire.

I don't know what awakened me. Perhaps it was Jemma's scream. But before I even knew I was awake I was on my feet, pistol in hand, and headed toward her tent.

Bobby Suggs was on top of her, one hand covering her mouth, the other holding a knife to her throat. Jemma's eyes were wide and she was using her hands to unbutton Bobby's trousers.

"Jus' get it out and stick it in," he growled. "Ya do it, or I'll cut ya. An' ever'body'll think some Rebs came in an' cut the throat of a run-away slave."

Jemma was sobbing beneath the hand that covered her mouth and between that and Bobby's threats and his grunting, he hadn't heard me slide into the tent.

I grabbed a handful of his greasy hair and yanked his head back, shoving the barrel of my pistol in his ear at the same time. "You cut that girl," I hissed, "and you're gonna hear one big boom and then you're not gonna hear anything ever again." I cocked the pistol to let him know I meant what I said.

"All right, all right, let me get offen her," he said.

"Drop the knife alongside of you."

He did so, and I picked it up and shoved it into my belt. Then I grabbed him by the back of his belt, dragged him off her, and out of the tent.

"What the hell's the matter with you?" Suggs snarled. "I was only givin' that nigger what they all want. I was jus'—"

Suggs never finished the sentence. The toe of my right boot caught him in the center of his chest and drove all the breath from his body. He fell onto his back gasping for air.

Abel and Johnny and a few other men came rushing up, wanting to know what had happened. Jemma came crawling out of her tent, her face streaked with tears. "He was gonna kill me, Massah Jubal. He was gonna do it fo' sure."

I turned to Johnny and Abel as Suggs continued to gasp for air. "I heard Jemma scream, and when I got to her tent I found that son of a bitch trying to rape her."

Johnny spun around in a circle. "Goddamn, Jubal, it weren't no rape. Them colored girls, they all lookin' for it all the time. Ya look at all the little kids runnin' aroun' these plantations an' most of 'em is half white. Ya think tha's cause they don't like spreadin' their legs fer a white man?"

I stared at Johnny in disbelief, wondering what had happened to the man I'd grown up with, the minister's son who might have been annoyingly mischievous, but who was never really mean.

"She's fifteen years old," I snapped. "She's a little kid who's trying to save herself from the Rebs."

"It don' matter with them," he shot back. "An' it don' matter how old they is. It's the way they was raised. Their own daddies give 'em a poke."

I stared at Johnny, then drew a deep breath. "Take Suggs back to his tent," I said. I glared down at the man, who had finally gotten his breath back. "You go near that child again and I'll put your sorry ass in front of a firing squad. You understand me, Suggs?"

"I understand you, Mr. Bigshot Corporal. An' you understan' this: I ain't gonna forget what you done. Kickin' me like a dog over some goddamn nigger bitch."

CHAPTER NINE

Walter Johnson was behind the counter when I got back to the store at six o'clock.

"Hello, Jubal," he called as I entered. "Rebecca tol' me ya might be stoppin' by. She said it had somethin' ta do with a friend a Johnny's."

"Yes sir, a man named Bobby Suggs who was with us in the war. Edgar Billingsley said he stopped by his farm about a week before Johnny died, asking where he could find him."

"Was he a tall fella—scruffy beard, kinda rough-lookin' all over?"

"That pretty much nails him down," I said.

"Yeah, I seen him then. He was standin' outside the store with Johnny, few days afore Johnny died. They looked like they was disagreein' about somethin' at first. Then Johnny started laughin' so's I figured it weren't nothin' serious. This Suggs fella, he came in later that day fer a plug a tobacco, but he din' say much, just paid his money an' left. I figured maybe he worked at the mill. They get a rough-lookin' group pickin' up jobs there from time ta time. Lot of 'em wear Union caps, so's I figure they're mostly war veterans." He shook his head. "I gotta tell ya, Jubal, a lot a strange boys come home from that war, some of 'em pretty scary. Makes me wonder what my Abel woulda been like if he made it home."

"Abel was the same boy you knew," I assured him. "The war never changed him."

Walter Johnson drew a deep breath. "Tha's good ta hear. He was always such a good boy. God, I loved him."

"He was the best of all of us," I said. "Always was."

The storekeeper drew another long breath and a smile passed over his face. It reminded me of the last time I saw Abel smile. "Ya been home yet?" he asked.

"No, I haven't."

"Well, Rebecca went down ta yer house a bit ago. Took ya a fresh baked apple pie, she did." His smile had widened. "She's a mighty good cook, that girl."

"I better get on home then, or my father will eat it all. Thanks for your help."

"Any time, Jubal. Any time at all."

Rebecca was seated at the kitchen table with my father. He had already cut himself a big slice of apple pie and was chewing happily.

"Dang," he said. "Thought I'd be able to finish off this whole pie afore ya got home. I guess ya better sit down an' have yerself a piece."

I thanked Rebecca for the pie, then went to the water pump and washed up before returning to sit between my father and her. She had already cut me a large slice of pie and, hungry as I was, I went straight to it.

"It's delicious," I said.

"Thank you." She lowered her eyes demurely. "We got two big barrels of apples in today, so I cooked up two pies before they were all gone. My father already ate the other one at dinner, and he was eyeing this one as well. Doc Pierce says he's not supposed to eat the way he does, says he's too heavy."

"So you brung it to us. God save Doc Pierce," my father said with a laugh.

"No, I was going to bring it to you anyway." Rebecca looked up at me and then turned her eyes away. "Well, I should get back to the store."

I pushed myself away from the table. "Let me give my horse some oats and I'll walk you on back," I said.

Out in the barn Rebecca stood beside me as I gave Jezebel a bucket of oats and fresh water. When I turned back to Rebecca, she slipped her arms around my neck and brought her lips to mine. "I'm sorry to be so forward, Jubal, but you know I was always a willful girl. I loved you before you went off to that awful war, and I still love you now, and I'm tired of waiting for you to tell me you love *me*."

I began to stammer a reply, but she wouldn't let me.

"And I don't want to hear anything about your arm and that it makes some difference between us." Her eyes were glittering, and in the dim light of the barn I couldn't tell if she was about to cry or if she was angry.

"I . . . I—"

Again, she cut me off. "I didn't grow up loving your arm, Jubal. I grew up loving you, and you grew up loving me too. I know you did."

My father was still seated at the table when I got back. "I couldn't come up with much on that Suggs fella," he said. "Railroad clerk says a fella fits his description asked directions ta Jerusalem's Landing, but he couldn't swear fer sure it was him. I checked some of the roomin' houses but they never seen him, so I don't think he's stayin' up in Richmond."

"I found him up on Lucie's woodlot," I told him. "Lucie took him on to take the place of a man who broke a leg."

"Ya seen him?"

"I tried to today, but he dodged me by slipping off into the woods."

"Ya think he took off fer good?"

"Can't be sure, but I don't think so. Anyway, I plan to be back there at sun-up just to make sure he doesn't. If he did I'll start running him down."

"I'll go with ya," my father said. "We have ta start chasin' him it'll be best there's two of us." He raised his chin toward the pie. "Cut yerself another slice," he said, grinning across the table at me. "Ya know, you'd be a pretty big fool not ta marry that girl. Iffen she'll have ya."

Jerusalem's Landing, Vermont, 1861

Johnny waved the newspaper about his head as he entered the Johnsons' store. "We got ourselves a war!" he shouted.

I was at the rear of the store with Abel, helping him stock some shelves for his father. I was home from school for the Easter observance and everywhere there was only one topic of conversation—the election of Mr. Lincoln as our new president, followed by the immediate secession of seven Southern states, making war seem inevitable.

Johnny brought the newspaper back to us and we were quickly joined by Abel's father and several other men in the store. "Those damn Rebels fired on Fort Sumter two weeks ago," Johnny said, holding the paper out for us to see.

"Where's Fort Sumter?" Abel asked.

"Says here it's in South Carolina, on the coast in Charleston harbor," Johnny said.

"Well, what's that mean ta us here in Vermont?" Abel asked.

"It's a challenge ta the Union," Johnny said. "All them fools seceded even afore Mr. Lincoln took office, now they's attakin' our forts, tryin' ta drive us outta what they claim is their country, the Confederate States of America. Oh, it's war fer sure, jus' like the newspaper says."

"Ya mean we have ta go down there an' fight?" Abel asked. He looked bewildered by the prospect.

"Could be," I said. "We'll have to wait and see what Mr. Lincoln can work out. But it sure doesn't look good."

Abel turned to me. "Are ya gonna go an' fight, Jubal?"

"I sure don't want to. But I don't know if I'll have a choice, if any of us will."

"You have a choice." It was Doc Pierce, who had come up to join us as we were talking. "You stay in school, Jubal Foster. Don't you let yourself become cannon fodder for a bunch of goddamn politicians." Doc's face had become beet-red as he spoke. Now he turned to Abel and Johnny. "You boys stay put too. This town don't need to lose its future to this madness."

Later, we went over to Johnny's barn to talk it over. We were all a bit grimmer now, after listening to Doc.

"Says in the paper that the army's gonna be sendin' out officers ta sign people up, that they'll even be comin' ta small towns like ours." There was still a bit of excitement in Johnny's voice. "Course we could go on up ta Richmond ta hear what they have ta say."

"I ain't in no hurry," Abel said. "I kin wait till they git here."

"You ain't anxious ta go off an' fight?" Johnny asked.

"What fer?" Abel countered. "So I kin go off an' kill some boy no older'n me over stuff I don' even understand?"

"Yer country's been attacked," Johnny said. "Don't that mean nothin' to ya?"

"I don' know what it means, 'cept that people I don' even know are gonna want me ta go off an' kill other people I don' even know." He shrugged at me. "Whaddaya think, Jubal?"

"I think what you're saying makes a lot of sense, Abel. But I also think we may not have a choice. Our country would end up pretty weak if it was split in two, and England would love to step in and take it back, one piece at a time. They already tried that about fifty years ago."

"So yer fer war," Johnny said, much more emphatically than I felt.

"No . . . I don't know what I am," I said.

"Well, ya better make up yer mind," Johnny responded. "Things are gonna start movin' awful fast."

"I guess we all better make up our minds," Abel said. "I jus' wish these damn politicians would leave us be."

Manassas, Virginia, 1862

We were sent out to probe the area north of Manassas, to make sure Lee's army wasn't planning to turn north and strike at Washington. We were only a single squad—ten privates, a sergeant, and a corporal—so we weren't looking for a fight with the Rebs. We just wanted to spy on them.

The sergeant was named Jim Lacey, a slender, bookish man who had been a schoolteacher in Pennsylvania, and who had left a wife and two small children behind when he'd joined up.

Lying behind a high embankment we could see the glow of fires and hear the faint murmur of voices coming from a Reb encampment about a hundred yards to the south.

Lacey explained that he had divided the squad between himself and me. "We're gonna move up on them on both flanks," he said. "Corporal Foster will take five men on the right flank and I'll take the remainder on the left. No shooting unless you have no other choice." He took out his knife. "Use your knives and make sure you hide any bodies. We want their officers to think those men deserted, so make sure you take their weapons with you. If you do have to open fire, beat it back here as quick as you can. The ten of us won't stand much of a chance against that many Rebs. So keep in mind that fighting's not what we're here for.

We're here to gather information, not to engage the enemy." He leaned over to me. "Try to see if they have any siege cannons. If they're going to move on the capital they'll have those with them."

We had decent cover as we moved down the slope toward the Reb encampment. The night was overcast and there was no moon to contend with, and the men had left their canteens and mess kits back at our camp to eliminate the clattering noises common to troop movements. We were carrying Spencer rifles, along with sidearms and knives. But we were no match for the thousand or so men camped ahead of us.

We crawled within fifty yards of the Reb camp and could make out sentries twenty yards farther in. They were spaced about fifty yards apart and as I studied them through a glass, they seemed unconcerned and a few appeared to be dozing. After beating us so badly they seemed to have few worries about a counterattack.

I motioned Abel up beside me. "There's a sentry sound asleep twenty yards ahead of us."

Abel squinted in the dark. "Yeah, I see him."

"I'm gonna crawl on up and take him out. That'll give us a hundred yards between the next two sentries, which should be enough cover to get inside their camp. We need a good look at what kind of armaments they have."

I crawled through the brush, Abel and the other men about ten yards behind me. The sentry had taken a position behind a large rock, and when I came within fifteen feet of it I could hear the faint sound of snoring. I held up my hand, ordering my men to stop, then rose to a crouch and slipped quickly behind the rock.

The sentry awoke as I moved in on him and started to reach for the rifle that lay beside him. But he never reached it. I slammed the butt of my Spencer into the side of his head, once, twice. The first blow hit with a cracking sound, the second much softer, and when I looked at the side of his head I could see blood and brain matter seeping out from under his gray cap.

I waved the others up and handed the Reb's rifle to Abel. "Drag the body out of here and find a good place to hide it. Cover it up with thick brush so nobody finds him till long after we're gone. Then wait there for us. We'll come out the same way we went in, so it should be easy for you to join up with us. But if you hear shooting, just head on back and meet up with Lacey and the rest of the squad."

"I ain't gonna leave ya behind, Jubal."

I took hold of Abel's sleeve. "It's just better not to waste time lookin' for each other in the dark. We'll meet back where the squad split up."

He reached down and grabbed the sentry's collar. "Damn," he whispered, "he don't look much older'n sixteen."

I had tried not to look at the sentry's face, just as I'd tried not to look at the faces of the other men I'd killed. After my first battle at Hoke's Run, a sergeant had warned me against it. To do so, he claimed, would invite those men into your dreams for years to come.

I looked into Abel's eyes and saw the deep sadness that resided there. I suddenly wished that I felt that sadness myself, but I no longer did, and I wondered which was worse: dreaming about the men you'd killed, or not caring that you had.

I left the sentry post with three men and we crawled quietly to the edge of the Rebel camp. The campfires were low now, the embers popping and crackling. We skirted the area and moved to the rear. There must have been a thousand men sleeping, most of them in bedrolls, some—officers, I supposed—in tents. We reached a corral where the horses were bedded down. They were not cavalry mounts, but horses used to pull artillery and supply wagons. Moving behind the corral we located the artillery pieces. There were siege cannons, mostly twelve-pound howitzers with a few three-inch ordnance and ten-pound Parrott rifles mixed in. Beside them were the wagons carrying their shells. None of the wagons were guarded.

I looked through two wagons before I located a box of dynamite and a coil of fuse. The men were staring at me as though I'd lost my mind.

"We're gonna blow these wagons," I whispered. "We'll set the fuse long enough to give us time to work our way back the way we came. We'll go nice and slow, so we don't wake anybody up. When it blows there'll be so much confusion and panic with all these canisters of grapeshot going off, nobody will think to come after us."

One of the men glanced at me nervously. "The sergeant said not to engage the Rebs," he whispered back. "Now you plannin' to blow up his camp."

"We didn't know we were going to find an unguarded gift like this, and we're sure as hell not gonna pass it up."

We rigged the explosives and returned to the edge of the camp and slowly began to work our way out. I wanted to go back through the empty sentry post and I urged the men to crawl as quickly as they could without making any noise. When the wagons began to explode we'd get up and run full-out for cover. I only hoped that Lacey and his men wouldn't find themselves in the middle of it.

The first explosion lit up the sky, and as grapeshot began to rain down on the sleeping Rebs I could hear shouts of pain and fear. I got to my feet and urged the men forward and we ran as fast as we could. A few shots rang out from the sentry positions to our right and left but there was little hope of hitting men running full speed in the dark. Ahead, I saw Abel rise from behind a fallen tree and he waved us forward wildly, then joined us as we raced past him, toward the position where our squad had split in two.

"I hid the body real good," he said as we ran.

"Doesn't matter," I answered. "They know we were here."

He started to laugh. "Yeah, they sure do, don't they?"

We both looked back over our shoulders and saw another plume of fire belch into the air.

"It's like the Fourth of July," Abel said, laughing as he ran on.

Lacey was waiting with the others when we got there, panting and out of breath.

"Jesus, what in hell's name did you boys do?" he asked.

"The Rebs left us a present of some unguarded ammunition wagons," I said, still struggling to regain my breath. "There were siege guns and what other artillery they did have doesn't really matter. There's no ammunition left."

He shook his head and now he too started to laugh. "You boys earned yourselves a medal for this one. And I'm gonna see that you get it."

CHAPTER TEN

My father and I were in Billy Lucie's dooryard a good half hour before sunrise. Mrs. Lucie invited us in for a steaming cup of coffee and both husband and wife listened quietly as my father explained why we were there.

"Oh Lord, I sure hope it don't turn out that I hired the man who kilt the poor reverend's son," Billy said. He shook his head and turned to me. "I figured it was somethin' serious when you axed me what time the men started up work in the morning. But I didn't wanna push ya fer yer reasons. Figured ya'd tell me when ya was ready."

I knew Lucie harbored some concern that I hadn't trusted him the previous day, which wasn't the case. The Lucies were members of Reverend Harris's church, and I had been concerned that Billy might demand some answers from Suggs if I told him about my suspicions. Sitting in his kitchen now I decided not to tell him that part of it. I simply explained that I had wanted to keep Suggs as calm as possible and not send him fleeing in the night.

"Oh, he ain't gone no place," Lucie said. "Not unless he went on foot. All the boys keep their horses in my barn, and when I went out to give 'em oats this mornin' his was in its stall like always. God, I hope he din' have nothin' ta do with that killin'. I don' think I'd be able ta face the reverend agin iffen he did."

"Well let's go on up an' talk ta him, see what he has ta say fer him-self," my father proposed.

"I'll go on up with you," Billy said.

The men were just rousing themselves when we reached the bunkhouse and Billy went on inside to give them their work orders as he did each morning. Coffee was brewing on a fire outside and the men began mak-ing their way to it, tin mugs in hand.

When Bobby Suggs stumbled out he immediately saw my father and me seated on our horses.

"You always was a persistent sumbitch, Jubal Foster," he said. He rubbed the back of his hand across his mouth. "Mind if I git some coffee afore I gotta listen ta ya?"

"Get it, and bring it over here so we can talk."

He did as he was told, then looked up at me and at my father. "Who's this here fella?" he asked.

"He's my father, and he's the town constable."

"Howdy do," Bobby said.

"We got some questions fer ya, son," my father began. "First of all, why'd you run off when Jubal was up cheer yesterday?"

Bobby snorted. "Din' wanna talk ta him. Knew him durin' the war and din' much like him." A smile exposed badly decayed teeth. "Or maybe I thought he was plannin' on kickin' me agin cause he thought I was havin' some sport with some nigger whore."

My father dismounted his horse, walked over, and took Suggs by the arm, leading him away from the others. He glanced up at me. "Follow along, Jubal, but stay up on yer horse in case you gotta run this fella down."

"I ain't runnin' no place. I ain't got no reason ta." Suggs tried to pull his arm free, but it was useless. My father's hand was like a large vice and when he wanted to hold onto someone, he held on. I'd seen him do it many a time.

"You tell us 'bout Johnny Harris, an' ya tell us true," my father said. "I even think yer lyin' ta me, yer ass is gonna be locked up in the sheriff's jail up ta Richmond."

"Johnny was my frien'," Suggs whined. "I come here ta Vermont ta visit him. I sure had no call ta do him harm."

"He was such a friend, why weren't you at his funeral?" I asked.

"He was buried afore I even knew he was dead," Suggs answered. "I was movin' aroun' lookin' fer work in the loggin' camps hereabouts, an' I was sleepin' out at night cause I din' have no extra money fer a room."

"Why din' Johnny put you up?" my father asked. "Even if his folks din' want you in the house, there woulda been room fer ya in the barn. An' I never heard of Reverend Harris turnin' anybody away."

"Din' wanna impose on 'em," Suggs said.

I laughed at the comment, couldn't help myself.

Suggs glared at me. "It's true, Foster, whether ya wants ta believe it or not."

I climbed down off my horse and walked up to him. "You're a goddamn liar," I snapped. "You were a liar ever' day I knew you during the war, and you're still a liar."

"You better be careful what yer sayin', cause I don't care iffen you's a one-arm cripple or not. An' I sure don' care iffen yer some half-cooked lawman. Ya call me a liar one more time we gonna have at it."

My father jerked Suggs around so hard his feet almost left the ground. "Ya lemme hear any more of that cripple talk, there ain't gonna be enough left of ya ta have at it with nobody. Ya understan' me, son?"

"All right, all right. I jus' had enough a yer boy durin' the war. I ain't needin' any more of it now." The whine was back in Suggs's voice.

"Ya jus' answer our questions," my father growled. "Ya kin start with tellin' us what the hell brought ya up ta Vermont."

"I was lookin' fer work," Suggs stammered.

"You live in goddamn Pennsylvania, Suggs," I countered. "It's a long way to come to look for a job choppin' down trees."

"There ain't no work in Pennsylvania." Some of the color left Suggs's cheeks, as though he'd suddenly realized he was heading for more trouble than he'd thought. "Look, all us boys come home from the war all at once, an' there jus' wasn't enough work fer ever'body. Then I remembered Johnny tellin' me what a great place he was from. How nobody was rich, but ever'body lived good in this here valley he grew up in. But all I could remember was that it was up near the Canadian border an' had some kinda name from the Bible. So I headed up this way, an' when I axed about a town with a Bible name they sent me ta this place called Jericho, but that weren't it. Then some folks tol' me about a place in the mountains called Jerusalem's Landing, so I come here. An' sure enough, this was the place Johnny'd been talkin' 'bout."

"Abel Johnson's father saw you talking to Johnny outside his store. Said you seemed to be mad about something and that Johnny just laughed at you. What was that about?"

A sly look came to Suggs's eyes, as though he'd found something he could use to deflect our attention. "We was talkin' about a man named Rusty LeRoche," he said. "I was up there lookin' fer work on his woodlot, an' he was ready ta take me on. Then he axed me what brought me up ta the mountains, and I mentioned I was a frien' of the minister's son from back in the war and I'd come up ta visit him. Hell, I thought that'd stand me in good stead, minister's son an' all that good shit. Well, it sure don't. LeRoche hears that an' he tells me Johnny's nothin' but a no-account sumbitch, minister's son or not, and iffen I'm his friend I must be a no-account too, an' he throws me offen his land without so much as a mind you be, sir."

My father had let go of Suggs, who was now just standing there, shuffling his feet.

Billy Lucie walked over and joined us. "Everythin' all right cheer?" he asked.

My father nodded. "Yer man here is tellin' us what brought him up to these mountains. Ain't found no reason not ta believe him . . . yet." He let the last word hang and turned back to Suggs. "But I'm tellin' ya this, son. Afore ya leave this here town, ya better come in an' let us know. Ya try ta slip away," he raised his chin toward Lucie, "an' Billy here will come and let us know. Ain't that right, Billy?"

"Right as can be," Billy said.

My father placed a heavy hand on Bobby Suggs's shoulder. "I hear that ya left without stoppin' by, I promise ya every lawman in Vermont will be lookin' fer ya. An' Jubal here an' me is gonna be ridin' up yer tail till we find ya."

Suggs glanced at Billy and me, and then back at my father. "I ain't goin' no place," he said. "Leastways, not till the loggin' season's finished."

My father and I thanked Billy and headed back down the mountain single file.

"Ya think he's lyin'?" my father asked when we reached the road below.

"Bobby Suggs couldn't tell the truth even if it would help him," I said.

"What was all that about ya kickin' him?" he asked.

I told him about the incident in camp, about young Jemma and Bobby trying to rape her.

"Ya did good ta stop him. Iffen ya shot him he woulda deserved it, goin' after a helpless child like that. Sounds like Rusty LeRoche was a smart'n ta throw him offen his land."

I had told my father about Johnny's trouble with Rusty, so Bobby's tale about Rusty had not surprised him.

"Looks ta me like Rusty's still our strongest suspect," he added.

"There's something about why Bobby Suggs is here that he's not telling us," I said. "Until I know what that is, I'm not ready to put him aside."

My father nodded. "Ya always had good instincts, Jubal. Ya follow up on whatcha feel in yer gut. Rusty'll still be here iffen this Suggs fella proves not ta be our man."

Jerusalem's Landing, Vermont, 1861

The fife-and-drum corps headed down the town's main street, stopping in front of the Johnsons' store where an officer and several of his men had set up a recruiting table.

"Hot damn!" Johnny shouted, following his words with a whoop. "I never expected nothin' like this."

Abel was grinning at him. "Me neither. Way they's stirrin' ever'body up, them Rebs oughta be shakin' in their boots."

I glanced around us. The army had put up posters the week before, announcing that a recruitment officer would be here today, and the whole town appeared to have gathered, even some folks from outlying farms. I'd heard the sawmill had even shut down so its men could hear what the army had to say.

Rebecca came up beside me and slipped her hand in mine. She leaned up to my ear. "Come take me for a walk," she said. "I don't want you listening to these men who want all you boys to go off to war."

I smiled down at her. "I have to hear what they say, Rebecca. It's about our country."

Before I could say more a tall, handsome army captain, flanked by a sergeant and a corporal, held up his arms for silence.

"Folks, my name is Captain John Lawrence, and if you'll just give me a minute of your time I'll tell you about the dangers that are facing our beloved nation."

Lawrence was dressed in a blue uniform dappled with a gold braid and a broad-brimmed blue hat. He was wearing a saber and a sidearm, and his insignia showed him to be a cavalry officer. He held up his arms again, cocking his head to one side, his neatly barbered beard giving him an air of great authority.

"The nation has been attacked!" he shouted. "A cowardly and un-provoked attack at Fort Sumter that sent good, wholesome American boys to their graves. Now the Confederate Army is massing in Virginia within striking distance of our nation's capital. And they have left us no choice but to let loose the dogs of war.

"So why am I here in the peaceful village of Jerusalem's Landing? you ask." He paused to gaze out over the crowd, stopping to stare at each young man he saw. When his eyes lighted on me, Rebecca squeezed my hand tightly, holding onto me as though his stare might pull me from her.

"I am here because the nation needs its young men to step forward and take the fight to the Rebs." He raised a warning finger. "And don't you doubt for a moment that if we don't take it to them, they will bring it to us."

The crowd began to buzz and he held up both hands again to silence them. "Oh, I know. You say that Vermont is so far from South Carolina. It is so far from Washington where our new president, Mr. Lincoln, struggles to hold our nation together. But I tell you this: If the Confederate Army overruns the nation's capital, they will not stop there. They will move on to Maryland and Pennsylvania, claiming they need to protect their flanks. Then they will move into New Jersey and New York for the same reason. And what sits across Lake Champlain from New York? Vermont sits there, my friends. Yes, once the Rebs overrun New York, they will head to Vermont, because they know our history. They know how Ethan Allen and his Green Mountain Boys attacked the British when they occupied New York, how they drove them out of Fort Ticonderoga, and those Rebs will know that they, too, will always be in danger as long as Vermont is free."

He began to pace. Then he stopped, removed his hat, and placed it over his heart. His voice became softer. "Oh, some say it will surely take time. And they are right. The Rebs may not be here for a year or more." Now his voice began to rise again. "But unless we defeat them now, and defeat them in Virginia and South Carolina and Georgia, we will surely have to defeat them here. And it will be a bitter fight. Farms and villages will be ravaged and burned, you can be certain of that. And to this I say no, never, not here, not in Vermont! I say let the burning take place in the South. Let those who started this war be the ones who pay that bitter price." Lawrence paced back and forth before his audience, his eyes again stopping on each young man.

"And how shall we do that? How shall we guarantee that the war is not brought to our doorstep? You know the answers to those questions— Ethan Allen answered them for you in 1775, almost one hundred years ago. We shall do as he did by taking the battle to the enemy." Lawrence drew a long, deep breath, as if he, himself, were girding for battle. "Right now our brave generals are bravely holding off the Rebel troops. And we must send our boys to help them. And if we do this we shall never have Vermonters awaking to find Rebel troops marching down our streets. No, never. Instead it will be those in the South, the ones who started this conflict, who will awaken to find Union troops standing in their dooryards. And that day will begin when you young men step up to this table behind me and pledge your honor to the Union cause, when you step forward to join those of us who already serve, when you join hands with President Lincoln to preserve our nation by joining his Army of the Republic."

Wild applause and shouting followed the captain's speech, and the fife-and-drum corps immediately began to play. Several of the older men in town stepped forward to shake his hand and to clap the backs of the young men who moved up to the table.

Rebecca clasped my hand so tightly it began to go numb. "Don't you sign your name, Jubal Foster." She glanced about her. "Where is Abel?" she asked no one in particular. "Where is my brother?"

Abel came pushing through the crowd, trailing Johnny in his wake. "We're gonna do it," he announced. "Me and Johnny both. We're gonna sign up ta defend the Union, just like the captain said. Are ya gonna come with us, Jubal? You gotta, ya know. We gotta do it all together, just like we always done."

Slowly I nodded my head. I believed what Captain Lawrence had said. Not all of it, not the part about Rebel troops marching down Vermont streets. But I believed we had to stop this secession if we hoped to preserve our nation, and to do that we had little choice but to invade the South and stamp out this new Confederate government.

Rebecca was staring at me. "Jubal, I don't want you to go, I don't want any of you boys to go." Her eyes filled with tears as she looked from me to her brother to Johnny. "I don't want you all going off to get killed for something I don't even understand, for something *you* don't understand."

"We know what we're doin', Rebecca," Abel said. He was grinning at her; then he seemed to notice she was crying and he reached out and stroked her arm.

She pulled away from him. "You're just boys," she snapped.

"We're twenty-one, or we will be soon," Johnny said. "That sure makes us men as far as I'm concerned."

The tears began to flow down Rebecca's cheeks. "Go ahead. Go sign your damned paper and go off and get yourselves killed. Just do it. Do it."

She spun on her heel and pushed her way through the crowd. I watched her go and I wanted to follow after her, but I remained rooted to the ground.

"Let's sign up," Johnny said.

"Yeah, come on, Jubal, let's do it." Much of the enthusiasm had left Abel's voice and I noticed that he too was following his sister's retreat. Then he brought his eyes back to me and slapped my shoulder. "Let's do it," he said again, more strongly this time.

Manassas, Virginia, 1862

Our artillery commenced shelling the Rebel encampment shortly after dawn, and since they had no ammunition left to respond to our volleys they began to beat a speedy withdrawal. We were lying along a rise watching the Rebs retreat, Abel, Johnny, and I. Johnny had missed our little adventure the previous night, having been assigned to a different detail, and Abel took great relish filling him in on our intrusion behind enemy lines. He made it sound like we had fought the Third Battle of Bull Run and that this time we'd won.

Sergeant Jim Lacey came up and slid down beside me. "How does it feel to see a Rebel retreat that you boys caused single-handedly?"

I smiled at him. "It wasn't quite that grand. There was a lot of blind-ass luck involved, including those Rebs being dumb enough to leave their ammunition wagons unguarded."

"That's what most of war is, a lotta blind-ass luck," Lacey said. "And if you're real, real lucky you even get to walk away alive."

"Are we gonna follow 'em?" Johnny asked.

"We're gonna shadow them with one column just to make sure they don't pick up a new supply of ammunition and turn back on us."

"Are we part of the column?" I asked.

"No, we are bonafide heroes, according to the generals, so we get to rest up for our next bit of daring do."

Abel and I started to laugh and then Johnny joined in. Abel jabbed a finger in Johnny's direction. "Why's he here restin' with the heroes? He was on litter duty at the field hospital, tryin' to get under the skirts a one of them nurses."

"Just mighta got there too, fer all *you* know," Johnny said. He grinned knowingly and fluttered his eyebrows. "Those poor nurses git tired an' like ta git them a poke or two when all the work's done."

"The only thing you been pokin' is yer hand," Abel replied.

Lacey slapped each of us on the back. "Come on, boys, let's go get us some chow. We got us an easy night for a change. You won't even be pullin' sentry duty."

"Holy shit," Abel said. "Those generals must really like us."

"Enjoy it while you can," Lacey said. "One thing's for certain: it won't last."

A large group of slaves had fled nearby plantations and had formed an encampment of their own adjacent to ours. They followed us whether we won or lost a battle, and I supposed they knew they had no other choice. Running farther north alone risked capture by Rebel forces who had been known to shoot the runaway slaves they encountered. Conversely, returning to their plantations assured they would at the least be whipped mercilessly before being returned to slavery.

The most disturbing thing to me had been hearing our own officers talking about driving the escaped slaves off, claiming they were a burden on our supplies and that they slowed our troops. How they slowed us I could not fathom. We never brought them with us; they simply followed at a distance, rejoining us when we stopped each night. And we did not feed them. They fed themselves from what they gathered and stole along the march, and their cook fires always smelled far better than ours. Some of their men even fought beside us in skirmishes using weapons they had plucked from the field.

Now, sitting under the shade of an ancient oak, my mind and body were soothed by the strains of "Swing Low, Sweet Chariot" that drifted up from the Negro encampment. Like all their music it was sweet and mournful at the same time. It spoke of suffering and yet was joyful. Above all, it told of a people who were enslaved but undefeated.

Josiah came and joined Abel and Johnny and me, his work at the hospital finished for the evening. He had been coming by almost every night and I suspected that the young slave girl Jemma was the reason.

"Do you ever get to talk to many of the runaway slaves?" I asked, as he slid down next to me.

"Time ta time," he said. "But ta be honest I have trouble understandin' mos' of 'em. They don'ts talk like Northern Negroes. It's like they swallows the words they say right as they sayin' 'em."

"You think they're a burden on us?" I asked.

"Don' see that they is. Why you axe me that?"

"I heard some officers bitching about them. It just surprised me."

"You mean big-time officers?"

"One was a general." I laughed. "You can bet the other officers agreed with him."

Josiah offered up his own laugh. "They damn well better agree wit him. They know what's good fer 'em. You gotta 'member, Jubal, they's white men we talkin' 'bout. You ain't never gonna hear mos' white men sayin' nothin' good 'bout black folk. We all jus' lazy, thievin' no-accounts."

"That's whatcha are," Johnny chimed in. "We all know that. It's 'bout time ya fessed up ta it."

"Johnny Harris, I don' know how ya got ta be a preacher's son. Ya musta been adopted." Josiah threw back his head and laughed again.

"You watch out," Abel joined in. "You'll give him ideas, an' afore long he'll be tellin' us how his momma found him floatin' down a river in a reed basket, an' how it's gonna be his job now ta lead us ta the promised land."

"I'm jus' gonna do the will of my Father in heaven," Johnny intoned.

The sound of the first shot sent us all scrambling for our weapons. Sergeant Lacey came running across the compound. "The Rebs are after our ammunition!" he shouted. "They wanna do the same thing we did last night. Grab your rifles and head back to the wagons."

We raced between rows of tents, staying low to make ourselves harder targets. When we reached the wagons three Rebs lay dead on the ground, along with two of our men who had been on guard duty. Lacey ran forward and began pulling fuses from the dynamite that had been stuffed in each wagon. As he reached the last wagon a shot rang out, spinning him around and throwing him to the ground. Johnny dashed past him and yanked the last fuse free and then threw himself down behind the wagon wheel.

Abel and I saw the Reb who had shot Lacey at the same moment and we opened up together, firing our sidearms until we saw his body pitch forward.

"Make sure he's dead," I ordered. "And watch out for others. I'm gonna see how bad Lacey was hit."

I crouched down beside the sergeant. He was on his back and his eyes were wide and unseeing, his face filled with surprise as he stared up at an empty black sky. The minie ball had caught him on the left side of his chest, and I'd seen enough men on the battlefield to know that the exit wound in his back would be as large as my fist.

A lieutenant came up beside me. "Is he dead, corporal?"

"Yes sir."

"How'd it happen?" he asked.

"He was pulling fuses from the dynamite the Rebs had planted in our ammunition wagons," I explained. "They shot him when he was going for the last one."

"Was it you who got that last one?"

"No sir, Private Harris got it." I inclined my head toward Johnny, who had come up beside us.

"Good work, private." The lieutenant looked back at me. "Your sergeant was a brave man."

"Yes sir," I said, wondering if that would give any comfort to his wife and children when they learned they would never see their husband and father again. Then I thought of the previous night, and I wondered if Jim Lacey would still be alive if I had not done what I had.

CHAPTER ELEVEN

It was Saturday night and I was sitting at my kitchen table reading Harriet Beecher Stowe's novel *Uncle Tom's Cabin; or, Life Among the Lowly*. Critics said its powerful narrative proved false all Southern justifications of slavery. I had heard about the novel long before war broke out. It had been discussed extensively at the university. But the pressure of my studies had kept me from reading it then. Now, having experienced slavery with my own eyes, I wanted to do so; wanted to see how well Mrs. Stowe had captured the cold-hearted callousness of one man's enslavement of another.

A knock at my back door brought me to my feet and I reached for my pistol and moved toward it.

"Who's there?" I called.

"It's Doc, Jubal. Open up."

I stuck the pistol under my belt and swung the door back and Doc stepped into the kitchen, immediately taking notice of the pistol. "Good thing you've got that," he said. "Somebody's movin' around in the Harris's barn, and it's not Virgil or his missus. They're out of town, visiting family."

"Let me wake up my father, and we'll go down and have a look."

"I'll leave it to you, then," Doc said. "I'm too old and fat to start chasing house breakers. But if I hear any shooting I'll be over with my scattergun."

* * *

My father dressed quickly, strapped on his own pistol, and followed me out the door. "Probably some kids who know the Harris's are out of town, an' decided to mess about in their barn. But we gotta check an' see. Be jus' our luck to have Johnny's killer come back lookin' fer somethin' he thought he left behind."

We reached the parsonage within minutes and my father leaned in, speaking quietly: "You go aroun' one side of the parsonage an' I'll go aroun' t'other. Let's be as quiet as we can, but if ya run inta any trouble sing out so's I know where ya are. I'll do the same. I don't want us ta go shootin' at each other."

My father and I came up on the front entrance of the barn together, each of us taking one side of the wide door. I could see a lantern inside the barn, moving slowly toward the rear. There was a tall figure behind it, definitely not a child.

We stepped into the barn together, one to each side of the doorframe, our pistols drawn.

"This here's Jonas Foster, the town constable," my father called out. "I'm here with my deputy an' I need ya ta turn aroun' slow an' easy; then walk on over ta the door holdin' that lantern high so's we can see who ya are. There's two pistols leveled on ya so don't do nothin' foolish."

"I ain't got no gun," a voice called back. "I'm comin' to ya nice an' slow."

I recognized the voice, and as the dark figure inched closer Bobby Suggs's scraggly features came into view. My father recognized him as well and he guided Suggs outside with a wave of his pistol, leaving me to follow behind him.

"Whatcha doin' in my minister's barn?" my father demanded.

"I'm jus' lookin' fer somethin' I left here."

I came up behind him and ordered him to place his hands behind his head. Then I holstered my pistol and ran my hand along his body, until I finally found his knife in his right boot. I tossed it on the ground at my father's feet.

"An' what was it ya left cheer?" my father asked.

"Jus' an ol' satchel with some clothes in it," Suggs said. "There was a wool shirt that I wanted. It's getting' a bit cold up on Mr. Lucie's woodlot, 'specially at night, an' I wanted the shirt ta keep myself warm." Suggs had turned so he could see both of us and his eyes were darting from one to the other like a cornered weasel. And like a weasel I knew he could be dangerous, so I kept my hand on the butt of my pistol.

"You had on a wool shirt when I saw you up on Lucie's woodlot the other day," I said. "Red-and-black check if I remember correctly. That's not good enough to keep you warm?"

"It's dirty an' it was gettin' a bit ripe," Suggs answered. "Can't deny a man a clean shirt, can ya, Jubal?"

"We can deny him comin' inta a man's barn when that man ain't home," my father snapped.

"I knocked on the front door," Suggs pleaded. "When nobody answered I figgered it was okay, since the reverend done tol' me ta stop by anytime. I figgered he wouldn't mind, an' I din' wanna ride all the way back ta Mr. Lucie's woodlot then have ta come back down agin later."

"Did ya think ta come down an' see me or my son?" my father asked.

"What fer? It was jus' my clothes I was after."

My father stepped in closer to him. "You tellin' me ya din' know that this here barn is where Johnny Harris was murdered?"

Suggs spread both hands out at his sides and shook his head. "No, I din'. I swear it. I din' know nothin' 'bout Johnny gettin' killed in this here barn."

"Bullshit," I barked. "You want us to believe those men up at the woodlot don't know every detail of what happened? They're as gossipy as a bunch of old church ladies."

"I'm tellin' ya true, I din' even hear 'bout Johnny gettin' kilt till he was already buried in the ground, an' I put off comin' back fer my stuff outta respect fer his ma an' pa."

I took hold of his shirtfront. "Suggs, you are a first-class liar. You were a liar and a thief and a rapist when I knew you back in the war, and you haven't changed one bit. Where's your horse?"

"Tied up inside the barn."

"Why inside?" my father demanded. "You wanna make sure nobody knew you was here? A man had nothin' ta hide woulda left his horse tied out front."

"I wanted it ta have some water fer the trip back ta Lucie's place. Figured there'd be water here inna barn."

My father shook his head. "Man's got hisself an answer fer everythin', don't he though?"

I spun Suggs around. "Go get that horse and walk him out here real slow."

I followed Suggs inside the barn and watched him as he took the horse's reigns and led him outdoors. There were saddlebags behind the saddle and I told him to pull them down. When he did I saw the brand CFA on the horse's haunch.

"Stole this horse from the Rebs, did you?" I said.

Suggs glared at me. "Tha's right. Figured they owed it ta me fer the time I spent in their stinkin' prison. Man who owned 'em was layin' dead onna groun'. Was one a them Rebs din' wanna stop fightin'."

"So you shot him and took his horse."

"Seemed like the right thing ta do."

I wanted to draw back my fist and slam it into his face. "Was the war over when you shot him?" I asked instead.

"Was fer him," Suggs said.

"Answer the goddamn question," my father snapped.

"I don' know iffen the surrender were signed then or not. An' when that Reb reached fer his gun it din' matter ta me."

I opened the saddlebags, rummaged through them, and found nothing but an old Navy Colt that Suggs had brought home with him.

"Mr. Lucie don' allow no guns up at the woodlot," Suggs said, when he saw the pistol in my hand. "Says he don' want us shootin' each other. So's I keep it in there."

"You git on yer horse and git the hell outta here," my father said. "You come down in the daylight an' look fer yer things. An' ya do it when Reverend Harris is home an' gives ya permission ta go inta his barn."

"When'll he be back?" Suggs asked.

"Late next week. I catch ya here afore then, I'm gonna lock you up with the sheriff up ta Richmond."

We watched Suggs ride off and then started back to our house.

"I know ya don' believe what he said, but there really ain't much ta hold him on. What do ya think he was lookin' fer?" my father asked.

"I don't know," I said. "But I learned during the war not to believe anything that man says. I'm going back to search that barn again tomorrow."

———

Jerusalem's Landing, Vermont, 1861

Reverend Harris stood high in his pulpit, hands spread at his sides as he looked down at us with pride. We were all wearing our new uniforms, all a rich, deep blue with shiny brass buttons, our blue field caps in our laps. We were leaving today for training, a march up to Richmond, then aboard a train that would take us down to Fort Ticonderoga, about seventy miles south in New York State.

Johnny and Abel and I were seated together. It seemed right to me that we were all going off to war together. Ever since we were small children we had been together most every day. We had gone to school together, gotten into mischief time and time again, gone to dances and church socials, and, as we grew older, prowled the woods searching out deer and rabbit, bear and grouse. The bond between us was one of brothers and I believed we would fight to the death for each other if that time ever came.

Strangely, the war to me was a different matter. I believed in its basic cause, keeping the Union together and ending slavery. I had been raised believing in those things. Reverend Harris was a staunch abolitionist and he had regularly railed from his pulpit about the evil of one man owning another. My father had agreed with him and I had grown up knowing that from time to time black men and women were sleeping in the Harris's barn, protected by my father as they readied themselves for the final trip up into Canada. It had seemed abhorrent to me, even as a child, that men and women had to flee their own country just because their skin was different from mine.

But still, the idea of killing for those beliefs seemed equally abhorrent. I would be freeing one class of man from the evils inflicted on him because he was born black, and to do so I would be taking the lives of other men because of the accident of their place of birth. The illogic madness of it came back to me again and again, but there was no resolution I could find.

We bowed our heads as Reverend Harris gave us his benediction, and then stood as the choir sang "Nearer My God to Thee." Our detachment was seated together on one side of the sanctuary, our friends and family on the other. I looked across as the choir sang and found Rebecca staring back at me. Like many of the other women, there were tears in her eyes. The men, by and large, gazed back at us with prideful stares. The emotions of the women were the wiser of the two, but I would only come to know that later.

At the end of the service we came together in the center aisle, each of us joining with our family and friends this final time. My father was with the Johnsons, so it was easy for me to be with both him and Rebecca, and I suspected he had planned it this way. He had a strong place in his heart for her.

We passed through the church doors, pausing to shake Reverend Harris's hand. When Johnny came through just ahead of us, the reverend stopped and hugged his son fiercely, the pride in what his son was doing quite evident.

My own father and I had talked quietly over breakfast. He had concluded our conversation simply.

"I know yer a brave boy . . . no, a brave man," he had said. "An' I want ya ta know that whatever ya have ta do, I'll support ya. But I want ya ta keep yerself safe, Jubal. I don't need ya bringin' home no medals. I just need ya ta bring yerself home."

It had been an awkward conversation, but one that was beautiful to me. Knowing my father loved me was a blessing I wished all men and boys could have.

We stepped out onto the grass in front of the church, and I watched as Mrs. Johnson held Abel tightly and stroked his cheeks. Rebecca hugged him, holding so long and so tight that his face began to redden with embarrassment.

When Rebecca turned to me, she stepped forward and put her arms around my waist. "I'll write to you every week, Jubal Foster, and I expect you to write me back." She raised herself up on her toes and placed her lips next to my ear. "I love you, Jubal," she whispered. "You keep yourself safe, and you come back to me. I don't want a life without you, so you make sure you bring yourself on home as soon as you can."

"I will," I said. "I can't imagine a life without you."

She leaned up again and kissed my lips. It was a lingering kiss that announced to everyone that there would be a life for us together when this war ended.

The sergeant who had been sent down to collect us ordered us into formation and started us off toward Richmond. I peered back over my shoulder and saw Rebecca and my father standing with the others waving us off.

"Eyes front," the sergeant growled, his face only inches from my own.

We marched on. When the sergeant moved to the rear of the column Abel spoke to me out of the side of his mouth.

"Saw ya kissin' my sister," he said.

"Wasn't the first time. And it sure as hell won't be the last."

Abel threw back his head and laughed.

"Quiet in the ranks!" the sergeant shouted.

We marched on.

Groveton, Virginia, 1862

I was promoted to sergeant to replace Jim Lacey, and based on my past success with the ammunition wagons was given the job of leading a reconnaissance unit to probe enemy lines. My lieutenant, a New Yorker named George Lewis, told me that the general staff felt we had been surprised too often by the cleverness of Stonewall Jackson and Robert E. Lee, and they had adopted a plan for constant reconnaissance to blunt that problem. As I sat in camp watching Jemma sew on my stripes, I wondered what they expected me to do other than stumble about the woods and fields between our two lines in hopes of uncovering hidden Reb positions and troop movements.

Abel slid down next to me. I had made sure both he and Johnny were assigned to me, along with some other men I had faith in. I had also asked for Josiah, but had been told that Negroes could not be assigned to regular units. It was a question of not offending the white soldiers, who likely would object to fighting alongside colored troops. Lieutenant Lewis said the general staff also had no faith in the reliability of Negro troops.

I hadn't argued, having learned by now there was no point disputing any position the army took. I also knew the lieutenant's first reason was undoubtedly true—I'd heard enough anti-Negro remarks within our own ranks. But the second reason I found laughable. Josiah had been assigned to the hospital unit, and as such was expected to crawl out under heavy Reb fire to drag our wounded to safety, hardly a job for an *unreliable* Negro.

"So now that yer a big-time sergeant, what plans ya got fer us?" Abel asked.

I looked at him and grinned. "Well, I thought we'd start off with you polishing my boots."

"In a pig's ass. I let ya kiss my sister without thumpin' yer sorry self, but tha's as far as it goes. By the way, I got a letter from her. Did you get one?"

I patted my hip pocket. "Got it right here."

"Wanna let me read it?"

"I don't think so."

"Too much mushy stuff, huh?"

"Could be."

"Damn. This keeps up, I could end up havin' ya as a brother-in-law."

I smiled, but didn't respond.

Abel waited to see if I'd say anything, then went on: "So what're we gonna do in this here new unit? An' when're we gonna do it?"

I raised my chin in the general direction of the Reb lines. "We're gonna wander around in the woods out there and see if we can find those gray-coated bastards. We're going out tonight. They want us to check up on a place called Brawner's Farm. It's just south of Stony Ridge where we attacked Jackson's troops and got our tails kicked."

"Oh, tha's real good," Abel said. We're goin' back without the 60,000 men we had the first time an' see if we can do better." He paused to smile at me. "An' you gonna lead us."

"That's about it."

Abel started to laugh softly. "I ever tell ya how *grand* it is bein' parta this Grand Army of the Republic?"

We were laid up in a stretch of narrow woods that ran along the southeastern bank of Catharpin Creek. There was a wide field ahead of us, a field were men had died by the hundreds only days before. I had a long glass fixed on the main house on Brawner's Farm. There were sentries surrounding it, making me certain there were officers inside—high-ranking officers by the number of men standing guard.

"Damn, I wish we could get closer," I hissed.

Johnny was lying beside me. "We're damn well close enough," he whispered back. "Ever' time we get too close to them Rebs they try ta stick a bayonet in our gullets."

I could see by the glow of small fires that there were two encampments—one south of the farm, and another to the north. "We'll just wait to see who comes out of that house and where they head," I said. I had six men with me, stretched out in a line about ten feet apart. I had sent two more with Abel to scout an unfinished railroad spur that ran below Stony Ridge. The general staff wanted to know if it was complete enough to carry any trains that might be used to replenish Lee's supplies. One of the great advantages the North had was an extensive rail system that kept men and ammunition flowing, along with replacements for artillery pieces lost in battle. The South was often forced to move equipment by wagon, and that usually left their forces at a tactical disadvantage. Now they were struggling to correct that problem, but building railroads and fighting a war at the same time was an almost insurmountable task. Our generals intended to keep it that way.

Abel returned about an hour later and slid in next to me. "That railroad's lookin' pretty good," he said. "They got a bridge finished that takes the tracks over Bull Run, an' they's guardin' it like it was made a gold. Looks like they're plannin' a second bridge for wagons an' men, but it ain't near bein' finished yet."

"Sounds like something our generals might want to blow up," I said.

"Well, they better send a whole lotta men," Abel replied. "Those Rebs fer sure look like they wanna hold onta it."

"Don't ya go gettin' any ideas 'bout blowin' it up yerself," Johnny whispered.

"Can't," I said.

"Why's that?" Abel asked.

"Didn't bring any dynamite."

"Well, that's sure the first smart thing I heard ya say today," Johnny said.

"Amen to that," Abel added.

Thirty minutes later we saw a group of six officers exit the farmhouse and stand briefly under the side lamps that illuminated the front door. I fixed my glass on them, moving from one face to the other. Three of the men had generals' stars on the collars of their tunics. The others wore the insignias of a colonel and two majors. The general who stood in the center of the group bidding farewell to the others was a short man with a white beard who I recognized from newspaper photos as Robert E.

Lee. The second general had a long black beard, and from descriptions I'd read I guessed him to be Stonewall Jackson. The third general stood in the shadows and I couldn't even guess at his identity.

I drew a deep breath, and then told Abel and Johnny what I was seeing through the glass.

"Damn," Johnny said. "We had us a howitzer and a canister of grapeshot we could pretty much end this damned war right here."

"Yes, indeedy do," Abel said.

I laughed softly and nudged Abel in the ribs. "I can't believe what I'm hearing. First you guys say thank you Lord that I haven't got any dynamite. Now you want a howitzer so you can blow Robert E. Lee to kingdom come."

Abel and Johnny both started laughing.

"Seems like a good idea ta me," Abel said.

CHAPTER TWELVE

Jerusalem's Landing, Vermont, 1865

I was back in the Harris's barn by seven the next morning, searching for the bag of clothing Suggs had claimed he was looking for the previous night, as well as anything else I might have overlooked during my initial search. Suggs's story just didn't make sense. If he had needed another wool shirt, or a jacket to cut the chill up on Lucie's woodlot, certainly he could have borrowed one from another logger, or even Lucie himself, then come into town on Sunday when Reverend Harris was most likely to be at home, and collect his missing bag. Foregoing that, Suggs could have purchased a new wool shirt at the Johnsons' store. The more I thought about it the more it annoyed me. His story, patently a lie, was one he'd thought I was gullible enough to swallow. I was new to the job my father had handed me, and certainly feeling my way, but the idea that Bobby Suggs considered me stupid to boot . . . I paused in my musings, forcing my anger aside. Suggs *was* looking for something, and he had come late at night because he wanted to do it secretly. Had he hidden something in the barn? Something he had used to kill Johnny?

"Find anything?"

It was my father. He had stopped just inside the barn entrance.

"Not a thing. I've even looked up in the rafters, and behind the troughs and feed boxes."

"You have breakfast?"

"No."

"I did. I had a big slice of apple pie. But don't ya worry, I left ya the last piece. It's a touch small," he said with a smile.

"It's good pie."

"Oh, yes. Ya need ta find ya a woman who kin cook like that."

"You already told me that."

"I just wanted ta make sure ya heard me." He paused. "So whaddaya think that sumbitch was lookin' fer? A weapon he used to kill Johnny and left behind?"

"It could be that simple, I suppose. What bothers me is why he came up here to Vermont in the first place."

"Said he came here lookin' fer work. He could be tellin' true on that one. From what I read in the newspapers there ain't a lotta jobs aroun' now that the war's over."

"Well, Vermont is a long way from Pennsylvania, a long way to come for a job chopping down trees."

"Probably was lookin' fer somethin' better, but this was all he could get," my father said. "Was him an' Johnny big-time friends durin' the war?"

"They became friends toward the end . . . I'm not sure *friends* is the right word. Johnny spent a lot of time with Suggs before they were captured." I wanted to tell my father exactly what had happened as the war reached its final stage for Johnny and Abel and me, the vicious depravity that enveloped both sides, a depravity that had crippled me and cost Abel his life and that seemed to swallow Johnny whole. But to do so would rob my father of what he had. The memory of three boys who had grown up in our small Vermont village, one his own son, the others children of men and women he had known most of his life.

"Could be Johnny had somethin' Suggs wanted an' wouldn't give it up, an' he's still looking fer it," my father suggested.

I tried to get my thoughts around that. "What could Johnny have had? Both he and Suggs were in a Confederate prison for almost a year. When Johnny was freed he was in such poor health the army discharged him and sent him home. I have no idea what happened with Suggs."

"Ain't likely the Rebs let Johnny keep anythin' a value in that prison."

"All right for me to come in?"

My father and I turned and found Doc standing in the doorway.

"Come ahead," my father called. "We ain't doin' no good. Maybe you'll bring us some luck."

"How'd that turn out last night?" Doc asked as he came over to us. "I saw from my window that you found some fellow in here. Saw you let him ride off, so I figured it wasn't anything serious."

My father took off his hat and waved away a fly that was buzzing around his face. "Yeah, it was that Suggs fella that came up here a week or so back ta visit Johnny. Said he was lookin' fer a satchel with some clothes in it that he'd left here. Jubal thinks it's a cock-'n'-bull story, an' I'm kinda leanin' toward that idea myself."

"I never met this Suggs, but I saw him with Johnny one time. He looked a bit rough around the edges."

"Did you notice them arguing?" I asked. "Walter Johnson said he saw Suggs getting a bit hot under the collar while he and Johnny were outside his store, but that Johnny just laughed at him and walked away."

Doc shook his head. "Nothin' like that. I only saw him that one time, and I didn't know who Suggs was until Edgar Billingsley told me he had stopped by his farm asking where Johnny lived. That one time I saw him, Suggs seemed to be following Johnny around, but Johnny didn't seem to be paying him much mind."

"And that was right around the time Johnny was killed," I said.

Doc nodded. "About a week before."

General John Pope stormed back and forth in front of his tent, raging at his subordinate officers, while Lieutenant Lewis and I stood off to one side. The lieutenant had brought me to the general's tent to report what I had seen at Brawner's farmhouse. The gathering of Lee and Jackson and the others seemed to hold little interest for Pope. What he ranted about now was the advanced state of the new rail line and bridge construction over Bull Run.

"The fact that I wasn't told about this immediately after our last battle is tantamount to treason!" he shouted. "We had troops in the area under Fitz John Porter's command, and yet they found no reason to report back that this bridge had been completed. It is obviously Lee's intention to connect this new rail line with the Manassas Gap Railroad, which if successful will give him a steady supply of munitions for his advance on Washington."

I watched Pope bark at his men who all stiffened under his tirade. One general, Brigadier Alpheus Williams, stood glaring at Pope, who as a major general outranked him. Finally Williams seemed unable to stand Pope's words any longer and stepped forward.

"If you recall, General Pope, the men in the vicinity of that bridge construction were under heavy bombardment by enemy artillery at the time. With grapeshot flying about, decimating their ranks by the hundreds, I doubt that any had time to note the level of bridge construction that had been achieved."

Pope stopped in his tracks and turned slowly to face General Williams. Pope was a thick-bodied man with a heavy black beard and piercing eyes that seemed as black as his hair. Williams, by contrast, was shorter and less physically intimidating, his light-brown hair and matching beard bearing a somewhat foppish mustache that extended a good four inches from his cheeks. Yet Williams stood his ground as if ready to do battle with his superior officer.

"If *you* recall, General Williams, troops under my command were able to blow Stone Bridge on the Warrenton Pike."

"I do recall that, sir," Williams said. "I believe it prevented Rebel troops from pursuing your *retreat* here to Centreville." He had spoken the word retreat with a note of contempt.

A major came up to Pope before the snapping and growling could continue and handed him a communiqué. Pope read it and leveled his gaze at the others. "It appears that Jackson's army is attempting a flanking move to interpose his troops between our forces and Washington."

He walked over to a map set on a table in front of his tent. He jabbed a finger into the center of it. "If we move quickly we can engage him here at Chantilly and stop him." He stared across the map at Williams. "We will finish this discussion later. Now you must get your troops ready to march."

Lieutenant Lewis grabbed my arm and steered me away from Pope's command post.

"Is it always like that?" I asked as we hurried away. "Do they always snarl at each other?"

"It is with Pope," Lewis said. "His officers hate him, but don't you go and let the men know that, Foster. It wouldn't be good for morale."

The rain began shortly after we formed up to march, a heavy, beating downpour that quickly drenched our tunics and turned the road to mud. My unit had been assigned to General Edwin Sumner's brigade, which was being sent to reconnoiter the movement of Stonewall Jackson's troops. Our squad would be the point unit and move forward until we encountered Jackson's lines, then send back intelligence to the brigade.

"Why the hell ain't they usin' cavalry for this like they always do?" Johnny asked as he huddled in his wet clothes.

"The lieutenant said the cavalry is too exhausted," I explained. "Their horses are near broken-down. So we're taking their place."

"I'm damn well near broken-down too," Abel said. "We fought like wild animals at Manassas and then beat a retreat back here ta Centreville. Then they sent us out ta Brawner's Farm ta see what them Rebs was up ta an' how close that new railroad was ta bein' ready. Now we got this. Well, damnit, I'm tired an' I'm soakin' wet. An' I'm also hungry as hell. I bet those cavalry horses got their oat buckets hangin' off their noses right now. So where the hell's *our* food?"

I agreed with everything Abel had said, but it didn't matter. My job was to shut them all up and get them moving. "You'll eat when we make camp," I said. "Now we gotta move, so stow the complaints and let's get on up and join the column."

Abel stared at me with a look of disbelief. "Damnit, Jubal, I liked it better when ya was jus' a private an' bitched along wit the rest of us."

I liked it better too, I thought, but kept it to myself. "Let's move!" I shouted.

CHAPTER THIRTEEN

Walter Johnson, as church deacon, was conducting the Sunday service for Reverend Harris, who had taken his grieving wife to visit relatives in New Hampshire. The minister was due back at the end of the week, but as my father explained, it was likely his wife would remain with the comfort of her family.

I glanced across the aisle where Rebecca sat with her stepmother Mary. I knew Rebecca would prefer to be seated elsewhere, and had her father not been at the pulpit, she would be with her friends. But to have left her father's new wife alone in the pew would be taken as an insult by our neighbors—an insult to her father as well as his new wife—and that was something Rebecca would never do.

Walter Johnson was a clumsy speaker and it was painful to listen to him, but he was wise enough to recognize his limitations and had kept his sermon short and given the bulk of the program over to the choir.

At the end of the service church members greeted each other in the aisles, sharing the gossip of the week, then moved outside to the front lawn. I found Rebecca and guided her to a spot under a shaded tree. All about us, younger children played games of tag, or keep-away with someone's cap, and it reminded me when she and I, together with Johnny and Abel, had done the same. It was not all that long ago, but to me it seemed a lifetime.

"I need your advice," I said at length.

Rebecca's eyes widened. "I'm shocked, but delighted. What can I do?"

"I need to speak to your father's wife about . . . well, about her relationship with Johnny, as well as anything she knows about Bobby Suggs."

"I thought she already told you she didn't know anything about Suggs."

I nodded slowly.

"You don't believe her," Rebecca said.

"No, I don't. Not if she was as involved with Johnny as you say. She would have asked him about Suggs, and I believe he would have told her something."

She licked her lips nervously. "Could you do it when my father isn't there? I don't want him hurt, and if he knew why you were talking to her, and what you were asking after, it would be more than he could bear."

"I can't promise you he'll never know. I can only promise that I'll do my best not to cause him pain."

Rebecca looked away, then turned back to me. "Did you see him in church today, Jubal? The way he would peek down at her while he was conducting the service, his eyes searching for her approval? He loves her so much. If he ever learned what she did with Johnny, it would break his heart."

"I'll be as discreet as possible," I said. "And I promise I'll do everything I can to keep him from finding out about their . . . relationship." I studied her face, noting the doubt I found there. "When would I find her alone?"

"Mondays are best," Rebecca said. "Every Monday morning my father takes the buckboard up to Richmond to meet the train and collect the store goods we've ordered. Then he does his banking and heads on home."

"So he'll be gone tomorrow?"

"Yes. He usually leaves right after breakfast. Mary runs the store while he's away. If you want, I'll be sure to be in the store tomorrow morning so she'll have no excuse not to step outside and speak to you."

"That would be a great help," I said. "I'll come to the store at eight."

My father and I left the church and headed for Billy Lucie's woodlot. It was eleven o'clock and the air was crisp and cool, and most of the leaves had lost their color and begun falling to the ground. Within the next few weeks winter would be upon us and moving about the countryside would become more difficult. When snow came the village would be isolated until teams of horses pushed wide, wooden wheels along the roads. The wheels were filled with water to give them weight and they compressed the snow into a hard-packed layer that allowed travelers to move about again in wagons and on horseback.

We turned onto the Gorge Road and off to our right the river began to pick up speed as it headed to the first series of waterfalls that would send it crashing down into the gorge.

"It's good to be home, to be back in the places I knew as a boy," I said.

My father smiled. "It's good ta have ya home. I have ta admit, it scared me pretty bad when I heard 'bout Abel. I jus' sat there an' wondered what had happened ta ya, if they'd be writin' ta me next. You'd tol' me in yer letters how ya all was in the same unit and was always together. I jus' had this awful feelin' 'bout it. Then when the letter come sayin' ya'd been wounded, I got Doc ta write our own letter tryin' ta get them to ship ya home ta the hospital in Burlington where Doc was workin'." He drew a long breath. "An army doctor wrote back ta Doc tellin' 'bout yer arm an' sayin' ya was too bad off ta be moved, an' that scared the hell outta me all over agin."

"It worked out. I'm back now."

We rode for a bit before my father spoke again. "Ya don' talk much 'bout the war. Sometimes I wanna ask ya 'bout it, but I don' wanna press ya."

Nearly a minute passed in silence. "I guess I don't really know what to say about it. It was a terrible thing to be part of, an ugly, senseless thing. Oh, I knew all the reasons we were fighting. I knew we had to preserve the Union and end slavery, all of it. But the thing was it was never about that during the battles we fought. It was about keeping the other side from overrunning us and killing us. When we were fighting in those battles I'd see a soldier from the other side and he looked like any boy or man I might have known here in Vermont. And he *was* the same. He wasn't shouting out things about keeping the Negroes in chains, or about ending the Union. He'd seen the same things I had. He'd seen his friends blown apart by artillery fire or dropped by minie balls or stabbed by a bayonet or saber, and the only thing he wanted was to stay alive and go home to his family just like me."

"Did ever'body feel that way?"

"Everybody I ever talked to; all the decent ones. There were some on both sides who wanted to kill every enemy soldier they could, just like there were some who wanted to raid every house they passed, kill any civilian who got in the way. But they would have been like that war or no war. Armies aren't too particular about who they hand a gun to."

"What about yer officers?" my father asked.

"The officers . . ." I paused to think about that. "I guess the lower-ranking ones were just like the rest of us. Those higher up, the ones who decided where and when we fought and with how many men, well, they kind of seemed to have their eyes on the history books. How history would view them, how the people would think of them, and how they'd be rewarded for what they did. And did they ever snipe at each other."

"How so?"

I told him about the confrontation I'd witnessed between Generals Pope and Williams just before the battle at Chantilly Plantation.

"Well, Pope lost his army after that battle. It was merged into the Army of the Potomac under General George McClellan, and Pope was shipped out west and pretty much forgotten."

"What'd ya think of General Pope?" he asked.

"I didn't see him but that one time," I answered. "But what I saw of him I didn't like."

We reached Billy Lucie's dooryard and dismounted. He came out on the porch and invited us in for coffee.

"The missus an' me din' go ta church this mornin'." He lowered his voice. "Ta be honest, the missus don' care much for it when Walter Johnson tries ta preach." He gave my father and me a wink. "I don' much care who it is, God help me, I jus' don' like any kinda preachin'."

My father laughed dutifully and told Billy we were there to talk to Bobby Suggs. He explained that we had found Suggs in the Harris barn the previous night, claiming he was looking for a satchel of clothing.

Billy just shook his head. "He shoulda stuck with findin' his clothes."

"Why is that?" I asked.

"Cause he dragged his sorry ass home jus' a coupla hours ago all beaten ta hell," Billy said. "After he left you folks he musta ridden up ta Sherman Hollow. He tol' me Rusty LeRoche caught him with his daughter Chantal, an' beat the tar outta him." Billy smiled. "Suggs said he woke up in Rusty's woodlot this mornin' an' dragged hisself to his horse. I guess Rusty jus' thumped him good an' proper an' left him out there fer the coyotes ta find. Maybe it'll teach him ta keep his britches buttoned, but I doubt it."

"Any point in us tryin' ta talk to him?" my father asked.

Billy shrugged. "Ya got plenty of time fer a cup of coffee. I don' think he's goin' anywhere fer a while. Probably up there layin' in his bunk."

We rode up to the bunkhouse an hour later and, as Billy had predicted, found Suggs snoring in his bed. My father had to lightly kick the sole of his foot three times before Bobby stirred enough to open one eye.

"Why ya kickin' me?" he asked. Slowly, he opened the other eye, then added: "Don't it look like I been kicked enough fer one day?"

"This happen after you left the Harris barn?" I asked.

"Tha's right." He drew a heavy breath. "Have some mercy an' lemme sleep."

"Who did this ta ya?" my father asked, letting Suggs know there would be no rest until our questions were answered.

"It was that crazy man, Rusty LeRoche."

"Whatcha do ta make him that mad?"

Suggs gave my father a contemptuous sneer. "I stopped by ta see his daughter. Las' time I was there she tol' me where her room was an' which window I could tap on ta git her ta come out. So I did it, an' sure enough she came out. But two minutes later so did her daddy, all pissed off an' comin' out the door, still pullin' on his britches an' growlin' like a damn bear."

"And he thumped you," I said.

Suggs glared at me. "I never even had no chance ta fight back. He came at me wit an axe handle and swung at both my elbows before I could even raise my hands. It hurt so bad I din' wanna do nothin' but lay down an' cover up my head."

From the look of his face Suggs had been equally unsuccessful at covering his head. The left side was a deep purple and swollen to twice its normal size.

"Sounds ta me that ya pretty much got whatcha deserved," my father said.

"So he jus' gits away with it, an' a war veteran like me . . ." He paused to glare at me. "A war veteran with medals as good as your'n jus' gits beat on anytime some backwoods trash feels like doin' it."

My father shook his head in disbelief. "My God, man, ya was on the man's property well after dark, tryin' ta get in his daughter's britches. Ya know that girl's only seventeen years ol'."

"Ol' enough where I comes from," Suggs said.

"Seems like Mr. LeRoche doesn't agree with you." It did my heart good seeing Suggs battered all to hell, but I fought to keep it out of my voice. "We looked for your satchel," I said, changing tack. "We didn't find it. Why do you think that is?"

"How the hell do I know?" he growled. "Maybe the reverend or his missus took it inta his house. Maybe Johnny did. I left it there afore he died."

I smiled down at him. "We'll check on that when the reverend gets back."

"Go right ahead. Go an' investigate where my satchel is. You'll find out I'm tellin' ya true." He did his best to glare at me again, but with his misshapen face it didn't quite come off. "You gonna investigate Rusty LeRoche?"

"Investigate him for what?" I asked.

"For beatin' the hell outta me!" he shouted.

"Seems ta me ya was trespassin' . . . jus like ya was at the Harris's barn," my father said.

"Maybe I'll take a ride up to Sherman Hollow and see if Mr. LeRoche wants to sign a trespass complaint," I said.

Suggs laid back and gave me an open-mouthed stare. "I don't believe this. This is bullshit, an' you is shovelin' it real heavy right on top a me."

"Sorry ya feel that way, son," my father said. "We got a little problem with a murder we're tryin' ta solve. So I guess you'll jus' haveta put
up with us fer a spell. An' like we tol' ya afore, don' plan on goin' no
place until we tell ya yer free ta travel."

Chantilly Plantation, Virginia, 1862

"I knows dat Chantilly Plantation," Jemma said. "So's I kin help ya. Dat's
da place I'z at till I runs away." She had come to me when the column
had camped for the night. She had climbed aboard one of the wagons
before we left and had hidden herself away until we stopped. I looked at
her now in disbelief, surprised she had followed. We were moving into
unsecured territory. Should she be caught she'd at best be whipped and
enslaved again. At worst she could be hobbled or even hung.

"Jemma, it's too dangerous for you to be here, but I don't know how
to get you back to our main army. They may have even moved by now.
If the Rebs catch you—"

"I'z hadda come, an' I'z knows I kin help ya, Massah Fosta."

I had told Jemma repeatedly not to call me master, but it was something she'd done her entire life with white men, a habit that was apparently too difficult to break.

She hesitated and bent in closer to me. "Dere's dis tunnel dat runs
outta a root cellah da's back by da cabins da darkies lives in. It runs on
back inna woods. Ya goes in back dere an' dat tunnel will bring ya right
up close so's ya can see ever'thin da's goin' on in da big house." She
hesitated a moment. "When ya dere you's kin do somfin' fer Jemma iffen ya wants."

"What's that, Jemma? What can I do for you?"

"Massah, my sistah, she still dere. Her name's Alva. Ya kin git a
darkie ta bring her to ya, an' den ya kin bring her back ta me. She be
lil'; she don' takes up no room at all."

I let out a deep breath. I tried to think how I'd feel if someone I loved, a child, was enslaved, and I thought, like Jemma, I'd risk anything to free them. I didn't want to dash her hopes but I doubted we'd be able to help her. I reached out and touched her shoulder. "I don't know if we'll get to the plantation, but if we do, and if I can find this tunnel without endangering the men, I'll see what can be done for Alva."

Jemma grabbed a twig from the ground and smoothed out a patch of dirt. "I makes ya a map shows how ta fine dis tunnel," she said. "It be real easy, Massah Fosta. Real easy."

We found Jackson's army encamped on a hill just southeast of Chantilly Plantation. My ten-man reconnaissance unit had struck out just before nine o'clock in a steady downpour and had finally located the Rebs at midnight just as the rain ended. My map identified the place as Ox Hill and showed the plantation just beyond. Circling the location on the map, I handed it to one of my men.

"You get this back to the brigade so they'll know where to attack in the morning." I turned to Abel and Johnny. "I want you two to come with me. The rest of you stay here and keep watch on the encampment. If for any reason they move before dawn, you send word back to the brigade. We should be back long before that, but in case we aren't . . . well, you know what to do."

"Where we goin'?" Johnny asked.

"We're going up to the plantation. I suspect the officers will be taking their comforts there, and we'll also be able to see if more troops are laying back in support."

"How we gonna get up close to that plantation without gittin' our asses blown off?" Abel demanded.

I smiled at him. "My ass isn't as big as yours, so I'm not worried.

Besides, Jemma told me a way to sneak in close to the house without being seen."

"How the hell did she know that?" Johnny asked.

"She was a slave here," I said simply.

They were suddenly silent. It was the first time we'd been confronted with a place where someone we knew had been enslaved.

We came to the copse of pine just north of the main house where Jemma claimed the entrance to the tunnel was hidden. We had skirted the plantation but had not come upon another body of Reb troops, save a small detachment of cavalry guarding the main plantation house. It confirmed my suspicions that the ranking officers had taken up residence in the house.

Inside the copse of trees an old castaway door lay on the ground, partially covered in vines and debris.

"The tunnel's supposed to be under that door," I said. "She claimed the slaves dug it as a way to get far away from the house when they tried to escape. It leads into a root cellar, and we should come up against the back of a chest that we'll have to push out of the way. The root cellar is right next to the slave quarters behind the main house."

With Abel's help I removed the brush and vines covering the door and pulled it off to one side. There was a hole beneath large enough for a man to fit through, but I had no idea how far it dropped. I got down on my belly and leaned into the hole and lit a match. It appeared to be about a six-foot drop, and there were some boards fitted into the dirt walls to use as a ladder. I handed Abel my Spencer rifle and dropped into the hole, then turned back and told him to pass me all three rifles, after making sure they were unloaded. I grinned up at him. "Don't need another hole in my ass cause you got clumsy."

I leaned Abel and Johnny's Spencers against the wall, took my own, dropped to my knees, and began to crawl forward. The tunnel was about four feet high and the walls were barely wide enough for my shoulders to fit through. As I crawled I could hear some animals scurrying ahead and assumed the tunnel had become home to a pack of wood rats. I didn't want to think of what else might have scurried or slithered inside and quickly came to the realization that I would never make a living as a miner.

It felt as though I'd been inching forward for more than an hour, although it couldn't have been more than ten minutes, when I came up against a solid wood surface. I laid down my rifle and pushed as hard as I could. Slowly the wood moved back, and I found myself facing the interior of a large root cellar. I pushed the wooden chest to one side, then stepped into the cellar proper. Abel and Johnny crawled out behind me and began looking around.

Johnny immediately started searching for food; he found a jar of peaches, opened it, and began eating them using his knife as a fork. Abel followed suit. "Damn, these are good," he said.

"Make sure you take the empty jar out of here when we leave," I said. "We don't wanna let on there's a tunnel back there, and we sure don't wanna get some fieldhand whipped for stealing peaches."

The root cellar was cool and dark, and when I opened the outside door warm humid air hit my face. I peered up at the house. There were about a dozen horses tied together and I guessed they belonged to the men who were guarding Jackson and his senior officers. As I watched for a sentry patrol, an old Negro came shambling out of the nearest slave cabin, using a single crutch to propel him toward a battered outhouse with a door that hung loosely on one hinge.

I ducked back into the root cellar. "We got a job to do," I said to the others. "Jemma's little sister is here, and Jemma wants her to be free like she is. I told her we'd get her out if we could."

I had expected them to object, but nothing came. Finally Johnny nodded his head. "Yeah, let's do it," he said.

"You betcha," Abel said. "Let's get her the hell outta here."

I smiled at both of them. "Okay. Johnny, you cover us from this door. Abel, an old Negro man just went in the outhouse. We're gonna have him show us where this child is."

We cut across the rear yard and reached the outhouse just as the old man came out. He was painfully thin and his clothes were little more than rags. He had tightly curled white hair and a scraggly white beard and one of his ankles had been hobbled—smashed by a hammer so he could not walk without the support of a crutch. It was something, I'd learned, that was often done to slaves who'd been recaptured after running away. I clamped a hand over his mouth and raised a finger to my lips. He nodded beneath my hand, his eyes wide and terrified.

"Father, we're friends of Jemma, a girl who used to work here. Did you know her?" I whispered.

He nodded his head beneath my hand and his eyes grew calmer. I took my hand away.

"We're here to get her sister. A girl named Alva. Do you know her, and can you take us to her?"

A sense of pride swept through the old man's face and his back seemed to grow straighter. "I knows her," he whispered. "Y'all come wit me."

He led us to the third cabin in a row of weather-beaten structures and turned back to us. "Y'all wait."

Abel and I crouched down beside the door he had entered, giving ourselves as much cover as possible. He was back within two minutes, a little girl no more than seven or eight standing beside him, rubbing sleep from her eyes.

The old man bent down and placed his hands on her shoulders. "You go wit dees mens, Alva. Dey gonna take ya ta Jemma."

The little girl nodded, still sleepy. She had large brown eyes and the same creamy complexion as her sister. The old man leaned over and kissed her cheek. "You's gonna be free, girl." There were tears pooling in the corners of his eyes.

Abel handed me his rifle and scooped the girl up and pressed her against his chest.

"Thank you, sir," I said.

"Y'all go fight dem Rebs," he whispered. "Y'all fight dem and make us all free."

CHAPTER FOURTEEN

Reverend Harris came home early on Monday morning, several days before he was expected. He had left his wife with relatives, in hopes they could help her overcome her grief, and when he answered my knock it was clear he could have used the help himself. In the short time since Johnny's funeral he seemed to have fared badly. His eyes were sunken from lack of sleep and there were deep fissures at the corners of his mouth. His hair seemed whiter than I remembered and his clothing hung loosely on his body. He appeared to have aged ten years in the short time since his son's death.

"I'm sorry to disturb you, Reverend Harris," I began.

He waved my comment away. "I'm always pleased to see you, Jubal." He smiled weakly. "We were called to this church when Johnny was three years old. That's twenty-three years ago, and you've been part of my church family all that time. Come in, and tell me how I can help you."

I followed him into the sitting room where Johnny's body had been laid out in his Army of the Potomac uniform. The room had a closed-up, musty smell and I wondered how much it had been used since Reverend Harris had buried his only child.

I was guided to a horsehair sofa and the pastor took a Queen Anne chair directly across from me.

"Are you familiar with a friend of Johnny's from the war, a man named Bobby Suggs?" I asked.

"Yes, I am. But I'm not certain he was a friend of Johnny's."

I was surprised by his comment. "Why do you say that?"

"Well, I was here when he arrived in town, and I must confess that Johnny didn't seem all that pleased to see him. I overheard this Suggs boy asking Johnny if we could put him up for a few days, and Johnny said flat-out there wasn't any room for him here. He even told him he couldn't stay in the barn, and when I asked Johnny about it later he was adamant that he did not want this Suggs fellow staying anywhere near him." Reverend Harris placed his forearms on his knees and leaned forward. "It was such an unchristian act that it shocked me. We have never turned anyone away from this house, even travelers who we didn't know."

"Did he and Johnny have any kind of argument?"

"I wouldn't call it an argument, but I saw them talking a bit intensely about something, although I couldn't hear what it involved. It was my impression that Suggs was getting a bit agitated. It seemed as though he wanted a response from my son, and was upset that Johnny just dismissed whatever they were talking about."

"My father and I found Bobby Suggs in your barn on Saturday night. He claimed he was looking for a satchel that had some of his clothes in it."

Reverend Harris sat back. "Yes, I have that satchel. Johnny told him he could leave it in the barn while he searched for work. When my wife heard that, she insisted the satchel be brought into the house. We get field mice in the barn this time of year and she was afraid they'd get into the satchel and ruin whatever was inside.

"How long ago was this?"

"About a week before Johnny . . . passed on."

I was disappointed to hear that Suggs had been telling the truth, but still clung to the fact that he and Johnny had argued before Johnny was killed. "I'd like to look at the satchel," I said. "I'd also like to look around Johnny's room, just to see if I can find out what he and Suggs were arguing about."

"Of course, you're welcome to look at anything that might help you find my son's . . ." He struggled to finish the sentence. "Find the person who killed my boy." He paused and looked at me with a sense of urgency. "But please understand, Jubal, I really can't say they were arguing. I never heard *what* they were saying; I only noted their demeanors toward each other."

"I understand. Walter Johnson noticed the same thing outside his store. He said it seemed as though Suggs was demanding something and Johnny just laughed at him. So I'd like to look around to put my mind to rest."

Reverend Harris went into another room and returned with a carpetbag satchel. I opened it and rummaged inside. It was stuffed with clothing, including the wool shirt Suggs had told me about. There was also a map of Vermont, and I opened it and noted some crude penciled lines marking his route—first to Jericho, a town to our north, and then to Jerusalem's Landing.

I returned the maps to the bag and told Reverend Harris that Suggs would be stopping by later in the week to pick it up. Then I asked him to take me up to Johnny's room.

The room Johnny had lived in most of his life overlooked the rear of the house and the woods beyond, and I recalled how he often told Abel and me about the deer he saw moving through the trees, claiming he could sit in his room with a rifle and keep his family in venison the whole year through if his father would let him.

I hadn't been in Johnny's room for years, but I could not see much that had changed from the time when the three of us sat there planning our boyish adventures.

I turned to Reverend Harris. "Is there a special place where he kept things?"

"I don't know. Johnny was a bit standoffish when he returned." Tears began to well up in the reverend's eyes and he glanced away. "I always attributed it to the prison he'd been in. I've read that the men who were captured lived very primitive lives in the Confederate prisons, desperate lives, and that those who weren't dying of disease were slowly starving. The article said they became men who fought over scraps of food and who hid the barest of necessities from each other. It said they had to, or whatever they owned would be stolen. It was a question of survival." His voice broke but I couldn't tell if it was because of the suffering he knew his son had endured, or because of the way he had changed when he returned home. He walked to the door and turned back to me. "My son, he wasn't the same boy who left our home four years ago. All those things that happened to him, all those things . . ." He drew a deep breath, choosing not to finish the thought. "Please take all the time you need, Jubal. I'll be downstairs working on next Sunday's sermon. Let me know when you're finished."

I sat on the edge of Johnny's bed just as I had so many times in the past, this time thinking of what lay ahead for Reverend Harris and his wife. The reverend, at least, appeared to recognize how much his son had changed. But he didn't know the half of it. He didn't know what a monster his son had become, and I wondered if I could do my job and find Johnny's killer, and keep him from ever finding out.

I searched Johnny's room. His Navy Colt was under his pillow, fully loaded, and I took it out, removed the cylinder, and placed it in the drawer of a bedside table.

I found several pictures we'd had taken by one of the many photographers covering the war, realizing I had prints of some of the same photos. The early ones showed the three of us together, smiling and looking very proud in our new uniforms. Those that came later showed battered men with drawn faces and fearful eyes. Some of Johnny's photos included Suggs and the other men he had joined up with, a group of men as monstrous as he became himself. At the bottom of the stack of pictures there was one more, one I had not expected to find, one that did not come from the war. It was of Mary Johnson, and the inscription on the other side read: *From Mary, to Johnny with love.* I put the photo in my jacket pocket.

In the back of Johnny's closet I found a loose floorboard and I pried it up. Inside there was a gold pocket watch and some women's jewelry, things I assumed he had stolen on one of the scavenging raids he regularly conducted with Suggs and their gang. I was surprised he hadn't sold the items yet. Perhaps he hadn't had the opportunity, or perhaps he wanted more time to pass so it wouldn't be obvious they were stolen goods taken during the war. Like most of the men who pilfered the plantations that fell under Union control, he had made little secret of it whenever he returned to camp, but perhaps he had wanted to appear more civilized now that he had come home.

I left the watch and jewelry on the bed stand and went downstairs to find Reverend Harris. I located him in his small study at the rear of the parsonage and knocked lightly on the open door.

"Ah, Jubal," he said, looking up. "Are you finished? Did you find anything?"

"I found Johnny's pistol. It was loaded, so I removed the cylinder and put it in his bed stand. I also found a watch and some jewelry that I expect he planned to give to you and your wife. I left it upstairs as well."

He seemed to swell with pride at the thought of his son having hidden away gifts for his parents. "He was a good boy. In the end, he was a good boy."

I just thanked him and left.

Washington, DC, 1862

We had taken up defensive positions outside Washington, although none of our reconnaissance patrols indicated any attack was coming. The Battle of Chantilly had been like so many others, one that ended with no clear winner, only death and suffering on both sides. Based on the report my unit had sent back about the location of Stonewall Jackson's troops, General Pope had sent two brigades under Generals Isaac Stevens and Philip Kearny to block Jackson's advance. Despite being heavily outnumbered, Stevens chose to attack Ox Hill across a grassy field at the center of the Rebel column. The attack was initially successful, routing one Confederate brigade and flanking another before being driven back by a counterattack. General Stevens was killed during the assault, shot through the head by a Rebel sniper.

Next, General Kearny attacked and maneuvered close to the Confederate line and engaged in fierce hand-to-hand combat until the fight stalled. The general apparently became confused during the battle and rode into the Confederate lines and was also killed. The Union Army then withdrew to Germantown, but Jackson's forward progress had been stopped. General Pope, meanwhile, fearing that Jackson might quickly regroup, withdrew to defensive positions around Washington, where he was heavily criticized for showing a lack of leadership and initiative in the field. A short time later he was relieved of his command and his Army of Northern Virginia was dismantled, its men absorbed into General George McClellan's Army of the Potomac.

To us it was all the same. The only difference was the name of the general sitting behind the lines deciding how many of us would be killed or maimed. Few thought the change from Pope to McClellan would have any real bearing on their lives. All they knew was that right now they were free of the carnage for a week or two while they guarded Washington from an attack that would never come.

Josiah had come up to join us, all the wounded having been moved into the main military hospital in Washington, the field surgeons and nurses and litter-bearers given a chance to rest up before the battles resumed.

Jemma and her sister Alva had remained close to us, and Josiah was showing great interest in both of them, feeding Jemma and the eight-year-old child stories about the beauty of Vermont—while never mentioning the long, cold winters—and the freedom everyone who lived there enjoyed regardless of their color. The latter was only partially true, of course. Like everywhere in the North, many Vermonters considered Negroes inferior, and while their children played and attended schools with white children, while they shopped freely in white-owned stores, Negroes were only hired for the most menial of jobs, and were forced to live separately from whites in places with names like Nigger Hill or Nigger Road or Nigger Hollow.

Abel and Johnny and I were enjoying the cool of the morning when Josiah came and sat beside us. Jemma was back by the campfire, brewing us coffee, and Josiah's eyes went straight to her.

"She takin' good care a ya," he said. "She be grateful 'bout how ya saved her sister."

"That lil' girl Alva's about the prettiest thing I ever seen," Abel said. "But she keeps callin' me Massah Abel, no matter how many times I tell her not ta."

"Jemma tol' me that slaves gets beat they don' call all white men massah."

"Maybe ya should tell her that don' happen here, that she don' have ta call us that," Johnny said. "Makes me feel like a damn Reb when she does it." He laughed. "If my father ever heard her, he'd pro'bly have a stroke, all the evils-of-slavery sermons he's given."

Josiah shrugged. "I tol' her. I guess it's jus' hard ta give up whatcha done all yer life."

Jemma came with two cups of steaming coffee, followed by little Alva who was carrying two more.

Alva gave one cup to Josiah and the second to Abel. Then she sat down next to Abel and laid her head against his arm. Abel had carried her back through enemy lines, holding her pressed against his chest the whole time. When he had finally handed her over to a sobbing Jemma, he stood there with a big grin spread across his face, all the weariness of battle draining away.

I smiled at him. "You got yourself a girlfriend, Abel," I said.

He smiled back at me. "Wish I could wrap her up an' take her home. My momma would spoil her real good."

I winked at him. "Maybe Josiah will do that for you."

Josiah smiled at Jemma. "Jus' might," he said. "If I kin talk her inta it."

I looked at Jemma and saw that she had lowered her eyes and that a faint blush had come to her light-brown complexion.

It was midafternoon and we were still lazing about. Josiah had taken Jemma and Alva for a walk, promising to find a shop that sold sweets. I was just about to nod off to sleep when Bobby Suggs came up and squatted down in front of Johnny.

"Some of the boys tol' me 'bout this sportin' house they found back there in town," he said. "Claim the ladies is real eager fer a good time an' weren't chargin' more'n a couple a dollars. I was thinkin' maybe I'd take a walk in an' give it a try. Any a you boys interested?"

Johnny perked up and looked over at Abel and me. "Well, what you boys think?"

"I sure would like ta be with a woman," Abel said. "But I sure ain't big on the idea of bein' with a whore who's been poked by half the regiment."

Suggs scoffed at him. "Well, maybe one of them fancy ladies who lives in town will invite ya over ta test out her bed." He turned to me. "How about you, *sergeant?*"

"I don't think so, Suggs. I've got some letters to write and some sleep to catch up on." I gave Johnny a questioning look.

He popped up to his feet. "Well, I'm gonna have me a peek," he said.

"You boys be careful," I warned, staring straight at Suggs. "The things you get away with out in the field will get you locked up here in Washington."

Suggs held his hands out to his sides in an image of innocence. "Why, sergeant, all I wants is a little lovin'." He grinned at me. "An' maybe a drink or two."

It was well past midnight when Johnny returned to camp. It was a hot night and he lay on top of his bedroll and stared up at the sky.

"Have yourself a good time?" I asked, keeping my voice low. Abel lay on my other side snoring lightly.

Johnny didn't look at me. "It didn't turn out too good," he said. "The ladies was okay, a little older'n I expected, but okay."

"So what was the problem?"

"Bobby got hisself all liquored up, then got inta a big fight with one a the whores—claimed she laughed at him when he took off his britches—an' before I knew what was happenin' they was callin' the police an' we was runnin' out the door an' down the street. I din' think whores would be callin' the police, them doin' somethin' illegal an' all, but Bobby says they pay the police fer protection, an' if the police catch ya, they take their clubs ta ya real good."

"You know exactly what Suggs did?" I asked.

"He jus' said he gave the whore what she deserved. I figured he musta hit her. When he came ta get me he said we hadda get outta there fast, an' that the police would grab me if I din' hightail it with him, cause the whores knew we came there together."

"You should stay away from Suggs," I said. "Sooner or later he's going to get caught, and I don't want to see you getting dragged down with him."

"Oh, Bobby ain't bad. He jus' gets a little wild sometimes. 'Specially if he's been drinkin'."

"I don't know him like you do," I said. "But what I do know, I don't like. He comes across like backwoods trash, and I haven't seen anything from him to change my mind."

"You jus' gotta get ta know him," Johnny said. "He's a pretty smart fella in his own way."

I rolled over and closed my eyes. "See you in the morning." Next to me Abel continued to snore peacefully.

The next morning we were cleaning and polishing our gear when a lieutenant I'd never seen before approached us.

"We're looking for two men, sergeant, who were in an altercation at a certain type of establishment last night."

I glanced at Johnny and noticed he had paled.

"What exactly did these boys do?" I asked.

"Well, this was a house of ill repute, and a pretty sleazy one at that, if you know what I mean. According to the police, one of our boys got upset and took a knife to a lady, cut her up pretty bad. The police said he was trying to slice her face, but he was so drunk she was able to fend off the attack. Her arms and hands got slashed up pretty bad. Afterward he ran off with another fellow he came there with. We were asked to get the names of any of our men who were out of camp last night so the police can talk to them."

I stared back blankly. "Far as I know all my boys were in camp," I said. "We're pretty worn out. Everybody's sort of resting up."

"I understand, sergeant." He took my arm and led me away from the others. "We're not terribly concerned about this whore, but we have to go through the motions for the sake of appearances. If any of your men know anyone who might have been involved, they should tell them to keep their heads down. General McClellan is a very moral man, and he would not appreciate having a member of his army involved."

When the lieutenant left I pulled Johnny aside. "You better keep out of sight for the next few days," I said.

"What about Bobby?" he asked.

I gave him a long, hard stare. "I don't care what happens to Suggs. He's not part of our squad, and if I have anything to say about it, he never will be. You just lay low and let Suggs take care of himself."

"Yeah, I will." As I turned to go Johnny grabbed my arm. "I din' know he cut her," he said. "He had blood on his arm, but I thought he only punched her. I appreciate whatcha done fer me."

"Make sure I don't have to do it again," I said. "And make sure Suggs understands I didn't do any of it for him. If it were just him, I would have turned his ass over to the lieutenant and let him get what he deserves."

"Bobby ain't a bad man, Jubal. He really ain't."

"He cut a woman with a knife because she laughed at him. Yes, Johnny, he's a bad man. He's a very bad man."

CHAPTER FIFTEEN

When I left the parsonage I crossed the street to the Johnsons' store. As Rebecca had promised, Walter Johnson had already left for the Richmond railroad station to collect his incoming goods. Inside the store, Rebecca and Mary were behind the counter dealing with two customers with yet another waiting to be served. I went to the dry goods table and busied myself with a pile of winter shirts. This time Mary didn't cast any nervous glances my way, as she had the previous time I was there, likely assuming that I wanted to see Rebecca. Over the past few weeks the gossip mill had been churning about Rebecca and me, fueled by the ladies of the church and, I had no doubt, by my own father. I was the one person who seemed to know the least about it.

But in this instance it served me well. Since my interrogation skills were at best minimal, the chance to catch Mary Johnson off-guard could only be a benefit. I waited until the last customer had left before I approached the counter.

"Hello, Jubal," Rebecca said with a smile.

I smiled back. "Hello." She was wearing the simple white dress I liked so much, and as always it brought out her reddish-blond hair and her soft green eyes.

"Good morning, Jubal," Mary said, bringing me back.

"Good morning. I wonder if I could have a moment of your time . . . in private?"

Mary Johnson's eyes flicked nervously toward her stepdaughter. "Oh, Jubal, you can talk to me in front of Rebecca. That will be fine."

"It would be best if I could speak to you alone." I put a note of firmness in my voice to let her know there was no other option.

"Oh, Mary, go ahead with Jubal. I can watch the store alone."

Rebecca had closed the door on any further excuses, and Mary smiled weakly. "Why don't we go up to our sitting room? I have some coffee on the stove and we'll be more comfortable."

I followed Mary up the stairs to the Johnsons' apartment. The door opened into a short hall with a coat closet, then directly into a wide area that included a large sitting room with a dining table off to one side and a kitchen directly beyond. To the rear, as I knew from childhood, there were three bedrooms, the one in which I had spent the most time now sadly empty.

Mary hurried toward the kitchen. "Let me get you some coffee. How do you take it?"

"Black is fine," I said.

"All you young men came home from the war drinking black coffee, it seems. I just . . ." She seemed to catch herself, as though what she had said had given something away, then she moved ahead quickly. "It just seems that whenever you young men get coffee in the store you don't need any cream for it. Seems odd in a community with so many dairy farms."

"There wasn't much cream on the battlefield," I explained, as she returned to the room with a mug of coffee. "We just got used to not having it."

She gestured me toward a chair and took one opposite, her hands held in two tight balls in her lap. "Now, what can I help you with?"

"I need to talk to you about your relationship with Johnny Harris," I said simply.

Mary shifted in her chair. "Well, as I told you before, I hardly knew him, except for the times he came into the store. There really isn't much I can tell you."

"Mrs. Johnson, Mary, I know your relationship was much deeper than that. I'm not looking for details; I'm looking for things you might know, things that might help me find Johnny's killer."

She had been shaking her head as I spoke. "No, you're mistaken. I don't know who could have told you these things, but I assure you they are hateful lies. My God, if my husband ever heard them—"

"Mary, I specifically waited until he was away for just that reason. I don't want to cause you any problems. I don't want to embarrass you in any way." I spoke the words slowly and deliberately, ending with: "But I need to know whatever you can tell me."

"Jubal, I assure you—" She stopped as I took the few steps that separated us. I reached into my jacket pocket and withdrew the photo I had taken from Johnny's room. I handed it to her.

"I found this when I searched Johnny's room."

She stared at the photo, her lips trembling.

"There's an inscription on the back," I added.

I watched as she turned the photo over and read what she had written: *From Mary, to Johnny with love.*

Her hands began to tremble as she took a deep breath and began to sob. I pulled a clean handkerchief from my pocket and pressed it in her hand. Making any woman cry has always been an abomination to me, filling me with guilt beyond all measure.

"He was the devil," she managed between tears. "He was the devil come to earth. But, God forgive me, I loved him." She looked up at me. "He was so sweet at first. He made me feel young and alive. But it was all a joke to him. It wasn't like that at first. He didn't show that side of himself then. It came out gradually. But when it did it was horrible.

He thought it was funny to seduce the wife of a man he had known all his life, a woman who would have been the stepmother of his boyhood friend. In the end he just laughed at me, and told me that Rebecca would be next. He said he would have her too, because he knew she loved you, and he wanted to see you suffer."

My body stiffened as the words flowed from her mouth, and I remembered the confrontation Johnny and I had had shortly after I returned home, the temptation I'd felt to kill him then and there.

"I know what Johnny was like," I said. "I saw him change during the war, watched him become the monster that came home."

"Will my husband find out?" she asked at length, breathing deeply.

"Not from me. And not from anyone else if I can stop it. Walter has had enough pain. He doesn't need this added to it." I paused, letting what I had said sink in. "Tell me about Bobby Suggs."

Mary pressed my handkerchief to her lips, then sat up straight and got control of her breathing. "Johnny was afraid of him," she began. "Oh, he wouldn't show it when Suggs was there, but when we were alone he told me that Suggs hated him, that it was about something that had happened during the war, and that Suggs had come to Vermont to cause him harm." She looked at me fearfully, and it made me wonder if she were about to utter a lie. "Johnny told me he might have to kill him."

Sharpsburg, Maryland, 1862

We had been on the tail of General Robert E. Lee's army for more than a week when it finally crossed the Virginia border and entered Maryland, the South's first incursion into Northern territory. Emboldened by his victory at the Second Battle of Bull Run, Lee intended to defeat the Union on its own ground, thus demoralizing all who sympathized with the Northern cause. But Lee had another motive as well. Virginia's farms had been stripped of food and he believed that the citizens of

Maryland might welcome Confederate forces and willingly supply his troops with much needed stores. Thus his 55,000-man army marched into the state singing "Maryland, My Maryland," only to find the citizens hiding in their homes.

When he realized that General McClellan was pursuing him with 75,000 men, Lee took up defensive positions behind Antietam Creek, and prepared to fight what was to become the bloodiest single-day battle in the nation's history.

Since there was no need for reconnaissance, my squad was returned to its regular unit to join in the pursuit of Lee's forces. As we crossed into Maryland, people emerged from their homes to cheer us, a stark contrast to the citizenry of the South, who hid behind locked doors, or occasionally hurled insults, or even shot at us as we passed.

"I feel like a hero," Johnny announced as the three of us trudged along together.

"All them cheers means we're marchin' through Northern territory," Abel said. "Which also means that Lee's takin' the fight ta our front door."

"I still like bein' taken as a hero fer a change," Johnny said. "It's a helluva lot better then lookin' over yer shoulder all the time, thinkin' some old lady with a pistol might take a shot at ya from her kitchen window. God Almighty, I can't believe how scared I am sometimes."

"You just be careful if we ever march past any Washington whorehouses," I said.

"Damn, you ever gonna let me forget that?" Johnny whined.

"Hell no," I replied.

"Why should we?" Abel said. "When yer ninety years ol' an' sittin' in yer rockin' chair, I plan ta come bother ya about it."

"If I get ta be ninety—hell, if I even get home—I won't care whatcha bother me with," Johnny snapped back.

* * *

General Hooker, who now had charge of our corps, ordered us into battle against Lee's left flank, which proved immediately vulnerable. We charged in, several thousand troops strong, and drove the Rebs back. The battle swirled about us for hours, sweeping back and forth across a wide expanse named "Miller's Cornfield," bodies piling deeper every time we crossed it, each side showering the other with artillery fire. We were bombarded by artillery under General Jeb Stuart to the west, and Colonel Stephen Lee to the south, his canister rounds firing from batteries across from Dunker Church, driving us back time and again in hales of grapeshot. Each time, Union forces returned fire with nine batteries of powerful twenty-pound Parrott rifles, which decimated advancing Reb troops in what became known on the Reb side as "Artillery Hell." On one advance General Hooker spied the glint of Rebel bayonets hidden in the cornfield and immediately called a halt; then he directed four artillery batteries to open fire over the heads of his crouching troops.

As we watched, the cornfield exploded with round after round, and when we resumed our attack we found stunned Reb forces scattered throughout the cornfield and we beat them over the heads with rifle butts and stabbed them with bayonets, the fighting too close at hand to risk firing a weapon. Our men then fought our way to Dunker Church, crashing through Reb fortifications, destroying their artillery batteries, and leaving the church mostly in ruin. When we finally stopped to rest, bodies lay all about us, Reb and Union alike, and the air was filled with the smell of blood and gunpowder and death. The following morning Lee continued to skirmish with McClellan, as he removed his battered army south, crossing the river back into Virginia.

While Lee fought his way home we were sent out to move through the bodies and search for any who were still alive. Word had come down that there were 23,000 casualties on both sides, and as my unit moved through the piles of twisted and torn bodies the shock of the carnage seemed overwhelming.

Abel walked beside me, shaking his head. "Jubal, we only got nine hundred folks livin' in Jerusalem's Landing," he said. "We got more bodies 'n that right cheer in this field."

We found one boy lying next to a split rail fence under the bodies of two others. He was still alive but had suffered a severe stomach wound and was moaning in pain. We lifted the corpses off him—one Union, one Reb, both as stiff as cordwood. Then we eased him onto one of the stretchers we had brought with us. He begged us for water, his lips dried and cracked, but we knew better than to do more than wet his lips and tongue.

"Damn," Johnny said. "Give the boy more water."

"He's got a belly wound. He'll die if we do," Abel said.

"Well, I'll tell ya, Abel. If ya ever find me like that, ya give me all the water I ask fer." Johnny shook his head and turned away. "I hate this goddamn war. I hate the stink of dead bodies. I hate seein' pieces a men layin' about, not knowin' which body they came off of. I thought I knew what this war was all about when we started out, but now I don't know what anythin' is about. It's jus' killin' an' more killin', an' I'm sick ta hell of bein' part of it."

I let Johnny rant, knowing he needed it. I waved for the wagon we had brought with us, and when it came forward we loaded the wounded soldier on board.

"We better get him to the field hospital," I said. "Abel, you come with me." I turned to Johnny, wanting to give him something to do. "Johnny, you take the rest of the men and look for more wounded. You're in charge. We'll be straight back with the wagon. We'll look for you due west of here."

The field hospital was a mile up the road at Grove Farm, the same encampment where General McClellan had set up his headquarters. As we drove our wagon into the camp we were stopped by a squad of heavily armed men, with a cavalry detachment fanned out behind them. A stocky sergeant with a thick red beard stepped up to the wagon, his hand on the grip of his holstered sidearm.

"Where you from and where you goin'?" he barked.

"We're from General Hooker's corps," I answered. "We're bringing in a wounded man we found near Dunker Church. I have a squad out there now looking for others."

The sergeant walked around to the back of the wagon, wincing at what he saw. "Looks bad. Better get him to the field hospital. It's up a piece to the left. Yer gonna see somethin' up there yer gonna havta keep quiet about."

"What's that?" Abel asked.

"President Lincoln is up at field headquarters meeting with General McClellan."

"Jaysus!" Abel yelped.

"We're here to keep him safe," the sergeant said. "Yer not talkin' 'bout him bein' here'll help."

"We'll keep our mouths shut," I said.

I started the wagon again and headed up a narrow dirt track.

"Ya think we'll get ta see him?" Abel asked.

"I don't know. I sure would like to," I said.

I pulled off at a sign directing us to the hospital. Across the dirt track was the large tent that housed McClellan's field headquarters, surrounded by a cluster of small tents. Abel and I strained our necks but we couldn't see anyone who resembled the president.

"Look for someone who's taller than most and who's wearing a stovepipe hat," I said, turning my attention back to the horses. "It's how he looks in all the pictures I've seen."

We reached the hospital and jumped down and hurried to the rear. As we pulled the stretcher from the wagon a tall, bearded man in a stovepipe hat stepped from the hospital tent. Josiah Flood was beside him, and once outside the president stopped and placed a hand on his shoulder.

As we approached the entrance, President Lincoln turned to look at us. He was a giant of a man, and his face was worn with enough creases to make you think he had seen all the troubles in the world.

"Is this boy badly hurt?" he asked in one of the softest voices I'd ever heard.

"Pretty bad, Mr. President," I said.

"Better get him inside."

As we passed, Mr. Lincoln reached out a hand and let it brush lightly against the boy's cheek. "They're going to take good care of you, son," he said in a near whisper.

"Damn," Abel muttered as we passed into the tent. "I never even got to salute the president."

"When we get back outside maybe you'll still get the chance."

We placed the stretcher down where we were told and were quickly brushed away by a heavyset nurse. "Go find some more," she said, ordering us out.

We hurried outside just in time to see the president joining a cluster of officers outside McClellan's field headquarters. Josiah still stood there watching him. Abel and I went up to him.

"So what'd the president say ta ya?" Abel asked.

Josiah turned toward us and I could see there were tears in his eyes. "When he was inside talkin' to the wounded boys, he was cryin'," Josiah said. "There was tears jus' rollin' down his cheeks. Then he seen me, an' he axed me where I was from an' how long I been fightin'. He put his hand on my shoulder an' he walks me outside cheer, an' then he tellin' me how he was signin' a paper tomorra tha's gonna make all colored folks as free as I is. Tha's when you boys come up."

I looked back toward McClellan's field headquarters and saw that the general and his staff were gathered next to the president as a photographer prepared to take their portrait.

That picture will be in the history books one day, I thought. Then I thought about the paper the president planned to sign tomorrow, a paper that would make all Negroes free men. It was a good thing, but it would sure raise hell in the South.

CHAPTER SIXTEEN

It was shortly after suppertime the following Friday when I saw Bobby Suggs ride up to the parsonage. I was standing outside the Johnsons' store talking with Rebecca. I had avoided her most of the week, not wanting to face the questions I knew she would ask about my conversation with Mary Johnson. Tonight I had gone to the store to pick up my father's weekly ration of pipe tobacco and she had followed me outside.

"Jubal, I need to know what Mary told you," she began.

It was just then that Suggs pulled up in front of the parsonage and dismounted.

"I'm gonna have to talk to him," I said, raising my chin toward Suggs.

"That's fine," she responded. "Then you can come right back here and take me for a walk. Unless you're going to reject me because I'm brazen enough to ask you to."

I smiled at her. I couldn't help myself. "I've known you since you were a little girl and you were brazen then. Why would I expect anything different from you now that you're a grown-up woman?"

Rebecca glanced down at her shoes, and when her head came up again she too was smiling. "And don't you forget it," she said.

Suggs came out of the parsonage carrying his carpetbag and began securing it to his horse.

"Got what you came for, eh?" I said as I approached behind him.

He cast a disdainful look over his shoulder and continued with his task. "I hear ya been ridin' up ta Lucie's woodlot durin' the week jus' ta make sure I'z still there," he said after a while.

"Maybe I just wanted to make sure you hadn't died from that thumping Rusty LeRoche gave you." I had run into several loggers while I was at Billy Lucie's house and knew the word would get back to Suggs. It was fine with me; I wanted him to know I was watching him and would be on his trail if he tried to leave.

"Didn't know ya worried after me like that," Suggs said. He finished his task and turned to me. "Ya really think I had somethin' ta do with Johnny gettin' kilt?"

"The thought has crossed my mind."

"Maybe ya oughtta be lookin' in the mirror, ya wanna find yerself a killer." He sneered at me and held my eyes.

"So you think I killed Johnny?"

"Coulda been you. Johnny tol' me how ya threatened him when ya came home. Tol' me ya put yer pistol right under his chin."

"Johnny had a good imagination," I said.

"Oh, ya denyin' it?"

I stepped in close, wishing I had two good hands I could use on him. "I don't need to deny anything to you, Suggs. But I do want to know what *you* were threatening Johnny about."

He gave my words a derisive snort. "I guess I'm jus' like you, Constable Foster. If somebody done tol' ya that, well, I'm sayin' they's got a good imagination too."

"Well, I sure am hearing it. Seems Johnny told his lady friends all about you, about how you were bothering him. You want to tell me what it was about?"

Suggs threw back his head and laughed. "Johnny'd tell a woman anythin' he thought she wanted ta hear," he said. "Anythin' that'd get her ta spread her legs."

I took him by his shirtfront and drove him back against his horse. "You should be careful what you say about the women of this town," I whispered. Then I drove my knee up into his crotch and felt a great rush of foul breath exit his lungs.

I let Suggs go and watched him crumple to the ground. "Have a nice ride back to Billy Lucie's place," I said as I turned and crossed the road to the Johnsons' store.

"What did you do to that man?" Rebecca whispered.

"I gave him a lesson in manners." I took her arm and started down the road, heading for the bridge that crossed the river.

"Why?"

"He made some disparaging comments about the women of this town."

"Who in particular?"

"Just the women in general."

She turned back and watched Suggs struggle to mount his horse. "Then you should go back and kick him again," she said.

I laughed and took her elbow as we continued down the road. "One kick a day is enough."

"And what if he'd said it specifically about me?" she asked.

I fought the smile but couldn't keep it down. "Well, then I'd still be kicking him."

We crossed the bridge and followed the river until we found a flat rock. I removed my jacket and spread it out to protect her pale blue dress and then sat beside her. Below us the heavy rush of water assured me our voices would not carry.

"You want to know what Mary told me?" I said matter-of-factly.

"Yes, I do." Her voice sounded slightly nervous, but there was an edge of determination as well.

"It wasn't much more than what you already told me," I said. "But I promised her I would do my best to keep it secret."

"She admitted her relationship with Johnny?" Rebecca's eyes were filled with anger over this confirmation of her father's betrayal.

"She acknowledged their relationship was more than it should have been. I didn't ask for details and she didn't offer them." I looked down at my hand, suddenly wondering where my other hand had gone. It was something that happened at the oddest of times and it always made me feel foolish.

"What were you asking her, then?"

"I wanted to know what Johnny told her, anything he said about being afraid of anyone, afraid someone might try to harm him."

"Did he mention this man you just . . . kicked?"

"His name is Bobby Suggs, and yes, Johnny mentioned him, at least according to your father's wife." I had consciously avoided referring to Mary Johnson as her stepmother ever since she had become so angry when I had.

"Do you think he killed Johnny?"

"I don't know. But I know he's capable of it."

"From the war?"

I nodded. "Some of our men did things there that were pretty monstrous. Suggs was one of them."

"Was Johnny another?"

"Yes, he was."

She hesitated, almost as if she were afraid to ask her next question. "Did Abel ever do anything like that?"

I stared at her, shocked that she would even ask. "No. Never," I said.

She let out her breath, relieved to hear me say it aloud. She looked down in her lap and then back at me. "I wouldn't have believed you if you said he had."

She reached over and placed her hand on my cheek, then leaned up and kissed my lips softly. "I love you, Jubal." She leaned back and stared into my eyes. "Do you love me?"

"Yes," I said. "I think I always have . . . but . . ."

She raised her hand to my lips and stopped me from saying more. "Will you walk me home?" she asked.

As we approached the store a wagon came toward us down the main road, spewing up a column of dust. I stared at it, hardly believing what I saw. Josiah was behind the reigns and seated next to him were Jemma and her sister Alva. Josiah pulled to a stop beside us.

"Jemma, Alva, what a pleasant surprise," I said.

"We jus' come onna train, Massah Jubal," Jemma said.

"It was wunnerful," Alva added.

"Josiah done sended us tickets. We gonna live here wit y'all," Jemma said.

Josiah sat there with a broad smile spread across his face.

"Why didn't you tell me?" I asked.

"I wasn't sure she'd come," Josiah said.

Jemma leaned her head against his shoulder.

I gestured toward Rebecca. "This is Rebecca. She's Abel's sister."

"How do, Miz Rebecca?" Jemma said. "I'z so sorry 'bout yer brudder. He was da one dat save my sista, him an' Massah Jubal an' Massah Johnny."

"Thank you for your sympathy," Rebecca said. "Abel wrote me all about you." She turned to Alva. "Especially you, Alva. You're just as beautiful as he said. Welcome to Jerusalem's Landing."

"We gots ta git goin'," Josiah said.

"Come back down later, so I can introduce the ladies to my father." I looked at Jemma and Alva in turn. "But you both have to stop callin' people massah," I added.

"And come to the store too," Rebecca said. "My brother wrote my father about you both and I know he'd like to meet you."

"I tanks ya fer da welcome, Miz Rebecca," Jemma said.

"Just call me Rebecca, please."

"We be back down," Josiah said. "Maybe t'nite, but fer sure tomorra."

As the wagon pulled away, Rebecca commented, "That little girl, she's lovely, just like Abel said."

I nodded. "He loved that little girl. He told me he was going to bring her home for your mother to spoil."

"And now she's here," Rebecca said. "Now I can spoil her."

Centreville, Virginia, 1862

We were part of a detachment sent off to guard the final construction of the Centreville Military Railroad. Our unit was now under the command of General Ambrose Burnside, who had replaced General McClellan as commander of the Army of the Potomac. According to the newspapers, President Lincoln had been displeased by McClellan's "lack of initiative" in pursuing the Confederate Army following Lee's defeat at Sharpsburg. Instead, McClellan had chosen to regroup and replenish his supplies, allowing Lee's battered army to escape to the south.

Now, as far as I could tell, Burnside was doing the same thing, but it was fine with my men and me. We were encamped on a high hill that overlooked the entire valley, with a clear view of any advancing enemy forces. To this point there had been none, and we contented ourselves with quiet patrols of the town and the surrounding countryside and with warm campfires at night to take the chill off the November evenings.

We had just finished breakfast when Bobby Suggs came into our camp looking for Johnny, quickly pulling him aside and jabbering at him. When he walked back to our campfire Johnny's face was filled with consternation. "Bobby says the talk is that we'll all be headin' south in a week or so. He says we're gonna join up with the rest of the Army of the Potomac fer a big push on ta Richmond, an' that Lee is massing his troops at Fredericksburg to stop us."

We were sitting about twenty-five miles west of Washington. Fredericksburg was another fifty miles south, and Richmond another fifty miles beyond that. The railroad we were guarding could easily be connected with another rail line that would bring our supplies straight in behind us to support an assault on Fredericksburg.

"What Bobby's saying makes sense," I noted. "The newspapers say that Mr. Lincoln wants us to give 'em hell."

Johnny's shoulders slumped. "Yeah, well, let Mr. Lincoln give 'em hell. I thought we'd get this railroad duty longer'n that," he said.

Abel let out a loud belch and grinned. "You know what they say, Johnny. If the officers see ya gettin' comfortable, they gonna change what yer doin'."

Johnny shook his head. He was clearly depressed over the news. He inclined his head toward Suggs, who was still standing off to one side. "Bobby's goin' on a patrol aroun' some of the farms. He asked me to go with him. That okay with you?"

Bobby had been made a corporal for reasons that mystified me and now had charge of a group of men who looked about as trustworthy as he did. But Johnny seemed to need a diversion. "That's all right with me," I said. "We're going on patrol in the town about two hours from now. Try and join up with us."

Johnny nodded. "Shouldn't be a problem ta git back by then, less we run into some trouble."

"Watch yourself," I said.

When Johnny had left, Abel brought me a cup of coffee. "Ya think Suggs knows what he's talkin' about?" he asked.

I shrugged. "It makes sense, given what I've read in the papers. The papers claim that Mr. Lincoln replaced McClellan because he thought he was too cautious."

Abel snorted. "Hell, at Antietam they sez there was 2,000 Union boys killed and 9,500 wounded. That sure don't sound very cautious ta me. Far as I'm concerned they kin get a helluva lot more cautious than they was."

I sat sipping my coffee and thinking about all the Union bodies we had carried off for individual burials, and the mass graves that had been dug for the Rebel dead. The Reb casualties had been only half of our own, despite the fact that their forces had been greatly outnumbered. But the worst thing for me had been the wounded—Reb and Union alike. The field hospitals were like charnel houses, the screams of agony filling the surgical tents as men's limbs were cut from their bodies without benefit of anything more than a shot of whiskey to ease the pain. I'd come to hate each time I had to bring a wounded soldier there, its dirt floors always slick with blood, the air rife with the stench of open wounds and burst bowels, and when I was finally sent away from our main encampment and its field hospital, I had left with a sense of relief, as though I had escaped from that one small part of the horrors we lived with day after day, week after week.

Abel and I and the remainder of my squad began our patrol at noon. We had been given a section of town that ran along the main road and included the church and most of the stores. The road itself was narrow and made of well-packed, heat-hardened dirt. The Rebs had fortified the area the previous year, and again during the spring, using the existing railroad to supply its troops. Now it was in Union hands and we were doing essentially the same thing, the only difference being that we were doing it under the hate-filled eyes of die-hard Virginians.

I kept my men spread out as we walked through the town, half on one side of the street, the other half on the other, with a good five paces between each man, each rifle brandishing a bayonet. The men knew to keep their eyes on the windows, especially those on a second floor or attic, but there had been only a few instances of sniping, each of which had ended with a Reb soldier or sympathizer being captured or killed.

As we passed a grocery store a one-armed man wearing a battered Reb field cap spat a wad of tobacco juice at the foot of one of my men and quickly found a bayonet pointed at his throat.

The man seemed as battered and beaten as his hat, his loose sleeve flapping in the breeze, his tired blue eyes glaring all the hatred he could muster. He had not shaved in days, and he had not washed his face. He was a sad sight, but he remained defiant.

"You gonna use that there bayonet, bluebelly?" he sneered. "Killin' a one-armed man oughtta be jus' 'bout yer speed. Probably go 'bout stabbin' our wounded boys on the battlefield. Oh yeah, I seen yer kind do it lotsa times."

I stepped in and pushed the bayonet up. "Let it go," I said to my man, whose name was George Sutton.

"He spits at me one more time, he's gonna be one dead Reb," Sutton said. He was young, not even twenty, and he'd just been sent to us as a replacement.

I looked at the man and spoke softly. "You lose that arm in the fighting?" I asked.

He gave me a curt nod. "But I killed me some bluebellies afore they got me," he said gruffly.

"We've all killed ourselves some boys," I said. "Too many, on both sides. We don't need you to be killin' us, or us to be killin' you. You did your part, so let's leave it be."

The man glanced at his empty sleeve and then back at me, the hate even heavier in his eyes. "I don't need yer pity, bluebelly. Y'all kin save it fer yer own."

"Fair enough," I replied. "Let's keep moving, men."

When we reached the church there was a group of woman standing outside. They were of varying ages, from elderly to quite young. One of the younger women raised her nose as we approached. "Momma, we should be goin' on home," she said. "There's a powerful bad smell comin' our way."

Abel, always the jester, couldn't resist. He stared at the young woman open-mouthed. She was tall and slender, with ringlets of brown hair cascading to her pale blue dress, her dark blue eyes and high cheekbones the epitome of Southern womanhood.

"What's it that smells so bad, young lady?" he called.

The woman turned and looked down her nose at him. "It smells a bit like Yankee, which is one step lower than pig."

"Ooh-ie!" Abel shouted. "I guess some of us done forgot ta take our baths. Sorry 'bout that, ma'am."

The young woman smiled in spite of herself, and as we moved past I saw Abel wink at her, causing the woman to spin on her heel.

I walked up beside him. "Abel, you will definitely get yourself shot one of these days."

"Oh Lordy, if I have to go, I'd sure like it to be a beautiful woman who does me in. Tha's sure 'nuff a lot better'n bein' kilt by some old Reb smells as bad as I do."

We checked the areas behind the stores, some of which had barns and storage sheds, for any contraband that might have been smuggled in and stashed away, but the area seemed clear. On the way back the man who had spit at one of my men was gone, and I halted the squad and told them they could go into the stores provided they went two at a time. Several of the men, Abel and I included, went into the grocery store to see if there were any foodstuffs we could buy.

The interior of the store was dark and cool with a middle-aged man and woman standing behind the counter. Abel went right up to them, and started off by telling them that his mother and father ran a store not unlike this one, except that it was up in northern Vermont.

"This sure 'nuff reminds me of home," he said. "Ya got any food we kin buy?"

The woman stared at him, unsmiling. The man twisted his mouth unpleasantly. "Ain't much that hasn't already been stolen," he said.

"We ain't lookin' ta steal nothin'," Abel said. "We get anythin', we'll pay ya fair an' square, jus' like we'd do at home."

I walked up beside him. "My men don't pilfer," I said. "Anything they take, they'll pay for."

The woman let out a breath through her nose, giving her strong opinion about my promise of payment; the man just shifted his weight.

"We got some country ham, but it's a bit salty fer Yankee tastes," he said. "An' we got some soda crackers, some coffee, a few eggs. Tha's 'bout it, far as food goes."

"Ya got any candy?" Abel asked, his voice filled with expectation.

The man reached under the counter and took out a jar half-filled with peppermint sticks that looked a bit stale and worse for wear.

"Oh, yes," Abel said. "Lemme have a coupla them. I ain't had no candy in the longest time."

The man extended the jar and Abel took two sticks.

"That'll be two cents," the man said.

Abel grinned at him and placed two pennies on the counter. "Sorry, but I only got Union money."

"It'll do," the storekeeper said, his expression remaining rigid.

Abel and I went outside and stopped on the porch.

"He sure wasn't a very friendly sort," he said.

"Makes me wonder if maybe he and his wife lost somebody in his war." I looked Abel in the eye. "Imagine how your father and mother might be if *they* lost someone, and some Reb soldier came waltzing into their store."

"Yeah, I never thought of it that way. But I sure as hell hope it weren't me they lost. Or Rebecca neither." He wiggled his eyebrows. "Then ya couldn't be my brother-in-law."

We met up with Johnny an hour later. He came up the street with a burlap sack slung over his shoulder, his rifle held down at his side.

"What have you got there?" I asked.

He grinned at me. "We went by this farm, had some chickens run-nin' aroun' in the yard. There's two less chickens runnin' now."

"I hope you paid the farmer."

"Weren't nobody there," he said.

"Prob'ly hidin' from Yankee thieves," Abel said.

Johnny chuckled at him. "Got me a pair of nice warm gloves too. When yer hands are all froze-up this winter, mine'll be nice an' warm."

"Glad to hear it," I said. "What else did you and Suggs pilfer?"

"It ain't pilferin', it's the spoils a war. These folks run off an' leave their stuff behind, if I don't take it somebody else'll come along an' *poof*, it'll be gone."

Abel made a show of scratching his chin. "I wonder what yer daddy would say about that."

"Well, when I get home, I'll ask him," Johnny said. "In the mean-time I aim ta have a full belly an' warm hands."

"That's straight from the mouth of the preacher's son," Abel re-sponded. "An' I say amen to that."

CHAPTER SEVENTEEN

I was seated at the kitchen table going over some fence line disputes that my father and I would have to resolve in the coming week, along with some past-due taxes we needed to collect. We had fallen behind in our regular work because of Johnny Harris's murder, and our regular work was what paid our bills. As my father had explained last night, we had to hunker down and do it if we planned to eat next month.

He had just come in to the kitchen, which was also our makeshift office, when someone began pounding on our back door.

"My Lord, somebody sure wants ta knock that door down," he said, pouring a mug of coffee. When he had finished he went to the door and opened it and was immediately confronted by Chantal LeRoche.

"I need ta make a complaint agin' my papa," she said without preamble.

"Well, ya bring yerself inside an' tell us what this here is all about," my father replied.

I stood as Chantal approached and pulled a chair away from the table. "Please sit down," I said.

Her hair was combed along her cheeks and she was wearing a simple brown dress that buttoned to her throat, and I thought it was the first modest clothing I had seen her wear. Right now she stared at me as though no one had ever shown her any display of manners before.

"My oh my, now ain't you the gentleman, Jubal Foster," she said as she approached the table.

"My boy's been ta college," my father said. "Talks real fancy an' knows his manners. He's been teachin' me, but ya know what they say 'bout ol' dogs."

My father couldn't stop himself from grinning, and Chantal realized he was having his fun with me.

"Please sit down," I said again.

She took a chair and my father sat next to her. "Now what's this all about, lil' girl?"

"First off, I ain't no lil' girl. I'm seventeen," she said. "Second off, my papa keeps on beatin' the hell outta me." She pulled her hair back from the side of her face and offered up a sizable bruise as evidence.

"An' why's he doin' that?" my father asked.

"He don' want me walkin' or talkin' with any boys, but them boys come by anyways, even after he's run 'em off, an' he jus' gets madder'n the devil. An' if he can't get hold a them he takes it out on me."

"Well, ya listen to me, dear. I'm about yer papa's age, so we prob'ly see things pretty much the same way. An' I'm thinkin' that maybe he jus' wants ta keep ya from bein' taken advantage of." He gave her a long look. "Ya know what I mean?"

"I know whatcha mean," she said, stiffening. "But that ain't his biz-ness. Tha's my bizness."

"Well, dear, as long as ya live in yer papa's house, it's sure enough his business. Now, I kin go up there an' talk ta him, but iffen I arrested him fer hittin' ya, the judge is prob'ly gonna tell me I gone too far an' up an' send yer papa on home."

"Well, why don' ya arrest him for all the boys he beat up on? I know he beat up on Johnny Harris, an' maybe it was even him that went an' kilt that poor boy."

"What makes you think that?" I asked, interested now.

"I heard him talkin' ta my mama. They was talkin' low an' it was hard ta hear good, but I heard my daddy say how he caught up with Johnny an' gave him what fer. I'm thinkin' now that maybe it was more'n jus' a thumpin'."

"When was that?" I asked.

"Right afore I heard that Johnny was kilt."

I glanced at my father.

"Ya better go on up and have a talk with Rusty," my father said. "I'll take care of our other business."

"I ain't goin' back home," Chantal snapped.

"Where ya goin'?" my father asked.

"I don' know, but I can't go back."

My father scratched his head. "Well, there's Mrs. Edwards, I suppose. She rents out rooms ta drummers an' timber buyers who are passin' through."

"How much she charge?" Chantal asked.

"Coupla dollars a week, I think. But she gives ya breakfast an' dinner. Kin ya afford that?"

"I got some money," she said. "Not much, but some. I needs ta get ta Burlington an' get me a job at the mill."

"How did you get here?" I asked.

"I took one a Papa's horses. If yer goin' up there I'd 'preciate it if ya'd take it back ta him."

"You know I'm going to have to tell him what you told us," I said. "I don't expect he'll be very pleased about that."

Chantal gave out a little huff. "He'll be madder'n a hornet. You ain't gotta tell him where I'm at, do ya?"

"I'll tell him you said you were headed for Burlington."

She gave a curt nod. "I'd be pleased if ya told my momma that I'll write ta her," she said.

"I'll tell her."

* * *

I left Chantal in my father's care, tied Rusty's horse to my saddle horn, and headed up to Sherman's Hollow. The wind had picked up and I could feel a hint of winter in the air. Within weeks, certainly by Thanksgiving, the snow would be deep around us, signaling that it was time for us to get out and shoot our winter deer. I smiled at the thought, and at the idea of the coming holiday. Thanksgiving was only declared a national holiday two years ago, and already Vermonter's were using it to mark the true start of winter. "As if we had to," I said to my horse Jezebel, thinking that snow up to your hind end should be enough of a signal in itself.

When I pulled into the LeRoche dooryard Mrs. LeRoche came rushing out her front door, wringing an apron with her hands. "Did ya find Chantal?" she asked. "Is she hurt?"

"She's fine," I said. "She asked me to bring your horse back and to tell you she'll write to you."

"Where is she?" Mrs. LeRoche was somewhere in her early-to-mid forties, although she looked a bit older. She had graying brown hair and doelike brown eyes that she had given to her daughter, and I could see that she had once been a handsome young woman. She smoothed out her apron over a well-worn calico dress and looked suddenly relieved.

"She told me she was going to Burlington to look for a job," I said. "She also said she didn't want her father to know where she was."

"I won't tell him," she snapped. "Damn that man and his temper."

"She's going to take a room with Mrs. Edwards, until she can get herself into Burlington."

"It's good she's getting off on her own," she sighed. "It's time. She an' her papa are like a cat an' a dog." She looked up at me. "But he loves her. He jus' don' know how ta handle her. I kep' tellin' him that nobody knows how ta handle a girl that age, but he din' believe me."

"Chantal told my father and me that he gave Johnny Harris a thumping right around the time Johnny died. She said she overheard him telling you that."

Mrs. LeRoche pressed her lips together. "She ought not be talkin' bad 'bout her papa. It's what the Bible says, an' she knows it."

"Did he tell you that?" I asked.

She stared me down. "Tha's somethin' you gonna have ta talk ta Rusty about. I don' know nothin' else 'bout it."

"Is he out in his woodlot?"

"He is."

I untied the horse and handed down the rope.

"Thank ya fer bringin' our horse back, an' fer tellin' me 'bout Chantal," she said. "I'll be ridin' inta town tomorra ta see her."

She didn't say it, but I suspected she'd wait until Rusty had headed out to his woodlot before she went into town.

I followed the sound of axes until I found Rusty and his sons, along with two hired hands, felling a stand of tall pines. As I did on my last visit, I tied Jezebel well away from any falling timber and walked to where the men were working.

Rusty saw me approaching and guided me off to one side.

"You sure do a lotta movin' about fer a fella with one arm," he said, watching me to see how I'd taken his jibe.

I bristled inwardly but otherwise let it pass. "I brought your horse back. Your daughter left it at our place."

Now it was Rusty's turn to bristle. "Where's she at?" he demanded.

"She said she intended to head on in to Burlington to look for work."

"An' how's she supposed ta git there?" He paused to work his mind around his own question. "Prob'ly goin' with one a them lil' skunks what's always sneakin' up ta see her," he said. "Damn."

"She's pretty upset about you beating on her," I said. "She even talked to my father about arresting you."

"I hope he done set her straight on it," he rasped.

"He did." Now I paused. "But I'm not sure I agree with him." Before he could respond I hurried on. "She also told us that she overheard you telling your wife that you went after Johnny Harris right around the time he turned up dead, that you claimed you gave him what for. Exactly what was that, Mr. LeRoche?"

Rusty squared on me, fists clenched and ready before he stopped himself. "So my own little girl's tryin' ta buy me a trip ta the gallows, is she?"

"I need you to tell me about the fight you had with Johnny Harris," I said, keeping my hand close to my sidearm.

Rusty let out a snort. "Yeah, I went after the sumbitch. Caught him saddlin' his horse up in his barn and grabbed him by the back of the neck an' the britches. Planned on givin' him the beatin' of his life." He looked down at my hand hanging next to my Navy Colt. "Well, the lil' sumbitch did the same thing you's thinkin' 'bout doin'. He pulled out a sidearm an' stuck it in my face an' tol' me he'd send me straight ta hell iffen I din' get outta his barn right quick."

"And when was this?" I asked, wondering what had made Johnny nervous enough to carry a sidearm. LeRoche? Suggs?

"We got inta it right afore he turned up dead." Rusty kicked the ground in front of him. "Tha's whatcha wanted ta hear, ain't it? But I'm tellin' ya one thing more: I din' kill that boy. Thought about it, but never done it."

"Do you have a small cant hook?" I asked. "Not the big ones they use at the lumber mill, but the smaller kind?"

"I got one." Rusty narrowed his eyes.

"I'd like to take it with me," I said.

"What fer?"

"I want to have it checked for blood."

He chuckled. "I'll get it fer ya." He walked over to a supply wagon and pulled a small cant hook from the rear.

He walked back to me, holding it along his side, and I suddenly realized that all he would have to do is thrust it forward and drive it into my chest and I'd be dead, killed the same way I thought Johnny had been killed.

"Better if ya git up on yer horse an' I'll hand it up to ya," he said.

"Thank you. I'll return it to you as quick as I can."

"Ya do that," Rusty said. "An' ya hear where my daughter's got off ta, ya let me know that too."

———————

Fredericksburg, Virginia, 1862

Christmas was only two weeks away and it was hard not to think of home, to think of Rebecca and my father, and the beauty of the snow-covered hills and mountains that came to us each winter in Vermont.

"We should all be sitting in front of a fire, sipping a hot mug of cider," I said.

"Or out shootin' a turkey or a deer fer Christmas dinner," Abel said.

"Ya remember the blind up behind my house?" Johnny asked.

"Hell yes," Abel answered. "We took a lotta bucks off that ridge."

"We sure did," I said. I looked at Johnny. "You remember the time you kept me from falling off that steep drop?"

"Sure do. Figure ya still owe me fer that one." Johnny laughed. "Hell, if I hadn't grabbed hold of ya, ya prob'ly woulda broke both yer legs an' crippled yerself up an' missed this here war."

"Never thought of it that way," I said. "If it hadn't been for you, I'd probably be sitting at home, holding hands with Rebecca. I guess I do owe you."

Abel slapped his thigh. "Ya gonna shoot him now, or wait till later?"

"I'll wait," I said. "Maybe some Reb will do it for me."

We were gathered just below Marye's Heights, about five hundred yards from a long stone wall the Rebs were using as a fortification. A heavy fog shrouded the open field before us, and our backs were to the Rappahannock River, which we had crossed late last night on one of the three pontoon bridges our engineers had built. If we had to withdraw under fire, those same bridges would become choke points that could lead to a slaughter.

The armies of Generals Longstreet and Jackson were spread out before us, with Robert E. Lee in overall command of 73,000 of the Rebels' best troops—seasoned, aggressive men, the type of army President Lincoln expected us to be. For our part we had General Burnside in command of three "Grand Divisions" totaling 114,000 men, with General Edwin "Bull" Sumner on the right flank, General Joseph Hooker in the center, and General William Franklin facing Stonewall Jackson's army on the left.

As we awaited orders to attack, General Sumner opened a withering artillery attack on Fredericksburg to clear it of any Reb units and snipers. More then 5,000 shells were fired into the city and its western ridges from 220 artillery pieces set up on the eastern side of the Rappahannock. Sumner then ordered 10,000 men into the city to clear it of all remaining enemy troops and to burn whatever stores they found, while 10,000 more guarded them from any frontal assault by Longstreet's army. My unit was part of that guard element, and as I watched our men loot and burn the city it reminded me of histories I had read of ancient Vandals sacking European towns and villages.

"My God, look at them boys," Johnny said, pointing to a group not far from us, some fifty men gathered outside a large store. "Look at their pockets. They's stuffed with money and God knows what else that they's taken. Why in hell are we jus' standin' here?"

"Cause them's our orders," Abel said.

Johnny turned to me, a pleading expression on his face.

"Abel's right," I said. I raised my chin toward the ridges to the west. "Longstreet's army is up there. He decides to send them down and defend the city, somebody better be here to stop him."

As we watched, our men lit torches and began moving down the street, smashing windows and setting one store after another afire. People fled into the streets, men and women, young and old, and some were shot down as they ran, while others headed for the river in hopes of finding an escape.

"There ain't gonna be nothin' left ta defend," Johnny said.

I watched our troops as they continued to loot and burn the city, ashamed of what I was witnessing, feeling impotent, knowing there was nothing I could do to stop it.

The main battle began at eight thirty the next morning. Despite a heavy fog that covered attacking and defending forces alike, General William Franklin sent two divisions into a gap in Stonewall Jackson's defenses. When the fog lifted at ten o'clock, Jackson's artillery opened up, pinning the Union troops. A two-hour artillery duel ensued, and in the end Franklin's assault was stalled.

My men and I lay huddled in a ditch listening to the seemingly endless roar of exploding shells to our left. At eleven o'clock the order came to begin our own assault on Marye's Heights where some 10,000 Rebel troops were entrenched behind a long, winding stone wall. Our assault came one brigade at a time, for a total of sixteen individual charges. My unit was somewhere in the middle, and as we advanced up the steep hill we found ourselves stepping on and over hundreds of our own troops who had gone before us.

Halfway up the hill the Rebel fire became withering, cutting down one line of our men after another. I shouted for my men to take cover behind our own dead and wounded, and we lay there firing up at the defenders behind the stone wall that sat more than a hundred yards above us.

I crawled down the line, checking my own men, telling them to make their shots count and to keep track of their ammunition. When I reached Abel he stared at me, his eyes glazed with fear.

"This here boy I'm layin' behind was alive when I dropped down," he said. "I give him some water, an' two more minie balls that were meant fer me near took his head off."

"Stay down. They have to order a retreat soon," I said. "This is insanity."

Johnny crawled up beside us. "Why the hell ain't they hittin' that ridge with artillery?"

I turned back behind us, and raised my chin toward the other side of the river where the Union artillery was positioned. The entire area in front of it was covered by fog. "They can't see where to shoot," I said. "If they simply opened up they'd be just as likely to hit us."

Johnny spit out ahead of him. "This war is jus' one big pile a shit," he said. "An' the generals we got are jus' wadin' through it with their heads up each other's hind ends."

"Amen to that," Abel said.

Behind us I could hear another brigade moving up the hill and I shouted out to my men: "When they reach us, join up with them and move on toward the wall!"

My men waited until the initial wave of the new assault passed them, then rose and followed up the hill. We had gone no more than twenty yards before we were pinned down again behind our own dead and wounded.

We remained there until three thirty when General Griffin's brigade renewed the attack. This was followed by General Humphrey's brigade at four p.m., both of which were repulsed by the Rebels. The final assault by General Getty's brigade came at dusk, but it too stalled before reaching the stone-wall defenses. In all, sixteen assaults had taken place and all had failed, before General Burnside finally called it off.

Night came with our troops still pinned down on the hill leading to the Heights, no one able to move or to help our own wounded because of continuing enemy fire. We lay there and listened to our dying men call out for help, but each time one of our numbers tried to move forward, he too became one of the dead or dying.

Abel crawled up beside me. "I can't stand listenin' ta these boys callin' out fer help," he said.

"You better stand it," I snapped, my anger bursting forth. "If you don't we'll be listening to you. You rise up too far and you'll make a perfect silhouette against the night sky behind you. They've got sharpshooters up there who can pick your fat ass off easy as pie."

Abel stared at me, confused by the harshness of my words. "It's jus' hard, Jubal. It's jus' hard."

I reached out and grabbed his arm and shook it. "I know it is. But damnit, I don't want to be writing Rebecca, telling her that her brother isn't coming home. You keep your head down. If there was a chance in hell that we could help those boys I'd go out there with you. But there isn't. There isn't any chance at all."

I lay there throughout the night, listening to the wounded call out in pain, begging for someone, for anyone to help them. At regular intervals our officers ordered us not to sleep, warning that enemy marauders were moving among the dead and wounded, bayoneting and clubbing anyone they found. I only saw one instance of it. I was lying behind a man whose head had been blown from his body when some thirty yards out I saw a figure rise up, his bayonet poised to strike. I fired a single shot at the center of his chest and I heard him grunt as his body flew back.

The next morning we were still pinned down, as Burnside considered yet another assault. There was no food and we were low on water, and I called out to my men, ordering them to take canteens from the dead and pass them down the line. Finally, by afternoon, Burnside became convinced that the battle was lost and he asked Lee for a truce to attend to his dead and wounded.

We learned later that Lee had graciously agreed and that night our army retreated across the river with our casualties. Burnside's folly had cost us 12,000 men—killed, wounded, and captured—while Reb casualties totaled 5,300, most of them from the early assault on General Jackson's position. Our sixteen assaults against Longstreet's forces on Maryre's Heights had cost between 6,000 and 8,000 Union casualties, while killing or wounding no more than a few hundred Rebs.

CHAPTER EIGHTEEN

Doc took some scrapings from the end of Rusty LeRoche's cant hook and placed them under his microscope. Then he placed the pointed blade beneath the lens, turning it carefully as he studied every portion of it.

"There are some faint traces of blood," he said. "But I can't tell if it's human or animal blood. And I don't have the equipment here to do anything more with them. I'll have to take the specimens in to the university and have proper tests run." Doc set the specimens aside. "You think Rusty might have done it?" he asked.

I shrugged. "I'd pretty much written him off, and then his daughter came to see us, wanting us to arrest him for beating on her. Then she started in about the boys he'd beaten for coming to see her, and claimed she had even overheard Rusty telling his wife that he had a run-in with Johnny and 'gave him what for.'"

"All this according to Chantal," Doc said.

"She admitted the conversation between Rusty and her mother was very low and hard to hear."

"Not very good evidence," Doc said.

"No, it's not. I confronted Rusty and he admitted having a set-to with Johnny in his barn, but insisted he didn't kill him. Said Johnny pulled a Colt on him before he could do anything and told him to get out. What bothers me is that the first time I spoke to Rusty he told me he hadn't gone to Johnny's house, that he was waiting for him to come back up to Sherman Hollow."

"So Rusty lied to you," Doc said. "Does that surprise you when you're asking questions about a murder? It tells me that Rusty's every bit as sly as I always thought he was. But being smart enough not to put your head closer to a noose doesn't make you a killer."

"So you don't think Rusty is the type to do Johnny in?"

"I didn't say that," Doc replied. "I wouldn't put a killing past Rusty at all. Especially if he was real angry. Man's got a temper like a bull in rut. Tell you what does bother me. Him saying that Johnny was carrying a sidearm. That doesn't sound right." He glanced down at my weapon. "Most folks don't go walking around with guns in Jerusalem's Landing. Not unless they're headed out to the woods."

"Or unless they think someone's coming after them," I added.

"Yes, a man might keep a gun close to hand if he thought that." He stared at me for a long moment. "You, for example. I think it's good for you to carry one, especially if you're getting close to Johnny's killer. Anyone else, beside Rusty, you think Johnny might have been concerned about?"

"Bobby Suggs, maybe. Or it could have been somebody we haven't even come across yet. Johnny hurt a lot of people since he came back. And from what I've been told, he planned on hurting more before he was finished."

Doc drew a deep breath. "Lord, that is not the boy I knew all those years. What happened to him?"

He went off to a glorious war, I thought, knowing I could not say the words aloud, not even to Doc.

"Why don't I take the specimens in to the university?" I said instead. "It will save you a long trip."

"Fine with me," Doc responded. "Let me give you a name at the medical school and a letter of introduction."

* * *

I stopped at the store to pick up some buttermilk. One of the few good things that came out of the war was learning a Southern recipe for fried chicken that required an overnight soak in buttermilk. I had cooked it for my father, and now he asked for it whenever the thought of chicken crossed his mind.

Rebecca was working behind the counter when I asked for the buttermilk.

"Are you cooking chicken for your father?" she asked.

"How in heaven's name did you know that?"

"Oh, he was in here one day when somebody else was buying buttermilk and he started bragging on you, telling everybody what a good cook you are." She gave me a coy smile. "I think he was trying to convince me that you'd be a good catch for a husband."

I could tell my face was beginning to take on color, a fact that only seemed to intensify Rebecca's pleasure. Her eyes drifted to the envelope in the front pocket of my shirt.

"Have you been to the post office in Richmond?" she asked.

I shook my head. "It's a letter of introduction Doc gave me for someone at the medical school. I'm taking some evidence in to him tomorrow."

"You're going into Burlington?" she said with excitement. "Can I go with you? Oh please, Jubal. There are some things I need to buy at a store there. And I promise I won't delay you. I know just what I need and if you bring me to the store I can get it while you're seeing the person at the medical school."

It would mean taking our buggy instead of just riding Jezebel, but it would also give me Rebecca's company for a three-hour trip.

"I'll want to leave early in the morning," I warned.

"You just tell me when to be ready and I'll be standing out front," she said.

* * *

We started out at six thirty the next morning. It was cool and crisp, a typical fall morning in the mountains. I had brought a blanket to keep Rebecca warm, and she had brought a basket of food, saying that we could eat a picnic lunch on the way home and save the cost of stopping at a roadside tavern. If I ever told my father, he'd point to it as another good reason she'd make a man a fine wife: she was considerate *and* thrifty.

Rebecca placed the blanket across her lap and moved closer to me so I could share it if I chose, but feeling her that near to me was enough to increase my body temperature a few degrees.

We drove past the Gorge Road and up the small hill that led into Richmond, and I thought of Bobby Suggs at Lucie's woodlot, wondering what was keeping him here with winter fast approaching. Certainly whatever he had expected from Johnny Harris was long past, and the lumbering season was coming to an end.

"What are you thinking about?" Rebecca asked.

"That man Suggs," I said. "He's up there on Lucie's woodlot and I was wondering what really brought him here and why he's stayed."

"But you told him to stay, didn't you?"

"Yes."

"And I thought you said you'd go after him if he tried to leave."

"That's true too."

"Well?"

"I don't have any reason to hold him, so if it ever went before a court I'm pretty sure the judge would slap me down and turn him loose."

"So you've been bluffing?"

"Yes, and Suggs isn't stupid. He knows we could make it hard on him, but he also knows we can't keep him here unless we come up with some pretty strong evidence against him."

"So why *is* he staying?"

"That's the question. Why is he?"

"Maybe he's really interested in Chantal LeRoche. Maybe she's why he's staying."

I had told Rebecca about Suggs's run-in with Rusty, and her romantic mind was now spinning it into something else.

"All the young men around here are interested in Chantal," I said.

"And why is that?" She had turned on the seat and was looking at me intently.

"Because Chantal is interested in every one of them," I said.

"Are you interested in her?"

"No."

"Why aren't you?"

"She's too young, and even if she was older she's not the type of woman I'm attracted to."

Rebecca sat quietly for a moment. "I bet she's attracted to you," she finally said.

"I'm certain she is."

"Why do you say that?"

"Because I wear pants and I'm under forty. I think that's all it takes to spark Chantal's interest."

We rode on in silence for several minutes before Rebecca turned to me again. "What kind of woman are you attracted to?" she asked.

I looked at her and smiled. "I think you already know the answer to that."

We followed the Winooski River from Richmond and on through Williston and into the outskirts of Burlington. Winooski was an Abenaki Indian name for the wild onions they had found growing along the banks of that particular river. The Abenaki were a part of the Algonquin Nation, a peace-loving people who had been in Vermont when the first white settlers had arrived. They were noted hunters and trappers and fishermen, and the river had been a favorite campsite, especially at the point where it emptied into Lake Champlain. Unlike other members of the Algonquin Nation, they had never attacked the settlers they encountered.

As we left the foothills of Richmond behind, the terrain flattened out into farmland used primarily for dairy cattle and the rough crops needed to sustain them. We passed through gently rolling hills with hundreds of cows watching us pass.

"They always look so curious when they see people," Rebecca said.

"It's where their food comes from. They're watching to see if we're bringing anything."

She laughed. It was a warm, beautiful laugh, one I knew I'd be happy listening to for many, many years.

"I'd find that easier to believe if those *cows* were bulls," she said. "Men are always looking for someone to feed them."

We entered Burlington shortly before nine thirty. The University of Vermont was located on a high promontory that looked down on Lake Champlain and the Adirondack Mountains beyond. The city itself was at the base of a long, gentle slope that ended on the banks of the lake.

"Do you think the store will be open?" I asked.

"It should be."

I drove down into the city, following Rebecca's directions. The store was on Church Street, a wide shopping street that ran parallel to and three blocks above the lake, and came to an abrupt end at a stately brick church with a towering white steeple. It was a lady's apparel store that also sold dressmaking materials. I told Rebecca that my errand might take an hour or more and suggested she check back at the store on the hour and the half hour should she finish before I returned.

"Don't worry about me," she said. "There's plenty for a country girl to look at if you're held up."

I drove back up the hill to the university and went directly to the medical school, a three-story brick building that faced the university's quadrangle. As I tied up Jezebel to a hitching post I watched students cross the quad and enter the medical building, headed for the next hour of classes, and I felt a sudden sense of loss at not being among them. Had I not gone off to war I would have graduated from the university by now, and would likely be studying medicine with these same students. The thought brought a twinge in my missing limb and I glanced at my empty sleeve as another thought slipped across my mind. It envisioned a sign posted on the building's front door: *One-armed would-be doctors need not apply.*

The man Doc had sent me to see was Dr. William Evers, a tall man in his late fifties with flowing white hair and square-cut spectacles that magnified intelligent gray eyes. He had come out of his office to greet me and stood before me reading the letter Doc had written.

When he finished he looked up at me. "Do you have the specimens Brewster sent along?"

I withdrew a cloth-wrapped parcel from my pocket. Doc and I had removed the cant hook blade from its shaft to make it easier to deal with. I handed it to Dr. Evers. "I appreciate your help with this," I said.

"Happy to do it, constable." He glanced at my empty sleeve. "The war?" he asked.

"Yes sir. A place in Virginia called the Wilderness."

"Yes, I remember reading about it. That was one of the bloodiest battles of the war, was it not?"

"They all seemed pretty bloody when you were in the middle of them," I said.

"Yes, I'm sure they did."

We started down a flight of stairs into the basement. "Did Brewster tell you that we worked together in the hospital here, tending to the boys who were shipped home?"

"He doesn't much like to talk about his work at the hospital," I said. "He says it sends him to the brandy bottle when he does."

"Mmm." Dr. Evers nodded. "Yes, indeed. He also wrote that he's been urging you to finish up your undergraduate degree—says you left it to go off to war—and to enroll in medical school. He feels you have a natural aptitude."

I looked pointedly at my empty sleeve. "Not much point in thinking about medical school."

We had reached the basement and Dr. Evers stopped and took hold of my good arm. "Don't despair because of that," he said. "I have a friend who lost an arm and a leg and he returned to practice using a prosthesis for each missing limb. The devices are fairly primitive but he overcame that. There is no reason you cannot do the same." He let go of me and turned and continued down the hall. "Anyway, if you decide you want to try, finish up your undergraduate degree and come see me. Brewster has nothing but high praise for you. Now, let's have a look at this specimen."

The laboratory was next to the dissection room where the school's cadavers were stored. When I'd been a student there were endless tales about grave robberies and bodies being slipped in the school's back door by professional body snatchers. A student could always get a young lady to draw in close by walking her past the rear of the school and pointing out the basement door.

It took Dr. Evers less than half an hour to reach a conclusion. "It's blood all right, reptile blood. I'd venture a guess that someone used the instrument it came off of to kill a snake or a turtle, something of that sort." He shrugged. "Of course, it could have been used on a human first. I can't think of a better way to obscure evidence. Wash down the blade, then use it again on some animal. Our tests aren't sophisticated enough to separate the two. So we'd only be able to see whichever was dominant."

I thanked Dr. Evers for his time and told him I'd give serious thought to returning to the university. "I didn't realize how much I missed it until I came here today."

He smiled. "I look forward to seeing you again. Give my best to that old scallywag Brewster."

"I will."

It was quarter to eleven when I pulled up in front of the store. Rebecca was not waiting for me, so I tied Jezebel and went inside.

A heavyset woman behind a counter smiled at me. "Are you Constable Foster?" she asked.

"Yes ma'am, I am."

"Well, the young lady you're looking for said to tell you she'd be back at the time you'd agreed on. She just went up the street a bit. Her parcels are here behind the counter if you'd like to take them."

"Thank you. I'll put them in our buggy and wait outside."

The woman smiled at me, a bit flirtatiously, I thought. "We're you in the war?" she asked, trying not to look at my empty sleeve, but failing.

"Yes ma'am, I was."

"I'm glad you got home safe," she said, her voice filled with sincerity.

I looked at her for a long moment. "Thank you," I said.

I loaded Rebecca's parcels into the buggy and glanced up and down the street. There were a number of shoppers going in and out of stores, several students standing outside a bookshop, and a group of men wearing battered Union caps and jackets, who were harassing passersby, some making comments the others would laugh at, several extending their caps in open requests for money. I climbed into the buggy just as the church at the top of the street began to peal out the hour. On the stroke of eleven I saw Rebecca moving toward me with another parcel tucked under her arm. She smiled when she saw me and quickened her pace.

Across the street two men broke away from the group of former soldiers and began crossing at an angle to intercept her. I climbed down from the buggy and started toward her. They reached her two steps ahead of me and I heard one of them say: "Hey, sweet lil' girl, don' go runnin' off, stay an' talk ta a gen-u-ine war hero."

I stepped in front of the two men and took her elbow. "Shopping all finished?" I asked.

"Yes. We better get on home." Her eyes flashed nervously toward the two men.

"You go on and get in the buggy," I said. "I'll be right there."

Rebecca started toward the buggy as one of the men called after her: "Hey, lil' girl, you like fellas with one arm, I kin chop one off fer ya."

The second man started to guffaw and I turned to face them both. "I think you should go back to your friends and leave the lady alone," I said.

The man who had called after Rebecca sneered at me. "Well, now maybe yer girlfriend wants ta get herself a *whole* man."

I stared at him without speaking until the sneer began to fade. He glanced at the pistol on my hip and the bit of badge that showed under my tan canvas coat.

"You a police officer?" he asked. "Cause if ya are, I ain't breakin' no law talkin' ta that girl. I'm jus' sayin' maybe she'd like a man what's got all his parts."

I took a step toward him and he began backing away. "If you want to keep all those parts you're so proud of, you better start moving," I said.

"All right there, officer. We leavin', jus' settle yerself down."

He grinned at me as they began to move away; then they turned and headed across the street. I noticed that the men they'd been standing with weren't even watching them. They were content with their own games of harassment. I walked back to the buggy, untied Jezebel, and was climbing up to the seat when the man called out again.

"Hey, lil' girl! Ya come on back when yer policeman friend ain't aroun', an' I'll show ya what a man's got all his parts kin do."

I turned the buggy and headed back toward Main Street and the long hill that would take us past the university and to the road home. Rebecca reached out and gently touched my arm. "Don't pay those men any mind, Jubal. They're such sad souls, out begging in the street the way they are."

I gave her a weak smile. "What did you buy?" I asked.

"Oh, so much. Material for several dresses, buttons, bows, everything I need. But I spent much too much money," she added. "I just couldn't help myself. Everything was so beautiful."

Like you, I thought, as I turned Jezebel onto Main Street and started up the hill, still trying to keep the soldier's words out of my mind.

It was nearing one o'clock as we approached the Williston–Richmond line. Rebecca turned to me and said simply: "I am starving, Jubal. Please, let's find a place to stop."

I turned the buggy onto a narrow dirt track that I had taken before. My father and I had fished there and I knew the path went about fifty yards, crossed the railroad tracks, and entered a small stand of pines that stood next to the Winooski River.

"This is a lovely spot," Rebecca said as I pulled up next to the river so Jezebel could drink. When she had finished I hitched her to a tree, helped Rebecca down, and spread our blanket on a soft bed of pine needles. I removed my gun belt and jacket and placed them in the buggy.

"I have a jug of cider. If you set it in the river I think it would chill quickly," Rebecca said.

I did as she suggested as she began spreading the contents of her picnic basket out on the blanket. There was a large piece of cheddar, a loaf of bread, some apples, and a jar of rhubarb preserves. She put two plates out along with knives and forks and smiled at me. "It's a good, healthy meal," she said.

"Yes, it is." I looked at the wedge of cheddar and thought back to the time Abel had convinced his father to buy a new brand from a drummer passing through town. The drummer had given him the Roman candle, the firework we had set off on the Fourth of July, nearly burning down the town's bandstand.

"What are you smiling about?" Rebecca asked.

"Do you remember the time we almost burned down the town bandstand?"

"Of course. It was horrible."

"It all started with a wheel of cheddar cheese," I said, telling her how Abel had schemed with the drummer to get the firework.

She laughed softly, but there was also a tear in the corner of her eye. It began to run along her cheek and she reached up and brushed it away.

"I'm sorry," I said. "I didn't mean to make you sad."

She smiled. "You didn't. When I think of Abel I always think what a wonderful man he became and what a shame it is he never had children of his own. He would have been a wonderful father."

"Yes, he would have. I wish you could have seen him with little Alva."

"I would have liked that," she whispered. "It was so perfect, growing up the way we did. You and Abel and Johnny and Josiah. And me as the tagalong little sister." She reached out and cut us each a slice of cheese, then quartered an apple and cut two thick slices of bread. "God, how I wish that war had never come, and we were all alive and together the way we were." She stopped and stared at me. "If you had it to do again, would you still go off to fight?"

It was a question I'd asked myself many times. "No, I wouldn't. And I would have argued like the devil to keep Abel and Johnny from going too."

We ate our lunch, enjoying the warm sun that filtered through the pines and the gentle breeze that came in off the river. When we had finished, Rebecca repacked the picnic basket and I placed it in the buggy. As I turned to retrieve the blanket she came up to me and slipped her arms around my neck.

"Jubal Foster, I am tired of waiting for you. I love you, and I know you love me, and I want you to show me right here, right now." She stared into my eyes, then raised herself on her toes and brought her lips to mine. Then she turned and led me back to the blanket. She sat down and gently pulled me down beside her. "Make love to me, Jubal," she whispered. "I've waited my whole life and I don't want to wait any longer."

I lowered my eyes. "Maybe that fella in town was right," I said, my voice cracking. "Maybe it would be better for you to have a whole man."

She reached up and placed her hands on my cheeks. "Stop it, Jubal. I'm in love with you. I always have been, and it's you I want, not one particular part of you; just you."

We lay beside each other, my one arm holding her, both of hers wrapped around my waist. We dozed, satiated with each other, and I wondered what I had done to deserve what she was offering me. She stirred and reached up and kissed my cheek.

"You know you have to marry me now," she whispered. "If you don't my father will come after you with a gun."

I pulled her closer. "He won't have to do that," I whispered back.

———

Chancellorsville, Virginia, 1863

We had spent four months on reconnaissance patrols trying to keep track of Lee's army and determine where Union forces could best attack him again. General Joseph Hooker had been placed in charge of the Army of the Potomac, while General Burnside, following his failure at Fredericksburg, had been banished to the Western Theater where he would not command troops involved in either the defense of Washington or the all-important defeat of Lee's forces.

Fearing an attack on Richmond, Lee had divided his forces, a fact we reported back to General Hooker's subordinates in early February. Convinced our information was inaccurate, we were sent out again and again to reconfirm it. Finally, in late March a captain from the newly established Bureau of Military Intelligence accompanied us and was shocked to discover that Lee had truly scattered his forces throughout Virginia, including 15,000 men under General James Longstreet, who had been sent to Norfolk to guard against a Southern push against Richmond. When brought the news, Hooker realized that he had 133,000 well-rested and fully provisioned troops, while Lee's army now numbered under 61,000 poorly supplied men—men who were often hungry and badly clothed. The army's intelligence bureau, using spies recruited among the Southern populace, along with information gathered from prisoners, deserters, slaves, and fleeing Southern refugees, also learned that Longstreet had been relegated to scouring the countryside seeking provisions from farmers and planters, who themselves were nearly destitute.

Once all that information had been gathered, Hooker decided on a move against Chancellorsville in Spotsylvania County, a gateway that would lead directly to Richmond, the seat of the Confederacy.

As we waited for orders to move on Chancellorsville, we continued our forays south, keeping track of Lee's scattered forces, carefully avoiding any engagements with Rebel troops that might give away our plan to attack.

Coming in one night we were greeted by Jemma and Alva with warm cups of coffee. Josiah had been urging them to leave camp and travel with any of several small detachments headed for Washington. Once there they could wait out the war in safety.

"I see you're still here," Abel said, as he accepted a cup from Jemma. "Josiah's right, ya know. You'd be a lot safer in Washington, and ya could even get paid work in a good household there."

"I wants ta stay wit y'all," Jemma said.

"Josiah said he'd come git ya when the war's over," Abel said. "An' I know he's a man keeps his word."

Jemma looked at me and I nodded agreement. "It would be safer for Alva," I said.

"Alva don' wanna leave Massah Abel. She say he saved her an' she gonna stay wit him."

"See, Abel, it's all yer fault," Johnny said. "These girls'd be sittin' pretty in Washington it weren't fer this mysterious hold ya got on 'em." Johnny waggled his fingers to emphasize Abel's powers over them. His clowning made Abel and several other men laugh.

"We'll be leaving for a battle soon," I said, trying to bring the subject back to their need to leave the war zone. "And it won't be safe for you to follow.

"I goes wit Josiah when de moves da hosp'l."

"But Josiah wants you and Alva to go to Washington," I argued.

Jemma just smiled at me. It was a beautiful smile and it told me that any further argument would be a wasted effort.

* * *

Our forces moved out on April 27, crossing the Rappahannock River, then the Rapidan River near Germanna and Ely's Fords, bringing our various corps together outside Chancellorsville on April 30.

Heavy fighting began the following day, and as we prepared to begin our assault Abel nudged me and pointed above our heads, where an aerial balloon floated across enemy lines. We had heard of the new balloon corps that had been formed to report on the size and dispersal of Rebel forces. Once viewing those forces through long telescopes while remaining out of firing range, the balloonists would drop messages to waiting couriers, who would ride back to Hooker's command post and relay the information.

We had been told by our officers that Hooker was employing the tactic to provide more accurate information that would allow our troops to initiate flanking attacks, thereby avoiding the direct frontal assaults that had ended in bloodbaths at Antietam and Fredericksburg.

When Lee surprised everyone by dividing his forces, Hooker ordered our corps to push through in an area known as the Wilderness, a large, nearly impenetrable region of scrub pine and thickets so dense it rendered our superior artillery useless. We were to keep the Rebs from establishing a foothold there, so we moved forward to try to push back the smaller Confederate force.

"Damn," Abel shouted across an opening in the dense brush, "I think we're gonna win ourselves a battle here, boys!"

As we charged ahead under light resistance, an officer rode up and ordered us to stop our advance and move to the rear.

I grabbed his stirrup when his horse drew near. "Why the hell are we retreating?" I demanded. "We finally got these Rebs on the run."

The officer yanked his foot and ripped the stirrup from my hand. "You saw what happened to us at Fredericksburg when we engaged in a frontal assault," he snapped. "General Hooker is going to make Lee bring a frontal assault against us and give him a taste of his own tactics. Now do what you've been told, sergeant, and get your men moving."

We took up defensive positions around Chancellorsville, an insignificant hamlet that was little more than a large mansion and a few scattered houses at the junction of Orange Turnpike and Orange Plank Road.

Our corps, some 15,000 strong, spent the morning digging defensive positions in preparation for the Rebel attack that General Hooker was trying to promote. To our right, General Oliver Howard commanded 11,000 additional troops guarding against any flanking attack the Rebs might make. Far to our left, the balance of our army, nearly 75,000 men, were prepared to slaughter any major assault by Confederate forces that came out of the dense Wilderness. According to our reports, all we needed now was an all-out attack by Lee's army and victory would be assured.

I had learned over the years of fighting that war involved periods of intense terror, followed by the horror of what we had done, and what had been done to us, followed again by a seemingly endless period of boredom while we waited for the terror to return. Now we were nervously enjoying the boredom.

"Maybe Lee'll be too smart ta attack us," Johnny said. "If he's been kickin' our butts by layin' back an' waitin' fer us, why in hell's name would he change it now?"

"I hope he does attack," Abel responded. "I think I'd like it a lot better staying right cheer behind this trench wall an' takin' potshots at the Rebs as they come at us, instead a runnin' up some hill inta their teeth like we done at Marye's Heights over ta Fredericksburg. That was a livin' hell."

"Either way there's going to be Southern boys trying to kill us," I said. "So make sure your weapons are cleaned and loaded and that you've got enough cartridges for your rifles and sidearms."

"Yes, Mother," Johnny said, and grinned at me. "You sure do like bein' a sergeant, don't ya, Jubal?"

"Just do it," I replied, ignoring the jibe.

Actually, I did like having the rank. Not because I particularly cared about telling people what to do, but because it gave me some small degree of control over what was happening to me and the men I was fighting alongside. According to my superior officers, my only response was to be "yes sir, no sir, three bags full sir," every time they issued an order. But in the heat of an attack it did give me the ability to order my men to take cover when Rebel fire was at its most withering, or to order my squad to end an assault when the slaughter of enemy forces threatened to get out of control. I did not regard myself as a butcher, and I certainly did not accept the idea of becoming cannon fodder at the whim of some general. The rank gave me some ability to control both.

There were about five hundred yards between our forces and General Howard's troops, and I decided to go down the line with Abel and see what their exact position was. The men were on edge and I did not want them firing on our own troops if they moved toward us in the dark.

To reach Howard's position we cut back well behind the lines and moved down to a hill overlooking his position.

Abel pointed down at the 11,000 troops that stretched out before us. "They ain't got any trenches dug or anythin' else," he said. "An' best I kin see is all they got is two artillery pieces pointed out at that there Orange Plank Road where any flankin' attack is likely ta come from. Does that make sense ta ya, Jubal?"

"No, it doesn't." I thought about it and shrugged. "Maybe Howard is trying to lure a flanking attack in. Maybe he's got men hidden farther out where we can't see them."

"I sure hope so," Abel said. "Cause them boys down there sure look like sittin' ducks ta me."

It was three o'clock when we returned to our unit and there was still no sign of a Rebel attack. Josiah came up with three other litter-bearers and squatted down beside us.

"Where's Jemma and Alva?" Abel asked.

"They up at the hospital helpin' the nurses get ready," he said. He reached out and handed Abel a small item tightly wrapped in bandaging material.

"Wha's this?" Abel asked.

"Alva sent it fer ya," Josiah said.

Abel unwrapped the small parcel and held up a tiny doll. "An' wha's this?" he asked.

A wide grin spread across Josiah's face. "It's a voodoo doll ta protect ya in battle." He reached into his shirt and pulled out a similar doll. "Jemma gave me this un t'other day."

Johnny began waggling his fingers again and let out a low, mournful wail. "You really spooky now, Abel," he teased. "But I was you, I'd still keep yer head down—an' yer fat ass."

"I ain't got a fat ass," Abel said, grinning back at him.

"Oh, yes ya do," Johnny snapped back. "Tha's why I always stay behind ya. I use yer fat ass fer cover."

The sound of gunfire ended the bantering. It was coming from Howard's position off to our right. It was sporadic at first, and then became more sustained, lasting for almost an hour. Our officers ordered us to hold our position. The attack on Howard's position was certain to be a flanking attack they were well prepared to meet.

We were to concentrate on the attack that would come straight at us.

As we focused on the area in front of us, small elements of Howard's troops began to filter into our ranks. I grabbed a sergeant and asked him what had happened.

He raised his arms and let them fall helplessly to his sides. "We was jus' gettin' settled in fer dinner 'bout an hour ago. Even had our rifles stacked, figgerin' there weren't gonna be no fightin' today, it startin' ta get dark an all. Then all hell broke loose. Rebs from Stonewall Jackson's army came outta them woods screamin' like banshees, an' was all over us afore we could even git ta our guns. Some managed ta get away, some managed ta fall back an' set up a perimeter. But a whole passel of 'em got captured without firin' a shot—maybe three, four thousand—an' a whole bunch more got slaughtered. Now they orderin' us back over cheer."

I stared at him. "So you never dug in, and you didn't have any troops hidden farther away?"

He shook his head. "When we first got there I tol' my men ta start diggin' in, but an officer come along an' tol' us ta stop an' jus' keep our men ready ta move. Well, they're movin' now. Some ta the graveyard, some ta the hospital, an' a whole lot more ta a Reb prison."

No attack came that night and word came down the line that Stonewall Jackson had been wounded and that a renewed attack had been stalled while the Rebs assigned a new commander to take over his army. Still, our troops had little sleep that night, and when dawn broke we were laying behind our trench walls scouring the opposite tree line for any sign of Rebel movement.

The attack came at midmorning as forces under the command of General J.E.B. Stuart launched a massive assault all along the front.

Thousands of Reb infantry came pouring out of the woods which were now smoking and burning from heavy Union artillery fire.

"Make your shots count!" I shouted as our men opened up on the advancing Rebs. I took careful aim myself, and knocked down a man about a hundred yards out, too far to know if he was young or old or in between. He just flew back and I knew from the way he landed, arms and legs flapping, that he was dead before he hit the ground. I drew in a breath, let it out slowly, and fired again, and another Reb crumpled to his knees.

Artillery fire opened up behind us, howitzer canisters of grapeshot bursting about ninety yards away. I saw one man fly into the air, his leg torn from his body and going off in another direction. Still the Rebs kept coming, screaming their frightening Rebel Yell like savages. I saw one of our men rear up, preparing to break ranks and run, and I moved up behind him and slammed him back into the ground. I leaned forward and hissed into his ear, "You run and I will shoot you down. You are *not* gonna panic this line."

He glanced back over his shoulder and I could see he was no more than eighteen, nineteen years old. "I'm all right, sergeant. I'm all right now," he said.

I left him and went back along the line of men calling out encouragement I did not feel myself, then dropping down and firing again and again and again.

We were ordered to fall back an hour later and we abandoned Chancellorsville to the Rebs and took up a defensive position encircling a river crossing known as United States Ford, our last remaining open line of retreat. We fought there throughout the next day, repelling one Rebel assault after another in the bloodiest battle any of us had yet seen, and when the day ended our troops fell exhausted where they stood.

I moved down the line looking for wounded who needed attention, calling in Josiah and the other litter-bearers whenever I found one. One man was curled into a ball, his head pressed into the ground, and I reached down and turned him over to check for wounds. It was the boy who had nearly broken ranks the previous day. He stared back at me blindly, a gaping whole in his throat where a minie ball had cut off his life.

He might still be alive if you'd let him run, I told myself, knowing it was something I could not have done, grateful I would never have to explain to his family that their boy was dead because I made him stay and fight.

In the predawn hours we retreated back across the Rappahannock River, exhausted, with the smell of another defeat filling our nostrils. Officers rode up and down the line telling us we had not been defeated, that Lee had lost 13,000 of his 52,000-man force—men who the South could not replace.

Johnny, his face covered with grime, stared at me. "Tha's right, ol' General Lee can't call up more men ta take their place cause he ain't got 'em ta call up." He grinned bitterly. "Not like us. We got all the boys we need ta throw inta this slaughterhouse."

The next morning, while we were awaiting word that a truce had been called so we could cross the river and retrieve our dead, Bobby Suggs stopped by our camp and pulled Johnny aside. A few minutes later Johnny knelt down beside me and told me he wanted to go off with Suggs and some of his friends to "scrounge up" some extra provisions.

"If the Rebs can't find enough to feed their own men, what the hell do you expect to find?" I asked.

"They jus' ain't good scroungers like we are," Johnny said with a tired grin.

"Go on," I said. "But you hear the bugler blowing a ceasefire, it means we're going out to collect our dead, and I want you back to help us."

"I'll be back." Johnny winked at me. "I'll see if I kin git ya a bit of bacon, or somethin' ta make ya happier."

"Just get back when you hear the bugler," I said.

Josiah arrived at camp an hour later and came straight up to Abel and me. "Abel, ya gots ta get ta the field hospital," he said. "We got hit by a stray artillery roun', an' Alva gone an' got herself wounded."

I watched Abel's face turn pale. "How bad?" he asked, grabbing Josiah's shirt. "How bad is she hurt?"

"She ain't bad, jus' a flesh wound in her leg, but she in a lotta pain an' she callin' fer her Massah Abel."

Abel let out a long, relieved breath. He looked at me, his eyes pleading.

"You better go," I said. "And you tell Jemma this means she has to take Alva to Washington as soon as she's able to travel."

"I'll tell her," Abel said, and glanced at Josiah. "But she don' even listen ta him, an' he's promisin' ta marry her."

I smiled at Josiah, feeling a sudden release from the battle we had fought, feeling human again. "You sure you want to marry that woman?" I asked. "She is sure a handful of female."

Josiah grinned back at me. "She sure is, an' tha's jus' why I wants her."

CHAPTER NINETEEN

Doc sat across from us at our kitchen table. My father had invited him to sample my Southern fried chicken, and the two of them had polished off nearly a dozen pieces between them.

"The boy sure can cook," Doc said. "But unless you're gonna open up a fancy restaurant here in town, I still want to see you back in school."

"That's what your friend, Dr. Evers told me this morning," I said.

"He's a smart man. What else did he tell you?"

I told Doc about Evers's analysis of the blood samples, his discovery that the blood we had found had come from a reptile, and his theory that it could have been used to mask any earlier blood deposited on the cant hook. "You think Rusty LeRoche is smart enough to figure that out?" I asked.

Doc pursed his lips before saying, "Rusty's a sly, clever man. But do I think he'd know that we could identify blood traces with a microscope?" He shook his head slowly. "No, I do not. But I've been wrong before about these backwoods boys we got living out here, so don't put your faith in that."

"Coulda just happened that way," my father said. "He coulda used the cant hook on Johnny, then happened across a snake an' done it in with the same weapon. Not outta any plan, mind ya, jus' that it happened that way."

"I'll buy that one," Doc responded. "And Rusty's sure got the temper for it. If Johnny pulled a gun on him, like he told Jubal here, well, Rusty's just not the kind to run off just because he's looking down the barrel of a pistol. Might even make him madder."

"What about Suggs?" my father asked, picking at a pile of chicken bones still heaped on his plate. "You think he's the kind who'd have the stomach ta do Johnny in?"

"Suggs got used to killing in the war," I said. "We all did . . . I think for some it became a natural thing to do."

"An emotion that's hard to turn off?" Doc speculated.

I stared at him, thinking my answer through. "Yes, for some I believe it is."

I rode out to Rusty LeRoche's woodlot the next morning, the cant hook I'd taken from him tied to my saddle horn. Rusty was still at the house when I arrived, and he came out into his dooryard, his wife watching me intently from the door to their small cabin.

"Bringin' my cant hook back?" he greeted.

"Yes sir, and I appreciate you making it easy for me to do."

"Ain't got nothin' ta hide," he said curtly. "Din' do nothin' ta that boy. Should've, but din'." He cleared his throat. "Ya seen my Chantal?"

I glanced at Mrs. LeRoche and she abruptly returned to the house. "No, I haven't," I told Rusty truthfully.

"Well, ya do, ya tell her she's welcome back ta home. Tell her that her momma's pretty damn lonesome without her daughter 'bout the house."

"I will tell her if I see her. But I think that's doubtful."

"Well, you jus' tell her iffen ya do." He hesitated a moment, then added, "Ya through botherin' me 'bout this Harris boy gettin' kilt?"

"I'm still looking for the person who killed him," I said, deflecting the question.

"Well, ya ain't gonna find 'em cheer."

My father and I were getting ready to head out to a farm on the southern edge of town to resolve a fence dispute when Billy Lucie rode into our dooryard. We were just leading our horses out of the barn so he remained on his mount, sitting there like a large, round elf.

"Was headed over ta the mill ta collect some timber money I'm owed, and thought I'd better stop by an' see ya," he said.

"Somethin' wrong?" my father asked.

"Yer man Suggs lit out 'bout two hours ago," he said. "Since I was comin' down anyways, I thought I'd better stop by an' tell ya."

"You think he bolted?" I asked.

Billy gave me a noncommittal shrug. "Said he needed a day off an' was goin' on up ta Richmond ta git hisself a woman." He glanced at my father, then grinned at me, assuming we had both paid the ladies a visit or two. I had not, but saw no reason to say so. "They live right there near the railroad station, so I thought I better tell ya, jus' in case Suggs decided ta jump on a train an' git hisself outta Vermont."

"I guess I better take a ride up to Richmond and point him back down this way," I said to my father. "Can you handle the fence dispute without me?"

"Sure can. Unless ya think ya need me with ya," he said.

"No, I got Suggs."

Billy laughed and turned to my father. "The way Suggs bitches 'bout yer boy here, I ain't got no doubts that he kin . . . Go get the sumbitch an' boot his ass back down this away. I could use him back ta work."

I mounted Jezebel and started her toward the road when Billy raised a hand, stopping me.

"There's also a tavern up there the boys likes ta go to," he explained. "It's called Dooley's."

"I know it too," I said. "Thank you."

"Jus' leave that boy in one piece so's I kin git sum work outta him."

I could hear Billy laughing as I rode away.

As Billy described, the two women lived in small houses near the railroad station. They were only a few doors apart but I didn't see Bobby's horse tied up in front of either. I knocked on the door of the first house. It was answered by a slightly plump woman with cunning eyes. She was dressed only in a petticoat that had seen better days.

"Well, hello there, honey. Ya here lookin' fer a little tender lovin'?" She brushed back a lock of curly brown hair and stepped aside to give me room to enter. "The name's Jewel, iffen yer interested."

I gave her a friendly smile. "I'm sorry to say that's not what I'm looking for. I'm looking for a man named Bobby Suggs. I was told he might be here."

"Shoot, an' yer the first good-lookin' clean man I seen in a week." She offered up another coy smile. "I know Bobby from Dooley's Tavern, but he goes ta another lady in the trade. She's a few doors up. Goes by the name Ruby."

"Thank you," I said. "I appreciate the information."

"Well, ya come back now an' I'll give ya somethin' y'all really 'preciate. An' don' ya worry 'bout that arm none. I takes care of a lotta wounded soldier boys."

I knocked on the second door and was greeted by a slender woman with long, wavy blond hair. She was heavily made up, her cheeks painted an unnatural pink hue that contrasted with her bright red lips. She was dressed in a simple shift that seemed to be lacking any undergarments.

"Well hello, ya handsome boy. I'm Ruby." She smiled at me, revealing a missing lower tooth. "Ya here ta give me some mornin' lovin'?"

"I'm sorry," I said. "I truly wish I could, but I'm trying to find someone. A fellow named Bobby Suggs. I was told he might be here."

Ruby gave me her best smile. "Well, he left 'bout an hour ago. Boy near wore me out. You'll prob'ly find him up ta Dooley's Tavern, I'm guessin'. Ya sure ya don' wanna stay a bit?"

"I'm afraid not, ma'am. But thank you for the offer."

"Well, ain't you the gentleman. Ya come on back whenever ya wants ta. Ruby'll be here waitin' on ya."

I started to leave, then turned back. "This Bobby Suggs, he's someone you'd be safer to avoid," I said.

"Why is that, honey?"

"He's a bad man, a truly bad man."

"Well, I'll take that in account," she said with a smile. "But that's part a the trade. There's a lotta men come through this here door, an' I'm guessin' most of 'em ain't gonna make it through the pearly gates."

Dooley's Tavern was on Main Street, one block up from the railroad station and directly across from a small commercial hotel frequented by drummers who were passing through town. It was a small, dimly lit room with a long bar taking up the rear wall, and a scattering of scarred wooden tables and chairs on either side of the door.

Bobby Suggs was at the bar, his back to me, a mug of beer set out before him. I took the place next to him and ordered a beer for myself.

He jumped at the sound of my voice, his eyes glaring hatred.

"You followin' me aroun' now?" he snapped.

I remained silent, letting his surprise and anger play out.

"Are ya?" he demanded.

I took a sip of my beer and set the mug back on the bar, then turned slowly to face him. The barkeep was watching us, so I shifted my shoulders so the edge of my badge would show under my canvas coat. I didn't need any interference from outside sources.

I kept my eyes on Suggs. "Bobby, you were a loud-mouthed little shit in the army, and civilian life hasn't changed you any. Now, you give me that mouth again and I'm going to slap my gun upside your head, tie your skinny ass to your horse, and ride you down to the sheriff's office. You understand me?"

Suggs balled his fists in anger. "Ya din' have that badge I jus' might let ya try. Then break the one arm ya got left an' stomp yer ass inta the floor."

"Don't mind the badge, Bobby," I said.

"I don' beat up on cripples," he scoffed.

"Don't mind the missing arm, either. One's good enough to break your skinny neck."

"Whatcha want from me, Foster?" All the phony agression was gone out of him.

"I want your ass down in Jerusalem's Landing until I find out who killed Johnny Harris. I don't care if you need a woman. I don't care if you need a beer. You keep yourself close by or you're going to be dealing with me. Is that clear enough for you?"

"Man's got a right ta get on his horse an' ride somewheres," he argued.

"I hope you heard me," I said after a long pause.

"I heard ya."

"Then you get on your horse and head back. Billy Lucie needs you swinging an axe. Go swing one."

———

Fredericksburg, Virginia, 1863

We were bivouacked outside Fredericksburg on May 11 when we learned that Confederate General Stonewall Jackson was dead. The wound he had sustained at Chancellorsville had necessitated the amputation of one arm, but had not been considered life-threatening. Jackson, however, had contracted pneumonia while recovering, and six days later he succumbed to the illness. The irony, we now learned, was that Jackson had been wounded by his own men. He had been leading a small force on horseback, trying to determine if a surprise moonlight attack on Chancellorsville was possible, when he and his men were mistaken for Union cavalry and fired on as they returned to their lines. That and the loss of 13,000 Confederate troops were the two lone points of victory that had come from the battle.

My men and I were exhausted from the extended fighting at Chancellorsville, and were allowed nearly a week's rest before again being sent out on reconnaissance patrol. When that order finally came, we left camp two hours after dark and began scouring the Rappahannock River for abandoned boats that would take all ten of us across. By nine o'clock that night we had what we needed, and using a moonless sky we crossed the river in two skiffs, which we then hid in a patch of reeds for our return to camp.

Once on shore we moved slowly, dodging occasional Rebel patrols that had been sent out to watch our troop movements from the Chancellorsville side of the river. We found a small detachment of men encamped outside the hamlet, but saw no sight or sound of Lee's main force.

"So whatta we do now?" Johnny asked.

"We'll split into two groups: one will move out to the northern side of the hamlet, the other will stay here at the southern end. Then each group will move inland about two miles and see if we can find the main body of Lee's army."

"Hell, he's supposed ta have 70,000 men," Abel said. "They sure as the devil shouldn't be hard ta find."

"All right. Abel, you take four men and move out from here. I'll take another four and move to the northern side of Chancellorsville. We'll meet back at the boats in three hours. Nobody crosses until everyone is back." I turned to Johnny. "Pick three other men and follow me into those woods. We'll move on up to the Plank Road and head in from there."

We forged through a heavy patch of scrub pine for about a quarter of a mile, stopping every fifty yards or so to listen for any movement ahead. The bed of pine needles we treaded across kept our shuffling silent and secure. When we reached the Plank Road we kept to both sides, ready to dart into the trees if we heard any sounds coming toward us. About a half mile in, we came across what must have been the encampment of Stonewall Jackson's army, an open field of beaten-down grass and dead campfires. It was strewn with the litter his men had left behind, including papers and letters from the 4,000 Union troops they had captured and searched before marching them off to a Rebel prison.

"There ain't nobody here," Johnny said. "Look's like they left a small garrison to guard the hamlet and keep watch on us, and moved ever'body else out fer God knows where."

"If that's true, then the garrison's no more than a decoy to keep us in place while Lee takes his army somewhere else," I said. "We'll head another mile, a mile and a half, and see if we're right."

We moved slowly inland, following the line of march Jackson's army had taken, which appeared to be going directly toward the Shenandoah Valley, the preferred route Lee had used in the past when sending his army north and south. Once we were approximately two miles in, we turned back and headed toward the area Abel had been sent to explore. There we found the abandoned encampments of Lee's main force.

We worked our way back to the patch of reeds where our boats were hidden and found Abel and the other men holed up in some dense brush thirty yards from the river.

"You find anything?" I asked as my men and I moved up beside him.

"'Peers they all took off like a flocka geese," Abel reported. "Even their field hospital's gone. We found where their hospital wagons moved off from the others and headed toward Richmond, while the main body headed west."

"Toward the Shenandoah Valley," I said needlessly.

"'Peered like it ta me," Abel said.

Johnny grabbed my arm and pointed upriver toward the hamlet. A two-man patrol was headed our way, walking slowly with their rifles resting casually on their shoulders. They looked more like hunters out for jackrabbits. But the jackrabbits they were about to find were a bit more lethal.

"I want to take them prisoner," I said. "We'll bring them back for interrogation and find out what the hell is going on with Lee's army. So no shooting unless you have no other choice."

We split up and moved out, using the brush for cover. The two Rebs were talking, telling stories from home as best I could hear, but it was enough to distract them and, together with the moonless night, cover our movements.

When we were five feet from the riverbank we crouched down and waited, and as they started past we jumped up and leveled our weapons at them, ordering them to halt. One of the men stared at us wide-eyed and immediately dropped his rifle. The second spun on his heel and started to run directly toward me. I swung the butt of my rifle and caught him on the jaw, the blow throwing him back against a large rock. The crack of his skull hitting the rock was a loud, sickening, wet sound, and I knew before I even knelt down beside him that he was dead.

I approached the second man, who Johnny had forced to his knees, the barrel of his Colt pressed against his ear.

"How's that other boy?" he asked.

"Dead," I said.

"Oh, sweet Jesus," the prisoner said. "He was only fifteen."

I felt the bile rise in my throat, but forced it down and squatted in front of the other Reb.

"How old are you?" I asked.

"Sixteen," he said in a shaky voice.

"If you lived to be seventeen when would your birthday be?" I asked.

"In August," he said. His voice was hoarse with fear. "August 3."

"Well, son, if you tell us what we need to know, you're going to live to blow out the candles on your cake. You understand me?"

The boy nodded his head.

"Shit," Johnny said. "I wanna shoot this sumbitch. Don't tell 'em nothin', kid. I ain't kilt me a Reb all day."

"Put your pistol away, Johnny. Let's see what he has to say. Then we'll decide whether we kill him or not." I turned my attention back to the boy. "Where did General Lee's army go?"

The boy's lips began to tremble. "All I knows is what the talk about camp was. Ever'body was sayin' the army was headed north to take the fight back to Yankee territory."

"You sure about that?" I asked.

"Yes sir, I'm sure. It's what ever'body was sayin'."

"Okay. You're coming with us. We have some officers who'll want to talk to you. You don't give us any trouble while we take you across the river, you're going to live to have that birthday cake."

"I won't cause no trouble. I promise ya, sir, no trouble at all."

CHAPTER TWENTY

———————

Jerusalem's Landing, Vermont, 1865

Rebecca was wearing a blue dress and matching hat when I picked her up at the store on Sunday. I recognized the material from the purchases she had made during our trip to Burlington, and I marveled that she could fashion such beautiful clothing from the bolt of cloth and bows and buttons she had carried home that day.

"What are you staring at?" she asked. "You're looking at me as if you've never seen me before."

"Your dress," I said. "I'm just amazed that you could make it from all those things I loaded into the buggy a few days ago."

She made a slow, deliberate turn, showing herself off, then smiled up at me. "And a bonnet too. See what a clever woman you've set your sights on?"

"Are you certain I've set my sights on you?" I teased.

"Just remember . . ."

"Remember what?"

"That my father has a gun."

I took her arm and started across the road toward the church. "Then I guess I've set my sights on you," I said.

It was the first time I had taken Rebecca to a regular Sunday service, and we immediately became the source of repeated glances and whispers among the good ladies of the church. Such an act among our quiet country people normally marked the beginning of a courtship, and when my father entered the church and chose to sit with Walter and Mary Johnson it was, I'm sure, taken as a final seal of familial approval.

Even Reverend Harris smiled down on us when he took the pulpit to deliver his sermon, although the topic—"The Sins of the Flesh"— brought a few more glances from the women in the congregation and made me squirm a bit in my seat. I recalled that he had given that sermon, or something quite similar, many years before, when Abel and Johnny and I were just entering puberty. Off in the woods later that day we had spent considerable time wondering aloud about the meaning of that phrase, and even more about when we would be able to enjoy those mysterious and obviously delightful temptations.

At the end of service there were the usual greetings among those who lived in outlying areas and who seldom saw each other outside church, although several village women took special care to speak to Rebecca—hushed conversations held out of my hearing that were interspersed with occasional glances in my direction.

As we were leaving the sanctuary I leaned in close and whispered in Rebecca's ear: "I decided that it's not your father I have to worry about."

"Oh," Rebecca replied, raising her eyebrows. "And why not?"

"Because before he got to my front door, he'd have to fight his way through all the church ladies marching toward my house with torches."

Rebecca covered her mouth to suppress her laughter. "Don't you forget that either," she whispered back.

Reverend Harris greeted us at the door of the church. "It's nice to see you both together," he said as he shook my hand. "Jubal, I've been thinking about your investigation, and there's something I want to talk to you about. Could you stop by this evening after supper?"

"Yes sir. Would seven thirty be a good time?"

"It would, yes," he said, taking my hand again.

"I'll be there."

Rebecca had been oddly quiet, and as we stepped out onto the front lawn I led her aside. "You seem uncomfortable around Reverend Harris," I said.

She gave a small shake of her head and kept us walking away from the church. "I never know what to say to him," she said. "His son is dead, a boy I grew up with and knew as well as I knew you and my own brother. And I liked him, I liked him very much back then. I considered him my friend for all those years. But he came home a different person, and it was a person I learned to hate." She stared up at me. "I mean that, Jubal. I hated him, and I wasn't sorry when he died. I think I was even glad that he was dead, and I know I've told you that before and I know that it's an awful thing to say, and that it's wrong and maybe it's even sinful, but I can't help it. Johnny was a monster when he came back, and he killed my mother just as sure as if he'd pushed her into that river, and in my heart I know he deserved to die. So whenever I see Reverend Harris I see how sad he is, and I want to comfort him, but I'm thinking all those things and I don't know what to say." She shook her head more vehemently this time. "I just don't know what to say."

We began walking back toward the church. "I wish I was wise enough to tell you what to do," I said. "I feel the same way when I talk to him. I feel it for some of the same reasons, and also for other things I know about Johnny, things he did during the war."

"What did he do? I always thought that what happened to him at the Confederate prison had turned him into what he was."

"No," I said. "Johnny changed long before he got to Andersonville." I stopped and saw Bobby Suggs across the road, standing in front of the Johnsons' store watching us. As I met his gaze he raised one finger to the brim of his hat and then pointed it at me like a gun.

"That man makes my skin crawl," Rebecca said. "There's just something about him that's—"

"Evil," I cut in. "If he appears around you, stay well away from him. And then you come get me or you send for me as quick as you can."

"You make him sound very frightening."

"He's as bad as Johnny ever was," I said. "Maybe worse."

When I glanced back across the road, Suggs had mounted his horse and was riding away from us. He was headed in the opposite direction of Billy Lucie's woodlot, and I had no idea where he could be going.

"I made up a picnic lunch," Rebecca said.

"Shall we ride up to that place on the river?" I suggested, grinning.

"Oh, no." She lowered her voice to a whisper. "I do not intend to walk down the aisle with a big, fat belly. Besides, I invited Josiah and Jemma to come with us, and to bring little Alva too."

My smile widened. "That would have made Abel very happy," I said.

We had our picnic in a meadow that was dotted with red clover, buttercups, and Indian paintbrush, and after we had eaten our chicken and cheese and apples, and washed it all down with cold cider, the women went off to gather bouquets for their homes.

"Looks like Jemma plans to give a woman's touch to your ragtag old cabin," I said.

"Already has," Josiah said. "She done put curtains onna windows, a tablecloth onna kitchen table." He sighed. "My sista tried a few years back, but I woun't let her. But ain't no way I kin stop Jemma. Woman jus' looks at ya like ya crazy an' does what she wants."

We both started to laugh and Josiah leaned in close. "Looks like Rebecca's got her cap set on ya. How ya feel 'bout that?"

"I feel good." I tugged at my half-empty left sleeve. "I worried about this, about what it would be like coming to her this way, but it doesn't seem to matter to her. I don't understand it, but I'm damned happy she feels that way."

Josiah put a hand on my knee. "I'm gonna tell ya somethin', Jubal. An' I wants ya ta know I means it. Iffen I was ever needin' somebody ta watch my back, an' Jubal Foster was missin' one arm an' bowf legs, Jubal Foster'd still be the one I'd be wantin'."

"I feel the same way about you, Josiah."

We both jolted to the sound of a horse moving along the road below us.

"Is 'at who's I thinks it is?" Josiah asked. "It is. Tha's 'at sumbitch Bobby Suggs."

The women and little Alva were below us picking flowers, and Suggs reigned in his horse and sat watching them. When Josiah and I both stood, he shifted his gaze to us and raised his finger to his hat brim, but this time he made his shooting gesture at each of the women.

Rebecca had noticed the horse and rider and had raised a hand to her eyes to shield them from the sun. When she recognized Suggs, she froze. Despite the distance between us, I could see the fear on her face.

"Son of a bitch," I hissed as I took a step toward the road. But Suggs was already riding away.

Gettysburg, Pennsylvania, 1863

The officers in our new intelligence unit had interrogated our prisoner for most of the night, and the following morning had sent out a balloon to confirm the location of Lee's army. The report that came back said Lee was moving north through the Shenandoah Valley and could be expected to either turn toward Washington or move up into Pennsylvania.

General Hooker quickly put his army in motion, moving all 80,000 men north and keeping those troops between Lee and any quick turn he might make toward Washington. Throughout that march Hooker continued to send out balloons for reports on Lee's progress, and when his army passed into Pennsylvania he became certain that Lee had decided to take his campaign away from war-ravaged northern Virginia and into the Union's own territory, perhaps even as far as Harrisburg or Philadelphia. Speaking to his troops when they had finally encamped, Hooker expressed the belief that Lee was mounting his second attack into Union territory with the goal of coercing Northern politicians into giving up the war against the South. It was a plan, Hooker told his men, that he had no intention of allowing his enemy to achieve. But by the time we reached the outskirts of Gettysburg, Hooker found himself relieved of command in favor of General George Gordon Meade.

"We runnin' through generals like shit runs through a goose," Abel observed as we sat about awaiting our next orders.

We were stopped on a rise known as Cemetery Ridge, looking down on areas called the Peach Orchard, Rose Woods, the Wheatfield, and Devil's Den.

"Who the hell names these places?" Johnny snapped. "An' who the hell decided ta put us in a place called Cemetery Ridge? It's like somebody's tryin' ta bring us bad luck."

I had talked with our lieutenant and he assured me that the main body of Lee's army was well to our north, and that our position was a defensive one, needed to guard against any flanking action designed to cut off our supply route. It was something, he said, that might well keep us out of the bloodiest part of the coming battle.

I told this to our men in hopes of lifting their spirits, but had little success. They had seen what Stonewall Jackson's flanking attack had done to General Howard's forces at Chancellorsville, where some 6,000 men had been killed, wounded, or captured in an assault that lasted only a few hours. It was a demoralizing memory.

The initial fighting began on July 1, when the first elements of both armies fought for control of the low ridges to the northwest of the small farming town of Gettysburg. Those ridges, initially defended by a lone cavalry division, were quickly reinforced by two corps of Union infantry. But Lee threw overwhelming numbers into the battle, simultaneously assaulting Union troops from the north and northwest, breaking the hastily assembled Union lines and sending them on a retreat through the streets of the town. When the first day of battle ended, the retreating Union forces had taken up new positions in the hills just to the south of the town, not far from our own position. So now the battle had moved to us, and we reinforced our trenches and readied ourselves for a full-scale assault.

It came the following morning, as Rebel troops swarmed through the Wheatfield, Devil's Den, and the Peach Orchard. We were ordered to lower trenches located on the side of Cemetery Ridge under the cover of heavy artillery fire. Howitzer canisters filled with grapeshot exploded two hundred yards ahead of us as we moved to the lower trenches, firing as we ran, and I could see the bodies of Confederate troops being thrown back as explosion after explosion cut swaths across their ranks.

We passed through one level of trenches and moved to another, lower still, and set our defensive position. The Rebs pressed forward through the devastating artillery barrage and a steady stream of minie balls fired from our position. Thousands moved toward us in succeeding waves and Abel and I lay beside each other, loading and firing over and over again.

"It's a damn turkey shoot!" Abel called out over the roar of weapons. "I jus' can't figger out which side the turkey is on!"

Bullets slammed into the trench wall and whistled past our heads. Each time we fired we ducked down to reload and the buzzing sound of return fire passed over us. Each time I rose to shoulder level to fire another round I expected a minie ball to slam into my face.

I glanced up and down our line and saw the bodies of our men that had been thrown back across the trench, and I realized that while the Rebs were being slaughtered down below us, we were sustaining enormous casualties of our own.

By midafternoon we were ordered up to the next trench line which had been dug some fifty yards below the summit of Cemetery Ridge. Again Union artillery opened up, laying out an overwhelming barrage as we moved along the hill. Still, the Rebs kept firing and before I reached the safety of the trench I could hear bullets hitting the ground on each side of me. I hesitated at the top of the trench and waved my men forward, shouting at them to get to cover as quickly as I could. As I crouched there, shouting, something heavy slammed into my chest and knocked me over the trench wall. Flat on my back, I looked up into Abel's round, dirt-streaked face, and realized he had knocked me back into the trench.

"You stand out there like 'at, yer gonna get yer ass shot off," he said.

Abel had hit me like a freight train and I struggled to regain my breath. "I was just trying to get the men to cover," I wheezed.

Abel grinned. "The only damn fool wasn't scramblin' fer cover was the dumb-assed sergeant, ya silly sumbitch."

The fighting ended for the day as light faded from the sky, and when I took one last look down the hill below us, a sea of blue- and gray-clad bodies greeted my eyes. The words *slaughter* and *bloodbath* played across my mind, and still I knew the battle was not over. Off in the distance, in the area known as Devil's Den—a seemingly endless expanse of massive boulders and scrub growth—I could see Rebel forces reforming, and I knew tomorrow would bring yet another assault just as fierce as the one we had endured today.

That night we sat around a campfire, some men taking their turns on watch while others slept and still others told tales of the battle they had just fought. Abel and I sat silently, just grateful we were alive. Across from us one of our men played a mouth organ, sending the mournful wail of "Vacant Chair" down the line of men.

"Damn," Abel growled. "Don't be playin' 'bout the vacant chair at the table. Give us somethin' light an' happy, somethin' the men kin sing to."

The man switched in midmelody and took up the strains of "When Johnny Comes Marching Home."

"Now tha's more like it!" Abel shouted as he began to clap his meaty hands to the rhythm, while other men picked up the lyrics:

When Johnny comes marching home again
Hurrah! Hurrah!
We'll give him a hearty welcome then
Hurrah! Hurrah!
The men will cheer and the boys will shout
The ladies they will all turn out
And we'll all feel gay
When Johnny comes marching home.

The old church bell will peal for joy
Hurrah! Hurrah!
To welcome home our darling boy
Hurrah! Hurrah!
The village lads and lassies say

With roses they will strew the way
And we'll all feel gay
When Johnny comes marching home.

Get ready for the Jubilee
Hurrah! Hurrah!
We'll give the hero three times three
Hurrah! Hurrah!
The laurel wreath is ready now
To place upon his loyal brow
And we'll all feel gay
When Johnny comes marching home . . .

I left the campfire as the men finished the final stanza and then started it up again. I headed for the uppermost trench to take my turn on watch and give those who were there a chance to sing and relax, and I wondered if the Rebs could hear us; and if they could, I wondered what they thought about the men they had fought so fiercely that day, the same men they would try again to kill when the sun rose on the morrow.

The breaking dawn brought the Rebels en masse, thousands of them screaming their infernal Rebel Yell as they stormed out of the Devil's Den and surged back across a wide, open area that lay below Cemetery Ridge. Again our artillery opened fire, the canisters of grapeshot driving the Rebs back to the boulders.

Their officers urged them forward yet again, and I watched one, his saber raised high above his head, move to the front of the line to lead the charge. Five feet away a canister exploded and the last I saw of the officer was his saber—his arm and hand still attached—flying up into the air and falling to earth among the line of men to his rear.

As the Rebs came into rifle range I ordered my men to open fire. We were in the trench fifty yards below the summit, and our orders were to hold that position unless we were overrun, and then retreat back up to the final trench above.

Again, the Rebs approached in succeeding waves in what was to become known as Pickett's Charge, what the newspapers would call the most dramatic infantry assault of the war, some 12,500 Confederate troops led by General George Pickett in a desperate attempt to break through Union lines.

They came and they came, and when driven back they came again. But our men continued to hold, and I wondered if we had just grown tired of being beaten by Lee's forces, or if fighting on Union land had angered us enough to finally defeat the Confederacy's best troops.

Throughout the day ammunition boxes were dragged down the hill, the contents distributed along the line, and our men fired round after round into a gradually slowing Rebel force.

I stared down the hill, watching the Rebs struggle forward in vain, a thick cloud of smoke hanging above the ground like low cloud cover, the smell of burnt gunpowder filling our lungs with every breath. At three o'clock we received the order to attack, rising from our trench and starting down the hill, firing as we walked and ran and stumbled ahead. The Rebs retreated before us, first facing us and firing, then rushing back to the Devil's Den. I turned to wave my troops on and a great blow struck my lower side and spun me to the ground. Abel came up beside me and slid down next to me.

"Where you hit?" he asked, so out of breath he was barely able to speak.

I looked down and saw blood staining my britches along my right buttocks. Abel followed my gaze and started to laugh.

"I tol' ya that ya'd get yer ass shot off if ya wasn't careful." He ripped open my clothes around the wound. "Don' look like it went nowheres worse. But ya ain't gonna be sittin' or walkin' aroun' fer a while."

I started to push myself up but Abel gently motioned me back to the ground. "Jus' lay there till a litter-bearer comes by. That new lil' hole you got in yer ass ain't bad enough ta send ya home, but it sure as hell's gonna buy ya a few days layin' up an' restin'."

"But—"

Abel shushed me to silence. "I'll come visit ya in the field hospital." He winked at me. "I'll come more'n once if they got some pretty nurses ta look at."

CHAPTER TWENTY-ONE

I took Rebecca home at suppertime and spoke to Walter and Mary Johnson, warning them to keep a close eye on Bobby Suggs should he come into their store. If I hadn't agreed to meet Reverend Harris that evening, I knew I'd be out looking for Suggs that very minute. Josiah had even offered to go with me, and I'd told him that I planned to find Suggs in the morning and would be pleased to have him along if he had the time.

He had nodded slowly and said: "Don't go lookin' till I gits ta yer door."

I had a light supper with my father and told him about Reverend Harris asking to see me. He scratched his chin, thinking this over. "That's odd," he said. "Saw him at church jus' like ya did, an' he din' say anythin' ta me."

"You're welcome to come with me," I said.

"No, no. If he'd wanted me there, he'd of axed me. This sounds like somethin' he jus' needs ta talk ta ya about."

Reverend Harris opened the door to the parsonage and ushered me into the sitting room. It was a room I had grown to dislike, the same room where Johnny's body had been laid out in full uniform, his medals pinned to his tunic.

"Can I offer you some cider, Jubal?" Reverend Harris asked when I was seated.

"No, thank you, sir. I was at a picnic today and drank all the cider I can hold."

"I know, I heard about your picnic."

"Heard about it? How did you hear about it?"

"Bobby Suggs stopped by and told me," he said. "He's very concerned that you're out to do him harm. He came to me last week and told me you had confronted and threatened him in Richmond."

I steamed inwardly. "Bobby Suggs is a suspect in Johnny's murder," I said. "I was warning him to stay close to Jerusalem's Landing until we arrest someone for that crime."

"He told me there was another time when you tried to have him arrested; tried to have Johnny arrested too, but the military wouldn't do what you wanted."

I felt trapped. I had no intention of telling Johnny's father about the crimes his son had committed with Suggs and with others, or about my failed attempts to seek justice for what they had done.

"I did accuse Suggs of crimes while we were in the army," I said.

"And Johnny also?" There was a slight crack in Reverend Harris's voice.

"He's just telling you that to try and get you on his side."

"What did you feel he had done?"

"It's not worth talking about. Just be careful of him, Reverend. He's a dangerous man, and a bad one."

Reverend Harris gave me a tired smile. "It's my job, my duty, to help those who have fallen by the wayside."

"Well, this is a dangerous wayside, Reverend. Bobby Suggs was a killer in the army, a stone-cold killer. Please don't forget that."

"Many good men were forced to kill during that terrible war," he said.

"That's true, Reverend. But most men put it aside. Bobby Suggs enjoyed killing, even if the people he killed were unarmed civilians; he looked forward to it, and I don't think that feeling went away when the war was over."

___ __

Gettysburg, Pennsylvania, 1863

A hospital had been set up in the town of Gettysburg, and I was told I'd be confined there until my wound healed. The doctors warned that infection was now the greatest danger, that it was important to keep the wound clean and dry. I had also been told that I probably would not return to duty for several months; that General Lee had begun a tortuous retreat back into northern Virginia, with Union cavalry and ground forces harassing him every step of the way.

The Battle of Gettysburg had claimed some 50,000 casualties, half that number from each side. Our officers considered it a mortal blow for the South. Lee had lost 13,000 men at Chancellorsville, and now another 25,000 at Gettysburg, and he still lacked the ability to replenish his ranks. The South simply didn't have the men. The Union had also named General Ulysses Grant, the hero of the Vicksburg campaign, as overall commander of federal forces, and he was rumored to be on his way to Virginia to make a final assault on Richmond and end the war.

During my second day in the hospital Abel came to visit me, his tunic emblazoned with new corporal's stripes.

"They put me in charge of the unit till ya git yer ass back," he told me. "Johnny's madder'n a hornet with a hard-on. Says him and Josiah's the only boys from Jerusalem's Landing ain't got any rank."

"You keep an eye on him," I said. "Don't let him take up with Suggs and that crowd."

"I'll do what I kin. I 'spect we're gonna be pullin' out any day now. Lieutenant said soon as General Grant gits here we're gonna be all over wha's lefta Lee's army."

I didn't tell Abel that lieutenants seldom knew what they were talking about. I figured he'd learn that fast enough all by himself.

"They say I could be here a couple of months. They're worried about infection."

"Will ya join up with us after that?" he asked.

"Come hell or high water."

"By the way, I wrote ta Rebecca an' tol' her how ya was wounded an' all.'

"You didn't."

"I sure did."

"What exactly did you tell her?"

Abel smiled at me. "I tol' her ya went an' got yerself shot in the ass," he said. "Hell, Jubal, she's done got her cap set fer ya, an' her bein' my sister an' all—my only sister—I figgered she had a right ta know. Can't 'spect a gal to go marryin' a man's got two holes in his ass, an' her not knowin'."

"You son of a bitch," I hissed, stifling a chuckle. "I'll fix you for this. You can count on it."

I could still hear him laughing as he walked out of the hospital ward.

It was two months before I could walk without pain. There had been a small infection, but nothing serious. As I rehabilitated my wound I walked about the town and the surrounding countryside, my treks always seeming to end at the massive cemetery where those who died in the battle had been buried. The cemetery was on the summit of Cemetery Ridge where we had finally defeated Lee's forces. Each time I went there more fresh graves were in evidence. The wounded continued to die, the number of casualties growing and growing, and I thought about the families learning that their sons and husbands would never be coming home. I couldn't even begin to imagine what such a message would mean to my father.

Please don't let it be any of us, I silently prayed. *Please, God, bring Abel and Johnny and Josiah and me home again. And let this damnable war be over soon.*

It was autumn before I rejoined my unit. There had been a series of skirmishes along the Blue Ridge Mountains, all proving indecisive, as Union forces continued to harass Lee's retreating army. General Grant arrived and took overall command. My unit remained under General Meade, the only Union general to defeat Lee. Our officers claimed we were maneuvering Lee's army into a position where he would be forced to either commit all his forces to defend Richmond, or flee. Richmond, they claimed, would be a death knell for the Confederacy when taken, and Lee would have no choice but surrender. Meanwhile, our own troops were being rested, their supplies replenished, and my unit was marking time by making renewed forays into the surrounding countryside to keep track of enemy forces and pick up any Rebel deserters we could find.

On one such foray we came across what appeared to be an abandoned tobacco plantation, where I decided I could rest my men before pushing on. Clothing and shattered furniture were scattered about the yard in front of the main house, and as we entered we found much the same inside. I climbed the wide staircase and went inside the first bedroom I found. It too was ransacked and empty. But the second bedroom was not. There I found an elderly woman being cared for by an equally old Negro. The white woman wore bedclothes and appeared to be ill; the Negro woman was dressed in a tattered calico dress and had a white scarf tied around her head. She was rail-thin and easily into her sixties.

"Ain' nothin' leff," the Negro woman said. "Yer boys done took ever'thin'."

"Are there any other people here?" I asked.

"Jus' two slaves like me. Yer boys kilt ever'body else. Kilt dis lady's husband, took 'er granchil' off someplace. Girl was only fo'teen."

"You're not a slave anymore," I said. "President Lincoln freed all the Negroes."

The woman snorted. "He say da place we was suppose ta go? He say anythin' 'bout food ta eat an' a place ta sleep?"

"I don't know," I said.

"Din' think ya did." She looked at me as if I was some fool who had stumbled into her home.

"We can take the lady to a hospital," I said. "You can go with her if you want."

"She don' wanna go no place. Wants ta die right here inner house."

"You said Union troops did this. Were there Rebel soldiers here?"

"Ain' nobody but two ol' peoples an' a granchil'. Dem boys a your'n take ever'thin' dey kin an' den dey starts killin'."

I went downstairs and pulled Abel aside and told him about the two women upstairs and what the elderly Negro had said.

"There's been a lotta that," Abel commented.

"Who's doing it?"

"Lotta people. Bobby Suggs fer one, ya ask me." He held up his hands. "I can't prove it, but he sure does seem ta have a lotta stuff he's sellin' an' tradin'. Watches. Silver hairbrushes. All kinda stuff he sure din' git from home."

"Did you report it to the lieutenant?"

"He don' wanna know. Tol' me ta forget it. Says those things happen inna war."

* * *

Back at camp I went to see the lieutenant myself and got the same an-swer. He told me to send a wagon out to collect the old woman so we could give her medical care. I did as he said, but when the wagon re-turned the driver said the old woman was dead. I asked after the Negro woman and he just shrugged his shoulders.

"Don' have no idea where them niggers is goin'," he said.

The next day I saw Johnny talking with Bobby Suggs, and when they finished I pulled Johnny aside.

Once we were alone I pointed to the area outside camp. "You been going over there with Bobby Suggs?"

Johnny shrugged, feigning innocence, and asked what I meant, but his eyes had become suddenly defensive.

"Have you?" I demanded.

"Once or twice," he said.

"Is Suggs raiding houses out there?"

"I dunno if ya'd call it raidin'. We find an empty house, we check an' see if it's got any provisions. Ya know what I'm talkin' 'bout: bacon, ham, any preserves, stuff like that. Got myself a jar of cherry preserves a week back. It was sure good eatin'."

"We came across a house that had been ransacked. The old man who owned it was killed; his little fourteen-year-old grandchild was taken off someplace."

Johnny held up both hands. "Hey, I don' know nothin' 'bout any-thin' like that." His expression hardened. "Ya know, Jubal, some a these civilians yer so worried 'bout, they'll kill ya as soon as look at ya. While you was restin' up in that hospital, I seen a farmer take an axe ta one a our boys. Buried it in that poor boy's back, killed him dead away, then he screamed at us that he was gonna kill all the bluebellies he could. We shot him dead right where he stood. Anyways, this house ya went to, I ain't gonna shed no tears over it. Besides, it coulda been Reb deserters done what ya found; prob'ly was. There's a lot of 'em out there, an' most of 'em is starvin' an' pretty wild."

I nodded, still not convinced. "Yeah, it could have been. Just so it wasn't any of our men. You hear about anybody doing that sort of thing, you come let me know. Agreed?"

"Sure enough, Jubal. I hear anythin', anythin' at all, an' I'll come an' tell ya right off."

CHAPTER TWENTY-TWO

The morning chill forced me to turn up the collar of my coat, and the fallen leaves, coated with a heavy frost, crunched beneath my feet. I had taken a seat on my front porch to wait for Josiah when a wagon laden with cut timber passed along the main road on its way to the sawmill. Three men were seated on the back of the wagon, cant hooks laid across their laps, and as they passed one of the men turned his head away and pulled down the brim of his hat.

Josiah rode up minutes later and climbed down from his horse.

"Bobby Suggs just rode on by with a wagonload of Billy Lucie's timber," I said.

"T'was kind of 'em," Josiah said. "Saved us a long ride."

Josiah put his horse in our barn and we walked down to the sawmill. I went inside the shack that served as the main office and told Jesse Barton, the yard manager, that I needed to talk to one of the men unloading Billy Lucie's wagon in the rear yard. He glanced at my half-empty sleeve and told me to be careful, that those big pieces of timber could roll off the wagons without warning. I wanted to tell him that my legs could still move as fast as they ever could, but knew it would be a waste of time, so I just smiled and thanked him.

I had a set of handcuffs in my jacket pocket and I took them out and tucked them into my belt so they were visible. I had little hope of using them, and they were more for intimidation than anything else.

"You gonna lock his ass up?" Josiah asked.

"If he gives me a reason. Right now I just want him to know I can, and that I'm thinking on it."

"I wish ya would," Josiah said. "I'd ride alla way ta Richmond wit ya if ya done it."

Josiah hated Suggs as much as I did, but why shouldn't he? He had been with me at Spotsylvania and had seen what Suggs and Johnny and the others had done.

"Betta yet," he added, "ya oughtta jus' take 'em out ta the woods an' bury the sumbitch. Snow's comin' soon, so's the varmints won' find 'em till spring."

Bobby had his back to us so he didn't see us approaching, and when he finally turned we were standing only five feet away. The sight startled him, bringing a smile to Josiah's face.

Suggs glared at Josiah. "What you smilin' at, nigger?"

Josiah took a step toward him. "White trash is always makin' me smile," he said. His body was coiled and waiting for Suggs to make a physically aggressive move.

Suggs turned quickly to me. "What do ya want? Ain't ya bothered me enough?"

"I haven't even begun to bother you," I said.

Suggs was holding the long handle of his cant hook in both hands, and I knew it would take little effort to swing it toward me and stab me in the chest.

"Put your hook down and come over to that stack of lumber behind me. I want to talk to you privately," I said.

"You kin talk ta me right cheer," Suggs spat.

His hands tightened on the cant hook and I pulled my coat back to make my pistol more accessible. It also gave Suggs a good look at the handcuffs tucked into my belt. "Last chance, Bobby," I warned.

"You gonna arress me?"

"Depends on you, Bobby. You do as you're told, you might be back to work in ten minutes. You don't, I promise you your day's gonna be one long misery."

Suggs cursed and dropped his cant hook to the ground, then walked past me, stopping again at the stack of cut lumber.

Behind us the heavy saw started up and began to chop the first of the tall pines from Billy Lucie's wagon. It was a high screeching sound, and sawdust floated into the air as the raw timber was cut into long white boards.

I gestured for Bobby to go to the other side of the lumber stack to cut down on the noise. He hesitated at first, but finally complied. He seemed to realize that I was just looking for an excuse to hand him a bit of the misery I had promised.

"All right, what do ya want?" He shouted out the words to be heard over the high-pitched wail of the saw.

"I didn't like the little games you were playing yesterday, Bobby."

"Wha' games?"

I took a step in, bringing myself close enough to grab him. "Following us around." I turned my hand into a gun and pointed it at him. "Trying to intimidate Abel's sister."

"'At girl was the fat boy's sister?"

I lashed out with the back of my hand and struck his face as hard as I could.

Suggs staggered back, his hat flying off, and Josiah grabbed his hair and yanked his head back. He had pulled a hunting knife from the sheath on his belt and had the blade pressed against Bobby's throat.

"Lemme cut this sumbitch's head off," he hissed.

Bobby's eyes widened in terror and, afraid to turn his head, he desperately tried to watch Josiah out of the corner of one eye. "Git him off me," he begged. "This black bastid's gonna cut my throat."

"I expect he will, you keep calling him a black bastard," I said. "I happen to know for sure that Josiah's momma and daddy were married. Are we going to have any more of your games?"

"No, no games." He again tried to look down at the blade pressed to his neck. "He's cuttin' me. He's cuttin' me! I kin feel the blood."

I peeked at Bobby's throat and saw a line of sweat running down his neck.

"You're just sweating like the pig you are, Suggs." I took his shirt front and Josiah moved the knife away, but kept it ready in his hand. I brought my mouth close to his ear, taking in the rank odor that came off his body. "And you smell like one," I added. I straightened up, holding him at arm's length. "I'm going to tell you this once. You ever again say anything like that about Abel Johnson, and I will cut your throat myself. Do you understand me?"

"I unnerstan'." He pulled back and straightened his shirt. "You been affer me fer a long time, Jubal. Ya even tried ta git me in trouble wit the army. Johnny too. Oh yeah, he tol' me all 'bout it when I got cheer. I din' know it afore, but he did, an' he tol' me. But ya couldna prove nothin' then, an' ya ain't got no proof 'bout nothin' now. So you best be leavin' me alone."

"You want me to leave you alone?"

"Tha's right."

"Not on the best day of your miserable life," I said.

Josiah and I walked back to the house, saying very little until we got there.

I turned to face him and placed a hand on his shoulder. "You are one scary man," I said. "I thought Bobby Suggs was going to wet his pants."

"Wouldna been able ta tell iffen he done it," Josiah said. "Man smells as bad as he does. You looked like you was gonna kill 'em when he said 'at 'bout Abel."

I slowly nodded my head. "You and I both know what he did. He killed Abel, sure as we're standing here."

Now it was Josiah's turn to nod his head. "Yessir, he sure did. Him and Johnny Harris bowf."

Rapidan River, Virginia, 1864

We were camped along the banks of the Rapidan River, only a few miles from Chancellorsville and a few more from Fredericksburg. There were a number of small units, mine among them, scouting the woods and farmlands to see if Lee's forces would try to reestablish his army in the area. The people who lived in that region of Virginia had been among the most rabid supporters of the Confederacy, taunting us whenever we moved through the area, even taking the occasional shot as we marched past. Now, with Lee's defeat at Gettysburg and newspaper reports about the devastation General William Tecumseh Sherman was wreaking across the deep South, a mood of inevitable defeat seemed to permeate the population. Some store owners and tavern keepers had even begun to trade openly with Union troops, appearing to want good relations with an army that seemed certain to become an occupying force.

There were still many, of course, who were determined to fight us to the end. We came across one at a rope ferry set up on the river. When we arrived, ready to cross, the operator told us boldly that he only ferried Confederate troops and Confederate citizens, that Yankees could either go twelve miles downriver to the bridge, or swim.

The man was short and skinny with scraggly gray hair and beard and several missing teeth, someone who clearly preferred to keep any form of civilization at a safe distance—what we would call a "wood-chuck" in Vermont.

"Sir, I am standing here with ten men who are armed to the teeth, and you are telling me we can *swim* the river if we want to cross to the other side. Am I right about that?"

Abel walked up beside me.

"Tha's what I'm sayin'," the ferry operator replied.

I pointed at a large tree about ten yards from the ferry. "Now, if I stood you against that tree and lined up my men as a firing squad, do you think you might change your mind? Because if you didn't we could just shoot your cantankerous old ass and pull ourselves across, now couldn't we?"

The ferry operator, who looked to be in his sixties, spit a wad of tobacco off to one side. "Ya'd waste that many bullets?"

"We're from the North," I said, exasperated. "We have a helluva lot of bullets."

"Better use 'em then, cause I ain't takin' ya."

Abel started to laugh. "I don't think yer scarin' 'em, Jubal."

Johnny joined us. "What the hell is goin' on?"

"This ol' geezer says he won't take us across. Says we kin swim," Abel said.

Johnny removed his sidearm and cocked the hammer. "I'll jus' shoot the damn Reb an' we'll do it ourselves."

I placed my hand on the barrel of Johnny's pistol and pushed it down. "Put the Colt away," I said. I glanced at a ramshackle cabin off to my left, assuming it was a shelter, maybe even a place the old man used as a home. I turned to Abel. "Take him over to that cabin and tie the dumb son of a bitch up . . . Maybe some Rebs will come along and cut you loose. Or maybe they'll just take what you've got in your pockets. I don't really care. You are a crazy old man and I don't have time to fool with you."

The old man spit out another wad of tobacco juice and grinned at me. "Yankee," he said, "y'all kin go shit in your hats."

Abel started to laugh again. "Son . . . of . . . a . . . bitch," he said. "Ever'body in the South is crazy as hell."

We took a southerly route through a region of small farms and rundown plantations. We were just east of the area known as the Wilderness, almost all of it now badly scarred by the artillery duels that had taken place there.

We met another unit coming toward us on the same road. Their sergeant explained that they had crossed the river farther south and were now working their way north. I noticed he was commanding the group Bobby Suggs and his friends were a part of, and that Johnny was standing off to one side talking to them.

The sergeant said his name was Riddle and claimed he had seen nothing but a small group of what appeared to be deserters. "Took off inta the Wilderness when they saw us," he said.

"We've come about ten miles since we crossed on the rope ferry north of us," I reported. "We haven't seen even that much activity."

I wished him luck and called to my men. They assembled quickly, all but Johnny, and I had to shout for him again before he pulled himself away from Bobby Suggs. They were too far away to be sure, but Suggs seemed to be showing Johnny something that he quickly returned to a pocket when he saw me watching.

"We're going to push into the Wilderness and head south another five miles or so," I explained when Johnny had finally joined us. "Then we'll head back to the river and cross at the stone bridge. We should be back at camp by suppertime."

As the men started to cross an open field, headed for the dense scrub forest that lay ahead, I moved up beside Johnny. "What did Suggs have to say?" I asked.

Johnny shrugged his shoulders. "Nothin' much. He was jus' tellin' me how borin' the patrol was so far. Sounded like they been havin' the same luck as us."

"What was he showing you?" I had grown suspicious of anything Suggs did.

"What're ya talkin' 'bout?"

"He was showing you something. I just wanted to know what it was."

Johnny shook his head. "T'was an ol' Reb compass he found. Said he thought it might fetch a price, but if not, he was gonna keep it as a war souvenir." He hesitated a moment. "Ya sure do got a bug up yer ass 'bout Suggs. How come?"

"I don't trust him," I said. "I don't trust him as far as I can spit."

We moved through the Wilderness, my men keeping line of sight to the man on their left, the brush so thick in places that we could be no more than five feet apart to still maintain eye contact. I spread the men out where I could do it safely, but those places were few and far between, and I didn't want any of my men lost, and I certainly didn't want them mistaken for a Reb and shot.

I gave up after five miles and cut back to the east, reckoning that we could reach the river in another two miles or so. As we came out of the thick brush there was a moderate-sized farm up ahead, and I decided to make for it so the men could replenish their canteens and take a much needed rest. When we drew closer the devastation was apparent. The first body we came across was a young black woman, clearly a slave, her dress pulled up and the bodice ripped, exposing both her breasts and vagina. She had been raped and strangled and her brown eyes bulged from her face and her tongue protruded from her open mouth. She was no more than sixteen or seventeen.

I reached down and touched her cheek. It was cold. I lifted her arm and found it still limber; there was no sign of stiffening.

Abel and Johnny came up beside me. "She's only been dead a few hours," I said.

"Musta been them Reb deserters," Johnny said. "I heard they treat runaway slaves pretty much like this."

"This girl was no runaway," I countered. "She was here on this farm." I turned to Abel and saw the hurt in his eyes. He was thinking of Jemma and little Alva, I guessed. "Pass the word to the men to keep an eye out. They see anybody, Reb or Union, they're to keep their rifles trained and ready until I have a chance to question them."

"What are we gonna do 'bout her?" Abel asked.

"We'll bury her before we leave," I said.

We found three more women who'd been raped and killed, along with two children whose heads had been bashed in, probably by rifle butts. One of the children, a little girl no more than four, had been hit so savagely that there was nothing left of her small face.

Inside the house we found a white man and woman, both somewhere in their fifties. The man lay in the hallway. He'd been shot and then bayoneted repeatedly. The woman's body was in the dining room. She appeared to have been shot while running away, her body having skidded across the bare wood floor after she fell, leaving a swath of blood behind her.

I checked them both and found that, like the Negroes outside, their deaths had been fairly recent.

Johnny came down the stairs from the second floor. "Whoever done it cleaned the place out pretty good," he said. "Even dumped the mattress on the floor. I guess they was lookin' fer any money these folks had hid." He was staring at the woman's body as he spoke. She was about the same age as his mother, but he didn't seem to make the connection. A few years ago he would have, I thought.

"We'll bury them all before we pull out," I said.

"Damn, we gonna miss supper we do that," Johnny objected.

"We'll bury them all," I repeated sternly. "Tell the others and get started."

I went outside and began checking the bodies again. I gently turned over the body of a small boy, maybe seven or eight years old. His smooth brown face was frozen in pain and his hands were balled up in two small fists. He had been stabbed repeatedly in the chest and stomach. I guessed it had been done with a knife, not a bayonet, because the wounds did not go entirely through his small body.

I reached out to open his hands so I could fold them across his chest. As I opened his right hand a brass button fell to the ground. It held the letters *U.S.* I picked it up. It was identical to the one on my own tunic. I placed it in my pocket.

We returned to camp shortly after seven, and while the men scrounged what food they could find, I went to our lieutenant's tent and asked permission to speak with him. He was new to the unit, having fought in the Western campaign under General Grant. There, he had been severely wounded and had lost his right arm. It was rumored among the other junior officers that he had begged to keep his commission and return to the fighting. The rumors claimed he was seeking revenge against the Rebs for the loss of his arm. He was from Ohio and his name was Arthur Nettles.

"What did you find out there, Foster?" Lieutenant Nettles asked. I told him about the absence of any Rebel troops, although I had come across a Sergeant Riddle who claimed to have seen some deserters. Then I told him about the farm we had stumbled across and the evidence of rape and murder that we'd found there.

"Probably those Reb deserters Sergeant Riddle saw," he said.

I handed him the tunic button I had found. "This was in the hand of a dead young slave boy. He was no more than seven or eight."

He stared at it for several moments. "I'll look into it," he said. "What did you do with the bodies?"

"We buried them, sir. I can show you where."

He ignored my offer, saying: "Good, good. It was the Christian thing to do."

"My men and I can give you statements about the number and the conditions of the bodies," I offered, unwilling to let it go.

"I'll get back to you on that, sergeant. Thank you for bringing this to my attention." It was a dismissal, so I saluted and left the tent.

I returned to my unit and found that Abel had brought me a plateful of food he had found somewhere. I thanked him and sat down next to him, exhausted, and began to eat.

"What'd the lieutenant say?" he asked.

I picked at the food on my plate. "We buried the bodies, and the lieutenant is about to bury my report."

Abel shook his head. "It ain't right."

"No," I said, "it's not. But there isn't much in this war that is."

I found Sergeant Riddle the next morning and told him what my men and I had come across. He just nodded and made no comment.

"I guess you didn't stop at that farm," I said.

"Passed more'n a few farms, but din' go inta any less we saw somethin' 'spicious aroun' 'em. We saw anythin' like 'at, we'd check fer Rebs. From what ya tell me, this 'un din' show any life at all."

"You see any other Union troops?"

Riddle shook his head. "Jus' you boys."

I told him about the Union tunic button I'd found in the boy's hand.

He took a deep breath. "Lemme tell ya somethin', Foster. My men been fightin' fer months, some of 'em even been fightin' fer years. They seen their friends blown all ta hell, jus' like yer boys have. They seen 'em bayoneted by Rebs chargin' their lines. They been talkin' to a boy one minute, turned away, an' then found that same boy wit his head blowed off when they looked back. Far as I'm concerned, they wanna kill them some Reb lovers, I ain't gonna worry myself 'bout it."

"These were children, small children, and slave women. The couple inside the house were older. I didn't see any weapons laying near them."

"Whoever done it prob'ly took the knives an' guns they had," Riddle said.

"And the children and the young women?"

"War's hard, Foster."

"Riddle, you tell your men that if I find them pulling off a raid like that, I won't stand by and tell them that war is hard. I will blow their asses to kingdom come."

Riddle nodded. "I'll be sure ta tell 'em, Foster. I surely will."

CHAPTER TWENTY-THREE

My father and I sat across the supper table from each other enjoying our final cup of coffee. My father lit up a pipe and waved away the initial cloud of smoke that encircled his head.

"I wanna axe ya somethin', Jubal."

"What is it you want to know?"

He took a drag on his pipe and blew out a perfect smoke ring. "You gonna axe that girl ta marry ya?"

"Rebecca?"

"Ain't seen ya moonin' over no other." He smiled broadly. "Are ya?"

"I'd like to."

"Thank the Lord I din' raise no stupid son," he said.

"I think she'll say yes."

He started to chuckle. "Say yes? She'll have ya hog-tied two minutes after ya open yer mouth. Girl's been plannin' on this fer years."

"You think Mr. Johnson will approve?" I glanced down at my empty sleeve.

"Don' ya worry 'bout that. I think he's plumb scared ya won't axe her. Only one worries 'bout that bum arm a yourn is you." He reached into his shirt pocket and placed two rings on the table. One had a small red stone in it; the other was a solid gold band. He slid them toward me.

I had never seen either before. "Were these—?"

"Your momma's," he said. "The one with the lil' ruby in it, I give ta her when she said she'd marry me. The t'other was her weddin' band. I been keepin' 'em for ya. Don' worry if they don' fit, we kin have 'em fixed up at the jewelers in Burlington."

I kept staring at the rings, visualizing photographs of the mother I only vaguely remembered, trying to imagine her accepting a ring from a much younger father, then later holding me in her arms with the wedding band on her finger.

"How do ya feel 'bout doin' it?" my father asked.

"I guess it scares me a little."

"Ya'd be a damn fool if it din'," he said. "Scary thing, takin' a wife. Yer all footloose an' fancy-free an' all of a sudden there's somebody else dependin' on ya." He took another long drag on his pipe. "Then comes a chil', an' tha's even scarier."

I smiled across the table at him. "You trying to talk me into it, or out of it?"

"Son, if I kin talk ya outta it, then sweet young Rebecca ain't the gal fer ya."

"You won't talk me out of it," I said. "I'll go see Mr. Johnson in the morning, and ask his permission to speak to Rebecca."

My father's eyes glistened with tears. It was the first time I had seen that happen. "I wish yer momma was here," he said. "She sure would be proud."

Everyone was in the store when I arrived the next morning. Rebecca and Mary were waiting on more than the usual number of customers and Walter Johnson was busy stocking shelves. Even Josiah had been hired to haul boxes of goods in from the barn.

"Looks like land office business," I said as I approached Walter. I nodded to Josiah as he dropped off a box containing sacks of dried beans.

"Folks'r jus' stockin' up fer the first snowfall," Walter said.

I waited until he'd placed the last sack of dried beans on the shelf. "I wanted to talk to you, Mr. Johnson. Privately, if possible."

"This 'bout Johnny Harris?" he asked.

"No sir. This is a personal matter that I need to speak to you about."

Walter Johnson's eyes brightened. "Best we go upstairs," he said. "Ladies kin handle the store." He went to the rear door and called to Josiah, who had gone for another sack. "I'm gonna be upstairs fer a bit, Josiah. You kin rest up a spell."

He ushered me into the upstairs parlor and offered me coffee, which I declined. I perched nervously on the edge of a small, fragile chair, which creaked under my weight. Walter took a heavy chair stuffed with horsehair and folded his hands across his protruding belly. As always I was taken by how much Abel had resembled him, and thought again that this was how he would have looked had he been allowed to live into his fifties.

"What kin I do fer ya, Jubal?" he asked.

I shifted nervously. "I don't know what else to do, except to come right out with it. I'd like your permission to ask Rebecca if she'll marry me."

A slow smile spread across Walter's face. He unfolded his hands, sat forward, and slapped his knees. "Damn, if that ain't wunnerful news. Of course ya have my permission ta ask her. I think we both know what her answer'll be." His smile suddenly disappeared. "God, I wish Abel was here ta see this day. Did ya know that he wrote ta me, tellin' me he thought he was gonna have ya as a brother-in-law when the war was over?"

"No, I didn't know about the letter, but he told me the same thing."

"He loved ya, Jubal. He loved ya like ya was his own blood."

"I know he did, Walter. I hope he knew I loved him too."

Walter forced the smile to return. "When do ya plan to . . . well . . . talk ta Rebecca?"

"I thought I'd see if she'd take a buggy ride with me this afternoon," I said.

"Ya got a pretty spot picked out, do ya?"

"Yes sir, I do."

He winked at me. "Well, I guess I better give her the afternoon off."

We went downstairs and found Josiah standing just inside the rear door.

"Time ta get back ta work, Josiah," Walter said. "Bring me in a barrel of coffee beans."

"Yes sir," Josiah replied, gesturing with his head that I should come outside.

I went out the back door and followed Josiah into the barn.

"What is it, Josiah?" I asked.

He led me to an area in the rear of the barn, where I could tell he had recently moved some goods. He pointed toward two remaining boxes. "Look behind them boxes," he said.

I did as he asked and saw an awl up against the barn wall.

"Looks like dere's dried blood on it," he said. "Blood startin' at the point an' goin' right up ta the hilt."

I took the neckerchief from around my neck and carefully wrapped up the awl and placed it in a side pocket of my jacket. "I'll take it to Doc Pierce," I said. "I need you to keep this between us. Just between us, nobody else."

"I unnerstan'," Josiah said.

I walked over to Doc's office. From the road I could see two women sitting in his waiting room, so I went to the rear door and let myself into his kitchen. When he ushered a local farm boy out of his office he saw me sitting at his kitchen table, and I heard him tell the next patient that he'd be just a minute or two. A moment later he took a chair across from me.

"You got a problem, Jubal?"

I took the neckerchief from my pocket and slid it across the table and watched as he carefully exposed the awl. He looked it over; then picked it up using the ends of the neckerchief and headed back to his office. "Come with me," he said.

I watched him as he placed the awl under a microscope and carefully examined it. He leaned back in his chair. "Looks like you'll be riding back into Burlington," he said.

"Blood?"

"Definitely, and my guess would be that it's Johnny Harris's blood. From the look of this weapon, the shape, the length of the blade, it's my bet that if we exhumed Johnny's body—which we may have to do—we'd find that it matches the wound in his chest and heart."

I stared at the awl but said nothing.

"Where did you find it?" he asked.

"Josiah found it while he was working in Walter Johnson's barn," I said.

Doc pursed his lips. "You think Josiah might have put it there, to throw suspicion off himself?"

I shook my head. "If Josiah killed Johnny he would have taken that awl out in the woods and lost it for good."

"I guess maybe the gossip was true," Doc said at length.

"What gossip is that?"

"Just remember this is gossip. It's nothing that I know for sure, but a few months back I overheard two women in my waiting room talking about Mary Johnson. They were talking about her marrying Walter, and her being only a few years older than Rebecca. Then one of them said that maybe Mary had found herself a younger man as well. She said Mary seemed to spend a lot of time talking to Johnny Harris."

I didn't respond. I just stared at the awl. A panicked woman might hide a murder weapon in her barn, hoping to get rid of it later, or believing that no one would ever find it. So might a cuckolded husband.

"I had a talk with Walter this morning," I said. "I asked his permission to speak to Rebecca, to ask her to marry me."

Doc leaned back in his chair. "Son of a bitch," he said. "What are you going to do, Jubal?"

"I'm going to ride into Burlington and show this awl to Dr. Evers."

Before I left town I stopped back at the store and told Walter Johnson that something had come up that made it necessary to ride into Burlington. "I'll have to put off speaking to Rebecca," I explained.

Walter looked at me with a hint of suspicion. "Must be somethin' pretty important," he said.

"Yes, it is." I hesitated, watching him for a reaction. "It's about Johnny's murder."

"Oh." He shifted his weight as if suddenly uncomfortable. "Well, it can't be helped, then," he said.

I reached the medical school shortly before noon. Dr. Evers was teaching an anatomy class in a large, elevated lecture hall, and I slipped inside and took a seat in the rear. There was a detailed drawing of the human body on the wall behind Dr. Evers, and a cadaver lay on a table set out before him. The cadaver had been opened from neck to pubis, the ribs pulled back to expose the vital organs. Evers was lecturing on the functions of the human heart. Using a pointer and the drawing behind him, he enumerated the various chambers of the heart, then invited the students to come up to the cadaver and view the atrium and ventricles.

I very much wanted to join them as they filed past the cadaver, but knew it would be inappropriate. So I waited patiently, taking what I could from the lecture and enjoying every moment of it.

When the class ended Dr. Evers waved me down. He was smiling broadly when I reached him. "You looked like you wanted to participate," he said.

"I did. Perhaps I'll be able to do so after I finish my degree."

"I hope so," Evers said. "Tell me, Jubal, do you have a family?"

"No sir, but I plan to ask a young woman to marry me."

"Good. I find married students are often more dedicated. We try to find work for them at the hospital and here at the school. They don't live well on what we pay, but they can get by if their needs aren't too great. We try to find work for the wives as well. Some people don't approve, but it's a bit easier if a medical student has a wife who's willing to help in that way."

I motioned at my empty sleeve. "And this?"

"There are artificial arms," Evers said. "They're not attractive and they're somewhat uncomfortable, but they do help to a degree. You just have to learn to overcome the handicap." He covered the cadaver and turned back to me. "Are you here about your murder?"

"Yes sir." I reached into my pocket and withdrew the wrapped awl.

Evers uncovered it and examined the blade closely. "Definitely blood," he said. "Let's go into the laboratory and see if it's human."

Doc Pierce sat at our kitchen table next to my father. I sat across from them. The awl lay between us on top of my open neckerchief.

"So Evers told you it was definitely human blood," Doc said.

"Yes, he said there was no question."

"An' if we dig Johnny up ya think y'all be able ta tell if this here awl was the weapon that kilt him," my father said.

"We could be ninety percent sure that it was," Doc said. "Or we could rule it out completely."

"We better talk to Virgil," my father said. "See if we kin git his permission ta dig up his boy without an order from the court. We wait too long an' the ground freezes, there won't be any diggin' till spring."

"I agree," Doc said. "I'll go with you and explain why it's necessary."

"That'd be good," my father said, then turned to me. "What'r ya gonna do, son? 'Bout Rebecca, I mean?"

"I'm still working that out." I tapped the side of my head. "Up here. I know what I want to do."

"Ya don' think it coulda been her, do ya?"

"No, I'm sure it wasn't," I said, a bit too vehemently.

My father and Doc looked at me, but said nothing.

"Maybe ya should wait," my father said. "I could talk ta Walter an' tell 'im that I axed ya ta wait, jus' till ya got yer college plans worked out."

"No, I'm going to see her tomorrow. I'll know what I want to do by then."

"Are ya gonna tell her what ya found?"

I stared at my father, trying to read his expression. "No," I said. "Not until I have to."

He looked relieved.

———

Spotsylvania County, Virginia, 1864

Lee's troops arrived at the Wilderness at the beginning of May. My men and I were out on patrol when another squad came toward us, moving fast.

I pulled their sergeant aside. "You look like you saw the devil himself," I said.

"Pretty near," he responded, "if General Lee counts fer the devil."

"Where'd you see him?"

"A way back, a few miles west of Chancellorsville. He's got fifty, sixty thousand of his Rebs diggin' in fer a fight, him ridin' up an' down the line on his big, white horse."

I grabbed his arm. "You better get on back and tell the officers so they can get a balloon up."

"What'r you gonna do?" he asked.

"I'll go and get a peek at them too. Our officers don't believe anything until they get at least three reports. I'll be an hour or two behind you."

Two days later General Meade moved his army across the Rapidan River at three separate crossings and converged on the Wilderness Tavern. The Rebs had used that site a year ago to launch their devastating attack on Union forces at Chancellorsville. General Grant, who was still in overall command, planned to set up his camps west of the old battle site and then move south, drawing Lee away from the quagmire of the Wilderness.

But Lee refused to comply. His forces were massively outnumbered—60,000 to 100,000—and he could not match the Union's artillery in either reliability or number. He desperately needed the near impenetrable terrain of the Wilderness to make the odds more equal.

The armies clashed for five days, first one and then the other pushing the opposing force back. In the last skirmish a brushfire broke out on the battlefield and we were forced to again listen to the wounded scream out in horror as they were burned alive.

Abel and I had pulled dozens to safety, to a small degree with Johnny's help, and when we awoke in the morning we found that the Rebs had pulled back. As I searched the abandoned battlefield the charred skeletons of those we had not saved were strewn about.

Abel crawled up beside me. "Johnny took off," he said.

"What do you mean, took off?"

"He ain't here. Neither is Suggs an' his boys. I checked jus' ta be sure."

I had started a small campfire and handed Abel a fresh cup of coffee. Josiah crawled in and squatted next to us. I poured him a cup as well.

"I hear ya say Johnny took off?" Josiah asked.

"That's what Abel says."

"Well, he better git his ass back real smart-like. I jus' heard some officers talkin' over ta the hospital. They says Lee's army is headin' ta a place called Todd's Tavern, an' our boys'll be headed after 'em soon. Johnny's ain't back, they gonna say he deserted, an' he's gonna find his-self standin' in front of a firin' squad."

"Whatcha gonna do?" Abel asked.

I thought if over before answering. "The lieutenant likes to send out patrols," I said. "I'm gonna see if he'll let me take a small squad to see where the Rebs have gone. He agrees, we'll see if we can find Johnny and drag his ass back here."

"An' if we can't find him we kin say he was on patrol with us an' we jus' got sep'rated somehow," Abel offered.

Josiah started to laugh. "You white boys is a sneaky bunch. I better go witcha jus' so's you be a lil' bit honest."

We headed south, keeping to the edge of the Wilderness to give our-selves some cover. To our left were open fields, laid fallow with their mostly abandoned farmhouses and plantations largely deserted. I had told the lieutenant that I'd take three men with me, Abel and Josiah and supposedly Johnny, and move south until we located the Rebel force we'd been fighting.

By midday we were several miles from the battlefield, and farther into the woods I could hear movement; at one point I thought I saw a flash of gray uniform. I had been warned to expect rearguard Reb patrols keeping track of our troop movements, as well as isolated howitzer batteries set up to slow any Union pursuit. We stopped at a large stone outcropping and Abel took my long glass and began scanning a small farm just east of us.

"There's blue uniforms in the yard outside that house," he said, handing me the glass.

I raised the glass and confirmed what he had seen. The field between us and the farmhouse was heavily overgrown and would offer decent cover. "Stay low crossing the field," I said. "We'll crawl up and see what's going on. But be careful. It could be a legitimate patrol. It could also be some of our boys out looting."

We could hear the woman begging when we got within fifty yards of the farmhouse. The words: "No, no. Please no," repeated over and over again, a man's gruff voice telling her to shut up.

We rose up from the weeds and high grass and rushed to the rear of the house, then moved cautiously to the side. From the open windows we could hear glass shattering and heavy objects being thrown. We came around to the front yard. The woman we had heard was laying on the ground with a man on top of her, his hand covering her mouth. He was raping her, while three other Union soldiers stood by and cheered him on.

We moved up on them, guns leveled, and I kicked the rapist in the side. He grunted and rolled off the woman. She was no more than seventeen, a fair-skinned mulatto girl, her face swollen and bruised where the man had beaten her. The soldier I'd kicked started shouting at me that I'd broken his ribs, and he was soon joined by the others who'd been urging him on.

"Shut your goddamn mouths," I growled. One man started reaching for his sidearm and I leveled my Spencer rifle at his chest. "Just one more inch toward that Colt and I'll send you straight to hell," I hissed. "Where's your sergeant?"

"Sergeant Riddle's dead," one of the men said. "Got hisself burnt up in the Wilderness."

Three men burst from the house, their rifles pointed straight at us. "You better be droppin' yer weapons," one said. "If ya don' yer the one's goin' ta hell."

"Put those rifles down," I barked. "I'm a Union sergeant and that's an order. Who's in charge here?"

Bobby Suggs came out behind the three men. He grinned at me and slowly drew his Colt sidearm. "I'm in charge, Foster. An' far as I kin tell you don' look like yer in any position ta be threatenin' my boys." He raised his pistol so it was pointed at my head. "So I think y'all better drop them rifles right quick."

The three of us stood our ground, and Bobby cocked his pistol. "I'll give ya ten seconds ta do like I said and git yer asses outta here. Ya kin take yer sidearms with ya, but yer rifles stay here. We ain't gonna have ya poppin' us off from that there tree line."

Johnny came out of the house holding a padlocked cashbox in his hands. "I found it," he said. "But that damn ol' man won't gimme the key." He glanced up and saw us for the first time. "Wha's goin' on?"

"We're 'bout ta shoot yer boys from Vermont, they don' drop them rifles an' git their asses outta here," Suggs said.

"You better do like yer told, Jubal."

"Johnny, what the hell's wrong wit ya?" Abel shouted.

"Shut up, fat boy," Suggs snarled.

"I can't help ya," Johnny said. "We got a right ta take what we find. An' you ain't got no right ta stop us. These people been feedin' these Rebs an' givin' 'em money fer ammunition. We're takin' what's left so

they can't give 'em no more. There ain't nothin' wrong wit that. Ya better drop them rifles an' git on outta here, or these boys'r gonna shoot
yer asses fer sure."

I stared at Johnny, dumbfounded. "You can live with this? Raiding
houses, raping women?"

He glared at me. "Yeah, I kin live with it, Jubal. Now git yer goddamn ass outta here."

We dropped our rifles and backed away toward the field. We were
maybe forty yards back in the overgrown field when the young girl
started screaming again.

I saw an elderly man and woman pushed from the house. Johnny
and Suggs were shouting at them, and the old man was shouting back
defiantly. I couldn't understand what they were saying over the girl's
screams, but Johnny was holding up the padlocked cashbox. Suggs
pulled his Colt and cocked it, and moments later Johnny did the same.
The old man shouted again and Suggs opened fire, spinning the man
around. Johnny fired and hit him again; then they both opened up on
the woman and I saw her body fly back.

Suggs then motioned to us out in the field. He shouted to his men
and they leveled their rifles at us.

"Hit the ground!" I yelled as their first shots whistled over our heads.

The first howitzer shell hit thirty yards behind us and grapeshot
cut through the weeds like a scythe. From the sound I could tell it was
coming from south of us, and I screamed at the others to get back to
the cover of the woods.

"There's too much field between us an' the woods!" Abel shouted
back. "The house would be better cover!"

"Suggs and his men will kill us if we try for the house," I stammered.
"Our only chance is the woods."

"Jubal's right," Josiah said.

"Stay low," I ordered.

The shooting from the house had stopped as Suggs and Johnny and their comrades took cover inside, and we stayed low to the ground and moved toward the woods, hoping the Reb artillery spotters would lose sight of us.

That hope ended as another shell hit, almost on top of us, and I saw Abel's body rise up in the air. I started toward him when another shell hit and I too was flying above the ground. When I hit back down all the air rushed from my lungs and I gasped for breath as I dragged myself toward Abel. He was on his back, his face ashen, his eyes filled with terror. There was a gaping wound in his belly and his intestines were spilling out of his tunic.

"Oh God, Jubal. Oh God, I wanna go home. I wanna see my momma an' my daddy an' Rebecca. Don' let me die here. Don' let me die." Abel began to cough and blood gurgled in his throat and started pouring from his mouth, and he took another gasping breath and his body bucked twice and then settled.

Josiah was next to me. "He gone, Jubal. An' yer hurt bad."

I peered down and saw that my left sleeve was covered with blood, and beneath the blood mangled flesh and bone were pushing through the fabric.

I ignored it and grabbed Josiah's shirt. "He's not dead!" I shouted. "We've got to get him back. Help me! Help me get him into the woods!"

"Ain't no use," Josiah said. He was tying a tourniquet around my arm and my vision began to cloud and the sky began to spin. The last thing I remember was Josiah hoisting me on his shoulder and beginning to run.

CHAPTER TWENTY-FOUR

Jerusalem's Landing, Vermont, 1865

I went to the Johnsons' store shortly after lunch and found Rebecca working behind the counter with her father.

Walter Johnson glanced at me cautiously. "You be needin' somethin', Jubal, or are ya jus' here ta see Rebecca?"

"I was wondering if I could steal Rebecca away for a few hours," I said. "It feels like a touch of Indian summer outside, probably the last we're going to have, and I thought we could take a buggy ride."

Walter's face broke into a wide smile. "Why sure, Jubal. That's if Rebecca's willin', of course."

Rebecca smiled at me. "Just let me get my bonnet," she said.

Jezebel was hitched up to the buggy and tied outside the store, and when Rebecca came out she stopped and put her hands on her hips. "So you had the buggy all hitched up and ready to go?" She turned to me and cocked her head to one side. "Pretty confident I'd say yes, weren't you?"

I smiled at her. "Let's say I was pretty hopeful, or maybe I thought that if you saw poor Jezebel all hitched up to the buggy it would make it hard to say no."

"That's a very slippery answer, Jubal Foster."

"Yes it is," I said. "Can I help you into the buggy?"

We drove west, following the line of the river, crossed over it at one point, and turned into the road that led up the side of Camel's Hump Mountain. There was an apple orchard and sugarbush about a half mile up, owned by a friend of my father's, and I pulled the buggy to the side of the road next to a field dappled with late-blooming flowers. I took a blanket from the buggy and helped Rebecca down and turned her toward the rising vista of the mountain as I slipped my arm around her waist.

"I've always thought this was one of the most beautiful places on earth," I said.

She pointed to the top of the mountain in the distance. "Look, there's snow on top of Camel's Hump."

I spread out the blanket and we sat down facing each other. "I'm going to hate not being in Jerusalem's Landing every day. I missed it so much all the years I was away."

Concern and surprise crossed Rebecca's face. "Are you leaving, Jubal?"

"I'm going to go back to school in Burlington. I want to finish my degree, maybe study medicine after that. Doc Pierce seems to think I have an aptitude for it, and a friend of his, a teacher at the school, said they'd give me a job so I could support myself."

"How . . . when will I see you?"

I reached out and took her left hand in my right. "It won't be much of a life for a time, but you'd make me very happy if you'd go with me."

"Go . . . go with you? I don't understand. What are you saying, Jubal?"

I reached into my pocket and took out the small ruby ring. "This was my mother's," I said. "I'd like you to wear it. And when you're ready . . . soon, I hope . . . I want you to marry me and come with me to Burlington." I slipped the ring on her finger. "Will you?"

She stared at me in disbelief. Then she stared at the ring and her face broke into a wide smile and she threw her arms around my neck and hugged me fiercely. "Oh, yes, Jubal," she said in my ear. "Of course I'll marry you. And I'll go anywhere you want."

Chancellorsville, Virginia, 1864

I awoke in a field hospital a few miles east of Chancellorsville. Josiah was sitting beside my cot. My mouth was dry and cracked but I managed one word: "Abel?"

"He dead, Jubal," Josiah said.

I squeezed my eyes shut and passed back into unconsciousness.

When I awoke again Josiah was gone. A nurse came by with a wet cloth and moistened my lips. She was a pretty young woman with brown hair and soft brown eyes that seemed very tired and full of the suffering she had witnessed.

"How are you feeling?" she asked.

"My arm hurts," I said.

"It will for a bit more," she said.

I glanced down and saw the bandages that swathed the stump that had been my left arm. I tried to raise my head, but couldn't. "Where is it?" I asked, surprised by the horror I heard in my own voice.

"The doctor had to amputate," she told me. "The wound was too severe."

"What did you do with it?" I demanded. My voice was a hoarse croak that I barely recognized.

The nurse wiped my forehead with a damp cloth; it felt cool and soothing. "Try to sleep," she said.

I knew very well what they had done with my severed arm. When on litter-bearer duty I had carried limbs out of our field hospitals and dumped them in the pits that had been dug for them, arms and legs and loose tissue, all piled together as though they were the remnants of some grotesque explosion in a human butcher shop.

I slipped into unconsciousness again, waking hours later with a start. In my dream I had seen my arm lying in a pit filled with limbs, the hands still attached to arms that reached out, the fingers grasping for whatever they could find, the severed legs straining to gain some purchase that would allow them to climb from the pit. Then Abel's body was dropped in and he turned and looked at my arm and I saw tears gather in his eyes. "I'm sorry, Jubal," he whispered. "I'll take yer arm home with me. I'll take it home an' I'll keep it fer ya. I promise, Jubal. I promise."

I shook my head, fighting the image away, and I gasped at the pain that surged through the remnant of my arm. It was dark outside and the odors that filled the tent were overpowering, deep pungent smells of rotting flesh and pus and excrement.

The man beside me moaned deeply and I saw that both of his legs were gone well above the knees and there were heavy bandages on one side of his face.

I felt a hand gently touch my shoulder and I turned my head and saw Josiah staring down at me.

"How ya feelin', Jubal?"

"Like shit," I croaked.

He smiled at me. "Now tha' sounds more like the man I knows."

"What happened to Johnny?" I asked. "Is he back in camp?"

Josiah shook his head. "Las' time I seen him, he was runnin' north, tryin' ta git back cheer, him an' Suggs an' them others too. Up ahead of 'em I could see the Rebs closin' in, but then I din' hear no shots, so I figgered they got 'emselves captured. I axed the lieutenant 'bout 'em an' he said they was prob'ly on the way ta some Reb prison."

"They should be dead, all of them. Johnny too."

"Yeah, they should."

"They killed Abel," I said, hearing the plea for vengeance in my own voice. "He'd be alive if they hadn't forced us out into that field." I closed my eyes. "Or if I hadn't taken us to that goddamn farmhouse."

"Ya did what was right, Jubal. An' ya was tryin' ta help tha' no-account Johnny too."

"I wish we'd never gone there," I said, my voice weak and distant. And a phrase my father had used when I was a small boy, a boy who was always wishing for impossible things, came back to me: *If wishes were horses, beggars would ride.*

I awoke the next morning to the sound of singing. It was a rich baritone voice and it was coming from the next bed, the soldier who had lost both his legs.

Rock of Ages, cleft for me,
let me hide myself in Thee;
let the water and the blood,
from Thy wounded side that flowed,
be of sin the double cure;
save from wrath and make me pure . . .

A nurse rushed over to his bed. "Corporal James, you must be quiet," she whispered. "You're waking the other men."

"I'm practicin'," James said. "I gotta practice if it's gonna work out."

"What are you practicing for?" the nurse asked.

"Fer when I git outta here. Fer when they sits me on that board with the wheels on it, so's I kin move myself aroun' with my hands. Ya see, I'll have ta earn my keep. I was a teamster afore the war, drove wagons at an iron mine way up in New York, near ta Buffalo." He let out a cold laugh. "Can't do that no more, an' singin' is the only other talent I got.

So, ya see, I figger I'll sit on my board an' move myself up an' down the street, singin' ta folks, an' they kin drop their pennies in my cup."

He started singing again and the nurse tried to hush him, but he ignored her. She shook her head and left, his voice following her:

While I draw this fleeting breath,
when mine eyes shall close in death,
when I soar to worlds unknown,
see Thee on Thy judgment throne,
Rock of Ages, cleft for me,
Let me hide myself in Thee.

The singing stopped and I turned to him. The barrel of a pistol was pressed under his chin and before I could shout a warning, James squeezed the trigger and the sound of the shot filled the tent.

Blood and bits of bone and brain covered the pillow and the bed-sheets and I turned away as doctors and nurses rushed needlessly to his side.

I closed my eyes and thought about my missing arm, wishing I could follow Corporal James on the journey he'd just begun. I bit down and squeezed my jaws together. *Not until you make them pay,* I told myself. *Not until Johnny and Suggs and the others pay for what they did.*

As I lay there I could hear the nurse begin to sob and another stanza of the same hymn that I'd known since childhood flowed through my mind:

Nothing in my hand I bring,
simply to the cross I cling;
naked, come to Thee for dress;
helpless, look to Thee for grace;

foul, I to the fountain fly;
wash me, Savior, or I die.

They had me sitting up three days later. The doctor said it was better for the healing process. By the end of the first week they had me on
my feet, claiming I needed to walk to regain my strength and balance,
and to keep blood clots from forming. They said pneumonia was the
greatest threat, and I needed to move about to keep my lungs clear. I
thought about Stonewall Jackson. He had died after his arm had been
amputated and pneumonia had set in. I thought he was a lucky man.

Josiah had gone off with the army. Grant had continued the fight at
Todds Tavern and Spotsylvania Court House, and when he finally dis-
engaged, Lee's forces were on the run, headed south toward Richmond.

Although the newspapers differed on the Battle of the Wilderness,
with some calling it inconclusive, and others—the Southern papers
mostly—claiming it was a tactical Confederate victory, our officers were
elated, insisting that Grant had won a great strategic victory and would
now pursue a war of attrition. Lee, they said, had been left with only two
choices: fight to the death, or surrender. In either event they claimed the
war would be over in less than a year. A year too late for Abel.

My father and Rebecca wrote every week. Everyone was crushed by
news of Abel's death and wanted to know anything I could tell them
about how he died and where his body had been buried. I did not know
what to say, so I said little, other than to tell them that Abel had been
buried at a military cemetery outside Chancellorsville, Virginia. They
also wrote that Johnny was a prisoner of war at Andersonville, and that
a prayer service had been held to thank the Lord for his survival and to
ask for his safe return to his family.

* * *

Two months passed before I was finally strong enough to go to Lieutenant Nettles to bring charges against Johnny and Suggs and the others. I found Nettles seated in his tent; my left arm was missing, just as his right arm was.

He ran his hand through his thick brown beard. "If we were twins we'd have a whole body, Foster." He grimaced at his own comment. "At least you can still salute with the proper hand. I feel like a fool using my left. What can I do for you, sergeant?"

"I'm here to press charges against a number of our men."

"What charges?" he asked, his eyes growing dark.

"Assaulting a superior officer, rape of a civilian woman, murder of two civilians, raiding and pillaging of a civilian home, and the murder of a member of the Union Army."

"Very serious charges, charges that would place these men before a firing squad if they were convicted. Do you have any witnesses?" the lieutenant asked.

"Yes sir. Myself and a litter-bearer named Josiah Flood."

"Is Flood a Negro?"

"Yes sir."

"You know this Flood well?"

"Yes sir. I grew up with him in Vermont, and know him to be an honest and honorable man."

"Tell me what happened."

I took a sheaf of papers from my pocket and laid it on his field desk. "I took the liberty to write it all down. I only know the names of two of the men, but I'm sure they'll reveal others under interrogation. I could also identify the others on sight. Unfortunately, they're all in Andersonville Prison."

"And right in the sights of General Sherman," the lieutenant said. "My bet is they won't be there too much longer." He picked up the sheaf of papers. "Let me read this, and consult my superiors. It may take a bit of time. The senior staff is concentrating on General Lee at the moment, but I assure you this will be read and acted upon."

CHAPTER TWENTY-FIVE

We dug up Johnny's body at night, when it was unlikely anyone would be passing by the cemetery. It was the lone condition Virgil Harris made. He did not want people telling his wife that the grave had been violated. He said it was more than the woman would be able to bear.

The cemetery had a stone crypt dug into a hill where those who died during the winter were stored until the ground thawed enough for burial. Josiah, my father, Doc Pierce, and I carried the wooden coffin there and placed it on a stone platform that lay against one wall. Lanterns were hung on the wall above the coffin to give Doc the light he would need.

"I feel like a grave robber," my father said, as he and Josiah fitted pry bars under the coffin lid and forced it up.

Johnny's body lay in the casket with a gold coin covering each eye, making his bloodless face seem even whiter.

"Wha's the money fer?" Josiah asked.

"It's an old custom," Doc said. "It actually started with the ancient Greeks and Romans, but they put the coins under the tongue. The English found that practice unpleasant, so they placed coins on the eyes instead."

"But what's the money fer?" Josiah asked. "It supposed ta keep the eyes closed?"

"It was for Charon," Doc explained. "He was the mythical ferryman who rowed the dead across the River Styx, taking them from the land of the living to the land of the dead. It was his payment for the service, and if he didn't get it the body of the deceased was forced to wander the banks of the river, looking for the pauper's entrance to the afterlife."

"I wonder why a Christian minister like Virgil would do that," my father said.

"His people were from England," Doc said. "Maybe he was just keeping with custom."

Doc unbuttoned Johnny's tunic and exposed his chest. Widely spaced sutures closed the incision from the autopsy and the lanterns made his pale, white chest appear to shimmer in the flickering light.

"Dis here is spooky," Josiah said. "I gonna be dreamin' 'bout dis fer a long time."

Doc took the awl and compared the long slender blade to the wound on Johnny's chest. "Looks like it fits perfectly," he said. "We'll have to check the interior wound."

Doc cut the sutures and pried the rib cage back. The ribs had been cut and spread for the autopsy and they moved easily, making a distinct sucking sound that sent a chill down my spine.

"Jesus," my father said, indicating it had done the same to him.

Doc took the awl again. All the organs had been removed and examined during the autopsy and lay inside the body cavity. They had begun to putrefy and a heavy odor of decay rose from the body, causing all but Doc to cover our noses and mouths. Doc picked up the heart and carefully slid the blade of the awl into the wound. He looked at us in turn. "It's a perfect fit," he said. "That makes it ninety percent certain this was the weapon the killer used."

My father, Doc, and I were seated at our kitchen table and a bottle of whiskey had been set out. We had returned Johnny to his grave and it left a pall hanging over us. I had seldom seen my father drink hard liquor, but I could tell he needed it to put aside the evening's work.

"Walter Johnson came ta see me this afternoon," my father said, trying to push other thoughts away. "He invited us ta supper next weekend ta talk over weddin' plans."

My father was avoiding the question he wanted to ask, but Doc stepped in and asked it for him.

"I'm real happy for you, Jubal," Doc began. "Please be certain of that. But I'm also worried. What are you going to do if it turns out someone in the Johnson household killed Johnny Harris?"

I tapped on the table. "The only evidence we have is the awl, our belief that it was the weapon that killed Johnny, and the fact that it was found behind some boxes in the Johnson barn. What we still need to find out is how it got there. Right now I can't answer that question. But one thing's certain: anyone could have thrown it behind those boxes. Anyone."

"You're right, son," my father said. "But there's also the talk that Mary Johnson was involved with Johnny. An' that could point a finger at both her an' Walter. Have ya talked ta either one of 'em?"

"I talked to Mary. She denied there was anything between them." The words burned in my throat. I had never lied to my father, not even as a boy. Now I had.

***

Chancellorsville, Virginia, 1864

Word came in November that General Sherman had put Atlanta to the torch and was now headed for Savannah and the sea. Jubilation filled the ranks. Everyone believed the South would now crumble before Sherman's marauding army and that he would march through the Carolinas leaving destruction in his wake. Within months he was expected to unite with Grant to deal the final crushing blow to Confederate forces.

My wounds had healed and I was working as a clerk at the field hospital. We were between battles with few new casualties coming in, and my job was limited to filling out discharge papers for those who were being sent home. I had expected to be sent home myself, only to be told that the loss of a single arm left me capable enough for clerical work, thereby freeing up a more able-bodied man for battle.

Lieutenant Nettles came to my small clerical tent while I was filling out papers for a man who had lost both an arm and a leg. The army had decided to send him home to his wife and child in New Jersey, even though his wife had written telling the army she could not care for him and insisting he be kept in a military hospital. Otherwise, she warned, they would leave her no choice but to turn him out to the streets.

Nettles picked up the papers and read quickly through them. "How does a woman like that live with herself?" he wondered aloud.

"How does the army?" I replied.

"The army is supposed to have a cold and calloused heart. It's the nature of the beast."

"Cold and calloused, even to its own men who have given so much?"

"Especially to its own men, and especially to those who are no longer useful." He tapped the side of his nose. "Why else would we take fine young boys and throw them into battles where we know many will be slaughtered? And all on the whim of politicians and generals."

"You're speaking treason, sir." I smiled at him, letting him know it had become my brand of treason as well.

"Come take a walk with me, Foster."

I followed Lieutenant Nettles outside. He was not a big man, and I towered over him, but he had a presence about him that commanded respect. His beard was fuller than the last time I'd seen him, his brown eyes a bit wearier. But he still walked with his shoulders squared and his back ramrod straight, almost as though he was defying anyone to think him a cripple. But, of course, there always would be those who would.

We stopped next to a large mound of dirt. "Do you know what this is?" he asked.

"It was a pit where they buried amputated limbs," I said.

Nettles nodded his head somewhat like a schoolmaster. "They filled this one up last May. It probably has your arm down there. They've dug two others since and filled them as well."

"Where is your arm, sir?" There was a touch of resentment in my voice. I didn't need to be reminded where my arm was.

"Vicksburg," Nettles said. "Our commander in chief, Mr. Lincoln, through the good offices of General Grant, allowed me to donate my arm to the greater good in beautiful Mississippi, a place best suited to alligators and cottonmouths." He turned away from the closed-over pit and faced me. "General Sherman's great success in Georgia has brought freedom to most of the men held at Andersonville Prison. A list of those freed was sent to Washington, which in turn informed the various units from which the men were captured. I learned last week that Johnny Harris and Bobby Suggs were among those freed. They were not in good shape. Conditions at Andersonville can only be described as horrendous. There was very little food and even less medical care, the Confederacy preferring to reserve its limited resources of each for their own men. I was informed that the men capable of travel were being sent home. Harris and Suggs were among them."

"What about the charges I filed against them?" I could feel the sudden anger radiating from my face.

"I asked that exact question. I had forwarded those charges to my superiors, urging they be acted upon." He drew a long breath, an angry one, I thought. "This morning I received a reply. There are to be no charges filed, no court martials, nothing. Our superiors feel that accusing federal troops of atrocities against civilians would only inflame hatreds at a time when we will be seeking to mollify a conquered people. They also feel that a trial that suggests Union troops deliberately caused the death of a fellow soldier and the serious wounding of a noncommissioned officer would only taint the great victory we are about to achieve." He placed a hand on my shoulder. "So nothing will be done. And nothing can be done on our part to change that fact. Of course, that doesn't stop you from seeking justice yourself," he said as he walked away from me. "Private Suggs hails from a small Pennsylvania town called Solebury, and I believe you know where Private Harris can be found."

General Lee abandoned Richmond on April 2, and the Confederate government followed his example and fled to Lynchburg. Lee led his army west, hoping to eventually join forces with Confederate troops in North Carolina where he could continue the fight. He got only as far as Appomattox Court House, where Grant and the Army of the Potomac cut off his retreat. Lee attempted to break through the Union lines, believing it was made up entirely of cavalry. When he realized that the cavalry was backed by two corps of Union infantry, he had no choice but to lead his army into a massacre or suffer the indignity of surrender.

Lee's surrender took place on April 9, and three days later Lieutenant Nettles came to my tent and handed me my discharge papers.

"Go home, Sergeant Foster," he said. "The war is over, or will be shortly, and all those who were seriously wounded are being discharged with the sincere thanks of a grateful nation." He clearly enjoyed the irony of his statement.

"Are you being discharged, sir?" I asked.

"The nation is not that grateful, Sergeant Foster. I have been reassigned to Washington where I shall be in command of a magnificent desk . . . undoubtedly in some delightful basement room of the War Department."

The next day I packed my few things, collected my separation pay, and arranged a ride to Washington where I could catch a train north. Before leaving, I borrowed a horse and rode to the cemetery where Abel was buried.

His grave was on a hillside that overlooked rolling Virginia hills. The countryside was still scarred by battles, spread out like a fallen man with deep wounds. But those wounds would heal—heal or be covered over and callused by time. There was a simple white wooden cross on Abel's grave, and I laid some wildflowers I had gathered at its base, then knelt and prayed for the boyhood friend I had loved more than I knew. Tears ran down my cheeks, but I ignored them, let them flow freely, knowing that Abel deserved tears at his gravesite, tears from someone who had loved him in life, something that his death so far away from home had denied him.

"I'm sorry I'm not taking you home with me," I said out loud. "Just as I'm sorry we won't become old men together, sitting in front of the store and telling tall tales of deer hunts and days spent fishing for trout. It's how it should have been." I lowered my head and closed my eyes. "I'll always keep you in my thoughts and my heart, Abel. And I promise you that I'll help Josiah look after little Alva." I reached down and ran my hand along the new grass that covered the grave, stroking it softly. "You were the best of us," I whispered. "You were always the best."

I took the train north to Philadelphia. It was April 14, Good Friday, and the station in Washington was crowded with holiday travelers and discharged soldiers like myself who were finally heading home.

I left the train in Philadelphia and rented a horse and rode north for Solebury. But it proved a wasted journey. When I arrived I was told that Bobby Suggs had left town nearly a month before and headed to parts unknown to look for work. I don't know what I would have done if I had found Suggs. But I knew I wanted to confront him and let him know that his villainy had not been forgotten. Perhaps I would have smashed him into the ground and beaten him until my strength was gone, and settled for that. Perhaps I would have killed him. I suppose it would have depended on what he said. I only knew that there was a deep and simmering rage inside me for both Bobby Suggs and Johnny Harris.

I returned to Philadelphia on Easter Sunday and found everyone I encountered in a state of shock and mourning. I learned that President Lincoln had been shot on Friday evening, only hours after I left Philadelphia for Solebury. A massive manhunt was now underway for Lincoln's assassin, an actor named John Wilkes Booth, and it made me consider that I, too, might well be the subject of another manhunt if I had found Suggs and made him pay for Abel's murder.

I sent a telegram to my father, telling him I was on my way home and when my train would arrive in Richmond. I also asked that he tell no one else about my return, explaining that I wanted time alone with him, time to adjust to being home again.

My train followed the Hudson River, passing through peaceful valleys that had seen nothing of the war, moving by the rising hills of the Catskill Mountains. Throughout the journey I thought of President Lincoln, of the brief encounter I'd had with the man at the field hospital outside Sharpsburg, the tears that had glistened in his eyes as he stroked the cheek of the wounded boy Abel and I were carrying. It was another sad waste in a war that, to me, had been nothing but waste.

We made stops in Poughkeepsie and Albany, and at each place discharged soldiers—many on crutches, many missing arms or legs—were greeted by waiting family and friends. Day became night and I changed trains the next morning at Saratoga and took a spur line across the Hudson and into southern Vermont. It was mid-April and the trees were just blossoming with new growth, giving the Vermont hillsides a renewed hint of pale green. As the train moved north we passed rivers and streams swollen by the snowmelt, and the roads that ran beside the tracks were thick with mud.

We stopped in Rutland and Brandon and Middlebury before moving north again, and suddenly Lake Champlain was just west of the tracks, a wide, shimmering expanse of blue water, beyond which rose the Adirondack Mountains in New York. I moved to the other side of the train and as the forests turned into fields I watched our own mountains appear: Mount Mansfield and Bolton and finally Camel's Hump, the foothills of which I and the people of Jerusalem's Landing called home.

The train stopped in Burlington and then turned east, passing through Winooski and Essex Junction, before finally arriving at the small red building of the railroad station in Richmond. I was exhausted from my journey, and my heart pounded in my chest as if I'd just run a great distance. I took a deep breath to calm myself while my mind raced through memories of all the days and nights I had laid in blood-soaked fields and forests, wondering if I'd ever see my home again.

I climbed down from the train carrying the one bag I'd brought with me and saw my father hurrying toward me, his smile so wide it seemed to cover his entire face.

"Oh God, oh God," he said as he pulled me to him. He stepped back, measured me from head to foot, looked at my missing arm, and then pulled me to him again. "Thank God you're home, son. Thank God Almighty you're home."

Jezebel was saddled and waiting for me outside the station. "I woulda brought the buggy," my father said. "But we never woulda made it with the mud. Kin ya ride okay?"

"Yes sir. I'm still a little clumsy with the arm missing and all. I have to get used to a new sense of balance. But I can ride."

"Does yer arm still hurt ya?"

"There's something the doctors call phantom pain," I explained. "Sometimes I'll feel pain in my hand or wrist or lower arm, where there is no hand or wrist or lower arm. Sometimes the stump hurts or tingles or itches like hell. But the wound is physically healed."

We rode on quietly, my father still smiling, his eyes lively and bright and pleased with the day. "What are ya goin' ta do with yerself, Jubal? Other than take a good, long rest, I mean. Have ya thought 'bout it at all? I mean such as goin' back ta college, somethin' like that?"

"I don't know. I suppose I'll need to find some work I can do for a start."

"Well, I been thinkin' on that. Doc Pierce has been after me ta ease up a bit. Says a galoot my age needs ta cut back iffen he expects ta reach a ripe ol' age. So I been thinkin' it might be good if ya became my deputy an' helped me with bein' constable. I gotta right ta hire a deputy under the town charter, an' it would sure be good ta work alongside each other, at least till ya decided whatcha wanted ta do."

I glanced across at him, wondering if this was some act of charity for his one-armed son, but decided to let it go for now. "I'd be pleased to help you," I said. "After I sleep for a few days . . . or weeks."

He laughed at that, knowing me better. "What about Rebecca? She talks ta me all the time 'bout when ya might be comin' home, 'bout any news I got from ya. Ever' time I see her she's got a question."

"I'll see her. I'll see Mr. and Mrs. Johnson too, to tell them about Abel."

"There's some bad news there," my father said. "A few months back Mrs. Johnson passed on. Fell inna river an' drowned." He hesitated several moments. "Fell, or jumped. Folks have different views 'bout that. Anyways, she never got over Abel dyin'. It hurt her deep down. Awhile back Walter Johnson took hisself a new wife. Lady from up here in Richmond. Lost her first husband in the war, she did. She's a bit younger'n Walter, a lot younger, really. He tol' folks he needed someone ta help with the store an' all. Got tongues a waggin'."

I felt as though I'd been hit in the belly. I had truly liked Mrs. Johnson. In many ways she'd been a mother to me. "I didn't know," I said.

"I guess the letters me an' Rebecca wrote ya never got ta ya afore ya left fer home."

"The mail was always weeks and weeks late, sometimes months. Then they'd all come in a rush." I peered off into the passing forest, thinking of the pain everyone I loved must have felt. "Poor Rebecca. First Abel, then her mother, and now her father finding a new wife."

"It's been hard," my father said. "Be soft with her when ya see her."

It was late evening when we rode through town. We passed by the darkened Johnson store, the only lights coming from their living quarters above it. The church and parsonage were also dark. We rode on the short distance to our home, dismounting outside the barn at the rear of our house. My father took the reigns of both horses and led them inside the barn.

"Go on inta the house, son," he said. "Won't take me but a minute ta tend ta the horses."

"Let me help you," I said. "If I remember right, old Jezebel likes to be combed down a bit while she's getting her water and oats."

We tended to the horses, and after a time my father brought up a question I could tell he'd been waiting to ask.

"Ya din' say anythin' 'bout wantin' ta see Johnny Harris. He never says much 'bout you, neither. There some bad blood goin' on there?"

"About as bad as it gets," I said.

He came around the side of my horse so he could see my face. "How so?"

"It's not something I'm ready to talk about. It will only bring hurt to people who don't deserve to be hurt more than they have been already." I studied my boots, hoping I had not already upset my father. "It's not that I don't trust you. It's just better this way. I hope you can understand."

"Course I do, son. Sometimes a man's gotta keep things inside fer a time. Jus' know that if ya ever feel a need ta talk 'bout it, ya jus' come an' let me know."

The next morning I changed into civilian clothes for the first time in four years. My father helped me pin up the sleeve of my shirt and coat, and dusted off my old Stetson hat and boots. He handed me a constable's badge that matched his own, told me to consider myself sworn in as his deputy.

"There's gonna be a service at church tonight fer President Lincoln," he said. "I reckon folks are gonna be mighty surprised ta see ya."

It was late morning when I gathered the courage to walk down to the Johnsons' store. Walter Johnson and a woman I assumed was his new wife were standing behind the counter. Walter was reading a newspaper and did not look up. The woman smiled at me. "Can I help you?" she asked.

"I'm here to see Mr. Johnson," I said.

At the sound of my voice, Walter Johnson's head snapped up and his eyes looked at me in wide disbelief. Then he hurried around the counter and put his arms around me, almost as fiercely as my father had the previous day. "Jubal, Jubal. Thank God you're home." He choked up momentarily and then turned to the woman behind the counter. "Mary, this is Jubal Foster. He was my boy's best friend. He was with Abel when he . . . when he died. Jubal, this is my wife. I guess you heard about Abel's mother."

"My father told me last night," I said. "I'm very sorry. She was a wonderful woman."

Walter nodded his head, his face suddenly filled with sorrow. "Abel's death was too much for her to bear," he said.

It was an awkward moment, broken when Rebecca rushed into the store. She stopped in her tracks when she saw me, her eyes wide and tearful. "I heard my father call out your name, and I couldn't believe it. And now you're here, standing right in front of me, and I still can't believe it."

"I came home late last night."

She rushed toward me and I stepped back awkwardly, moving the left side of my body away from her. The movement stopped her and she looked at me, confused and hurt. Walter didn't seem to notice and he turned to his new wife.

"Mary, could you watch the store alone fer a spell. I wanna take Jubal upstairs so we kin talk 'bout Abel."

The Johnson living quarters were just as I remembered them. I must have been smiling slightly, because Rebecca asked me what I was thinking about.

"All the time we all spent here when we were children," I said.

"It seems impossible that yer all not here," Walter said. "Have ya seen Johnny yet?"

"No, I haven't." I could hear the cold tone in my voice, and Rebecca appeared to have noticed it as well. Her father had not.

"Kin ya tell us 'bout Abel? he asked. "The army letter didn't say much, 'cept that he died durin' the Battle of the Wilderness in Spotsylvania County in Virginia."

"We were together," I said. "And Josiah Flood was with us. We were crossing a field when we were hit by an artillery barrage. Abel died next to me. His last words were that he wanted to go home to you"—I looked at Walter Johnson—"to his mother"—I turned to Rebecca—"and to you. Your name was the last name he spoke, Rebecca."

I gave them both time to weep and then Walter asked a choking, halting, sobbing question. "Where . . . where is . . . Abel buried?"

"In a military cemetery outside Chancellorsville, Virginia," I said. "I visited his grave before I headed home. It's very beautiful there, overlooking rolling green hills. Now that the war has ended it will become a very peaceful and restful place. I'll draw you a map so you can go and visit him."

"Is that where you were wounded, in the same field where Abel died?" Rebecca asked.

"Yes. The war ended for me there too. Josiah Flood carried me to the hospital. It was too late for Abel. He died in that field."

"Johnny said he was with ya," Walter said.

"Johnny was in a farmhouse about a hundred yards away. He and the men he was with were captured by Rebel troops." I paused, fighting to control my anger. "I'm sure he saw the artillery shells hit our position." I kept my voice cold and flat and emotionless.

Rebecca stared at me, as if she understood there was more that could be said. "Did you get the letter I wrote you about my mother's death?" she asked.

"No. It hadn't arrived before I left for home. I'm very sorry. She was always very kind to me."

"She loved you, Jubal. Just as we all love you," Rebecca said.

* * *

When my father and I entered the church that evening, people I had known all my life rushed up to us. Many of the older women had tears in their eyes as they welcomed me home; many told me how they had prayed for me; almost all looked at my empty sleeve with sadness.

Reverend Harris and his wife came to us before the service started, welcoming me home and explaining that Johnny had gone to visit a friend that evening but would be back later. When he took the pulpit, Reverend Harris began by praising the Lord for my safe return.

The service for President Lincoln had been going on for almost an hour when Mary Johnson arrived and took a seat next to her husband. Walter smiled at her and whispered something in her ear. Rebecca just stared straight ahead as the choir and the congregation began singing "The Battle Hymn of the Republic."

When the service ended I was again surrounded by well-wishers, and while I appreciated their kindnesses I very much wanted to get away and be off by myself. I worked my way to the door as politely as I could and thanked Reverend Harris for the service and for his kind words and finally stepped out into the cool April night. I had only taken a few steps when I heard Johnny's voice.

"Hail the conquering hero."

I turned and saw him leaning up against a maple tree. He seemed thinner than I remembered and his face had a pale, pasty look to it.

I walked up to him and stared into his eyes.

He sneered at me. "Did ya tell all the folks how you an' fat ol' Abel got ta meet President Lincoln at Sharpsburg?"

"No."

"Too bad, they woulda been *mighty* impressed. Jubal, ya look like ya wanna kill yer ol' friend. I know ya tried ta get me stuck in front of a firin' squad." The cold smile returned to his lips. "But that din' work out too good fer ya, did it?" He looked behind me at the people gathering outside the church. "Too many witnesses," he said. "Guess you'll havta wait till later."

"There's no rush," I replied coldly. "No rush at all."

Johnny let out a short, barking laugh and lightly cuffed the stump of my left arm. "Be easier if ya had two arms an' two hands," he said as he stepped by me and headed toward the parsonage.

Johnny was sitting on the front steps of the parsonage when I left my house the next morning. He watched me as I crossed the road and headed toward him; then he stood and walked around the side of the house and back to his barn. I followed him and saw him enter the barn. I walked up to the open door and stopped to allow my eyes to adjust to the change in light. I had put on my sidearm, letting my jacket conceal its presence, and now I pulled back the side of the coat so the Colt was more easily accessible.

"Well, well, the sergeant's got his pistol," Johnny said as I stepped into the barn. We were only six feet apart. There was a rifle leaning up against one of the stalls and Johnny's hand inched toward it. I took two quick steps forward and kicked it out of reach, then hit Johnny as hard as I could, driving him back against the side of the stall.

As he tried to regain his feet I hit him again, then drew the Colt and shoved it up under his chin and cocked the hammer. The two clicks it made sounded like explosions.

"Ya gonna kill me now, Jubal?"

I could hear the quiver of fear in his voice. It seemed to match the shaking of my hand and I drew the Colt back and lowered the hammer. Johnny was drawing a deep breath when I slammed the Colt against the side of his face, knocking him to the ground. Blood ran from a cut above his eye. I leaned down and stared into his face.

"Not yet," I said.

I picked up his rifle and unloaded it and threw it across the barn.

"You see, Johnny, one arm's good enough to handle a piece of dog shit like you."

Five months later, as I was saddling my horse, a recently returned Josiah Flood came and told me that Johnny Harris was dead.

CHAPTER TWENTY-SIX

I took Rebecca for a buggy ride the day after we exhumed Johnny's body. It was a bright, sunny day, the air brisk but carrying none of the winter that would soon be upon us.

Rebecca smiled as I turned into the road that led up to the base of Camel's Hump Mountain. "Are you taking me to that beautiful place— the place where you asked me to marry you?" she asked.

"Yes, I am."

"Why? Are you going to take back your ring?" she teased.

"I can't," I said. "Your father has a gun."

"I'm glad you remembered."

I pulled the buggy to the spot where I had proposed to her only a day earlier. "I need to tell you something," I said.

She looked at me curiously. "What is it?"

"We exhumed Johnny's body last night."

She was startled, trying to get her thoughts around what I had just told her. "W . . . Why?" she asked at length.

"We found the weapon that killed him," I said. "And we had to be sure it fit the wound on his body."

"Did it? Did if fit the wound? Where did you do it, where did you take his body?"

I told her and she shuddered at the thought of it.

"The weapon was an awl," I said. "The blade was covered in

dried blood. Josiah found it and came straight to me."

"How did he know it was blood?"

"Dried blood was something he saw every day for the past four years," I explained. "I took the awl to the university and confirmed that it was human blood, and when Doc reexamined Johnny's body the blade fit perfectly into the wound."

"That's horrible. Don't tell me any more, please."

"There's just one more thing you have to know," I said.

She stared at me, fearlessly.

"The awl was in the barn behind your father's store," I said. "Josiah found it while he was helping your father restock the shelves."

"Wha . . . What?"

I reached out and took her hand. The shock on her face was exactly what I had hoped to see.

"Are you saying someone in my family killed Johnny Harris?" she stammered.

"I'm not saying that. But if people hear that we found the murder weapon in your barn it's certain to create a great deal of suspicion." I paused, giving her time to understand what I was saying. "Did your father know about the relationship between Johnny and his wife?"

She shook her head vehemently. "No, I'm certain he didn't. I suspected there was something between them, but I didn't know for sure until you spoke to her. And I know my father. He's a very straightforward man. If he had known, if he had even suspected, he would have confronted Mary, and if she admitted it he would have gone after Johnny openly."

I could find no argument with her rationale. We were quiet for several moments, then she said, "If it was Mary, and it comes out, it will kill my father. He's lost so much; first Abel, then my mother. This . . . this would be more than he could bear." There was fear in her eyes now.

I picked up the reigns and started Jezebel in motion. "I don't want you to worry about this anymore," I said.

"What are you going to do?"

"When will your father be away from the store again?"

"Tomorrow," she said. "He'll be picking up supplies again."

"I want to talk to Mary."

"You think she killed Johnny, don't you? You think she killed him and hid the awl in our barn."

I very much wanted to ease her fear. "Anyone could have put the awl in your barn," I said. "Anyone at all."

Mary was alone in the store when I got there the following morning. It was ten o'clock. I had watched Walter drive his buckboard north toward Richmond, and then had waited half an hour to make sure he wouldn't return unexpectedly.

Mary gave me a warm smile when I came through the front door, but the smile disappeared when I asked if she could call up to Rebecca and have her take over the store for a short time. "I need to talk to you," I said. "And it's best I do it while Walter is away."

Rebecca came downstairs looking happy to see me, and it made my heart swell to glimpse the pleasure in her eyes. She rose up on her toes and kissed my cheek.

"We won't be long," I said.

"Take all the time you need." I noticed that Rebecca had not looked at Mary when she came downstairs, nor did she now.

"Do you want to go up to the parlor?" Mary asked. She too had consciously avoided making eye contact with her stepdaughter.

"No, I'd like you to go out to the barn with me. I need to show you something there." She seemed initially confused, but she held it in and followed me outside without objection.

I led her into the barn and walked her to the rear corner where Josiah had found the bloodstained awl. I removed it from my jacket pocket and opened the neckerchief in which it was wrapped. Mary gasped when I held it out to her.

"This is the weapon that killed Johnny Harris," I said simply. "We've had the dried blood examined at the university and we exhumed Johnny's body to make sure the blade of the awl fit the wound. All the results were positive, and Doc Pierce is certain that this was the murder weapon."

Mary's hands were trembling and I paused to draw the moment out. Then I stepped up to a box that sat next to the rear wall. "We found the awl behind this box. Someone threw it here to hide it."

"What are you trying to say, Jubal?" Her voice was shaking, and despite the chill in the air there was a visible line of perspiration on her upper lip. "Are you saying you think I hid it here?"

I stared at the earthen floor and toed the dirt with my boot. "I'm not trying to say anything in particular, Mary."

She began to shake uncontrollably. "He was terrible and vile," she blurted out. "He laughed at me, just laughed at me, and then he threatened to tell Walter that he'd been with me. He said he'd have to leave Jerusalem's Landing when he did, but that he planned to do it anyway. He said with him gone, the whole village would turn against me and Walter would throw me out with nothing. He said I'd be lucky if the townspeople didn't take a bucket of tar to me." She was sobbing, no longer able to control herself. I handed her a clean handkerchief and she wiped away some of the tears.

"I asked him what he wanted and he said he didn't want anything. He said I'd already given him what he wanted. Then he laughed at me again and promised me this time I'd get what I deserved. I asked him what he meant and he just laughed again, and told me I knew exactly what he meant. Then he slapped me across the face and he kept doing it. Once, twice, three times, more. Not hard really. It was for humiliation more than pain. We were in the barn and the awl was just there, and I . . . and I . . ." She squeezed the handkerchief between her hands and twisted it fiercely. "Later, after Johnny was dead, Bobby Suggs came to me and told me he knew everything about me." She was babbling now, unable to stop talking. "He said I had to tell him where Johnny had hidden it or *he'd* go to Walter and tell him everything—"

"Hidden what?" I asked, stopping her.

She seemed momentarily confused. "I thought I'd told you. It was why Johnny was afraid of him—why he thought he might have to kill Bobby."

"Slow down and tell me," I said.

"I'm sorry," she said. She took a deep breath and continued: "Johnny told me that he had something he'd brought home from the war and that half of it belonged to Bobby Suggs. But he said he had no intention of giving him his share, and that he'd told Bobby that. He said they argued and that Bobby had threatened to kill him, and that he'd had to use his gun, had to stick it in Bobby's face to drive him off. But he knew Bobby would be back. He said it was only a matter of time before he came after him, and when he did he wouldn't have any choice. He'd have to kill him."

"What was it that he had?" I asked.

"I don't know," Mary said. "Johnny wouldn't tell me. But he said he'd be able to live off it for a long time, maybe even use it as a stake to head out west."

"Did he tell you where it was?"

"No. He said the only people besides him who could find it were you and Abel. He said it was hidden in a place only you three knew about, a place the three of you had built when you were younger. Then he laughed and said that since Abel was dead you were the only one who would know where it was, but that you were too thick-headed to figure it out." She stared at me for a long time, her eyes begging me to understand. "Jubal, Johnny was a terrible man. Everybody tells me what a wonderful boy he was, but he wasn't like that anymore. He was cruel and vicious and hateful and he enjoyed hurting people. And I think Bobby Suggs is maybe even worse."

"I know," I said. "I know what Johnny was like, what Suggs is still like. On the day Abel died I saw them shoot down a man and his wife. They weren't armed, they were just proud and defiant, and Johnny and Suggs never gave them a chance; they just murdered them where they stood."

I felt no pity for the woman. Whatever happened to her she had brought upon herself, just as Johnny had brought about his own death. But in Mary's case being a fool didn't warrant the destruction of her life. And it was certainly no reason to bring pain to Rebecca or her father. I studied the earthen floor again, then took Mary's elbow and led her back toward the store. "Johnny would have killed you without giving it a thought," I said. "Consider yourself lucky he didn't." I held her eyes again. "Bobby Suggs would do the same. Stay clear of him."

When we reached the back door she stopped me and stared up into my face. "What's going to happen to me? What are you going to do?"

"Nothing's going to happen," I said. I saw relief course through her, and it angered me. My mind took me back to the night I told the Harris's that their son was dead; how Mary had accompanied her husband to help ease their pain, help them through that terrible night, and I recalled how Mary's hands had trembled violently as she reached out to Johnny's mother. Now she reached for the door and I took her arm and turned her back so we faced each other again. "Nothing is going to happen to you, unless you do something to hurt Walter or Rebecca," I said. "Or if you say anything that hurts Reverend Harris or his wife. If any of those things happen, you'll regret the day you met me, and you'll wish to God you had never heard of Jerusalem's Landing."

The next morning I headed for Billy Lucie's woodlot. I had asked Josiah to ride with me and to bring his rifle along.

The work crew had just gotten out of bed and was having their morning coffee when we rode up to their campfire. Suggs was sitting on the bunkhouse steps and he glared at us, but said nothing. I dismounted and walked over to him, and without warning, reached out, grabbed the collar of his shirt, and yanked him to his feet. Josiah angled his horse so his rifle took in the entire work crew.

"What the hell are ya grabbin' me fer?" Suggs yelled.

"I'm about to lock your sorry ass up for the murder of Johnny Harris," I said. I shoved him as hard as I could and sent him staggering across the dooryard of the bunkhouse.

"I din' kill nobody," he snarled.

"Really?" I leaned in close so the other loggers wouldn't hear me. "I seem to remember a farmhouse in Virginia where you and Johnny Harris slaughtered a man and his wife."

"That was the war!" Bobby shouted.

"The war. Oh, I see, it was the war. That's where unarmed civilians were fair game. That's the place where you could gun down a man and his wife because they wouldn't give you the key to the cashbox you and Johnny stole from their house. Abel and Josiah and I watched you do it, and if that artillery barrage hadn't started we would have blown your ass to hell right then and there."

"Ya tried ta git the army ta arress' me on that, an' they tol' ya ta forget it; they tol' ya there wasn't no evidence. It was jus' yer word and that nigger's word agin' Johnny's and mine."

Josiah raised the barrel of his rifle and smiled down at Suggs. "Ya call me a nigger one more time an' ya ain't gonna have ta worry 'bout Jubal arrestin' ya. The only thing ya'll havta worry 'bout is what hole yer bones is gonna rot in."

"Ya gonna let that . . . that sumbitch talk ta me like that?"

"I'm going to let him talk to you any way he wants. And you take one step out of line and I'm going to let him shoot you any *place* he wants. And if he misses, I'll shoot you myself."

"I won't miss, Jubal. I sure won't miss this piece a sorry white trash."

I heard a voice call out and watched Billy Lucie ride across the clear-cut. When he reached the campfire he dismounted, handed the horse's reigns to one of his men, and walked toward me. "Looks like maybe I'm gonna be shorthanded a man fer the day," he said.

"I'm afraid so," I replied. "He'll be packing up his things and coming with me. Does he have any weapons in the bunkhouse?"

"Ain't supposed ta," Billy said. "But I can't guarantee it." He raised his chin toward Suggs. "He's wearin' a knife on his belt."

I nodded. "Not for long. His horse still in your barn?"

Billy said it was. "An' his pistol should be in his saddlebags," he added.

"Will you collect his horse?" I asked Josiah. "And see if his pistol is there."

Josiah nodded and rode off.

I turned back to Suggs. "Throw the knife on the ground." My hand was on the butt of my pistol for emphasis.

Suggs did as he was told and I picked it up and pointed the blade at the bunkhouse. "Let's go pack up your stuff," I said.

When we were alone in the bunkhouse, Suggs turned to me "I din' kill Johnny," he said. "An' tha's the truth."

"I don't care who killed him. I just want someone to hang for it. And you've been elected."

"Wait." He held up his hands, palms facing me as though he were warding me off. "There's some money to be made cheer. A lotta money."

"Tell me about it," I said.

"Ya was talkin' 'bout that cashbox, the one me an' Johnny took from the farmhouse in Spotsylvania."

"That's right."

"Well, the only reason we went there was that we heard those folks had a big poke stashed away. Had it since afore the war started. We found it sure enough. All it took was puttin' a gun ta the man's head an' that woman opened up right quick. But when we found it the man wouldn't give us the key, an' we wanted ta be sure we got us the right cashbox. So I shot him in the leg, figgerin' the woman would come ta her senses. But then Johnny panicked an' shot her too. Killed her right where she stood, so I had ta kill the man, an' we ended up blastin' the lock off the box when that artillery barrage started up. An' jus' like we'd been tol', it was stuffed with money, and not that Confederate kind, but real money from afore the war started. An' they was big bills, hun'reds mostly. There hadda been $10,000 in there."

"Why didn't the Rebs take it when you were captured?"

Suggs grinned at me with yellowed teeth. "Cause I was too smart an' too quick fer 'em." He jabbed a finger into his chest. "Me, not Johnny. I buried that cashbox while Johnny was takin' cover in the farmhouse. He laid there under a kitchen table an' watched me do it. I figgered Johnny an' me, we'd come back after we got away from the Rebs. See, I wasn't gonna cheat him like he cheated me. But it din' matter, cause we din' git away. We ended up in Andersonville Prison instead."

"And when you were freed Johnny beat you back to the farmhouse and took the money for himself."

"Tha's right. We were moved to other prisons when Sherman's army got close, an' the one Johnny was in got overrun first. He was gone a good five days afore I even started out, an' by the time I got ta that farmhouse the only thing there was an empty cashbox all buried back up with a little note inside it that said I shoulda been quicker. I found out later that Johnny had already been discharged an' was headed home."

"So you followed him."

"After a spell. I went on home first but the more I stewed on it the madder I got, an' I decided that I was gonna travel up cheer an' git what was comin' ta me."

"And now you will," I said.

"Will what?"

"Get what's coming to you."

"Now jus' you wait a damn minute. I'm sayin' I'll share it with ya. The part that was supposed ta be Johnny's is all yers. All ya gotta do is let me take mine. Soon as I got it I'll hightail it outta here an' you'll never see my sorry self agin."

"But you don't know where the money is," I said. "If you did you'd already have taken it and run off."

"Tha's right, I don't know where it is. But you do. Johnny tol' me that hisself. He said the money was hidden in a place that you an' him an' Abel built when you was kids. I figgered it was some kinda clubhouse, or tree house, or somethin', an' I thought maybe he tol' that bitch that runs the store, the one he was givin' it to ever' time her husband looked t'other way. But if she knowed, I couldn't git her ta talk. I knew Johnny was gonna run her off, an' I figgered I'd wait a spell, then threaten ta tell her husband 'bout her an' Johnny if she din' fess up an' tell me what she knowed." His face suddenly soured. "But first I was gonna grab Johnny an' tie him up an' do a little persuadin' wit my knife ta git him ta tell me hisself, but I never got the chance. So I was jus' bidin' my time, waitin' ta go back ta that store lady."

"And now you figure you'll take me on as a partner."

He shrugged. "Money's money, an' we all kin sure use a nice little pile of it."

"But if I know where it is, why should I share it with you?"

He smiled at me. "Cause as soon as ya lock me up in that sheriff's jail, I'm gonna start off talkin' 'bout the pile a money Johnny came home with, an' how ya know half of it's mine, an' how ya got me locked up so's ya kin steal it fer yerself."

"What makes you think I want your damned money?"

"Shit, what man don' wanna big pile a money."

"Then why don't I just shoot you and go and get it?"

He showed me his yellow teeth again. "Cause you ain't no killer, Jubal. Oh, ya killed yerself plenty, but only cause ya had ta. The war taught some that killin' was killin' no matter what the reason. An' it taught us that killin' wasn't all that bad, that it was even good if it kept ya alive, an' better still if it could put somethin' in yer pockets. Johnny, he learned that real quick."

At that moment Josiah rode up to the bunkhouse with Bobby's horse trailing behind his own. He tied them up and came inside, rifle in hand, Suggs's saddlebags in his free hand.

"You find his pistol?" I asked.

He opened the saddlebag and withdrew a Navy Colt. I took it and stuck it in my belt. "Give him the saddlebags. He should be able to fit all his stuff in there and the carpetbag that's under his bunk."

Josiah walked over to the bunk and pulled out the carpetbag. "I better check this," he said. "Just ta make sure he ain't got another weapon stashed inside."

I watched him rummage through the bag until he finally pulled out a second knife. He stuck that one in his belt.

"All right, Suggs, pack on up and we'll head back to town," I said.

"Ya gonna arress' me or not," he demanded.

"We'll talk that over when we get there."

Suggs grinned at me.

"Hurry up," I snapped.

I went out on the porch with Josiah, took him aside, and spoke to him quietly.

"Tha's whatcha want?" he asked.

"That's what I want."

We rode on into town with my horse on Suggs's right and Josiah one length behind, his rifle lying across his lap. Suggs glanced back at him occasionally, but otherwise paid him little mind, certain I would let nothing happen to him until I had located the money.

When we got back to my house I put up Jezebel and tied Suggs's horse to a post. Then I thanked Josiah for his time and took Suggs inside. "You figgered out where the money is?" he asked as he dropped into a kitchen chair.

"I know where it is," I said. "It's several hundred yards up the ridge that runs behind the church. When we were kids we built a hunting blind up there, a very elaborate one made of large rocks and heavy timber, built to survive our winters. It's still there to this day."

"Well, why don't we go on up there an' git it," he said. "The sooner I'm outta this place the better I'll like it." He let out a soft laugh. "'Specially if I leave with my poke full a greenbacks."

"And the happier I'll be to see you gone," I said.

I stayed behind Suggs as we climbed the ridge, forcing him to speak to me over his shoulder. He was carrying the shovel I'd given him and I wanted to stay well out of its reach.

"Whatcha gonna do wit yer share?" he asked when we were halfway up the ridge. "I hear yer marryin' Abel's sister, that pretty lil' gal over ta the store. Oughtta have enough ta build her a nice house an' fix her up wit a fancy buggy. Them ladies sure do like a fancy buggy."

"What do you care what I do with the money, Suggs?"

"Jus' curious, tha's all. Me, I'm gonna head west, maybe find me a town that needs itself a nice saloon. Always thought I'd make a good biznessman, an' sellin' whiskey don't seem like a hard way ta make a livin'. Maybe put a few whores upstairs ta keep the customers happy." He let out a cackle. "Keep me happy too."

We reached the level area on the ridge where the blind stood. Suggs stopped and let his eyes roam the various outcroppings as if he were checking the area for wildlife. "Ya git many deer offen this ridge?" he asked.

"Some years yes; some years no. There's a stream up ahead that they water at, and there are two runways that they follow to move up and down the ridge. If you didn't give yourself away you had a chance."

"Sounds pretty much like a turkey shoot."

"You ever hunt deer, Suggs?"

"Naw. Never wanted ta freeze my ass off jus' fer a bit a meat."

"I didn't think so."

"Why's 'at?"

"Because deer hunting is never a turkey shoot," I said. "No matter how hard you scout them, no matter how smart you think you are, most days they leave you talking to yourself."

We walked to the blind and I circled it slowly. Fallen leaves had left a thick carpet on all sides and I directed Suggs to clear them away.

"Find a place that somebody's put a spade to in the last few months and start digging there," I said.

When all the leaves were removed we located an area near a large rock where the earth had been disturbed. Suggs started digging and when he was two feet down he hit something solid.

"Sounds like Johnny put the money in a new box," he said as he began to clear the area around a bit of black metal that showed through the dirt. Within five minutes he had uncovered a square metal box and pulled it free. There was no lock and he yanked back the lid and exposed a dozen stacks of currency. "Hallelujah!" he called out. "Bobby gives, Johnny takes it away, and then Bobby comes along and grabs it all back agin. It's almos' like readin' the Bible, ain't it?"

I placed my hand on the butt of my Colt. "Step back from the box," I said.

"What the hell ya mean? I jus' want my half an' I'll be headed on down this here ridge an' on my way west."

"I don't think so," I said. "I think you've got a date with a six-foot drop at the end of a rope."

Bobby stared at me, eyes wide and wild. "Ya think it's yers. Ya think yer gonna take it all fer yerself. I tol' ya, I din' kill Johnny Harris an' I ain't gonna hang fer it."

"I told you once, Suggs. I don't care if you killed Johnny or not. You killed Abel, you and Johnny both, just as sure as if you'd fired that howitzer shell yourselves. And you killed the people this money belonged to. You shot them down in cold blood and Johnny helped you do it. I tried to get the army to make you both pay for those murders, but the politics of it didn't fit their plan. Now Johnny's paid for what he did. And I don't care who killed him. He got just what he deserved, and it doesn't matter a good goddamn who the executioner was, just like it doesn't matter whether you swing for Johnny's murder or stand in front of a firing squad for killing Abel and those people in Spotsylvania County. Either way the books will be cleared."

I reached for my pistol and Suggs let out a roar and leaped forward, catching me off-guard as he swung the shovel in a wide arc. The shovel hit me on the shoulder and then glanced off the side of my head and I fell backward, stunned, my Colt only halfway out of its holster. Suggs reached down and snatched it from my hand, stood over me, and pulled the hammer back.

He started to laugh. "Well, ain't this nice. So all I gotta do is put one right through yer head, and then dig me a nice new grave."

I stared up at him as he raised my Colt, then watched as a hole the size of a small fist appeared in his throat, followed by the sound of the shot. Bobby's hands went to his ruined throat as blood gushed from the wound. He tried to level the Colt again, his hand waving back and forth. Then a second exit wound appeared in his chest and he pitched forward and fell facedown in the bed of leaves to my right.

I struggled to my feet, still dizzy, and looked down at the wounds in the center of Suggs's back and his neck. Then I glanced at the ridge and saw Josiah making his way down.

"You okay, Jubal?"

"I'm fine. Better since I thought to put you up on that ridge."

"Jus' like deer season," he said. "'Cept this time we was huntin' skunk."

I picked up the money box and held it out to him. "This is what it was all about," I said.

"Whatcha gonna do with it?"

"Next spring, right after Rebecca and I get married, I'm going to take her to Virginia to visit Abel's grave. While I'm there I'll find the relatives of the people Suggs and Johnny killed. I figure it's their money." I extended the box toward him again. "I don't think they'll miss it if you take some for yourself," I said. "Sort of a reparation payment for Jemma and Alva."

Josiah thought that over and shook his head. "It's bad money," he said. "It ain't no good ta start a life on bad money."

"You're a wise man, Josiah." I looked down at Bobby Suggs. "Let's go get Doc Pierce, so he can pronounce this son of a bitch dead."

EPILOGUE

Rebecca knelt before Abel's grave and wept.

It was a beautiful spring day, the skies clear and blue, birds flying from tree to tree, a gentle breeze blowing across the hilltop, brushing against our faces like the fingers of angels.

I gazed out across the valley. It was hard to believe that men had fought here, slaughtering each other by the thousands; that cities and villages had been destroyed, burned to the ground; that people's lives and fortunes had been lost in numbers too vast to even imagine, and all over questions the answers to which now seemed so obvious.

Newspapers both North and South had called it a grand and glorious struggle—a *good war* that had to be fought. As I watched Rebecca's shoulders heave in sorrow I knew those newspapers were wrong, and as I looked down at Abel's grave I understood that this *good war* had to some degree destroyed us all. Three boys grew up in our beautiful, peaceful village, and then they marched off to war. Four years later, one came back a cripple, one came back a monster, and one did not come back at all.

Rebecca stood and wiped away her tears. "Thank you for bringing me here, Jubal. You're a good husband and a good friend."

I slipped my arm around her and drew her to my chest. "I hope Abel is someplace where he can see us standing here," I said. "It would greatly please him to know how much he was loved."

A sudden breeze brushed against us, and I took it as a sign that my old friend had heard me.

Rebecca glanced up at me and smiled. "Are we going to that farmhouse now?" she asked.

I turned to Johnny's black metal box that now sat on the seat of our buggy. "Yes," I said. "We're going there now."

Kase-san and Yamada 1

story & art by Hiromi Takashima

CONTENTS

Kase-san and Pinks

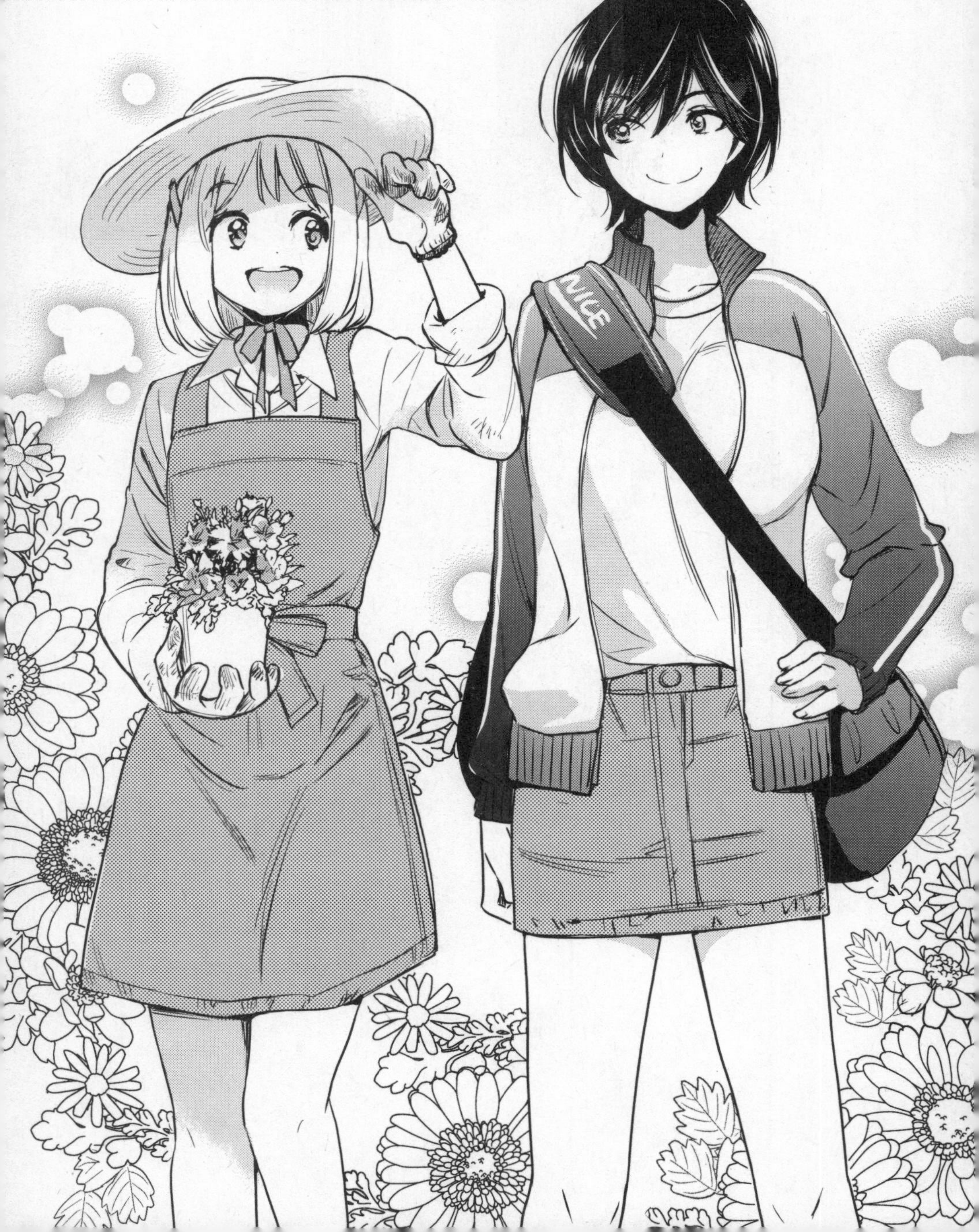
NICE

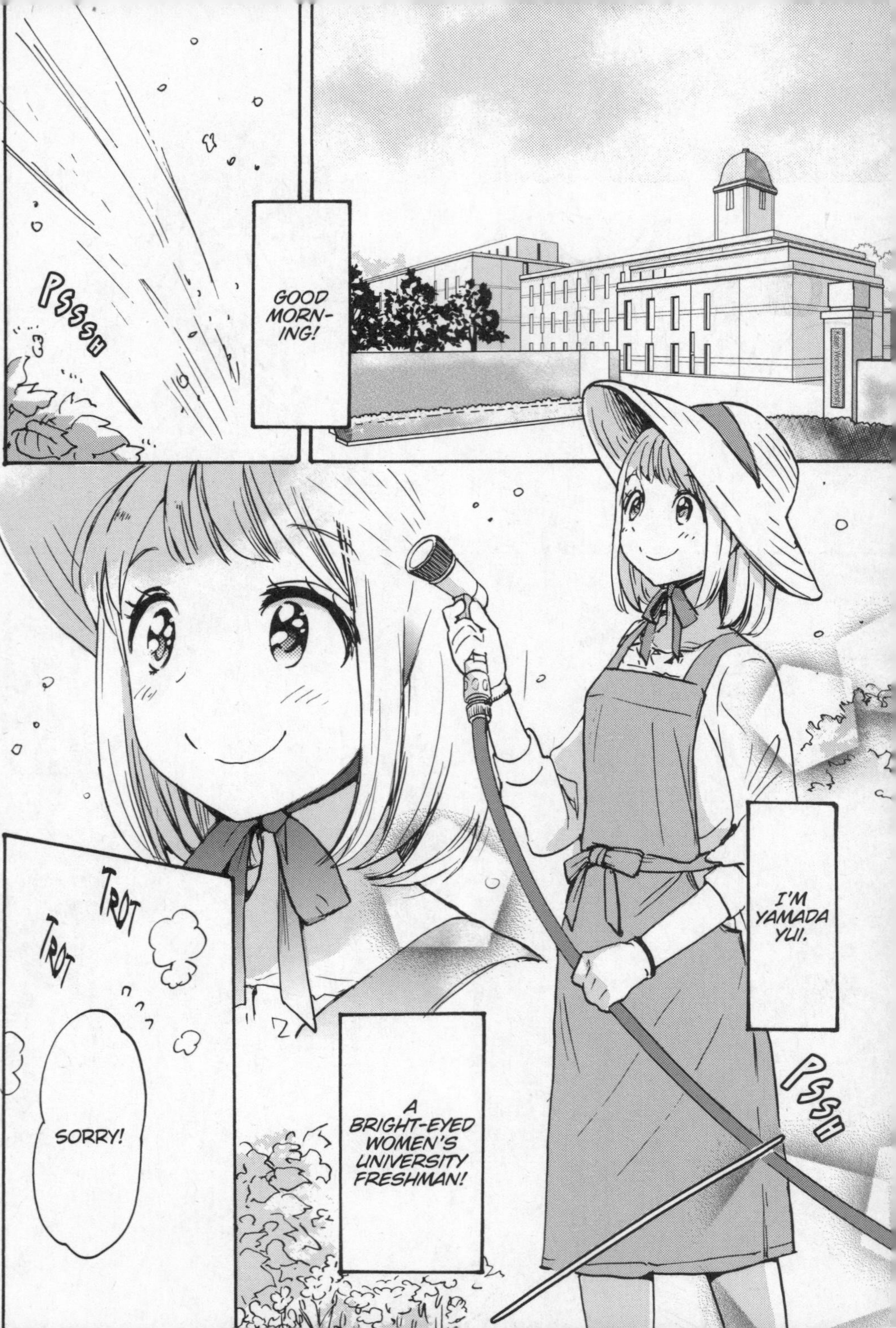
GOOD MORNING!
PSSSH
I'M YAMADA YUI.
PSSH
A BRIGHT-EYED WOMEN'S UNIVERSITY FRESHMAN!
TROT TROT
SORRY!

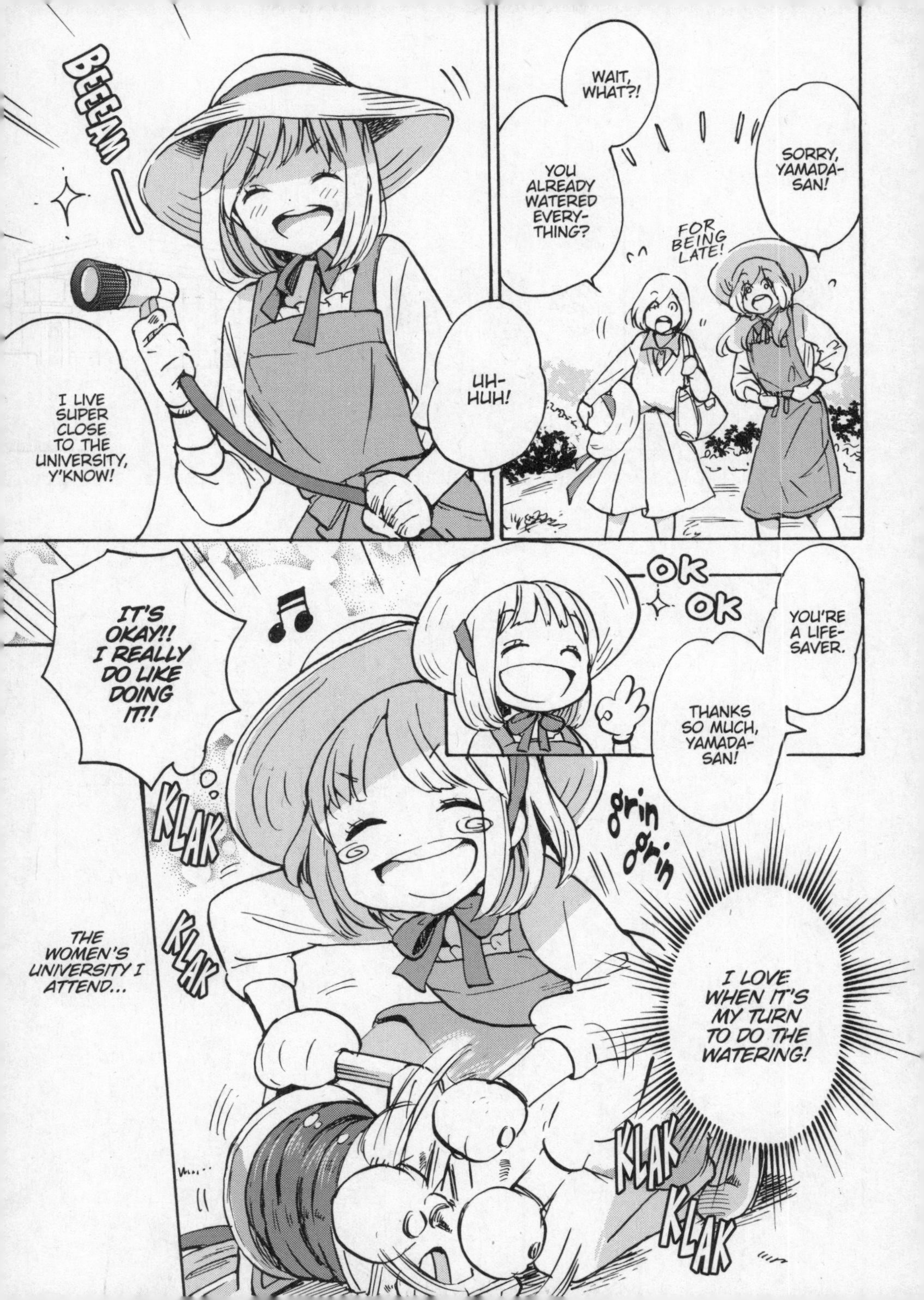

WAIT, WHAT?!
SORRY, YAMADA-SAN!
FOR BEING LATE!
YOU ALREADY WATERED EVERYTHING?
BEEEAM
UH-HUH!
I LIVE SUPER CLOSE TO THE UNIVERSITY, Y'KNOW!
YOU'RE A LIFE-SAVER.
THANKS SO MUCH, YAMADA-SAN!
OK OK
IT'S OKAY!! I REALLY DO LIKE DOING IT!!
grin grin
I LOVE WHEN IT'S MY TURN TO DO THE WATERING!
KLAK KLAK
THE WOMEN'S UNIVERSITY I ATTEND...
KLAK KLAK

AND SO EVERY DAY, WE WORK HARD AND GET A LOT OF HANDS-ON EXPERIENCE WITH FARM WORK AND GARDENING.

THERE ARE SEVERAL GARDENS AND ANNEX FARMS ON CAMPUS...

HAS A HORTICULTURE DEPARTMENT.

IT'S THE BEST!

I LEFT MY SMALL HOMETOWN TO COME STUDY HORTI-CULTURE.

I'M GONNA GIVE IT MY ALL AGAIN TODAY!

Woo!

※ She's on the outskirts of Tokyo, though.

TOKYO!

I THOUGHT IT WAS THIS BIG SCARY PLACE, BUT I'M TOTALLY OKAY WITH THIS!

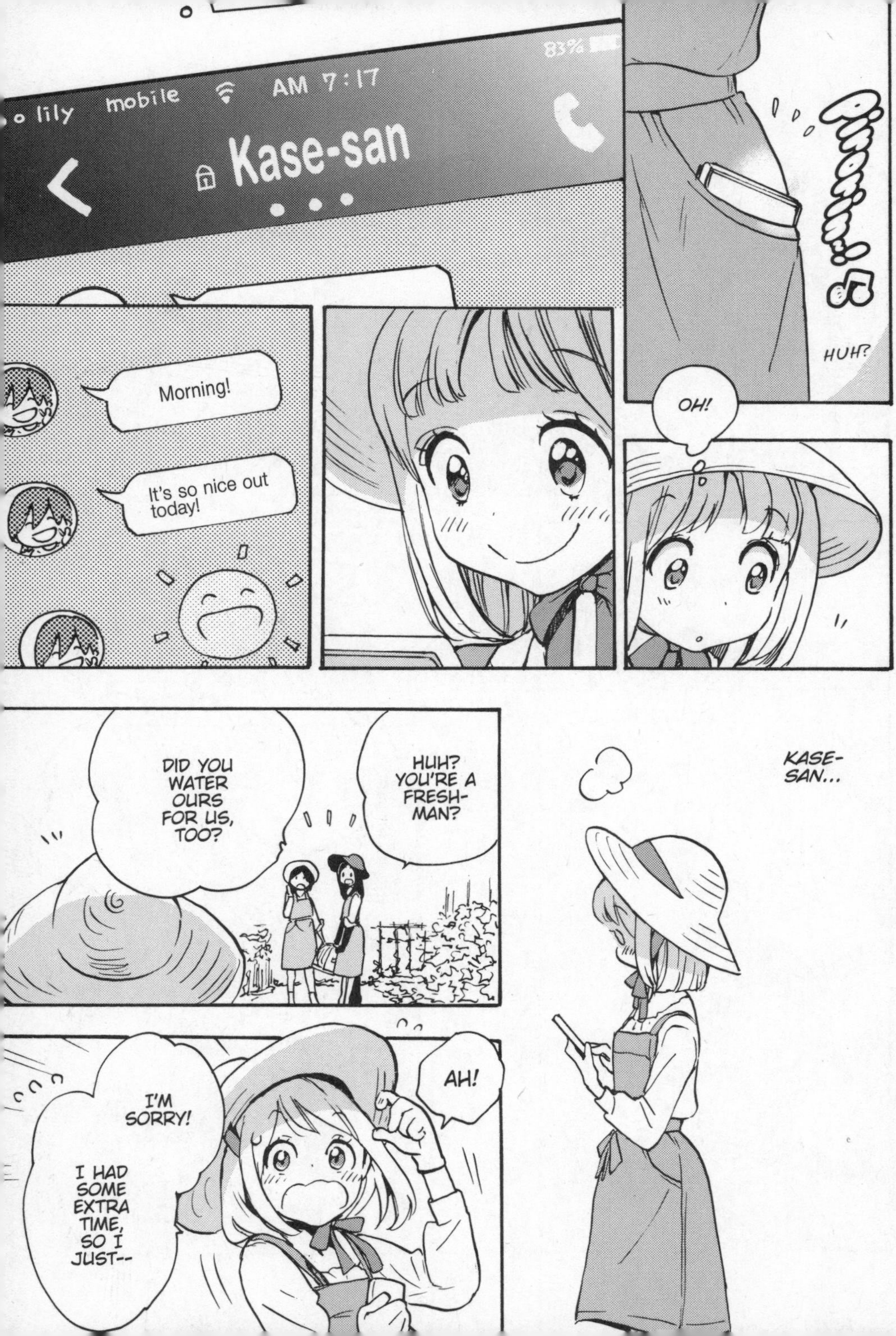
Pirorin!! ♫
HUH?
83%
lily mobile
AM 7:17
Kase-san
OH!
Morning!
It's so nice out today!
KASE-SAN...
HUH? YOU'RE A FRESHMAN?
DID YOU WATER OURS FOR US, TOO?
AH!
I'M SORRY!
I HAD SOME EXTRA TIME, SO I JUST--

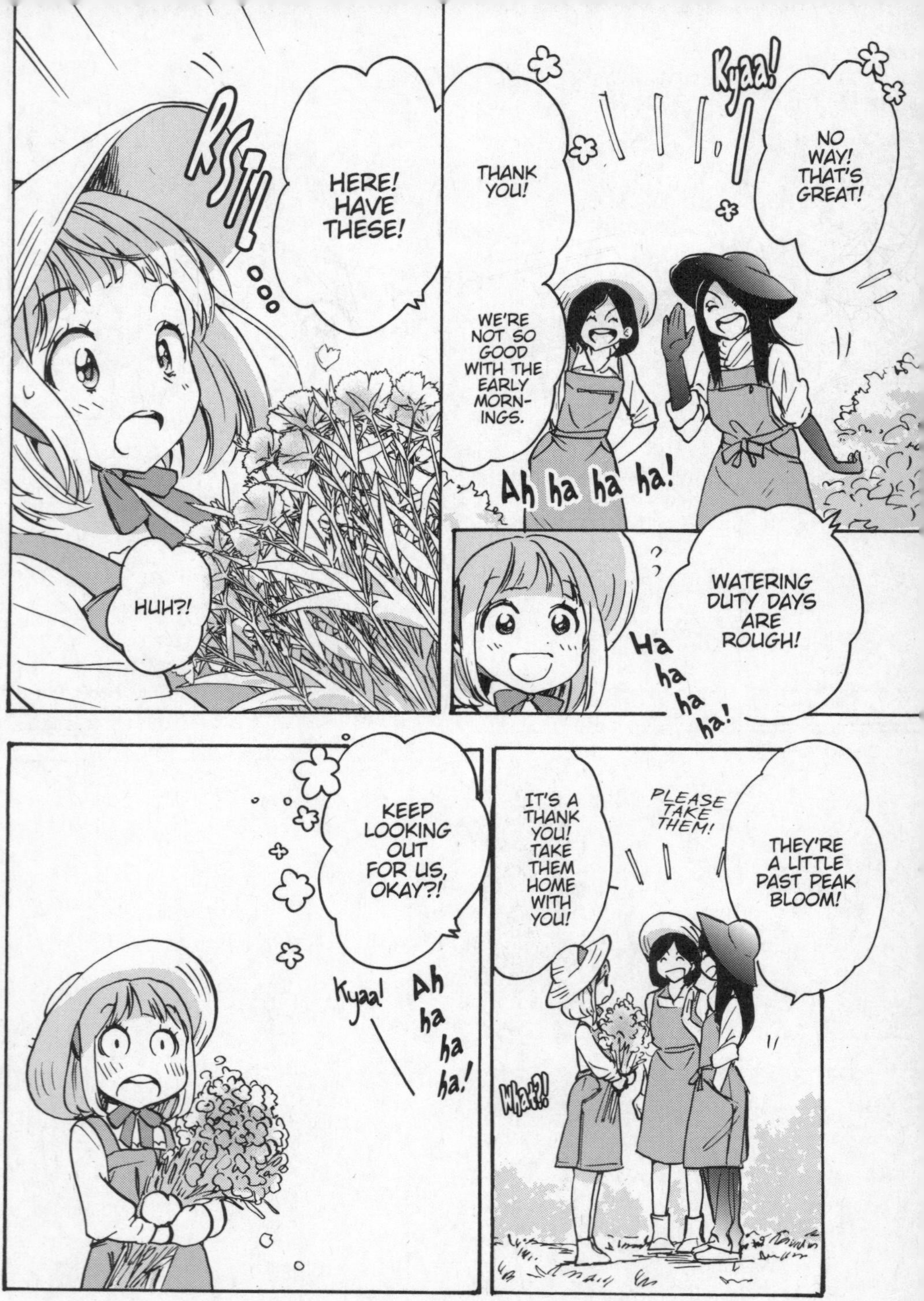
Kyaa!
NO WAY! THAT'S GREAT!
THANK YOU!
WE'RE NOT SO GOOD WITH THE EARLY MORNINGS.
Ah ha ha ha!
WATERING DUTY DAYS ARE ROUGH!
Ha ha ha ha!
RSTL
HERE! HAVE THESE!
OOO
HUH?!
THEY'RE A LITTLE PAST PEAK BLOOM!
PLEASE TAKE THEM!
IT'S A THANK YOU! TAKE THEM HOME WITH YOU!
What?!
KEEP LOOKING OUT FOR US, OKAY?!
Kyaa!
Ah ha ha ha!

PINKS...

"MORNING, KASE-SAN! IT'S REALLY NICE OUT TODAY!"

"THE FLOWERS ARE SO PRETTY!"

PAST SEVEN ALREADY, HUH...?

Snap

THERE'S A TON OF PEOPLE THOUGH

TOKYO'S AMAZING, TOTALLY DIFFERENT FROM HOME.

THE TRAINS COME RIGHT AWAY.

I CAN GET TO KASE-SAN'S UNIVERSITY IN ABOUT FIFTY MINUTES...

WITH A CHANGE OF TRAINS.

YOU CAN GET ANYWHERE YOU WANT IN NO TIME.

↗

EXIT

NIKKYO SPORTS UNIVERSITY

GYMNASIUM

SETAGAYA-DORI

NIKKYO SPORTS UNIVERSITY

'SUUUR!

'SUP!

scary!!

SO MANY PEOPLE IN TRACK SUITS!!

MY FIRST TIME AT THE SPORTS UNIVER-SITY!!

WHOA!

KASE-SAN HAS MORNING TRACK PRACTICE UNTIL EIGHT.

THAT NO MATTER HOW MANY PEOPLE IN TRACK SUITS THERE ARE...

I'LL BE ABLE TO PICK HER OUT RIGHT AWAY.

I'M CONFIDENT...

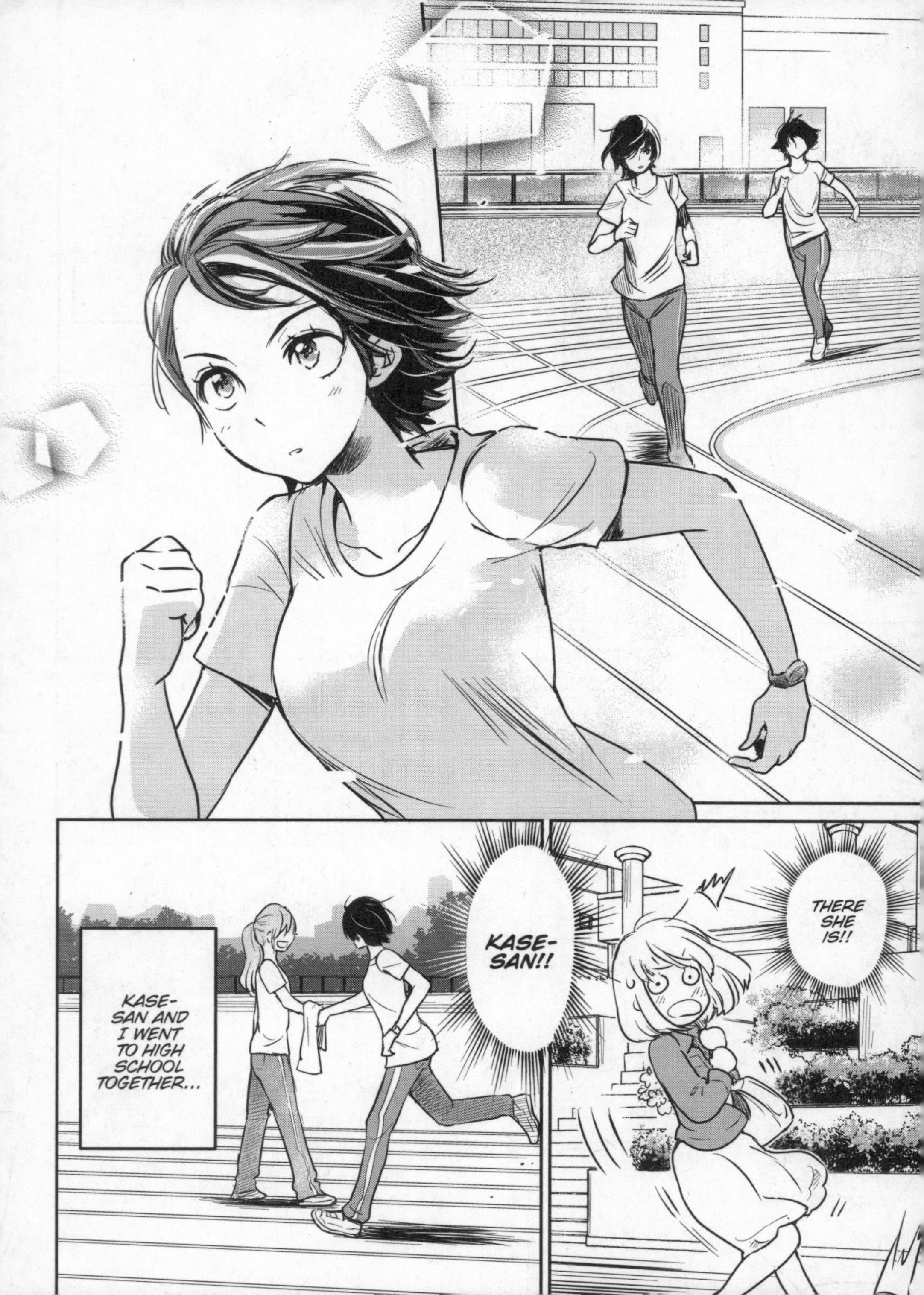
THERE SHE IS!!
KASE-SAN!!
KASE-SAN AND I WENT TO HIGH SCHOOL TOGETHER...

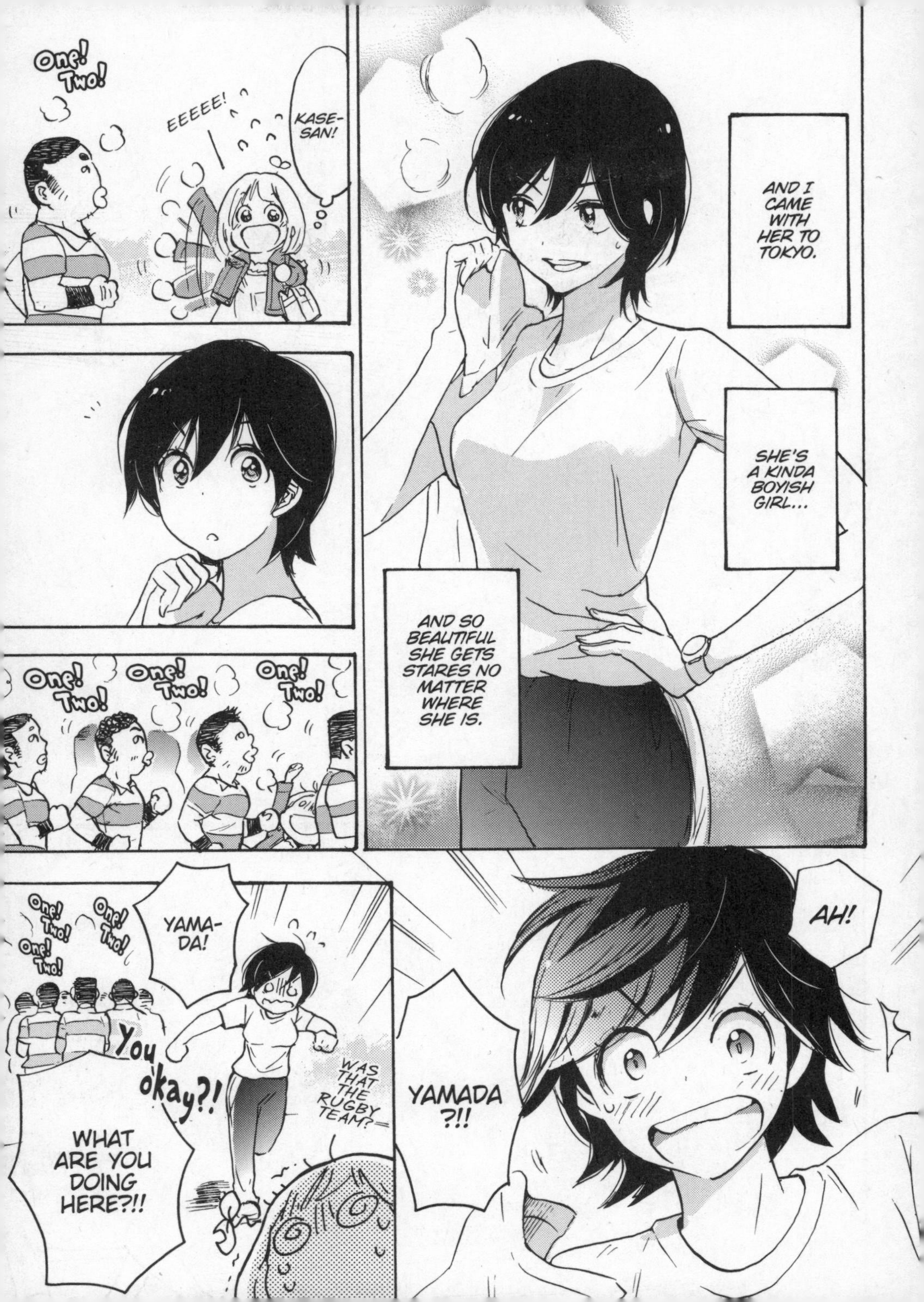
AND I CAME WITH HER TO TOKYO.
SHE'S A KINDA BOYISH GIRL...
AND SO BEAUTIFUL SHE GETS STARES NO MATTER WHERE SHE IS.
KASE-SAN!
EEEEE!
One! Two!
One! Two!
One! Two!
One! Two!
AH!
YAMADA?!!
WAS THAT THE RUGBY TEAM?
YAMADA!
You okay?!
WHAT ARE YOU DOING HERE?!!
One! Two!
One! Two!
One! Two!

THESE ARE FOR YOU!

M-MORNING, KASE-SAN.

HERE!

THANKS FOR YOUR LINE MESSAGE.

ばさ
RUSTLE

HUH?

AREN'T THEY PRETTY?

PINKS!

DECORATE YOUR DORM ROOM!

I WAS GOING TO SEND YOU A PICTURE, BUT THEN I FIGURED I COULD JUST BRING THEM TO YOU.

TH...

THANKS...

I GOT A TON OF THEM IN THE GARDEN EARLIER.

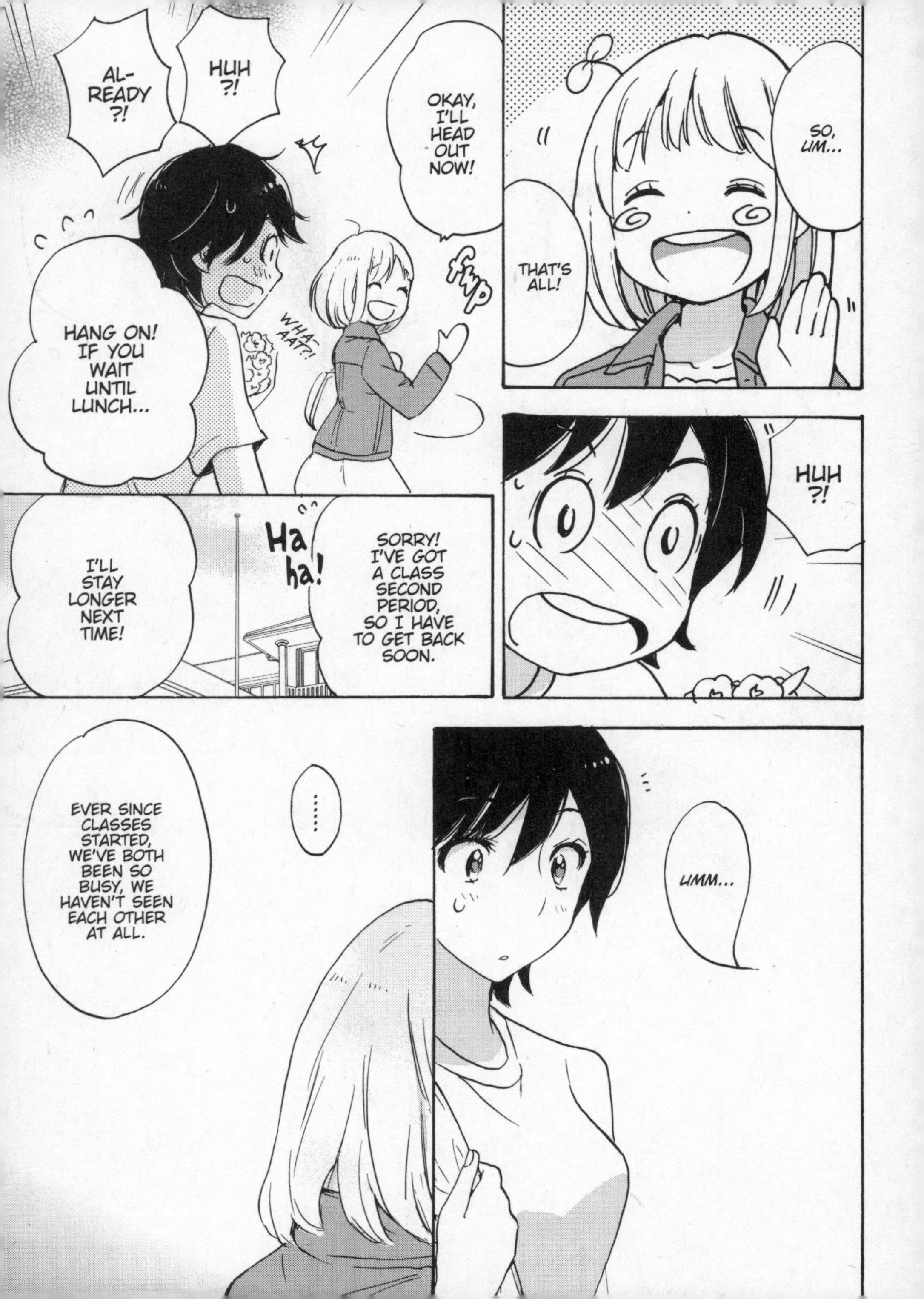
SO, UM...
THAT'S ALL!
OKAY, I'LL HEAD OUT NOW!
fwp
HUH?!
AL-READY?!
WHA-AAT?!
HANG ON! IF YOU WAIT UNTIL LUNCH...
HUH?!
SORRY! I'VE GOT A CLASS SECOND PERIOD, SO I HAVE TO GET BACK SOON.
Ha ha!
I'LL STAY LONGER NEXT TIME!
UMM...
......
EVER SINCE CLASSES STARTED, WE'VE BOTH BEEN SO BUSY, WE HAVEN'T SEEN EACH OTHER AT ALL.

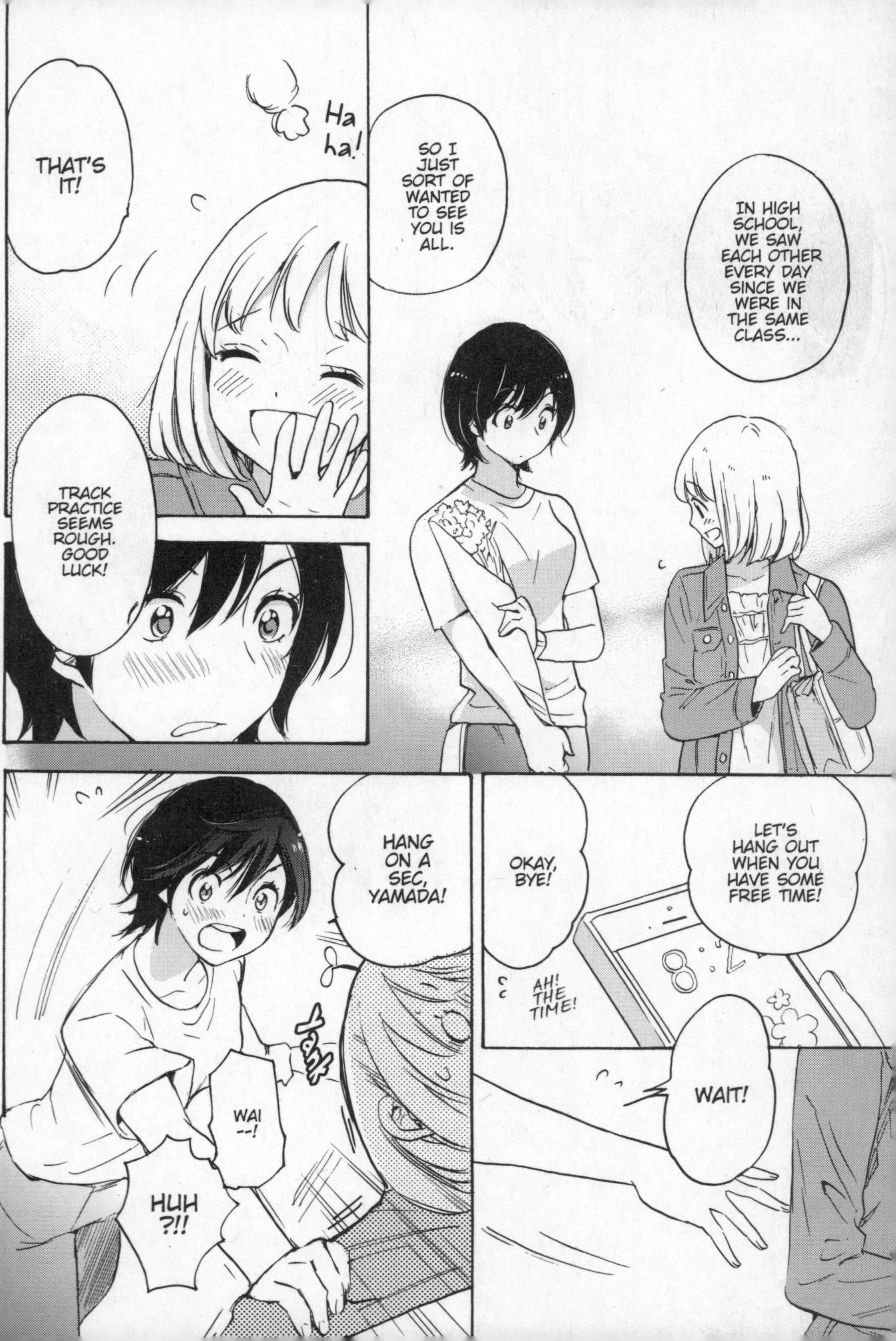
IN HIGH SCHOOL, WE SAW EACH OTHER EVERY DAY SINCE WE WERE IN THE SAME CLASS...
SO I JUST SORT OF WANTED TO SEE YOU IS ALL.
Ha ha!
THAT'S IT!
TRACK PRACTICE SEEMS ROUGH. GOOD LUCK!
LET'S HANG OUT WHEN YOU HAVE SOME FREE TIME!
OKAY, BYE!
AH! THE TIME!
WAIT!
HANG ON A SEC, YAMADA!
Yank
WAI--!
HUH?!!

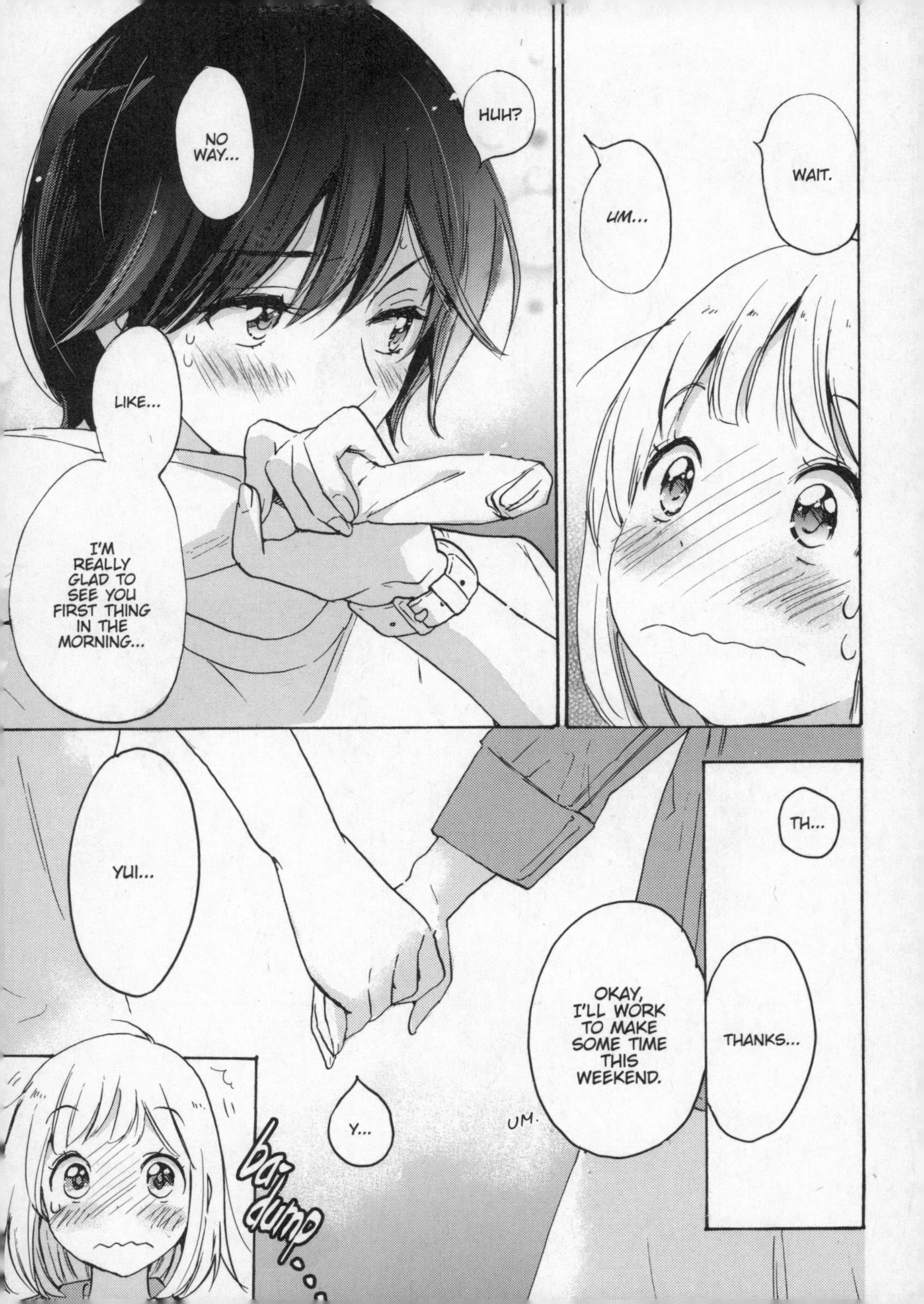
WAIT.
UM...
HUH?
NO WAY...
LIKE...
I'M REALLY GLAD TO SEE YOU FIRST THING IN THE MORNING...
TH...
THANKS...
OKAY, I'LL WORK TO MAKE SOME TIME THIS WEEKEND.
UM.
YUI...
Y...
ba-dump

HUH?

YAMADA'S OKAY, OKAY?

BUT...

THE WAY WE'VE BEEN IS OKAY, YOU KNOW? KASE-SAN...

YAMADA'S FINE, OKAY?

IT'S KINDA EMBARRASSING TO SUDDENLY BE CALLED BY MY FIRST NAME!

HUH?

AH!

YAMADA IS FINE, YOU KNOW?

shake shake

ttch ttch!

THANKS FOR THE FLOWERS.

SEE YOU THIS WEEKEND?

ttch!

GOT IT, YAMADA.

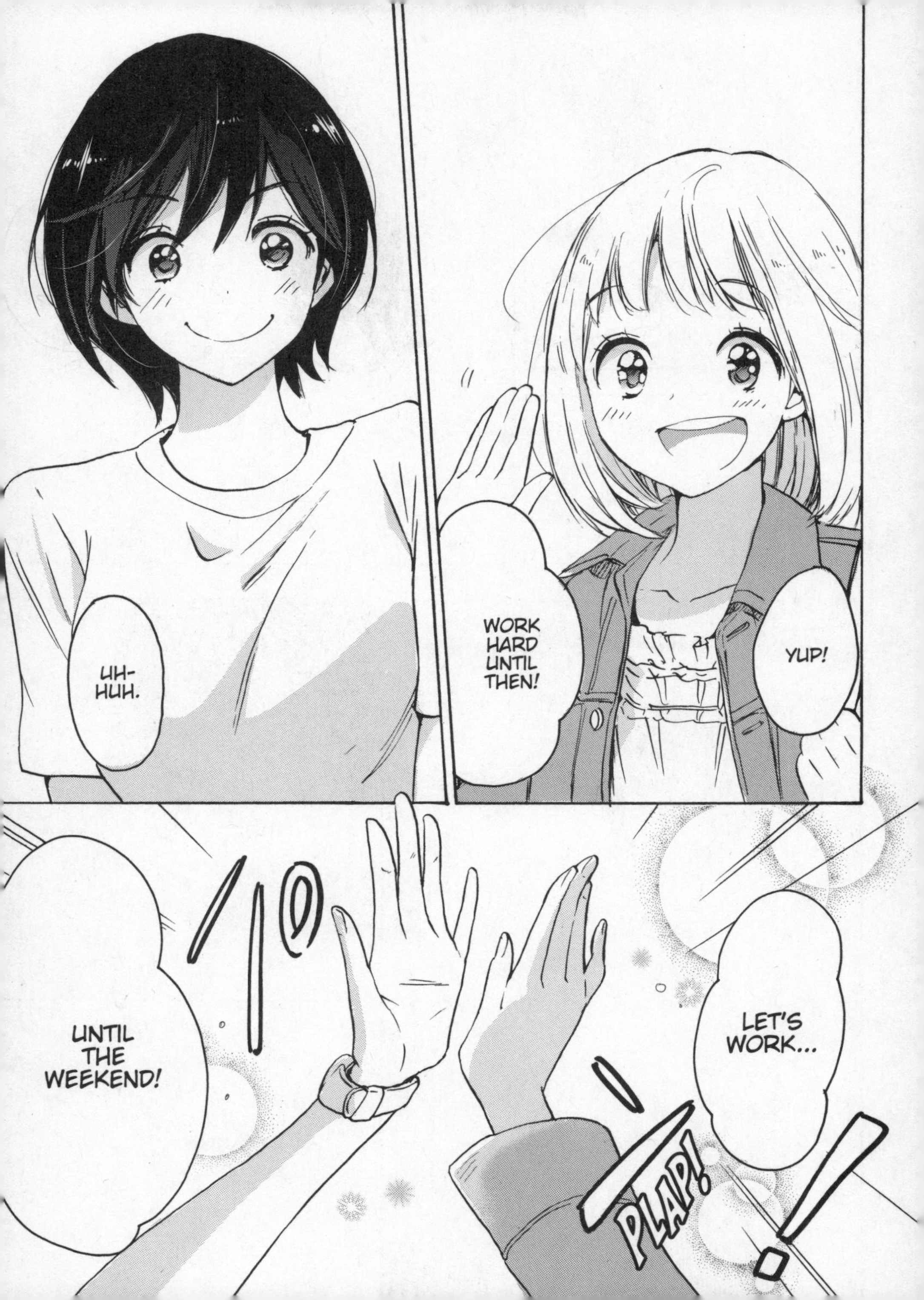
YUP!
WORK HARD UNTIL THEN!
UH-HUH.
LET'S WORK...
UNTIL THE WEEKEND!
PLAP!

ME AND KASE-SAN...

ARE BOTH GIRLS...

BUT WE'VE BEEN GOING OUT FOR AGES.

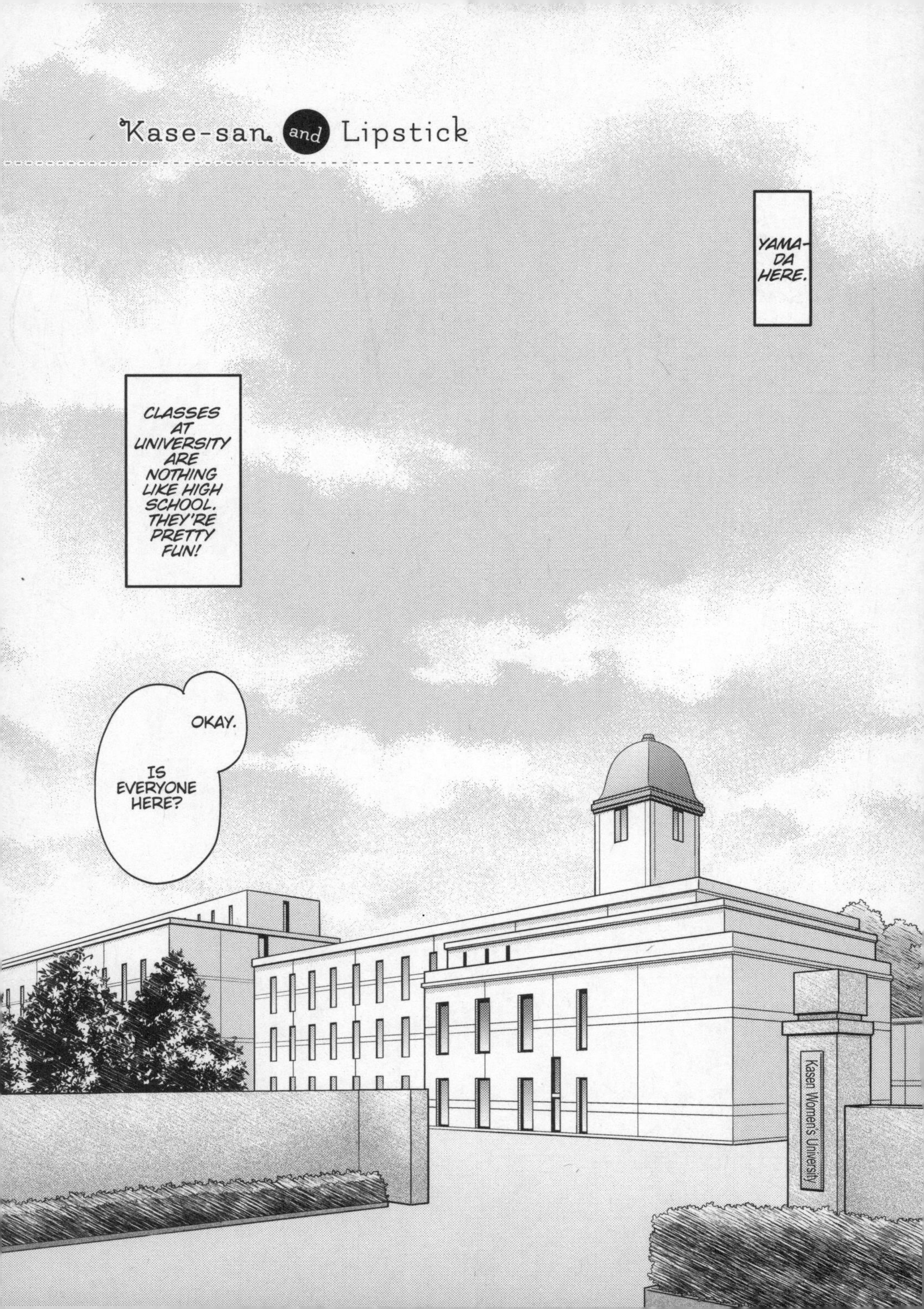
Kase-san and Lipstick
YAMA-DA HERE.
CLASSES AT UNIVERSITY ARE NOTHING LIKE HIGH SCHOOL. THEY'RE PRETTY FUN!
OKAY.
IS EVERYONE HERE?
Kasen Women's University

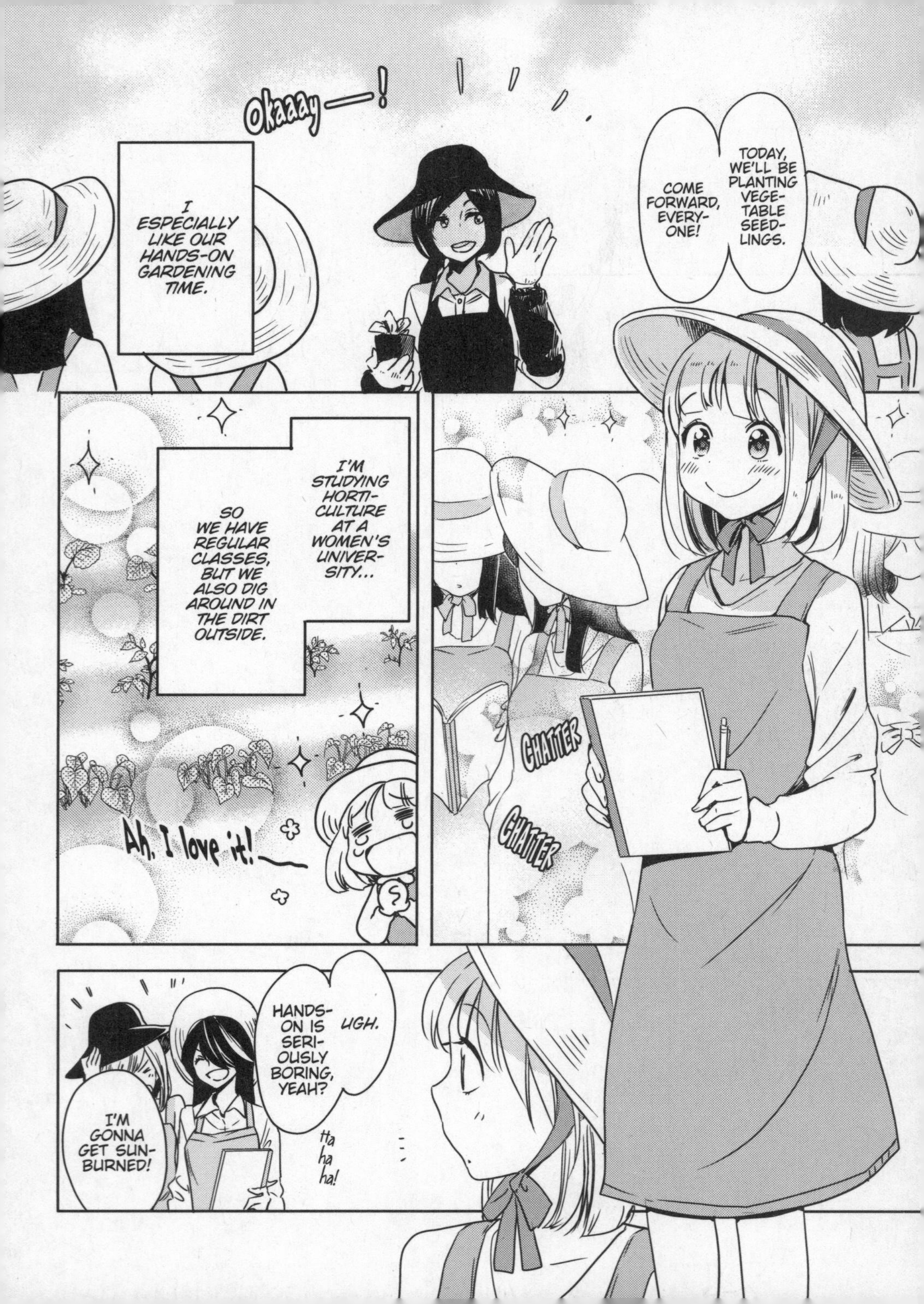
Okaaay—!
TODAY, WE'LL BE PLANTING VEGE-TABLE SEED-LINGS.
COME FORWARD, EVERY-ONE!
I ESPECIALLY LIKE OUR HANDS-ON GARDENING TIME.
CHATTER
CHATTER
I'M STUDYING HORTI-CULTURE AT A WOMEN'S UNIVER-SITY...
SO WE HAVE REGULAR CLASSES, BUT WE ALSO DIG AROUND IN THE DIRT OUTSIDE.
Ah, I love it!
UGH.
HANDS-ON IS SERI-OUSLY BORING, YEAH?
I'M GONNA GET SUN-BURNED!
Ha ha ha!

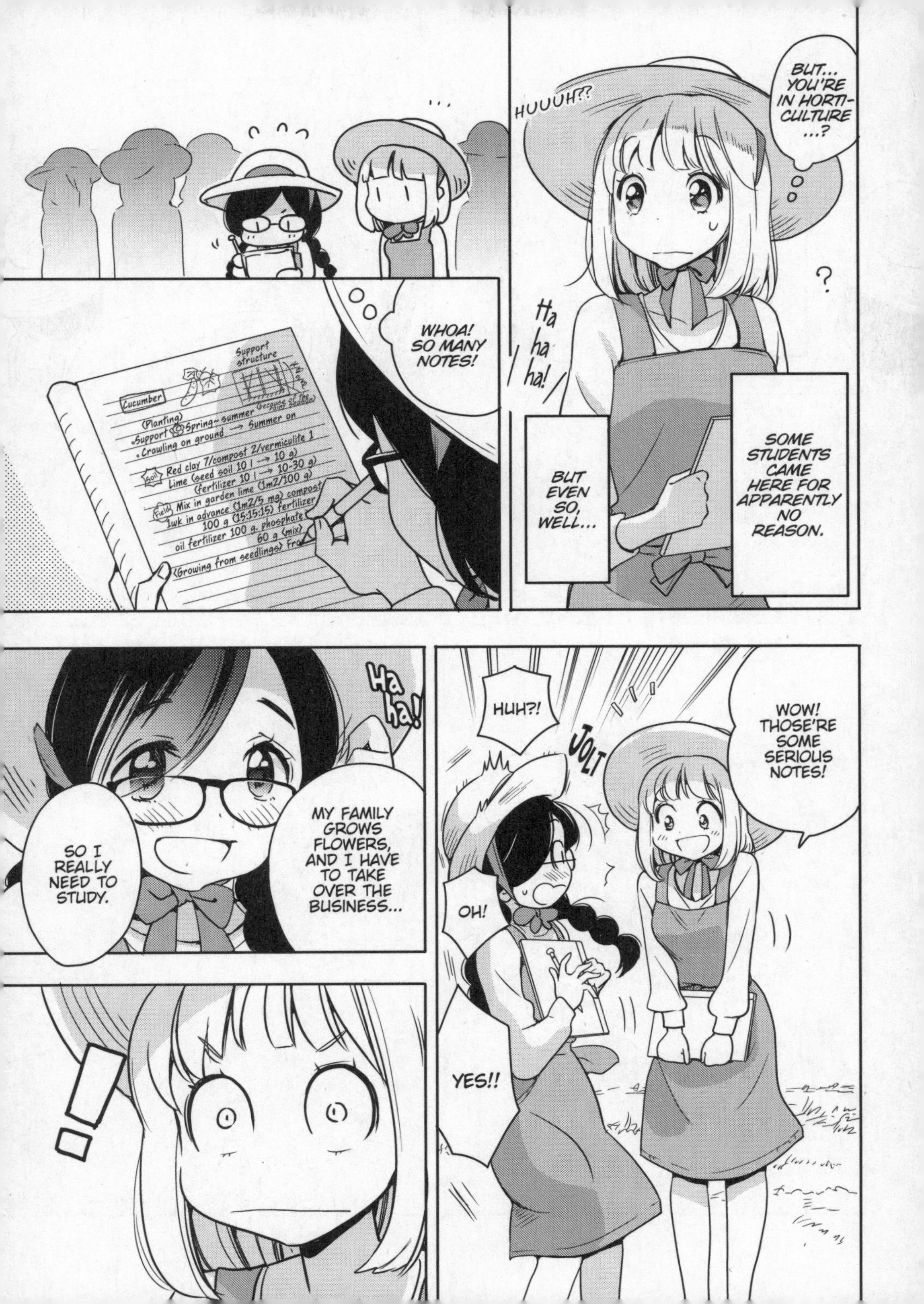

HUUUH??
BUT... YOU'RE IN HORTI-CULTURE ...?
?
Ha ha ha!
SOME STUDENTS CAME HERE FOR APPARENTLY NO REASON.
BUT EVEN SO, WELL...
...
WHOA! SO MANY NOTES!
Support structure
Cucumber
(Planting)
Support Spring~summer
Crawling on ground → Summer on
Soil Red clay 7/compost 2/vermiculite 1
Lime (seed soil 10 l → 10 g)
(fertilizer 10 l → 10-30 g)
Field Mix in garden lime (1m2/100 g)
1wk in advance (1m2/5 mg) compost
100 g (15:15:15) fertilizer
oil fertilizer 100 g, phosphate
60 g (mix)
(Growing from seedlings)
WOW! THOSE'RE SOME SERIOUS NOTES!
HUH?!
JOLT
OH!
YES!!
Ha ha!
MY FAMILY GROWS FLOWERS, AND I HAVE TO TAKE OVER THE BUSINESS...
SO I REALLY NEED TO STUDY.
!

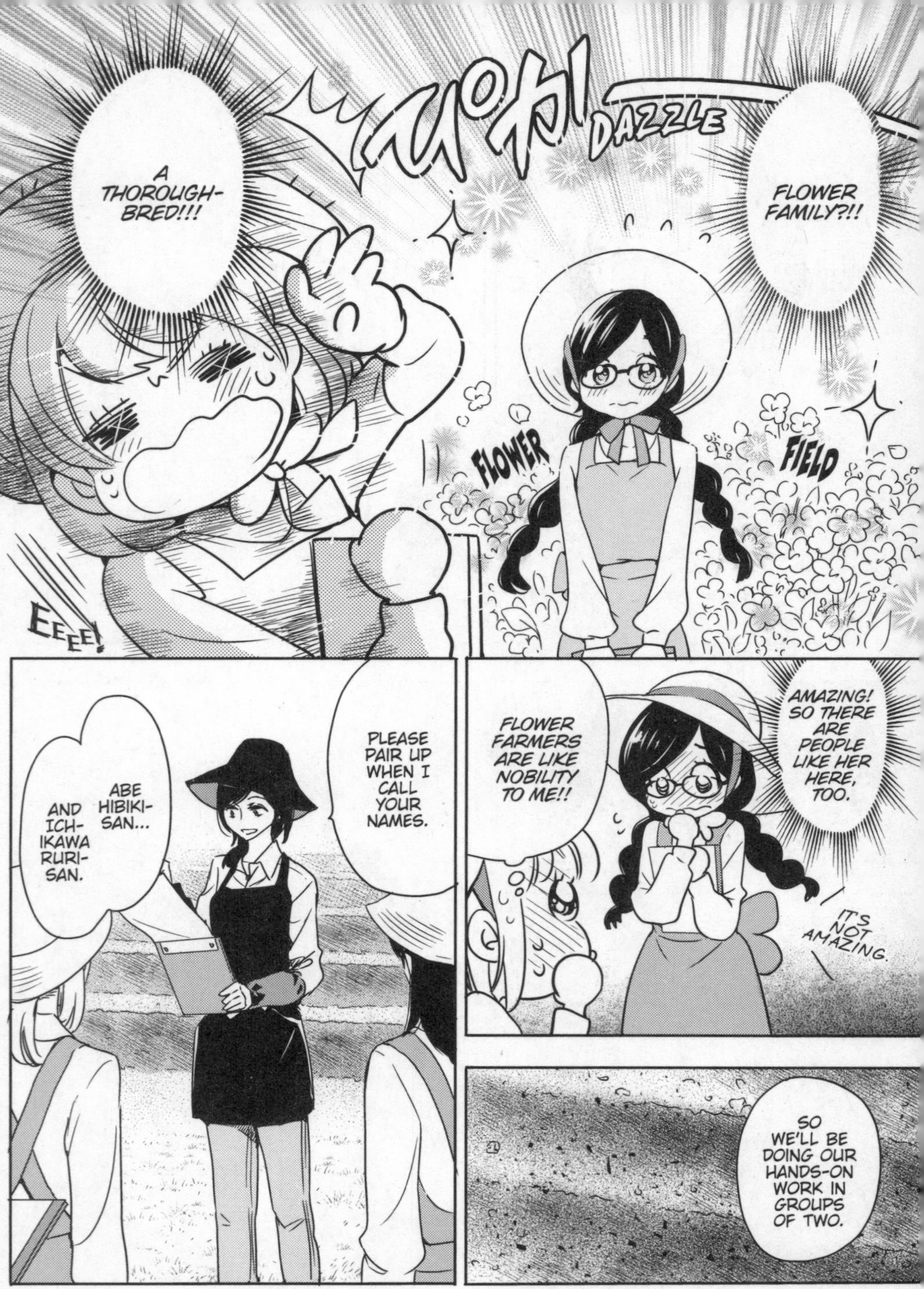
FLOWER FAMILY?!!
DAZZLE
A THOROUGH-BRED!!!
FLOWER FIELD
EEEE!
AMAZING! SO THERE ARE PEOPLE LIKE HER HERE, TOO.
FLOWER FARMERS ARE LIKE NOBILITY TO ME!!
IT'S NOT AMAZING.
SO WE'LL BE DOING OUR HANDS-ON WORK IN GROUPS OF TWO.
PLEASE PAIR UP WHEN I CALL YOUR NAMES.
ABE HIBIKI-SAN...
AND ICHIKAWA RURI-SAN.

YOSHIMURA HANA-SAN.

YAMADA YUI-SAN...

AND...

HA HA!

NICE TO MEET YOU, YAMADA-SAN!

I'M YOSHIMURA HANA!

BUT JUST HANA IS FINE!

HUH?

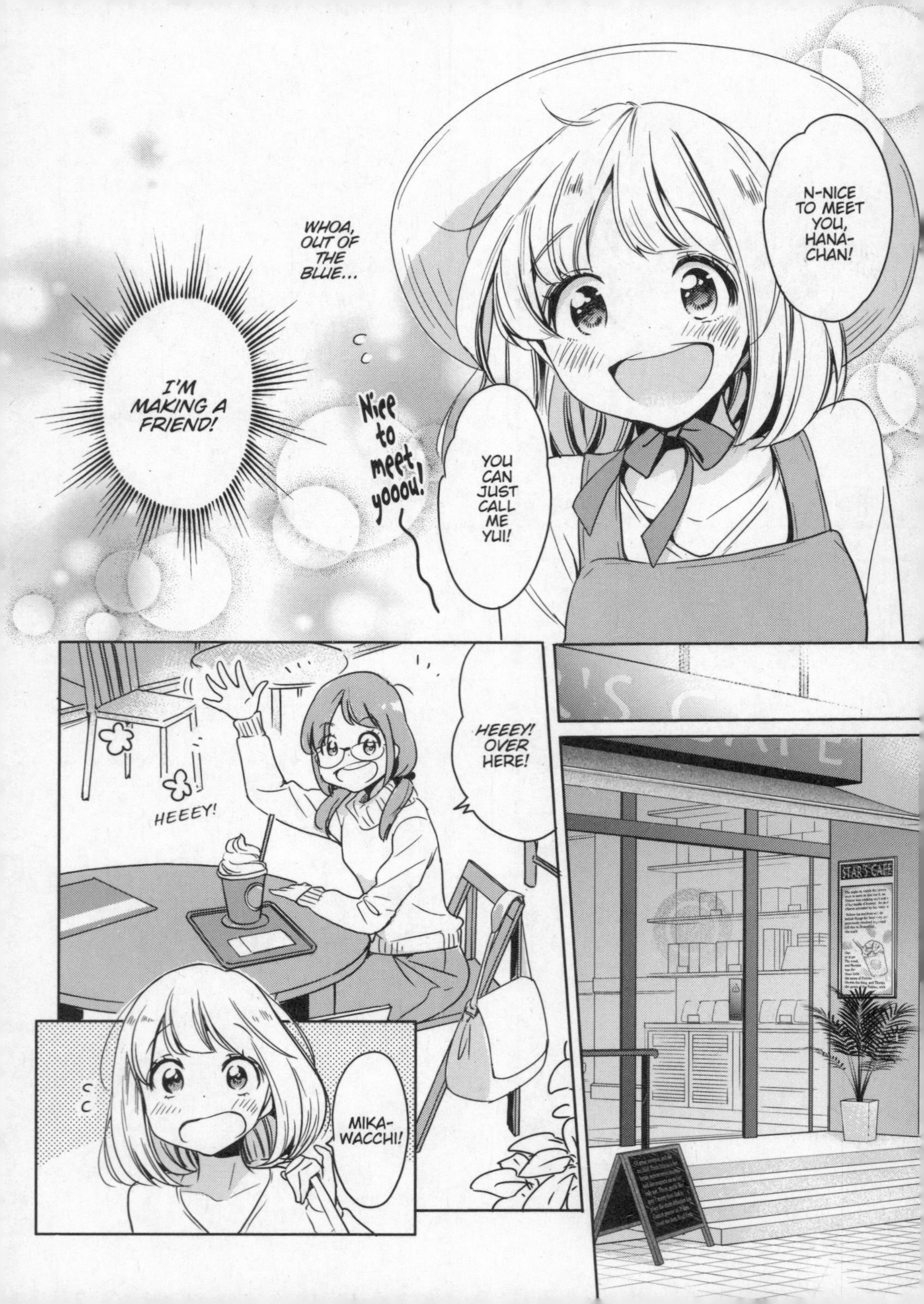
N-NICE TO MEET YOU, HANA-CHAN!
YOU CAN JUST CALL ME YUI!
WHOA, OUT OF THE BLUE...
Nice to meet yooou!
I'M MAKING A FRIEND!
STAR'S CAFE
HEEEY! OVER HERE!
HEEEY!
MIKA-WACCHI!

THE COUNTRY!

WELL, BACK HOME, THERE WAS JUST THE BUS OR THE ONE JR LINE.

Ha ha ha!

C'MON. YOU NEED TO GET USED TO THE TRAINS ALREADY.

I MADE IT!!

AHH!!

SHE GOES TO A TECHNICAL SCHOOL IN TOKYO NOW.

MIKA-WACCHI'S MY BEST FRIEND FROM HIGH SCHOOL.

NOT GONNA HAPPEN. I'M STILL FREAKED OUT BY ANYTHING OTHER THAN MY OWN STATION.

AND CHANGING TRAINS IS A WHOLE OTHER THING.

OH!

I'M JUST GONNA GET TEA.

WHOA! IT'S EXPENSIVE!!

AHH!

Menu

COULD HAVE A MEAL.

I CAN INDULGE THIS MUCH AT LEAST.

I'VE BEEN WORKING AT MY JOB NONSTOP SINCE I CAME HERE.

Mwah ha-ha-ha! ♪

HUH? WHAT'RE YOU DRINKING?

CARAMEL VANILLA CREAM FRAPPUCCINO WITH WHIPPED CREAM.

WHAT?

CARAMEL VANILLA CREAM FRAPPUCCINO WITH WHIPPED CREAM.

IS THAT A SPELL?

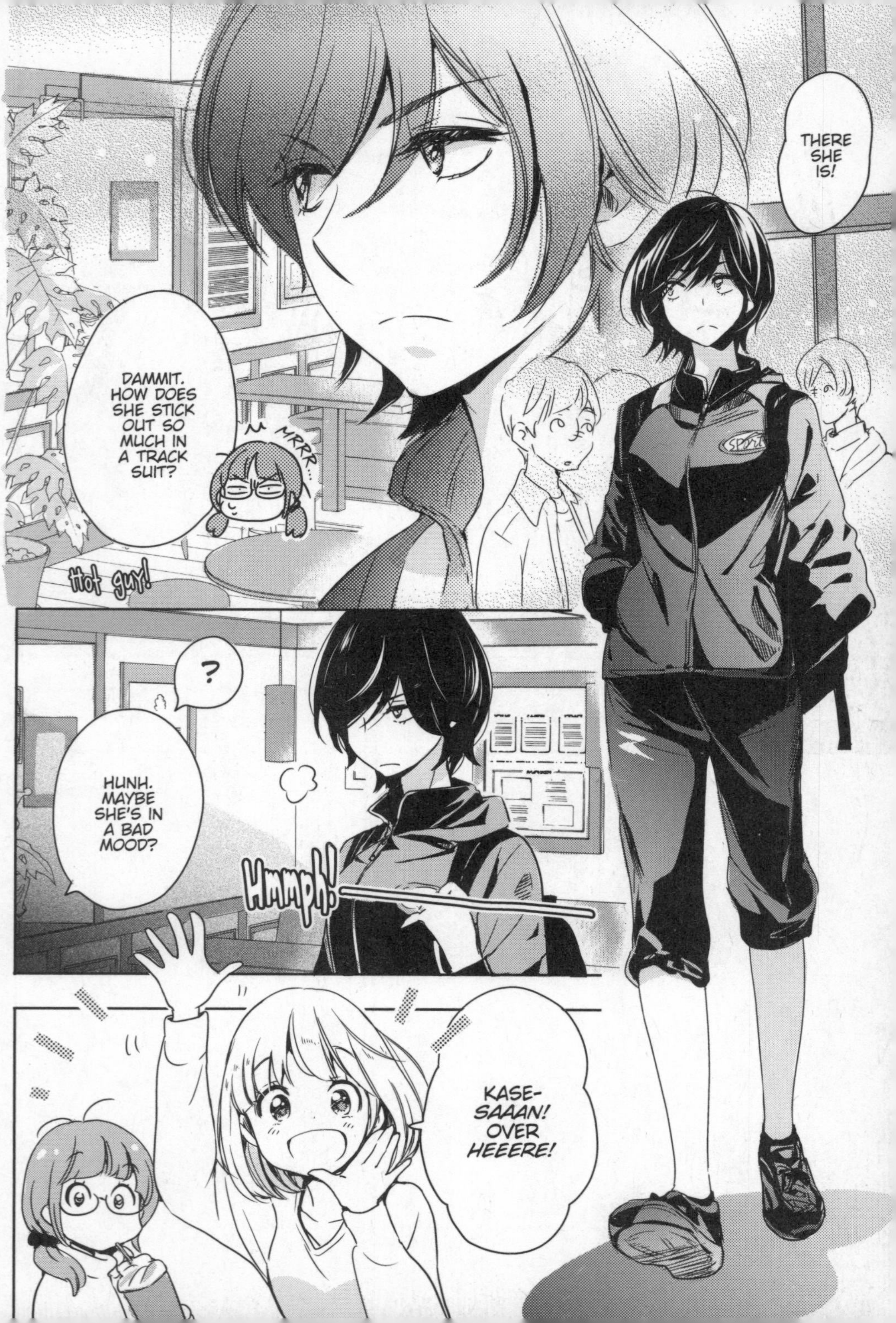
THERE SHE IS!
DAMMIT. HOW DOES SHE STICK OUT SO MUCH IN A TRACK SUIT?
MRRR...
Hot guy!
?
HUNH. MAYBE SHE'S IN A BAD MOOD?
Hmmph!
KASE-SAAAN! OVER HEEERE!

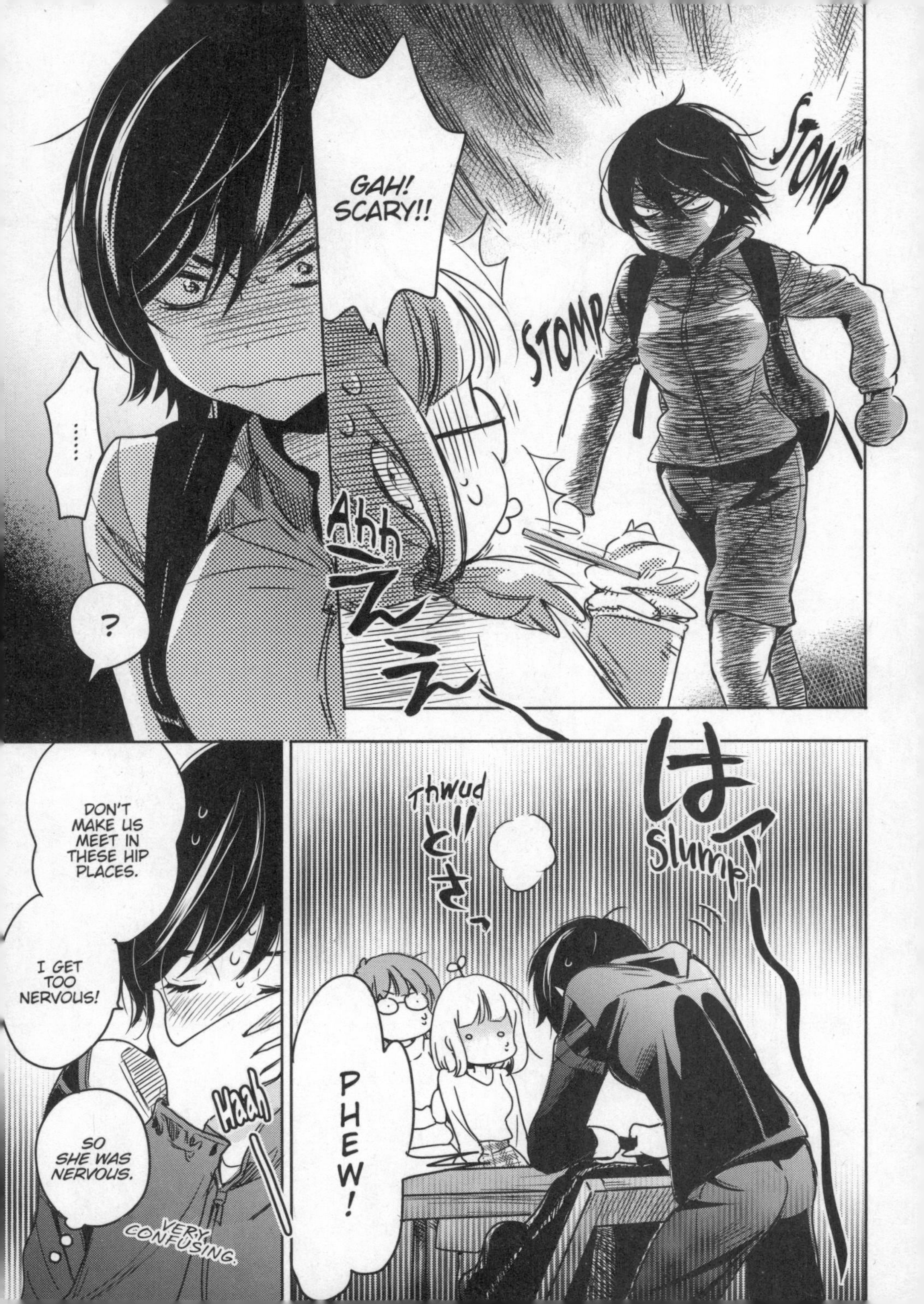
STOMP
STOMP
GAH! SCARY!!
Ahh
......
?
は
Slump
Thwud
どさっ
DON'T MAKE US MEET IN THESE HIP PLACES.
I GET TOO NERVOUS!
PHEW!
Haah
SO SHE WAS NERVOUS.
VERY CONFUSING.

BEEN A WHILE...

YAMADA.

YEAH-- AND I'M EVEN BUSIER NOW.

Ah ha ha!

I GUESS YOU WERE BUSY EVEN IN HIGH SCHOOL-- HUH, KASE-SAN?

PLUS, I'M IN THE DORM.

SERIOUSLY, I DON'T HAVE ANY TIME TO MYSELF!

IT'S BEEN FIVE DAYS.

THAT'S SEEING EACH OTHER!

HUH?

YOU DON'T SEE EACH OTHER?

JUST A MINUTE BETWEEN PRACTICES, LIKE TODAY.

EVEN IF WE DO, IT'S REALLY JUST FOR A LITTLE BIT.

STAR'S CAFE

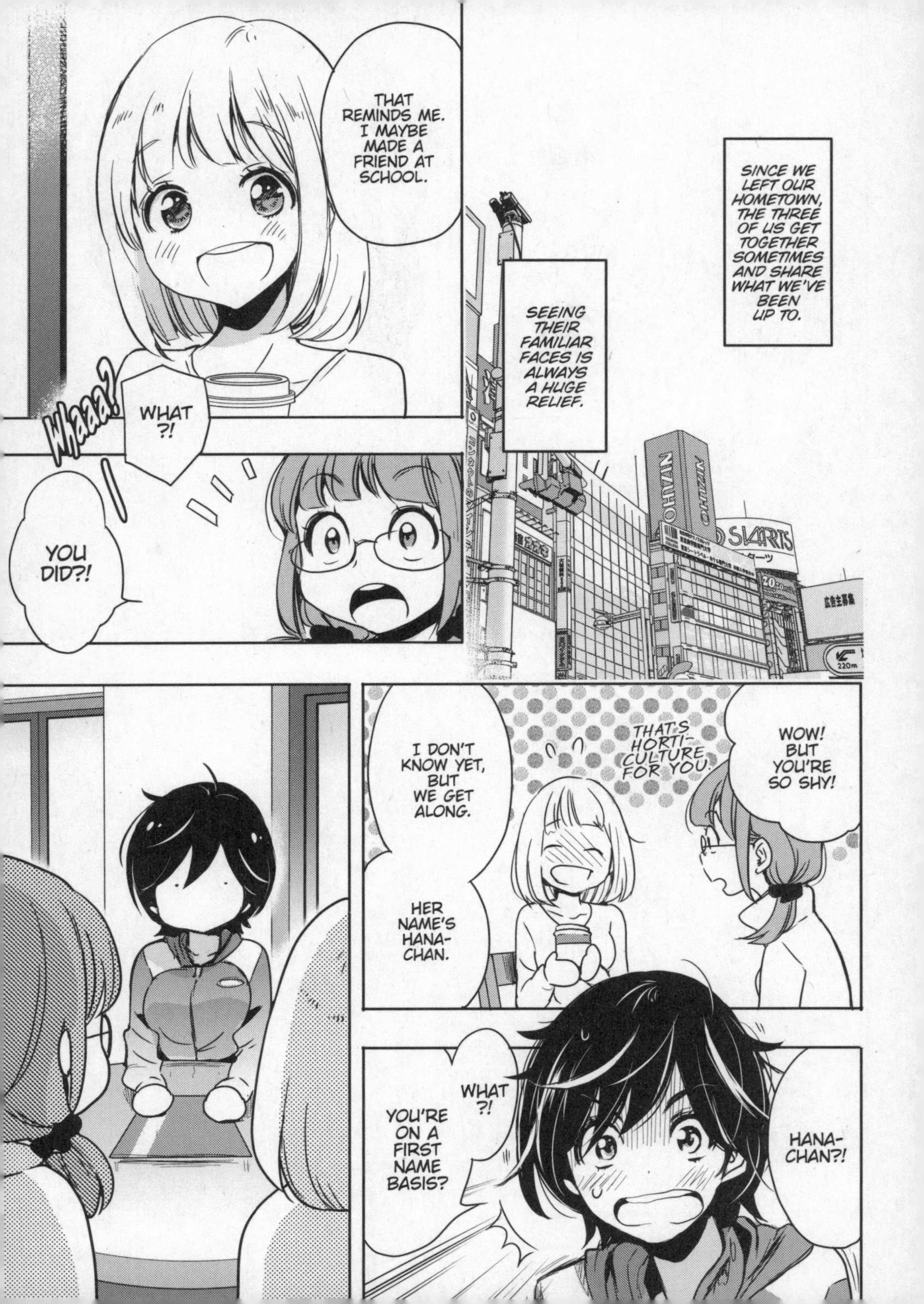
SINCE WE LEFT OUR HOMETOWN, THE THREE OF US GET TOGETHER SOMETIMES AND SHARE WHAT WE'VE BEEN UP TO.
SEEING THEIR FAMILIAR FACES IS ALWAYS A HUGE RELIEF.
THAT REMINDS ME. I MAYBE MADE A FRIEND AT SCHOOL.
Whaaa?
WHAT ?!
YOU DID?!
WOW! BUT YOU'RE SO SHY!
THAT'S HORTI-CULTURE FOR YOU.
I DON'T KNOW YET, BUT WE GET ALONG.
HER NAME'S HANA-CHAN.
HANA-CHAN?!
WHAT ?!
YOU'RE ON A FIRST NAME BASIS?

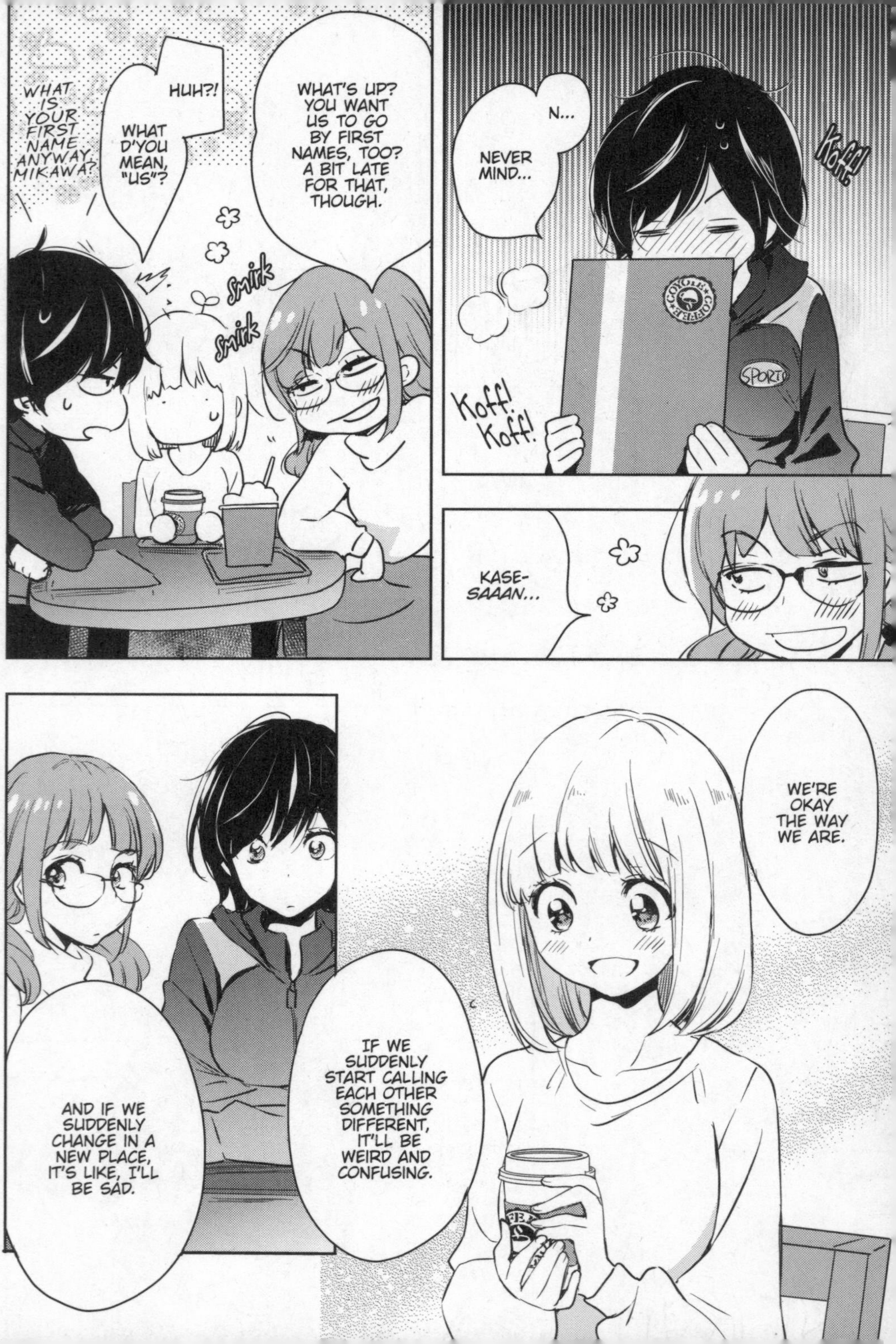
N...
NEVER MIND...
Koff!
Koff! Koff!
KASE-SAAAN...
WHAT'S UP? YOU WANT US TO GO BY FIRST NAMES, TOO? A BIT LATE FOR THAT, THOUGH.
HUH?!
WHAT D'YOU MEAN, "US"?
WHAT IS YOUR FIRST NAME ANYWAY, MIKAWA?
Smirk
Smirk
WE'RE OKAY THE WAY WE ARE.
IF WE SUDDENLY START CALLING EACH OTHER SOMETHING DIFFERENT, IT'LL BE WEIRD AND CONFUSING.
AND IF WE SUDDENLY CHANGE IN A NEW PLACE, IT'S LIKE, I'LL BE SAD.

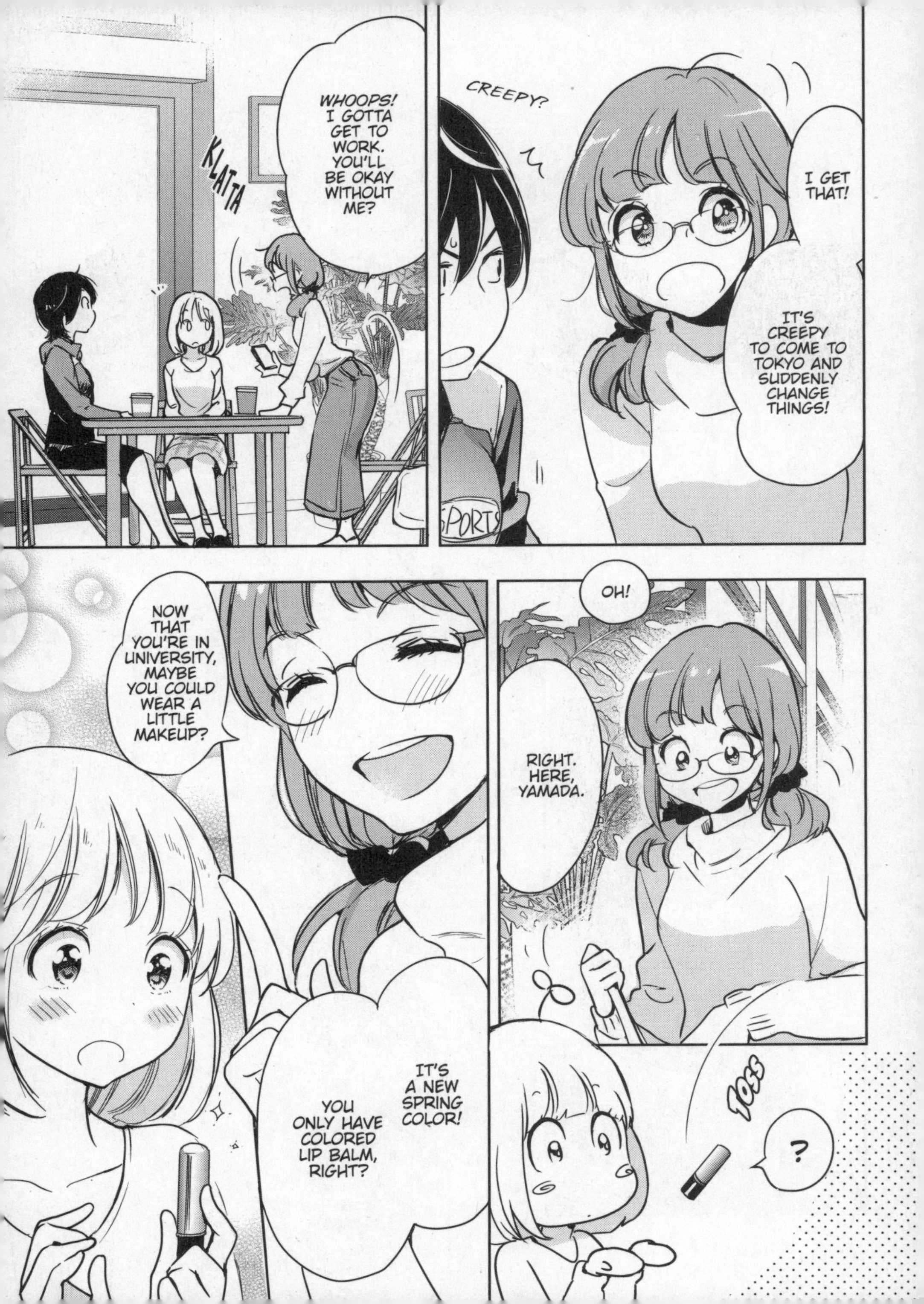
CREEPY?
I GET THAT!
IT'S CREEPY TO COME TO TOKYO AND SUDDENLY CHANGE THINGS!
WHOOPS! I GOTTA GET TO WORK. YOU'LL BE OKAY WITHOUT ME?
KLATTA
OH!
RIGHT. HERE, YAMADA.
NOW THAT YOU'RE IN UNIVERSITY, MAYBE YOU COULD WEAR A LITTLE MAKEUP?
IT'S A NEW SPRING COLOR!
YOU ONLY HAVE COLORED LIP BALM, RIGHT?
TOSS
?

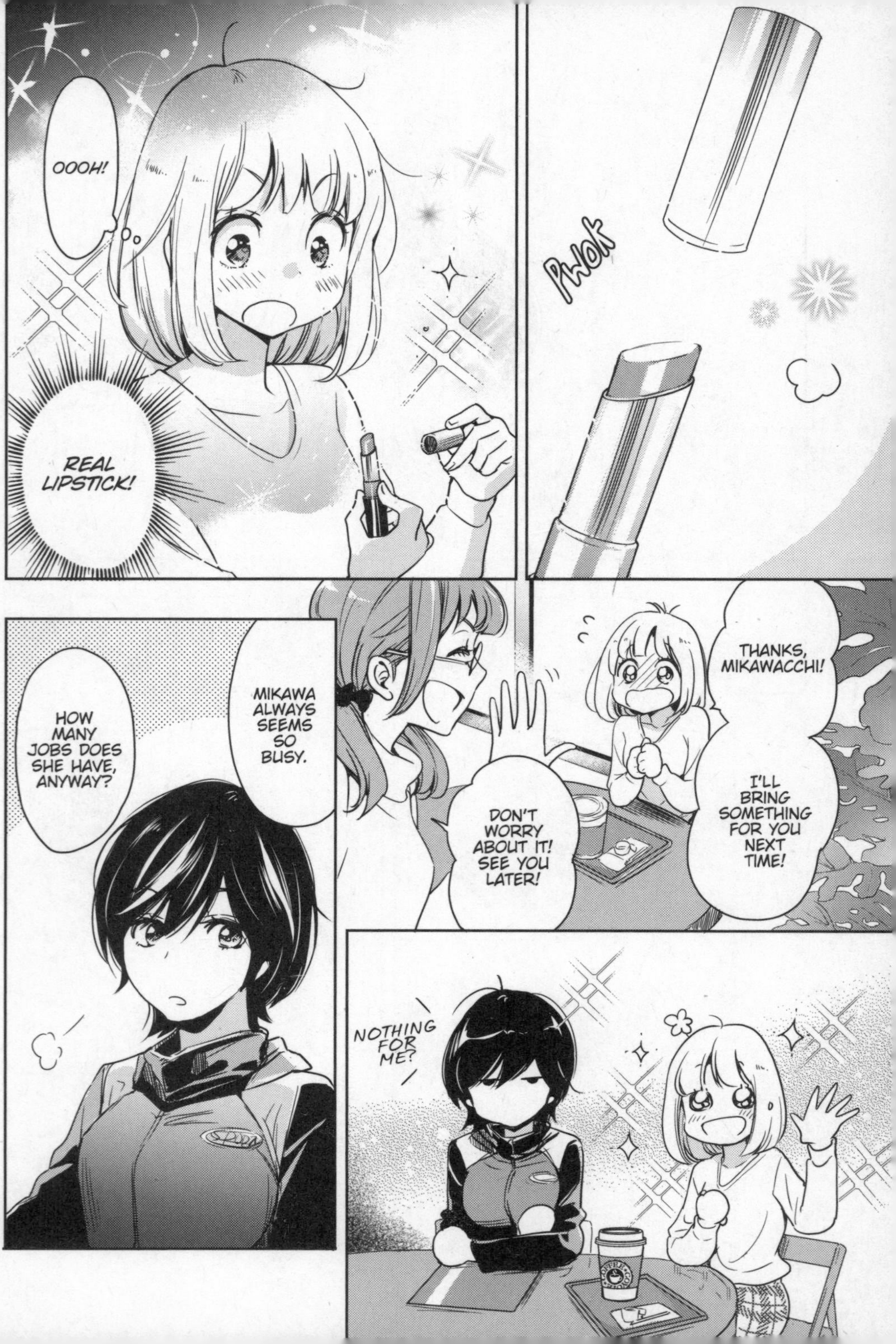
PWOK
OOOH!
REAL LIPSTICK!
THANKS, MIKAWACCHI!
I'LL BRING SOMETHING FOR YOU NEXT TIME!
DON'T WORRY ABOUT IT! SEE YOU LATER!
MIKAWA ALWAYS SEEMS SO BUSY.
HOW MANY JOBS DOES SHE HAVE, ANYWAY?
NOTHING FOR ME?

HUH?

YOU LIKE THAT KINDA STUFF, YAMADA?

YEAH...

WHY DON'T YOU PUT SOME ON THEN?

SO THAT'S IT, HUH?

Hmm?

WHAT?

HERE?!

Ha ha!

EVERYONE AT SCHOOL WEARS MAKEUP. THEY SEEM SO GROWN-UP!

I NEVER REALLY THOUGHT ABOUT IT, SO I WAS A BIT SURPRISED.

BUT THERE WERE GIRLS WHO WORE MAKEUP EVEN IN HIGH SCHOOL, RIGHT?

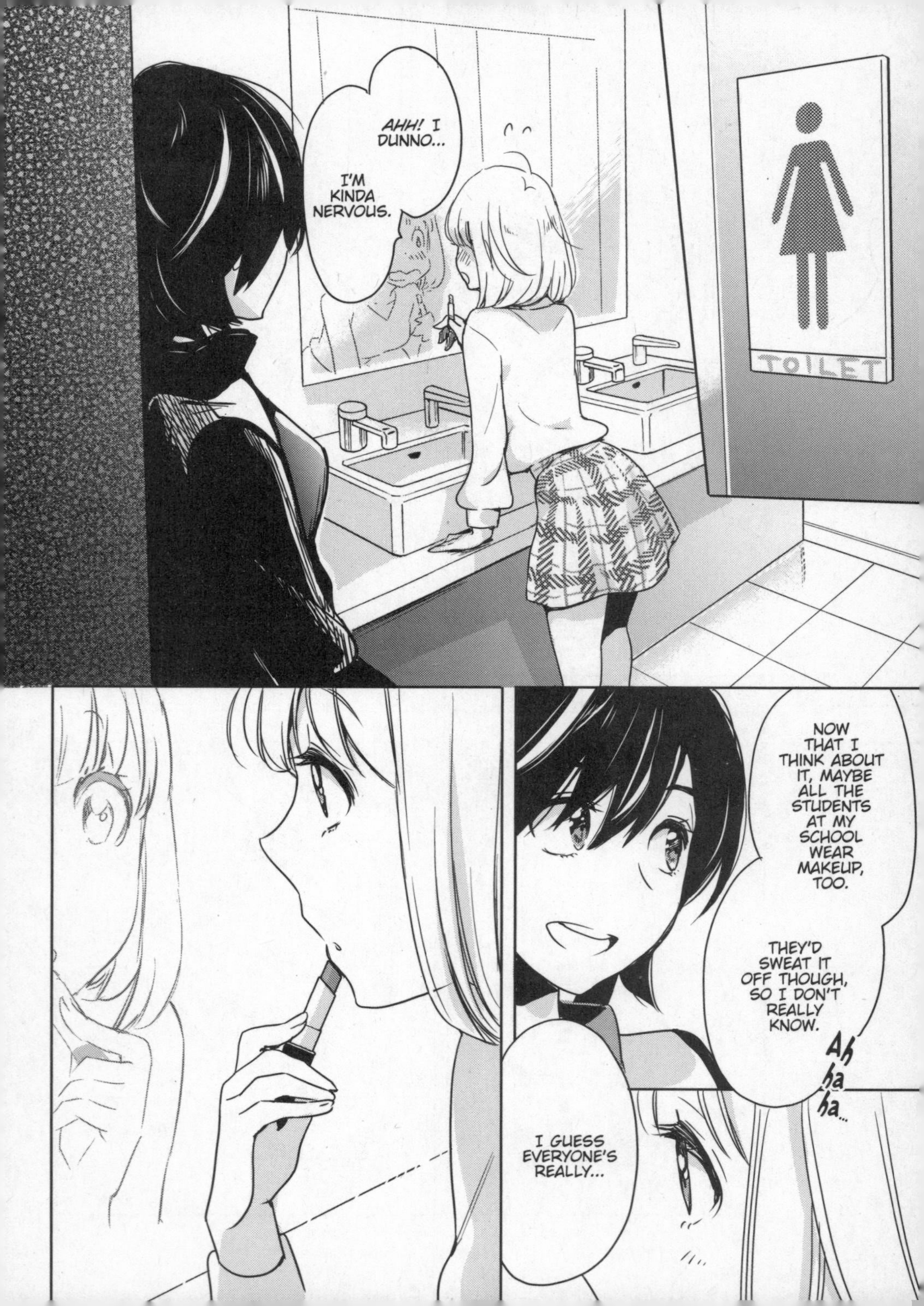

AHH! I DUNNO...
I'M KINDA NERVOUS.
TOILET
NOW THAT I THINK ABOUT IT, MAYBE ALL THE STUDENTS AT MY SCHOOL WEAR MAKEUP, TOO.
THEY'D SWEAT IT OFF THOUGH, SO I DON'T REALLY KNOW.
Ah ha ha...
I GUESS EVERYONE'S REALLY...

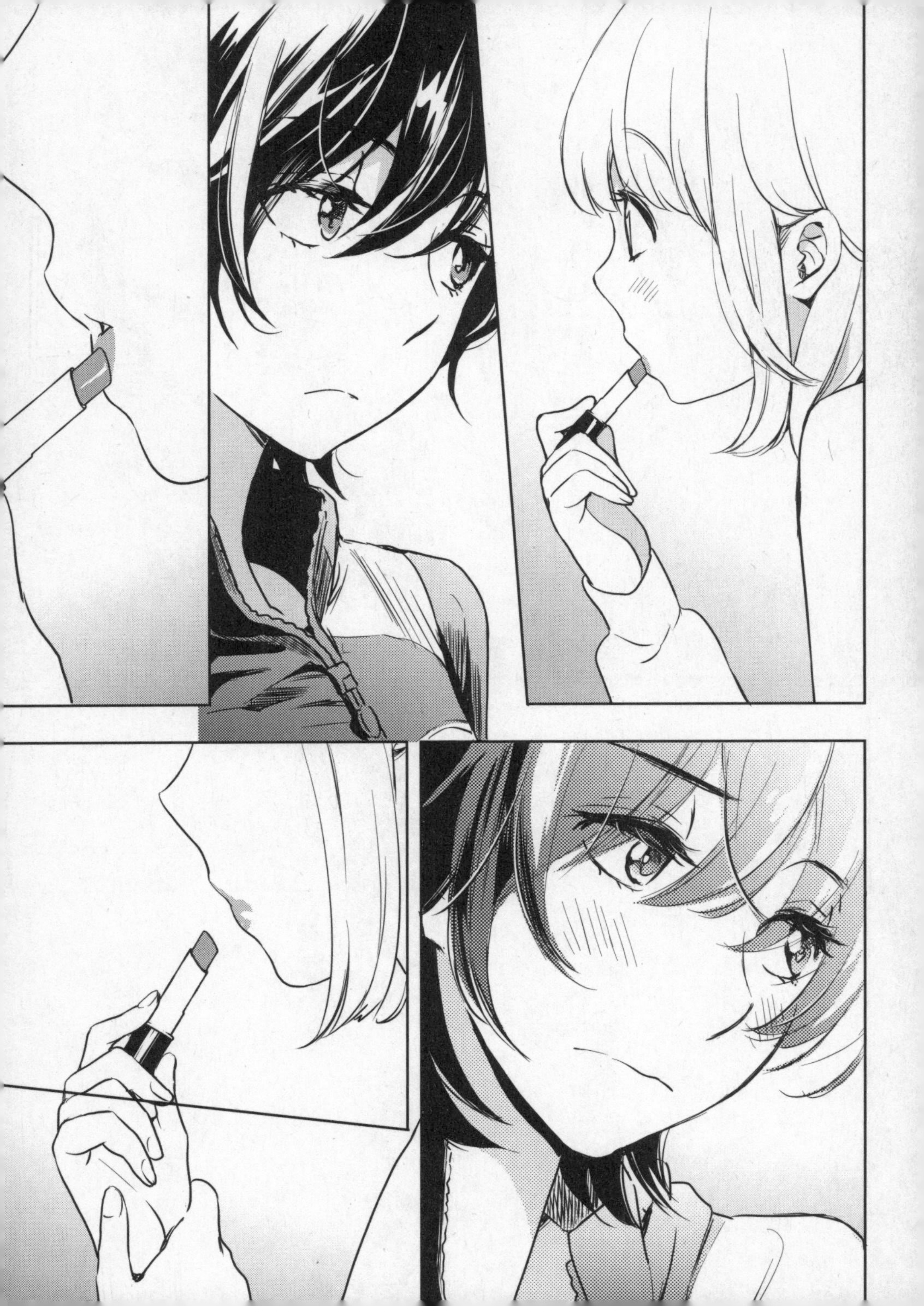

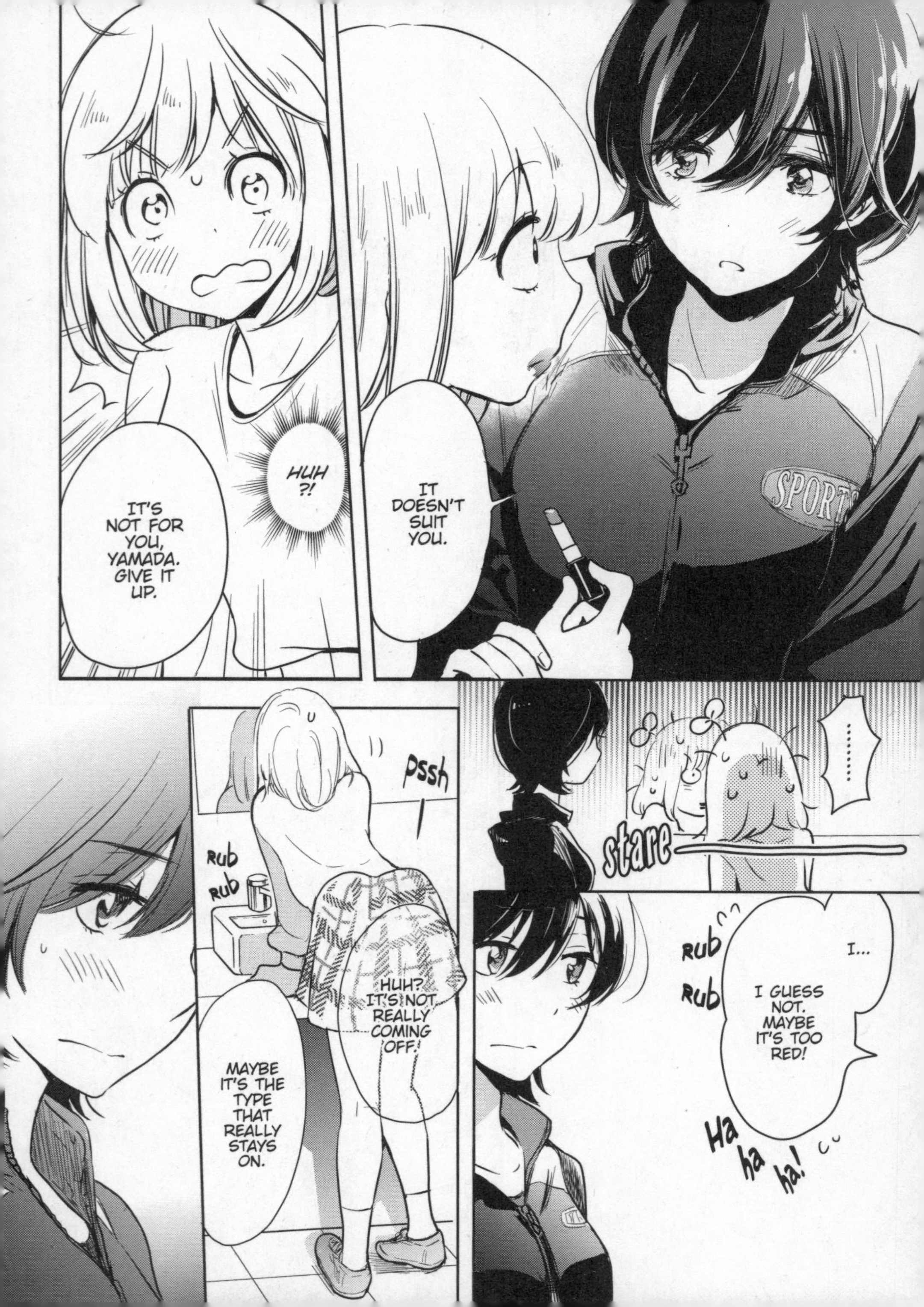
IT DOESN'T SUIT YOU.
HUH ?!
IT'S NOT FOR YOU, YAMADA. GIVE IT UP.
stare
I...
I GUESS NOT. MAYBE IT'S TOO RED!
Rub Rub
Ha ha ha!
pssh
Rub Rub
HUH? IT'S NOT REALLY COMING OFF.
MAYBE IT'S THE TYPE THAT REALLY STAYS ON.

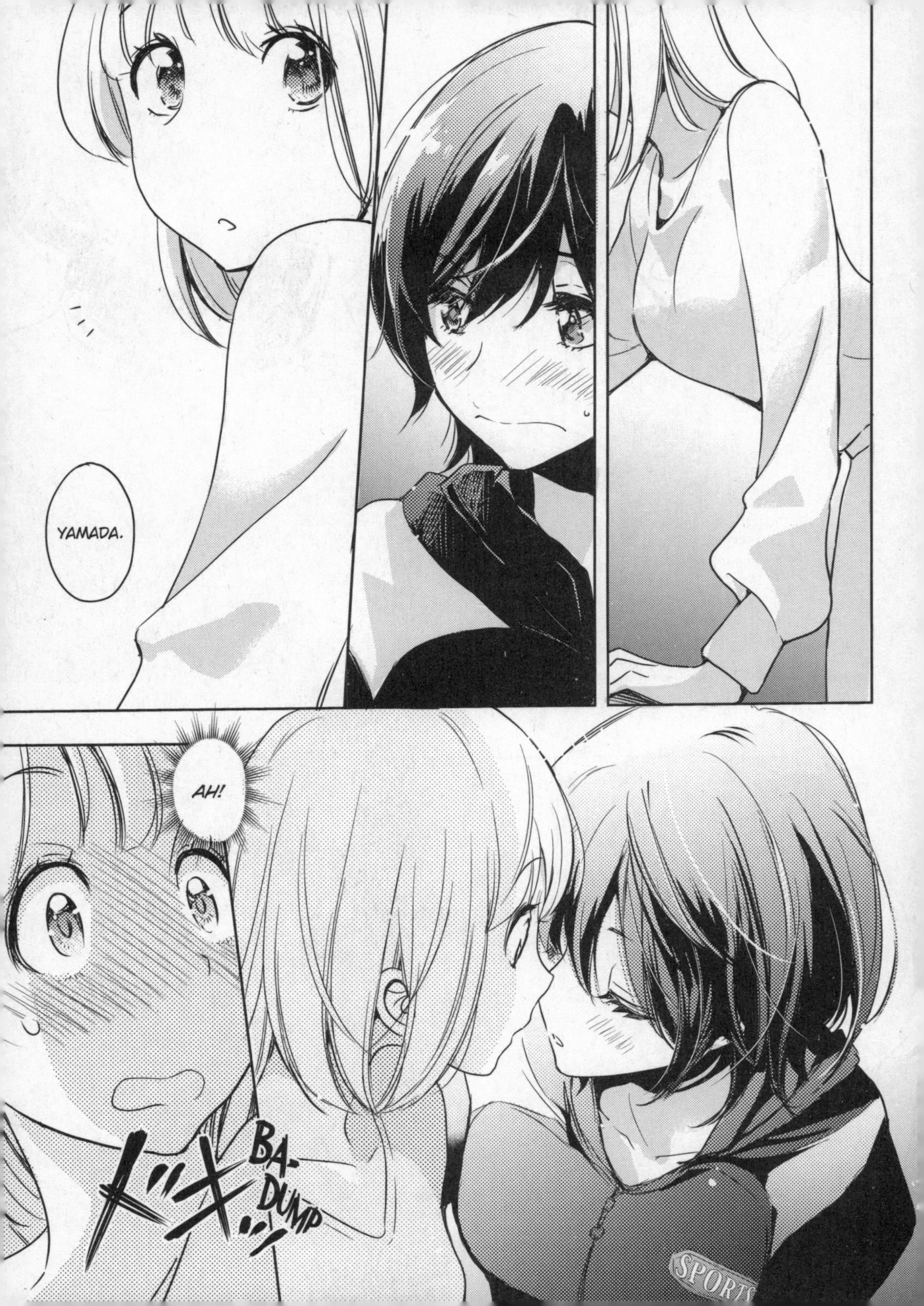
YAMADA.
AH!
BA-DUMP
SPORTS

SO THEN!

KA-CHAK

LEAP

Kya ha ha!

Ah ha ha ha ha ha!

OH! ARE THERE ANY EMPTY STALLS?

OH!

KASE-SAN! WAIT!

R... RIGHT.

GOOD LUCK AT EVENING PRACTICE.

S-SEE YOU LATER, KASE-SAN.

OH! HERE'S GOOD.

Komazawa Uni
Komazawa Park

40

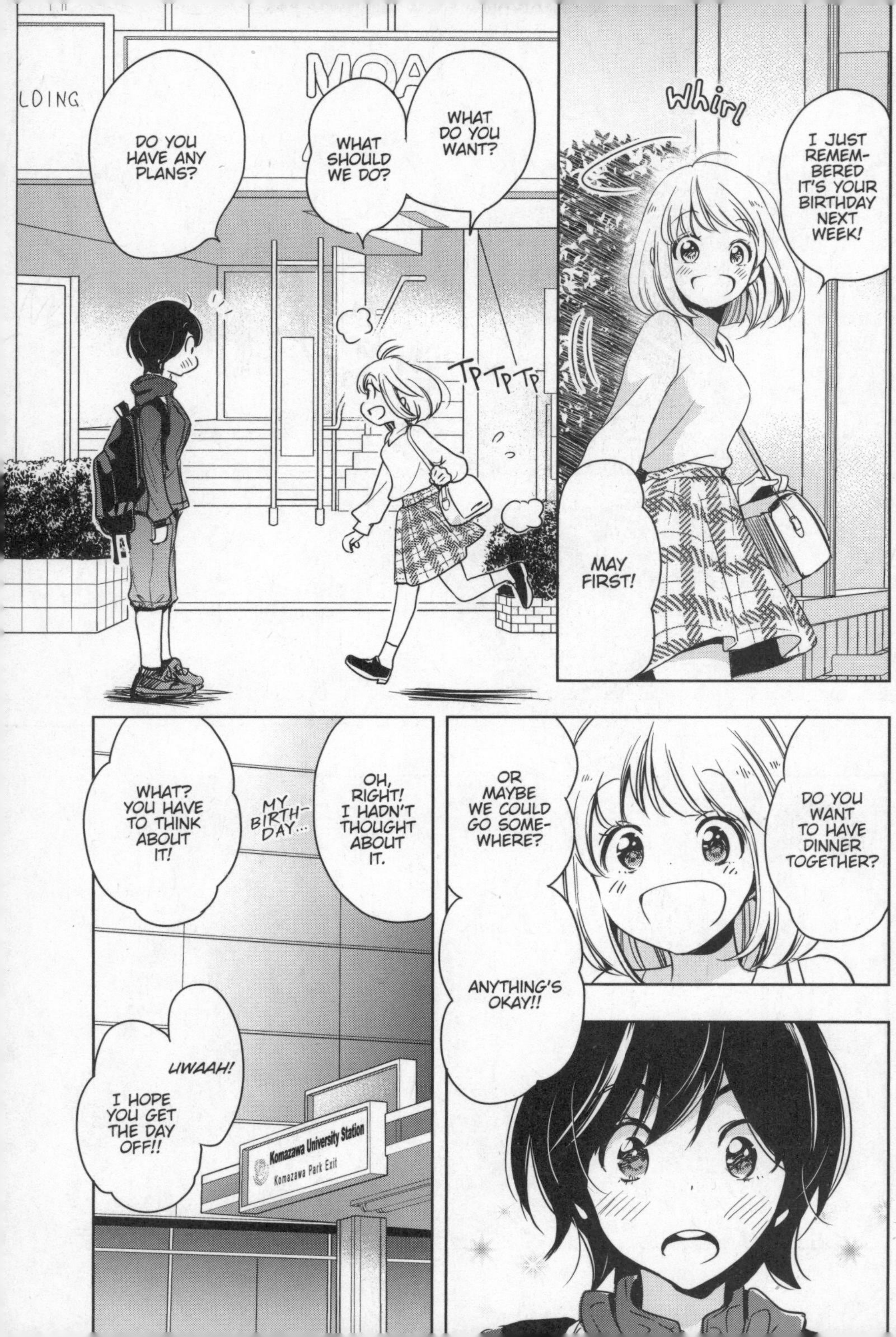
Whirl
I JUST REMEMBERED IT'S YOUR BIRTHDAY NEXT WEEK!
MAY FIRST!
LDING
MOA
WHAT DO YOU WANT?
WHAT SHOULD WE DO?
DO YOU HAVE ANY PLANS?
TP TP TP TP
DO YOU WANT TO HAVE DINNER TOGETHER?
OR MAYBE WE COULD GO SOMEWHERE?
ANYTHING'S OKAY!!
OH, RIGHT! I HADN'T THOUGHT ABOUT IT.
MY BIRTH-DAY...
WHAT? YOU HAVE TO THINK ABOUT IT!
UWAAH!
I HOPE YOU GET THE DAY OFF!!
Komazawa University Station
Komazawa Park Exit

IN HIGH SCHOOL, YOU ALWAYS HAD A MEET SOMEWHERE, SO YOU WEREN'T AROUND.

IT'S MAY, SO THE WEATHER WILL BE NICE. IT'D BE FUN TO GO SOMEWHERE!

HEY! LET'S GO SOMEWHERE TOGETHER!

OH! MAYBE I'LL PACK LUNCHES!

WE'VE NEVER CELEBRATED YOUR BIRTHDAY.

I'LL THINK ABOUT IT.

OKAY...

THANKS, YAMADA.

Eh heh...

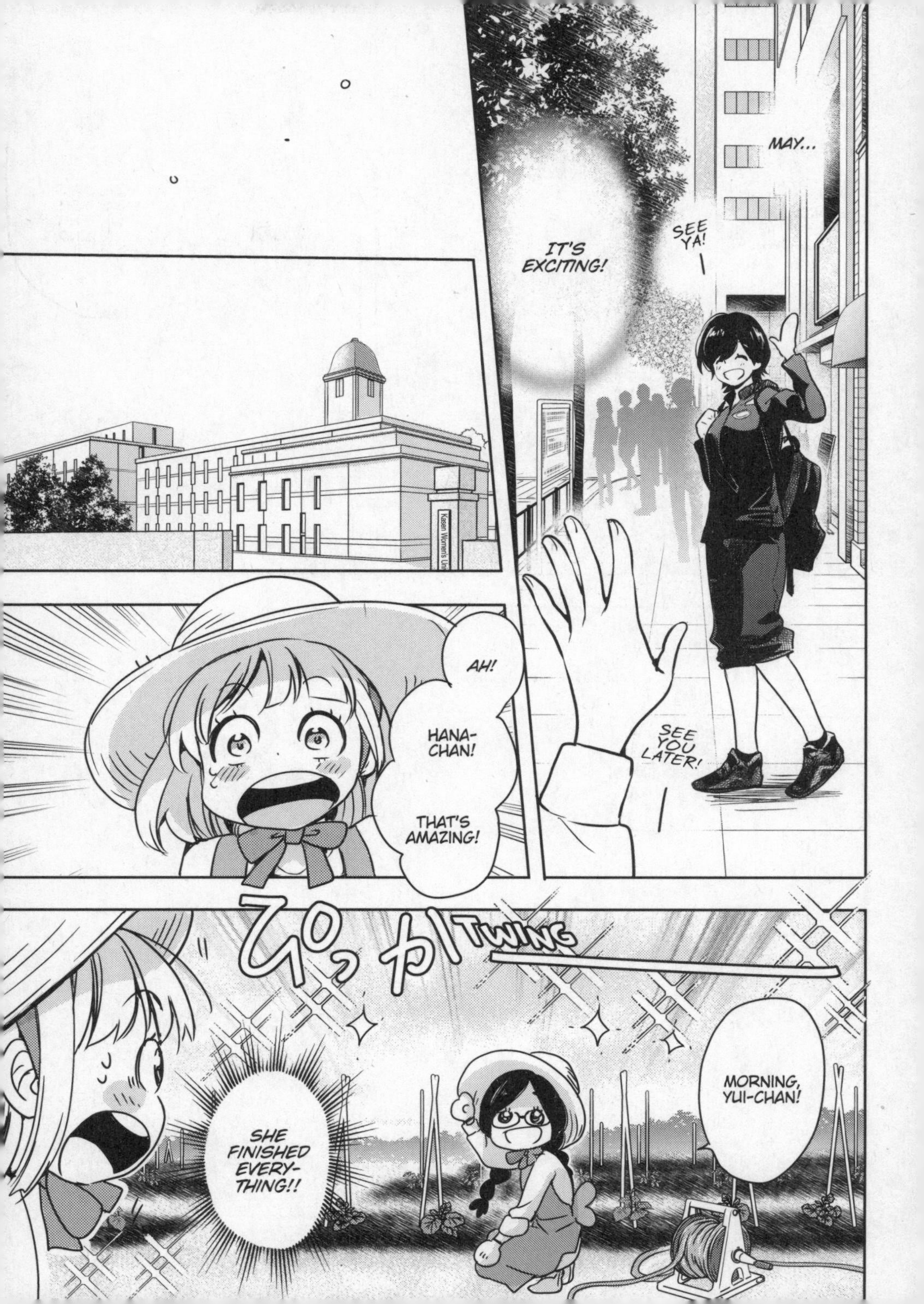
MAY...
SEE YA!
IT'S EXCITING!
Kasen Women's Uni
SEE YOU LATER!
AH!
HANA-CHAN!
THAT'S AMAZING!
TWING
MORNING, YUI-CHAN!
SHE FINISHED EVERY-THING!!

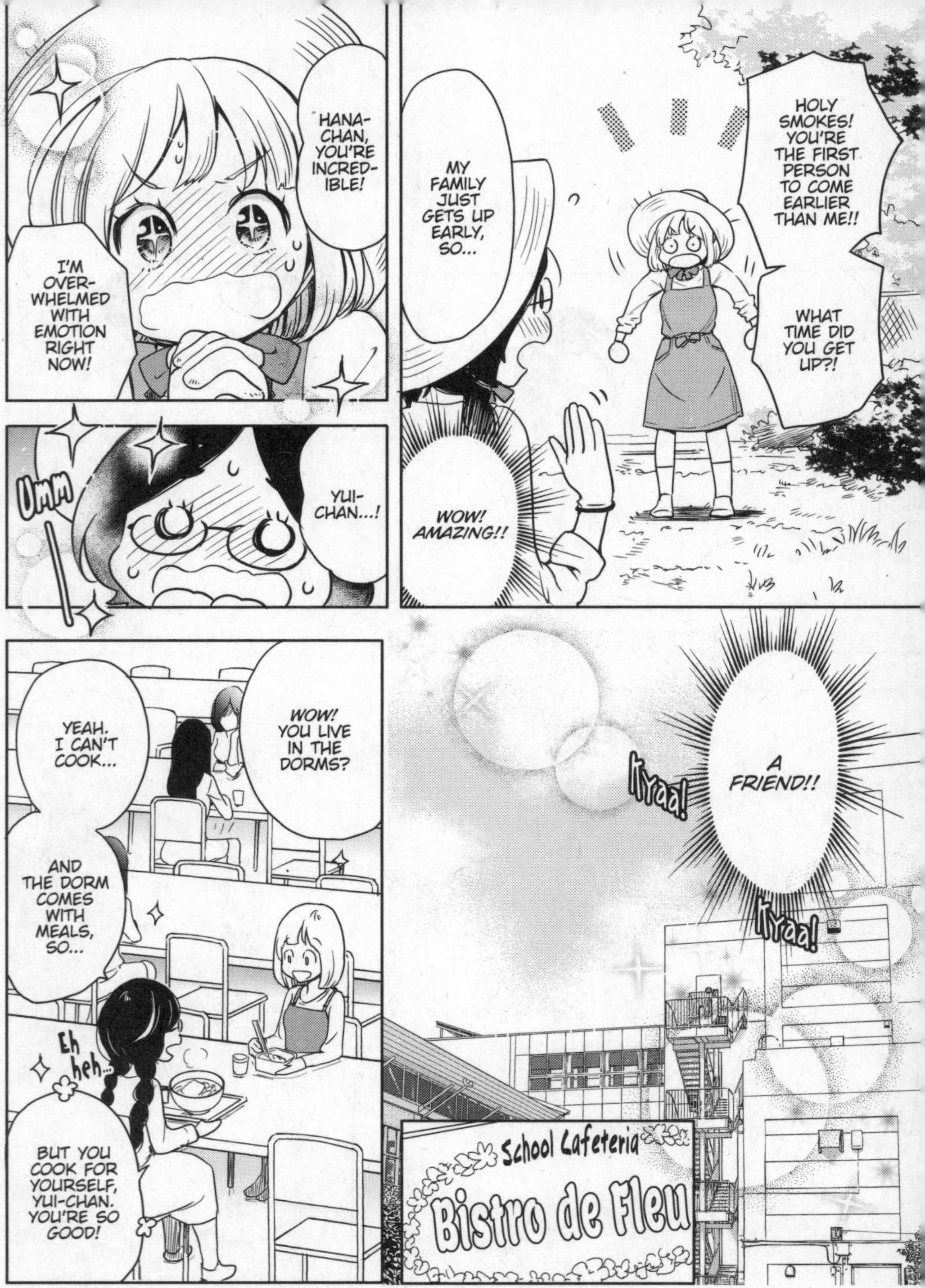
HOLY SMOKES! YOU'RE THE FIRST PERSON TO COME EARLIER THAN ME!!
WHAT TIME DID YOU GET UP?!
MY FAMILY JUST GETS UP EARLY, SO...
WOW! AMAZING!!
HANA-CHAN, YOU'RE INCREDIBLE!
I'M OVERWHELMED WITH EMOTION RIGHT NOW!
Umm
YUI-CHAN...!
Kyaa!
A FRIEND!!
Kyaa!
School Cafeteria
Bistro de Fleu
WOW! YOU LIVE IN THE DORMS?
YEAH. I CAN'T COOK...
AND THE DORM COMES WITH MEALS, SO...
Eh heh...
BUT YOU COOK FOR YOURSELF, YUI-CHAN. YOU'RE SO GOOD!

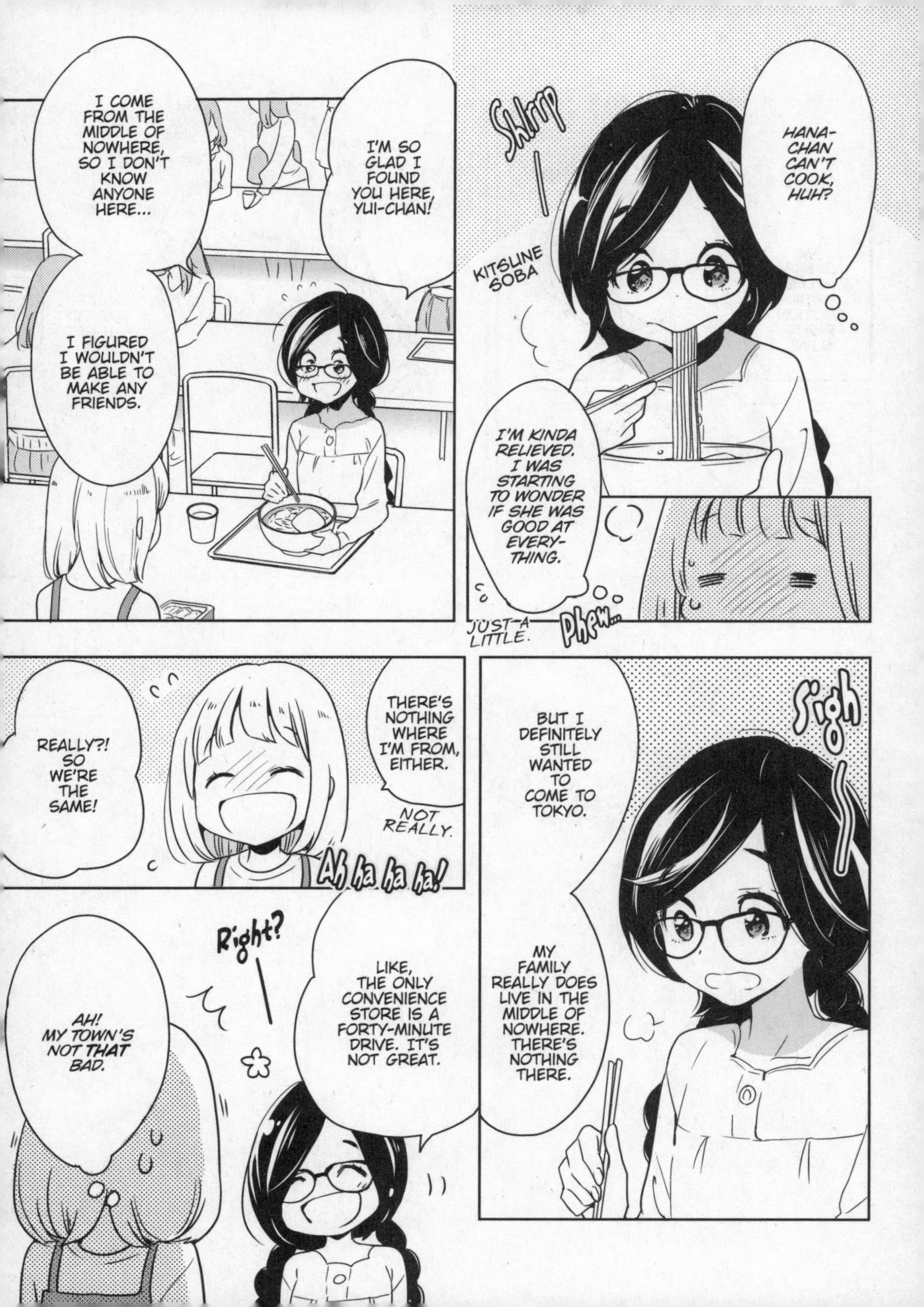
HANA-CHAN CAN'T COOK, HUH?
Shlrrp
KITSUNE SOBA
I'M KINDA RELIEVED. I WAS STARTING TO WONDER IF SHE WAS GOOD AT EVERY-THING.
JUST A LITTLE.
Phew...
I'M SO GLAD I FOUND YOU HERE, YUI-CHAN!
I COME FROM THE MIDDLE OF NOWHERE, SO I DON'T KNOW ANYONE HERE...
I FIGURED I WOULDN'T BE ABLE TO MAKE ANY FRIENDS.
Sigh
BUT I DEFINITELY STILL WANTED TO COME TO TOKYO.
MY FAMILY REALLY DOES LIVE IN THE MIDDLE OF NOWHERE. THERE'S NOTHING THERE.
THERE'S NOTHING WHERE I'M FROM, EITHER.
NOT REALLY.
REALLY?! SO WE'RE THE SAME!
Ah ha ha ha!
Right?
LIKE, THE ONLY CONVENIENCE STORE IS A FORTY-MINUTE DRIVE. IT'S NOT GREAT.
AH! MY TOWN'S NOT THAT BAD.

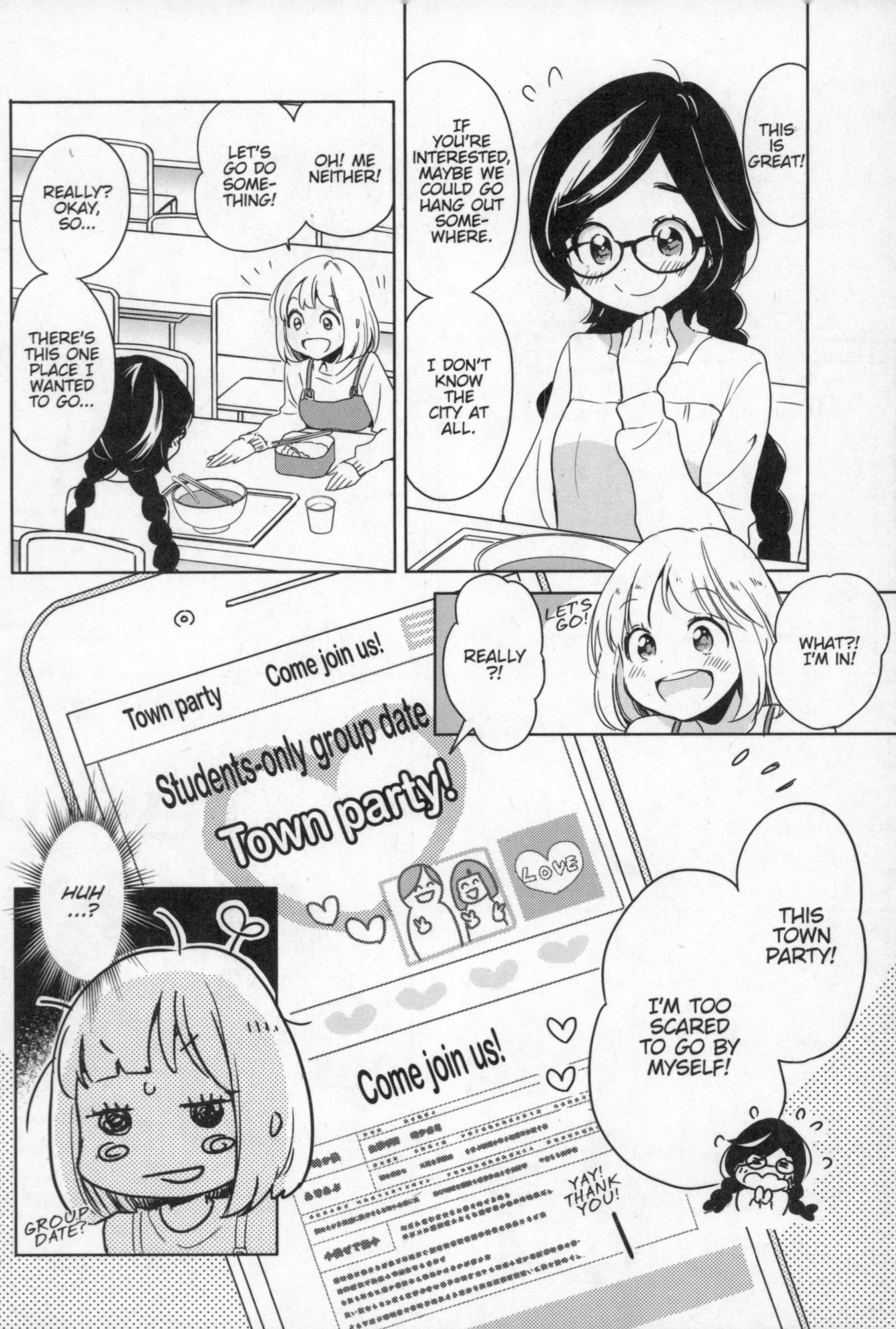
THIS IS GREAT!
IF YOU'RE INTERESTED, MAYBE WE COULD GO HANG OUT SOME-WHERE.
I DON'T KNOW THE CITY AT ALL.
OH! ME NEITHER!
LET'S GO DO SOME-THING!
REALLY? OKAY, SO...
THERE'S THIS ONE PLACE I WANTED TO GO...
WHAT?! I'M IN!
LET'S GO!
REALLY ?!
Come join us!
Town party
Students-only group date
Town party!
LOVE
THIS TOWN PARTY!
I'M TOO SCARED TO GO BY MYSELF!
Come join us!
YAY! THANK YOU!
HUH ...?
GROUP DATE?

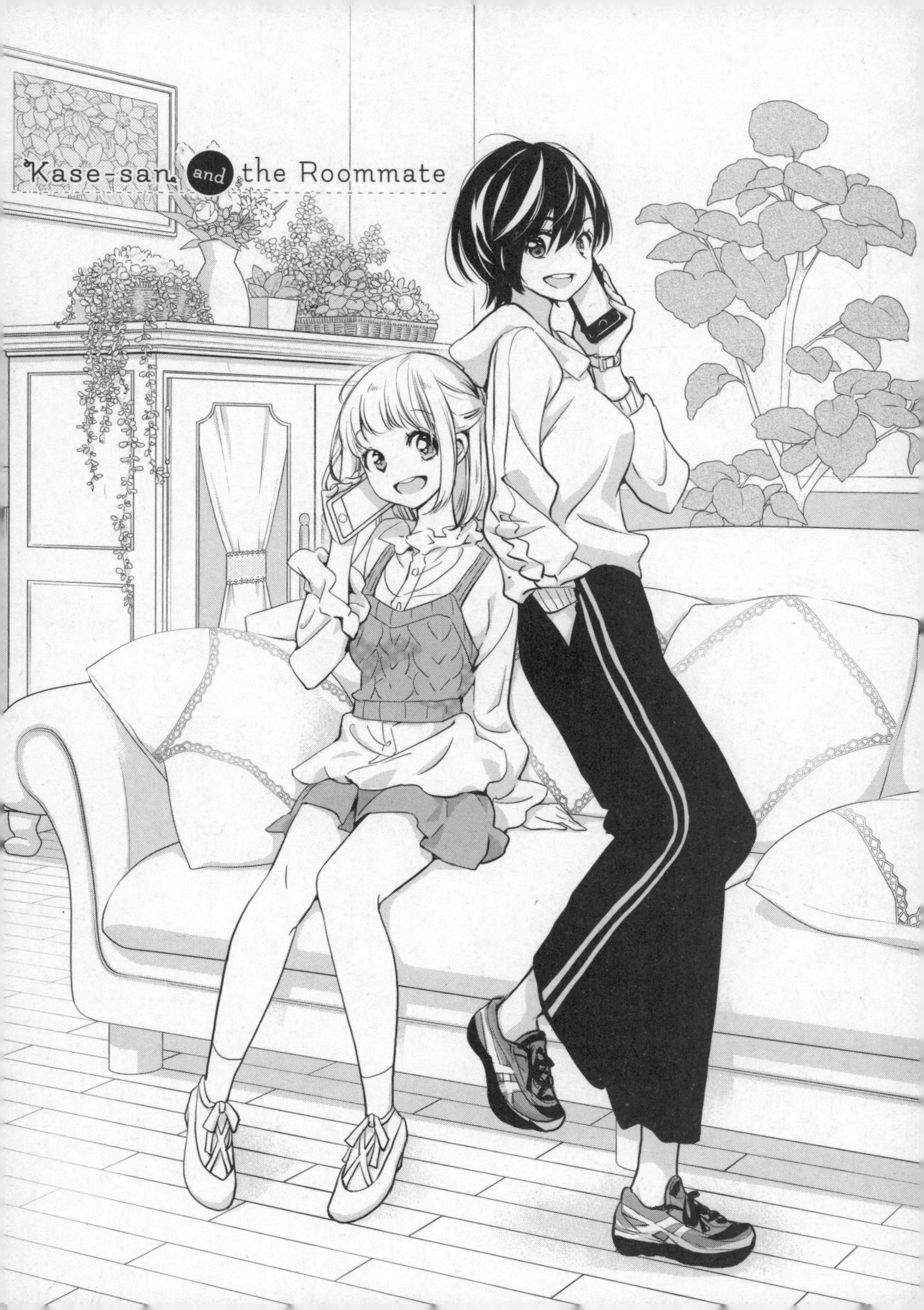
Kase-san and the Roommate

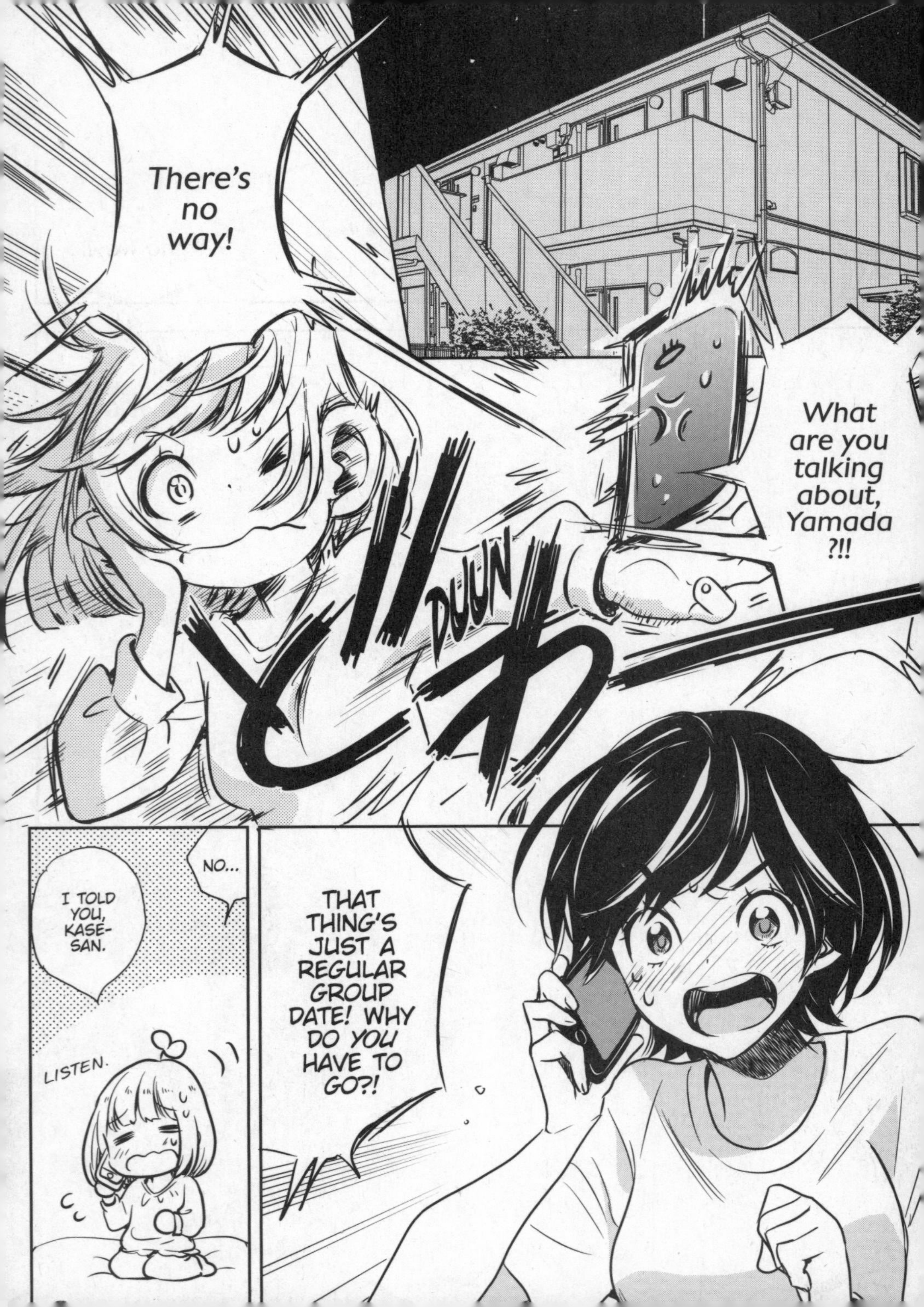
What are you talking about, Yamada?!!
There's no way!
DUUN
THAT THING'S JUST A REGULAR GROUP DATE! WHY DO YOU HAVE TO GO?!
NO...
I TOLD YOU, KASE-SAN.
LISTEN.

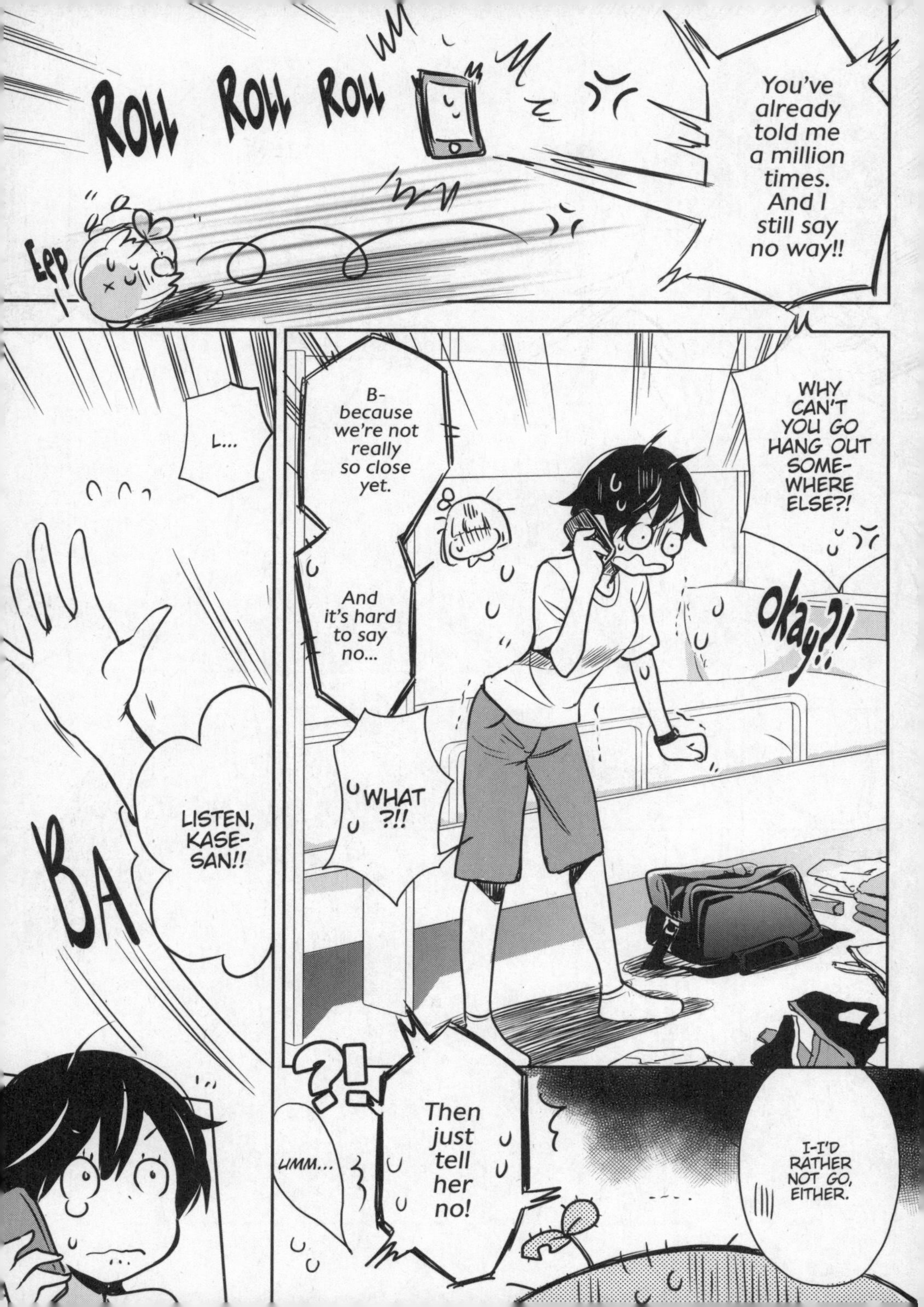

You've already told me a million times. And I still say no way!!
ROLL ROLL ROLL
Eep
WHY CAN'T YOU GO HANG OUT SOME-WHERE ELSE?!
okay?!
B-because we're not really so close yet.
And it's hard to say no...
L...
WHAT?!!
LISTEN, KASE-SAN!!
BA
I-I'D RATHER NOT GO, EITHER.
Then just tell her no!
UMM...
?!

I--!

THIS IS THE FIRST TIME I'VE EVER JUST TALKED TO A PERSON LIKE THIS.

THE FIRST TIME IN MY WHOLE LIFE!

SO, LIKE...

CLench

SHE JUST KEPT TALKING TO ME, SO WE MANAGED TO BECOME FRIENDS.

IT'S BEEN LIKE THAT FOR ME EVER SINCE ELEMENTARY SCHOOL.

FOR THREE YEARS, MIKAWACCHI WAS BASICALLY MY ONLY FRIEND.

AND THAT WAS ONLY BECAUSE WE SAT RIGHT BY EACH OTHER IN GRADE TEN.

AND IT'S MY FIRST FRIEND WHO LIKES THE SAME STUFF AS ME!

I WANT TO TRY AND MAKE IT WORK!

THIS IS THE FIRST TIME I'VE MADE A FRIEND ALL ON MY OWN!

BWAAAN

Yama-da...

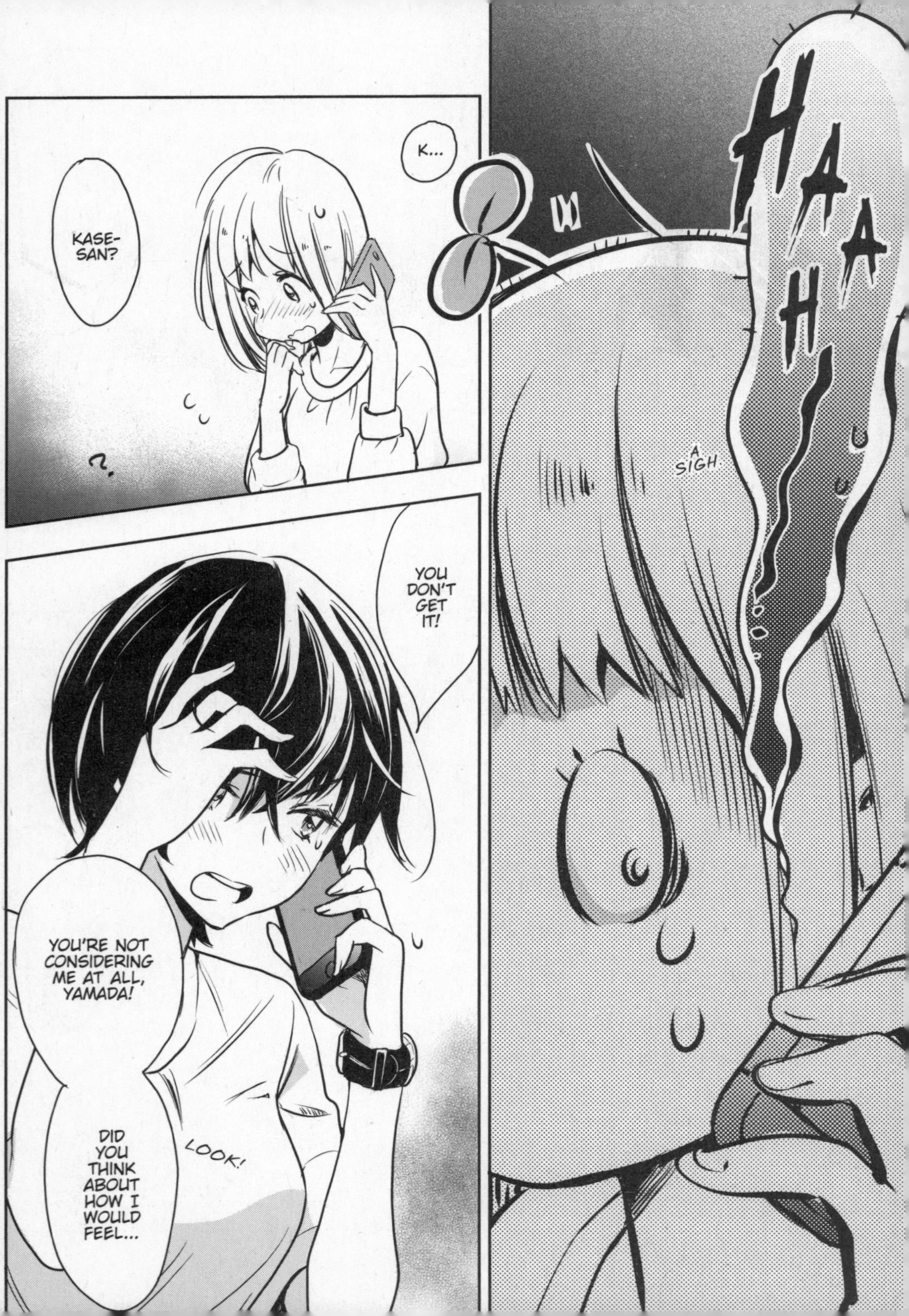
HAAH
A SIGH
K...
KASE-SAN?
YOU DON'T GET IT!
YOU'RE NOT CONSIDERING ME AT ALL, YAMADA!
LOOK!
DID YOU THINK ABOUT HOW I WOULD FEEL...

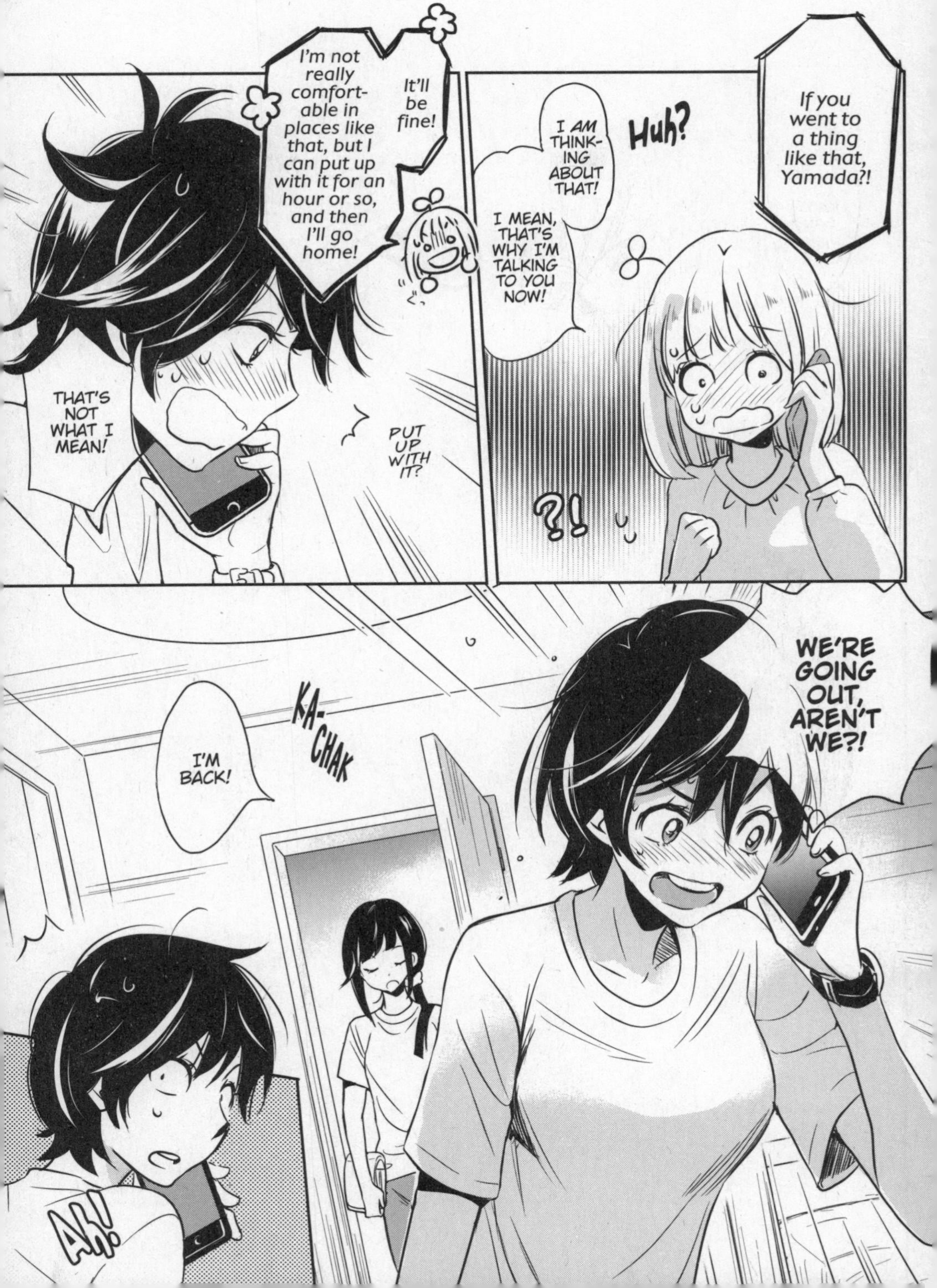
If you went to a thing like that, Yamada?!
Huh?
I AM THINKING ABOUT THAT!
I MEAN, THAT'S WHY I'M TALKING TO YOU NOW!
?!
It'll be fine!
I'm not really comfortable in places like that, but I can put up with it for an hour or so, and then I'll go home!
PUT UP WITH IT?
THAT'S NOT WHAT I MEAN!
WE'RE GOING OUT, AREN'T WE?!
KA-CHAK
I'M BACK!
Ah!

LIGHTS OUT IS AT ELEVEN, AND WAKE-UP TIME IS AT SEVEN.

KASE-SAN SHARES A ROOM IN A WOMEN'S DORM.

54

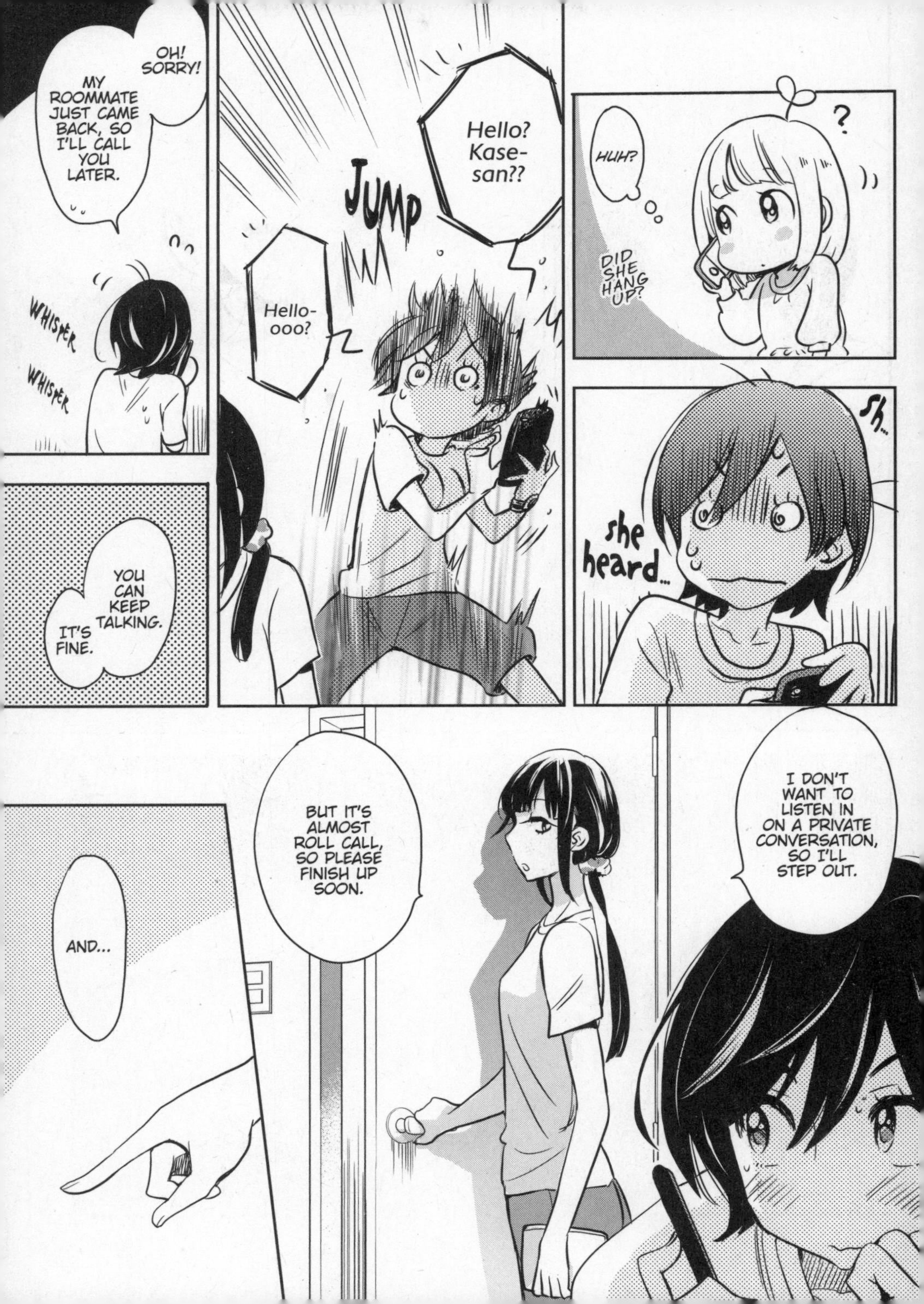
HUH?
DID SHE HANG UP?
Hello? Kase-san??
JUMP
Hello-ooo?
OH! SORRY!
MY ROOMMATE JUST CAME BACK, SO I'LL CALL YOU LATER.
WHISPER
WHISPER
sh...
she heard...
YOU CAN KEEP TALKING.
IT'S FINE.
I DON'T WANT TO LISTEN IN ON A PRIVATE CONVERSATION, SO I'LL STEP OUT.
BUT IT'S ALMOST ROLL CALL, SO PLEASE FINISH UP SOON.
AND...

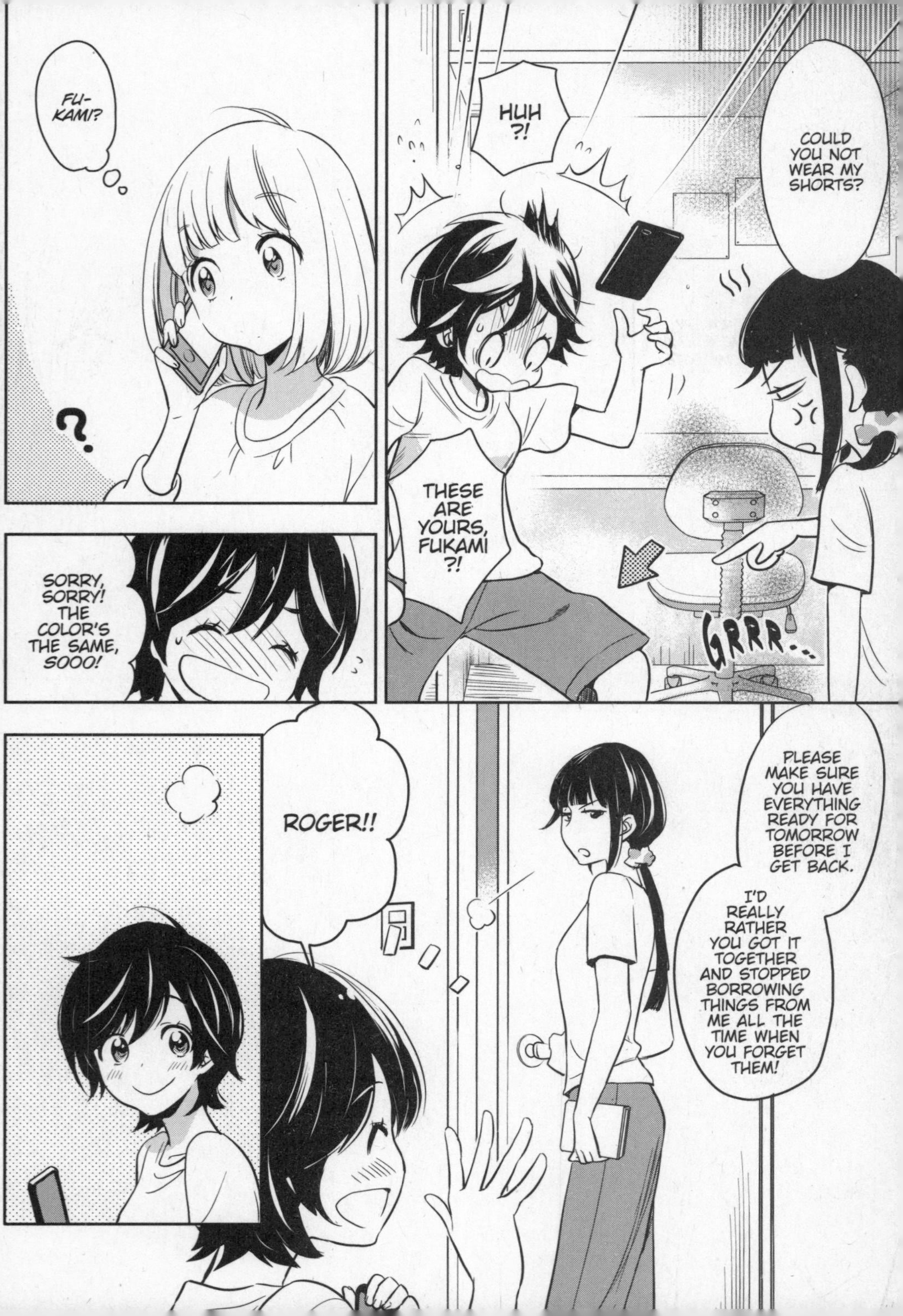
COULD YOU NOT WEAR MY SHORTS?
HUH ?!
THESE ARE YOURS, FUKAMI ?!
GRRR...
FU-KAMI?
SORRY, SORRY! THE COLOR'S THE SAME, SOOO!
PLEASE MAKE SURE YOU HAVE EVERYTHING READY FOR TOMORROW BEFORE I GET BACK.
I'D REALLY RATHER YOU GOT IT TOGETHER AND STOPPED BORROWING THINGS FROM ME ALL THE TIME WHEN YOU FORGET THEM!
ROGER!!

WHAT IS THIS FEELING?

I KNEW SHE HAD A ROOMMATE.

AND SHE SAID THEY HAD A BUNK BED.

HUH?

SLUMP...

.....

clench...

HELLO?

IT'S LIKE... I DON'T KNOW...

BUT HEARING THEIR VOICES...

I SUD-DENLY...

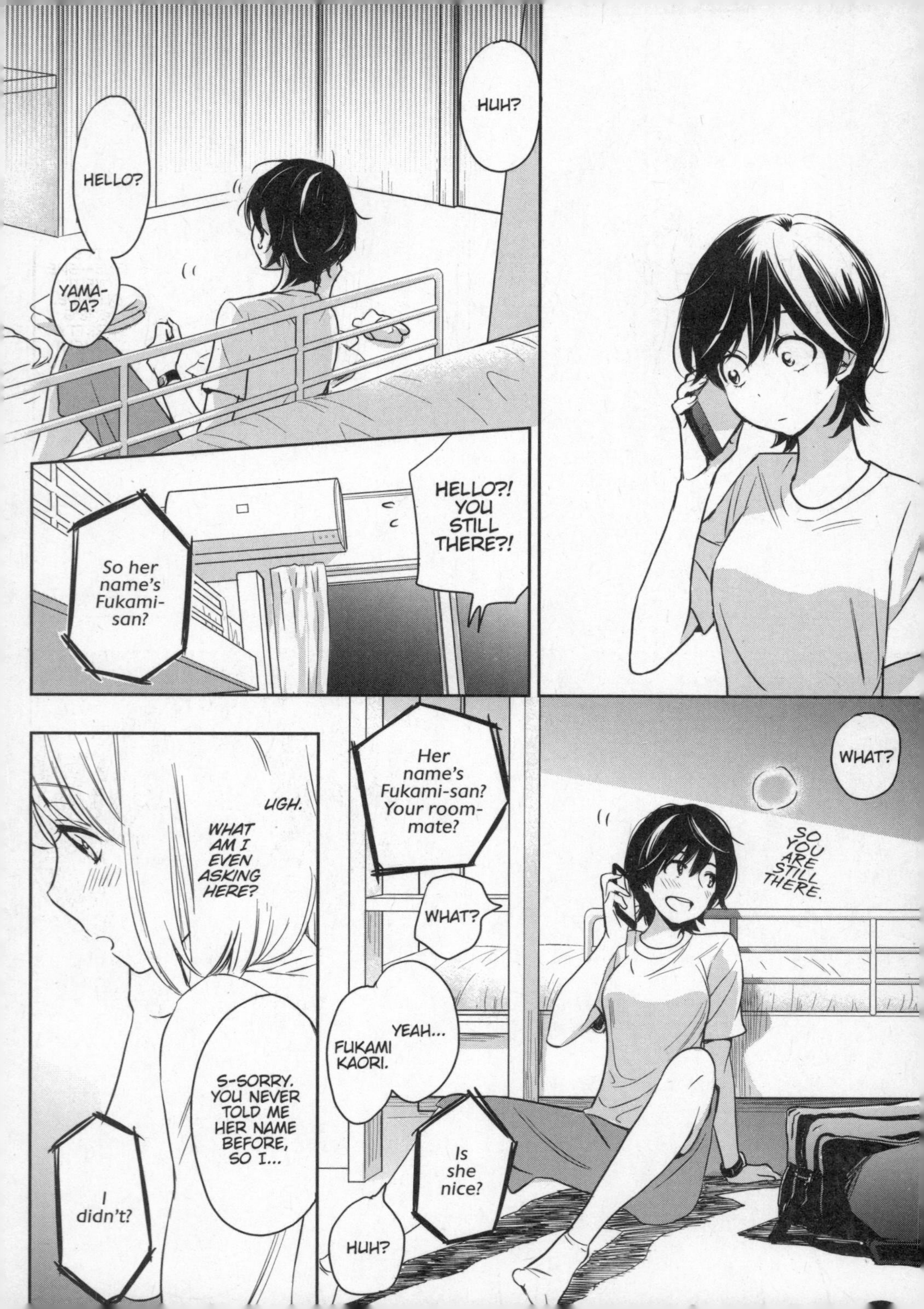
HUH?
HELLO?
YAMADA?
HELLO?! YOU STILL THERE?!
So her name's Fukami-san?
WHAT?
SO YOU ARE STILL THERE.
Her name's Fukami-san? Your room-mate?
WHAT?
YEAH... FUKAMI KAORI.
Is she nice?
HUH?
UGH.
WHAT AM I EVEN ASKING HERE?
S-SORRY. YOU NEVER TOLD ME HER NAME BEFORE, SO I...
I didn't?

HUH?

SHE'S PRETTY COOL. I DON'T REALLY KNOW HER, THOUGH.

BUT YOU CAN FORGET ABOUT HER, YAMADA.

AHAHAHA...

ANYWAY, SO GETTING BACK TO IT...

SHE'S COOL.

IT'S FINE--SHE WENT OUTSIDE. SHE'S PRETTY THOUGHTFUL.

I HEARD SOMETHING ABOUT GETTING READY...

DO YOU HAVE A THING TOMORROW?

What?

HUH? DUNNO. JUST REGULAR, I GUESS.

So you're pretty friendly...

AH...

I WON'T BE AROUND UNTIL NEXT SATURDAY-- SORRY.

AND THEN WE'VE GOT THE MEET AFTER THAT, SO I'M BASICALLY GONE THE WHOLE WEEK.

YEAH, WE'RE GOING TO NAGANO FOR THREE DAYS.

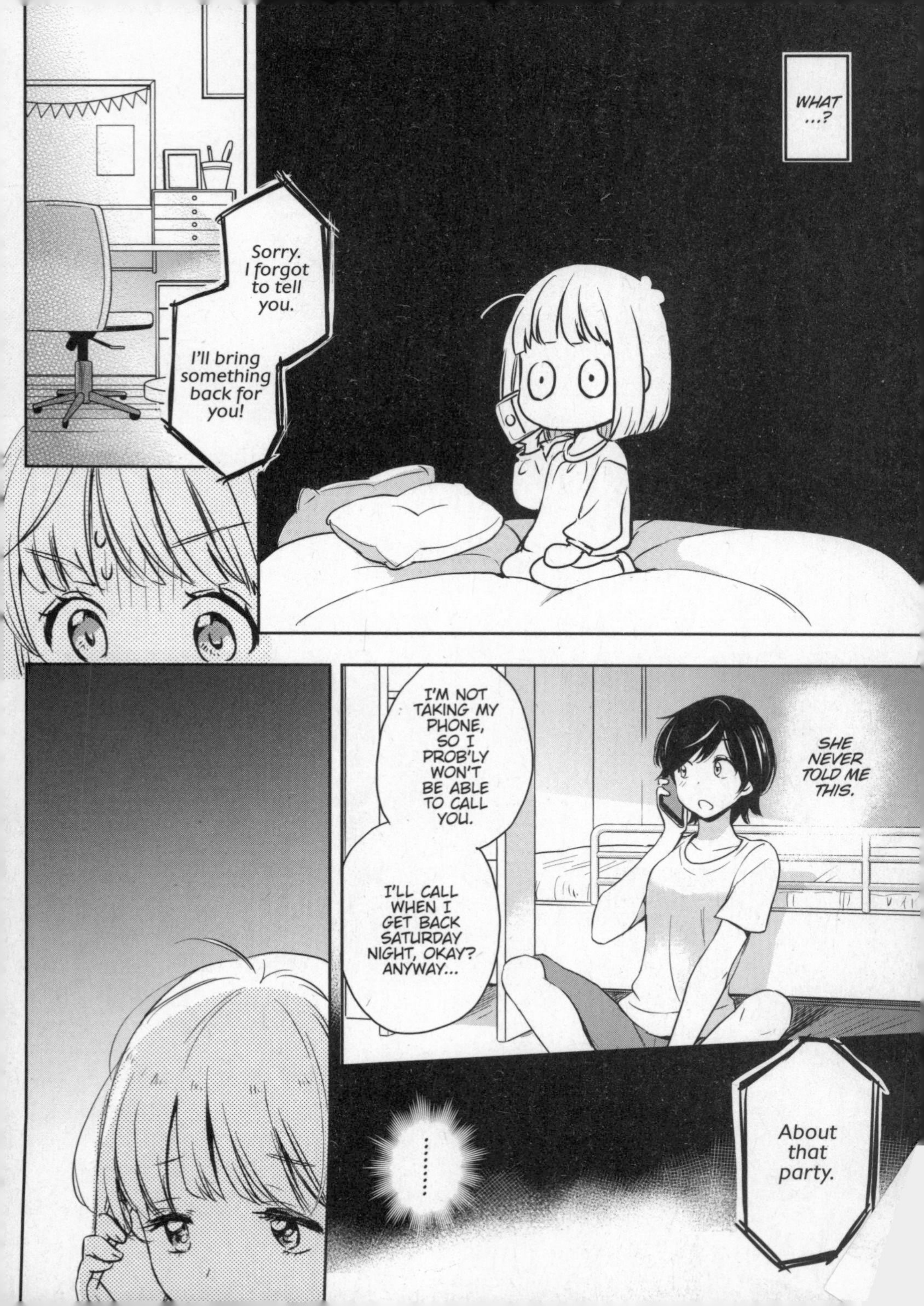
WHAT ...?
Sorry. I forgot to tell you.
I'll bring something back for you!
I'M NOT TAKING MY PHONE, SO I PROB'LY WON'T BE ABLE TO CALL YOU.
I'LL CALL WHEN I GET BACK SATURDAY NIGHT, OKAY? ANYWAY...
SHE NEVER TOLD ME THIS.
......
About that party.

I'M GOING.

HUH?

It's next Saturday. The town party.

IN IKEBU- KURO.

KASE- SAN...

I'M GOING TO GO WITH HANA- CHAN!

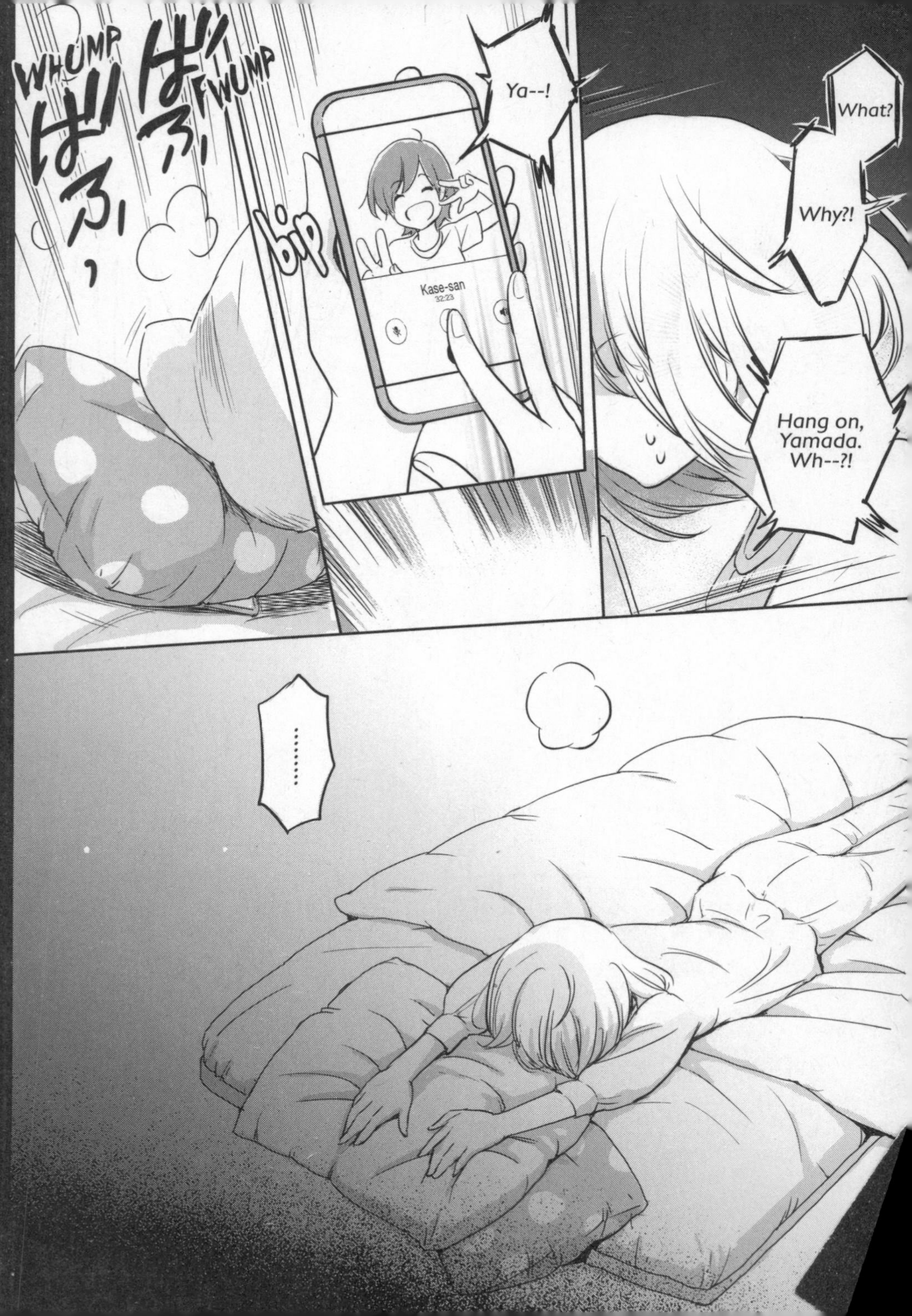

What?
Why?!
Hang on, Yamada. Wh--?!
Ya--!
Kase-san
32:23
bip
WHUMP
ばふ
FWUMP
ばふ
......

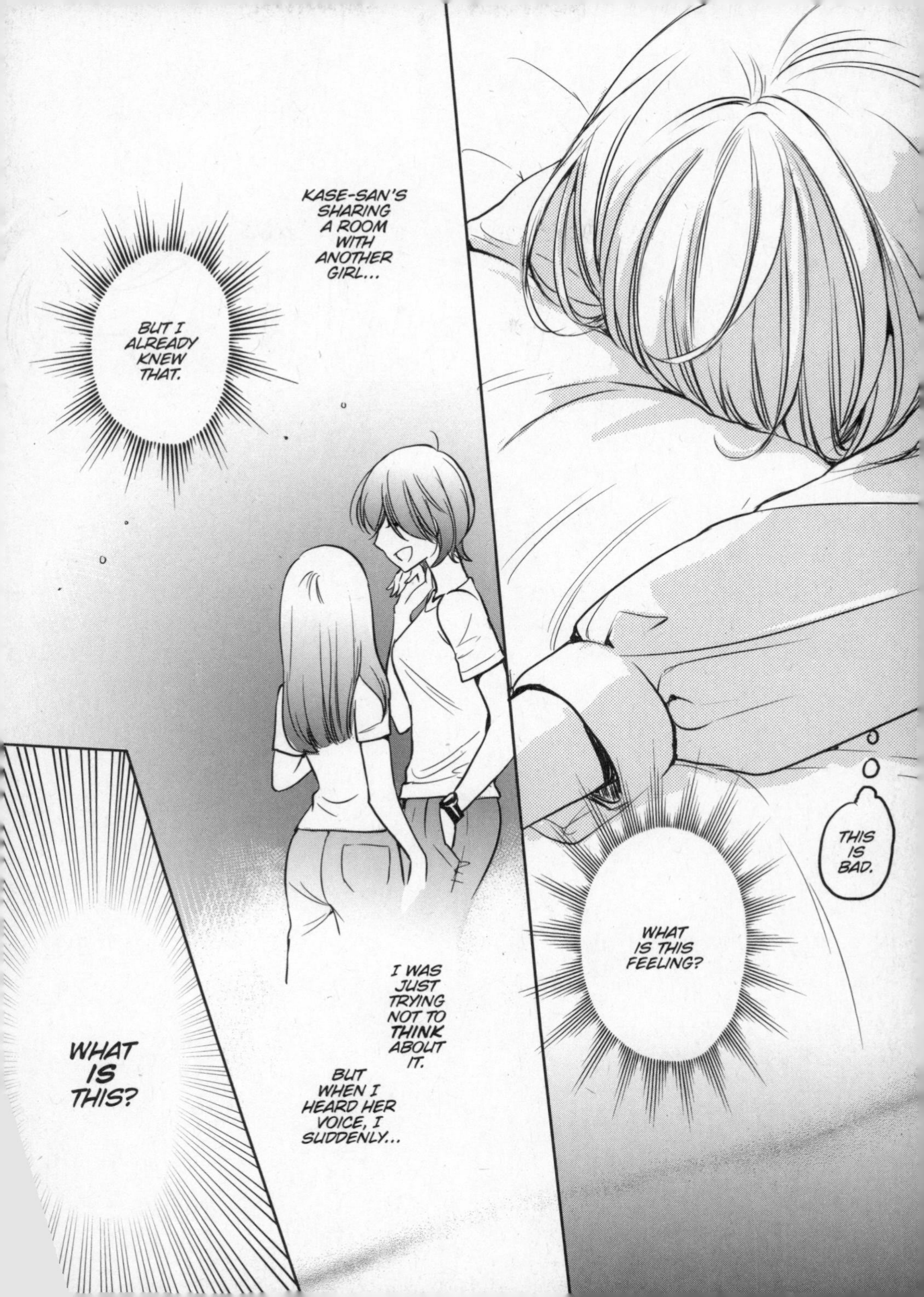
THIS IS BAD.
WHAT IS THIS FEELING?
KASE-SAN'S SHARING A ROOM WITH ANOTHER GIRL...
BUT I ALREADY KNEW THAT.
I WAS JUST TRYING NOT TO THINK ABOUT IT.
BUT WHEN I HEARD HER VOICE, I SUDDENLY...
WHAT IS THIS?

YUI-CHAAAN!

THE NEXT SATUR-DAY...

GETTING READY TOOK TOO LONG, AND NOW I'M LATE!

S-SORRY!

HUFF!

HUFF! HUFF!

HANA-CHAN?!

Y'AY

HUFF! HUFF! HUFF!

I GOT LOST, SO I JUST GOT HERE!

IT'S OKAY!

Ah-ha-ha!

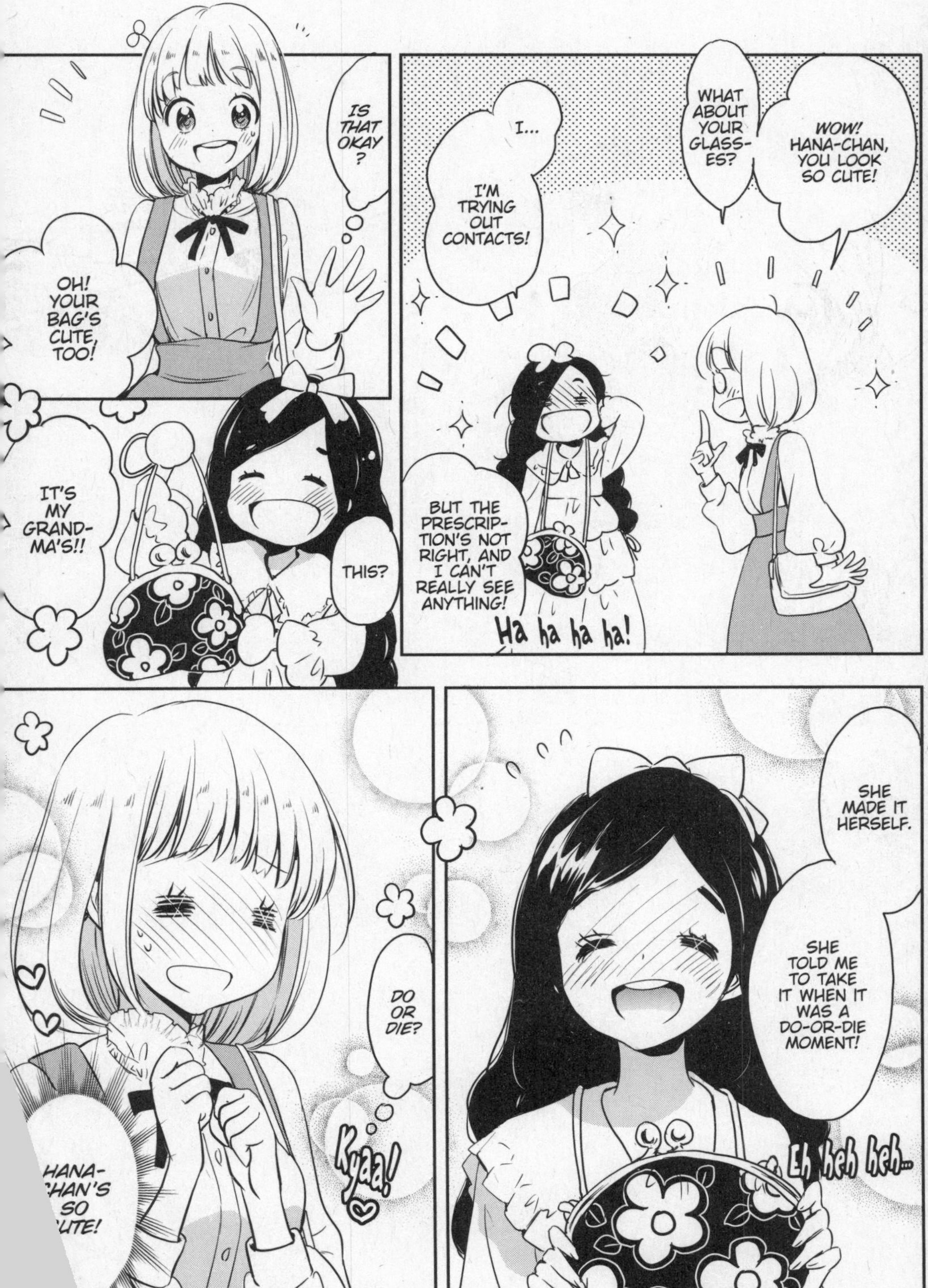
WOW! HANA-CHAN, YOU LOOK SO CUTE!
WHAT ABOUT YOUR GLASS-ES?
I...
I'M TRYING OUT CONTACTS!
BUT THE PRESCRIP-TION'S NOT RIGHT, AND I CAN'T REALLY SEE ANYTHING!
Ha ha ha ha!
IS THAT OKAY?
OH! YOUR BAG'S CUTE, TOO!
THIS?
IT'S MY GRAND-MA'S!!
SHE MADE IT HERSELF.
SHE TOLD ME TO TAKE IT WHEN IT WAS A DO-OR-DIE MOMENT!
Eh heh heh...
DO OR DIE?
Kyaa!
HANA-CHAN'S SO CUTE!

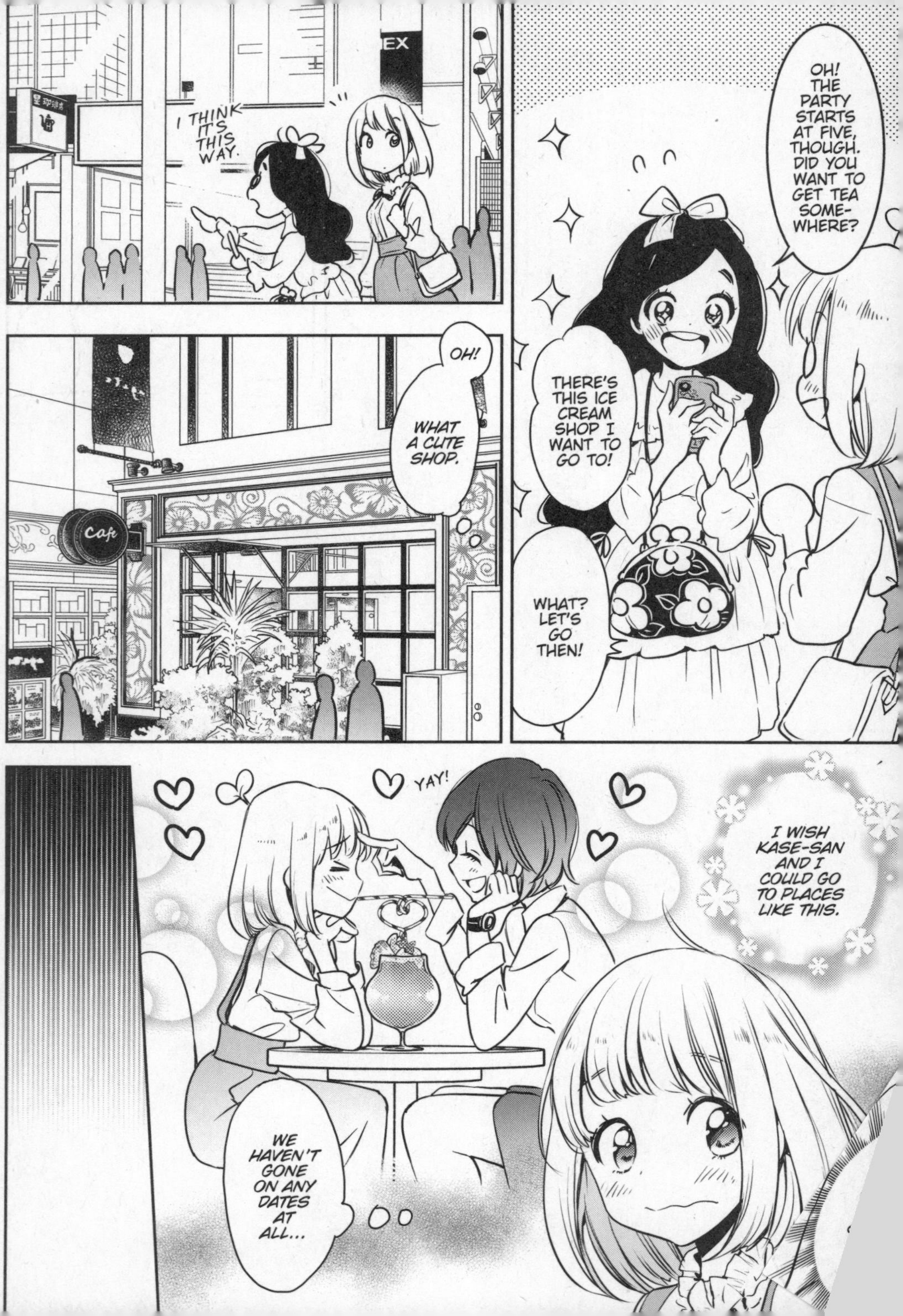
I THINK IT'S THIS WAY.
OH! THE PARTY STARTS AT FIVE, THOUGH. DID YOU WANT TO GET TEA SOME-WHERE?
THERE'S THIS ICE CREAM SHOP I WANT TO GO TO!
WHAT? LET'S GO THEN!
OH!
WHAT A CUTE SHOP.
Cafe
YAY!
I WISH KASE-SAN AND I COULD GO TO PLACES LIKE THIS.
WE HAVEN'T GONE ON ANY DATES AT ALL...

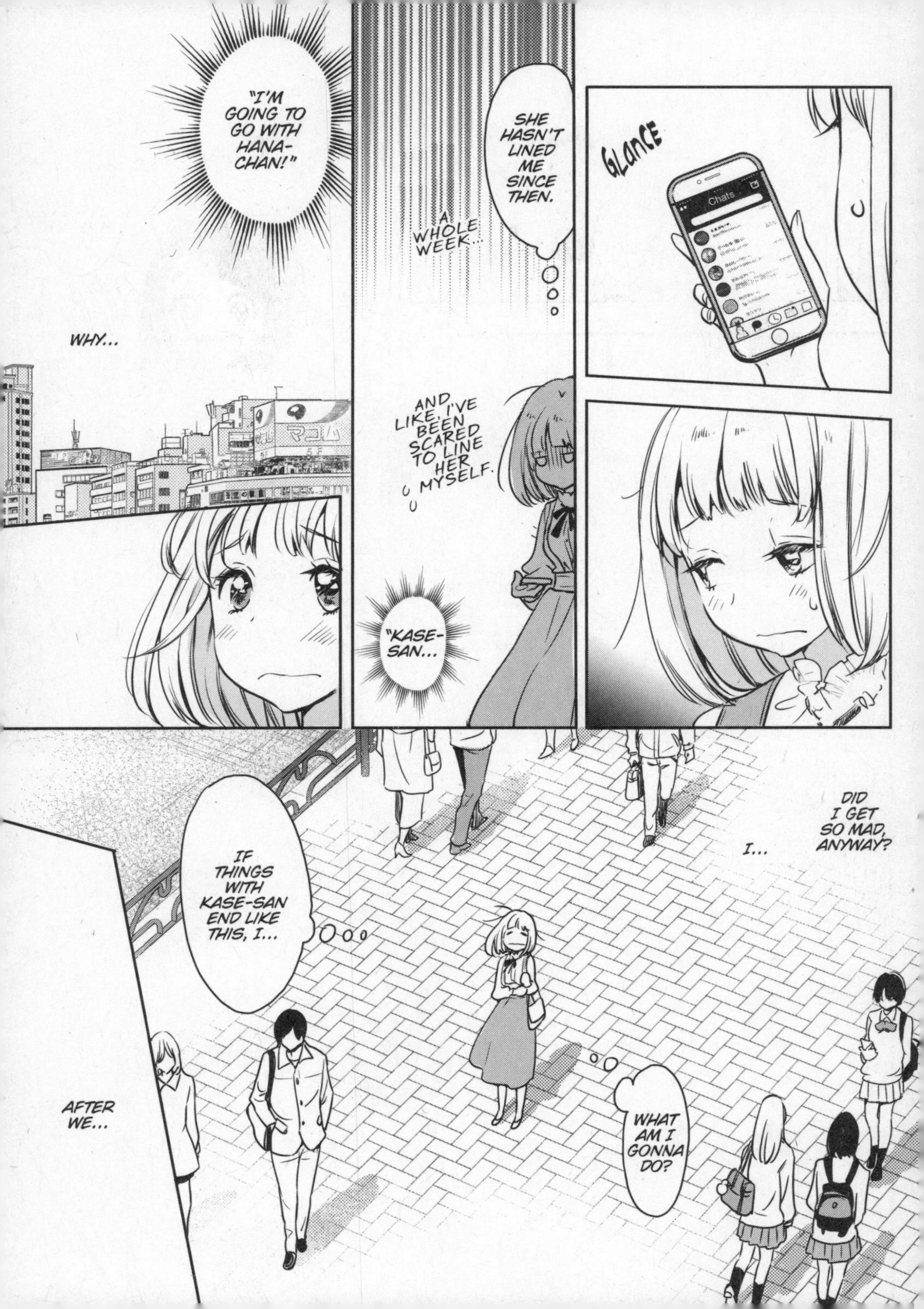
GLANCE
Chats
SHE HASN'T LINED ME SINCE THEN.
A WHOLE WEEK...
AND LIKE, I'VE BEEN SCARED TO LINE HER MYSELF.
"KASE-SAN...
"I'M GOING TO GO WITH HANA-CHAN!"
WHY...
DID I GET SO MAD, ANYWAY?
I...
IF THINGS WITH KASE-SAN END LIKE THIS, I...
WHAT AM I GONNA DO?
AFTER WE...

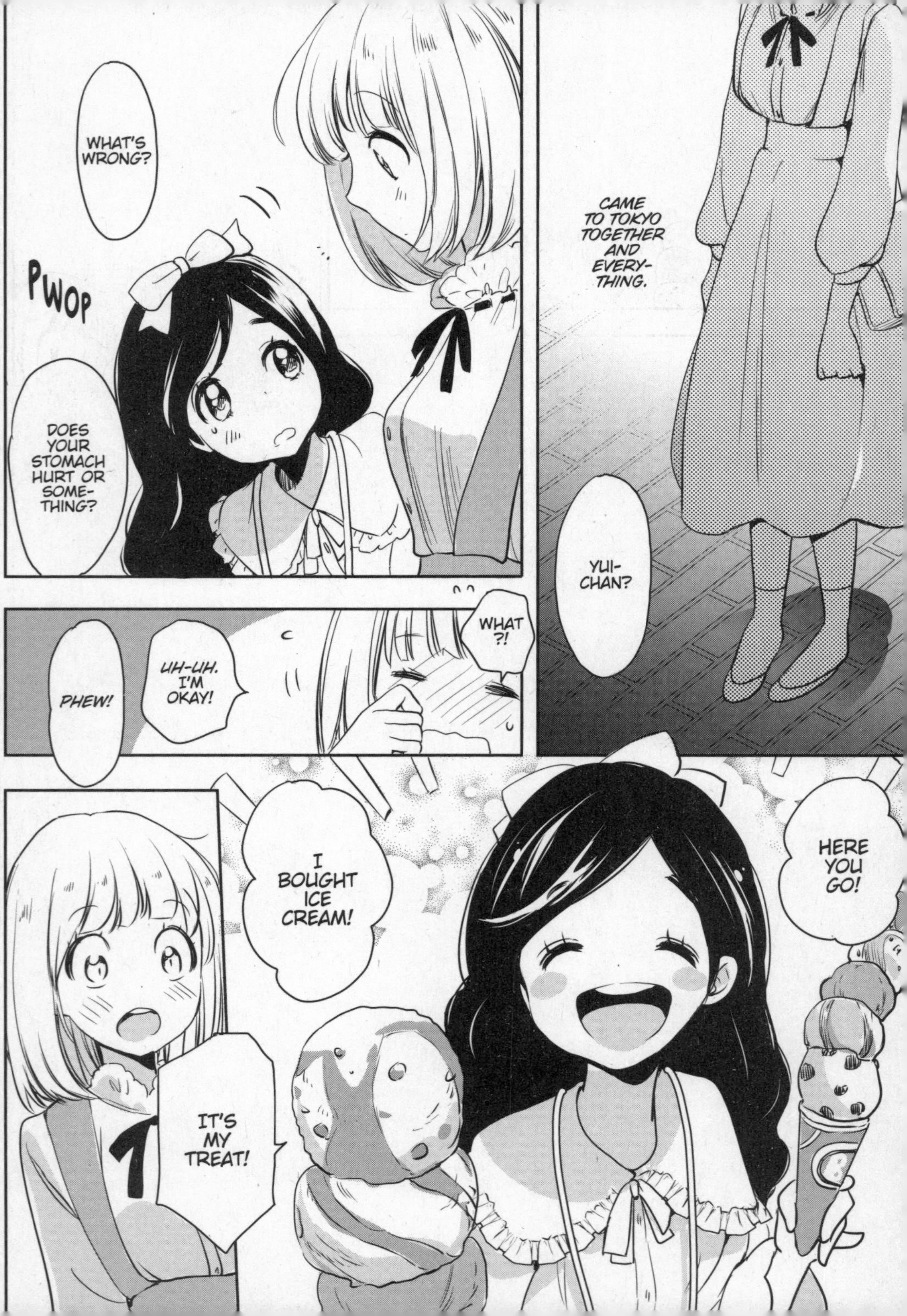
CAME TO TOKYO TOGETHER AND EVERY-THING.
YUI-CHAN?
WHAT'S WRONG?
PWOP
DOES YOUR STOMACH HURT OR SOME-THING?
WHAT?!
UH-UH. I'M OKAY!
PHEW!
HERE YOU GO!
I BOUGHT ICE CREAM!
IT'S MY TREAT!

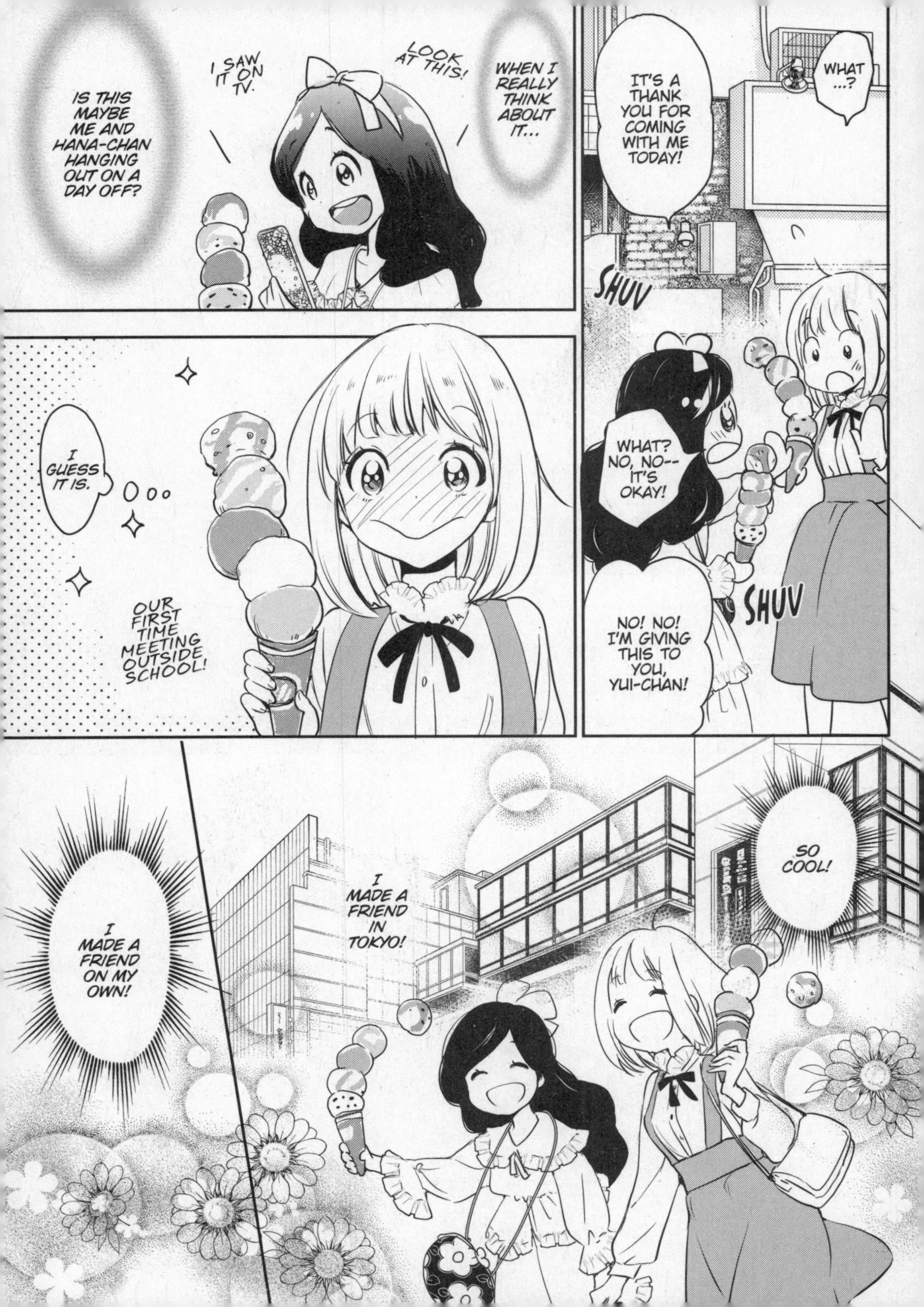
WHEN I REALLY THINK ABOUT IT...
IS THIS MAYBE ME AND HANA-CHAN HANGING OUT ON A DAY OFF?
LOOK AT THIS!
I SAW IT ON TV.
WHAT ...?
IT'S A THANK YOU FOR COMING WITH ME TODAY!
SHUV
WHAT? NO, NO-- IT'S OKAY!
SHUV
NO! NO! I'M GIVING THIS TO YOU, YUI-CHAN!
I GUESS IT IS.
OUR FIRST TIME MEETING OUTSIDE SCHOOL!
SO COOL!
I MADE A FRIEND IN TOKYO!
I MADE A FRIEND ON MY OWN!

TOWN PARTY!

IT SAYS TOWN PARTY!

Town Party

Time: 17:00~20:00

Free Drink

University/Graduate/Technical School Students aged 18-24 only.
Student ID Required.
※Alcohol will not be provided to underage students.

OH!

IT'S HERE, YUI-CHAN!

5:00 PM.

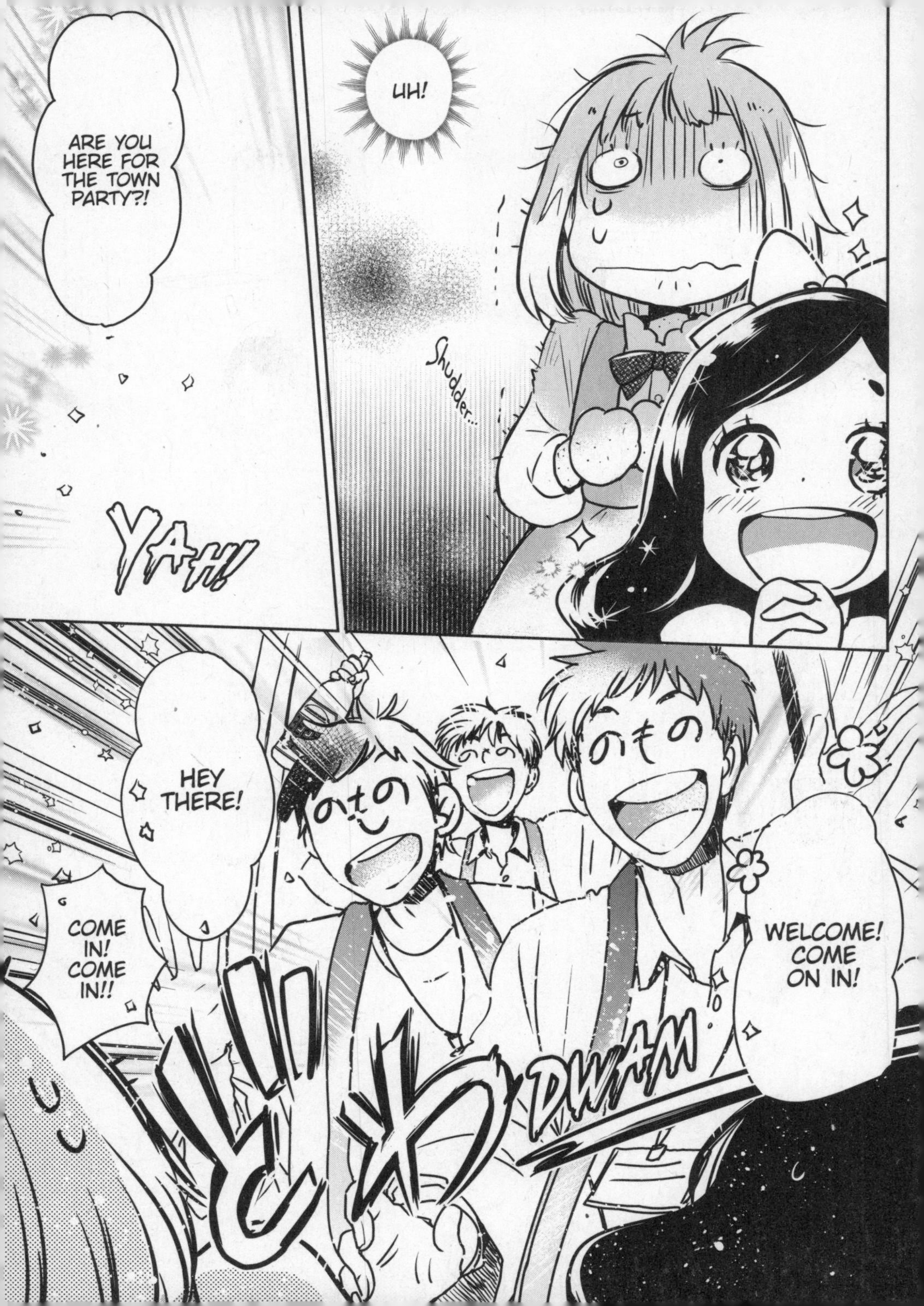
UH!
Shudder...
ARE YOU HERE FOR THE TOWN PARTY?!
YAH!
WELCOME! COME ON IN!
HEY THERE!
COME IN! COME IN!!
DWAM

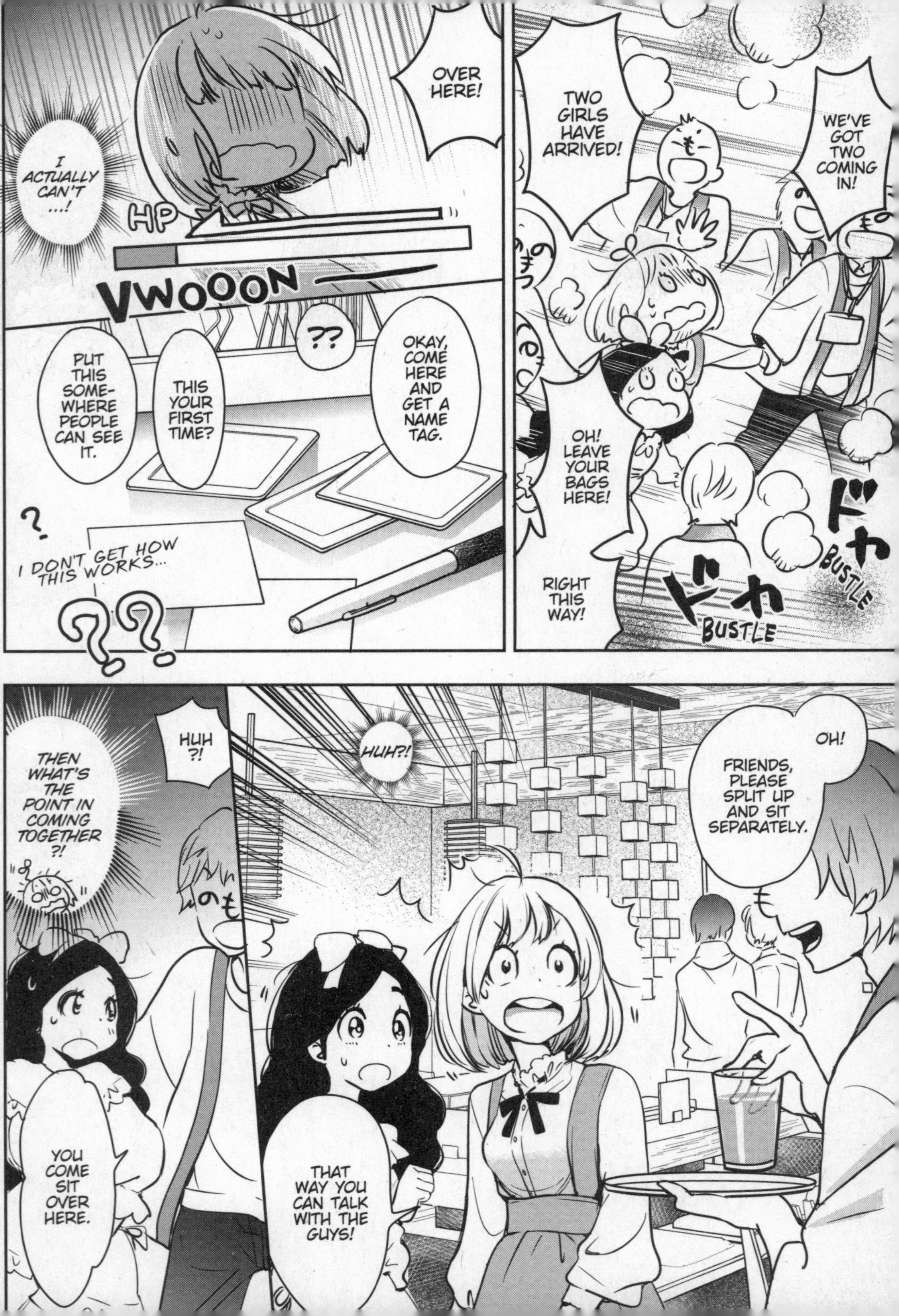
WE'VE GOT TWO COMING IN!
TWO GIRLS HAVE ARRIVED!
OH! LEAVE YOUR BAGS HERE!
RIGHT THIS WAY!
ドヤ
BUSTLE
ドヤ
BUSTLE
OVER HERE!
I ACTUALLY CAN'T ...!
HP
VWOOON
OKAY, COME HERE AND GET A NAME TAG.
??
THIS YOUR FIRST TIME?
PUT THIS SOMEWHERE PEOPLE CAN SEE IT.
I DON'T GET HOW THIS WORKS...
??
OH!
FRIENDS, PLEASE SPLIT UP AND SIT SEPARATELY.
HUH?!
HUH?!
THEN WHAT'S THE POINT IN COMING TOGETHER?!
THAT WAY YOU CAN TALK WITH THE GUYS!
YOU COME SIT OVER HERE.

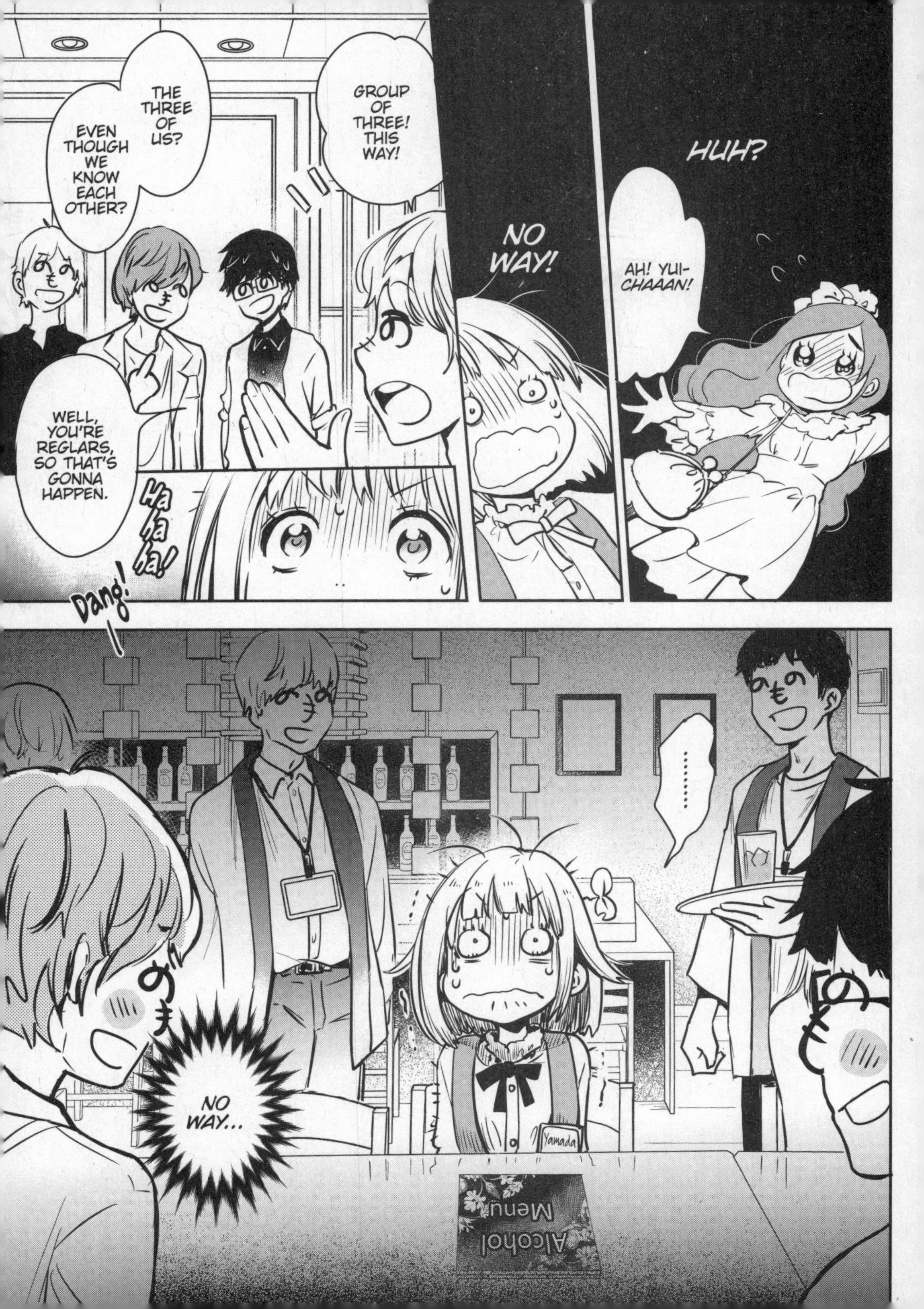
HUH?
AH! YUI-CHAAAN!
NO WAY!
GROUP OF THREE! THIS WAY!
THE THREE OF US?
EVEN THOUGH WE KNOW EACH OTHER?
WELL, YOU'RE REGLARS, SO THAT'S GONNA HAPPEN.
Ha ha ha!
Dang!
......
NO WAY...
Yamada
Alcohol Menu

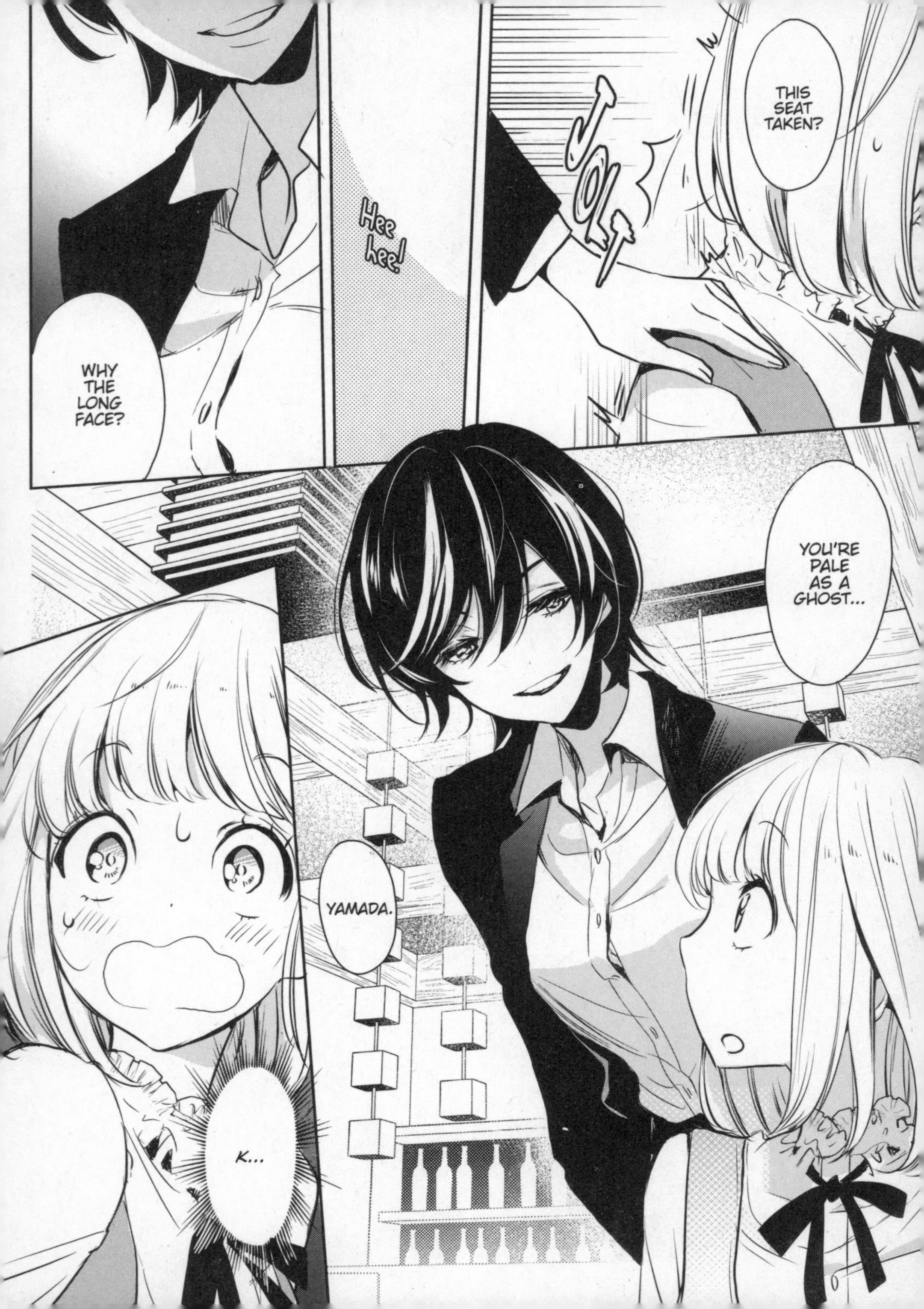
THIS SEAT TAKEN?
JOLT
Hee hee!
WHY THE LONG FACE?
YOU'RE PALE AS A GHOST...
YAMADA.
K...

Kase-san *and* Yamada ①

Kase-san and Yamada ①

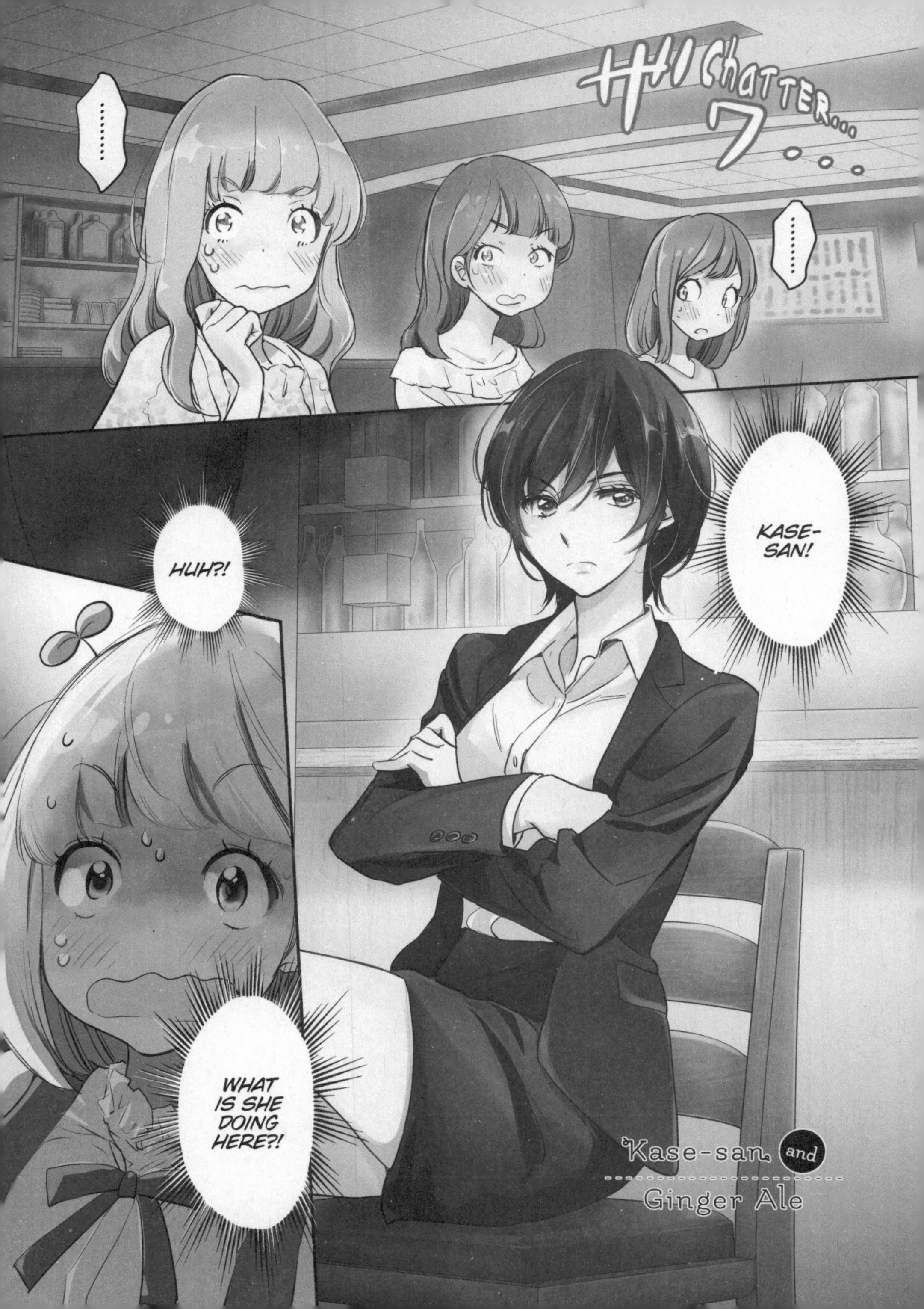
CHATTER CHATTER...
......
......
KASE-SAN!
HUH?!
WHAT IS SHE DOING HERE?!
Kase-san and Ginger Ale

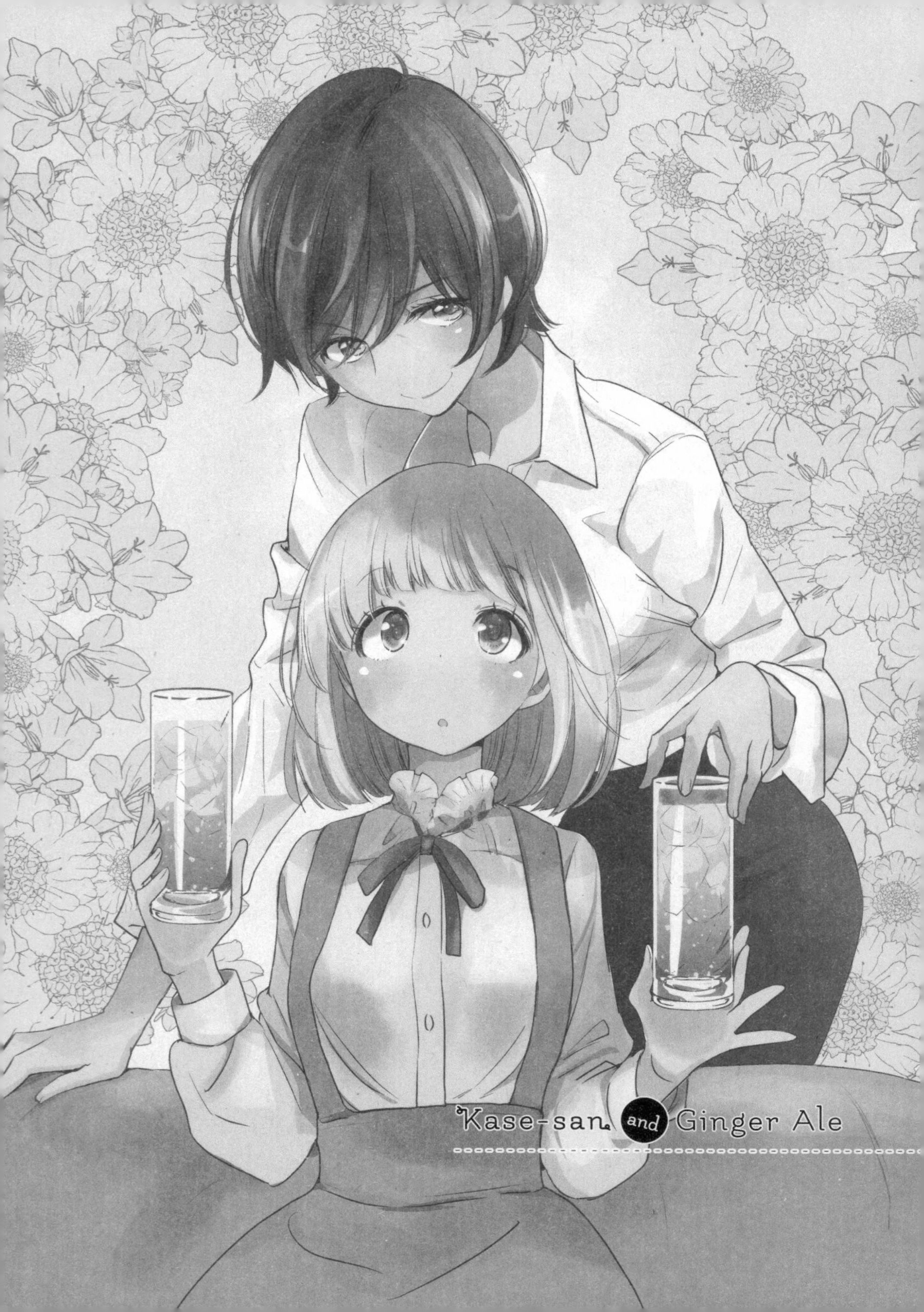
Kase-san and Ginger Ale

OF COURSE SHE'S A WOMAN...

A WOM-AN.

A WOM-AN.

Spoof

WHAT?

EXCUSE ME. ABOUT YOUR SEAT...

AREN'T THE WOMEN SITTING ON THIS SIDE?

WE DON'T KNOW EACH OTHER AT ALL.

OH, IT'S JUST WE'RE GETTING FRIENDS TO SIT APART FROM EACH OTHER.

WE'RE NOT FRIENDS.

Soft Drink Menu

Alcohol Menu

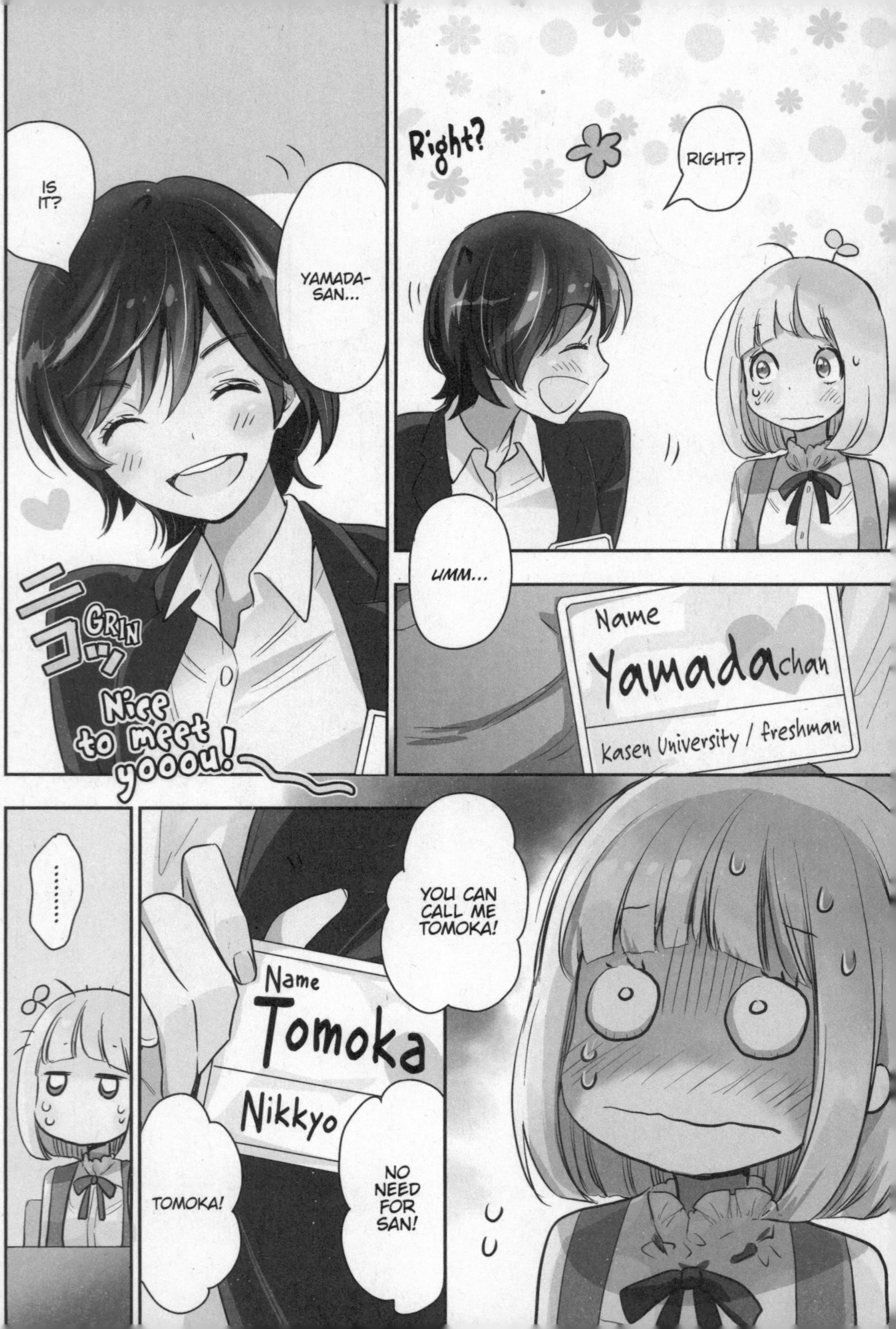
Right?
RIGHT?
UMM...
YAMADA-SAN...
IS IT?
GRIN
Nice to meet yooou!
Name
Yamada chan
Kasen University / freshman
YOU CAN CALL ME TOMOKA!
Name
Tomoka
Nikkyo
NO NEED FOR SAN!
TOMOKA!
......

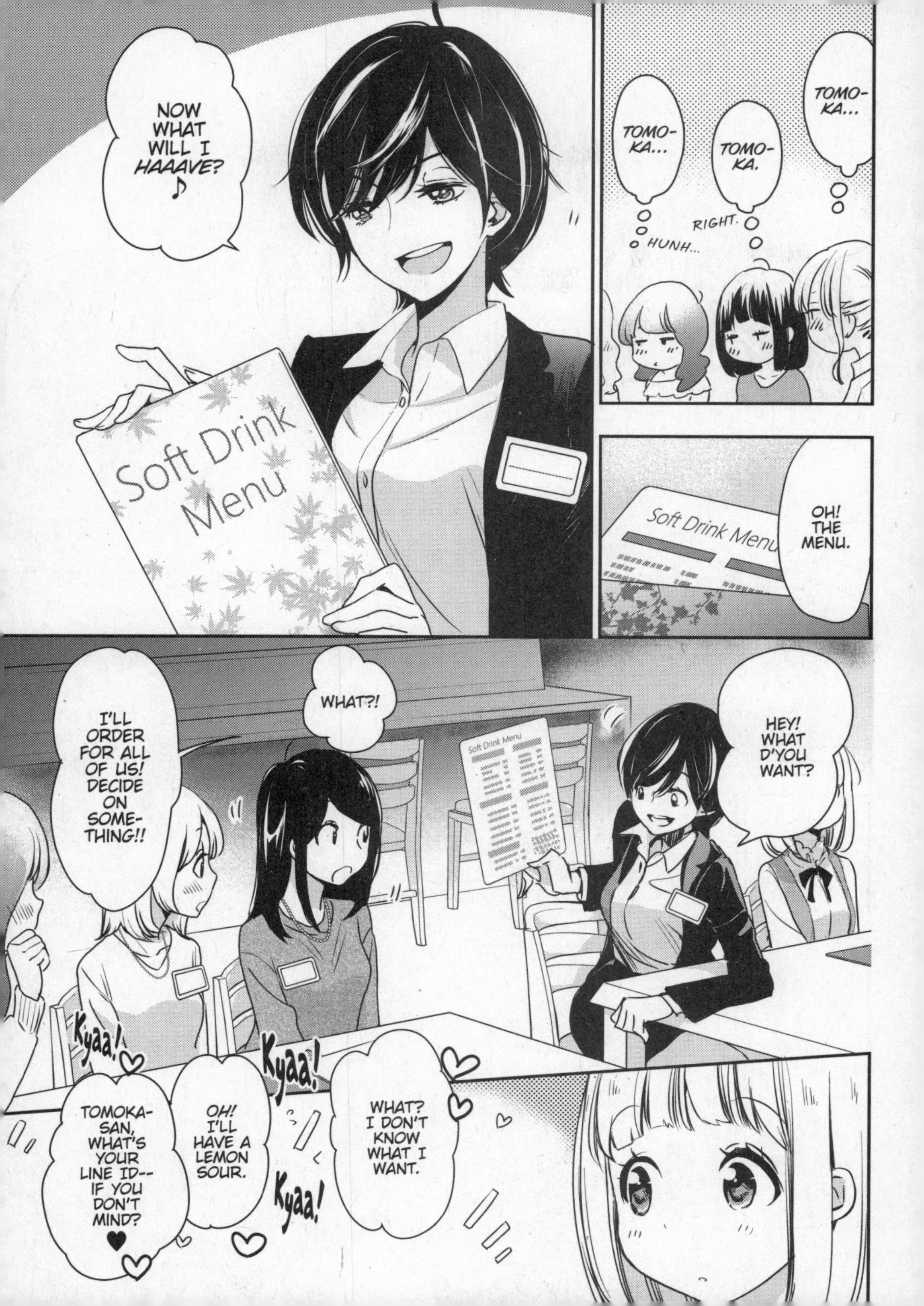
TOMO-KA...
TOMO-KA.
TOMO-KA...
RIGHT.
HUNH...
OH! THE MENU.
Soft Drink Menu
NOW WHAT WILL I HAAAVE? ♪
Soft Drink Menu
HEY! WHAT D'YOU WANT?
WHAT?!
I'LL ORDER FOR ALL OF US! DECIDE ON SOME-THING!!
Soft Drink Menu
Kyaa!
Kyaa!
Kyaa!
WHAT? I DON'T KNOW WHAT I WANT.
OH! I'LL HAVE A LEMON SOUR.
TOMOKA-SAN, WHAT'S YOUR LINE ID-- IF YOU DON'T MIND? ♥

COLD WIND

HEY, SO!

I CAN JUST TELL.

KASEN, THAT'S A WOMEN'S UNIVERSITY, RIGHT?!

ARE YOU IN ANY SCHOOL CLUBS, YAMADA-CHAN?!

WHAT?!

KASE-SAN'S MAD.

OH...

OH!

EXCUSE ME! WE'D LIKE TO ORDER HERE!

??

?

BWAN!

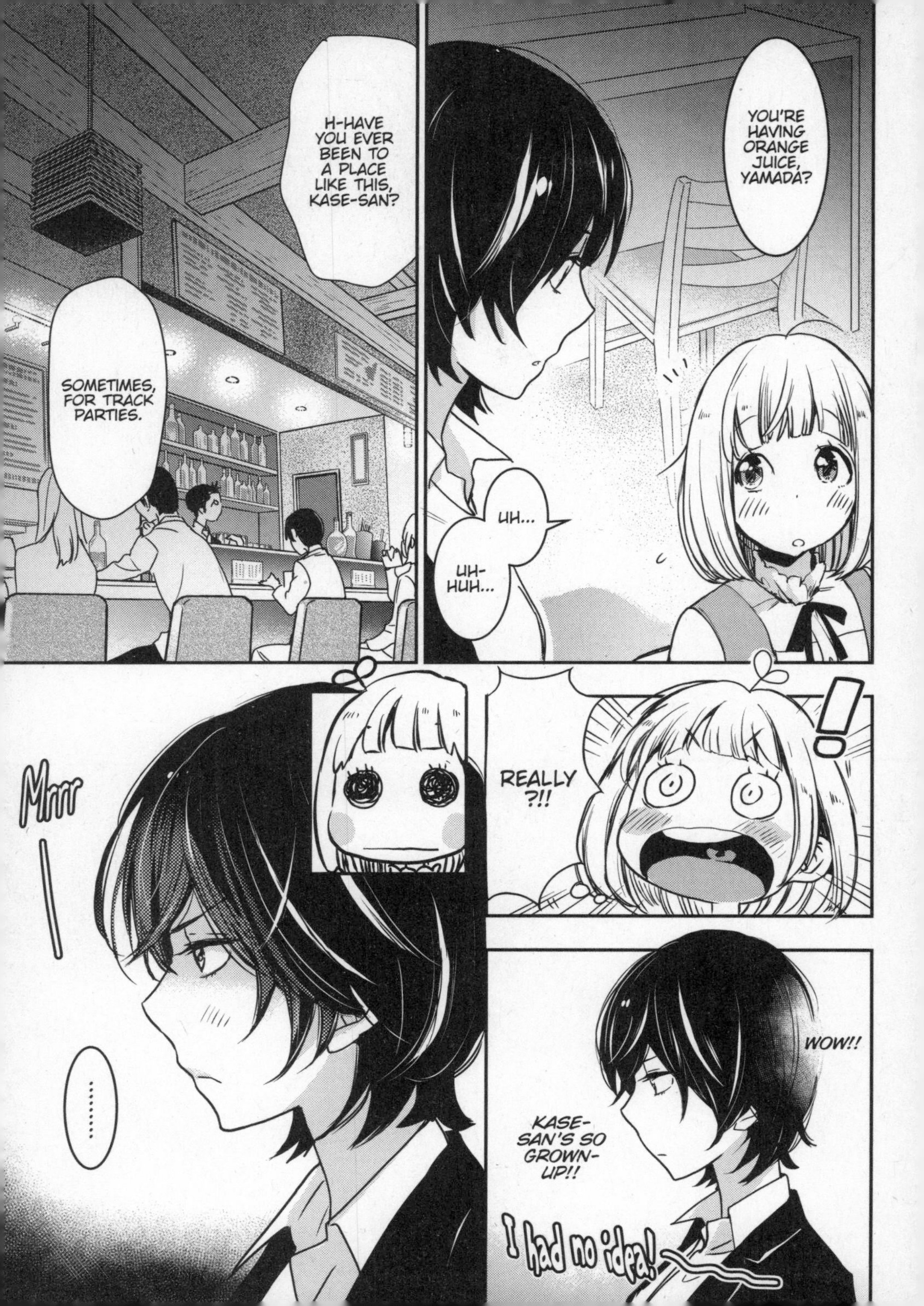
H-HAVE YOU EVER BEEN TO A PLACE LIKE THIS, KASE-SAN?
SOMETIMES, FOR TRACK PARTIES.
YOU'RE HAVING ORANGE JUICE, YAMADA?
UH...
UH-HUH...
REALLY ?!!
Mrrr
WOW!!
KASE-SAN'S SO GROWN-UP!!
I had no idea!

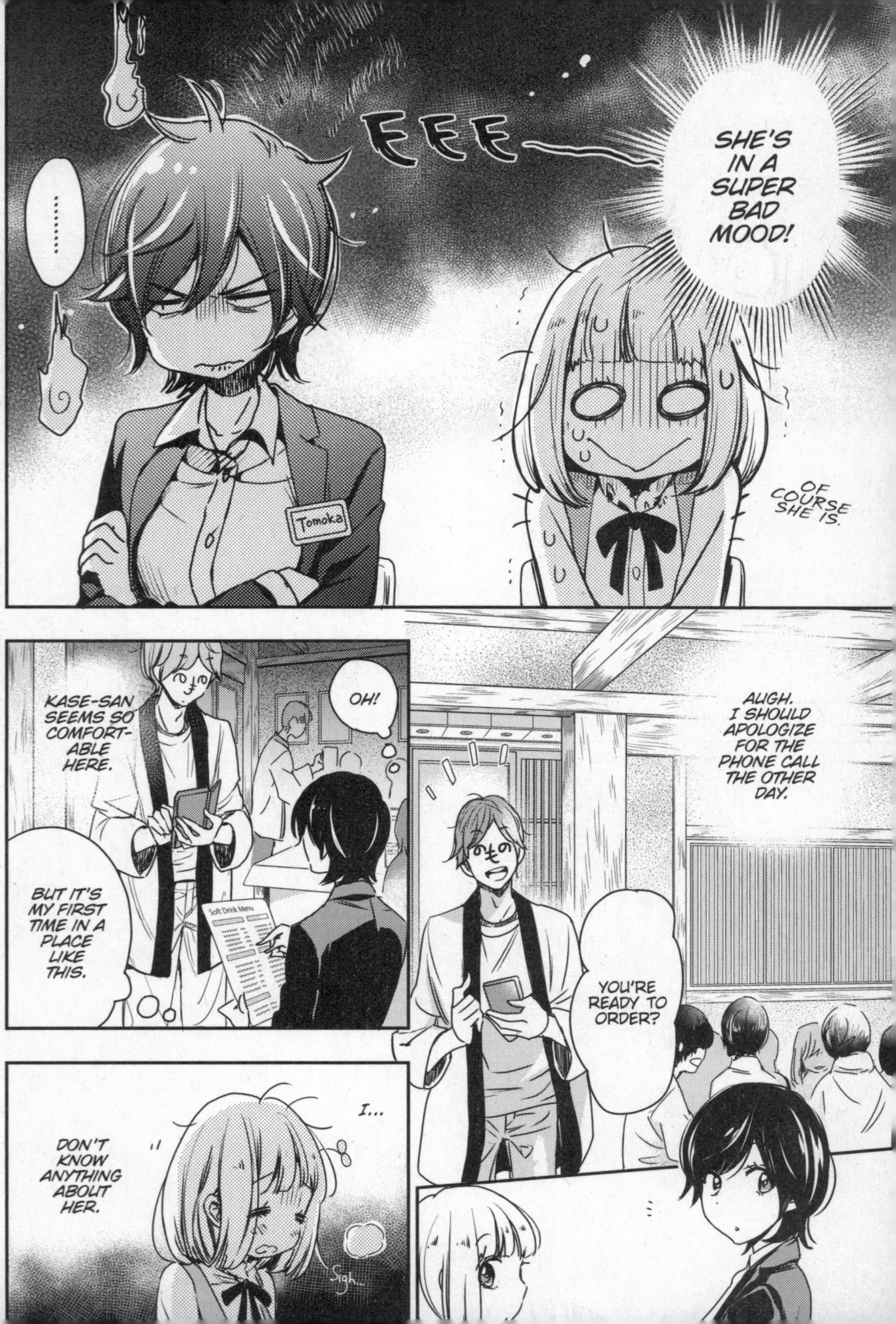
SHE'S IN A SUPER BAD MOOD!
EEE
......
OF COURSE SHE IS.
Tomoka
AUGH. I SHOULD APOLOGIZE FOR THE PHONE CALL THE OTHER DAY.
OH!
KASE-SAN SEEMS SO COMFORTABLE HERE.
BUT IT'S MY FIRST TIME IN A PLACE LIKE THIS.
Soft Drink Menu
YOU'RE READY TO ORDER?
I...
DON'T KNOW ANYTHING ABOUT HER.
Sigh...

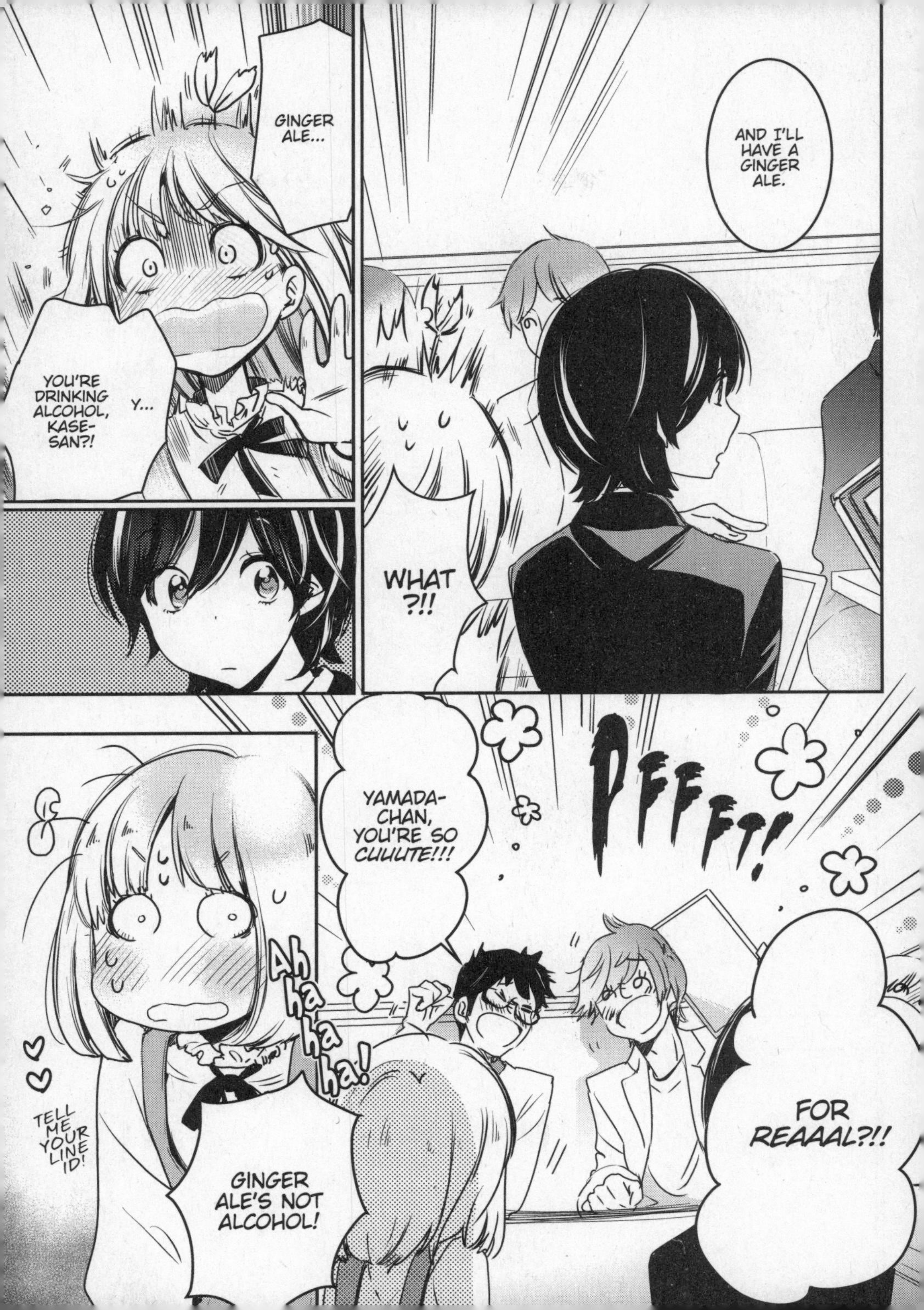
AND I'LL HAVE A GINGER ALE.
GINGER ALE...
Y...
YOU'RE DRINKING ALCOHOL, KASE-SAN?!
WHAT?!!
PFFFT!
YAMADA-CHAN, YOU'RE SO CUUUTE!!!
Ahahahaha!
FOR REAAAL?!!
GINGER ALE'S NOT ALCOHOL!
TELL ME YOUR LINE ID!

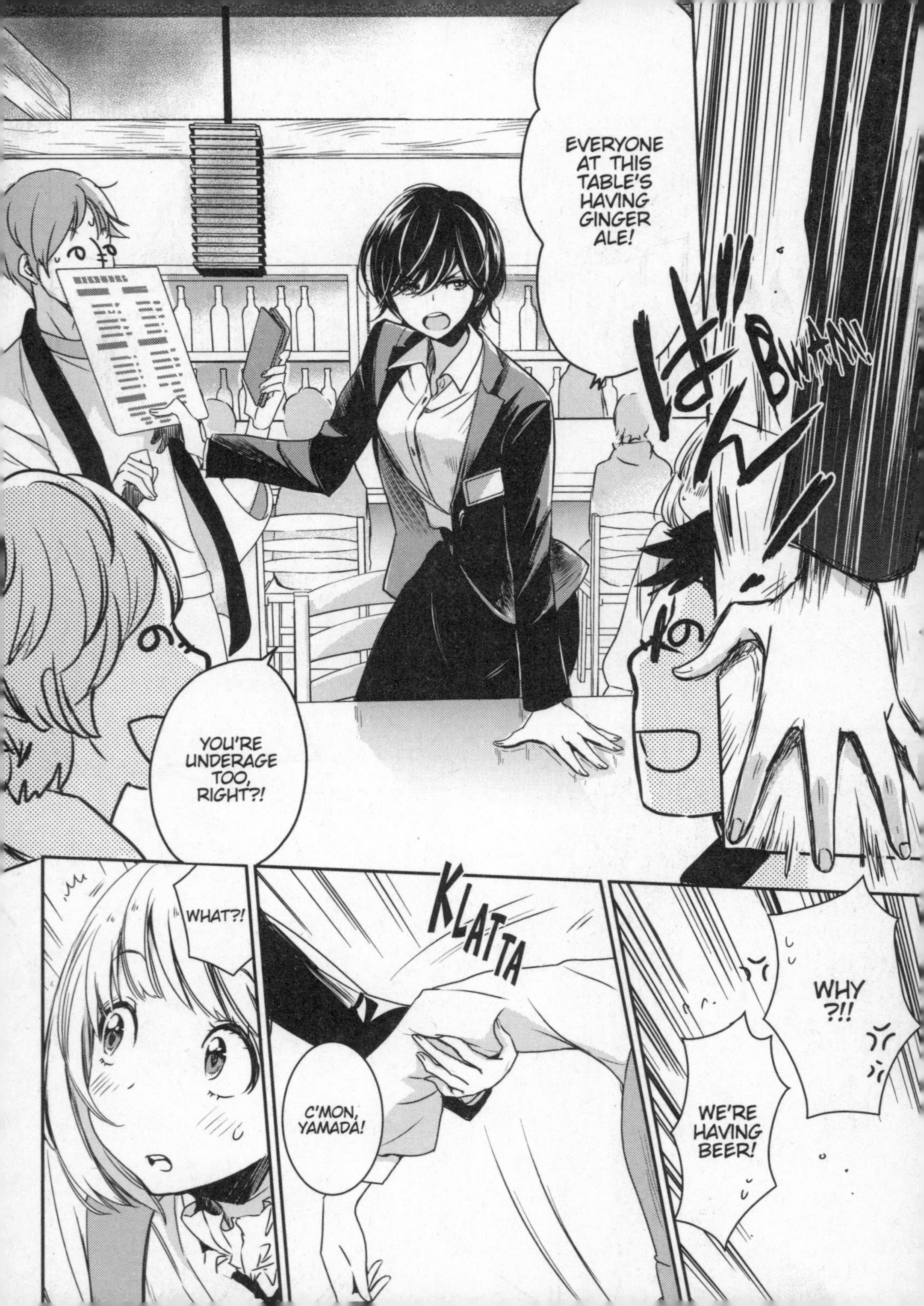
EVERYONE AT THIS TABLE'S HAVING GINGER ALE!
ばん BWAM!
YOU'RE UNDERAGE TOO, RIGHT?!
WHY?!!
WE'RE HAVING BEER!
KLATTA
WHAT?!
C'MON, YAMADA!

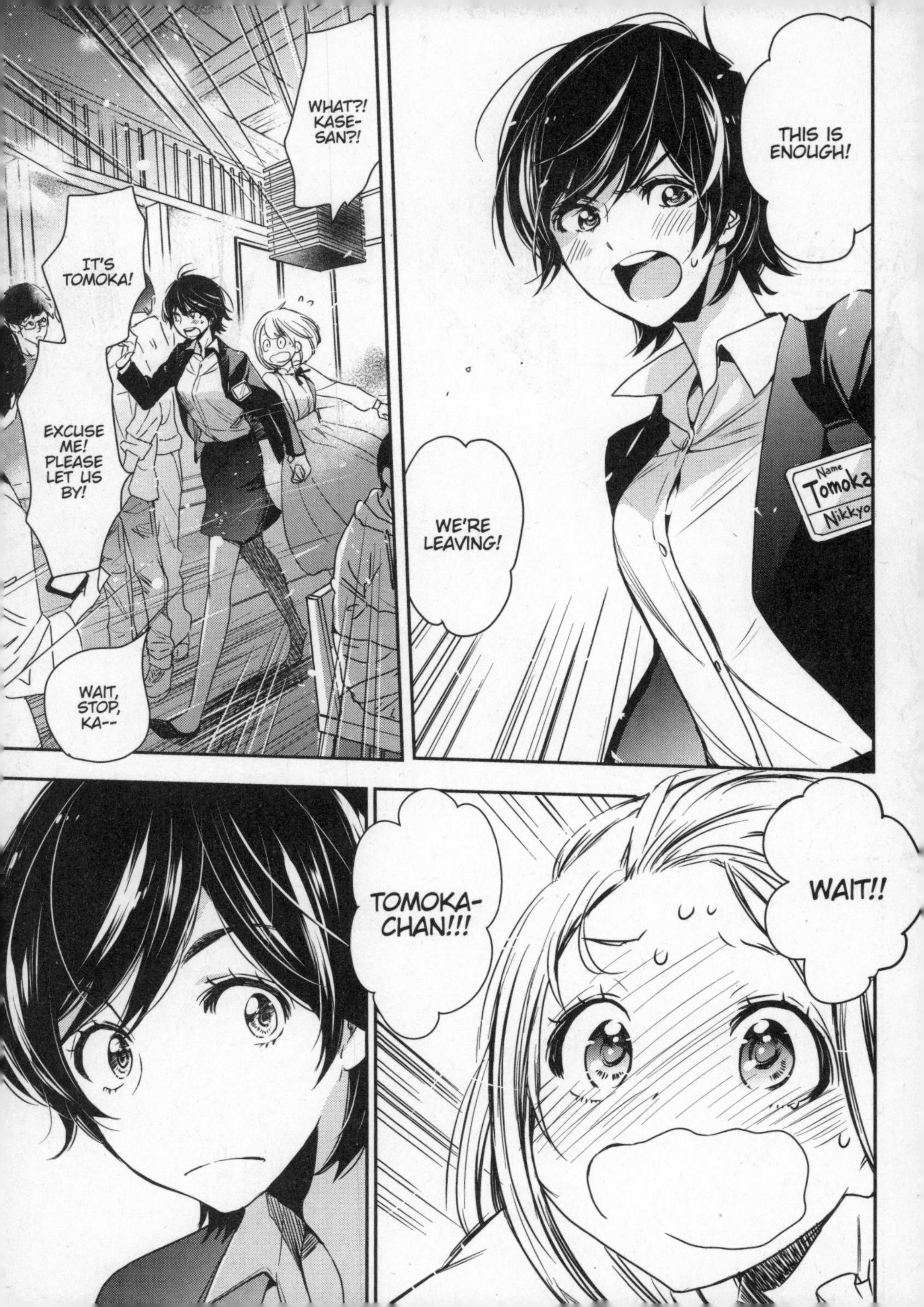

THIS IS ENOUGH!
Name
Tomoka
Nikkyo
WE'RE LEAVING!
WHAT?! KASE-SAN?!
IT'S TOMOKA!
EXCUSE ME! PLEASE LET US BY!
WAIT, STOP, KA--
WAIT!!
TOMOKA-CHAN!!!

Tomoka! Tomoka-chan Tomoka Tomoka-chan... Tomoka

SLAM
バム！

UM...

I CAME WITH HANA-CHAN, AND SHE'S STILL HERE. I--

S...

SO SMALL.

Hiring

Tomoka

BUMP...

HUH?

ARE YOU ENJOYING TOKYO...

YAMADA?

DID YOU COME TO TOKYO TO DO STUFF LIKE THIS?

DO YOU WANT A FRIEND THIS BADLY?

IS IT FUN TO COME TO A PLACE LIKE THIS AND PUT UP WITH IT?

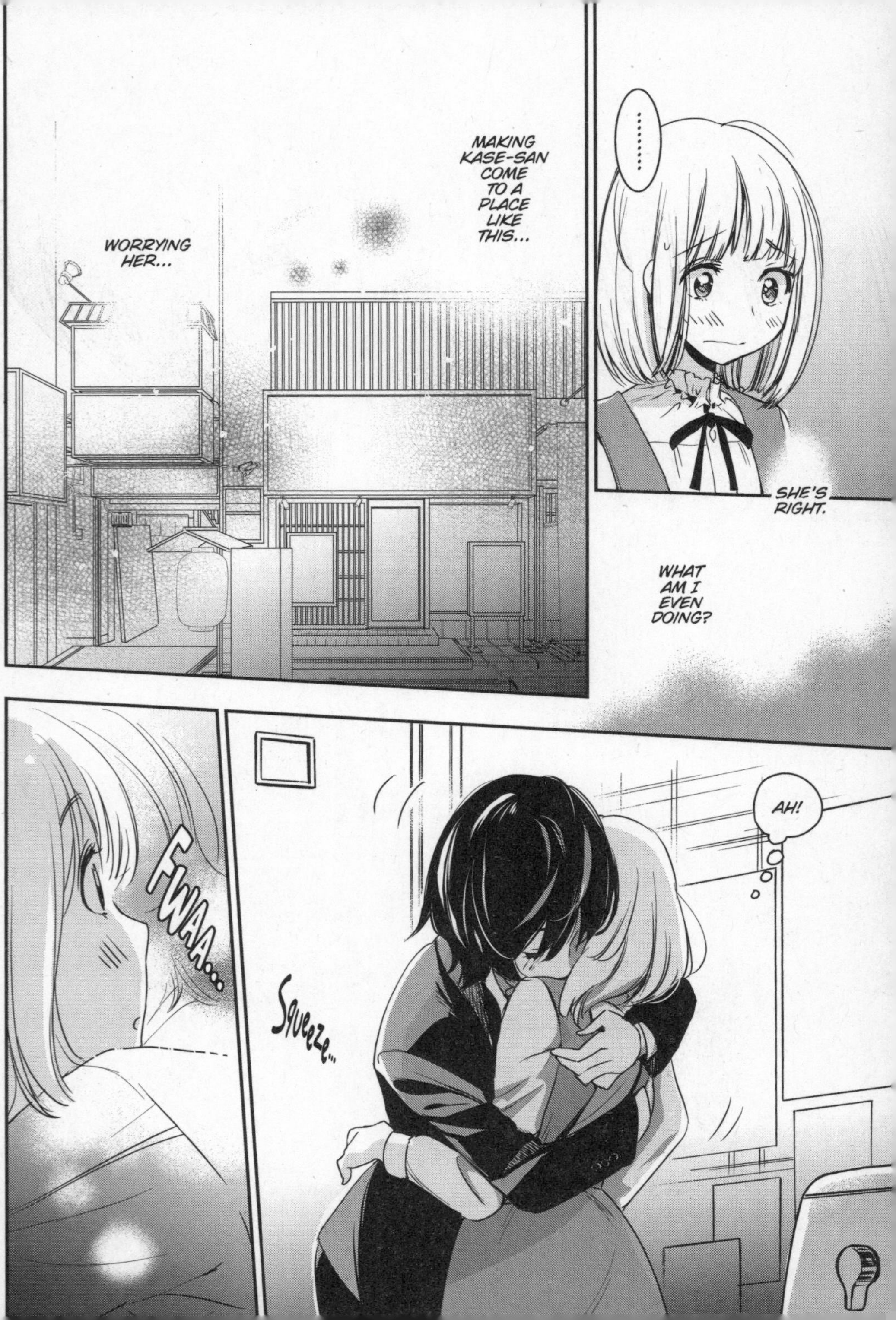
……
MAKING KASE-SAN COME TO A PLACE LIKE THIS…
WORRYING HER…
SHE'S RIGHT.
WHAT AM I EVEN DOING?
AH!
Squeeze…
FWAA…

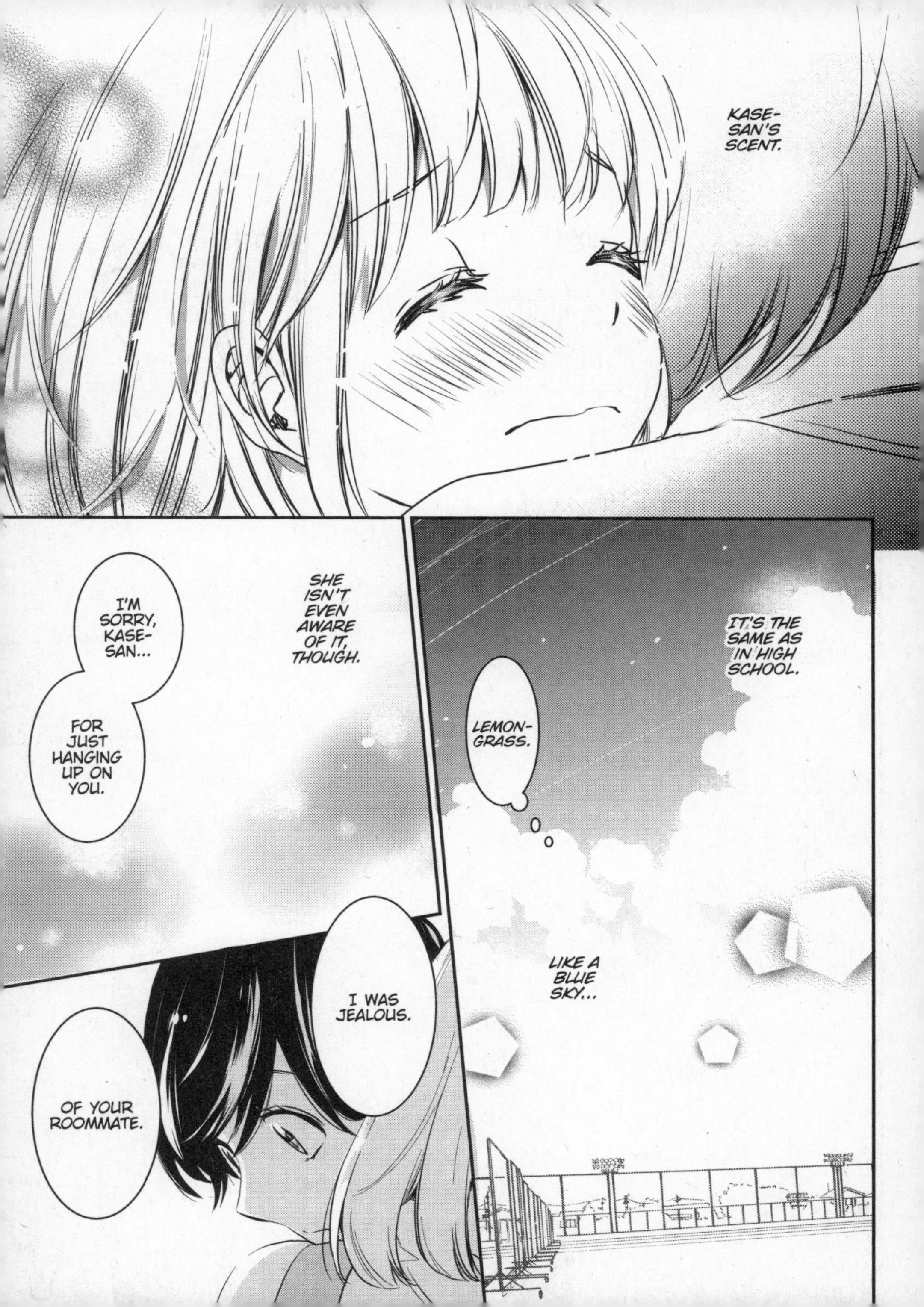
KASE-SAN'S SCENT.
IT'S THE SAME AS IN HIGH SCHOOL.
LEMON-GRASS.
LIKE A BLUE SKY...
SHE ISN'T EVEN AWARE OF IT, THOUGH.
I'M SORRY, KASE-SAN...
FOR JUST HANGING UP ON YOU.
I WAS JEALOUS.
OF YOUR ROOMMATE.

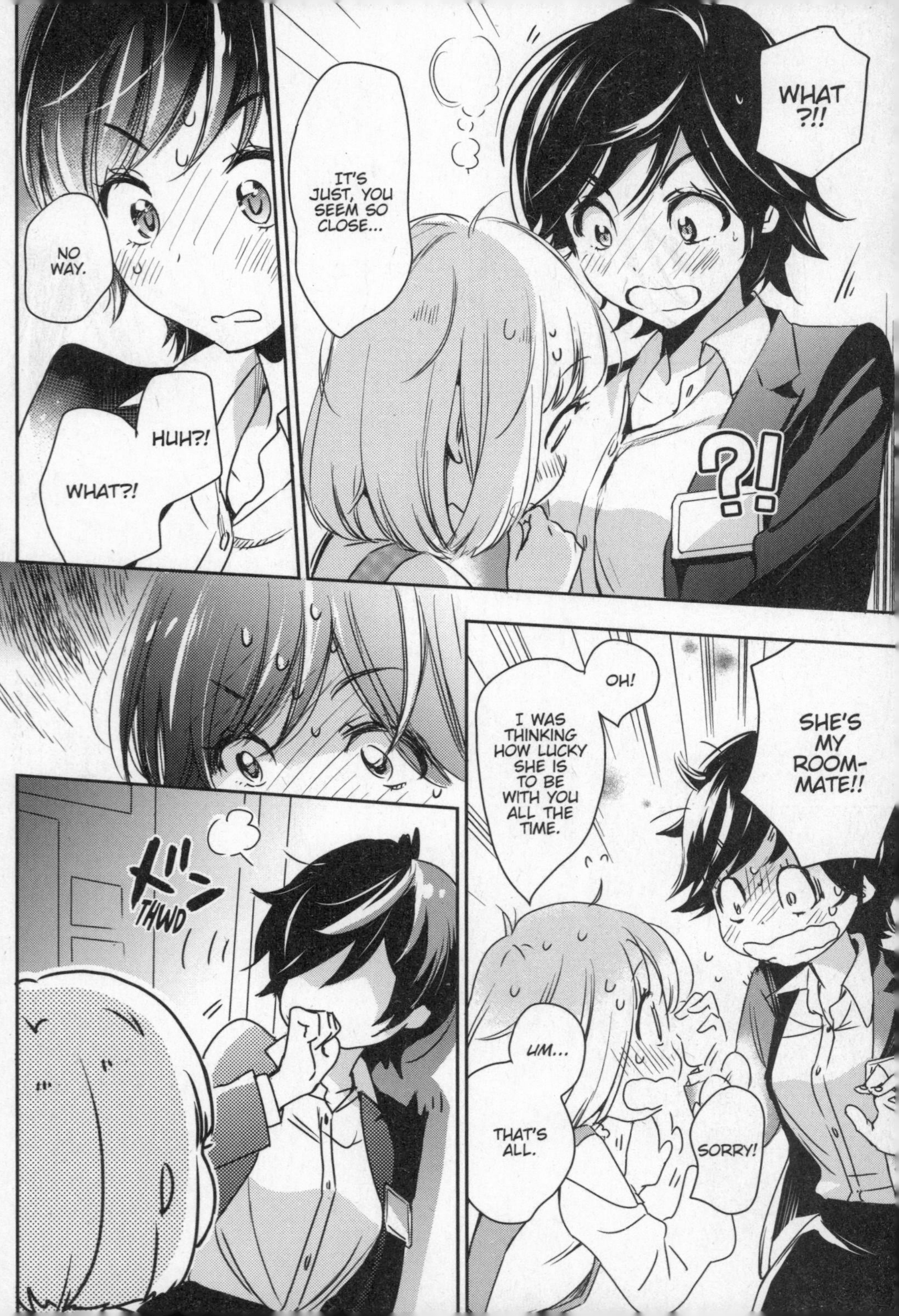
WHAT ?!!
IT'S JUST, YOU SEEM SO CLOSE...
NO WAY.
?!
HUH?!
WHAT?!
SHE'S MY ROOM-MATE!!
OH!
I WAS THINKING HOW LUCKY SHE IS TO BE WITH YOU ALL THE TIME.
UM...
SORRY!
THAT'S ALL.
THWD

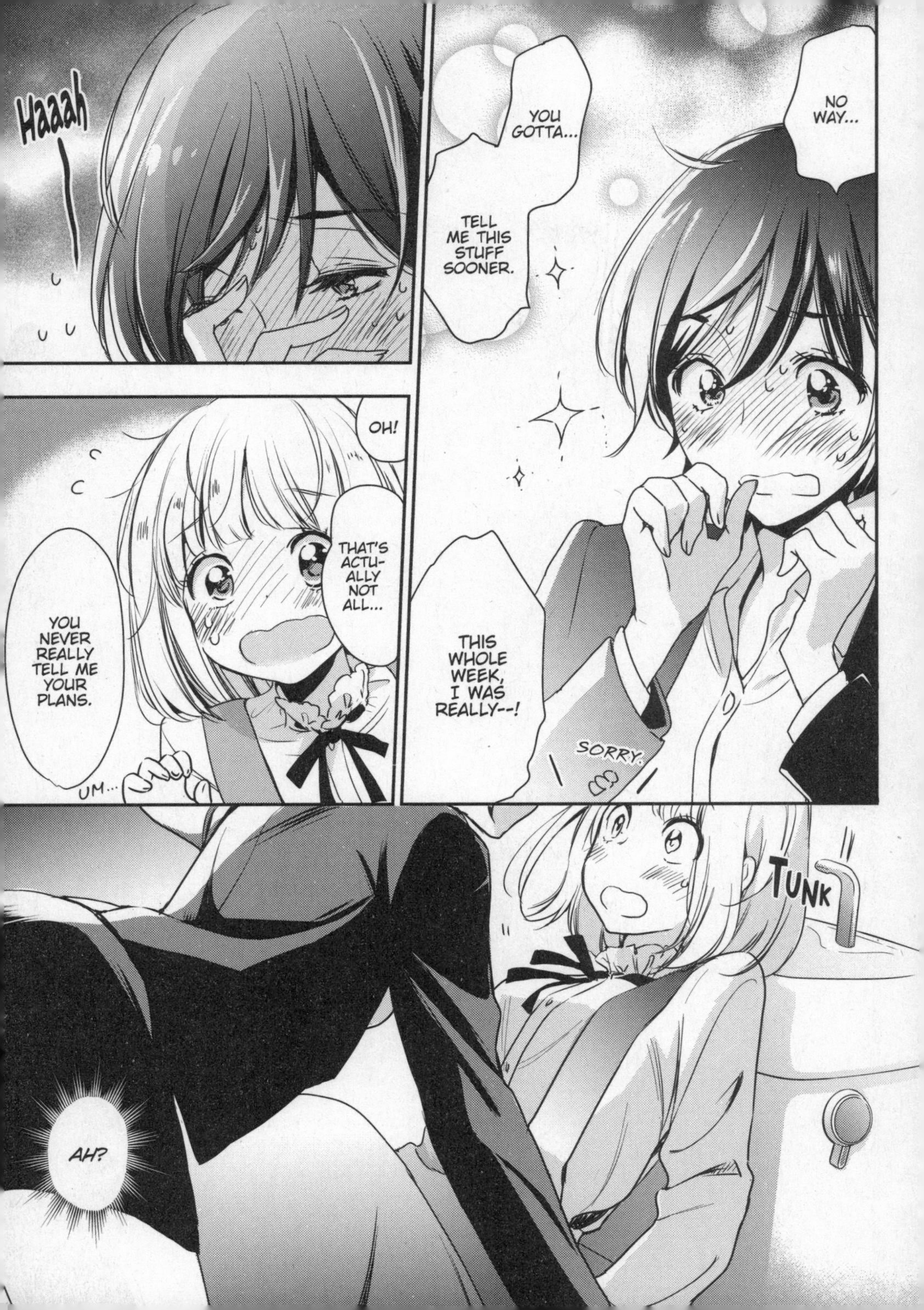
NO WAY...
YOU GOTTA...
TELL ME THIS STUFF SOONER.
Haaaah
THIS WHOLE WEEK, I WAS REALLY--!
SORRY.
OH!
THAT'S ACTU-ALLY NOT ALL...
YOU NEVER REALLY TELL ME YOUR PLANS.
UM...
TUNK
AH?

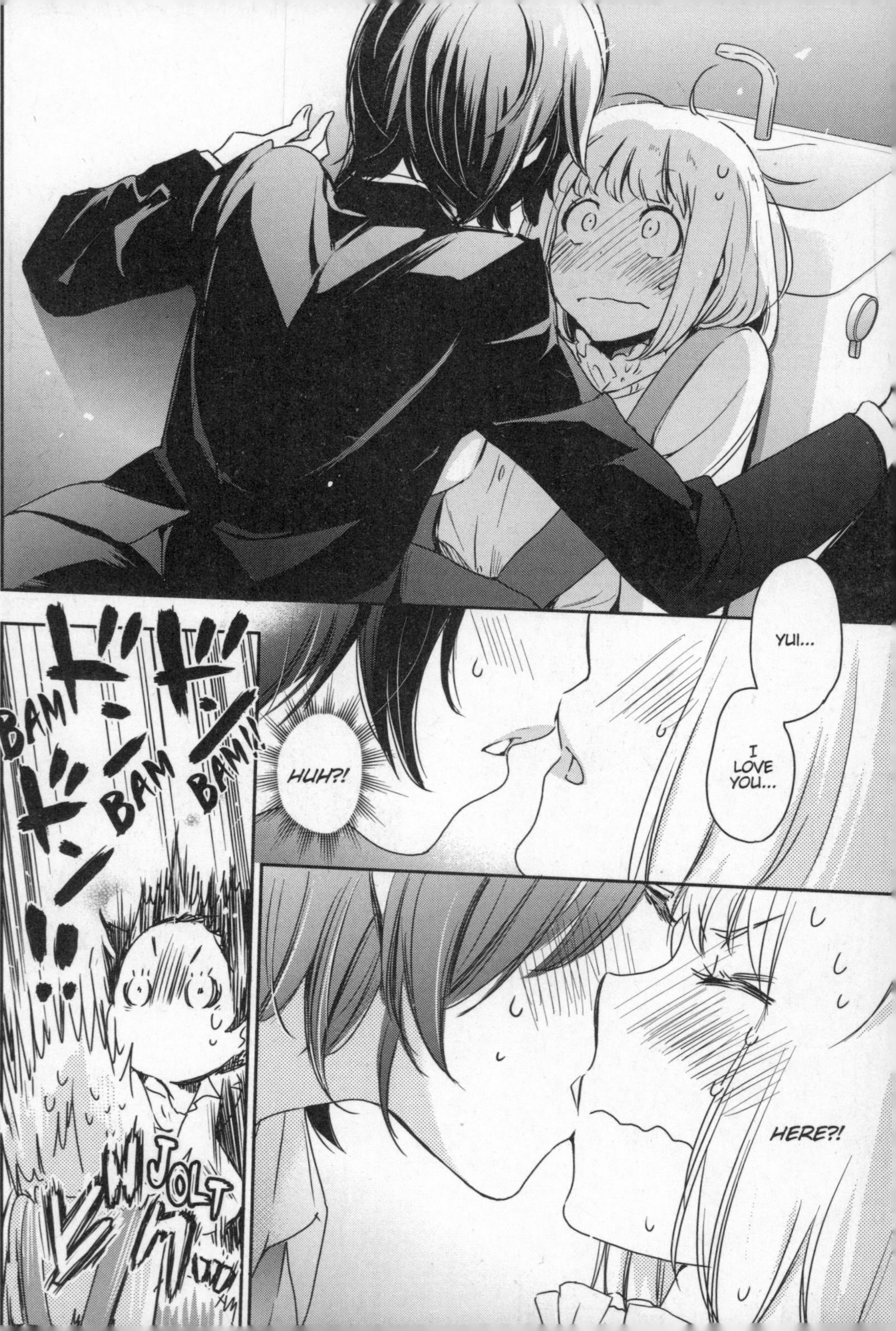
YUI...
I LOVE YOU...
HUH?!
BAM BAM BAM BAM!!
HERE?!
JOLT

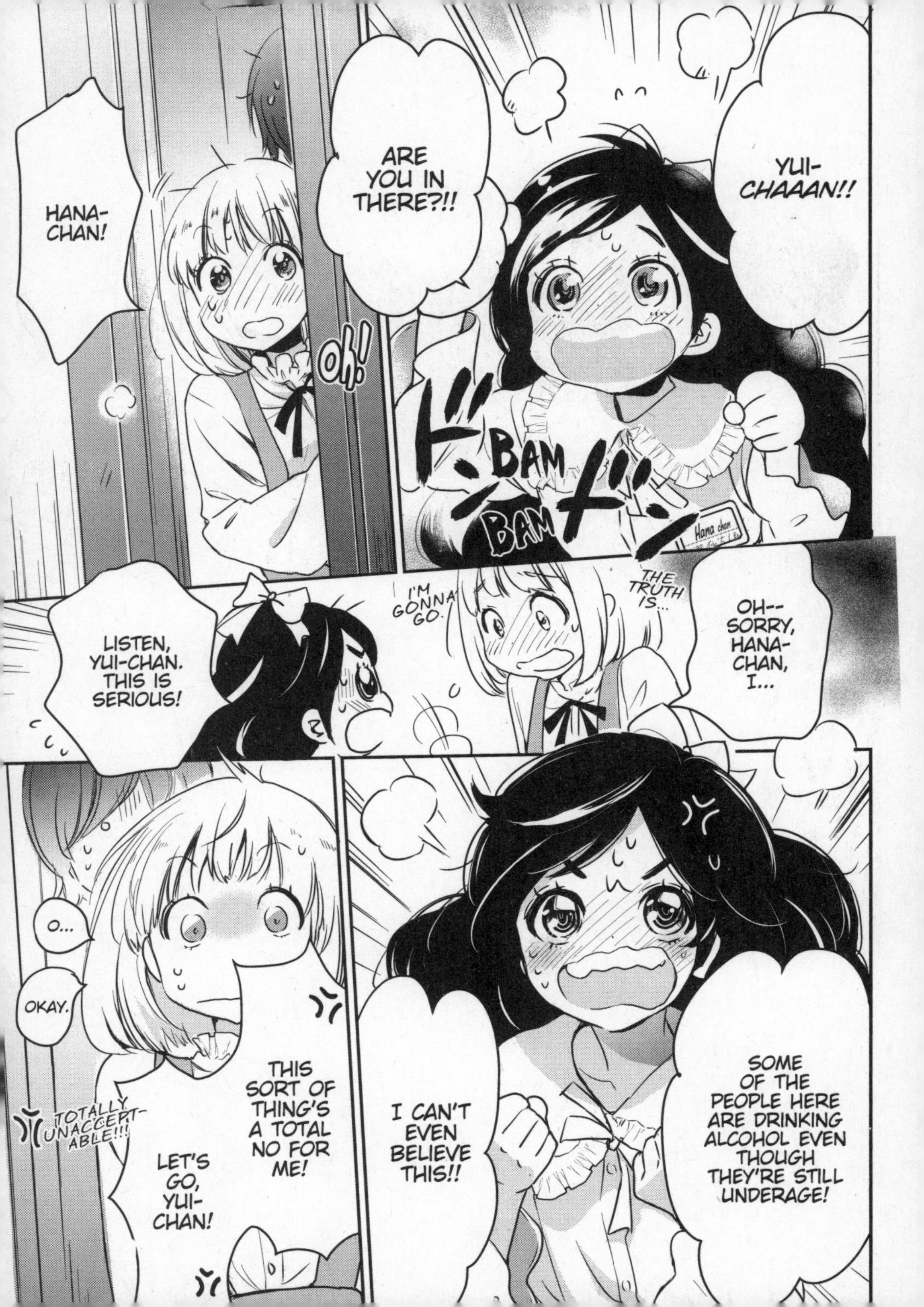

YUI-CHAAAN!!
ARE YOU IN THERE?!!
BAM BAM
Hana chan
HANA-CHAN!
Oh!
OH-- SORRY, HANA-CHAN, I...
THE TRUTH IS...
I'M GONNA GO.
LISTEN, YUI-CHAN. THIS IS SERIOUS!
SOME OF THE PEOPLE HERE ARE DRINKING ALCOHOL EVEN THOUGH THEY'RE STILL UNDERAGE!
I CAN'T EVEN BELIEVE THIS!!
THIS SORT OF THING'S A TOTAL NO FOR ME!
LET'S GO, YUI-CHAN!
TOTALLY UNACCEPTABLE!!!
O...
OKAY.

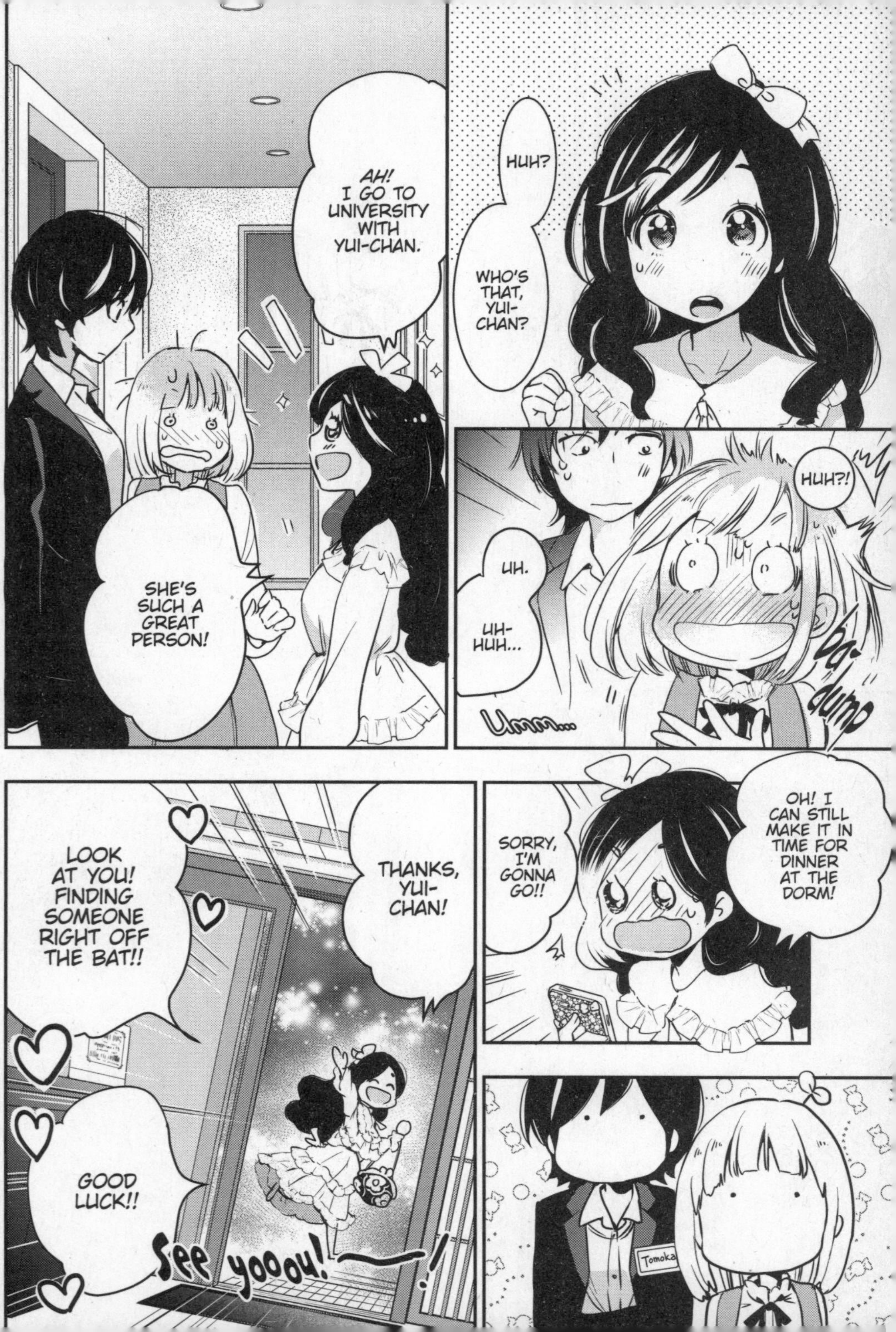
HUH?
WHO'S THAT, YUI-CHAN?
AH! I GO TO UNIVERSITY WITH YUI-CHAN.
SHE'S SUCH A GREAT PERSON!
HUH?!
UH.
UH-HUH...
Umm...
ba-dump
OH! I CAN STILL MAKE IT IN TIME FOR DINNER AT THE DORM!
SORRY, I'M GONNA GO!!
THANKS, YUI-CHAN!
LOOK AT YOU! FINDING SOMEONE RIGHT OFF THE BAT!!
GOOD LUCK!!
See yooou!—!
Tomoka

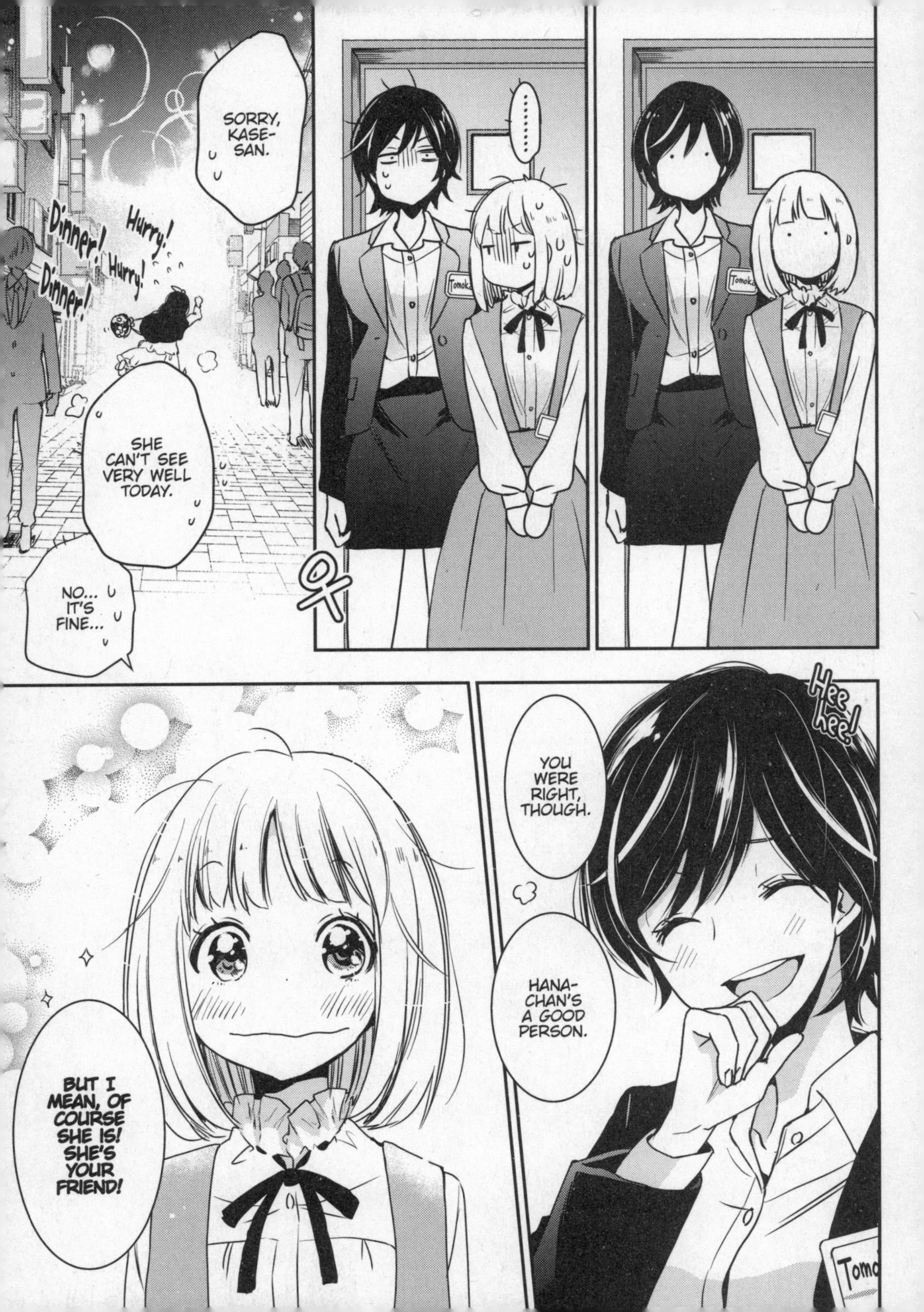
......
SORRY, KASE-SAN.
Hurry! Hurry!
Dinner! Dinner!
SHE CAN'T SEE VERY WELL TODAY.
NO... IT'S FINE...
Hee hee!
YOU WERE RIGHT, THOUGH.
HANA-CHAN'S A GOOD PERSON.
BUT I MEAN, OF COURSE SHE IS! SHE'S YOUR FRIEND!

SHE KINDA RESEMBLES YOU. (SAME STOCK.)

?

RIGHT?!

Hee hee hee!

WAAH!

I'VE NEVER BEEN HERE BEFORE. THE ROAD'S SO BIG!

THE EVENING'S NICE, BUT I'D LIKE TO COME DURING THE DAY, TOO!!

HEY, KASE-SAN?

THANKS FOR COMING.

I'M JUST ALWAYS WATCHING FOR THE OTHER PERSON'S REACTION.

BUT I WANT TO GET STRONGER. LIKE YOU, KASE-SAN!

FROM NOW ON, I'LL TELL YOU WHEN I'M UNHAPPY.

I'M PRETTY SURE THAT BEING A GROWN-UP MEANS YOU'VE LEARNED HOW TO SAY THAT KINDA STUFF.

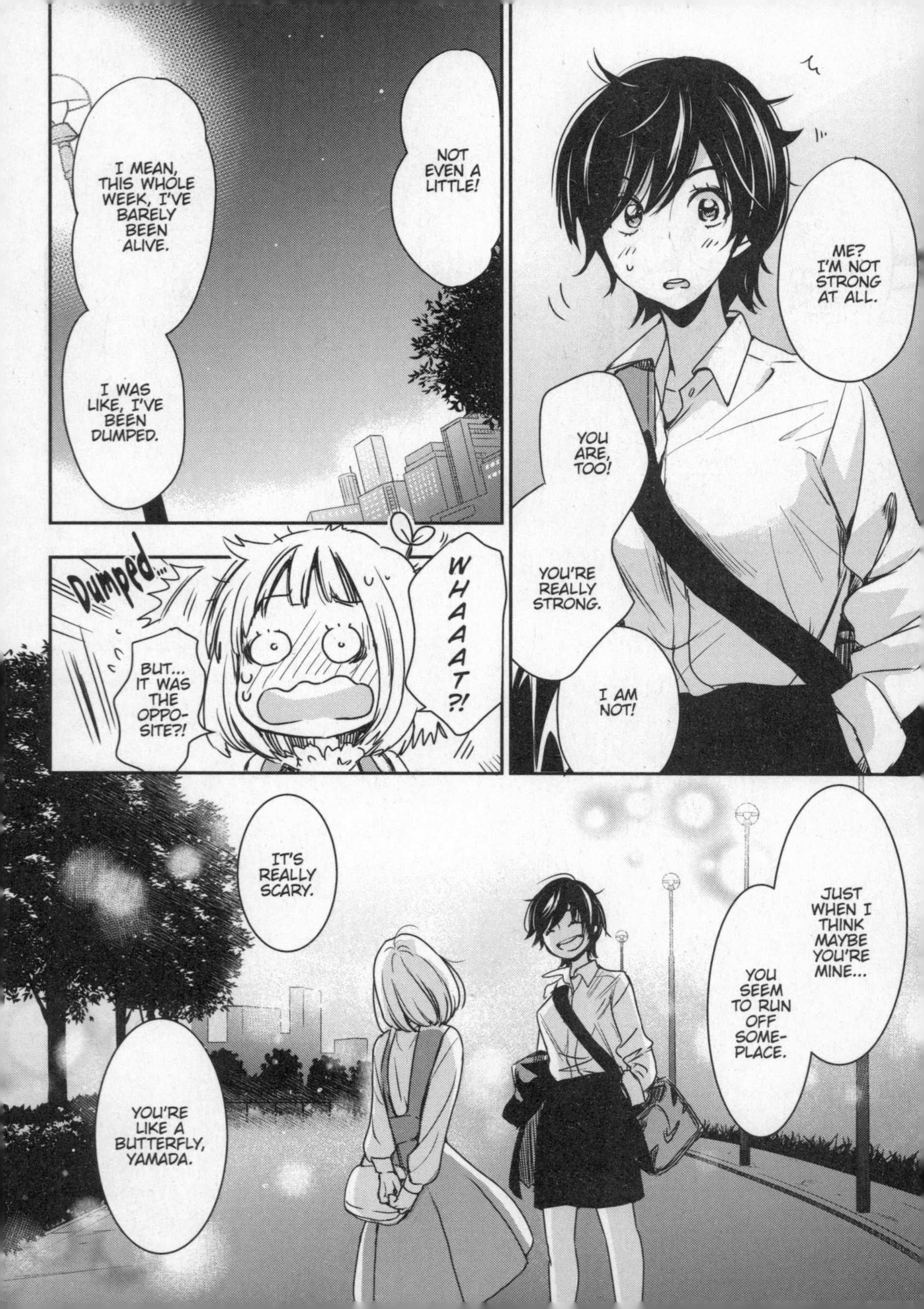
ME? I'M NOT STRONG AT ALL.
YOU ARE, TOO!
YOU'RE REALLY STRONG.
I AM NOT!
NOT EVEN A LITTLE!
I MEAN, THIS WHOLE WEEK, I'VE BARELY BEEN ALIVE.
I WAS LIKE, I'VE BEEN DUMPED.
WHAAAAT?!
BUT... IT WAS THE OPPOSITE?!
Dumped...
JUST WHEN I THINK MAYBE YOU'RE MINE...
YOU SEEM TO RUN OFF SOME-PLACE.
IT'S REALLY SCARY.
YOU'RE LIKE A BUTTERFLY, YAMADA.

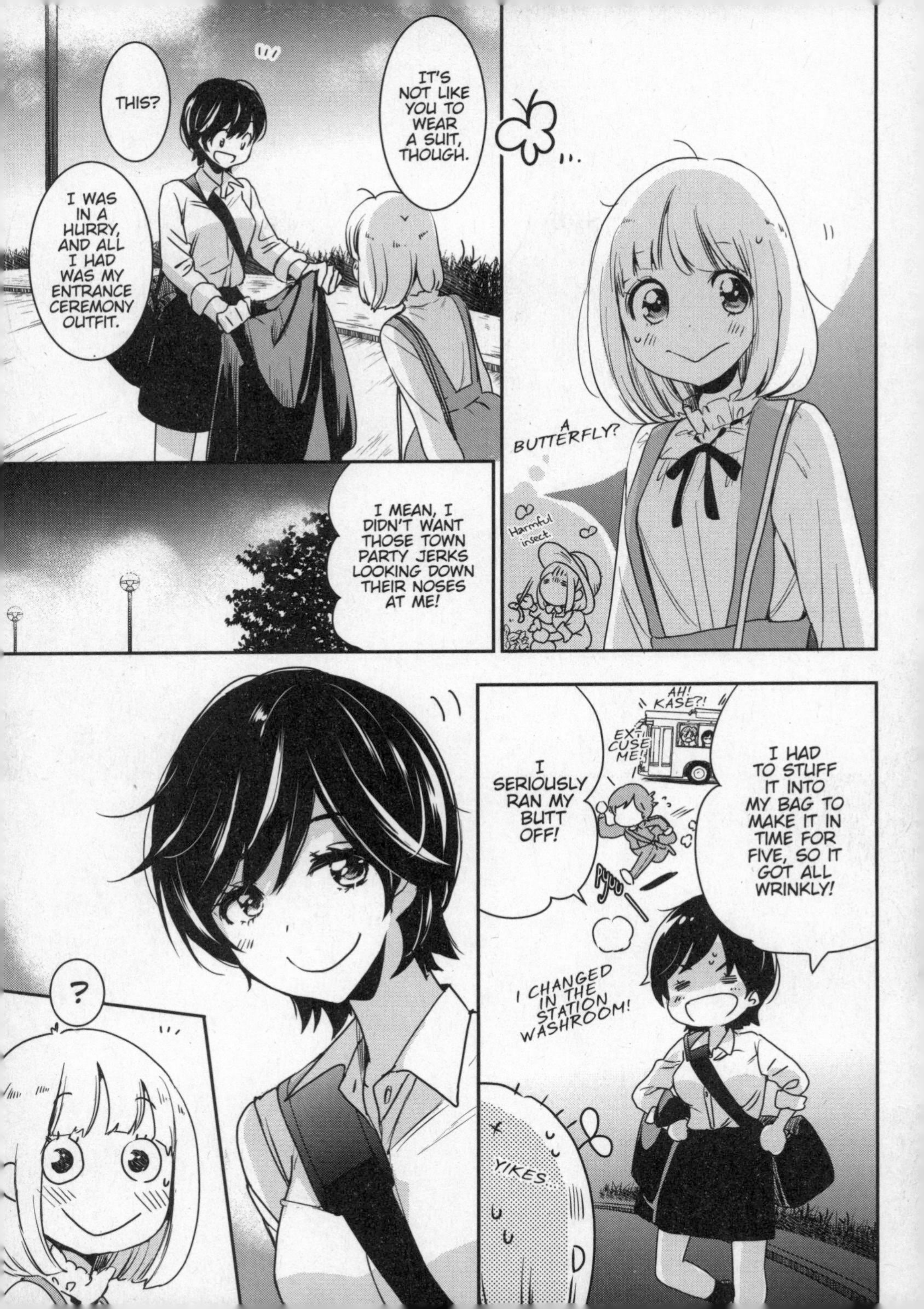
IT'S NOT LIKE YOU TO WEAR A SUIT, THOUGH.
THIS?
I WAS IN A HURRY, AND ALL I HAD WAS MY ENTRANCE CEREMONY OUTFIT.
A BUTTERFLY?
Harmful insect.
I MEAN, I DIDN'T WANT THOSE TOWN PARTY JERKS LOOKING DOWN THEIR NOSES AT ME!
I HAD TO STUFF IT INTO MY BAG TO MAKE IT IN TIME FOR FIVE, SO IT GOT ALL WRINKLY!
AH! KASE?!
EX-CUSE ME!
I SERIOUSLY RAN MY BUTT OFF!
PYUU
I CHANGED IN THE STATION WASHROOM!
YIKES
?

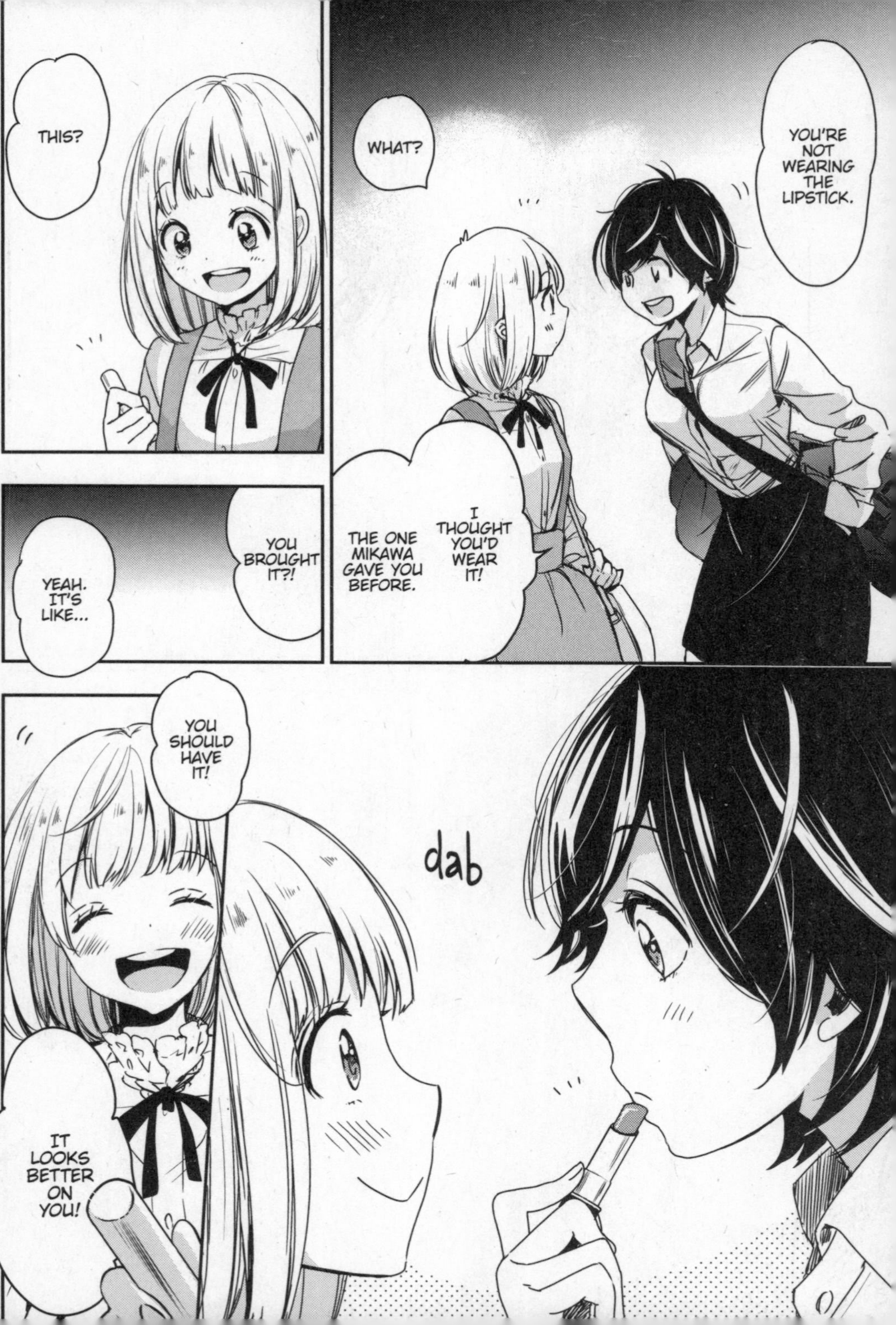
YOU'RE NOT WEARING THE LIPSTICK.
WHAT?
I THOUGHT YOU'D WEAR IT!
THE ONE MIKAWA GAVE YOU BEFORE.
THIS?
YOU BROUGHT IT?!
YEAH. IT'S LIKE...
dab
YOU SHOULD HAVE IT!
IT LOOKS BETTER ON YOU!

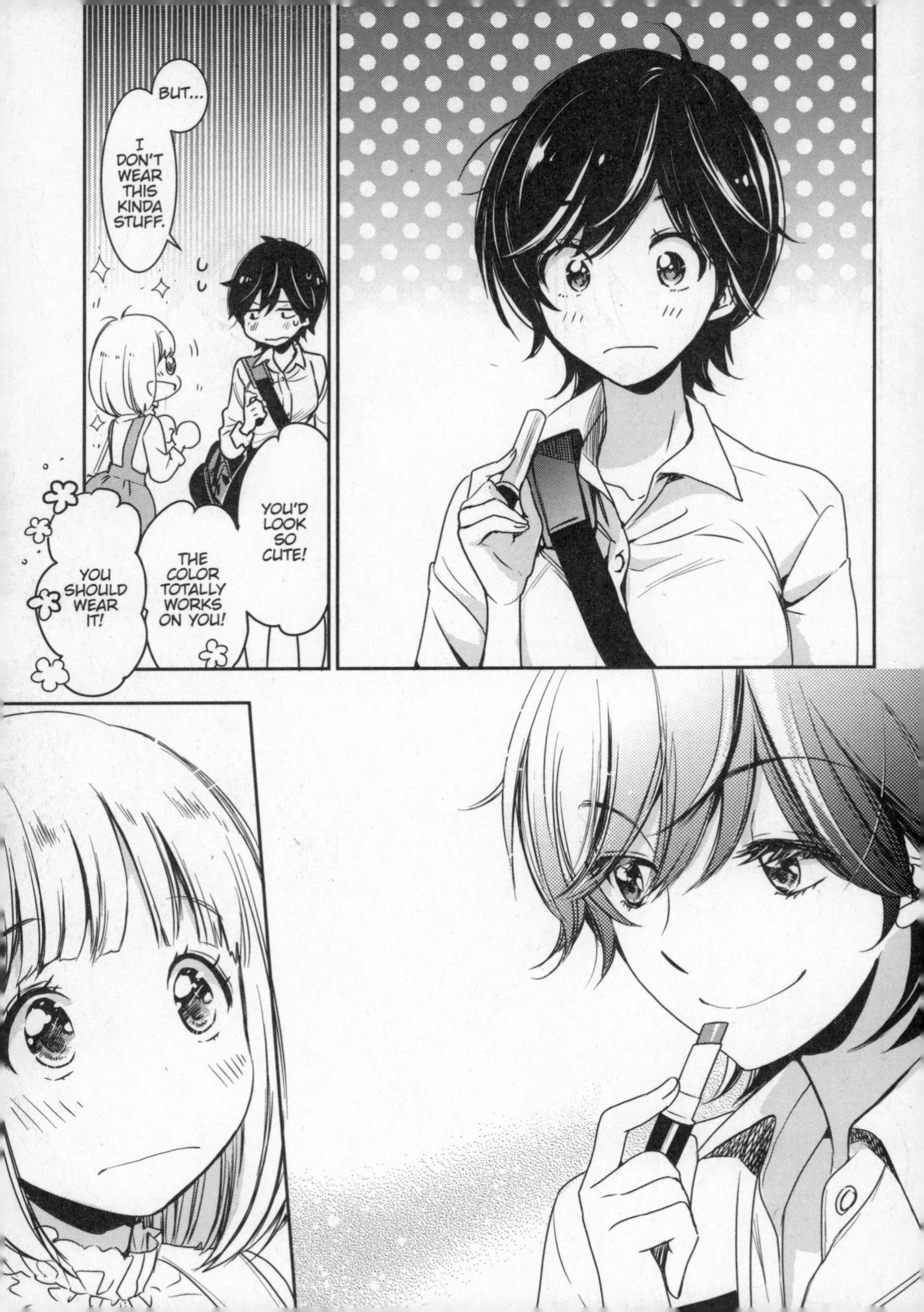
BUT...
I DON'T WEAR THIS KINDA STUFF.
YOU'D LOOK SO CUTE!
THE COLOR TOTALLY WORKS ON YOU!
YOU SHOULD WEAR IT!

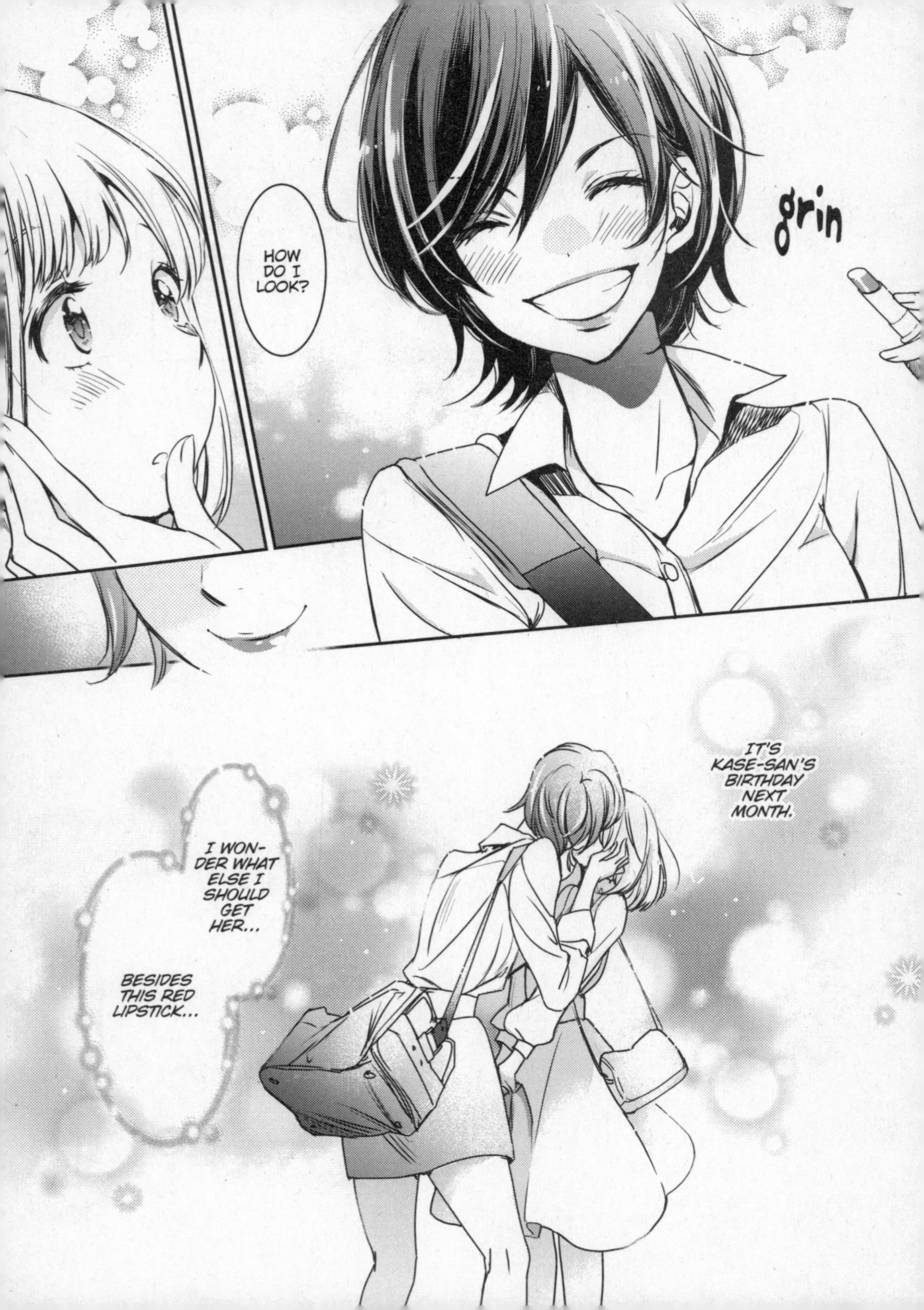
grin
HOW DO I LOOK?
IT'S KASE-SAN'S BIRTHDAY NEXT MONTH.
I WON-DER WHAT ELSE I SHOULD GET HER...
BESIDES THIS RED LIPSTICK...

Kase-san and the Bouquet

KASE-SAN'S
BIRTHDAY
IS MAY
FIRST.

CLAP!

PLEASE, YAMADA!!!

HELP OUT AT MY WORK!

I-I'VE NEVER HAD A JOB BEFORE.

AND I MEAN, OUT OF THE BLUE LIKE THIS...

IT'S A FLOWER SHOP!!

I'M NOT READY.

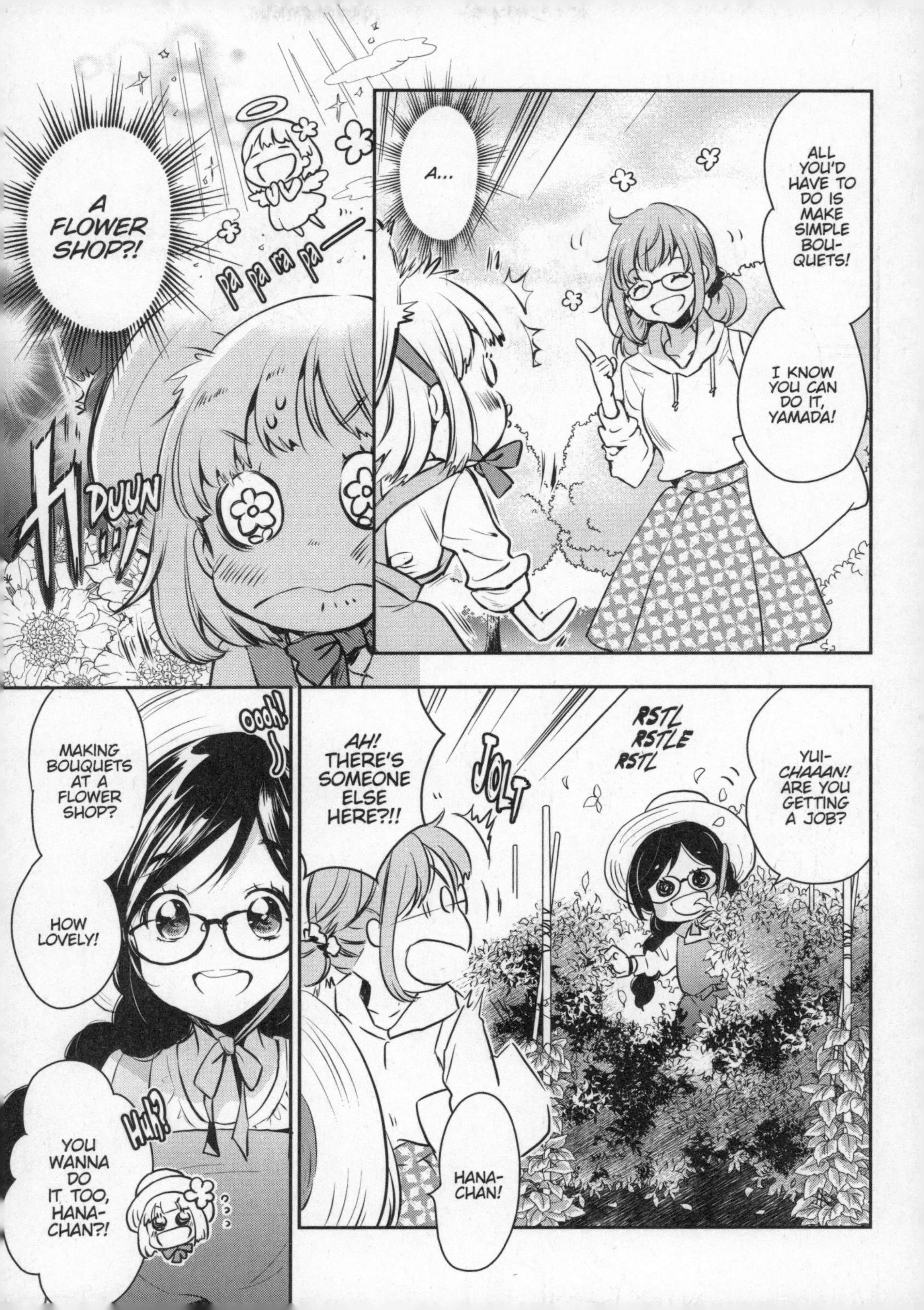
ALL YOU'D HAVE TO DO IS MAKE SIMPLE BOU-QUETS!
I KNOW YOU CAN DO IT, YAMADA!
A...
A FLOWER SHOP?!
pa pa ra pa—
HDUUN
YUI-CHAAAN! ARE YOU GETTING A JOB?
RSTL RSTLE RSTL
AH! THERE'S SOMEONE ELSE HERE?!!
JOLT
HANA-CHAN!
MAKING BOUQUETS AT A FLOWER SHOP?
oooh!
HOW LOVELY!
YOU WANNA DO IT TOO, HANA-CHAN?!
Huh?

YOUR
FRIEND.

HUH?
WHY IS
THIS
PERSON IN
HORTICUL-
TURE?

IF I GOT
A JOB, I'D
WANT TO
WORK AT
STARBUCKS
OR SOME-
THING.

I'VE HAD
MORE THAN
ENOUGH OF
FLOWERS...

OH!

SHE'S
ACTUALLY
A THOR-
OUGH-
BRED!

OF
GARDENING.

OH!

THAT
REMINDS ME.
KASE-SAN'S
BIRTHDAY
IS THE DAY
AFTER
TOMORROW,
YEAH?

HOW
ABOUT
YOU GET
SOMETHING
FOR HER
WITH YOUR
PAY?

YEAH?

YOU GET
SOME
SPENDING
MONEY,
PLUS IT'S A
CHANCE TO
OBSERVE
THE
WORLD!

HAVING
A
JOB'S
GREAT.

YOU HAD
A JOB IN
HIGH
SCHOOL,
TOO--
RIGHT,
MIKA-
WACCHI?

I'M
IMPRESSED.

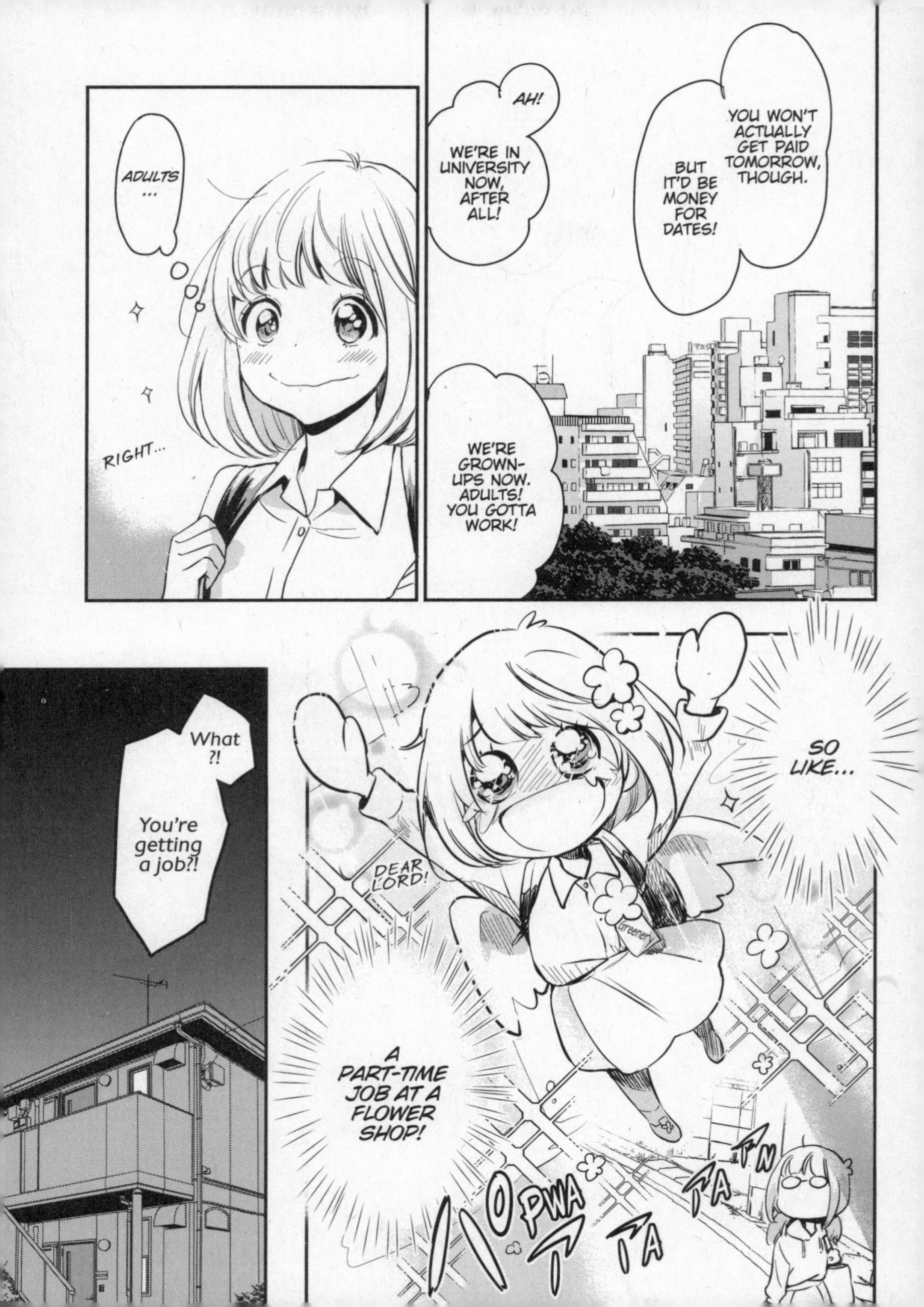

YOU WON'T ACTUALLY GET PAID TOMORROW, THOUGH.
BUT IT'D BE MONEY FOR DATES!
AH!
WE'RE IN UNIVERSITY NOW, AFTER ALL!
WE'RE GROWN-UPS NOW. ADULTS! YOU GOTTA WORK!
ADULTS ...
RIGHT...
SO LIKE...
A PART-TIME JOB AT A FLOWER SHOP!
DEAR LORD!
Greenery
PWA
TA TA TA TA N
What ?!
You're getting a job?!

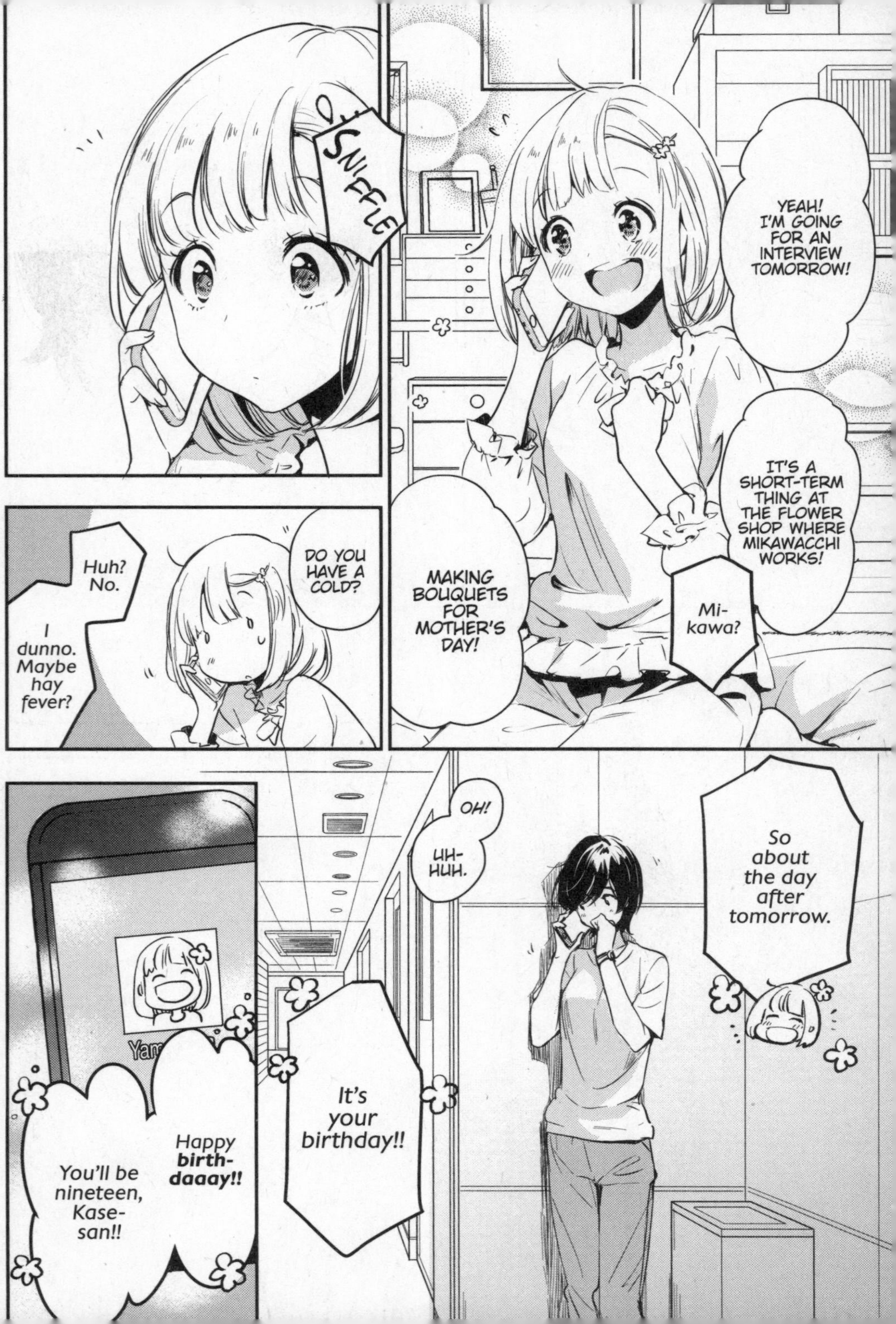
YEAH! I'M GOING FOR AN INTERVIEW TOMORROW!
IT'S A SHORT-TERM THING AT THE FLOWER SHOP WHERE MIKAWACCHI WORKS!
Mi-kawa?
MAKING BOUQUETS FOR MOTHER'S DAY!
SNIFFLE
DO YOU HAVE A COLD?
Huh? No.
I dunno. Maybe hay fever?
So about the day after tomorrow.
OH!
UH-HUH.
It's your birthday!!
Happy **birth-daaay!!**
You'll be nineteen, Kase-san!!

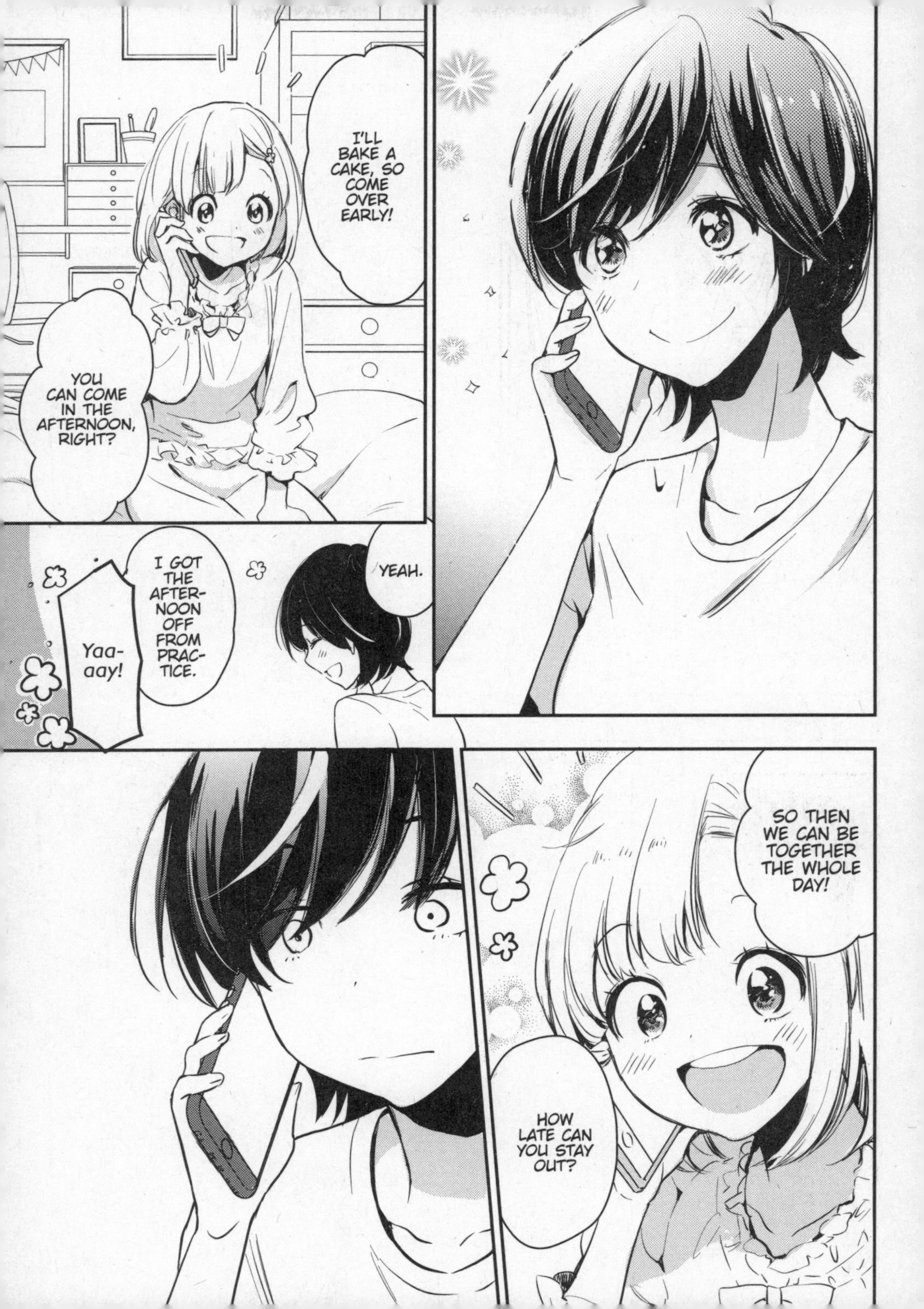
I'LL BAKE A CAKE, SO COME OVER EARLY!
YOU CAN COME IN THE AFTERNOON, RIGHT?
YEAH.
I GOT THE AFTERNOON OFF FROM PRACTICE.
Yaa-aay!
SO THEN WE CAN BE TOGETHER THE WHOLE DAY!
HOW LATE CAN YOU STAY OUT?

what time can I stay until?

Shmp...

HUH?

Fire Ex[

OH...

WH...

BUT LIKE, IT'S ONLY BEEN FOUR MONTHS, SO STAYING OVER MIGHT BE A NO.

OH!

WHAT ?!

BUT...

STAY OVER?!

WHAT?!

OH!

STAYING OVER?!

OH! UM...

MY PLACE IS SO SMALL.

UM!

THAT WOULDN'T WORK FOR ME EITHER. OR LIKE...

NO...

Byoing

KONK

GUESTS...?

And I don't have an extra futon for guests!

I'll have to be back before roll call, so maybe just the usual amount of time.

Hee hee!

MY DORM'S PRETTY STRICT.

But I'm excited!

Ha ha...

THANKS!

I'M REALLY LOOKING FORWARD TO THE DAY AFTER TOMORROW!

GOOD LUCK ON YOUR INTERVIEW, YAMADA!

I HAVEN'T GOTTEN TO HANG OUT WITH YOU IN A WHILE!

bip

IT REALLY HAS BEEN A LONG TIME...

SINCE WE GOT TO HANG OUT.

KASE-SAN...

KASE-SAN'S BIRTHDAY...

THE DAY AFTER TOMOR-ROW...

KA-CHAK

KASE-SAN, YOUR BIRTHDAY'S THE DAY AFTER TOMORROW, RIGHT?

YEAH.

I HEARD EVERYONE TALKING ABOUT IT.

BUT...

HAPPY BIRTH...

I'M NOT GOING TO GIVE YOU A PRESENT OR ANY-THING.

THAT'S OKAY, RIGHT?

AND I DON'T NEED ANYTHING WHEN IT'S MY BIRTHDAY. START WITH THAT STUFF, AND IT JUST NEVER ENDS.

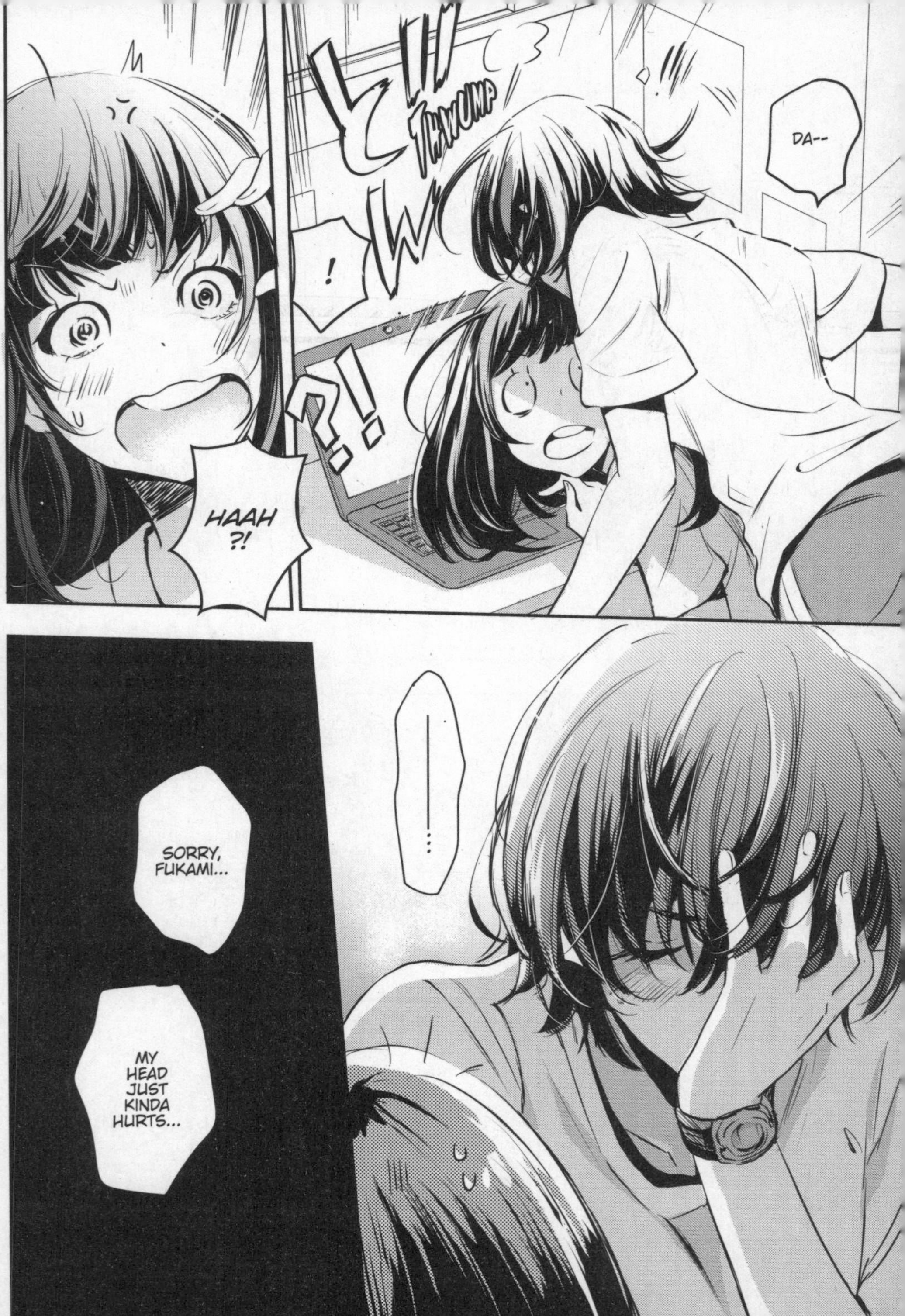
M
THWUMP
!!
DA--
!
?!
HAAH ?!
—......
SORRY, FUKAMI...
MY HEAD JUST KINDA HURTS...

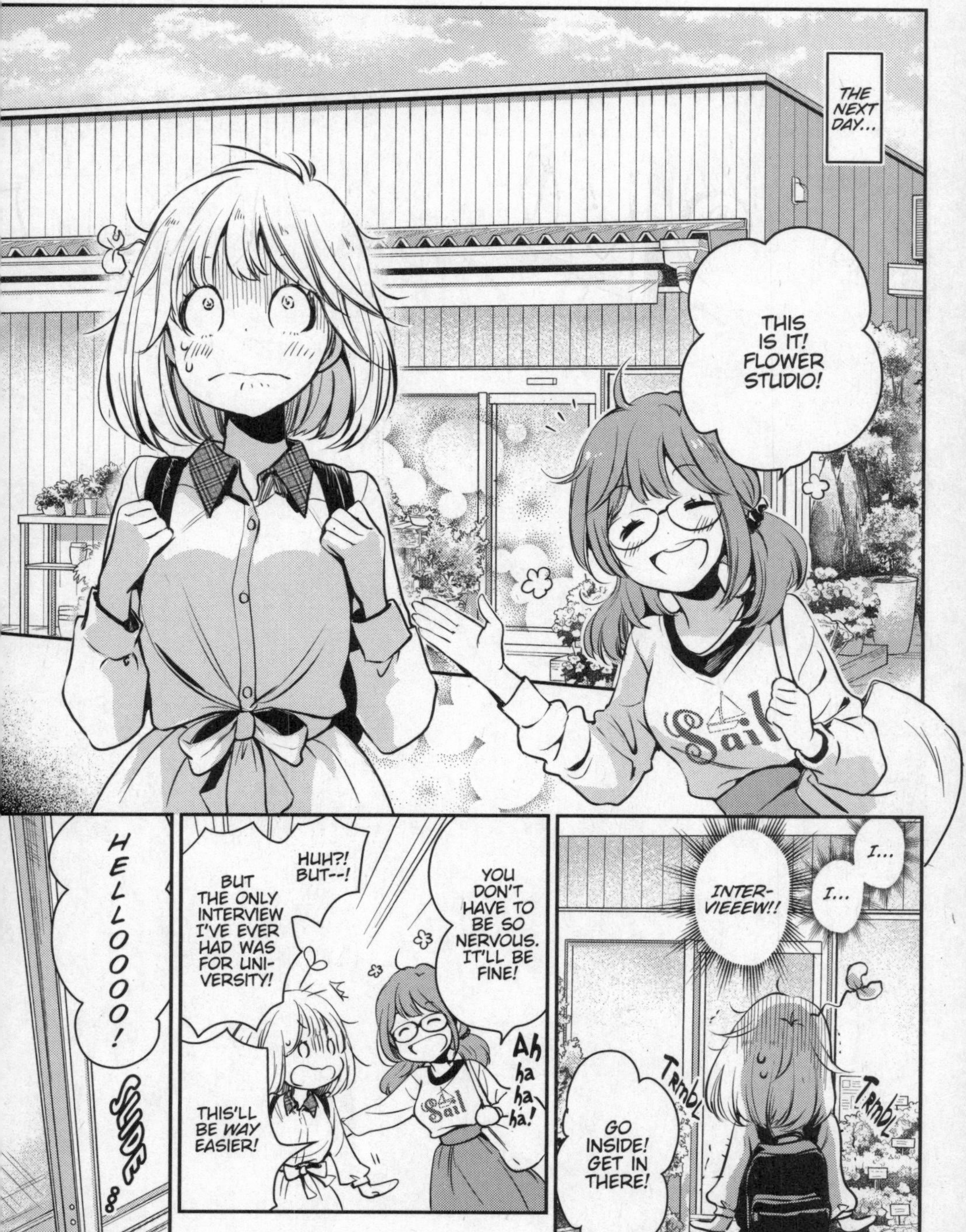

THE NEXT DAY...
THIS IS IT! FLOWER STUDIO!
I... I...
INTER-VIEEEW!!
TRMBL
TRMBL
GO INSIDE! GET IN THERE!
YOU DON'T HAVE TO BE SO NERVOUS. IT'LL BE FINE!
HUH?! BUT--!
BUT THE ONLY INTERVIEW I'VE EVER HAD WAS FOR UNI-VERSITY!
Ah ha ha ha!
THIS'LL BE *WAY* EASIER!
HELLOOOOO!

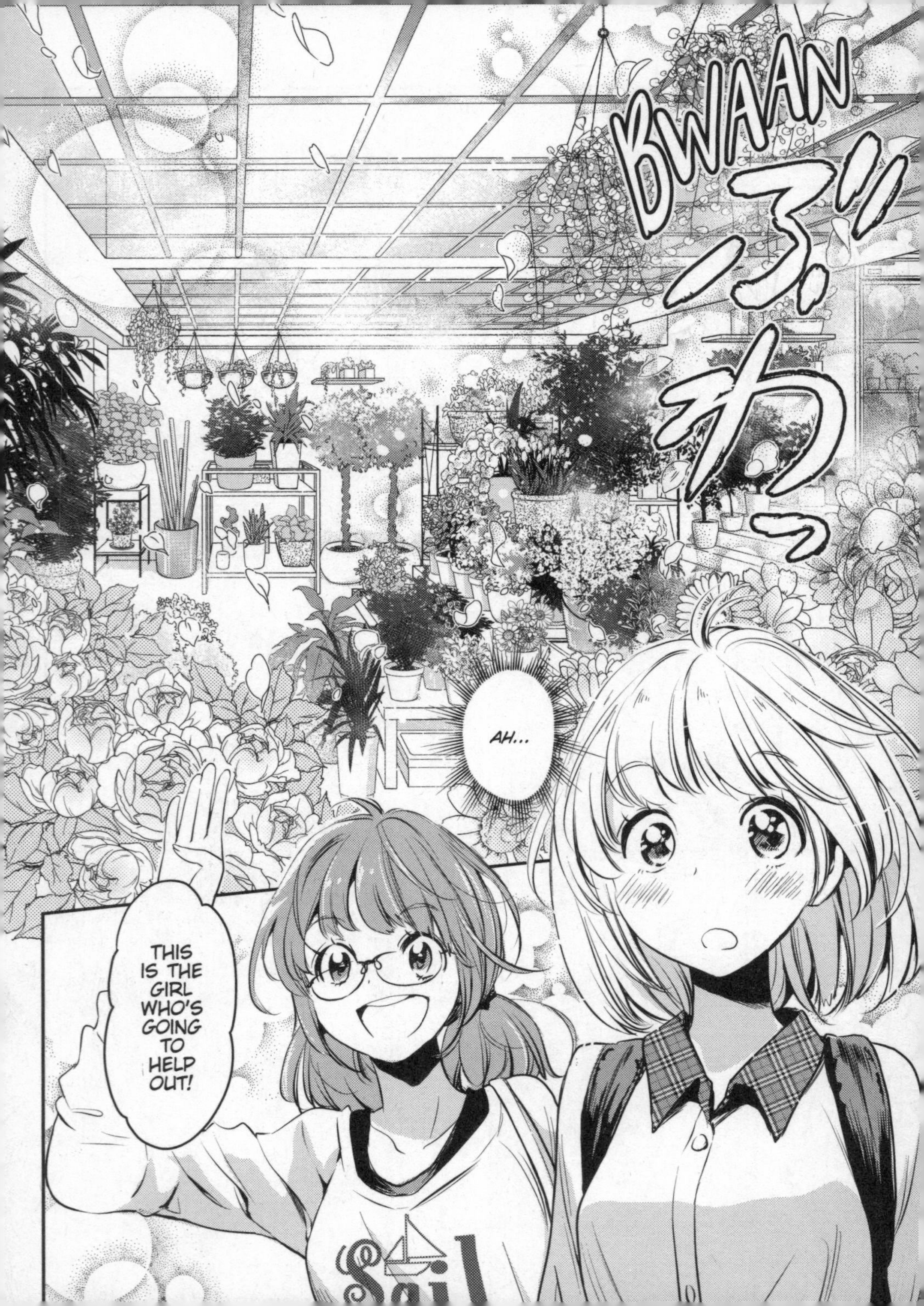
BWAAN
ぶわっ
AH...
THIS IS THE GIRL WHO'S GOING TO HELP OUT!

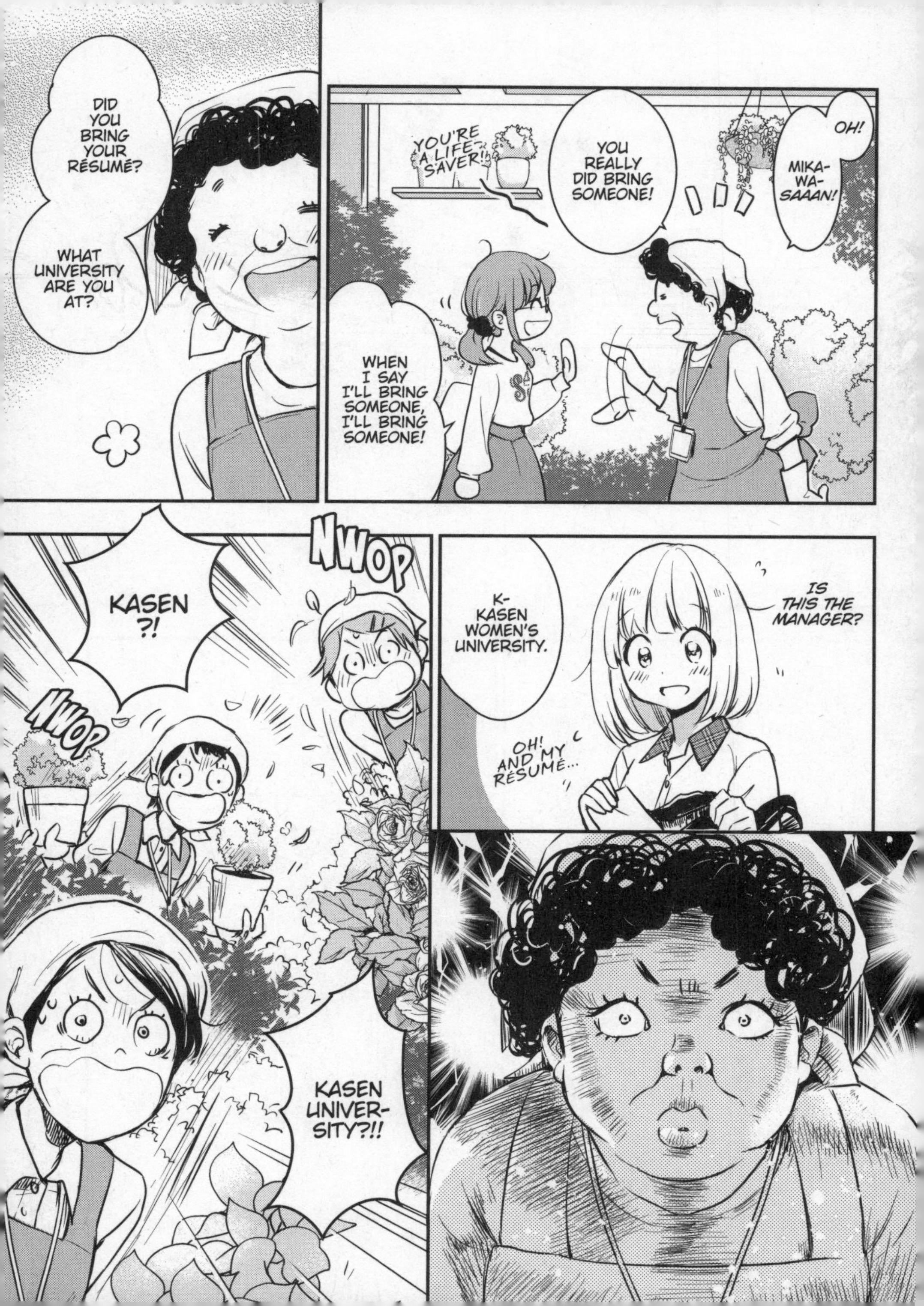
DID YOU BRING YOUR RÉSUMÉ?
WHAT UNIVERSITY ARE YOU AT?
OH!
MIKA-WA-SAAAN!
YOU REALLY DID BRING SOMEONE!
YOU'RE A LIFE-SAVER!!
WHEN I SAY I'LL BRING SOMEONE, I'LL BRING SOMEONE!
NWOP
KASEN ?!
NWOP
K-KASEN WOMEN'S UNIVERSITY.
IS THIS THE MANAGER?
OH! AND MY RÉSUMÉ...
KASEN UNIVER-SITY?!!

I GUESS THIS MEANS YOU'RE...

HIRED?

UM, MY RÉSUMÉ...

Waaaah!

Horticulture!

AMAAAZ-ING!!!

A BUNCH OF PEOPLE JUST QUIT, SO WE'RE SUPER SHORT-STAFFED.

I NEVER DREAMED I'D GET TO START TODAY! ♥

Ha ha ha ha!

thing thing

IT ALL WORKED OUT. THEY EVEN GAVE YOU A BOUQUET AS A THANK YOU!

WELL, THEY'RE BASICALLY THE SAME THING.

AND WITH MOTHER'S DAY COMING UP, WE'RE GONNA BE BUSY MAKING BOU-QUETS.

IT'S MORE LIKE A GARDEN CENTER THAN A FLOWER SHOP, HUH?

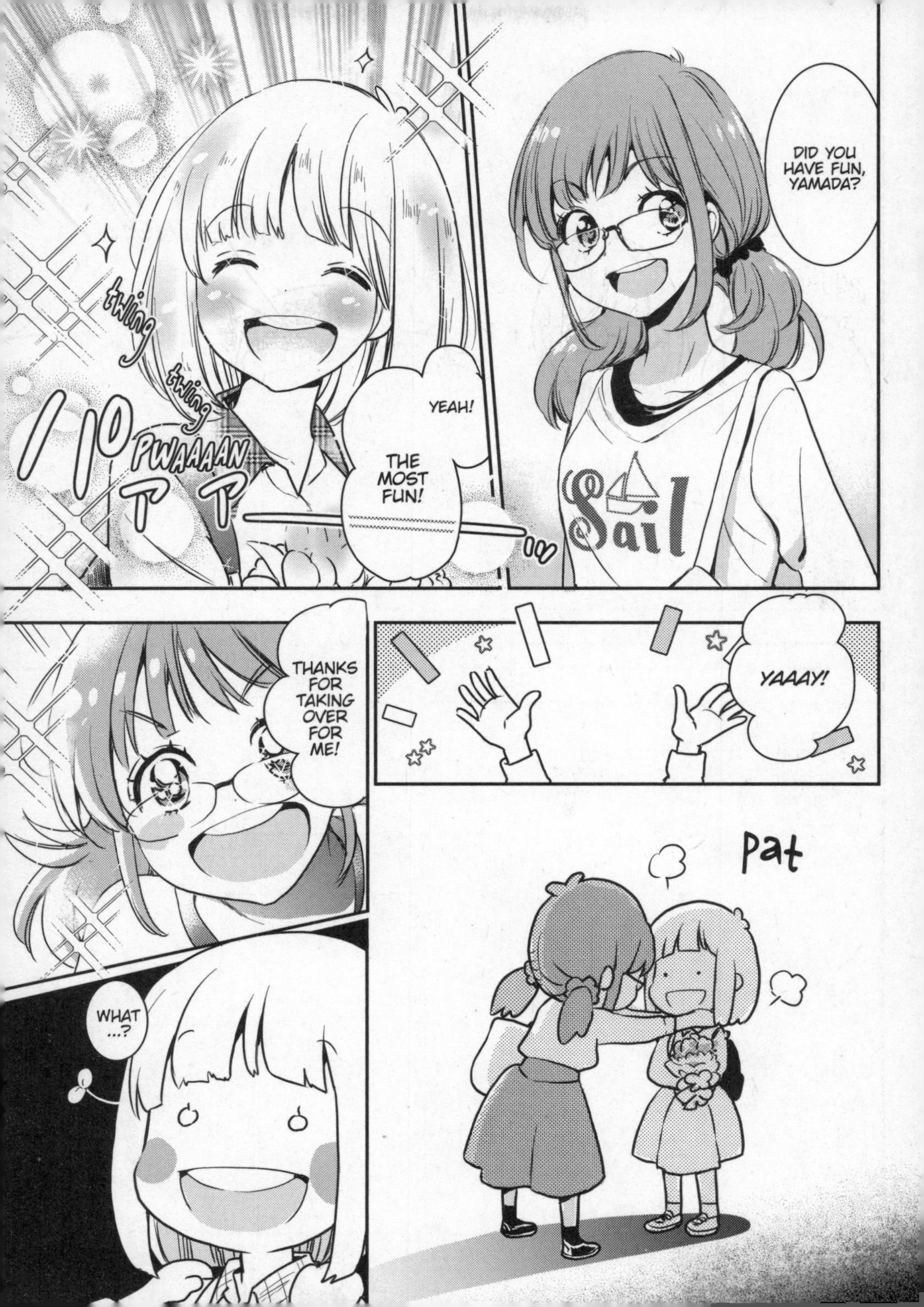
DID YOU HAVE FUN, YAMADA?
twing
twing
PWAAAAN
YEAH!
THE MOST FUN!
THANKS FOR TAKING OVER FOR ME!
YAAAY!
WHAT ...?
Pat

WHAT ?!!

I THOUGHT IT WAS SHORT TERM?!

I WANTED TO GET ANOTHER JOB, BUT I COULDN'T QUIT UNTIL I FOUND SOMEONE TO TAKE MY PLACE.

THANKS A LOT!

Ha ha ha!

I GOT THE JOB. ♥

I... GUESS IT'S OKAY.

IT IS A FAVOR TO MIKA-WACCHI AND ALL.

I got the

KASE-SAN...

122

THE SUN-SET'S...

SO BEAUTI-FUL.

I WONDER IF IT'LL BE NICE OUT TOMOR-ROW, TOO.

WOW...

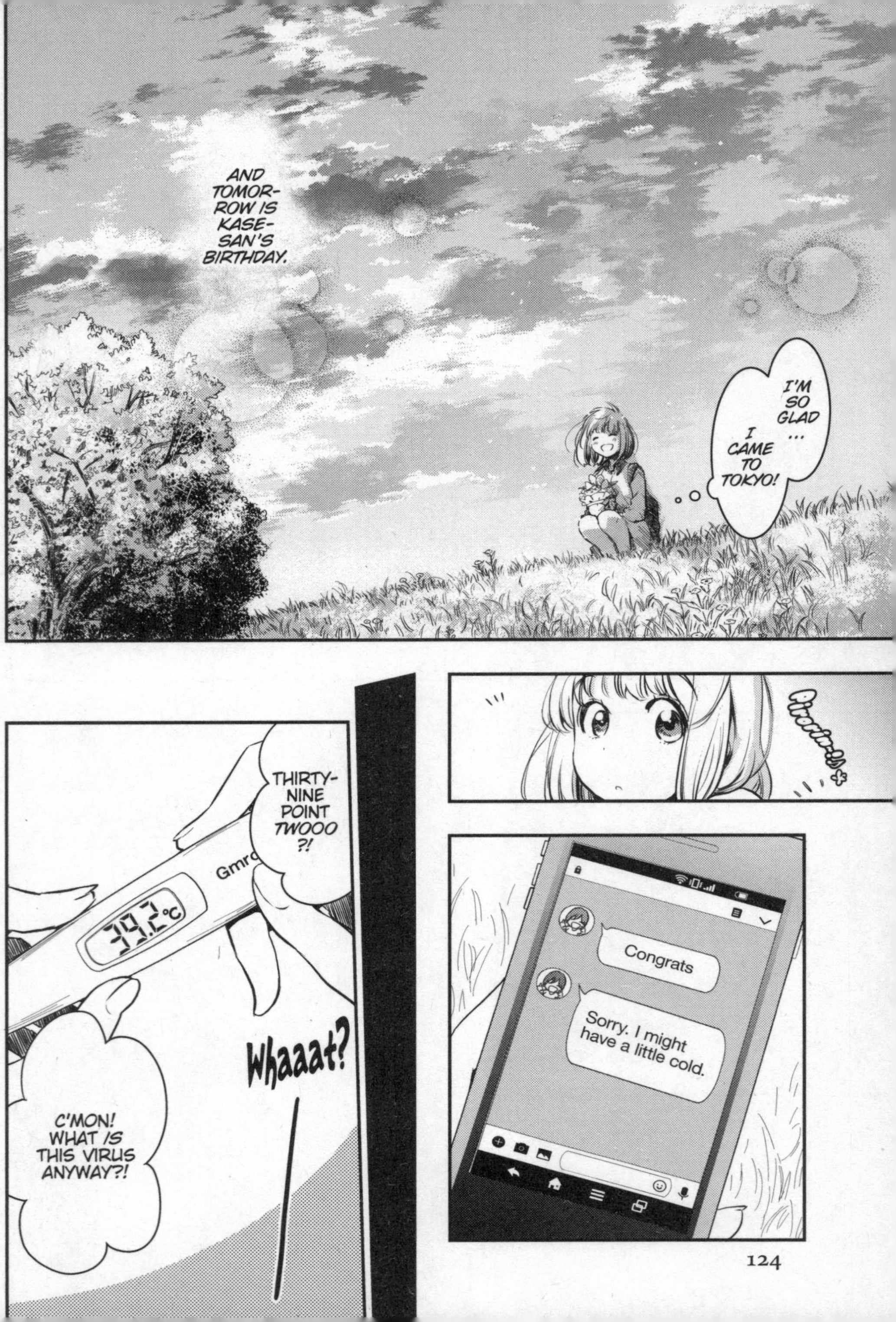
AND TOMORROW IS KASE-SAN'S BIRTHDAY.
I'M SO GLAD... I CAME TO TOKYO!
Congrats
Sorry. I might have a little cold.
39.2°C
THIRTY-NINE POINT TWOOO?!
Whaaat?
C'MON! WHAT IS THIS VIRUS ANYWAY?!

CRAP. THIS IS THE FIRST TIME IN MY LIFE I'VE EVER HAD A FEVER.

MY BODY FEELS LIKE LEAD.

THAT THE FEVER'S FROM OVERWORK AND I'M SUPPOSED TO REST.

WHAT'D THE DOCTOR SAY?

ARE MY MUSCLES GOING TO WITHER AWAY LYING AROUND LIKE THIS?

WHAT'S WITH THE GEAR?

YOU THINK I'LL BE ABLE TO MOVE TO- MORROW?

ANYWAY, I'M ONLY TRADING BUNKS TODAY.

WHAT ?!

THAT'D JUST CAUSE TROUBLE FOR EVERYONE ELSE!

I'LL GO GET YOU SOME DRINKS ...

BUT AFTER LIGHTS OUT, YOU'RE ON YOUR OWN.

I GUESS...

MRRR...

SHE'S ALREADY ASLEEP...

Snrr

"THAT'S NOT WHAT I MEAN!"

Snrr

Snrr

"WE'RE GOING OUT, AREN'T WE?!"

SOME-ONE...

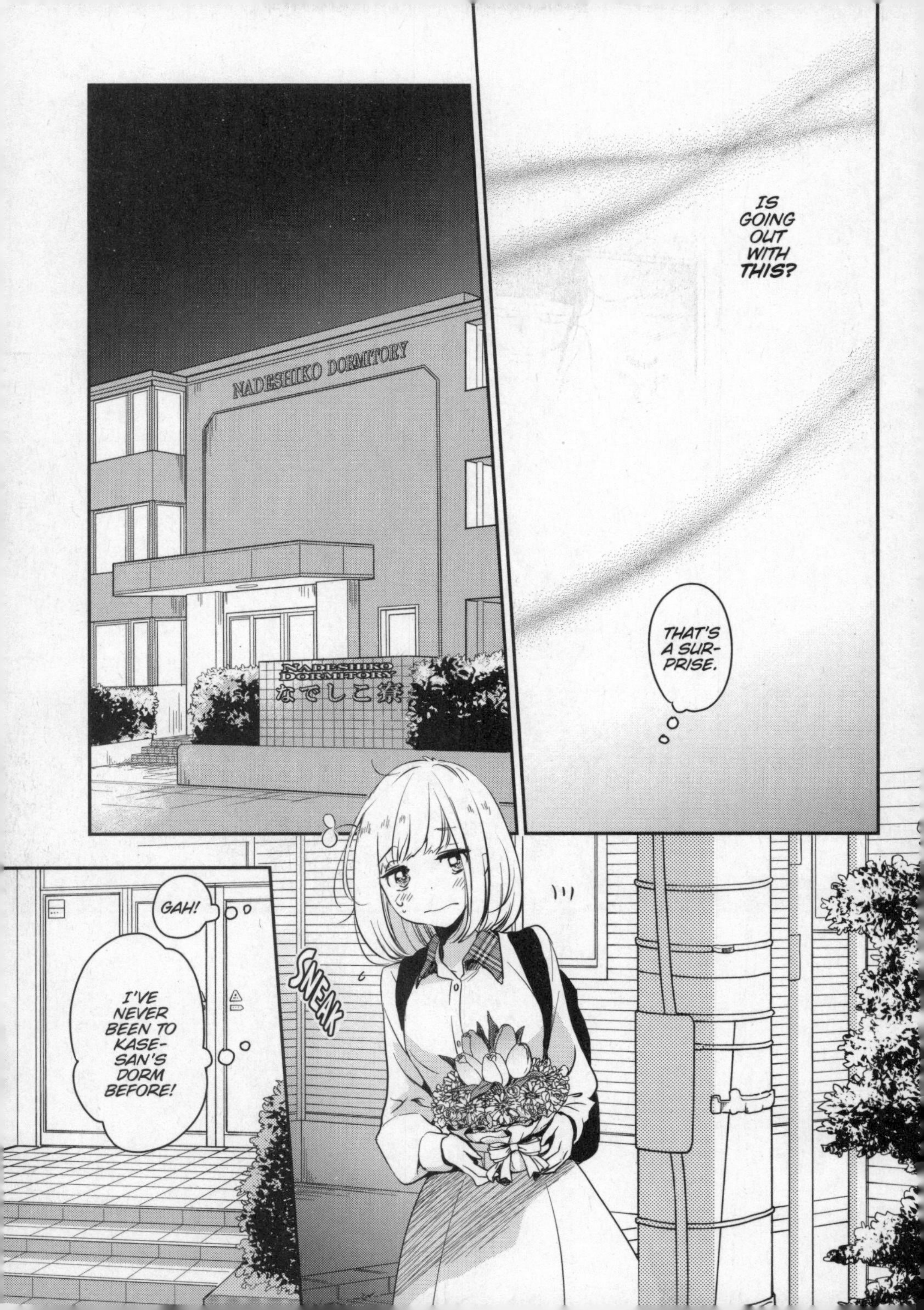
IS GOING OUT WITH THIS?
THAT'S A SURPRISE.
NADESHIKO DORMITORY
NADESHIKO DORMITORY
なでしこ寮
SNEAK
GAH!
I'VE NEVER BEEN TO KASE-SAN'S DORM BEFORE!

KASE-SAN'S NEVER HAD A COLD OR ANYTHING BEFORE...

Kase

I'll be a little late tomorrow. Sorry. 16:36

Are you okay?

16:37

THERE'S NO READ RECEIPT...

......

I WONDER IF SHE'S OKAY.

IF I WAIT UNTIL TOMORROW, IT'LL GET WILTY...

AND TOMORROW'S HER BIRTHDAY.

HUH? YAMADA-SAN!

INOUE-SENPAI!

Ah!

YAY!

WHAT'S UP?!

WHOA! IT'S BEEN AGES!!

HOW YA BEEN?!

A SICKROOM VISIT FOR KASE?

WHAT?

OOH! PRETTY FLOWERS!

UH!

FUKAMIII!

IS SHE DOING THAT POORLY?!

I GUESS SHE WENT TO THE DOCTOR THIS AFTERNOON. SAID SHE HAD A FEVER.

OH! HANG ON A SEC.

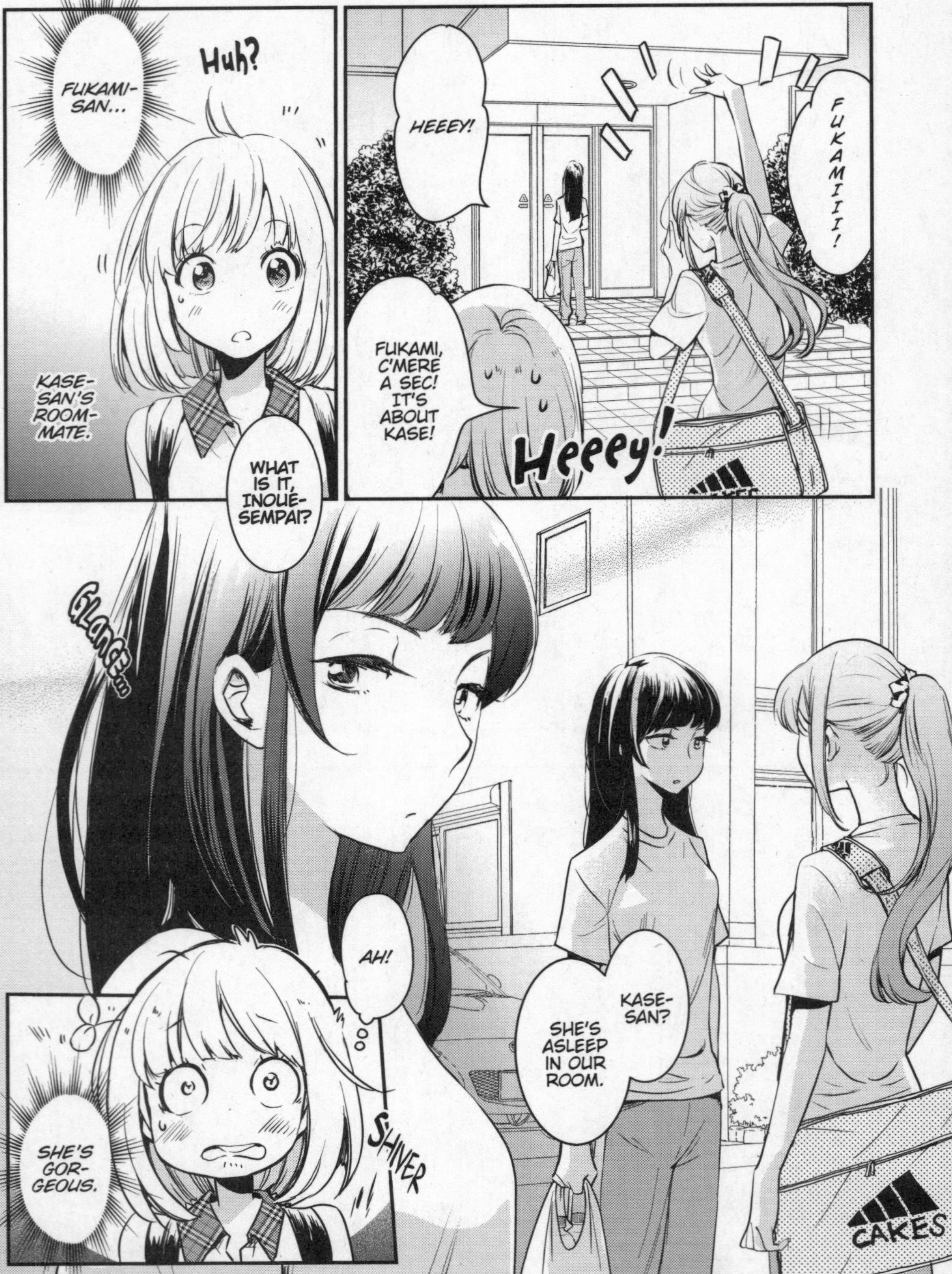

FUKAMIIII!
HEEEY!
FUKAMI, C'MERE A SEC! IT'S ABOUT KASE!
Heeey!
CAKES
FUKAMI-SAN...
Huh?
KASE-SAN'S ROOMMATE.
WHAT IS IT, INOUE-SEMPAI?
GLANCE...
KASE-SAN? SHE'S ASLEEP IN OUR ROOM.
CAKES
AH!
SHIVER
SHE'S GORGEOUS.

Kase-san and Yamada ①

Kase-san and Yamada ①

Kase-san and the Birthday

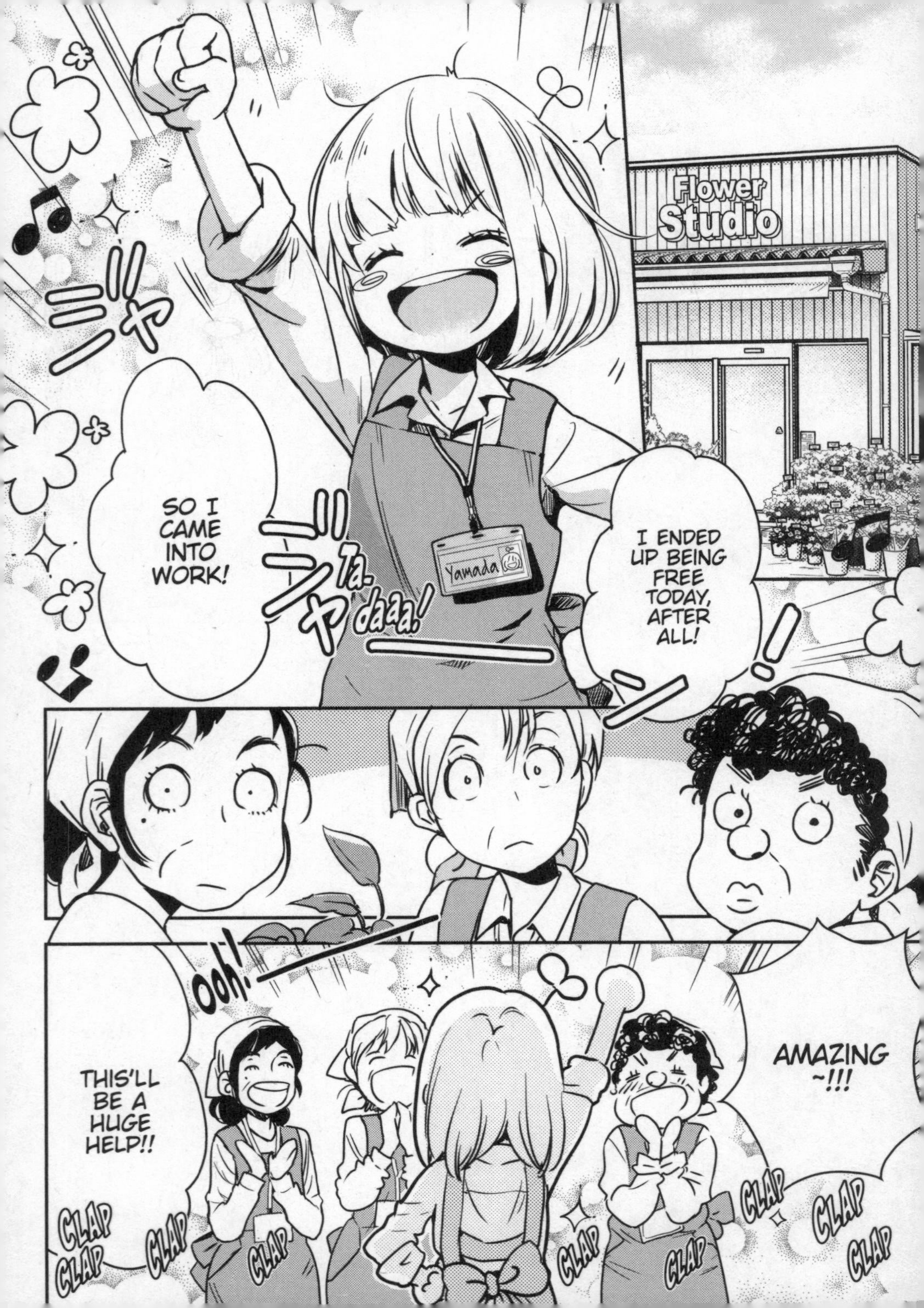
Flower Studio
I ENDED UP BEING FREE TODAY, AFTER ALL!
SO I CAME INTO WORK!
Yamada
Ta-daaa!
Ooh!
AMAZING~!!!
THIS'LL BE A HUGE HELP!!
CLAP CLAP
CLAP
CLAP
CLAP
CLAP
CLAP
CLAP

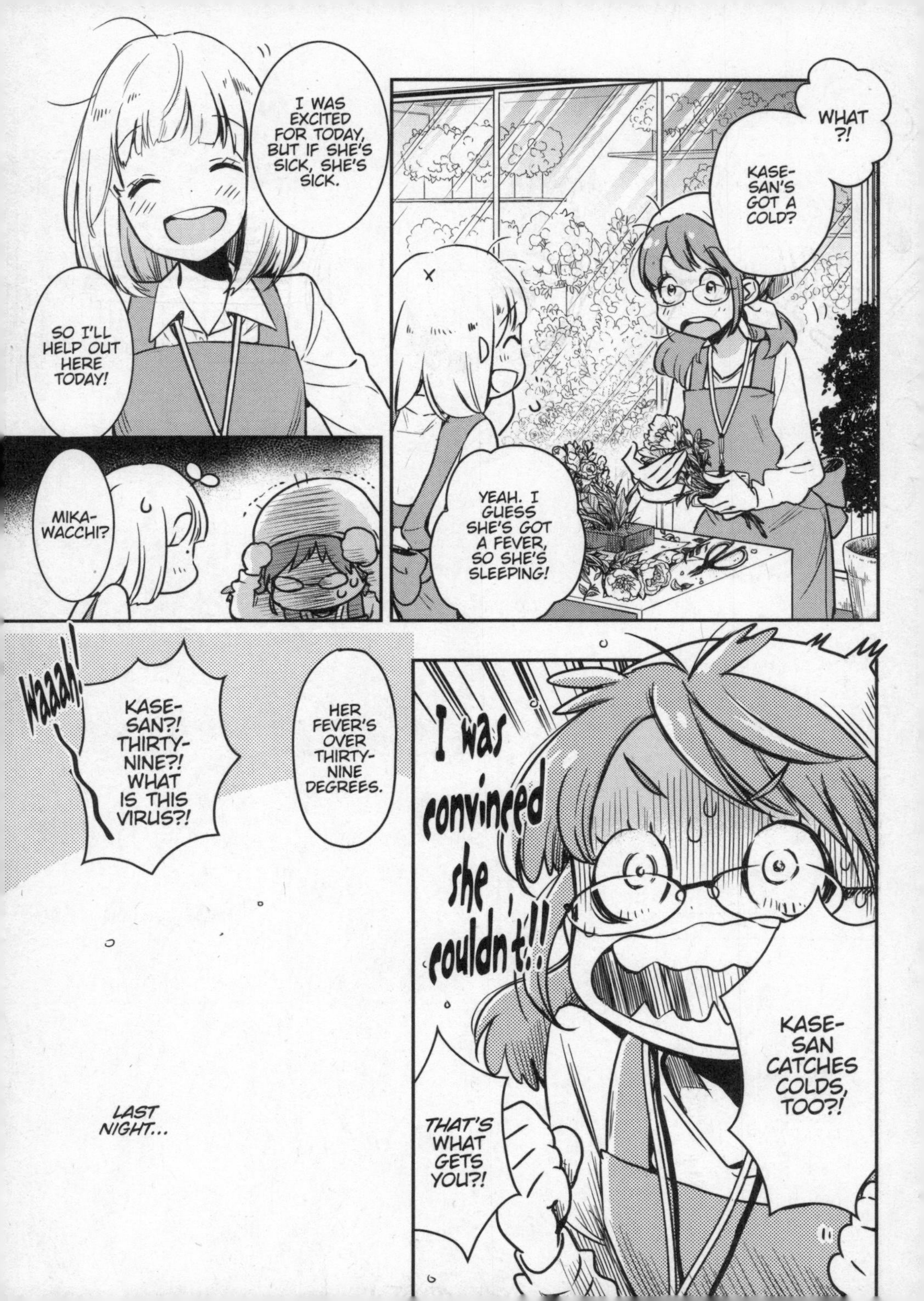
WHAT?!
KASE-SAN'S GOT A COLD?
YEAH. I GUESS SHE'S GOT A FEVER, SO SHE'S SLEEPING!
I WAS EXCITED FOR TODAY, BUT IF SHE'S SICK, SHE'S SICK.
SO I'LL HELP OUT HERE TODAY!
MIKA-WACCHI?
I was convinced she couldn't!!
KASE-SAN CATCHES COLDS, TOO?!
THAT'S WHAT GETS YOU?!
LAST NIGHT...
HER FEVER'S OVER THIRTY-NINE DEGREES.
Waaah!
KASE-SAN?! THIRTY-NINE?! WHAT IS THIS VIRUS?!

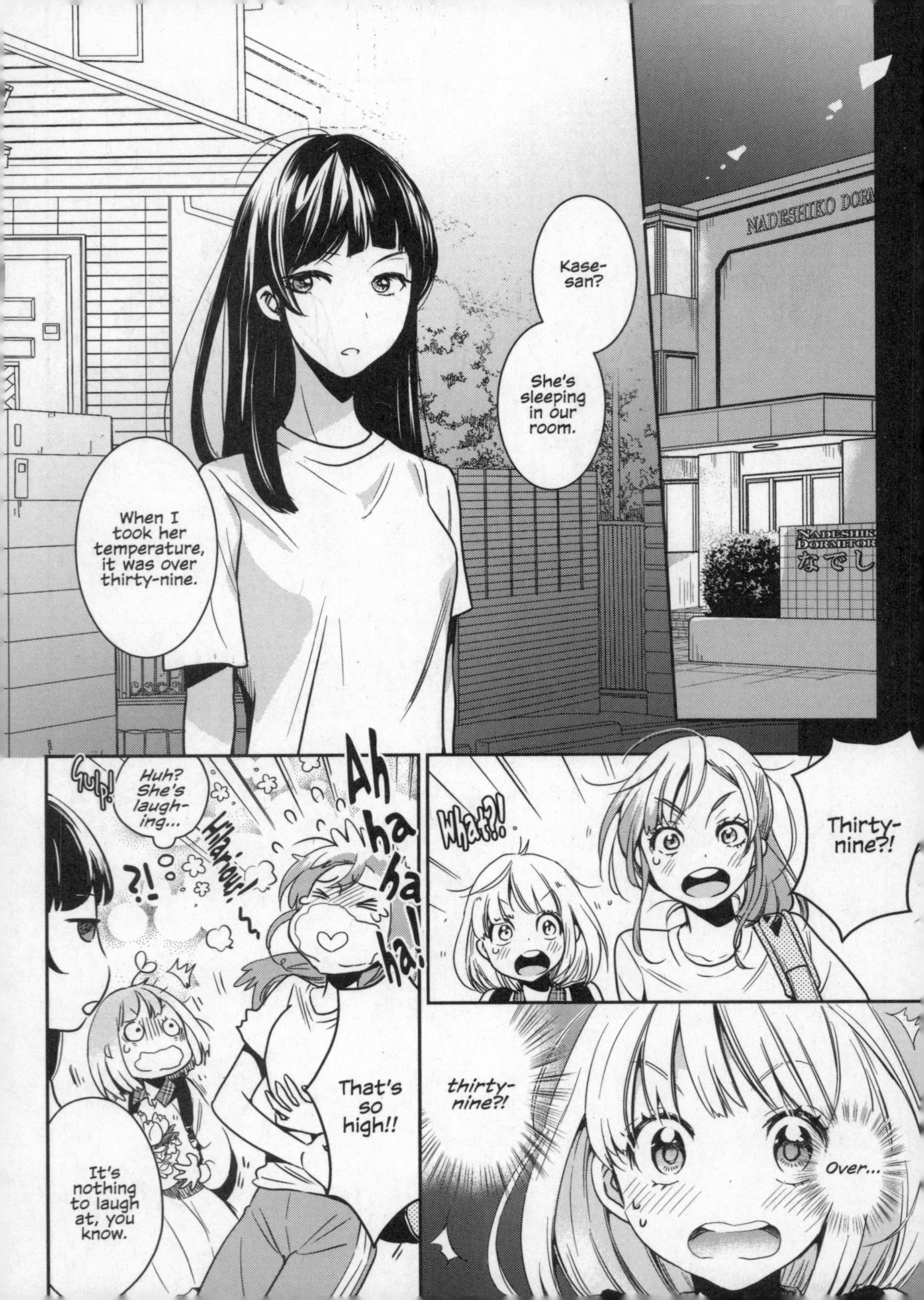
Kase-san?
She's sleeping in our room.
When I took her temperature, it was over thirty-nine.
Thirty-nine?!
What?!
Ah ha ha ha ha!
Hilarious!
Huh? She's laughing...
Gulp!
?!
Over...
thirty-nine?!
That's so high!!
It's nothing to laugh at, you know.

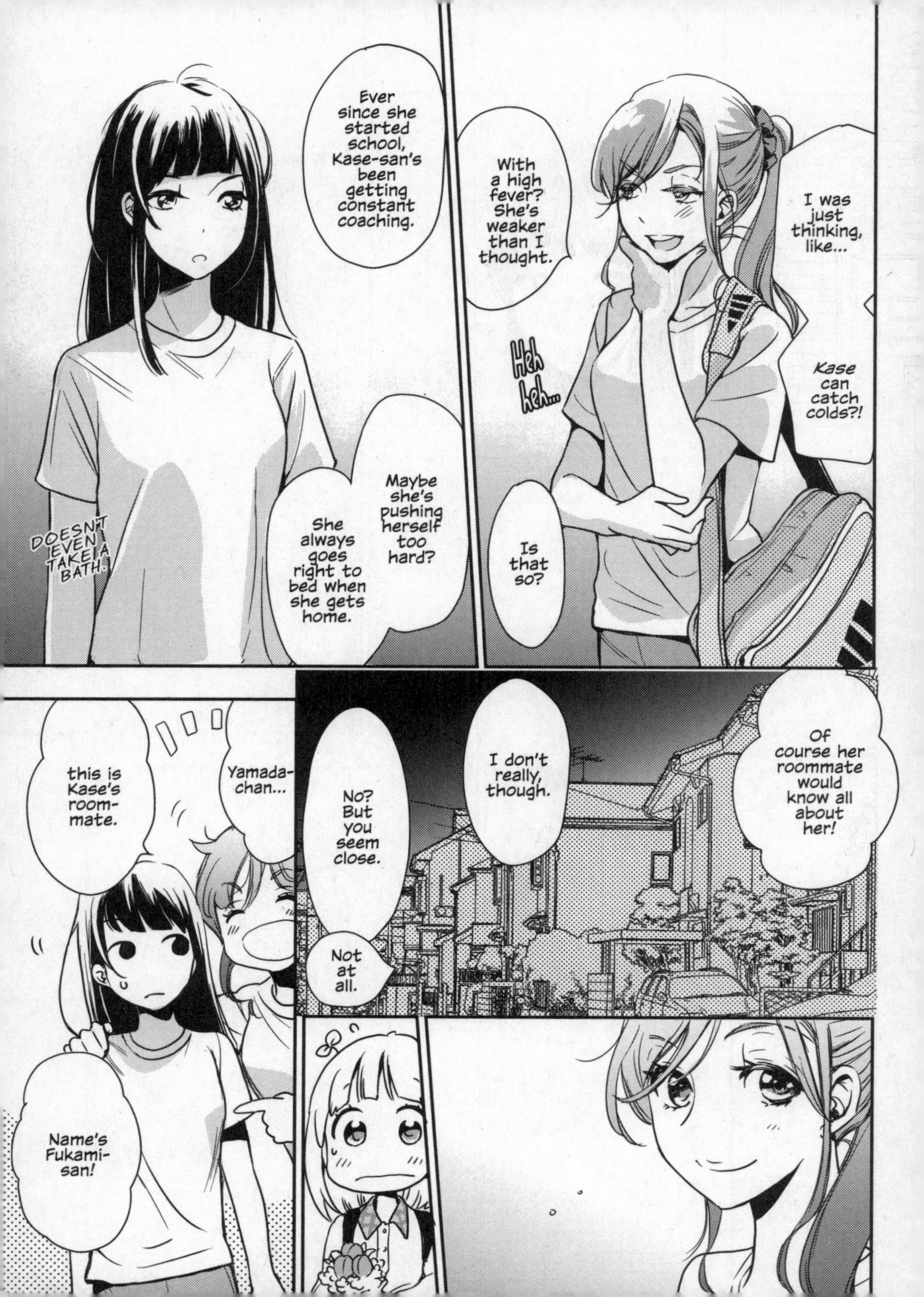
I was just thinking, like...
Kase can catch colds?!
With a high fever? She's weaker than I thought.
Heh heh...
Is that so?
Ever since she started school, Kase-san's been getting constant coaching.
Maybe she's pushing herself too hard?
She always goes right to bed when she gets home.
DOESN'T EVEN TAKE A BATH.
Of course her roommate would know all about her!
I don't really, though.
No? But you seem close.
Not at all.
Yamada-chan...
this is Kase's roommate.
Name's Fukami-san!

umm...

friend!

She came to visit Kase!

Yamada-chan is Kase's...

I know...

N...

nice to meet you.

It's fine. Don't bother!! I mean--!

What ?!

Gulp

WAKE...

Fukami, could you wake Kase up for a moment?

Tell her to get well soon.

But when she wakes up, please tell her we'll do it another time.

we're supposed to meet tomorrow.

W...

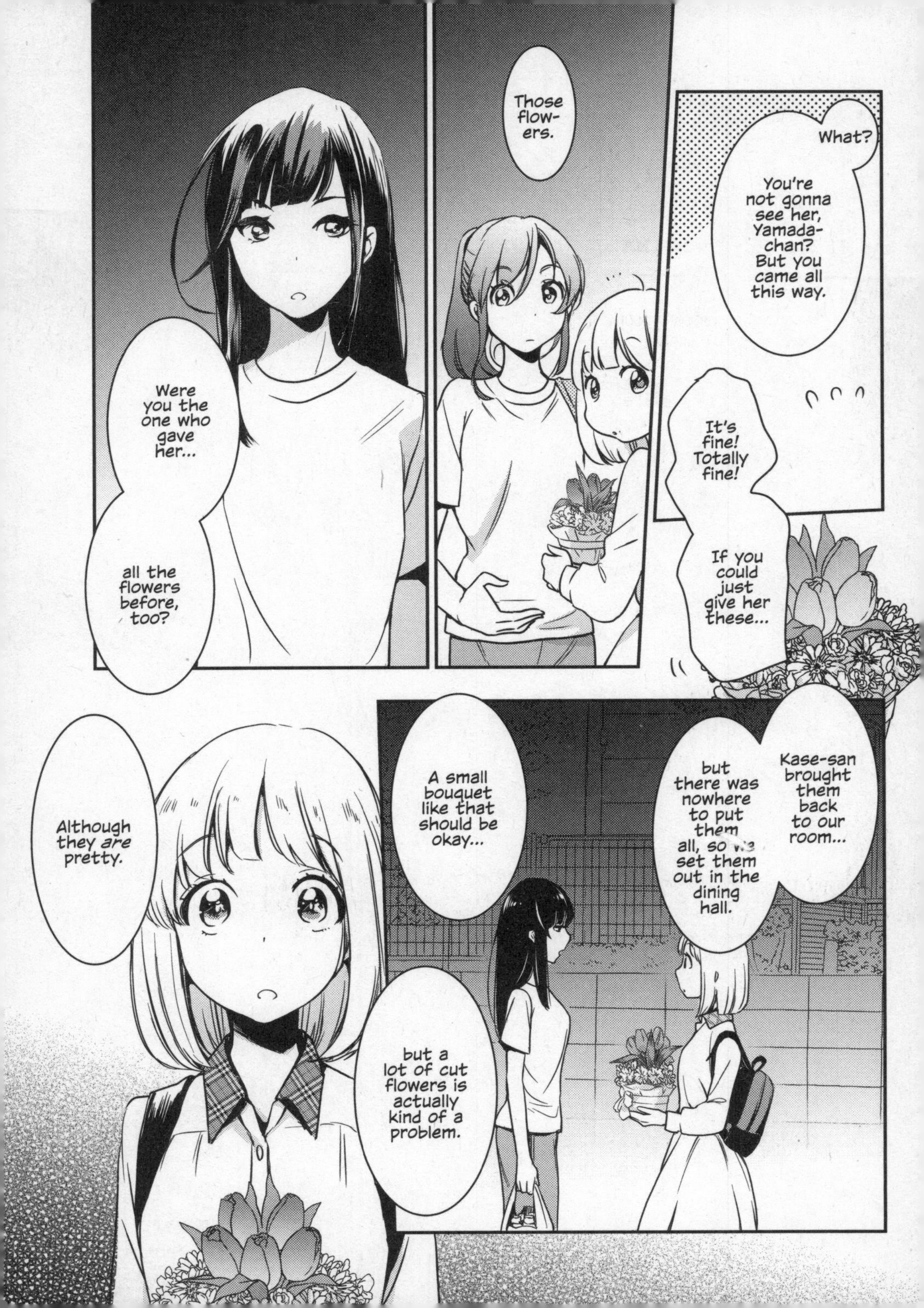
What?
You're not gonna see her, Yamada-chan? But you came all this way.
It's fine! Totally fine!
If you could just give her these...
Those flow-ers.
Were you the one who gave her...
all the flowers before, too?
Kase-san brought them back to our room...
but there was nowhere to put them all, so we set them out in the dining hall.
A small bouquet like that should be okay...
but a lot of cut flowers is actually kind of a problem.
Although they *are* pretty.

WHERE'D THAT COME FROM?

IT'S NOTHING...

AhH

THAT WAS YESTERDAY.

FLOWER

"WERE YOU THE ONE WHO GAVE HER ALL THE FLOWERS BEFORE, TOO?"

FUKAMI-SAN WENT OUT AND BOUGHT DRINKS...

I'M SO THOUGHTLESS.

FOR KASE-SAN, I GUESS.

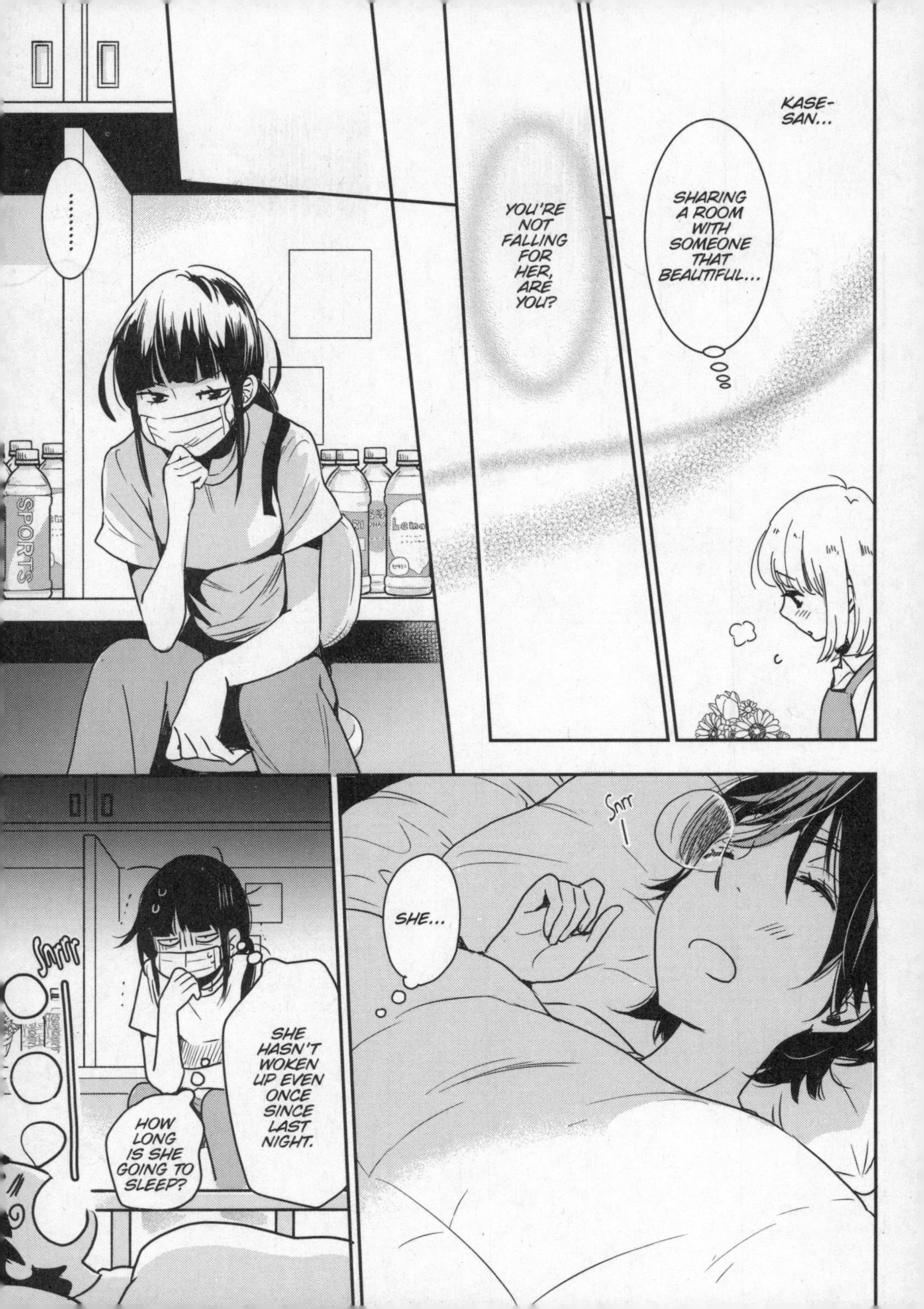
KASE-SAN...
SHARING A ROOM WITH SOMEONE THAT BEAUTIFUL...
YOU'RE NOT FALLING FOR HER, ARE YOU?
......
SPORTS
Snrr
SHE...
SHE HASN'T WOKEN UP EVEN ONCE SINCE LAST NIGHT.
HOW LONG IS SHE GOING TO SLEEP?
Snrrr

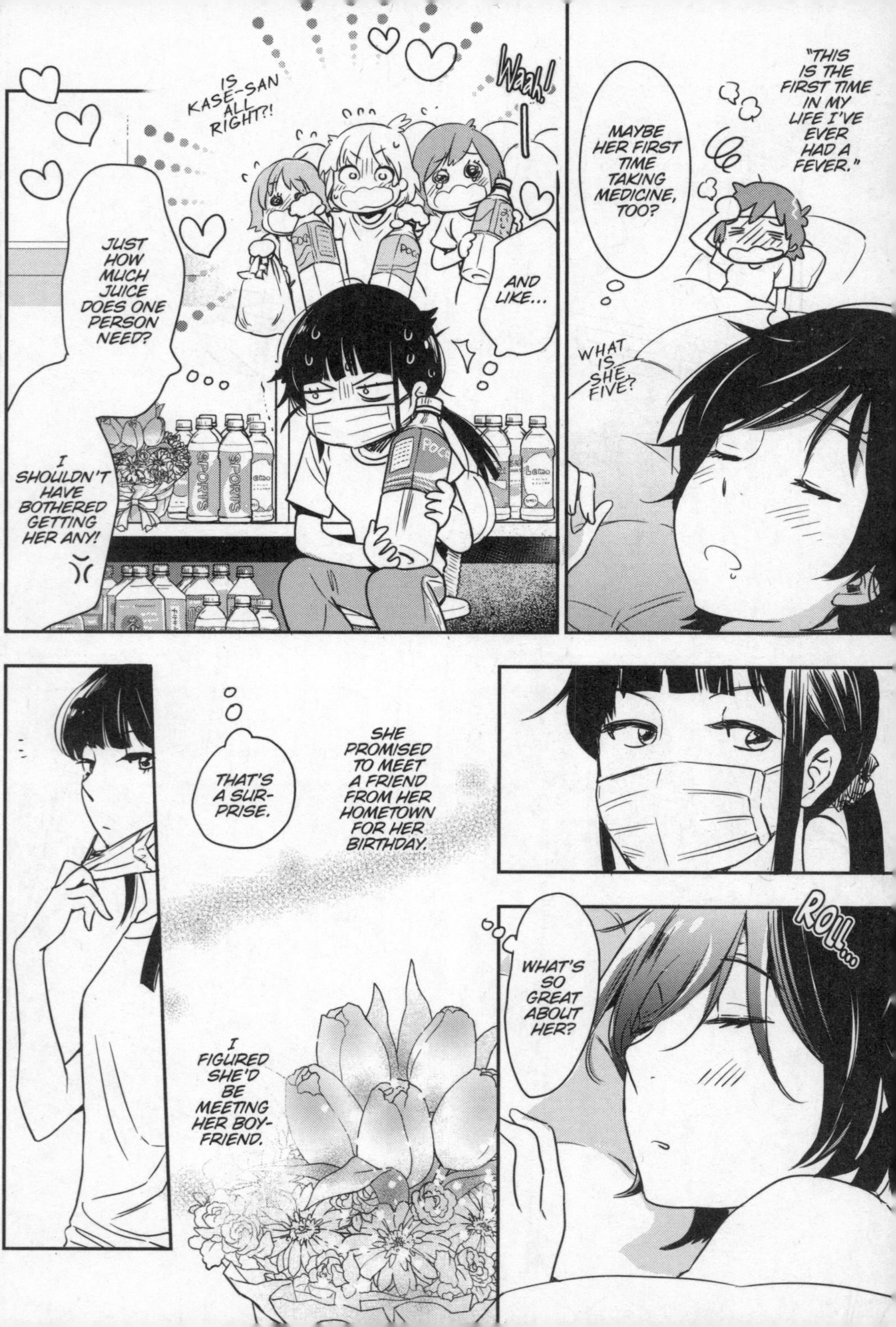
"THIS IS THE FIRST TIME IN MY LIFE I'VE EVER HAD A FEVER."
MAYBE HER FIRST TIME TAKING MEDICINE, TOO?
WHAT IS SHE, FIVE?
WAAH!
IS KASE-SAN ALL RIGHT?!
AND LIKE...
JUST HOW MUCH JUICE DOES ONE PERSON NEED?
I SHOULDN'T HAVE BOTHERED GETTING HER ANY!
SHE PROMISED TO MEET A FRIEND FROM HER HOMETOWN FOR HER BIRTHDAY.
THAT'S A SURPRISE.
I FIGURED SHE'D BE MEETING HER BOYFRIEND.
ROLL...
WHAT'S SO GREAT ABOUT HER?

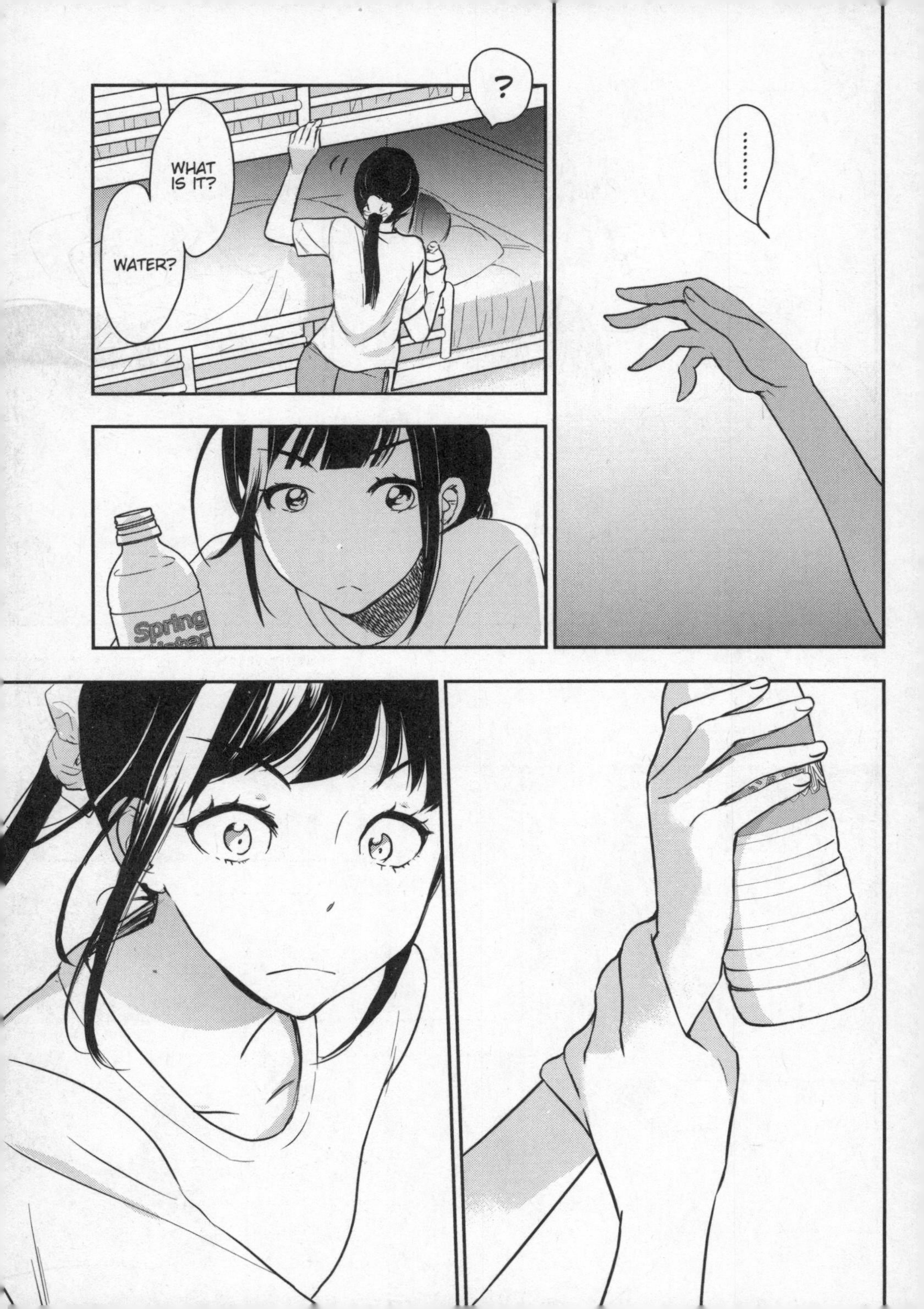

……
?
WHAT IS IT?
WATER?
Spring Water

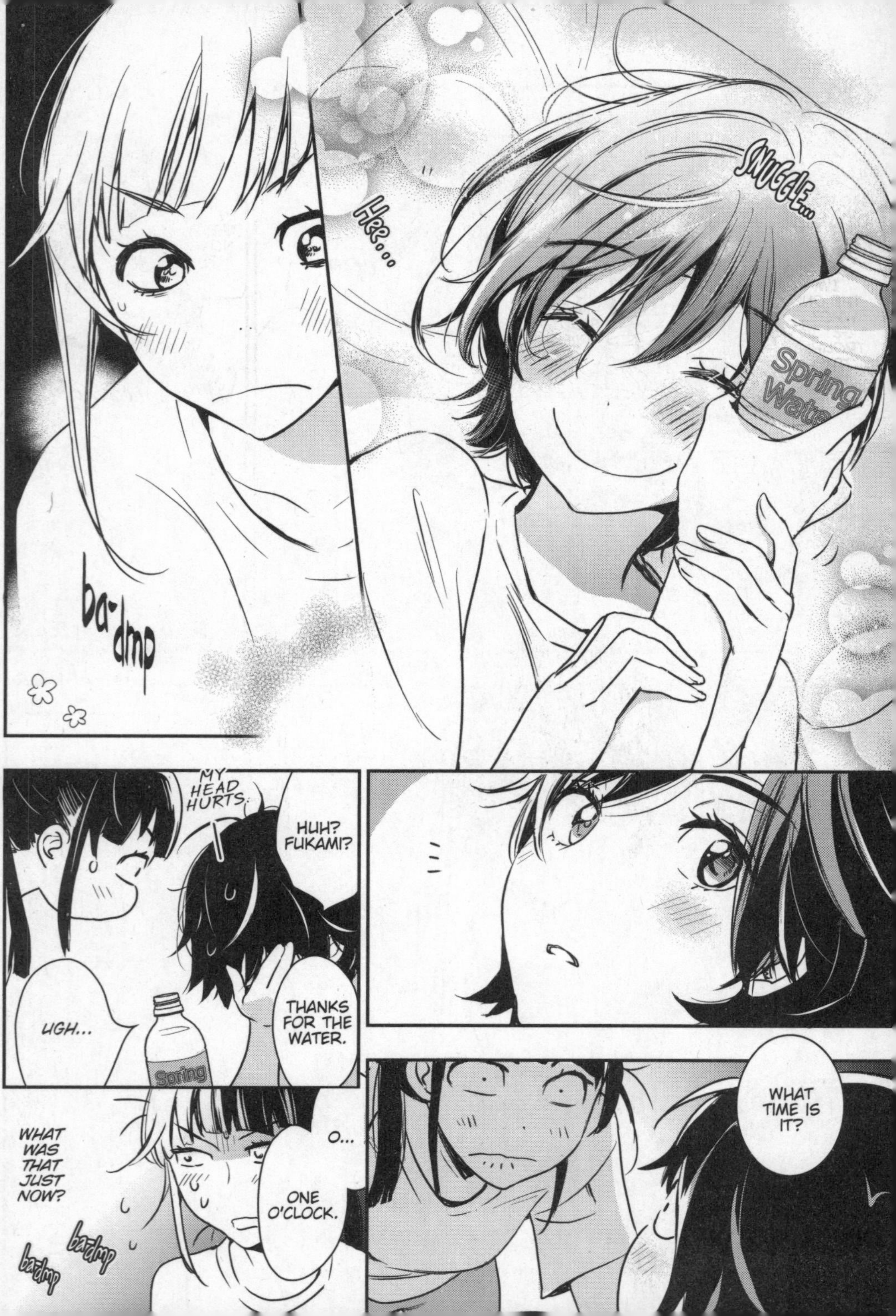
SNUGGLE...
Hee...
Spring Water
ba-dmp
HUH? FUKAMI?
MY HEAD HURTS.
THANKS FOR THE WATER.
UGH...
Spring
WHAT TIME IS IT?
O...
ONE O'CLOCK.
WHAT WAS THAT JUST NOW?
ba-dmp
ba-dmp

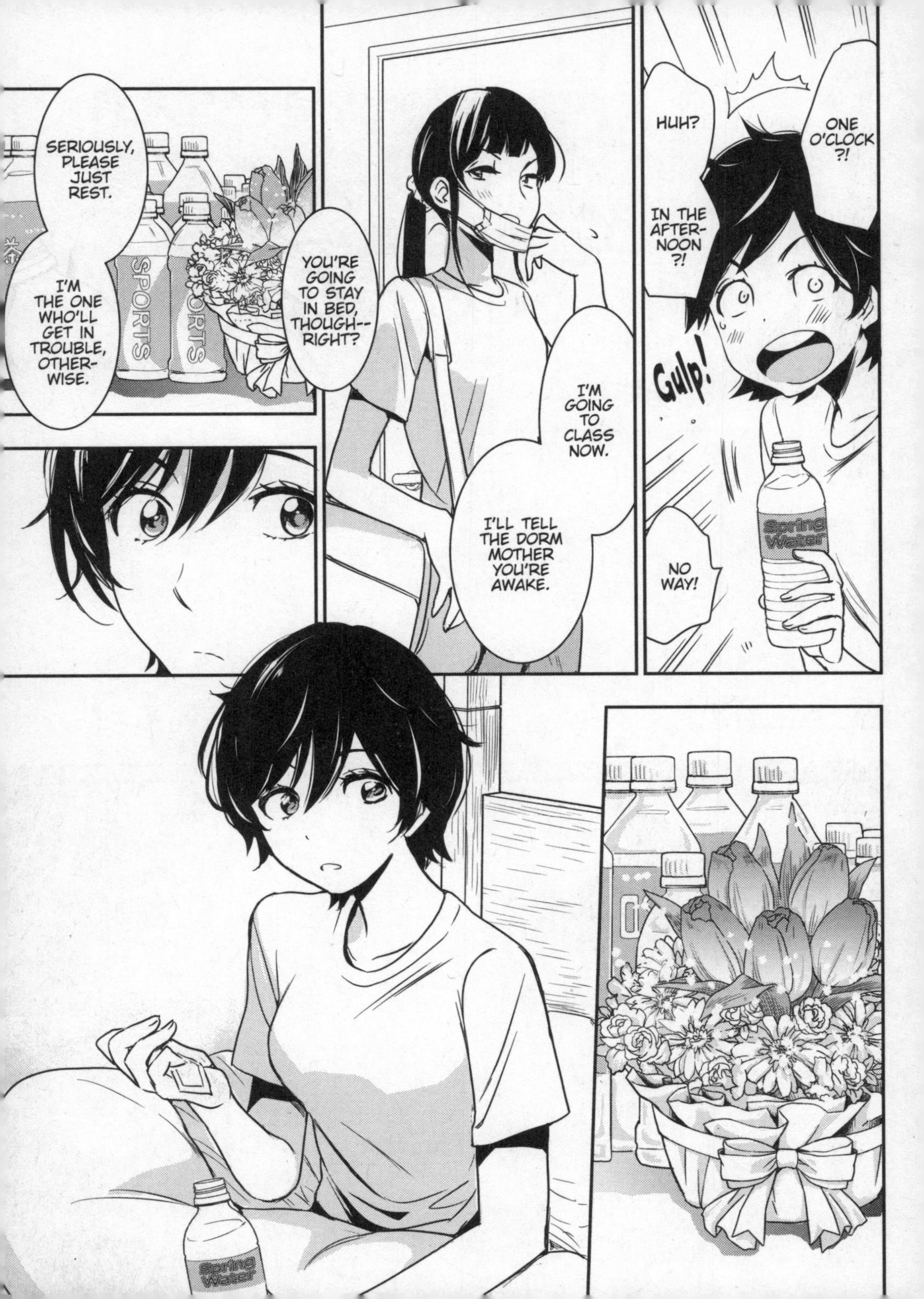
HUH?
ONE O'CLOCK?!
IN THE AFTERNOON?!
Gulp!
NO WAY!
Spring Water
I'M GOING TO CLASS NOW.
I'LL TELL THE DORM MOTHER YOU'RE AWAKE.
YOU'RE GOING TO STAY IN BED, THOUGH--RIGHT?
SERIOUSLY, PLEASE JUST REST.
I'M THE ONE WHO'LL GET IN TROUBLE, OTHERWISE.
SPORTS
SPORTS
Spring Water

MIKA-WACCHI WENT TO AN INTER-VIEW FOR HER NEXT JOB...

SO SHE SLIPPED OUT IN THE MIDDLE OF THE DAY.

SEE YA!

THANKS FOR STAYING LATE, YAMADA-SAN.

IT'S GREAT TO HAVE YOU WITH US.

THANK YOU! I'M GLAD TO BE HERE!

THANKS, MIKA-WACCHI...

FOR GIVING ME THE FLOWERS.

HOW TO SPEND THE DAY IF I HADN'T GOTTEN THIS JOB.

I WOULDN'T HAVE KNOWN...

I'M GLAD I HAVE THE FLOWERS.

......

YESTER-
DAY WAS
SO MUCH
FUN...

THE
WORLD IS
SO BIG
AND DARK
WHEN
YOU'RE
ALONE.

BUT
TODAY
WAS
DIFFER-
ENT.

I GOTTA
GET IT
TOGETHER.

AND
THEN
I HAVE
WORK
IN THE
AFTER-
NOON.

IT'S MY
TURN TO DO
THE MORN-
ING WATER-
ING AT
SCHOOL...

I GOTTA
GET OUT
THERE
AGAIN
TOMOR-
ROW.

19:48
Wednesday, May 1

25 minutes ago
LINE
What time do you work until? Can you call me?

Kase
32 minutes ago
LINE
until eight. Can you call me?

Kase

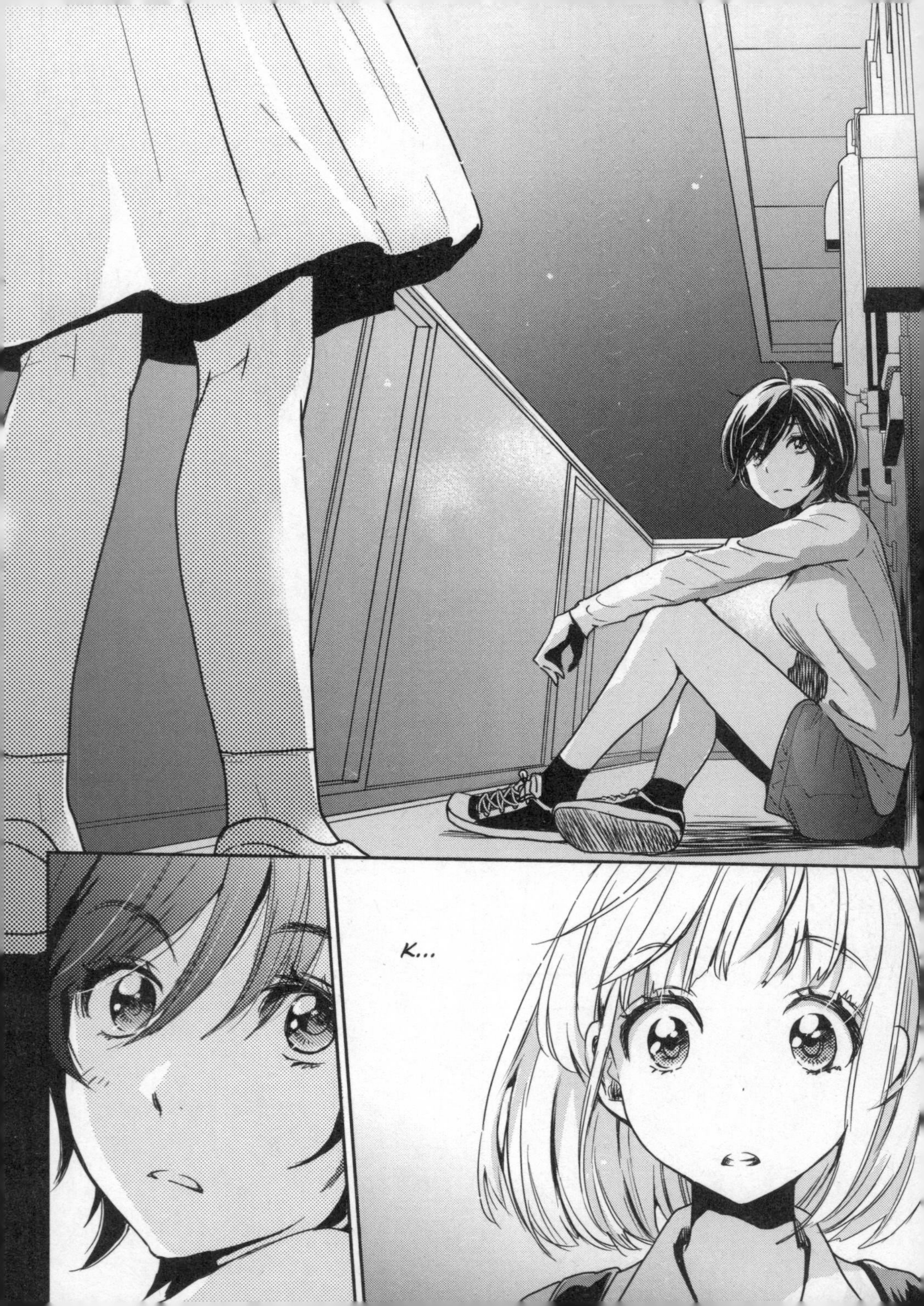
K...

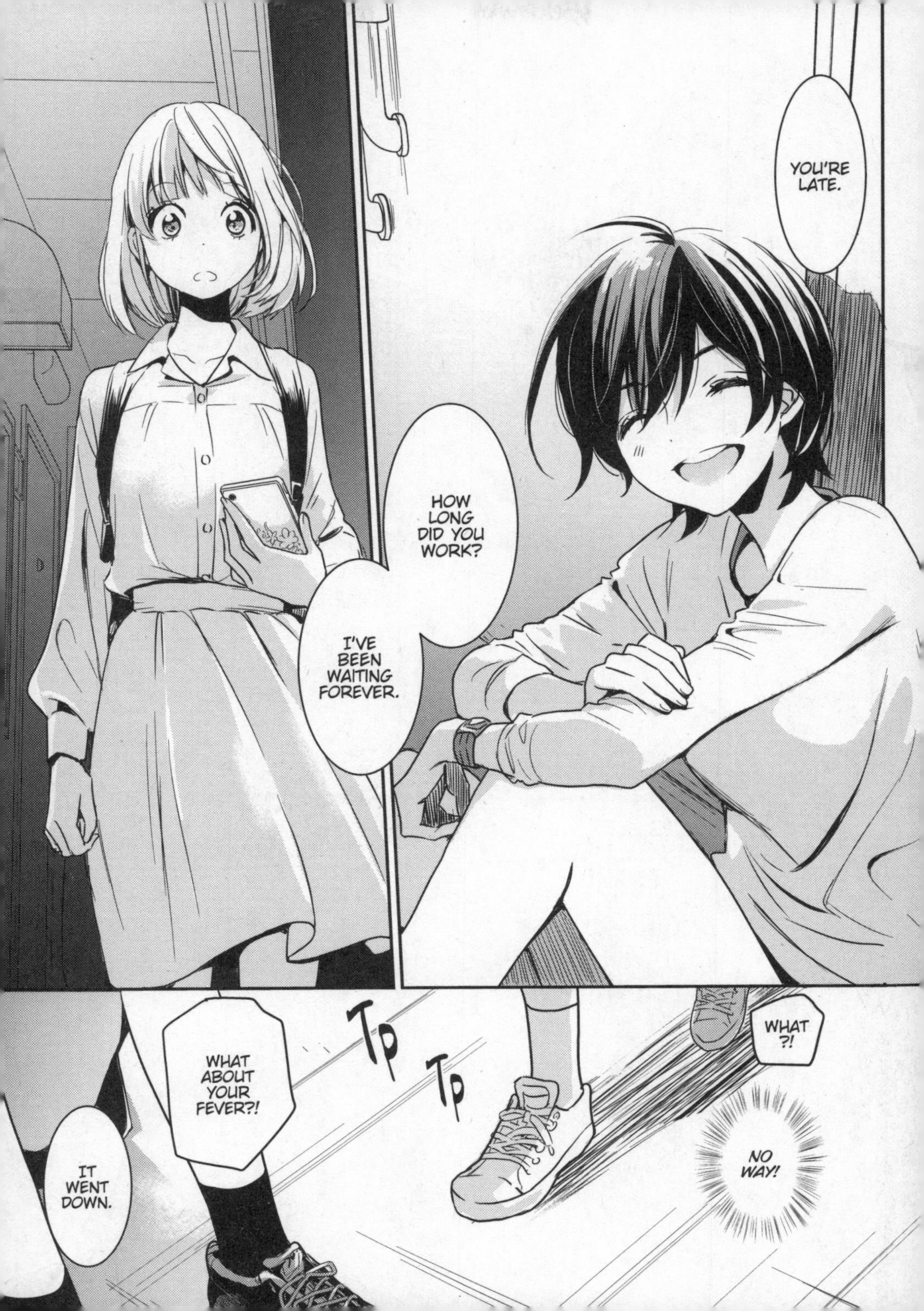
YOU'RE LATE.
HOW LONG DID YOU WORK?
I'VE BEEN WAITING FOREVER.
WHAT ?!
NO WAY!
Tp Tp
WHAT ABOUT YOUR FEVER?!
IT WENT DOWN.

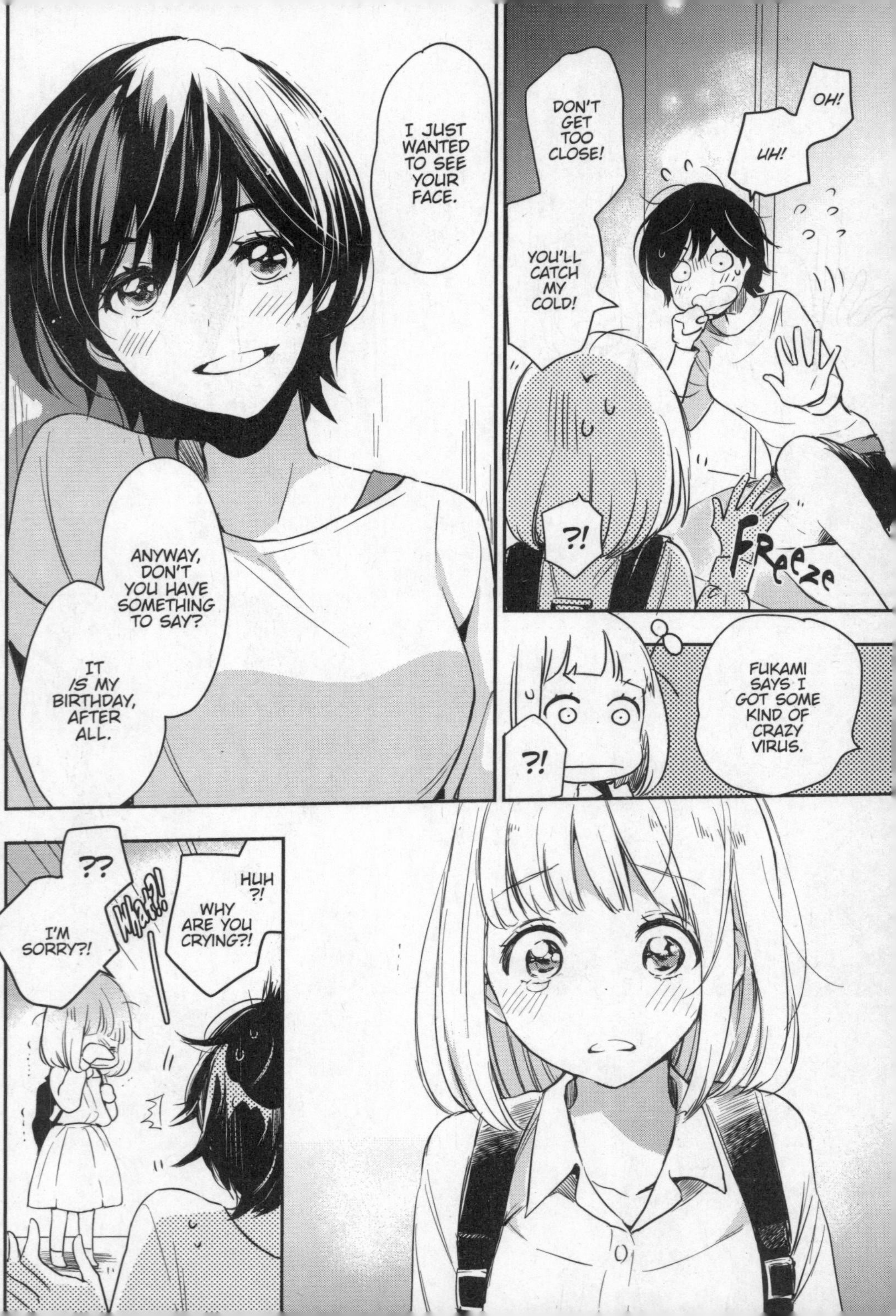

OH!
UH!
DON'T GET TOO CLOSE!
YOU'LL CATCH MY COLD!
?!
Freeze
FUKAMI SAYS I GOT SOME KIND OF CRAZY VIRUS.
?!
I JUST WANTED TO SEE YOUR FACE.
ANYWAY, DON'T YOU HAVE SOMETHING TO SAY?
IT *IS* MY BIRTHDAY, AFTER ALL.
HUH?!
WHY ARE YOU CRYING?!
What?!
??
I'M SORRY?!

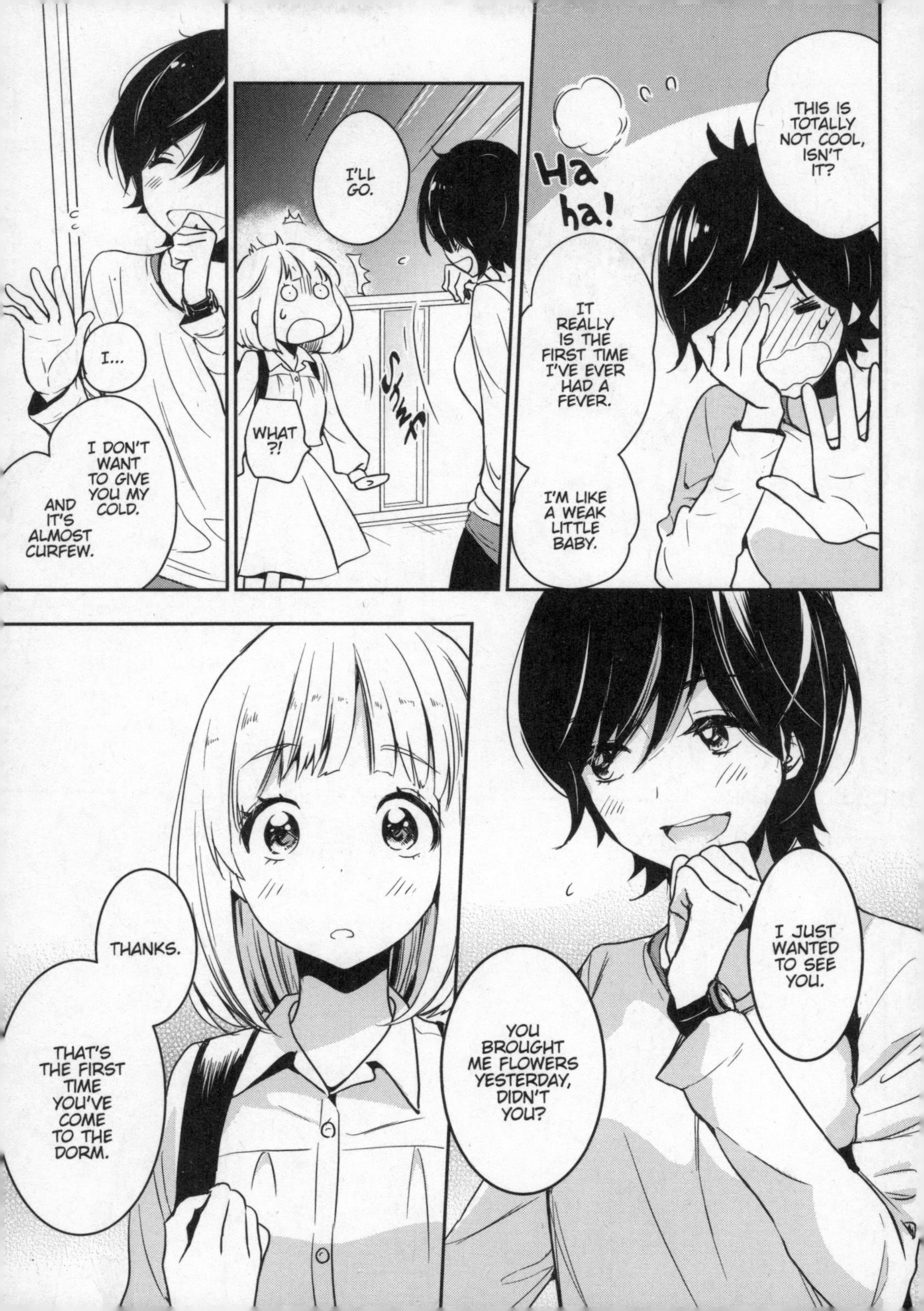
THIS IS TOTALLY NOT COOL, ISN'T IT?
Ha ha!
IT REALLY IS THE FIRST TIME I'VE EVER HAD A FEVER.
I'M LIKE A WEAK LITTLE BABY.
I'LL GO.
Shwf
WHAT ?!
I...
I DON'T WANT TO GIVE YOU MY COLD.
AND IT'S ALMOST CURFEW.
I JUST WANTED TO SEE YOU.
YOU BROUGHT ME FLOWERS YESTERDAY, DIDN'T YOU?
THANKS.
THAT'S THE FIRST TIME YOU'VE COME TO THE DORM.

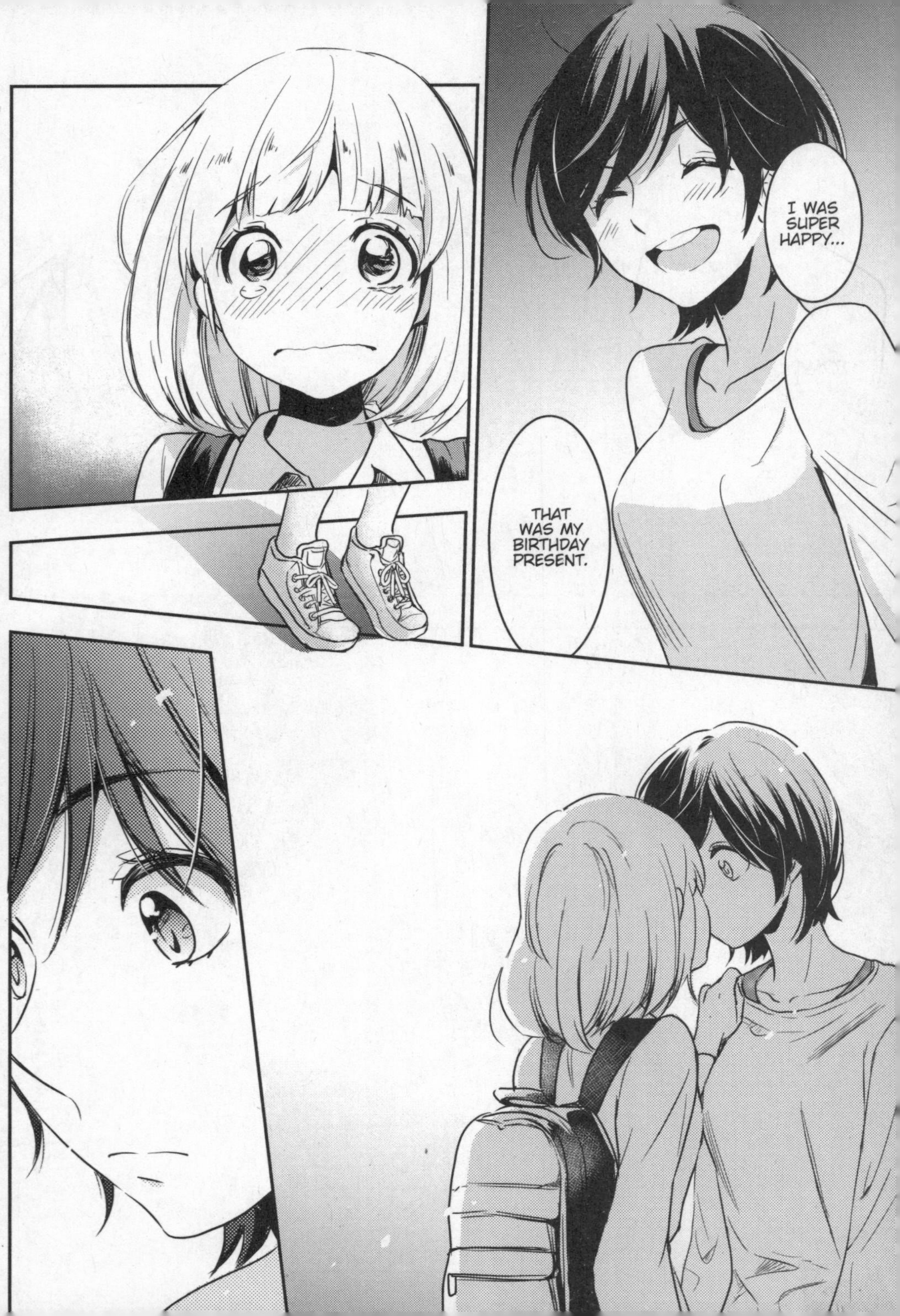
I WAS SUPER HAPPY...
THAT WAS MY BIRTHDAY PRESENT.

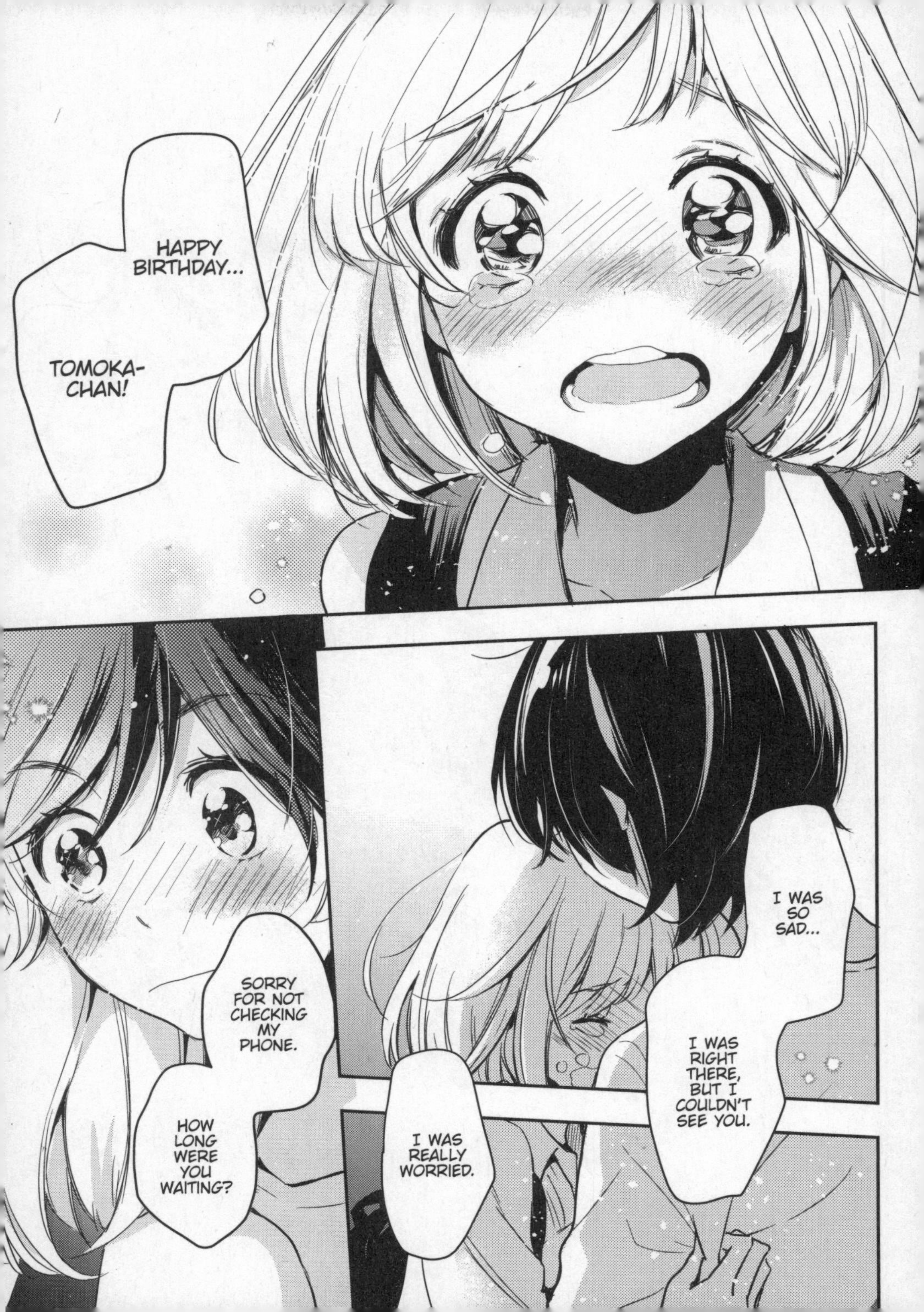
HAPPY BIRTHDAY...
TOMOKA-CHAN!
I WAS SO SAD...
I WAS RIGHT THERE, BUT I COULDN'T SEE YOU.
I WAS REALLY WORRIED.
SORRY FOR NOT CHECKING MY PHONE.
HOW LONG WERE YOU WAITING?

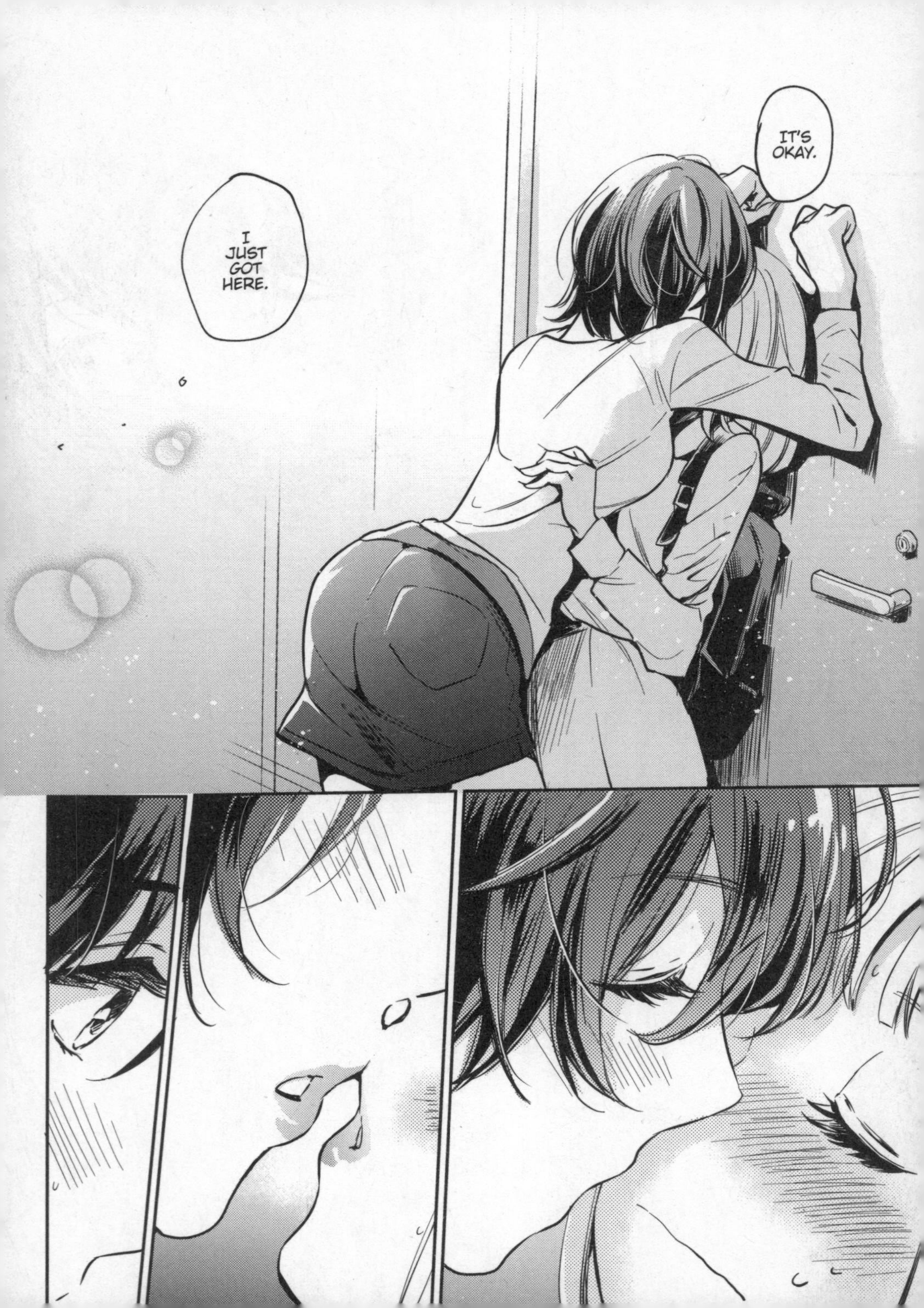
IT'S OKAY.
I JUST GOT HERE.

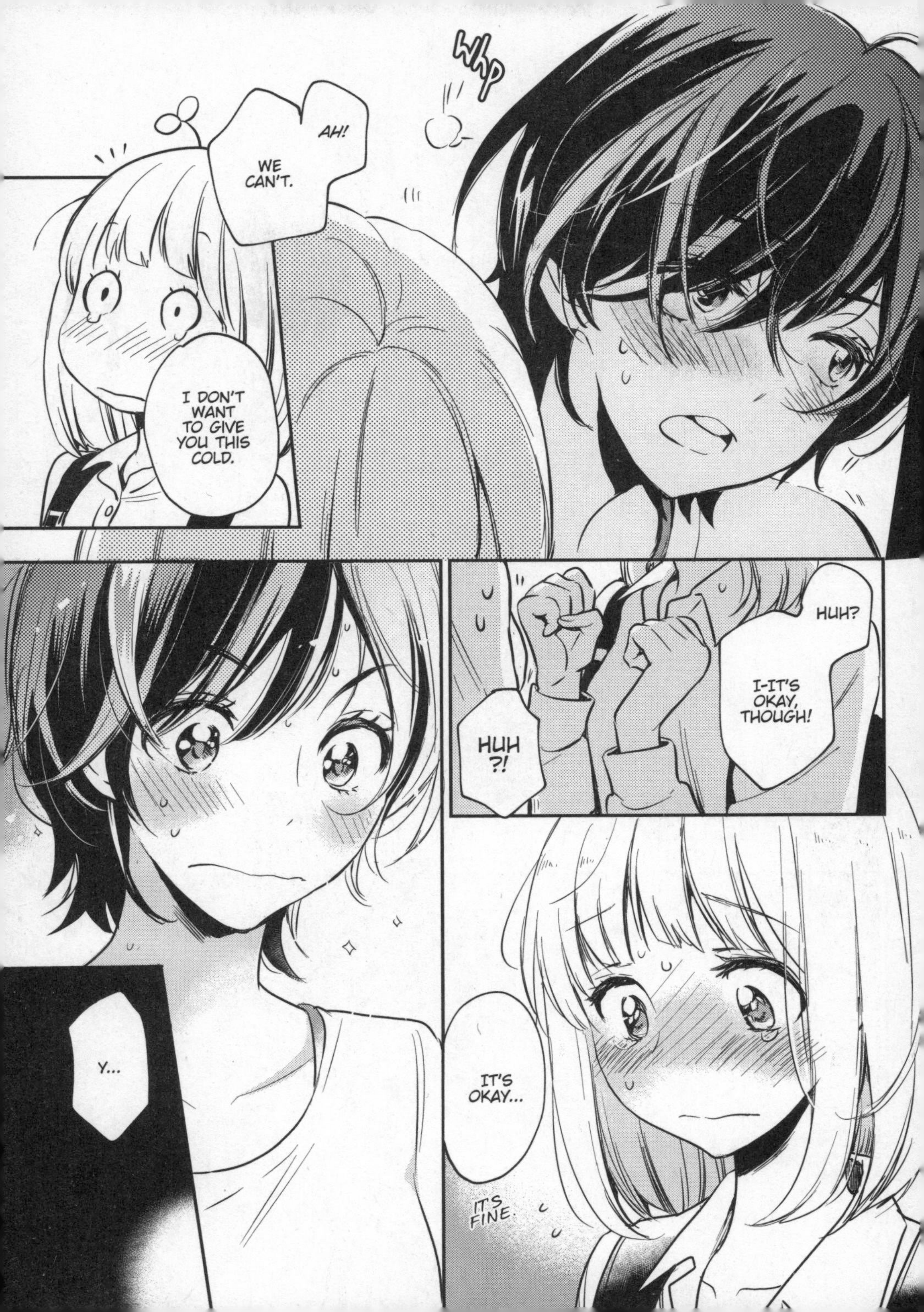
Whp
AH! WE CAN'T.
I DON'T WANT TO GIVE YOU THIS COLD.
HUH?
I-IT'S OKAY, THOUGH!
HUH ?!
IT'S OKAY...
IT'S FINE.
Y...

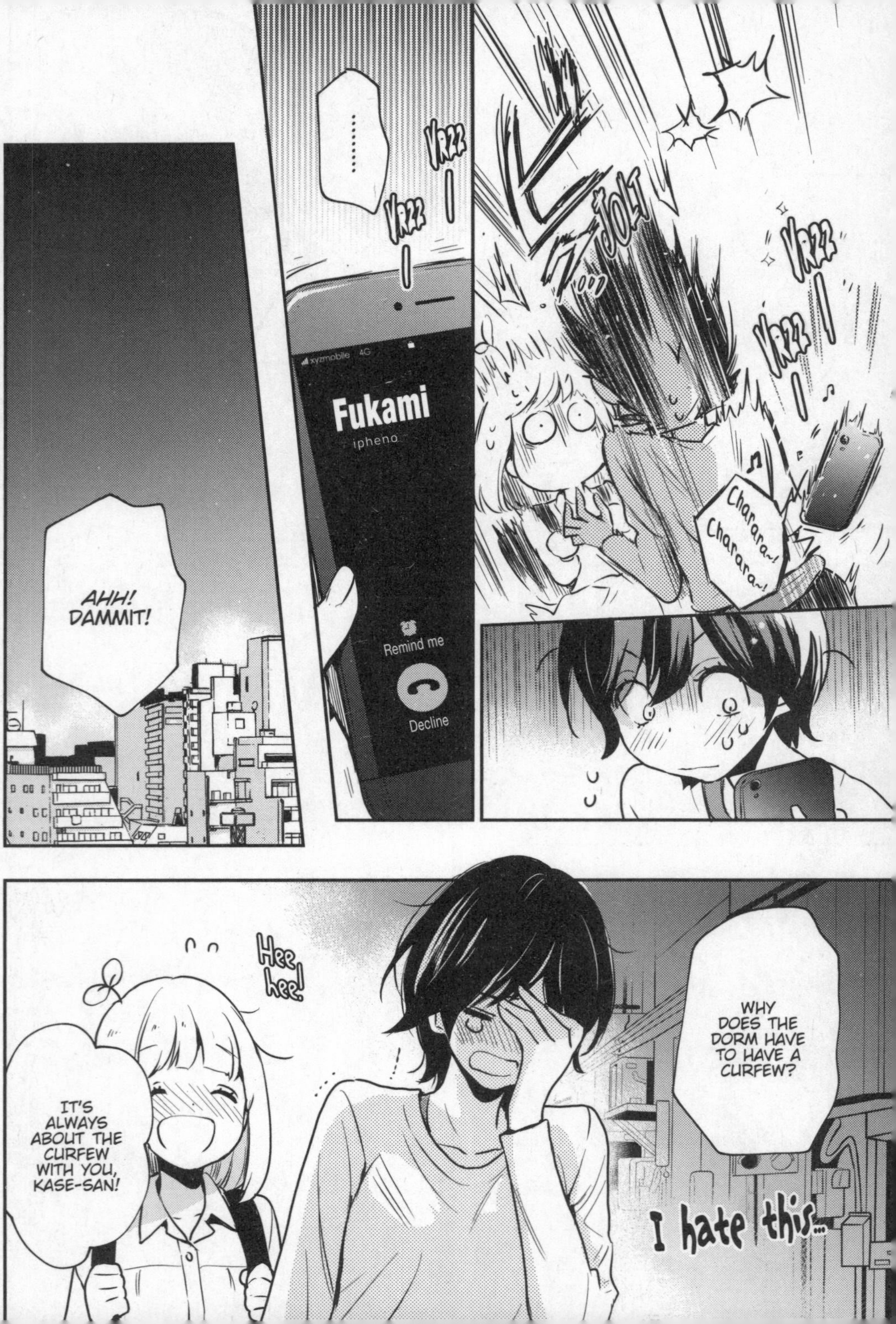
JOLT
VRZZ
VRZZ
Chararara~! Chararara~!
......
VRZZ
VRZZ
Fukami
iphena
Remind me
Decline
AHH! DAMMIT!
WHY DOES THE DORM HAVE TO HAVE A CURFEW?
I hate this...
Hee hee!
IT'S ALWAYS ABOUT THE CURFEW WITH YOU, KASE-SAN!

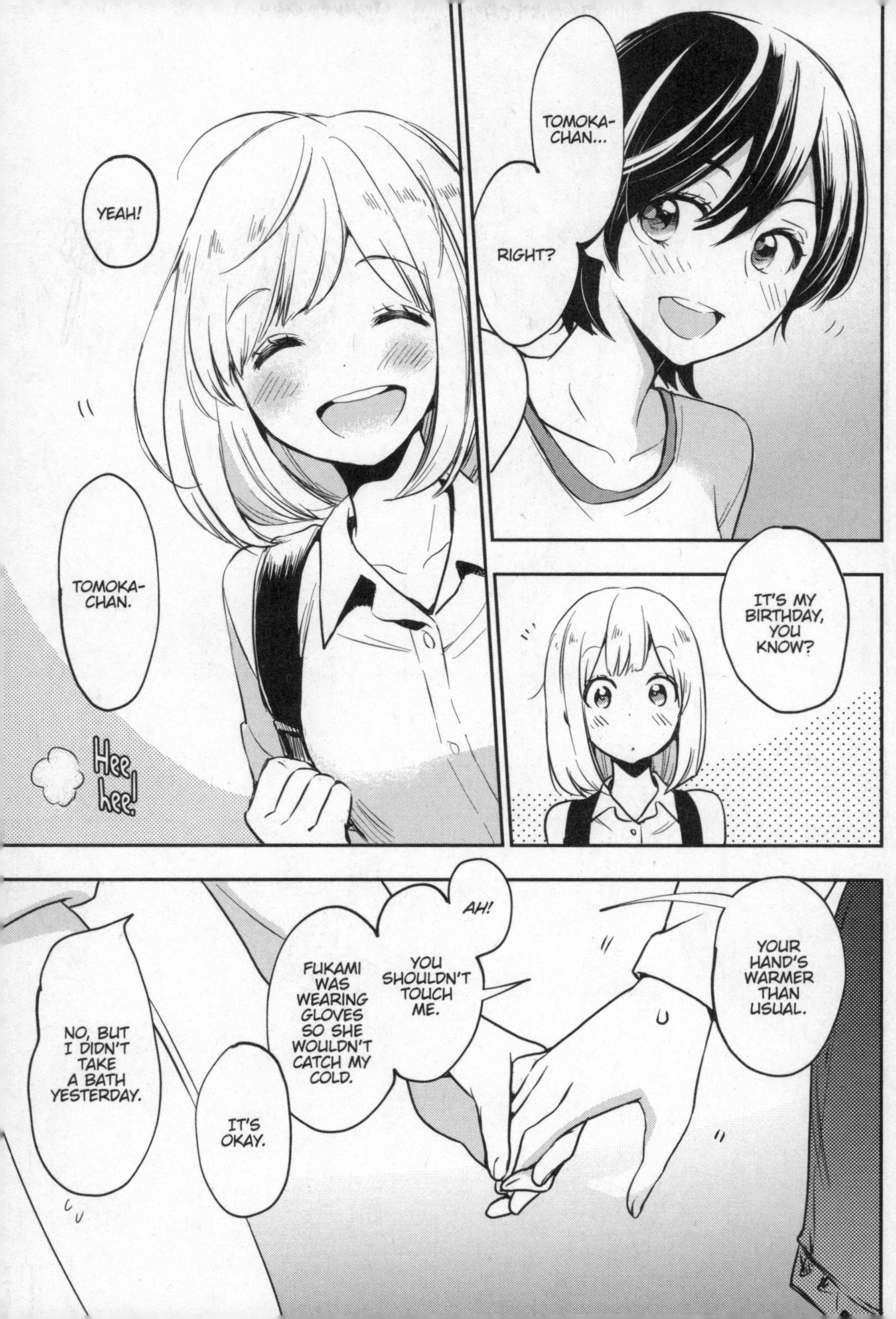
TOMOKA-CHAN...
RIGHT?
IT'S MY BIRTHDAY, YOU KNOW?
YEAH!
TOMOKA-CHAN.
Hee hee!
YOUR HAND'S WARMER THAN USUAL.
AH!
YOU SHOULDN'T TOUCH ME.
FUKAMI WAS WEARING GLOVES SO SHE WOULDN'T CATCH MY COLD.
IT'S OKAY.
NO, BUT I DIDN'T TAKE A BATH YESTERDAY.

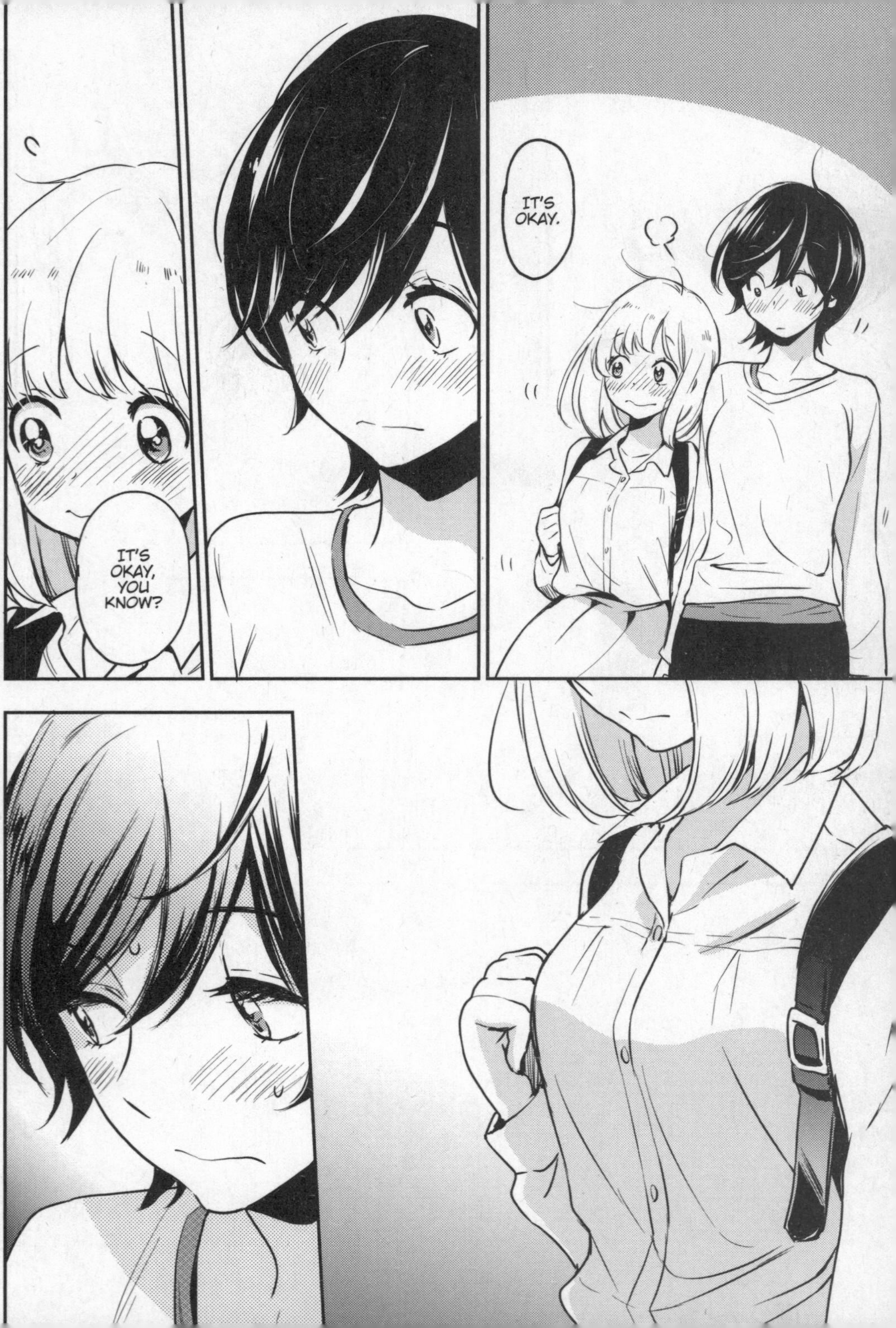
IT'S OKAY.
IT'S OKAY, YOU KNOW?

I'M FALLING APART.

EVERY DAY, I WANT TO SEE YOU SO MUCH...

AND THEN I JUST COLLAPSE.

Sniffle

I...

SHLUP...

I REALLY HAVEN'T BEEN ABLE TO TAKE ANY TIME SINCE SCHOOL STARTED.

NEVER THOUGHT I'D GET TO SEE YOU SO LITTLE, YAMADA.

ARE YOU SURE YOU'RE OKAY TO GET HOME ON YOUR OWN?

KEIO

Tick

I'M BEING SERIOUS!

THIS IS FOR REAL!

HUH?!

Hee hee!

YOU'RE SO FUNNY, TOMOKA-CHAN!

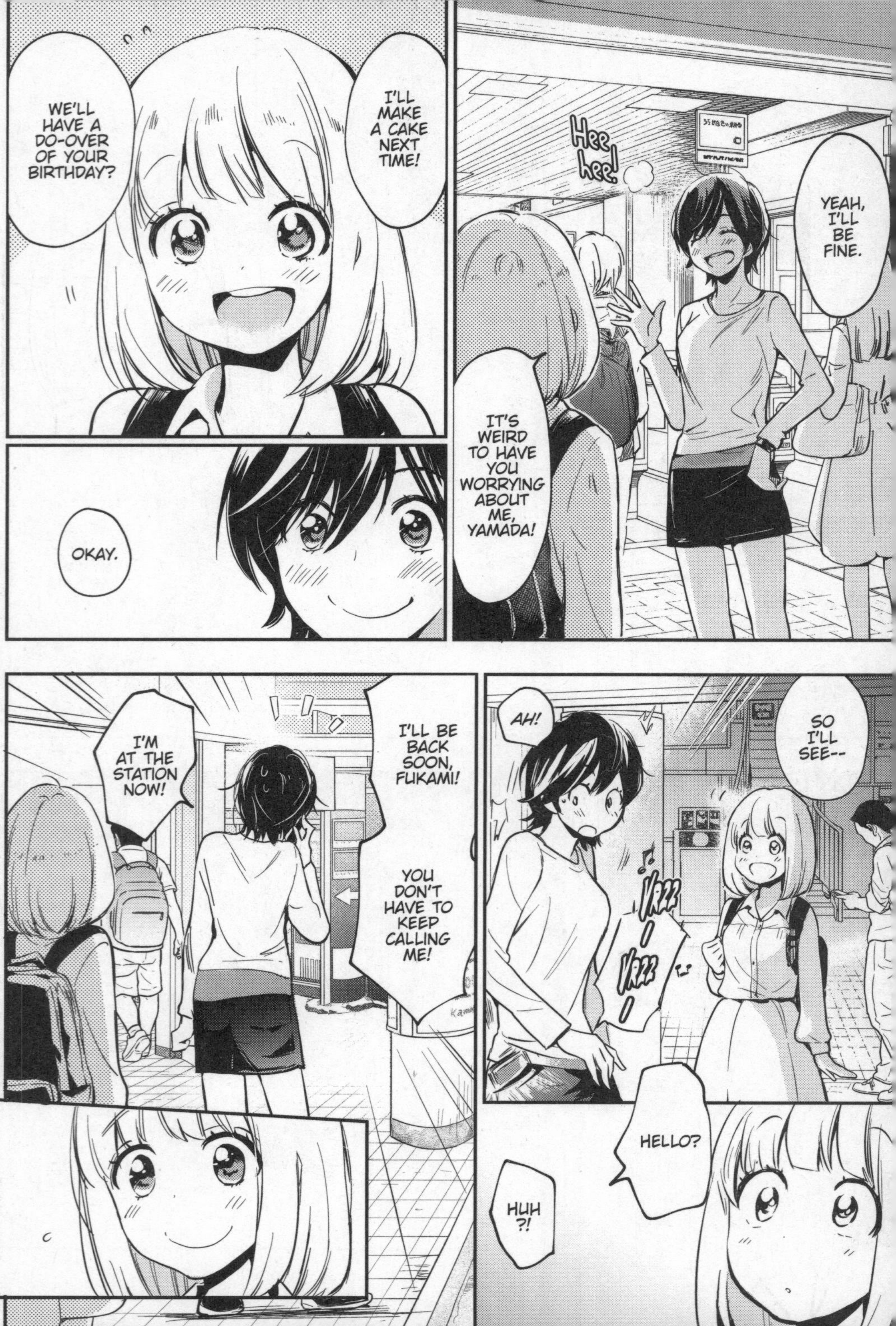

YEAH, I'LL BE FINE.
Hee hee!
IT'S WEIRD TO HAVE YOU WORRYING ABOUT ME, YAMADA!
I'LL MAKE A CAKE NEXT TIME!
WE'LL HAVE A DO-OVER OF YOUR BIRTHDAY?
OKAY.
SO I'LL SEE--
AH!
VRZZ
VRZZ
I'LL BE BACK SOON, FUKAMI!
YOU DON'T HAVE TO KEEP CALLING ME!
I'M AT THE STATION NOW!
HELLO?
HUH?!

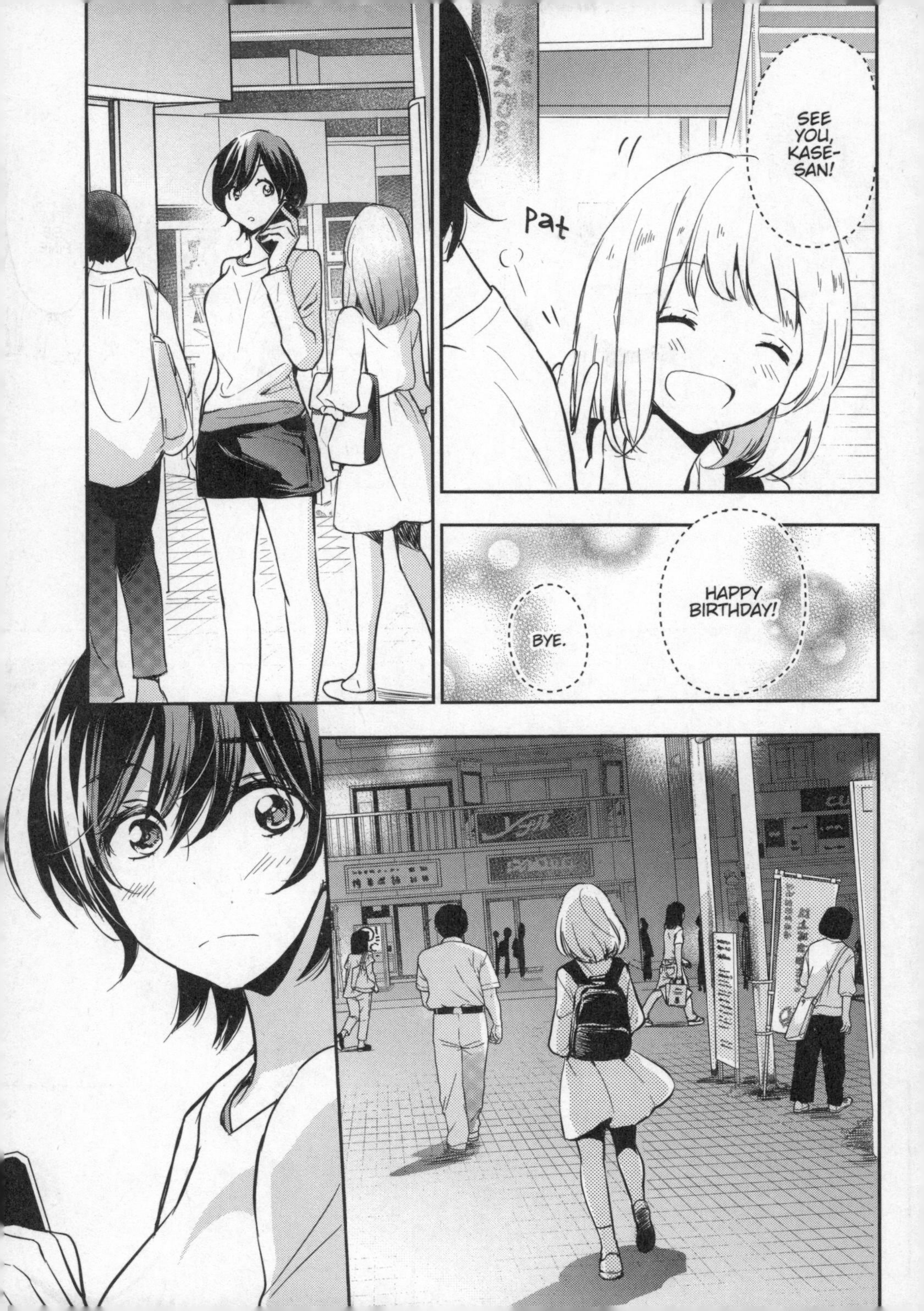

SEE YOU, KASE-SAN!
Pat
HAPPY BIRTHDAY!
BYE.

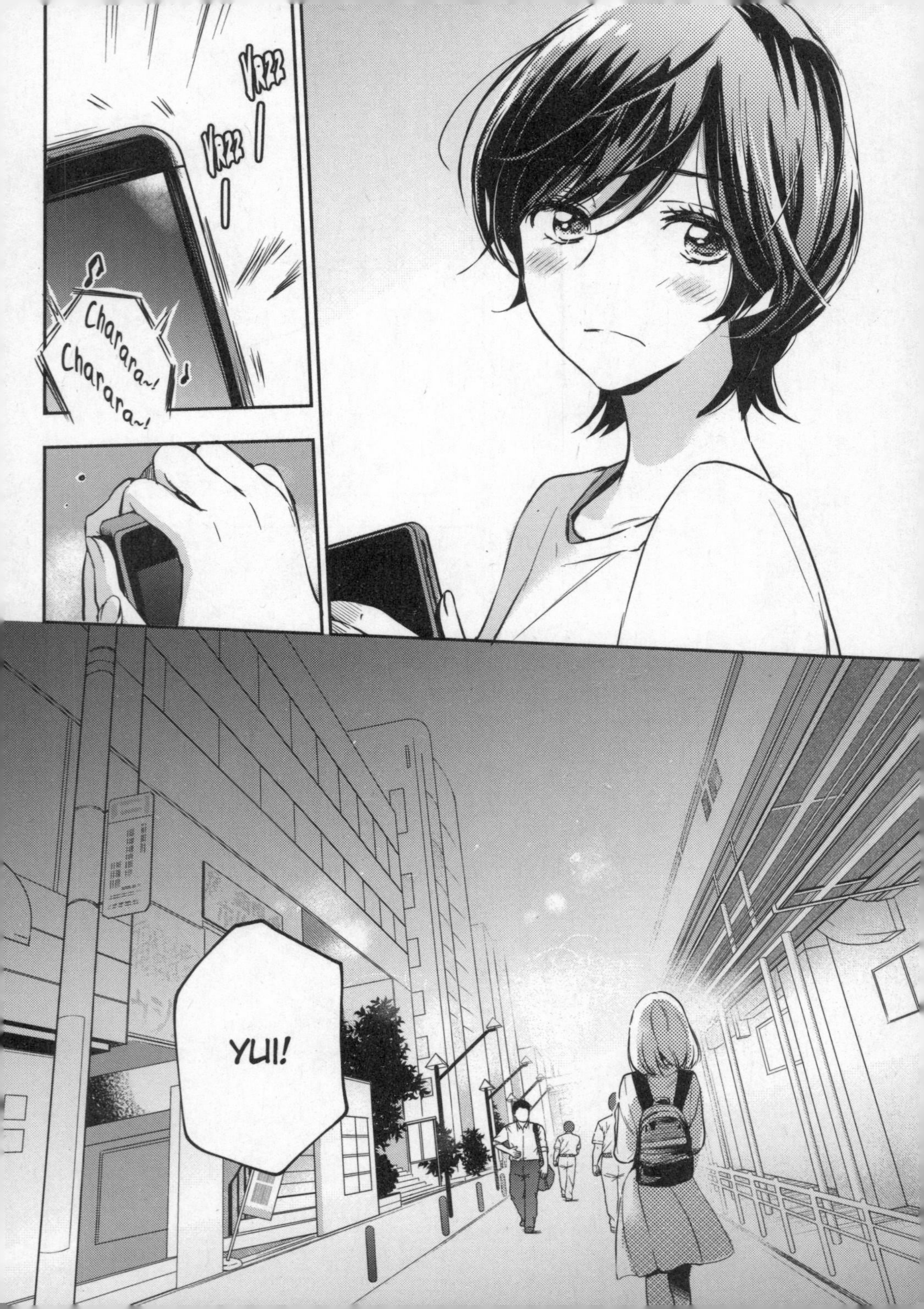

VRZZ
VRZZ
Charara~!
Charara~!
YUI!

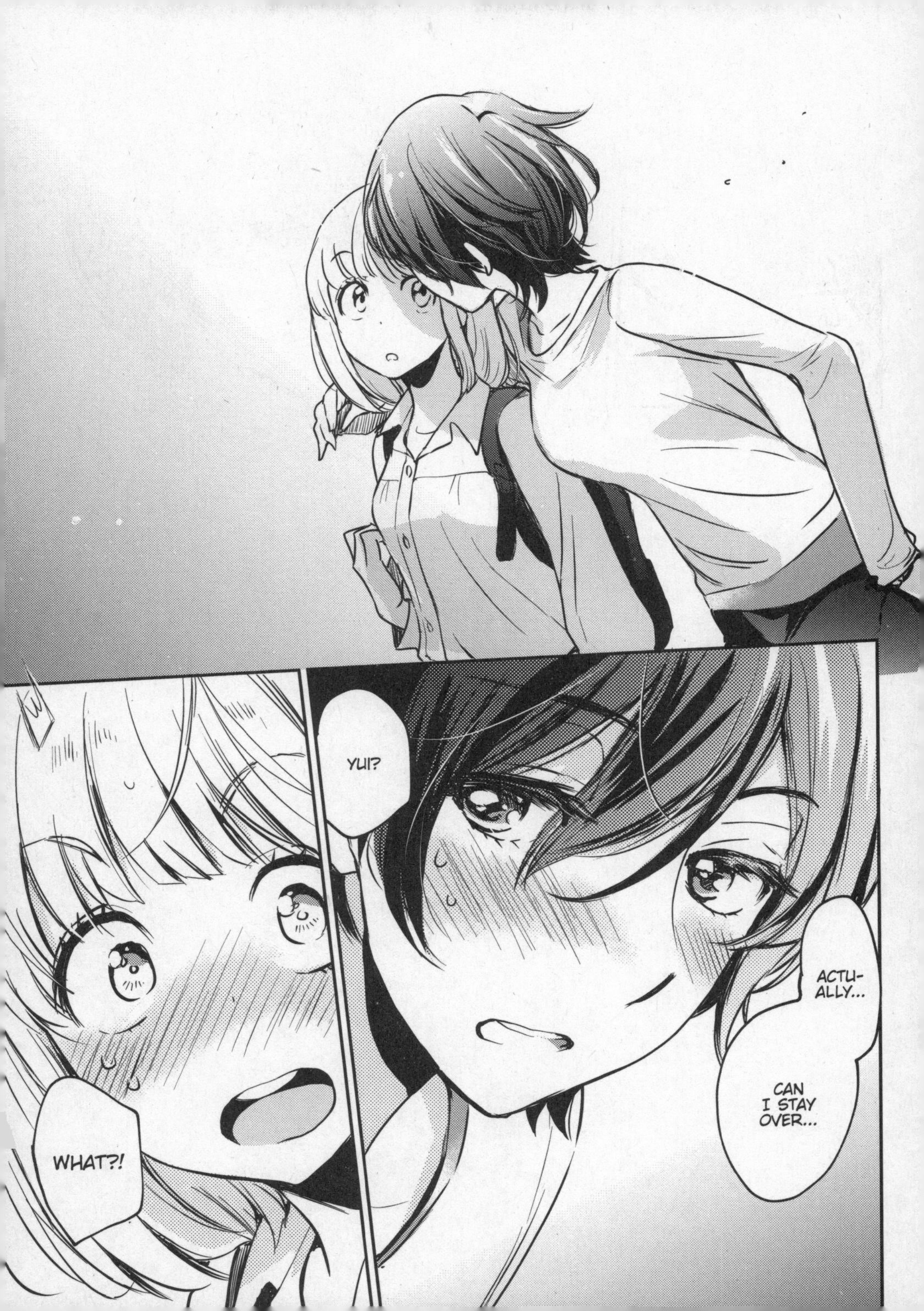
YUI?
ACTU-ALLY...
CAN I STAY OVER...
WHAT?!

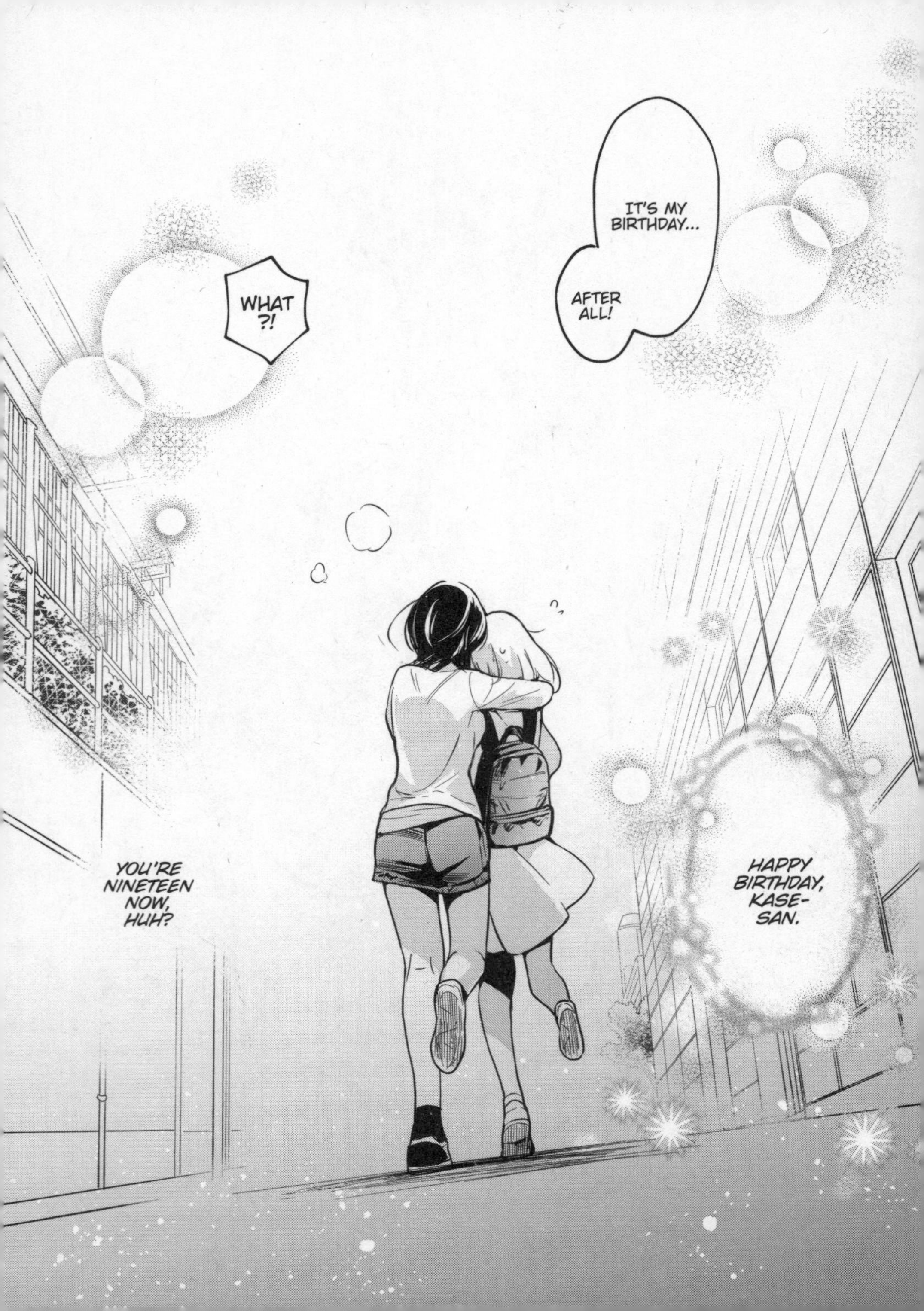
IT'S MY BIRTHDAY...
AFTER ALL!
WHAT ?!
HAPPY BIRTHDAY, KASE-SAN.
YOU'RE NINETEEN NOW, HUH?

Kase-san and Yamada ①

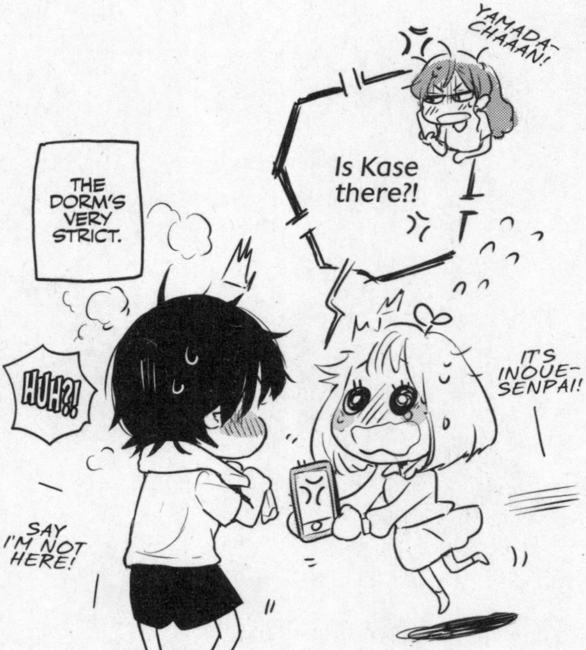
YAMADA-CHAAAN!
Is Kase there?!
THE DORM'S VERY STRICT.
IT'S INOUE-SENPAI!
HUH?!
SAY I'M NOT HERE!

Kase-san and Tokyo

Kase Tomoka (18) came to Tokyo at the beginning of February.

LET'S SEE...

ALL RIGHT. KASE TOMOKA-SAN, YOU'RE IN ROOM 203.

NADESHIKO DORMITORY

ガ！！KA-CHAK チャッ

NADESHIKO DORMITORY なでしこ寮

OH!

NICE.

YOU'RE SHARING A ROOM, SO BE NICE.

MM. WELL... JUST THE BARE MINIMUM.

IS THAT ALL YOU BROUGHT?

FROM DEKOYAMA PREFECTURE.

HIYA! I'M KASE TOMOKA...

HUH? YOU HAVE TO BUY THAT YOURSELF?

WHAT ABOUT SOAP OR DETERGENT?

I'VE HEARD ABOUT YOU.

YOU'RE FAMOUS.

FUKAMI KAORI.

COULD YOU USE THE SAME DETERGENT AS ME?

I HATE WEIRD SMELLS IN MY ROOM.

DUUN

Serve

Whee! ♥

HUNH! I AM? NICE TA MEETCHA!

298 YEN PER USE.

NO.

WHAT? YOU'RE GIVING THIS TO ME? THANKS!

Whee! ♥

Serve

I'M SORRY. COULD YOU JUST WASH YOUR HANDS?

HELLO? THIS IS KASE.

HALLWAY

Piru ru ru ru ru ru ru!♪

bip

2 FEB

					1	2
4	5	6	7	8	9	
11	12	13	14	15	16	
18	19	20	21	22	23	
25	26	27	28			

Oh! Kase-san?!

JOLT

VALEN-TINE'S...

YA-MADA!

IT'S ME!

Yay

siigh...

BUT I'M IN TOKYO!

Wow! Your voice sounds the same as when you're here!!

Heh heh!

I GUESS SHE'S ALREADY HOMESICK.

THE BIG EVENT IN FEBRUARY...

siigh

Sneak

UMM...

YAMADA, ABOUT THE FOURTEENTH THIS MONTH...

DID YOU NEED SOMETHING?

OH!

WHERE'S KASE?!

SHE'S OUT.

The fourteenth?

THIS IS FOR YOU. CHOCOLATE!

HERE! HAVE SOME CHOCOLATE!

LAST YEAR, WE MANAGED TO EXCHANGE VALENTINES.

LUCKY!

YOU'RE HER ROOMMATE?

I'm so scaaared! Freaking out!!

My exam's on the eighteenth, though?

Uwaaaah!

COULD YOU TELL HER HER **RIVAL** WAS HERE?

ER, I MEAN!

WHO ARE YOU?

I CAN'T SAY ANYTHING NOW!!

But I'm gonna try!!

It's so trivial in comparison!

Unh...

170

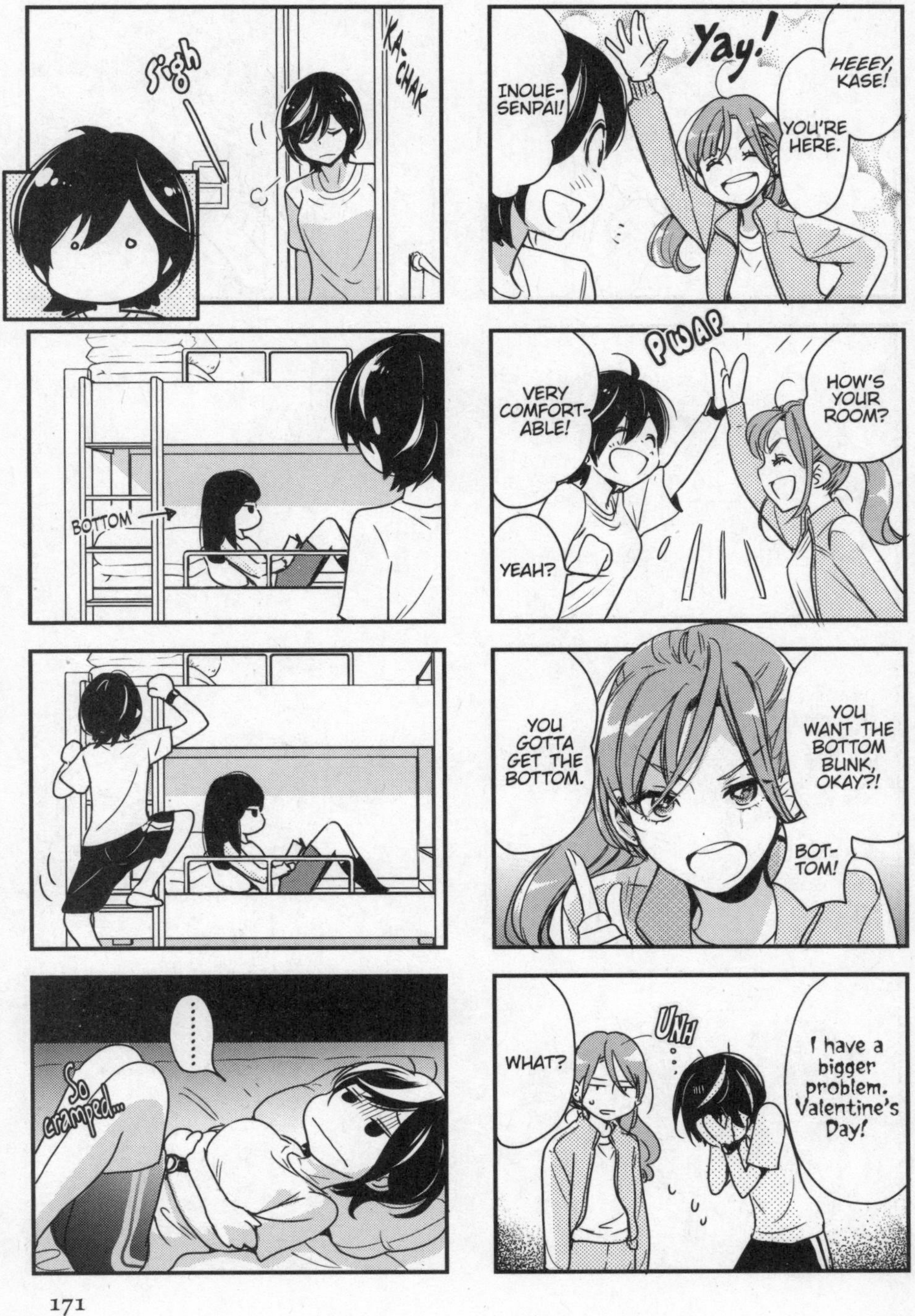
Yay!
HEEEY, KASE!
YOU'RE HERE.
INOUE-SENPAI!
PWAP
HOW'S YOUR ROOM?
VERY COMFORT-ABLE!
YEAH?
YOU WANT THE BOTTOM BUNK, OKAY?!
BOT-TOM!
YOU GOTTA GET THE BOTTOM.
I have a bigger problem. Valentine's Day!
UNH
WHAT?
Sigh
KA-CHAK
BOTTOM
......
So cramped...

THE FOUR-TEENTH.

KASEEE! HERE!

CHOCO-LATE FOR VALENTINE'S DAY!

Hngah?

HUH?

WHAT IS IT?

Kase

DON'T GET THE WRONG IDEA. IT'S ALSO TO CONGRATU-LATE YOU FOR GETTING IN HERE.

WHAT? THANK YOU!

?!

OKAY!

PAY ME BACK ON WHITE DAY!

Whee!

I GUESS IT'S OKAY.

THE TIMING'S JUST NOT GOOD THIS YEAR...

WELL... BUT...

PLAP

Slip

OWW.

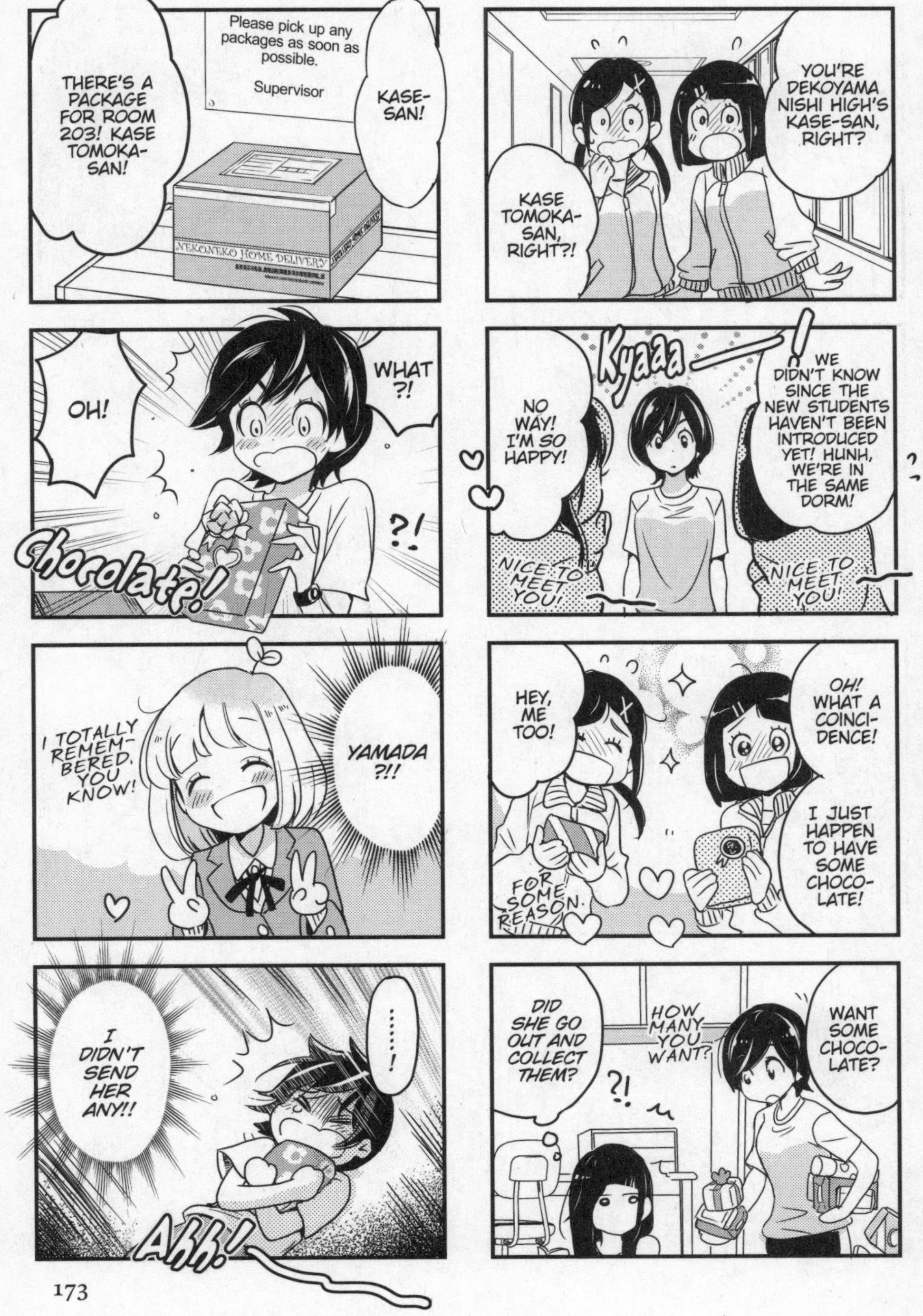
YOU'RE DEKOYAMA NISHI HIGH'S KASE-SAN, RIGHT?
KASE TOMOKA-SAN, RIGHT?!
WE DIDN'T KNOW SINCE THE NEW STUDENTS HAVEN'T BEEN INTRODUCED YET! HUNH, WE'RE IN THE SAME DORM!
Kyaaa—!
NO WAY! I'M SO HAPPY!
NICE TO MEET YOU!
NICE TO MEET YOU!
OH! WHAT A COINCIDENCE!
I JUST HAPPEN TO HAVE SOME CHOCO-LATE!
HEY, ME TOO!
FOR SOME REASON.
WANT SOME CHOCO-LATE?
HOW MANY YOU WANT?
DID SHE GO OUT AND COLLECT THEM?
KASE-SAN!
Please pick up any packages as soon as possible.
Supervisor
THERE'S A PACKAGE FOR ROOM 203! KASE TOMOKA-SAN!
NEKONEKO HOME DELIVERY
WHAT?!
OH!
Chocolate!
YAMADA?!!
I TOTALLY REMEM-BERED, YOU KNOW!
......!
I DIDN'T SEND HER ANY!!
Ahh!

What? Really?

I'LL PAY YOU BACK ON WHITE DAY!

Yaay!

I'VE NEVER GOTTEN WHITE DAY PRESENTS FROM ANYONE BUT MY DAD!

Piru ru ru ru!

Piru ru ru ru!

SO I'M OKAY WITH ANYTHING!

HE GAVE ME STUFF LIKE HANDKERCHIEFS OR CANDY OR MARSHMALLOWS.

Ha ha ha!

OH!

YAMADA!!

Hello? This is Yamada!

HANDKERCHIEFS, CANDY, AND MARSHMALLOWS...

Pay back...

UNH!

ARE ALL OUT!

THEY DID? I'M SO GLAD!

Your chocolates arrived! Thanks!!

174

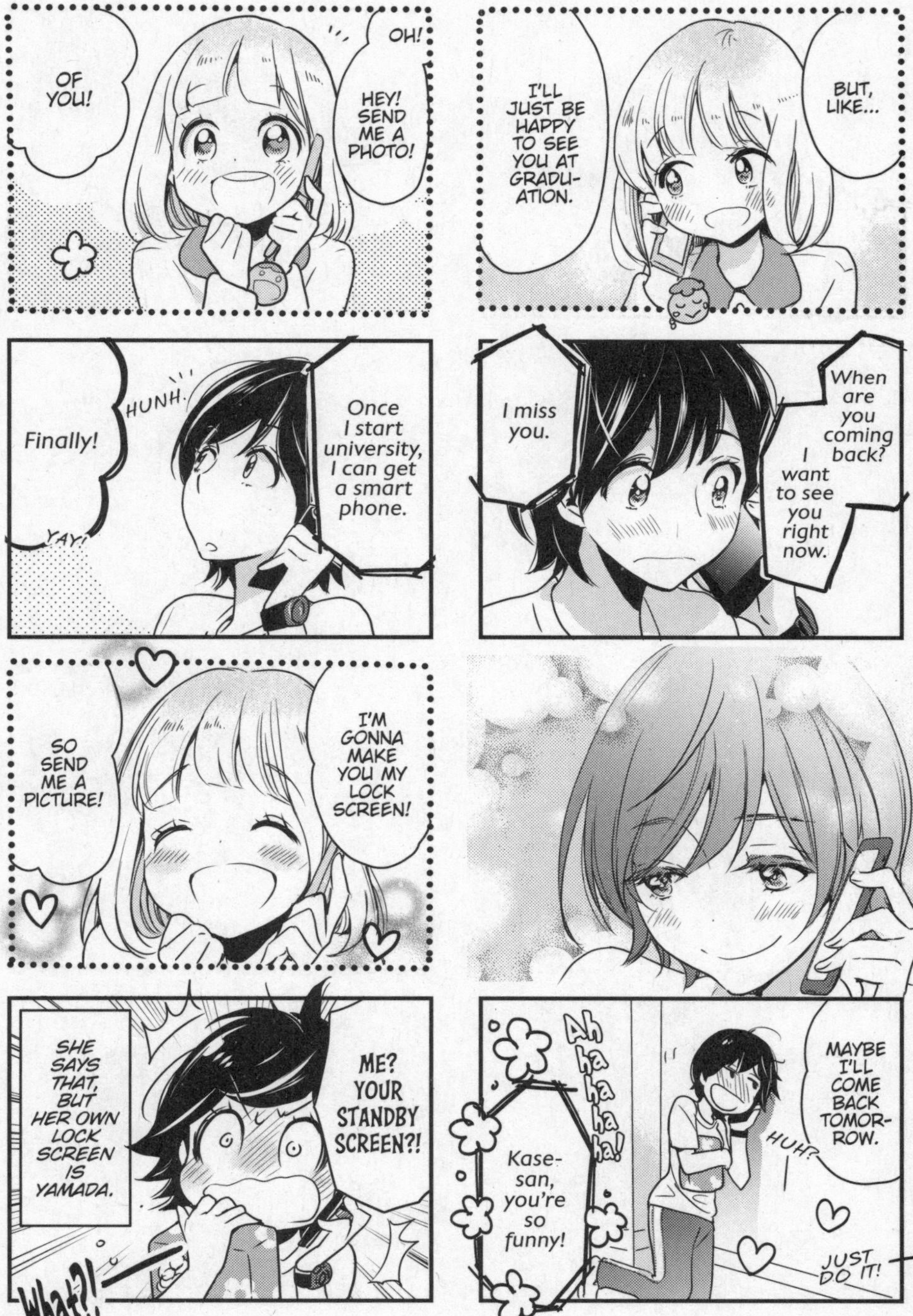
BUT, LIKE...
I'LL JUST BE HAPPY TO SEE YOU AT GRADU-ATION.
When are you coming back?
I want to see you right now.
I miss you.
MAYBE I'LL COME BACK TOMOR-ROW.
HUH?
JUST DO IT!
Ah ha ha ha ha!
Kase-san, you're so funny!
OH!
HEY! SEND ME A PHOTO!
OF YOU!
Once I start university, I can get a smart phone.
HUNH.
Finally!
YAY!
I'M GONNA MAKE YOU MY LOCK SCREEN!
SO SEND ME A PICTURE!
ME? YOUR STANDBY SCREEN?!
SHE SAYS THAT, BUT HER OWN LOCK SCREEN IS YAMADA.
What?!

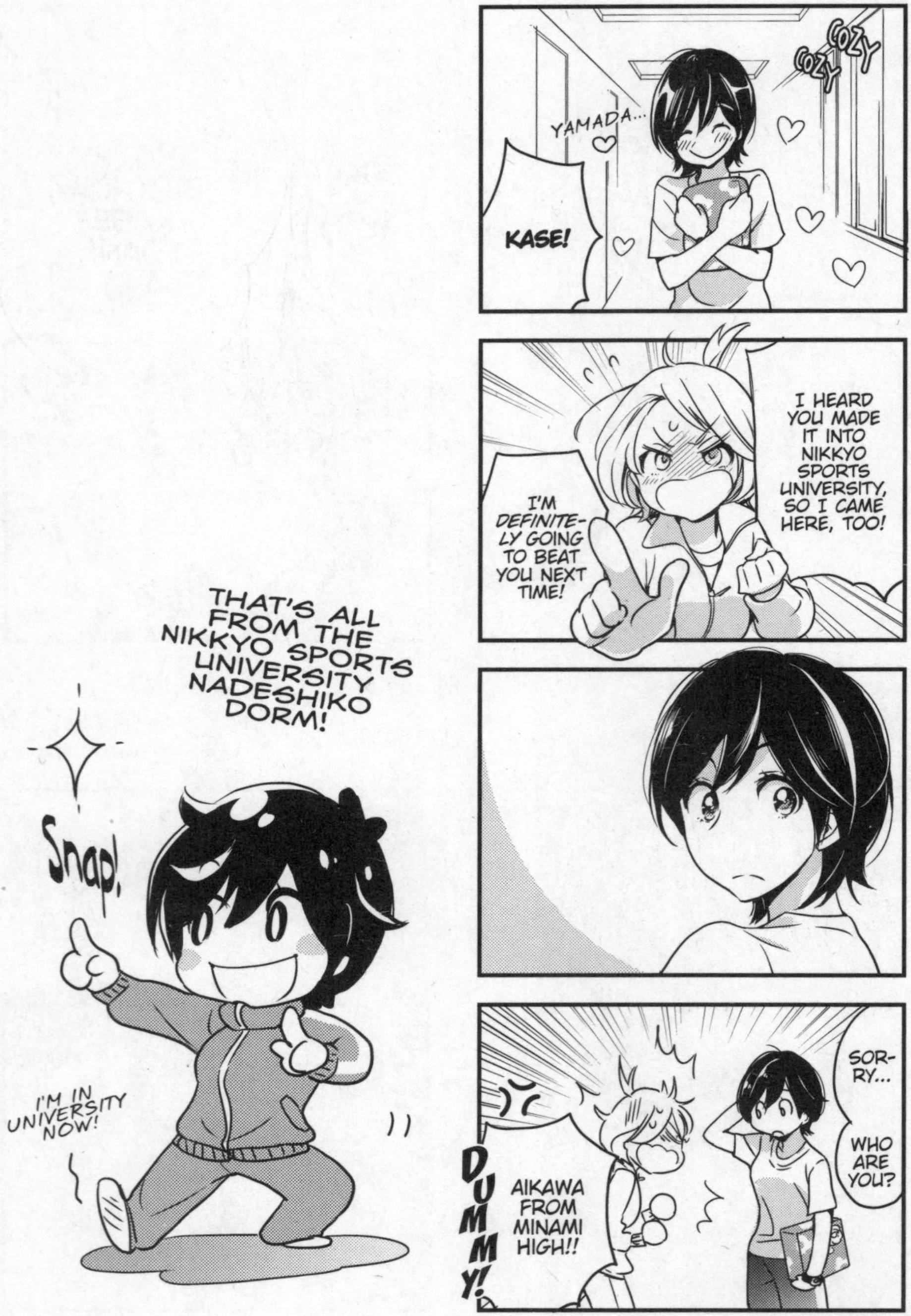

COZY COZY
YAMADA...
KASE!
I HEARD YOU MADE IT INTO NIKKYO SPORTS UNIVERSITY, SO I CAME HERE, TOO!
I'M DEFINITE-LY GOING TO BEAT YOU NEXT TIME!
SOR-RY...
WHO ARE YOU?
AIKAWA FROM MINAMI HIGH!!
DUMMY!
THAT'S ALL FROM THE NIKKYO SPORTS UNIVERSITY NADESHIKO DORM!
Snap!
I'M IN UNIVERSITY NOW!

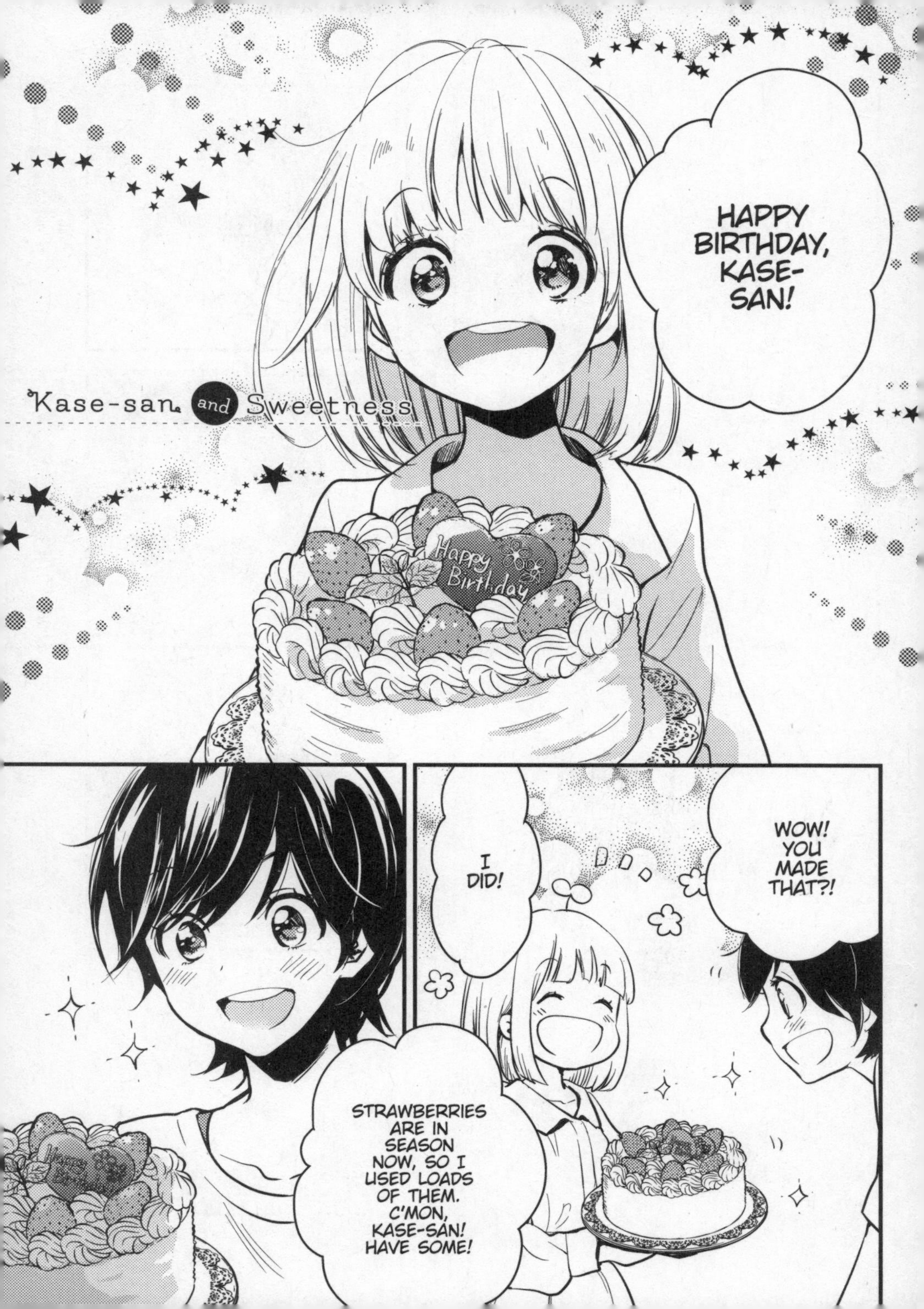

HAPPY BIRTHDAY, KASE-SAN!
Kase-san and Sweetness
Happy Birthday
WOW! YOU MADE THAT?!
I DID!
STRAWBERRIES ARE IN SEASON NOW, SO I USED LOADS OF THEM. C'MON, KASE-SAN! HAVE SOME!

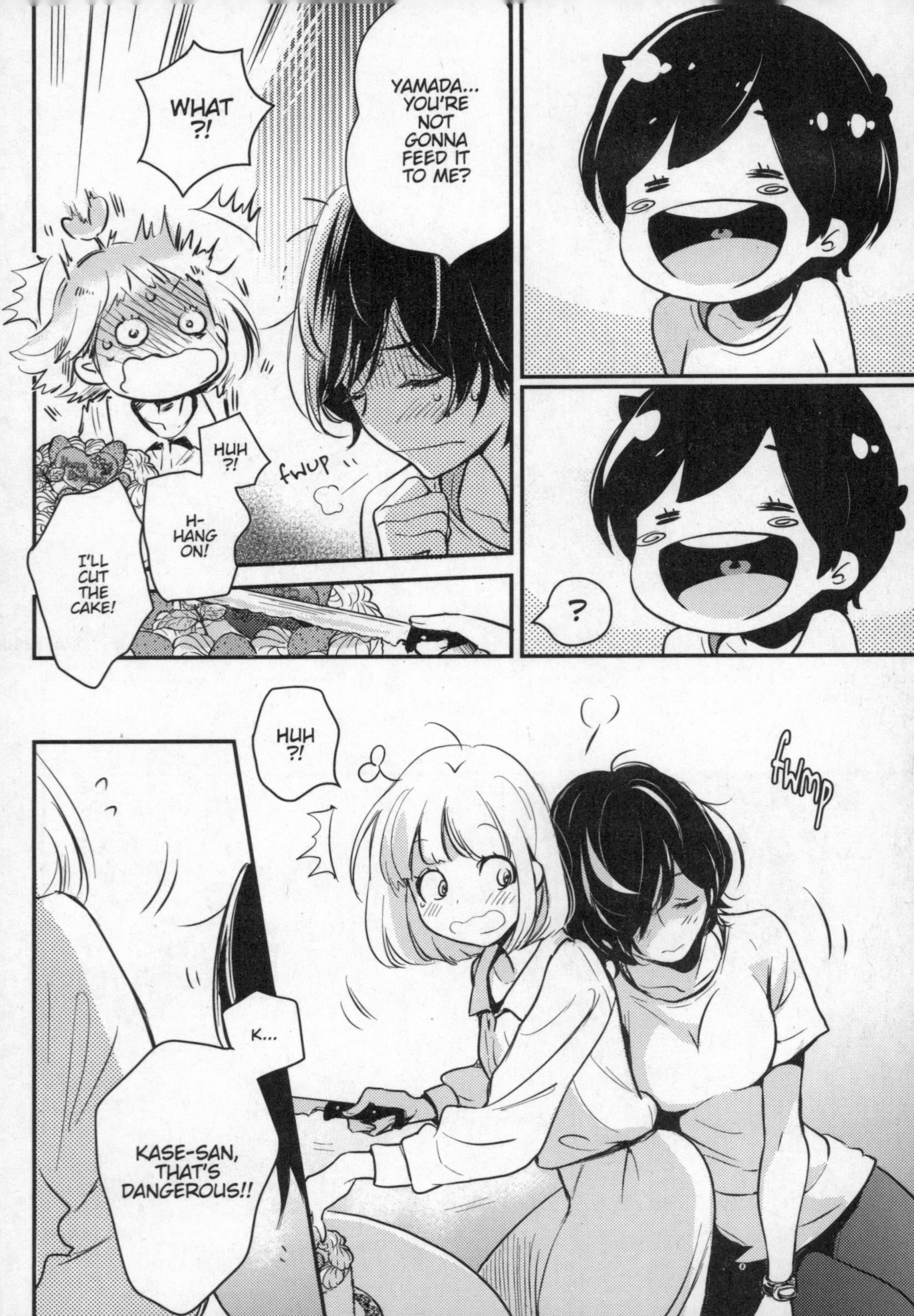
?
YAMADA... YOU'RE NOT GONNA FEED IT TO ME?
WHAT ?!
fwup
HUH ?!
H-HANG ON!
I'LL CUT THE CAKE!
fwmp
HUH ?!
K...
KASE-SAN, THAT'S DANGEROUS!!

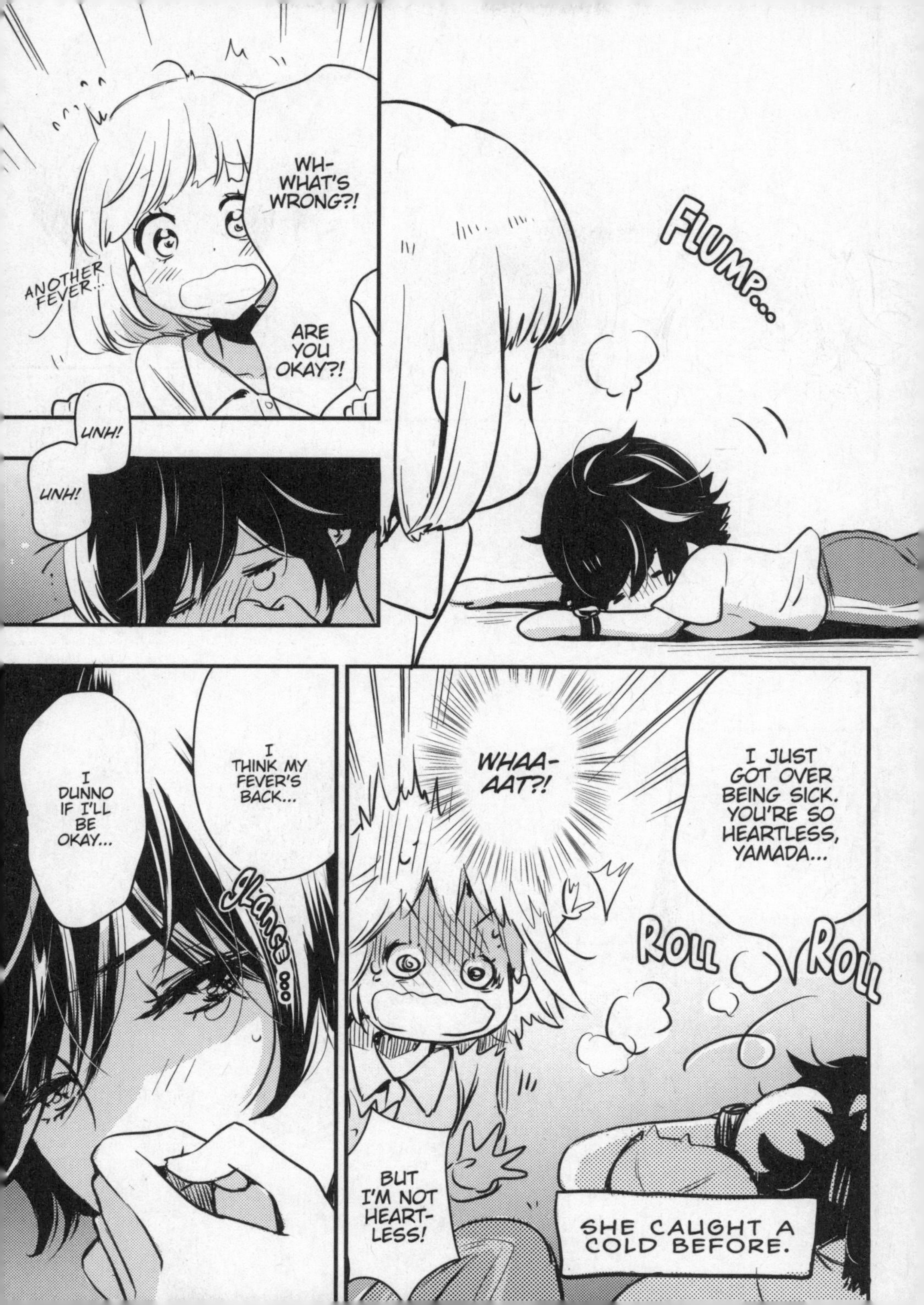
FLUMP...
WH- WHAT'S WRONG?!
ARE YOU OKAY?!
ANOTHER FEVER...
UNH!
UNH!
I JUST GOT OVER BEING SICK. YOU'RE SO HEARTLESS, YAMADA...
ROLL
ROLL
WHAA- AAT?!
BUT I'M NOT HEART- LESS!
SHE CAUGHT A COLD BEFORE.
I THINK MY FEVER'S BACK...
GLANCE...
I DUNNO IF I'LL BE OKAY...

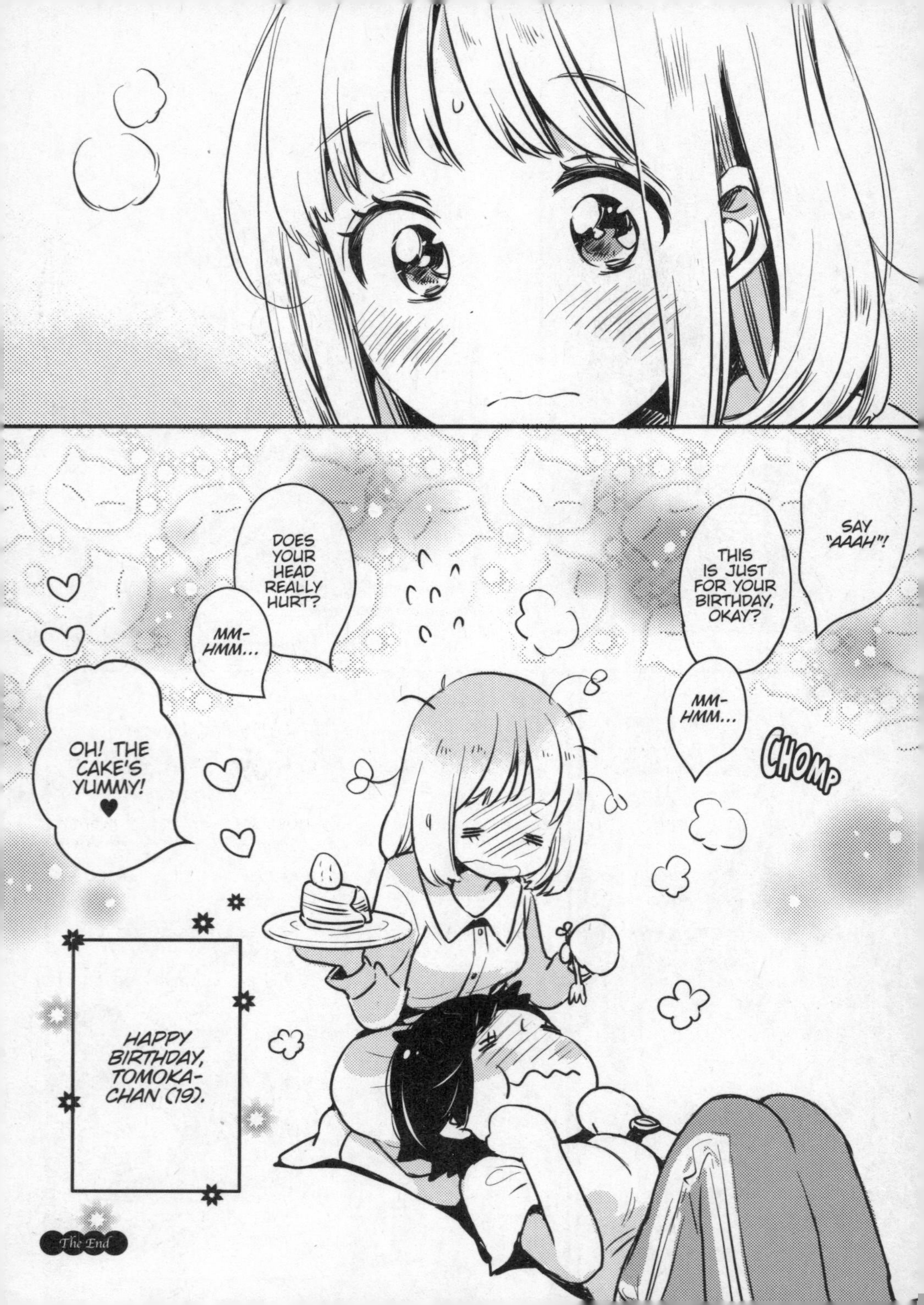
SAY "AAAH"!
THIS IS JUST FOR YOUR BIRTHDAY, OKAY?
MM-HMM...
CHOMP
DOES YOUR HEAD REALLY HURT?
MM-HMM...
OH! THE CAKE'S YUMMY! ♥
HAPPY BIRTHDAY, TOMOKA-CHAN (19).
The End

Kase-san and the Afterword

Hello!! So Kase-san and Yamada are in university now. *Wow!* Only a month passes in the whole book!!! (Kase-san's birthday is May First.) I'd like to see a little more of these two during the day next time. The scenes in this volume are mostly at night, which surprised me. Volume 2 will be summer, so there'll be fireworks and the beach and trips and part-time jobs!

I want to draw stuff that makes university seem fun. I hope you'll pick up Volume 2, as well!

The series is ongoing in *Wings*, by the way!

★ Hiromi Takashima (高嶋ひろみ)

Kase-san and Yamada

story & art by
Hiromi Takashima

①

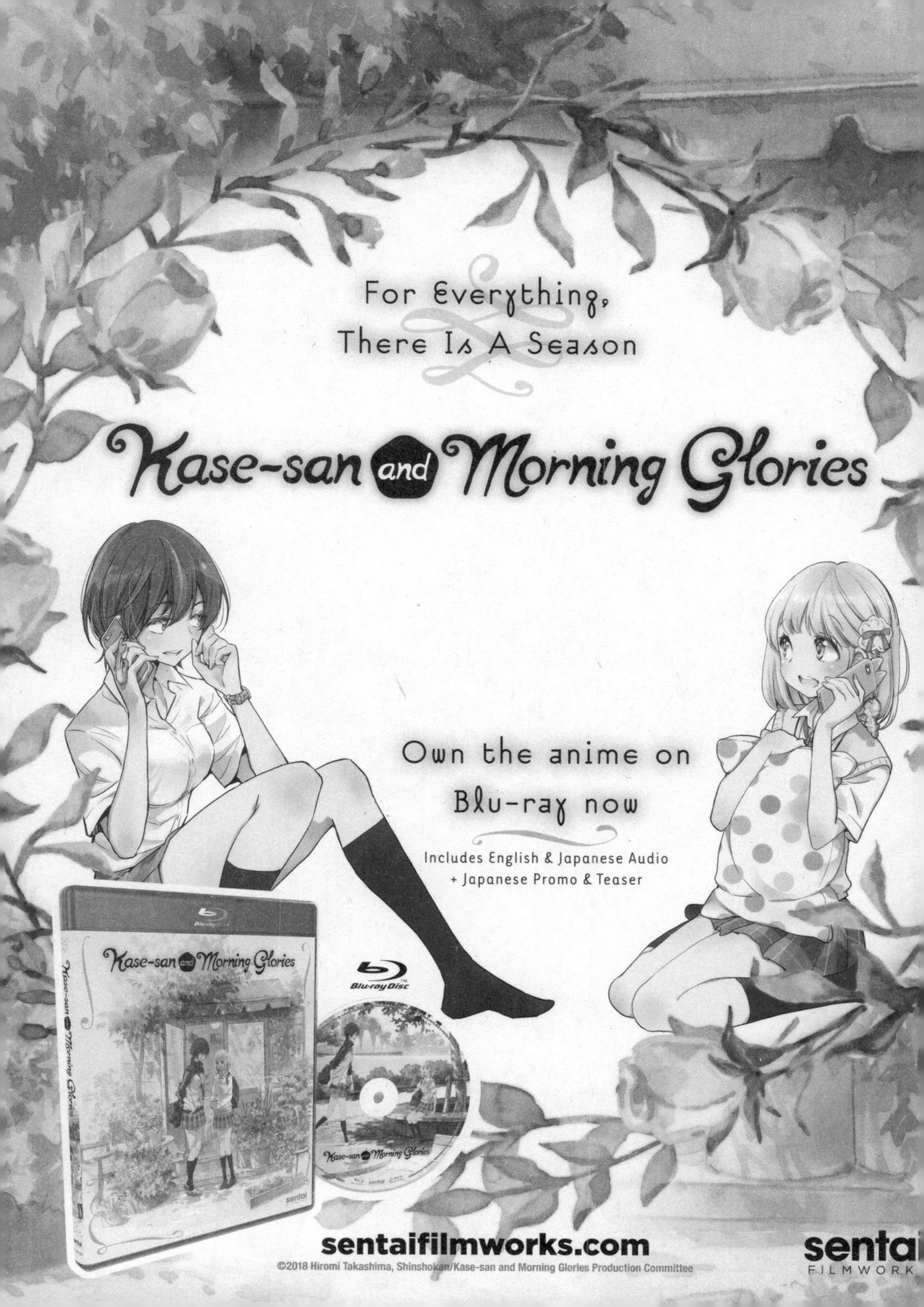
For Everything,
There Is A Season
Kase-san and Morning Glories
Own the anime on
Blu-ray now
Includes English & Japanese Audio
+ Japanese Promo & Teaser
Kase-san and Morning Glories
Blu-ray Disc
sentaifilmworks.com
©2018 Hiromi Takashima, Shinshokan/Kase-san and Morning Glories Production Committee
sentai

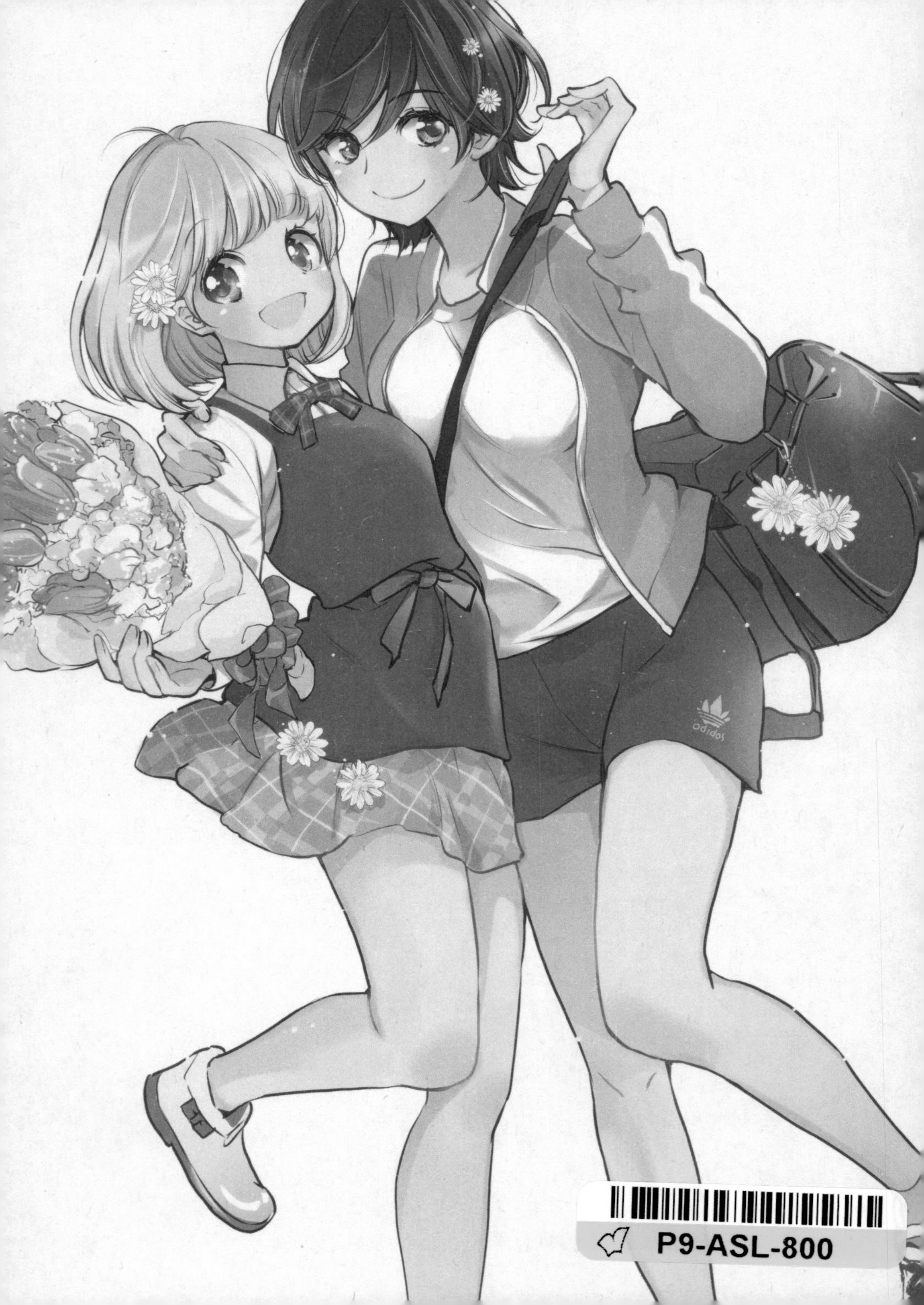
odidas